Gilbert's

LIVING WITH ART

ON THE FRONT COVER:
Pierre-Auguste Renoir. *The Swing*, detail. 1876.
Oil on canvas, entire work (shown here) 36¼ × 28¾″.
Musée d'Orsay, Paris.

ON THE BACK COVER:
The Swing, from Punjab Hills, India.
Kangra school, 19th century.
Ink and opaque watercolor on paper.
Victoria and Albert Museum, London.

Gilbert's

LIVING WITH ART

SIXTH EDITION

Mark Getlein

McGraw
Hill

Boston   Burr Ridge, IL   Dubuque, IA   Madison, WI   New York   San Francisco   St. Louis
Bangkok   Bogotá   Caracas   Kuala Lumpur   Lisbon   London   Madrid   Mexico City
Milan   Montreal   New Delhi   Santiago   Seoul   Singapore   Sydney   Taipei   Toronto

McGraw-Hill Higher Education

A Division of The **McGraw-Hill** *Companies*

GILBERT'S LIVING WITH ART

Published by McGraw-Hill, an imprint of The McGraw-Hill Companies, Inc. 1221 Avenue of the Americas, New York, NY, 10020. Copyright ©2002 by The McGraw-Hill Companies, Inc. Copyright ©1998, 1995, 1992 by Rita Gilbert. Copyright ©1988, 1985 by Alfred A. Knopf, Inc. All rights reserved. No part of this publication may be reproduced or distributed in any form or by any means, or stored in a database or retrieval system, without the prior written consent of The McGraw-Hill Companies, Inc., including, but not limited to, in any network or other electronic storage or transmission, or broadcast for distance learning.

Some ancillaries, including electronic and print components, may not be available to customers outside the United States.

This book is printed on acid-free paper.

3 4 5 6 7 8 9 0 DOW/DOW 0 9 8 7 6 5 4 3 2

ISBN 0-07-231726-4

Editorial director: *Phillip A. Butcher*
Sponsoring editor: *Joe Hanson*
Associate editor: *Allison McNamara*
Senior marketing manager: *David Patterson*
Lead project manager: *Susan Trentacosti*
Lead production supervisor: *Lori Koetters*
Coordinator freelance design: *Gino Cieslik*
Cover design: *Z Graphics*
Interior design: *Z Graphics*
Photo research coordinator: *Judy Kausal*
Photo research: *Robin Sand*
Illustrations: *John McKenna*
Layout designer: *Wanda Lubelska*
Lead supplement coordinator: *Cathy L. Tepper*
Media producer: *Shannon Rider*
Compositor: *GTS Graphics, Inc.*
Typeface: 10/11.5 *New Aster*
Printer: *R. R. Donnelley & Sons Company*

Library of Congress Control Number: 2001091171

www.mhhe.com

Gilbert's
LIVING WITH ART

To my parents
who taught me that art was important
and in memory of Frank Getlein
who showed the way

BRIEF CONTENTS

CONTENTS

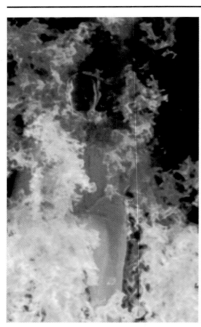

CHAPTER 9 The Camera Arts: Photography, Film, and Video 202

CHAPTER 10 Graphic Design and Illustration 242

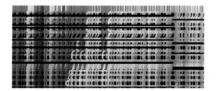

PART FOUR Three-Dimensional Media 254

CHAPTER 11 Sculpture 255

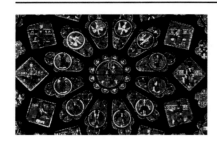

PREFACE

Living with Art is a basic art text for college students and other interested readers. It offers a broad introduction to the nature, vocabulary, media, and history of art, illustrated by hundreds of examples drawn from many cultures and across many centuries.

A Brief Word from a New Author

Beginning in 1985 and continuing through five editions, *Living with Art* grew from strength to strength under the inspired authorship of Rita Gilbert. Her impressive knowledge lightly worn, her personal insights, and her engaging style have introduced thousands of readers to art, in the process starting not a few of them on a lifelong interest in the subject. Being asked to continue her work was an honor, initially thrilling, then by turns intimidating and humbling as a deepening acquaintance with the text increased my respect for how thoughtfully it was put together.

Luckily, it soon became clear that I have inherited not only a wonderful book but also a wonderful and vocal community of dedicated instructors. The suggestions and criticisms of those who reviewed the fifth edition were my constant companions in planning this revision. In large matters, they spoke in remarkable unison; in smaller matters, they offered numerous intriguing ideas for artists, works, and topics that might be included. To all whose names are listed in the Acknowledgments section of this Preface, my thanks. I hope you enjoy finding your excellent advice reflected in these pages. E-mail has already brought lively and productive exchanges with several longtime users of this book, and I look forward to getting to know many more of you over the coming years as together we shape and reshape *Living with Art* to your needs.

Organization of the Text

As in previous editions, *Living with Art* is divided into five parts.

The three chapters of Part One provide a general overview of the subject, introduce basic concepts, and pose questions that encourage critical thinking about the nature of art and its role in society. The first chapter explores what it means to live actively with art, the origins of the artistic impulse, and some functions that artists fulfill. It also contains a discussion, newly expanded for this edition, about the act of looking and especially looking at art. Finally, the chapter touches on what it is to study art and how study can increase enjoyment. Chapter 2 poses the question "What Is Art?" Far from offering a definitive answer, the text encourages readers to examine their preconceptions by probing in turn the shifting definitions of the word *art;* the relationship of art to a person called an *artist* and the attendant issues of fame and monetary value; the connection between art and beauty and whether we can truly say what beauty is; the ways in which art can mirror, transform, or transcend the appearances of the visible world; and questions of how art can carry meaning, including formal relationships and iconography. Chapter 3 takes up the themes of art and touches on some of the purposes that artists have turned them to. With this edition, the themes have been broadened to embrace the full variety of the world's art, and examples have been chosen to encourage a lively dialogue across cultures and over time.

Part Two takes up the visual elements, first presenting them in detail, then examining how artists have organized them into art, how this organization structures our experience of looking, and how a sensitivity to the elements and their organization can help us to see more fully and to experience art in a more rewarding and meaningful way. Part Three covers two-dimensional media and devotes a chapter each to the most common categories—drawing, painting, prints, camera arts, and graphic design. In Part Four the same detailed coverage is applied to three-dimensional media—sculpture, crafts, architecture, and environmental design.

Part Five is a brief but comprehensive history of art. These materials now begin with a chapter called "Ancient Mediterranean Worlds," covering the art of that region from the Paleolithic era through the overlapping and interrelated civilizations of Mesopotamia, Egypt, the Aegean, Greece, and Rome. The remaining chapters trace the formation of Europe and the subsequent development of Western art to the present day. Interrupting this story on the brink of our modern era are three chapters, new to this edition, that look at the historical development of art beyond the West. (These chapters are discussed more fully later in this Preface.)

Illustrations

As in previous editions, *Living with Art* is lavishly illustrated in full color throughout. Every image available in color appears in color. Thirty illustrations have been added to this edition in order to represent a broader range of contemporary and world art, bringing the total to some 700 images. Many appear a second time in miniature as part of the unique Related Works feature that links the history chapters to the rest of the text. We have made every effort to obtain the best possible transparencies, and we have reviewed and color-corrected each image during the production process to ensure that the reproductions are as faithful to the originals as four colors of ink on paper can be.

Boxes

Boxed features in *Living with Art* focus on four broad topics.

"Artists" presents single-page biographies of noted artists. Each biography includes a portrait of the artist (often a self-portrait), a brief life history, and a quotation. New to this edition are biographies of Maya Ying Lin and Olowe of Ise.

"Art People" focuses on individuals who have played important roles in the world of art. They include collectors, a biographer, an artist's relative, art patrons, and even a thief.

"Art Issues" explores controversies surrounding restoration, censorship, public art, and the removal and display of artworks from tombs. An issue new to this edition is "Presenting the Past," which touches on the ideological nature of museums through a brief look at the Gare d'Orsay and a painting by the arch-academic William Bouguereau. Also new is "Who Is an Artist?" which takes up issues raised by outsider art, folk art, and other vernacular forms.

"Crossing Cultures," highlighting artistic contact and exchange across cultures, is new to this edition. Subjects are the influence of Japanese prints in Europe, Primitivism and European Modernism, European characters in African masquerades, and the influence of Hellenistic art on the early Buddha image.

Maps, Time Lines, Pronunciation Guide, Glossary, Bibliography

As in previous editions, maps are integrated into the history chapters of Part Five. Key cities, sites, and works mentioned in the text are indicated on the maps. A comprehensive fold-out time line of world art is packaged with the book, with thumbnail illustrations linked to a clear chronology. The Pronunciation Guide for unfamiliar names (both people and places) is found after the last chapter. Words that appear in **bold** at their first mention in the text are listed and defined in the Glossary at the back of the book. A Bibliography provides suggestions for further reading.

New to the Sixth Edition

Increased Attention to Art from Beyond the West

Numerous examples of art from beyond the West have been newly selected and integrated into the first four parts of the book, exposing students to the rich variety of the world's artistic traditions. Care has been taken to choose the finest and most representative works, to present them with a sense of their cultural context, and to introduce them in a pedagogically useful way. Even readers who do not progress to the history chapters will become acquainted with such characteristic forms as Chinese landscape painting, the monumental narrative reliefs of India, the Buddha image and its iconography, Islamic calligraphy, Olmec jades, Mayan ceramic figures, African masquerades and sculptures, American Indian basketry and ledger drawings, Japanese prints and folding screens, and much more.

Contemporary artists from beyond the West have been included as well, underscoring the continuing vitality of regions and cultures too often considered only for their "traditional" arts. Among these artists are Indian photographer Raghubir Singh, Australian Aboriginal printmaker Lin Onus, Chinese installation and performance artist Cai Guo Qiang, Senegalese painter Fodé Camara, Malian photographer Seydou Keïta, Iranian-born video artist Shirin Neshat, American Indian painter Jaune Quick-to-See Smith, and Japanese video and performance artist Mariko Mori.

Finally, Chapter 21 in the fifth edition, "Art Around the World," has been reconfigured as three expanded chapters that examine in turn the arts of Islam and Africa (Chapter 18); of India, China, and Japan (Chapter 19); and of the Pacific and the Americas (Chapter 20). Many of the illustrations in the rest of the book link up to these chapters with the unique Related Works feature, enabling an economical yet remarkably complete overview.

More Contemporary Art

One of the most rewarding tasks of art appreciation is to introduce students to the art of their own time, the art that speaks from and to their experience most directly. To this end, new examples of recent art have been integrated throughout the first four parts of the book, and Chapter 22, "Art Since 1945," has been expanded to include such topics as feminism and postmodernism. Contemporary artists represented for the first time in this edition include Bill Viola, Sandy Skoglund, Felix Gonzalez-Torres, Rebecca Purdham, Christian Schumann, Janine Antoni, Enrique Chagoya, Kerry James Marshall, Robert Gober, Louise Bourgeois, Matthew Barney, Terry Winters, Luis Jiménez, and Kiki Smith.

Sustained Attention to Photography

Over the past fifteen years, photography has been fully accepted into museums and taken on increasing importance in contemporary artistic practice. With this edition of *Living with Art*, examples of photography have been integrated into the chapters of Parts One and Two. In addition, an expanded section on "Photography and Art" in Chapter 9 examines how the medium found its way both as an art and into art, while a section on "The Photo Image and Printmaking" appears as a coda to Chapter 8. Photographers new to this edition include Manuel Alvarez-Bravo, Henri Cartier-Bresson, W. Eugene Smith, Eliot Porter, Robert Frank, Flor Garduño, Paul Strand, Sebastião Salgado, Duane Michals, and Andres Serrano.

Increased Representation of Architecture

In response to reviewers' requests, the chapter on architecture has been broadened to include important works and structural systems from beyond the West, and the historical chapters of Part Five now pay greater attention to developments in architecture and include plans of key buildings. Important works new to this edition include the Nanna Ziggurat at Ur, the Funerary Temple of Hatshepsut, Alberti's Church of Sant'Andrea, Borromini's San Carlo alle Quattro Fontane, Byodo-in, the Inner Shrine at Ise, Nanchan Temple at Wutaishan, the Great Mosque at Djenne, the Friday Mosque at Isfahan, the Kandariya Mahadeva temple at Khajuraho, Renzo Piano and Richard Rogers' Pompidou Center, and Frank O. Gehry's Guggenheim Museum Bilbao.

The fascinating Guggenheim Museum Bilbao has been singled out for more extended representation, and aspects of it appear in several chapters. Included are a preliminary gestural drawing, a dramatic interior view, the exterior in close-up and in full, a scale model and plans, and a downloaded screen from Catia, the computer program used to aid construction. The discussion of the Parthenon, formerly dispersed in a similar way throughout the book, is now concentrated in Chapter 14.

A Strengthened Western Core

As in past editions, the core of the book focuses on the Western tradition. The text has been revised to trace the outlines of this tradition more precisely, not only setting it against art from other traditions but also emphasizing how Western ideas about the nature and role of art have changed over the centuries. The illustration program has been thoroughly reviewed with an eye toward ensuring that artists are represented by their strongest and most characteristic works. Important works new to this edition include Picasso's *Three Musicians* and *Three Women at the Spring*, Monet's *Waterlilies at Dusk* and *Haystack at Sunset*, Matisse's *Joy of Life*, Holbein's *The Ambassadors*, Vermeer's *Woman Holding a Balance*, David's *Oath of the Horatii*, Thomas Cole's *The Oxbow*, Henry Ossawa Tanner's *The Banjo Lesson*, Manet's *Bar at the Folies-Bergère*, Mary Cassatt's *Boating Party*, Georges Seurat's *Bathers at Asnières*, Munch's *The Scream*, Wifredo Lam's *The Jungle*, Mondrian's *Broadway Boogie-Woogie*, and Judy Chicago's *Dinner Party*.

Student Resources

Please note: The supplements listed here and below in Support for Instructors *may accompany this text. Please contact your local McGraw-Hill representative for details concerning policies, prices, and availability as some restrictions may apply. If you are not sure who your representative is, you can find him or her by using the Rep Locator at www.mhhe.com.*

The Basic Student Package

Free to students with every new text:

> *Living with Art Core Concepts CD-ROM*—offers students essential study material on the key art elements and techniques. Each element is illustrated and enhanced with interactive exercises. Techniques are demonstrated and explained with brief video segments.
>
> The *Living with Art Time Line*—a fold-out chronology of concurrent events in culture and history.

The Expanded Student Package

Includes everything from the Basic Student Package as well as:

> *Design Overlays*—coordinated with the Projects Manual, these overlays clearly demonstrate the structure and composition of various works of art.
>
> *Projects Manual and Writing Guide*—exercises that both hone formal analysis and assist in the more complex process of writing about art.

Online Learning Center
www.mhhe.com/livingwithart

McGraw-Hill offers extensive Web resources for students with Internet access. Students will find the Online Learning Center of particular use with *Living with Art,* as for each chapter it offers chapter objectives, discussion questions, online testing, and interactive time lines. In addition, the site hosts links to promote getting involved in art and in conducting research on the Web.

Support for Instructors

Instructor's Resource Manual

McGraw-Hill offers an Instructor's Manual to all instructors who adopt *Living with Art* for their courses. The Instructor's Manual includes:

> A Transition Guide containing chapter outlines with topic headings and the accompanying illustrations, and an outline of the changes to the sixth edition to ease the way for users of the fifth edition.
>
> Examination questions, including multiple-choice, slide ID, true/false, and essay questions.
>
> Suggested Video and Multimedia Resources.

Computerized Test Bank

The test questions from the Instructor's Manual are available on Diploma™ Testing Software, a powerful but easy-to-use test-generating program.

Online Learning Center
www.mhhe.com/livingwithart

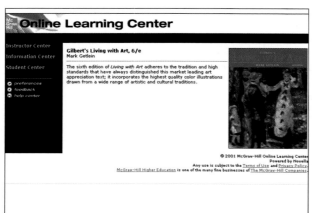

An Internet-based resource for students and faculty alike. The Instructor's Resources are password-protected and offer the complete text of the Instructor's Manual. To receive a password for the site, contact your local sales representative or e-mail us at art@mcgraw-hill.

Additionally, the Online Learning Center offers chapter-by-chapter quizzes for student testing. These brief quizzes are separate from those offered in the Instructor's Manual, they generate instant grades, and the results can be e-mailed directly to the instructor with the click of a button. This special quizzing feature is a valuable tool for the instructor who requires a quick way to check reading comprehension and basic understanding without using up valuable class time.

Slide Sets

Available to all adopters. Please call your local McGraw-Hill representative for details.

Acknowledgments

This book has been a collaborative effort of the most collegial kind. My gratitude and admiration flow first to the extraordinary staff at McGraw-Hill, who have offered every imaginable support and extended every possible kindness. I have been cheered by their enthusiasm, buoyed up by their energy, and inspired by their dedication and creativity. My earliest debt there is to editor Cynthia Ward, who put her faith in my ability to undertake this revision and with whom I hammered out its broad outlines. When Cynthia departed for the freelance life, I found myself in the expert hands of Allison McNamara, who coolly took over without skipping a beat. Allison combines, somewhat alarmingly, talents for organization, management, motivation, friendship, and humor with an excellent eye and the detached critical spirit of an ideal first reader. After watching her see this project through in all its byzantine complexity, I think she might consider running a small country. Gratitude gravitates as well to her associates Joe Hanson and Phil Butcher, to her assistant Ashaki Charles, and to marketing manager David Patterson, who has devoted untold energy to seeing that this new edition of *Living with Art* enters the world with both fanfare and follow-through. Surely David has other books to think about, but I would never know it.

The Herculean task of photo research seemed to sit lightly on the shoulders of photo researcher Robin Sand. Her resourcefulness and discerning eye are reflected everywhere in these pages. Robin was assisted, we believe, by the mysterious Robert, as well as by Julie Tesser, who bravely took over a group of problem cases. It was our special good fortune to have Yoshiko Nihei securing photos for us in Japan. Many of the treasures from Japanese temples and museums illustrated in this edition would quite simply have been unobtainable without her. Katherine Baker ingeniously tracked down a number of mysterious sources and contemporary artists, and Julia Ruxton and her colleagues at Calmann & King in London were generous about sharing sources for images from Africa and China. John McKenna oversaw the program of line art and furnished elegant new examples with his customary grace under the customary pressures.

The complicated process of transforming an unwieldy morass of manuscript, transparencies, drawings, and disk files into the beautiful book you hold in your hands was overseen by Susan Trentacosti and her associates in Burr Ridge. I am especially grateful to Gino Cieslik for his subtle update of the design and to copyeditor Leslie Anne Weber for her bold green pen, sharp eyes, and tactful queries. Fate smiled on us once again when Wanda Lubelska, who was responsible for the exceptionally fine page layouts in the fifth edition of *Living with Art*, agreed to bring her acute visual sensitivity to this edition as well.

A project of this intellectual scope exceeds the boundaries of any one person's competence, or at least it exceeds mine. It has been my privilege to draw on the expertise of many of the scholars and artists that I have come to know over the years. I am especially indebted to Peter Gallo for the boxes on outsider art, the Gare d'Orsay, and Maya Ying Lin; to Monica Visonà for the biography of Olowe of Ise; and to Herbert M. Cole for his advice on African art and for casting an eye over the finished chapter. Chu-tsing Li, Marylin M. Rhie, Anna Dallapiccola, Jim Whittaker, Kate Sibole, and David Damrosch graciously fielded questions about Ming court painting, Buddhist iconography, Indian art, photographic processes, and Mesoamerican civilization. Virginia Budney saved me from error and filled in many blanks through her efficient research and curatorial connections, and her experience as a sculptor and foundry worker proved invaluable in getting a grip once and for all on lost-wax casting. Many artists were generous with their time, and several had transparencies of their work made especially for this book. I have particularly profited from e-mail exchanges with Daniel Canogar and with Jennifer Ma of the Cai Guo Qiang studio. Wanda Glowacka patiently read through drafts of early chapters. Her encouragement was encouraging, and her silences pointed as effectively as any critique to weaknesses that needed attention. It will be a pleasure to repay the special debt I owe to Elise Engler. Fine artist, good friend, and peerless gallery-going companion, she patiently talked through many of the ideas presented in these pages and saw to it that food passed my lips when a round-the-clock schedule threatened to undermine both my health and my sanity.

Reviewer Acknowledgments

This book belongs to its users, whose needs and wishes give it form. I am especially grateful for the suggestions and criticisms of all who reviewed the fifth edition of *Living with Art*.

Fred C. Albertson, *University of Memphis*; Antoinette M. Aleccia, *Montgomery College—Rockville Campus*; Jean Audigier, *University of San Francisco*; Barbara Bernstein, *Fresno Pacific University*; Arlene Berrie, *Miami-Dade Community College*; Patricia J. Craig, *California State University*; Catherine Jones Davies, *Kirkwood Community College*; Shirley Dort, *Virginia State University*; Carole Drachler, *Mesa Community College*; Paula A. Drewek, *Macomb Community College*; Dwaine Greer, *University of Arizona*; Bertha Steinhardt Gutman, *Suffolk County Community College*; Cheryl M. Hamilton, *University of Wisconsin—Oshkosh*; Marleen Hoover, *San Antonio College*; Penny Jacoby Prince, *Georges Community College*; Soo Yun Kang, *Chicago State University*; Kathryn E. Kramer, *SUNY Cortland*; Leslie A. Lambert, *Santa Fe Community College*;

Robert Mansfield, *San Diego State University*; Gayle McCarty, *Hinds Community College*; Julie McGuire, *Georgia Southern University*; Helaine M. McLain, *Northern Arizona University*; Lynn Metcalf, *St. Cloud State University*; Sue E. Milner, *Eastern Wyoming College*; Percy North, *Montgomery College*; Christie Nuell, *Middle Tennessee State University*; Mallory Pearce Armstrong, *Atlantic State University*; Emma Gillespie Perkins, *Morehead State University*; Barry Phillips, *Odessa College*; Barbara Pogue, *Essex County College*; Dominic Ricciotti, *Winona State University*; Cherri L. Rittenhouse, *Rock Valley College*; Diego Sanchez, *Virginia Union University*; Nancy M. Shelton, *Old Dominion College*; Cheryl Souza, *Kapi'olani Community College*; Michael John Stone, *Cuyahoga Community College*; Sally A. Struthers, *Sinclair Community College*; Mary Frances VanPelt, *North Central Texas College*; Robert Wojtpwicz, *Old Dominion College*; Salli Zimmerman, *Nassau Community College*.

We would also like to thank the readers of previous editions, whose counsel continues to enlighten the text. They include Judith Andraka, *Prince George's Community College*; Mary Alice Arnold, *Appalachian State University*; Gisele Atterberry, *Illinois State University*; Michelle R. Banks, *Memphis State University*; Ross Beitzel, *Gloucester County College*; Kyra Belan, *Broward Community College*; John Bell, *Blue Ridge Community College*; Catherine Bernard, *City College of New York*; Barbara Bernstein, *Ashland University*; David Bertolotti, *GMI Engineering and Management Institute*; Sarah Burns, *Indiana University*; Carole Calo, *University of Massachusetts*; Roger Churley, *Southwestern College*; George Arnott Civey III; Brian Conley, *Golden West College*; David Cooper, *Butte College*; Shelley Cordulack, *Millikan University*; Jerry Coulter, *James Madison University*; Patricia Craig, *California State University, Fullerton*; Larry Dellolio, *Camden County College*; Beverly Dennis, *Jones County Junior College*; Christina Dinkelacker, *University of Memphis*; Betty Disney, *Cypress College*; Richard T. Doi, *Central Washington University*; Henry Drewal, *Cleveland State University*; Steve Eliot, *Broward Community College*; Robert N. Ewing, *California State University, Fullerton*; Kathy Flores, *New Mexico State University*; Elisabeth Flynn, *Longwood College*; Leonard Folgarait, *Vanderbilt University*; Lynn Galbraith, *University of Nebraska*; Douglas George, *University of New Mexico*; Larry Gleeson, *University of North Texas*; Dwaine Greer, *University of Arizona*; Paul Grootkerk, *Mississippi State University*; Janis Hardy, *Georgia College*; Sharon K. Hopson; Susan Jackson, *Marshall University*; Ralph Jacobs, *Mankato State University*; Andrew Jendrzejewski, *Vincennes University*; Rebecca Jones, *University of Texas—Pan American*; Soo Yun Kang, *Chicago State University*; John Keller, *Harding University*; Karen Kietzman, *College of St.Francis*; Jan Koot, *California State University, Long Beach*; Cher Krause, *West Texas A&M University*; Nell Lafaye, *University of South Carolina*; Pamela Lee, *Washington State University*; Anne Lisca, *Santa Fe Community College*; Robert Llewellyn, *Frostburg State University*; Kathleen Lobley, *Butler University*; Carolyn Loeb, *Central Michigan University*; Walter Martin, *Concordia University*; James May, *University of Nebraska*; Robert McGrath, *Dartmouth College*; Timothy McNiven, *Ohio State University*; Lynn Metcalf, *St. Cloud State University*; Joseph Molinaro, *Broward Community College*; Tim Morris, *University of Central Arkansas*; Lois Myuskens-Parrott, *Richland College*; Susan Nelson, *Indiana University*; Jo Anne Nix, *Georgia College*; Christie Nuell, *Middle Tennessee State University*; Pamela Patton; Lawrence Rakovan, *University of Southern Maine*; Helen Phillips, *University of Central Arkansas*; Robbie Reid, *Foothill College*; Dominic Ricciotti, *Winona State University*; John C. Riordan, *State University of New York, College at Potsdam*; Isabelle Sabau, *Northern Illinois University*; Diego Sanchez, *Virginia Union University*; Kathleen Schulz, *Raritan Valley Community College*; Barbara Kerr Scott, *Cameron University*; Claire Selkurt, *Mankato State University*; John Shaak, *California State University, Long Beach*; Michael J. Smith, *Southern Illinois University*; Ray Sonnema, *Georgia Southern University*; Sally Struthers, *Sinclair Community College*; Sandra Swenson, *University of Texas—Pan American*; Sharon Tetley, *Washington State Univer-*

sity; Thomas Turpin, *University of Arkansas*; Donald Van Horn, *Marshall University*; Barbara von Barghahn, *George Washington University*; Randy Wassell, *Colorado State University*; Kenneth Weedman, *Cumberland College*; Rochelle Weinstein, *Borough of Manhattan Community College of the City University of New York*; and Salli Zimmerman, *Nassau Community College*.

Mark Getlein

Gilbert's

LIVING WITH ART

PART ONE

INTRODUCTION

1.1 Brancusi's studio, as reconstructed 1977–90
at the Musée National d'Art Moderne, Centre Georges Pompidou, Paris.

CHAPTER 1

Living with Art

Our simplest words are often the deepest in meaning: birth, kiss, flight, dream. The sculptor Constantin Brancusi spent his life searching for forms as simple and pure as those words—forms that seem to have existed forever, outside of time. Born a peasant in a remote village in Romania, he spent most of his adult life in Paris, where he lived in a single small room adjoining a skylit studio. Upon his death in 1957, Brancusi willed the contents of his studio to the French government, which eventually re-created the studio itself in a museum (**1.1**).

Near the center of the photograph are three versions of an idea Brancusi called *Endless Column*. Pulsing upward with great energy, the columns seem as though they could go on forever. Perhaps they *do* go on forever, and we can see only part of them. Directly in front of the shortest, rightmost column, a sleek, horizontal marble form looking something like a slender submarine seems to hover over a disk-shaped base. Brancusi called it simply *Fish*. It does not depict any particular fish, but rather shows us the idea of something that moves swiftly and freely through the water, the essence of a fish. To either side of the columns are two versions of Brancusi's most famous work, *Bird in Space*. To the left, a version in bronze arches upward against a painted strip of wall; to the right, a ghostly version in white marble stands on a wooden base. Here again the artist portrays not a particular bird, but rather the idea of flight, the feeling of soaring upward. Brancusi said that the work represents "the soul liberated from matter."[1]

A photograph by Brancusi shows another, more mysterious view of *Bird in Space* (**1.2**). Light from a source we cannot see cuts across the work and falls in a sharp diamond shape on the wall behind. The sculpture casts a shadow so strong it seems to have a dark twin. Before it lies a broken, discarded work. The photograph might make you think of the birth of a bird from its shell, or of a perfected work of art arising from numerous failed attempts, or indeed of a soul newly liberated from its material prison.

Brancusi took many photographs of his work, and through them we can see how his sculptures lived in his imagination even after they were finished. He photographed them in varying conditions of light, in multiple locations and combinations, from close up and far away. With each photograph they seem to reveal a different mood, the way people we know reveal different sides of themselves over time.

1.2 Constantin Brancusi. *Bird in Space*. c. 1928–30. Gelatin silver print, 11¾ × 9⅜".
Musée National d'Art Moderne, Centre Georges Pompidou, Paris.

Living with art, Brancusi's photographs show us, is making art live by letting it engage your attention, your imagination, your intelligence. Few of us, of course, can live with art the way Brancusi did. Yet we can choose to seek out encounters with art, to make it a matter for thought and enjoyment, and to let it live in our imagination.

You probably live already with more art than you think you do. Very likely the walls of your home are decorated with posters, photographs, or even paintings you chose because you find them beautiful or meaningful. The buildings you live and work in, the clothes you wear, the furniture that surrounds you—all were designed by artists in specialized fields. When you notice with pleasure the way the sunlight casts shadows across the front of a building, you have made the architect's work live for a moment by appreciating an effect that he or she prepared for you. We call such an experience an *aesthetic* experience. Aesthetics is the branch of philosophy concerned with the feelings aroused in us by sensory experiences—experiences we have through sight, hearing, taste, touch, and smell. Aesthetics concerns itself with our responses to the natural world and to the world we make, especially the world of art. What art is, how and why it affects us—these are some of the issues that aesthetics addresses.

This book hopes to deepen your pleasure in the aesthetic experience by broadening your understanding of one of the most basic and universal of human activities, making art. It focuses on the Western tradition, by which we mean art as it has been understood and practiced in Europe and in cultures with their roots in European thought, such as the United States. But it also reaches back to consider works created well before Western ideas about art were in place and across to other cultures that have very different traditions of art.

THE IMPULSE FOR ART

What are the origins of art? Where does the urge to make art come from? Is it really, as claimed above, a basic and universal human activity? Before we begin to explore the diversity of the world's art, such basic questions present themselves. For answers, we might begin by looking at some of the oldest works yet discovered, paintings and structures dating from the Stone Ages, near the very beginning of the human experience.

On the afternoon of December 18, 1994, two men and a woman, all experienced cave explorers, were climbing among the rocky cliffs in the Ardèche region of southeastern France. From a small cavity in the rock they felt a draft of air, which they knew often signaled a large cavern within. After clearing away some rocks and debris, they were able to squeeze through a narrow channel into what appeared to be an enormous underground room, its floor littered with animal bones. Pressing farther into the cave, the explorers played their lights on the walls and made an astonishing discovery: the walls were covered with drawings and paintings (**1.3**)—more than three hundred images as they eventually found—depicting rhinoceroses, horses, bears, reindeer, lions, bison, mammoths, and others, as well as numerous outlines of human hands.

It was evident that the paintings were extremely old and that the cave had remained untouched, unseen by humans, since prehistoric times. The explorers agreed to name the site after the one in their number who had led them to it, Jean-Marie Chauvet, so it is called the Chauvet cave. What they did not realize until months later, after radiocarbon testing had accurately dated the paintings, was that they had just pushed back the history of art by several *thousand* years. The Chauvet images were made about 30,000 B.C.E. and are the oldest paintings we know. The paintings date from a time known

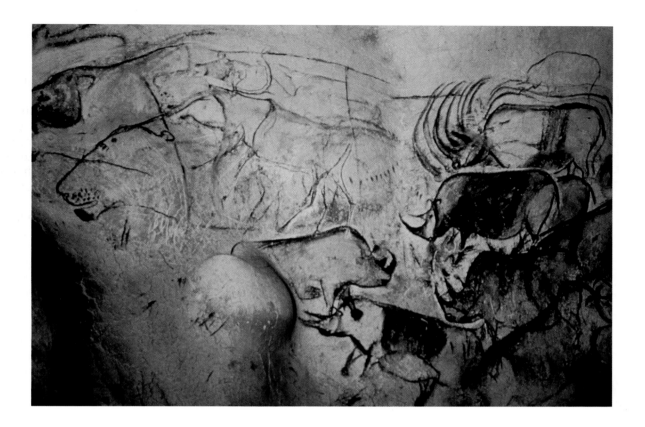

as the Upper Paleolithic Period, which simply means the latter part of the Old Stone Age. Archaeologists have formed some tentative conclusions about how the paintings were done. Pigments of red and yellow ochre, a natural earth substance, along with black charcoal, could have been mixed with animal fat and painted onto the walls with a reed brush. In powdered form, the same materials probably were mouth-blown onto the surface through hollow reeds. Many of the images are engraved, or scratched, into the rock.

More intriguing is the question of *why* the cave paintings were made, why their creators paid such meticulous attention to detail, why they did their work so far underground. The paintings clearly were not meant to embellish a dwelling space. The cave artists must have lived—slept, cooked their meals, mated, and raised their children—much nearer to the mouths of these caves, close to daylight and fresh air. Until the Chauvet cave was discovered, many experts believed that ancient cave paintings were done for magical assistance in the hunt, to ensure success in bringing down game animals. But several of the animals depicted at Chauvet, including lions and rhinos and bears, were not in the customary diet of early peoples. Perhaps the artists wished to establish some kind of connection with these wild beasts, but we cannot know for sure.

Art historians often point to cave paintings as the earliest art. Archaeologists disagree. They maintain that the concept of art arose much later and prefer to focus on the paintings as evidence of early human culture. Are the images art? It really doesn't matter. The most important and amazing thing is that they are images at all. The ability to make images is uniquely human. We do it so naturally and so constantly that we take it for granted. We make them with our hands, and we make them with our minds. Lying out on the grass, for example, you may amuse yourself by finding images in the shifting clouds, now a lion, now an old woman. Are the images really there? We know that a cloud is just a cloud, yet the image is certainly there, because we see it. Our experience of the images we make is the same. We know that a drawing is just markings on a surface, a newspaper photograph merely

1.3 Left section of the "Lion Panel," Chauvet cave, Ardèche Valley, France. c. 25,000–17,000 B.C.E.

1.4 Stonehenge. c. 2000–1500 B.C.E. Height of stones, 13′6″. Salisbury Plain, England.

dots, yet we recognize them as images that reflect our world, and we identify with them. The experience was the same for Paleolithic image-makers as it is for us. All images may not be art, but our ability to make them is one place where art begins.

The contemporary British sculptor Anthony Caro has said that "all art is basically Paleolithic or Neolithic: either the urge to smear soot and grease on cave walls or pile stone on stone."[2] By "soot and grease" Caro means the cave paintings. With "the urge to pile stone on stone" he has in mind one of the most impressive and haunting works to survive from the Stone Ages, the structure in the south of England known as Stonehenge (**1.4**). Today much ruined through time and vandalism, Stonehenge at its height consisted of several concentric circles of **megaliths,** very large stones, surrounded in turn by a circular ditch. It was built in several phases over many centuries, beginning around 3100 B.C.E. The tallest circle, visible in the photograph here, originally consisted of thirty gigantic upright stones capped with a continuous ring of horizontal stones. Weighing some 50 tons each, the stones were quarried many miles away, hauled to the site, and laboriously shaped by blows from stone hammers until they fit together.

Many theories have been advanced about why Stonehenge was built and what purpose it served. In the 20th century it was discovered that Stonehenge is oriented to the movements of the sun, and one American astronomer went so far as to propose that the monument served as a sort of calendar, measuring out the year and even predicting eclipses. Most experts remain skeptical of such elaborate theories. It seems likely that the site was used as a setting for public rituals or ceremonies, but beyond that nothing is certain. Perhaps, as Caro suggests, Stonehenge can do no more than stand as an example of how old and how basic is our urge to create meaningful order and form, to structure our world so that it reflects our ideas. This is another place where art begins.

Stonehenge was erected in the Neolithic era, or New Stone Age. The Neolithic era is named for the new kinds of stone tools that were invented, but it also saw such important advances as the domestication of animals and crops and the development of the technology of pottery, as people discovered that fire could harden certain kinds of clay. With pottery, storage jars, food bowls, and all sorts of other practical objects came into being. Yet much of the world's oldest pottery seems to go far beyond purely practical needs (**1.5**). This elegant stemmed cup was formed around 2000 B.C.E. in what is now eastern China. Eggshell-thin and exceedingly fragile, it could not have held much of anything and would have tipped over easily. In other words, it isn't practical. Instead, great care and skill have gone into making it pleasing to the eye. Here is a third place we might turn to for the origins of art—the urge to explore the aesthetic possibilities of new technologies. What are the limits of clay, the early potters must have wondered. What can be done with it? Scholars believe such vessels were created for ceremonial use. They were probably made in limited quantity for members of an elite group. This use of fine objects to signal or support social distinctions is also bound up in the history of art.

To construct images and forms that carry meaning, to create order and structure, to explore aesthetic possibilities—these characteristics seem to be part of our nature as human beings. From them, art has grown. In our society, art has long been made by specialists, people we call artists, just as medicine is practiced by doctors and bridges are designed by engineers. Yet as we have seen, the urge toward visual expression is part of being human and common to us all. Children, for example, come readily and naturally to making art. In 1989, over seventy-five children joined forces to paint a mural they called *Calle de Sueños (Dream Street)* on the blank wall of a Post Office in the East Harlem section of New York (**1.6**). The children ranged in age from five to fifteen, and most of them were homeless, living in city shelters or welfare hotels. Their mural project was supported by New York artist Brookie Maxwell, who had founded the Creative Arts Workshop for Homeless Children.

The children were as free with their colors and forms as with their dreams. A magical Oz-like urban landscape fills the mural, its buildings cheerfully topsy-turvy, its sunny colors as far as possible from the drab surroundings of the real inner city. And what were their dreams for the Calle de Sueños? The dreams of these children were straightforward: McDonald's; unlimited skateboards; free apartments, some meant only for children; no bedtime; no drug dealers; everyone friendly and happy; and, most poignant for these young artists, "Daddy Home." The children cannot create the world they dream of in real life, but they readily embrace the impulse to create that world in art.

Many adults, too, have felt compelled to create against all odds, even though they may have known very little about this concept we call art. James Hampton worked for most of his adult life as a janitor for the federal government, yet for many years he labored secretly on an extraordinary work

1.5 (left) *Stemmed vessel*, from Weifang, Shandong, China. Neolithic period, Longshan culture, c. 2000 B.C.E. Black pottery, thin biscuit; height 10½".

1.6 (right) *Calle de Sueños (Dream Street)*. 1989. Mural, mixed media; 100 × 50′.
East 124th Street, New York. Project of the Creative Arts Workshop in affiliation with Sheltering Arms Childrens Services 1989.

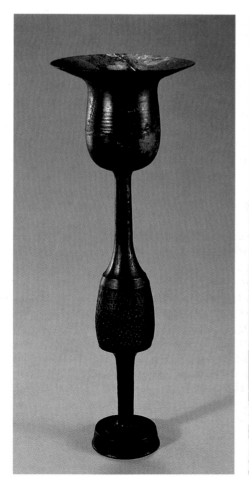

1.7 James Hampton. *Throne of the Third Heaven of the Nations' Millennium General Assembly.* c. 1950–64. Gold and silver aluminum foil, colored kraft paper and plastic sheets over wood, paperboard, and glass. 180 pieces, 105 × 27 × 14¹/₂′.
National Museum of American Art, Smithsonian Institution, Washington, D.C.

called *Throne of the Third Heaven of the Nations' Millennium General Assembly* (**1.7**). Discovered after Hampton's death in a garage that he had rented, *Throne of the Third Heaven of the Nations' Millennium General Assembly* represents his vision of and preparation for the Second Coming as described in the biblical Book of Revelation. Humble objects and cast-off furniture are here transformed by silver and gold foil to create a dazzling setting ready to receive those who will sit in judgment at the end of the world. Over the central throne are the words *Fear Not.*

We do not know whether Hampton considered himself an artist. He made art, and that is what matters. In our desire to classify things, we might call Hampton's work an example of folk or naive art, art made by people who are self-taught, who have not studied art techniques, art history, and art theory. In other words, they have not pursued the path that society has laid down for becoming a professional artist. Folk artists can produce works of great power and imagination, however, and the lines of division between folk art and other kinds of art are by no means clear. More important, folk artists fulfill the same roles in society as trained artists, though they may intend their art for a different audience. We look next at these roles.

WHAT DO ARTISTS DO?

Throughout history artists have served many functions, but their value and importance to society have remained basically the same. To begin with, artists fulfill practical roles, designing virtually every structure or object that is built or made. Today these activities are largely carried out by artists with specialized training such as industrial designers, architects, and fashion designers. Artists who work with images—painters, sculptors, and photographers—also fulfill practical roles, along with other roles that are less practical but perhaps even more valuable.

First, artists *record and commemorate.* They create images that help us remember the present after it slips into the past, that keep us in mind of our history, and that will speak of our times to the future. Illustrated here is a segment from a long painting that portrays episodes from a Chinese emperor's tour of the southern provinces of his realm in the year 1689 (**1.8**). Upon his return to the capital, the emperor commissioned a well-known painter named Wang Hui to oversee a team of court artists in creating a pictorial record of the trip. The result was a truly monumental work, a set of 12 scrolls, each around 58 feet long, recreating the journey in minute detail. In the segment illustrated here, the emperor (in the foreground beneath the yellow parasol) visits an important local shrine. For the emperor, the scrolls underscored the importance of his visit and served as an official visual record of it. For us hundreds of years later, the visit has very little importance. Instead, we are enchanted to find the past come to life before our eyes with a wealth of visual detail that no written account could match.

A second function artists perform is to *give tangible form to the unknown*. They portray what cannot be seen with the eyes or events that can only be imagined. An anonymous Indian sculptor of the 11th century gave tangible form to the Hindu god Shiva in his guise as Nataraja, Lord of the Dance (**1.9**). Encircled by flames, Shiva dances the destruction and rebirth of the world, the end of one cycle of time and the beginning of another. The figure's four arms communicate the complexity of this cosmic moment. In one hand, Shiva holds the small drum whose beat summons up creation; in another hand, he holds the flame of destruction. A third hand points at his raised foot, beneath which worshipers may seek refuge, while a fourth hand is raised with its palm toward the viewer, a gesture that means "fear not."

1.8 (above) Wang Hui and anonymous court artists. *The "Southern Tour" of the Kangxi emperor in 1689*, detail. c. 1693. Handscroll, ink and color on silk; 2'3" × 73'. Palace Museum, Beijing.

1.9 (left) *Shiva Nataraja (Lord of the Dance)*. 11th century. Bronze, height 43⅞". The Cleveland Museum of Art.

Looking at the statue in a museum, we can appreciate the sculptor's skill at handling this complicated pose so gracefully. When the statue was in use, however, it would have been almost completely hidden by silks and flowers draped about it—offerings to the deity who was believed to have taken up residence within. It is useful to remember that much of the art we find in museums originally played a direct and vital role in people's lives.

A third function artists perform is to *give tangible form to feelings and ideas*. These may be the artist's own personal feelings and ideas, but they may also be those of a larger group or culture. The statue of Shiva we just looked at, for example, gives tangible form to ideas about the cyclical nature of time that are part of the religious culture of Hinduism. The artist probably shared those ideas, but we cannot know for sure. Our society has come to place great importance on the individual, and we take it for granted that self-expression is fundamental to artistic creation, but this has not always been so. Throughout much of history, artists have expressed feelings and ideas on behalf of others.

In *The Starry Night* (**1.10**), Vincent van Gogh labored to create a visual equivalent for his feelings as he stood on the outskirts of a small village in France and stared up at the stars. Surrounded by halos of radiating light, the stars have an exaggerated, urgent presence, as though each one were a brilliant sun. A great wave or whirlpool rolls across the sky—a cloud, perhaps, or some kind of cosmic energy. The landscape, too, seems to roll on in waves like an ocean. A tree in the foreground writhes upward toward the stars as though answering their call. In the distance, a church spire points upward as well. Everything is in turbulent motion. Nature seems alive, communicating in its own language while the village sleeps.

Fourth and finally, artists enable us to *experience a way of seeing different than our own*. Through art we can live more than one life, see through more than one pair of eyes. Artists show us something new in the world. Like self-expression, newness and originality are valued very highly today in our thinking about art. Yet artists in other cultures and at other times would not necessarily have understood such ideas. For them, the goal of art was to continue the forms of the past.

1.10 Vincent van Gogh. *The Starry Night*. 1889. Oil on canvas, 29 × 36¼".
The Museum of Modern Art, New York.

VINCENT VAN GOGH
1853–1890

T HE APPEAL OF Van Gogh for today's art lovers is easy to understand. A painfully disturbed, tormented man who, in spite of his great anguish, managed to create extraordinary art. An intensely private, introspective man who wrote eloquently about art and about life. An erratic, impulsive man who had the self-discipline to construct an enormous body of work in a career that lasted only a decade.

Vincent van Gogh was born in the town of Groot-Zundert, in Holland, the son of a Dutch Protestant minister. His early life was spent in various roles, including those of theological student and lay preacher among the miners of the region. Not until the age of twenty-seven did he begin to take a serious interest in art, and then he had but ten years to live. In 1886 he went to stay in Paris with his brother, Theo, an art dealer who was always his closest emotional connection. In Paris Vincent became aware of the new art movements and incorporated aspects of them into his own style, especially by introducing light, brilliant colors into his palette.

Two years later Van Gogh left Paris for the southern city of Arles. There he was joined briefly by the painter Paul Gauguin, with whom Van Gogh hoped to work closely, creating perfect art in a pure atmosphere of self-expression. However, the two artists quarreled, and, apparently in the aftermath of one intense argument, Van Gogh cut off a portion of his ear and had it delivered to a prostitute.

Soon after that bizarre incident, Van Gogh realized that his instability had gotten out of hand, and he committed himself to an asylum, where—true to form—he continued to work prolifically at his painting. Most of the work we admire so much was done in the last two and a half years. Vincent (as he always signed himself) received much sympathetic encouragement during those years, both from his brother and from an unusually perceptive doctor and art connoisseur, Dr. Gachet, whom he painted several times. Nevertheless, his despair deepened, and in July of 1890 he shot himself to death.

Vincent's letters to his brother Theo represent a unique document in the history of art. They reveal a sensitive, intelligent artist pouring out his thoughts to one especially capable of understanding. In 1883, while still in Holland, he wrote to Theo: "In my opinion, I am often *rich as Croesus,* not in money, but (though it doesn't happen every day) rich, because I have found in my work something to which I can devote myself heart and soul, and which gives inspiration and significance to life. Of course my moods vary, but there is an average of serenity. I have a sure *faith* in art, a sure confidence that it is a powerful stream, which bears a man to harbour, though he himself must do his bit too; and at all events I think it such a great blessing, when a man has found his work, that I cannot count myself among the unfortunate. I mean, I may be in certain relatively great difficulties, and there may be gloomy days in my life, but I shouldn't want to be counted among the unfortunate nor would it be correct."[3]

Vincent van Gogh. *Self-Portrait,* 1889.
Oil on canvas, 25$\frac{1}{2}$ × 21$\frac{1}{2}$".
Musée d'Orsay, Paris.

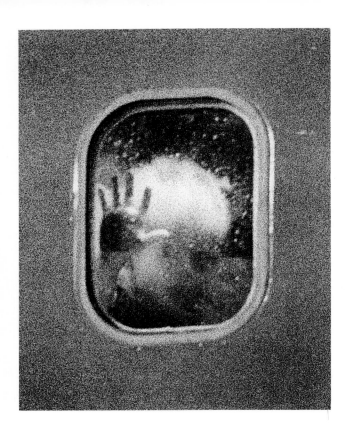

1.11 John Schabel. *Untitled (Passenger #3).* 1994–95. Toned gelatin silver print. 23¼ × 19¼". Courtesy the artist.

Newness and originality can make themselves felt in subtle ways as well as obvious ones. John Schabel found newness with a telephoto lens (**1.11**). Standing in an airport lounge on a drizzly day, he zoomed in on distant planes waiting to take off, photographing the passengers on board through the tiny airplane windows. Enlarged, the photographs have a grainy quality, as though they were made of gray mist. We have never quite seen ourselves this way before, so vulnerable and transitory. The technologies of air travel and photography made the view possible, but it took an artist to uncover its newness and to bring it to us.

CREATIVITY

The four works we have just looked at—Wang Hui's scroll, the figure of Shiva Nataraja, Van Gogh's *The Starry Night,* and John Schabel's *Untitled (Passenger #3)*—exist because an artist created them. Each work shows a different use for creativity. Wang Hui imaginatively reconstructed a journey that he did not take part in. The anonymous Indian sculptor made a traditional pose seem fresh and new. Van Gogh found a visual equivalent for his feelings as he looked at the night sky. John Schabel turned common technology to an uncommon purpose, and in doing so showed us something new.

Creativity is a word that comes up often when talking about art, but what is creativity exactly? Are we born with it? Can it be learned? Can it be lost? Are artists more creative than other people? If so, how did they get that way? Many writers and educators have tried to analyze creativity and determine what makes a person creative.[4] While the exact nature of creativity remains elusive, there is general agreement that creative people tend to possess certain traits, including:

- *Sensitivity*—heightened awareness of what one sees, hears, and touches, as well as responsiveness to other people and their feelings.
- *Flexibility*—an ability to adapt to new situations and to see their possibilities; willingness to find innovative relationships.

- *Originality*—uncommon responses to situations and to solving problems.
- *Playfulness*—a sense of humor and ability to experiment freely.
- *Productivity*—the ability to generate ideas easily and frequently, and to follow through on those ideas.
- *Fluency*—a readiness to allow the free flow of ideas.
- *Analytical skill*—a talent for exploring problems, taking them apart, and finding out how things work.
- *Organizational skill*—ability to put things back together in a coherent order.

We might keep this list in mind as we look at Alan Rath's delightful *Hound* (**1.12**). An ordinary wooden packing crate serves as the dog's body. Clearly this is no thoroughbred, just a good old hound dog. We have no trouble understanding that the wheels stand for legs. In fact, they seem better than realistic legs would have been for evoking the swift movement of a hound on the track of a scent. Far ahead of the body, two cathode-ray tubes each display a computer-animated image of a nose. Two noses? The noses seem to serve for eyes as well, which is just the impression we get when we watch a hound at work. Rath's sculpture looks something like a cross between a dog and a vacuum cleaner. But then, a vacuum cleaner also goes along with its nose to the ground, sniffing.

Certainly sensitivity must have made Rath an excellent observer of dogs in the first place. Flexibility, originality, and playfulness allowed him to see that a box could also be a body, and that the contrast between advanced computer technology and parts recycled from a junkyard would make us smile. Productivity and fluency allowed him to see how a dog could come of it all. Analytical and organizational skills enabled him to put the pieces together to make his sculpture.

The profession of artist is not the only one that requires creativity. Scientists, mathematicians, teachers, business executives, doctors, librarians, computer programmers—people in every line of work, if they are any good, look for ways to be creative. Artists occupy a special place in that they have devoted their lives to opening the channels of *visual* creativity.

Can a person become more creative? Almost certainly, if one allows oneself to be. Being creative means learning to trust one's own interests, experiences, and references, and to use them to enhance life and work. Above all, it means discarding rigid notions of what has been or should be in favor of what *could* be. Creativity develops when the eyes and the mind are wide open, and it is as important to looking at art as it is to making it.

1.12 Alan Rath. *Hound*. 1990. Wood, steel, aluminum, electronics, and cathode-ray tubes, 18 × 76 × 26″. Collection Walker Art Center, Minneapolis.

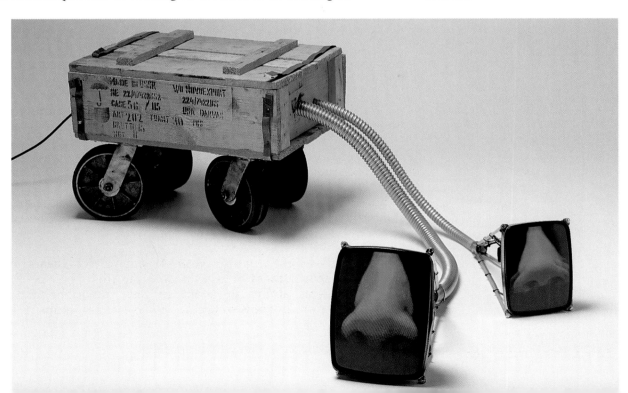

LOOKING AT ART

Art communicates to us primarily through our eyes. We look at art, and we try to find some meaning in the experience. If we are to begin to think about art more seriously, we might do well to become more aware of the process of seeing itself. What is it to look?

Science tells us that seeing is a mode of perception, which is the recognition and interpretation of sensory data—in other words, how information comes in our eyes (ears, nose, taste buds, fingertips), and what we make of it. In visual perception our eyes take in information in the form of light patterns; the brain processes these patterns to give them meaning. The mechanics of perception work much the same way for everyone, yet in a given situation we do not all see the same things. The human eye cannot take in all available visual information. Our world is too complex, and we are constantly bombarded with an incredible range of visual images. To avoid overloading our mental circuits, the brain responds only to that visual information required to meet our needs at one moment.

Suppose you are motoring along a busy street. Your eyes "see" everything, but what does your brain register? If you are the car's driver, you will see the traffic signs and lights, because awareness of such details is necessary. If you are hungry, your attention may be attracted by fast-food signs. If you are looking for a specific address, you will focus on building numbers and block out nearly everything else. It is easier to cope with our complex visual world if we simplify our perceptions and see according to our immediate needs.

In looking at art, we need to revise our habits of looking, for art asks us to take the time to register every detail. Images such as Edward Weston's *Cabbage Leaf* (**1.13**) seem especially made to help restore vision that has become dulled by habit. Gazing at the way the light caresses the gracefully arching leaf, we can almost feel our vision slowing down. As we continue to look, we become conscious of the curved object as a pure form, and not as a thing called "cabbage leaf" at all. It looks perhaps like the foam of a breaking wave, or a ball gown trailing across a lawn. There is surely nothing more common than a leaf of cabbage, and nothing more miraculous than this photograph of one.

1.13 Edward Weston. *Cabbage Leaf.* 1931. Gelatin silver print, 7½ × 9½".
Collection Center for Creative Photography, The University of Arizona, Tucson.

Earlier, we examined the statue of Shiva Nataraja, and the text drew your attention to the meanings of its hands and feet. But did you notice that Shiva stands on the back of a small demon, and that the circle of flames issues from the mouths of two dragons? Did you notice that two famous cartoon mice appear on a billboard in *Calle de Sueños*? That amid the sculptures in Brancusi's studio is a chair he carved for himself? "A picture is something which requires as much knavery, trickery, and deceit as the perpetration of a crime," said the French painter Edgar Degas.[5] We in turn need to be as observant as detectives.

Studies indicate that the brain is often more important than the eyes in determining what each of us sees as we move through the world. The brain's ability to control perception is obvious when we study ambiguous figures, such as the classic one reproduced here (**1.14**). When you first look at this drawing, you may see a white vase. Or you may see two dark profiles. Even after you have been made aware of the two images, you must consciously work at going back and forth between them. You can feel your brain shifting as it organizes the visual information into first one image and then the other. The important thing to remember as you shift your perception back and forth is that the visual image *always stays the same*. It is only your perception that changes.

The vase/profiles drawing is an example of a specific kind of relationship called figure and ground that is fundamental to the way we see. A **figure** is the object we distinguish. The **ground** is the backdrop we see it against. When we select the vase as a figure, it appears to move forward, while the dark ground recedes. We imagine that the ground continues in back of the vase, although we have no evidence for this. When we select the profiles as figures, they in turn seem to come forward and the white ground to recede.

In daily life we negotiate visually by focusing on figures. In looking at images as art, however, we need to be equally aware of both figure and ground. Henri Matisse used simple means to make this clear in *Venus* (**1.15**). Onto a white ground he pasted two cut pieces of paper painted blue. We

1.14 (left) Reversible vase-profiles, after Edgar Rubin.

1.15 (right) Henri Matisse. *Venus*. 1952. Paper painted with gouache, cut and pasted, 39⅞ × 30⅛".
National Gallery of Art, Washington, D.C.

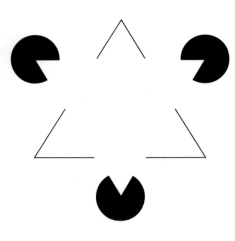

would expect to interpret these blue pieces as the figure, but instead they seem to carve a figure out of the ground itself, a figure of a woman. We watch the transformation, but can't say exactly where or how it occurs. Matisse was aware that every blue shape he pasted down also created a white shape, and he paid equal attention to how both were evolving as he worked. To see art as artists do, we too need to cultivate this way of looking.

If habits of perception can cause us to miss seeing all of what is actually present in a visual field, they can also cause us to see things that aren't there at all. If you look at illustration **1.16,** you will probably see a white triangle. Yet the triangle is not physically present. We see it because of the way the dark lines and circles are arranged. If you cover up the circles, the triangle disappears. It was there only because the brain tends to complete what is implied, supplying missing information to create the order it seeks.

One artist who explores such effects of perception is James Turrell, who makes art with light. We normally think of light as something immaterial that lets us see other things, but Turrell makes us perceive light itself as a substance. His goal is to make viewers conscious of the process of seeing and of the mind's role in it. In *Afrum-Proto* (**1.17**), we perceive a hovering cube of solid light. But the cube is an illusion we create from a carefully calculated shape of brilliant white light projected into a corner. Is the cube there? Like the face in the cloud mentioned earlier, it is there because we see it. We create the work of art by looking.

Joel Shapiro is another artist who plays with our tendency to find images. Made of rectangular units of wood or metal, his sculptures at first glance seem like children's blocks that are about to teeter and fall (**1.18**). Or is that a person? Did the artist mean for us to see a person there or not? What is a person doing projecting from the wall over our heads, attached by one leg? Shapiro's sculptures are like sophisticated stick figures, and as such they can perform all sorts of contortions that actual people could not manage. They can be touching or funny or sad or harrowing, even as all the while they hover on the verge of being nothing more than a few blocks of wood.

Why should we recognize a human figure in a stack of blocks? It doesn't really look anything like us. In the end, science does not completely understand how we recognize objects. For art, the benefit of our ability is that there are many effective ways to represent the world. In the hands of a skilled artist, blocks can speak to us about the human condition as eloquently as the most realistic sculpture imaginable.

1.16 (above) The triangle that isn't there.

1.17 (below left) James Turrell. *Afrum-Proto*. 1967. Quartz-halogen projection.
Courtesy the artist.

1.18 (below right) Joel Shapiro. *Untitled*. 1998. Oil paint on wood, 21 × 22 × 8″.
Courtesy PaceWildenstein Gallery, New York.

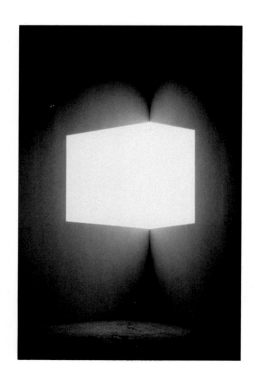

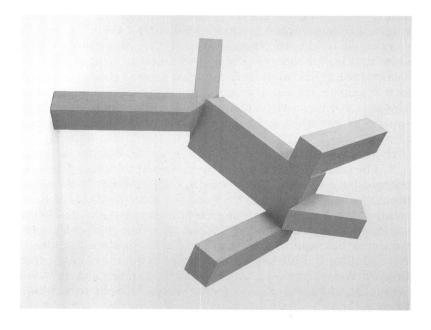

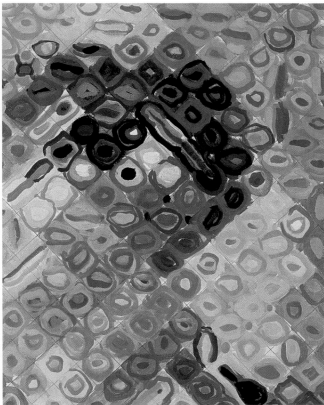

Shapiro's sculpture is, of course, a three-dimensional object. To understand its form completely we would have to walk around it and view it from every angle. The photograph shows only one view and reduces the three dimensions to two. Still, we understand a good deal about the form, for a photograph captures some of the clues we use to perceive objects in depth. We assume, for example, that the entire sculpture is painted in one shade of yellow, despite the fact that the photograph shows many shades. We understand that these shades result from the way the light is falling on the variously angled surfaces, and we use that information to help perceive the sculpture's form.

Taking into account how light reveals form was central to the Western tradition of painting for several hundred years. Today, the painter Chuck Close continues to explore the limits of how we perceive depth in a two-dimensional image. His chosen subject is the human head or, rather, a photograph of a human head, generally the face of someone he knows (**1.19**). His working method is to draw a grid over the photograph, then a grid with the same number of squares over a much larger canvas. He copies or interprets each square of the photograph, one at a time, ignoring the larger image and focusing solely on the information in the square. The image results as a byproduct of this activity. Over the years, Close has used progressively larger squares in his grids, and he has experimented with different kinds of marks to fill the squares. In *Bill* the grid is set diagonally, and each square is filled with loosely brushed lines, circles, dots, and squares in pure colors.

The size of Close's paintings—*Bill* is 6 feet in height—ensures that viewers will have the experience of confronting them from near enough to see nothing but a flat surface of colored markings (**1.20**). As they step back, a solid, three-dimensional image seems to emerge. "The idea was to make something that was so large that it could not readily be seen as an image," the artist has said, "and force the viewer to scan the image . . . as if they were Gulliver's Lilliputians crawling over the surface of the face."[6] Like Edward Weston, whose photograph of a cabbage leaf opened this discussion (see 1.13), Close wants to slow our vision down by presenting us with something we have to puzzle out, so that we take the time to truly see.

1.19 (left) Chuck Close. *Bill*. 1990. Oil on canvas, 6 × 5′. Courtesy PaceWildenstein Gallery, New York.

1.20 (right) *Bill*, detail.

DOROTHY AND HERBERT VOGEL

ART COLLECTORS ARE RICH. Art collectors are glamorous. Art collectors are members of the upper classes or the nobility, or else they are important business leaders. Everybody knows these facts, but apparently nobody bothered to inform Dorothy and Herbert Vogel of New York City. The Vogels—she a retired librarian, he a retired postal worker—are not rich, and their lifestyle is modest. They are the sort of people one can't help but call "ordinary." One fact about the Vogels is undeniably *extra*ordinary: They have been collecting art on an ambitious scale for more than thirty-five years.

Everybody in the fashionable art world of New York, it seems, knows the unfashionable Herbert and Dorothy. The Vogels attend as many openings as possible, they regularly visit several artists' studios, they study the art seriously—and they buy. Their small Manhattan apartment eventually became crammed to the ceilings with some seventeen hundred original works of art, emphasizing Minimal, Conceptual, and Postmodern artists. This collection was acquired almost entirely on Herbert's salary from the post office. Dorothy's income pays the couple's living expenses.

The odds against two such . . . well . . . *ordinary* people becoming important art collectors seem formidable.

Herbert, the son of a tailor, grew up in New York and started working for the post office after high school and the army. Dorothy, born in Elmira, New York, earned a master's degree in library science and took a librarian's job in Brooklyn. The couple met at a singles' party, dated for a year, then married in 1962. Their plunge into the art world was led by Herbert, who had taken some art courses at New York University, had made friends with young artists, and aspired to become an artist himself. Soon Herbert got Dorothy involved, and the two decided collecting would be more to their taste.

The Vogels began slowly. Rushing from their respective jobs in the evening, they would rendezvous in a subway station, then go off to a gallery to study the art and consider possible purchases. At first, dealers and gallery habitués wondered, "Who on earth *are* those people?" The Vogels do not look like one's usual image of collectors. Soon, however, their informed and persistent buying attracted attention; soon their appearance in a gallery created a stir. As their collection grew, so did their reputation. Artists accept them as friends because their love of the work is so sincere.

No doubt an important factor in the Vogels' success has been their single-mindedness. Dorothy and Herbert have no children, though they have turtles, fish, and cats in quantity. Nearly all their time is devoted to the collection. They are shrewd buyers, stretching their limited budget to the utmost.

The value of the Vogels' collection was demonstrated in 1992, when the National Gallery of Art in Washington announced it would acquire the collection as part purchase, part donation. Once the art was moved out for inventory, the Vogels had their apartment painted for the first time in decades—and went back to buying art.

Most people pretty much live out the lives they were born to, but Herbert and Dorothy Vogel obviously are made of stronger stuff. The postal worker and the librarian—together they invented a special life for themselves, a life with art. Seeing them, talking with them, one cannot doubt they are enjoying every moment of it.

Collectors Dorothy and Herbert Vogel at the exhibition "From Minimal to Conceptual Art: Works from the Dorothy and Herbert Vogel Collection," at the National Gallery of Art, May 29 through November 27, 1994.

STUDYING ART

We can take great pleasure in merely looking at art, just as we take pleasure in the view of a distant mountain range or watching the sun set over the ocean. But art, unlike nature, is a human creation. It is one of the many ways we express ourselves and attempt to communicate. A work of art is the product of human intelligence, and we can meet it with our own intelligence on equal footing. This is where study comes in.

The understanding of process—the *how*—often contributes quite a lot to our appreciation of art. Parts Three and Four of this book are largely concerned with this issue. If you understand why painting in watercolor may be different from painting in oil, why clay responds differently to the artist's hands than does wood or glass, why a stone building has different structural needs than one made of poured concrete—you will have a richer appreciation of the artist's expression.

Knowing the place of a work of art in history—what went before and came after—can also deepen your understanding. Artists learn to make art by studying the achievements of the past and observing the efforts of their contemporaries. They adapt ideas to serve their own needs and then bequeath those ideas to future generations of artists. The more you know about this living current of artistic energy, the more interesting each work of art will become. For example, Matisse assumed that his audience would know that Venus was the ancient Roman goddess of love. But he also hoped that they would be familiar with one Venus in particular, a famous Greek statue known as the *Venus de Milo* (see 2.4). Knowing the Greek work deepens our pleasure in Matisse's version, for we see that in "carving" his Venus out of a sheet of white paper he evokes the way a long-ago sculptor carved her out of a block of white marble.

An artist may create a specific work for any of a thousand reasons. An awareness of the *why* may give some insight as well. Looking at Van Gogh's *The Starry Night* (see 1.10), it might help you to know that Van Gogh was intrigued by the belief that people journeyed to a star after their death, and that there they continued their lives. "Just as we take the train to get to Tarascon or Rouen," he wrote in a letter, "we take death to reach a star."[7] The tree that rises so dramatically in the foreground of the painting is a cypress, which has often served as a symbol of both death and eternal life. This knowledge might help you to understand why Van Gogh felt so strongly about the night sky, and what his painting might have meant to him.

But no matter how much you study, Van Gogh's painting will never mean for you exactly what it meant for him, nor should it. An artist's work grows from a lifetime of experiences, thoughts, and emotions; no one else can duplicate them exactly. Great works of art hold many meanings. The greatest of them seem to speak anew to each generation and to each attentive observer. The most important thing is that some works of art come to mean something for *you*, that your own experiences, thoughts, and emotions find a place in them, for then you will have made them live.

CHAPTER 2

What Is Art?

When Auguste Rodin exhibited *The Age of Bronze* in Paris in 1877, his public had no doubt that it was art (**2.1**). The work was clearly a sculpture, a category of art. It was lifelike, faithfully mirroring the appearances of the natural world, which is what art was supposed to do. It was made of bronze, which was considered a "noble" material and thus worthy of art. It depicted the human form, which was held to be the most elevated subject for sculpture. It also had an excellent pedigree: viewers would certainly have recognized Rodin's debt to Michelangelo, especially his *Dying Slave* (see 11.22).

Yet the critics weren't sure they liked it. Why? For one thing, it looked a little *too* lifelike. People suspected Rodin of taking a mold of an actual person instead of creating the work himself. Worse, they couldn't tell what it meant, and they liked art that sent a clear message. In fact, Rodin had originally conceived a clearer work. At an earlier stage the figure had held a spear in its left hand and was called *The Vanquished*. Rodin had intended it as a tribute to the people of France, who had recently suffered defeat in a traumatic war on their home soil. Yet at some point Rodin realized that he wanted to send a more universal message, so he took away the spear and retitled the statue. Viewers would have understood the new title easily: the Bronze Age was one of the "four ages of man," the one in which injustice first entered the world and warfare began. It didn't matter. Critics still found the statue ambiguous, and that made them uneasy.

The assumptions about art that informed Rodin's world had been in place for several hundred years, but they would not last much longer. The 20th century saw radical changes in Western thinking about art, as artists sought out new subjects, new materials, and new forms of expression. The question "What is art?" became itself a subject for art. When Roni Horn exhibited *Thicket No. 2* in 1990, her public also had no doubt that it was art (**2.2**). But none of the criteria Rodin's public took for granted applied anymore. The work is not in a noble material, nor does it depict the human form. In fact, it does not seem to depict anything at all. It just *is*. It may not even be useful to call it a sculpture. *Thicket No. 2* evokes William Blake's famous poem "The Tiger," which begins, "Tiger, Tiger burning bright / In the forests of the night." The poem asks the disturbing question of whether the

2.1 Auguste Rodin. *The Age of Bronze*. 1875–77. Bronze, height 6'.
Albright-Knox Art Gallery, Buffalo, New York.

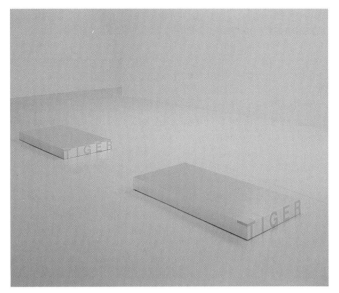

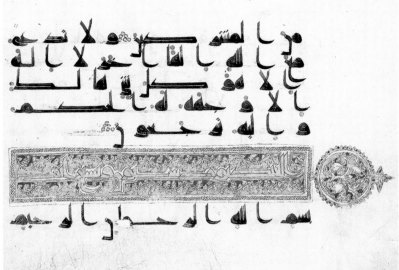

same God who made innocence could have made evil, and whether He took pleasure in it. Isolated on the floor in an otherwise empty white room, the two boxlike units have a menacing presence. The words seem to glow, burning bright, as the poem says.

The realization that written words are also images was new to Western art in the 20th century. Several non-Western cultures, however, elevated the written word to the status of art long ago. In the religious culture of Islam, for example, **calligraphy,** beautiful writing, is considered the most important of the arts (**2.3**). This is because the Qur'an, the holy book of Islam, is believed to be the direct, unmediated word of God. Since God's revelations were made in Arabic, the Arabic language itself became an object of attention and reverence. Styles of writing were codified according to strict rules. The page here, for example, is in a script style called Kufic. Calligraphers studied for years to achieve its spare and dignified rhythms.

People have considered different things to be art at different times and in different places. What distinguishes our experience of art today is that for us, all of those times and places have run together. Visiting a large museum you are likely to see on display works that come literally from all over the world and cover a time span of thousands of years. Each work is the product of an artist working within a specific culture at a specific historical moment, and thus each one answers to different assumptions about what art is. Some may not have been considered art in their day at all, but have had that status conferred on them by their presence in a museum, an institution which itself grows out of modern Western ideas about art. Furthermore, the art of our own time has become so diverse that if you were to visit all the galleries in a major city, you would be hard pressed to come up with a definition that covers everything you would see.

No wonder, then, that today the question of what is art and what is not can seem especially confusing. Yet *art* as a concept in Western thought has always been problematic. Its development has been neither clear, nor logical, nor consistent. During the Middle Ages, the formative period of European culture, *art* was used in roughly the same sense as *craft*. Both had to do with practical skill. Forging a sword, painting a picture, carving a cabinet—all of these were considered art. Beginning around 1500, during the period known as the Renaissance, painting, sculpture, and architecture came

2.2 (left) Roni Horn. *Thicket No. 2.* 1989–90. Plate aluminum with epoxy resin inlay, two units; 4¼ × 25¾ × 51½″ each.
Courtesy Matthew Marks Gallery, New York.

2.3 (right) Leaf from a Qur'an. Iraq(?), before 911. Ink, colors, and gold on vellum.
The Pierpont Morgan Library, New York.

to be seen as more elevated forms of art. Their prestige was such that the word *art* gradually attached exclusively to them, while other skilled activities became known as craft. During the 18th century, painting and sculpture were grouped together with music, dance, and poetry (and sometimes landscape gardening) as the *fine arts* on the principle that they were similar kinds of activities—activities that had no function other than to be beautiful or expressive. At the same time, the philosophical field of aesthetics came into being and began to ask questions: What is art? How can we tell if an image is art or not? Are we justified in applying our concept of art to other cultures? Can we apply it backward to earlier works in our own culture? What is the correct way to appreciate and understand art? Are there objective criteria for judging art?

Many answers have been proposed, but the fact that philosophers still debate them should tell us that the questions are not easy. This book will not give any definitive answers. Rather, it will present you with a broad range of works from the past that have been understood as art, and also with works by living artists that have been accepted as art by many people interested in art today. This exposure will broaden your understanding of the things that art has been and may help you to think more clearly about the most important question of all, "What is art for *me*?"

In trying to understand whether something is art or not, there are a number of questions we are likely to ask ourselves. Among the most frequent are, Who made it? Is it beautiful? Does it depict appearances faithfully? What does it mean? Such questions raise interesting issues about the nature of art and the value systems used to judge artistic quality. They also reveal some assumptions that most of us bring to art, assumptions based in ideas that we have inherited from the various uses of the word over the centuries. This chapter examines each question in turn.

ART AND THE ARTIST

Some artists' names are familiar to the public at large. Picasso. Michelangelo. Rembrandt. Leonardo da Vinci. Van Gogh. Mention any one of them, and your listener's brain will probably register "great artist." It follows, therefore, that any work made by one of these people must be "great art"—or, at the very least, unquestionably art. For those with a broader education or interest, the list of "genuine" artists would be much longer. Whether for good or ill, the verdict on "Is this art?" has much to do with another question: Who made it?

One of the most famous works in the Western tradition is the *Aphrodite of Melos* (**2.4**), popularly known as the *Venus de Milo* (Venus was the Roman equivalent of the Greek goddess Aphrodite). The ancient Greeks envisioned their gods in perfected and idealized human form. As the goddess of love, beauty, and fertility, Aphrodite was commonly portrayed as a sensuous nude. Here, her twisting pose may be explained by the theory that her missing arms once held a shield propped up on her raised knee. She would have been admiring her own reflection in it as in a mirror, her draperies slipping provocatively as she contemplated her beauty.

Ancient Greek ideals of beauty exerted a profound influence on later Western art, and the *Aphrodite of Melos* is one of the most important examples to have come down to us of an idealized female form. Who made it? We do not know. Artists in ancient Greece could become quite famous, and many names have survived, just not this one. Much of the world's art, especially art from the past, is anonymous. The names of the artists have been lost. It is useful to remember that we can consider a work to be art, and even great art, without knowing who made it.

2.4 *Aphrodite of Melos* (also called *Venus de Milo*). c. 150 B.C.E. Marble, height 6′10″.
Musée du Louvre, Paris.

Beginning in the Renaissance—with its admiration for painting, sculpture, and architecture—artists again could become famous. Today, the name of a famous artist functions for many people almost as a brand name, a guarantee of quality. You might hear someone say "That's a Picasso" just the way they would say "That's a BMW." But is everything an artist makes art? Our second female nude is by Edgar Degas (**2.5**). Much rougher than *Aphrodite of Melos*, it could almost be a sketch. In fact, it *is* a sort of sketch. Degas commonly worked out ideas for poses in his paintings by modeling small figures in wax. Toward the end of his life he grew almost totally blind, and modeling came to replace sketching as a way to explore ideas. Hundreds of figures were discovered in his studio after his death, many broken or unfinished or discarded. His executors salvaged as many as they could and had them cast in bronze. Many museums display them.

Are the figures art? Degas did not consider them to be finished works. He never intended to show them. They were merely ways to test out ideas and keep working. On the other hand, everything that comes from the hand of an artist like Degas is interesting, because it lets us see his mind at work. Would we be as interested in these works if they were by someone we had never heard of? Probably not. But the very fact that they have been displayed has caused them to have an influence that Degas could not have foreseen. Younger artists found their rough quality interesting and began to conceive of sculpture in new ways. An artist may not always have the last word on what is seen as art and what is not, even in his own work.

To consider the opposite case, is a work *not* great art because a master artist *didn't* paint it? For generations a painting called *The Polish Rider* (**2.6**) was thought to be a work by Rembrandt and was considered one of the

2.5 (above) Edgar Degas. *Dancer looking at the sole of her right foot.* Bronze, height 19½". Tate Gallery, London.

2.6 (left) Rembrandt(?). *The Polish Rider.* c. 1655. Oil on canvas, 3′10″ × 4′5⅛". The Frick Collection, New York.

jewels of the Frick Collection, a distinguished small museum in New York City. But now Rembrandt's authorship of this painting—and of numerous other paintings—is in question.

Over the years various experts have tried to determine how many genuine Rembrandts there are in the world. Estimates have ranged from a high of 614 to a low of 48. In 1982 a group of five scholars known collectively as the Rembrandt Research Project, based in the artist's home city of Amsterdam, began work trying to find a definitive answer. Using modern scientific methods, considering such subtleties as brushwork, use of colors, and handling of anatomical forms, the R.R.P. studied paintings thought to be by Rembrandt and presented its conclusions. The task is truly daunting, because judgments of quality are always subjective and unreliable. Nevertheless, the R.R.P. persevered, and for many museums and private collectors the news was bad. The R.R.P. "deattributed" their prized Rembrandts.

Among the deattributed paintings, there is no question of forgery or attempt to deceive. With older paintings it is simply difficult to know for sure who painted them and when. A pupil of Rembrandt's, Willem Drost, is now thought a likely candidate as artist of *The Polish Rider*. Whatever the truth, the effect of deattribution is dramatic. Another Rembrandt work, which came up for auction in 1988, was expected to bring ten million dollars. After the R.R.P. turned its thumbs down, the painting was sold for $800,000—or 8 percent of its previous value.[1]

Through all this questioning, we must remember, *the paintings remain the same*. No matter who painted *The Polish Rider*, it is a splendid, masterful picture. Yet crowds of tourists, who once would have elbowed each other to get a glimpse of it, will now pass it by, looking for the "real" Rembrandts.

Why would a painting one day worth ten million dollars the next day be worth only a fraction of that? Clearly there is something contradictory about our attitudes toward art. On the one hand, we claim that art has an intrinsic value. We often talk of this value as spiritual or expressive or communicative or even therapeutic. In this sense we are encouraged to think that art cannot be valued in monetary terms. Yet art is bought and sold all the time, and it often seems indistinguishable from a luxury object such as a rare antique or a one-of-a-kind designer dress. High prices paid for art regularly make headlines, and readers are regularly fascinated or outraged by them. During the 20th century, many artists also became troubled by the relationship between art and money, and by how money defines an audience for art. Robert Watts' *Rembrandt Signature* (**2.7**) is a pointed example of art that responds to these issues. It is nothing more or less than the great painter's

2.7 Robert Watts. *Rembrandt Signature*. 1965/1975. Neon, glass tubing, Plexiglas, transformer, 13 ½ × 44 × 5 ⅛".
Courtesy Robert Watts Studio Archive.

signature, presented in neon as a work of art in its own right. If this is where value really lies, Watts seems to be saying, then this must be the art.

An artist who took a more ambiguous stance toward art, money, and fame was Andy Warhol. Two subjects he returned to again and again were glamour and celebrity—the modern phenomenon of being famous just for being famous, and not for any particular accomplishment. He himself was both a famous artist and a celebrity. *Diamond Dust Shoes* (**2.8**) portrays what for many is a seductive symbol of status and glamour, handmade designer shoes. Like Watts, Warhol seems to be suggesting that if this is what we value, it must be important enough to portray in art. Unlike Watts, however, he presents the painting itself as a luxury object, with lollipop-colored shoes materializing from a gray ground of glittering diamond dust. Is this a criticism of our society or a love letter to it? Art or advertisement? Art *about* advertisement? Warhol was notoriously reticent about what his art might mean. He positioned himself as a kind of reporter, giving us the facts of contemporary life while seeming to make no judgment about them. "If you're not making money with your art, you have to say it's art," he once said. "If you are, you have to say it's something else."[2]

2.8 Andy Warhol. *Diamond Dust Shoes*. 1980. Synthetic polymer paint, diamond dust, and silkscreen ink on canvas. Courtesy The Andy Warhol Foundation for the Visual Arts.

ANDY WARHOL

1928–1987

J. WYETH

WHEN FRIENDS RECALL the most visible and colorful of the Pop artists, they often remark that he was two people. There was Andy Warhol—media celebrity, high priest of commercial and show-business imagery, wearer of bizarre white wigs, leader to an entourage of quirky New York types, maker of sexually explicit cult films. Then there was Andrew Warhola—child of struggling Czech immigrants, devout Roman Catholic, prolific worker, introvert often paralyzed by shyness, adoring son who, as an adult, brought his mother to live with him for twenty years.

Warhol, born Warhola, grew up in Pittsburgh and attended Carnegie Institute of Technology. After graduation in 1949 he moved to New York, where he launched what would become a highly successful career as a commercial artist. Over the next ten years his employers included most of the chic fashion magazines and elegant Fifth Avenue stores, for which he designed advertisements, promotional pieces, and window displays. He was also—ironically, in view of his later adventures—one of the illustrators for the first edition of *Amy Vanderbilt's Complete Book of Etiquette.*

By 1960 the artist and his style had found each other. Warhol, the gifted commercial artist, slipped into Pop, the "fine art" style of commercial images, without missing a beat. For a decade Pop would remain a dominant art wave in the United States, and Warhol sailed on the crest of that wave. The themes with which he is most closely associated appeared repeatedly in prints and paintings: Marilyn Monroe, Elizabeth Taylor, Jackie Kennedy, and, of course, the famous Coke bottles and Campbell's soup cans.

A turning point in Warhol's career occurred in 1963, when the artist moved into a new studio in New York. A friend decorated the entire space in silver paint and aluminum foil, a large group of acquaintances and admirers and hangers-on converged, and thus was born—the Factory. At the Factory Warhol continued his enormous output of prints, paintings, and sculptures. At the Factory he directed the production of many avant-garde (some would say outlandish) films, featuring actors with names like Viva, Ultra Violet, and International Velvet. And at the Factory, in 1968, a woman who announced herself as the founder of SCUM (Society for Cutting Up Men) shot Warhol and nearly killed him.

Many observers felt that Warhol ran out of steam after the shooting, that his art no longer showed the edge and excitement it once had. Nevertheless, he worked steadily, developing his familiar themes and some new ones, until his death at age fifty-eight, of complications following gall bladder surgery.

Warhol often liked to say he was a "machine." He claimed to be devoid of emotion or feeling, just a machine that produced a product, called art, in a place called a Factory. One of his much-quoted statements sums this up. "If you want to know all about Andy Warhol, just look at the surface: of my paintings and films and me, and there I am. There's nothing behind it."[3]

James Wyeth. *Study for a Portrait of Andy Warhol.*
Gouache on paper.
National Portrait Gallery, Washington, D.C.

2.9 Felix Gonzalez-Torres. *Untitled (U.S.A. Today)*. 1990. 300 pounds of candies, individually wrapped in red, silver, and blue cellophane; dimensions variable. Courtesy Andrea Rosen Gallery, New York.

More recently, Felix Gonzalez-Torres responded to the realities of the art market by making art that could be sold but whose purpose was to be given away. Among his works were stacks of large posters. The stack could be viewed as a sculptural form, but viewers were also encouraged to take as many posters as they wanted. The stacks were replenished each night. Other works consisted of heaps of wrapped candies (**2.9**). Like the posters, the candies formed a sculptural mass, but intrepid viewers were not stopped when they grabbed a handful.

What is sold in such works is the right to reproduce the posters and stack them to a specified height, or the right to arrange a specified weight of a certain kind of candy a certain way. Each time they are shown, the works are dispersed yet again among their viewers. Gonzalez-Torres was aware that he was trying to have the best of both worlds, both selling art and giving it away, but he recognized also that to stay outside of the mainstream art market altogether would have been to have no career at all, or to have been easily ignored or dismissed.

The issues of art, artists, fame, and value are not easy ones to resolve. As much as they may trouble us as viewers, artists also question them, and many have made them a part of their work. Yet is owning a work of art the same as possessing it? Here Gonzalez-Torres' sculptures reveal some of their other meanings, for do we not always "take something away with us" from a work of art when we look at it? We take away the experience, which exists in our memory, where in the end all experience exists. We come to possess a work of art gradually, by looking at it repeatedly, thinking about it, and learning about it. It does not matter who owns it.

ART AND BEAUTY

Beauty is deeply linked to our thinking about art. Aesthetics, the branch of philosophy that studies art, also studies the nature of beauty. Many of us assume that a work of art should be beautiful, and even that art's entire purpose is to be beautiful. But what beauty is, and where in a work of art it can be found, are interesting questions.

Few of us would be prepared to argue that Quinten Massys' *Grotesque Old Woman* is a beauty (**2.10**). Withered with age, she still plays the flirt, dressing in ridiculously outdated fashions and holding up a rosebud to advertise her charms. The painting once formed a pair with a portrait of an equally ugly old man, who is shown rejecting her advances. How could that woman possibly think she is desirable? How could that man possibly think he deserves any better? Massys resorts to ugliness to paint a biting satire of pride, vanity, and human folly. An image of a beautiful woman would not have conveyed his message at all. If we want art to have the freedom to address all aspects of the human experience, we cannot limit it to beauty.

On the other hand, would you still find this woman ugly if she were your beloved aunt, a kind and generous woman who had always loved you, who had taken care of you since you were a child? Does beauty lie solely in appearances? The question is posed again by Van Gogh in *Shoes* (**2.11**). Battered and dirty, placed on a humble tile floor, the shoes reflect a life of hard physical labor. Van Gogh paints them with infinite respect, his hundreds of short brushstrokes exploring and describing their surfaces as though at that moment they were the most important objects in the world. There is no question that the shoes we looked at earlier by Andy Warhol (see 2.8) are more attractive, more desirable, and more glamorous. But which are more beautiful?

In discussing the paintings by Massys and Van Gogh, we focused on the beauty of the woman and the shoes themselves. But in fact we are not

2.10 (left) Quinten Massys. *Grotesque Old Woman*. c. 1510–20. Oil on wood, 25 ¼ × 17 ⅞″.
The National Gallery, London.

2.11 (right) Vincent van Gogh. *Shoes*. 1888. Oil on canvas, 17⅜ × 20⅞″.
The Metropolitan Museum of Art, New York.

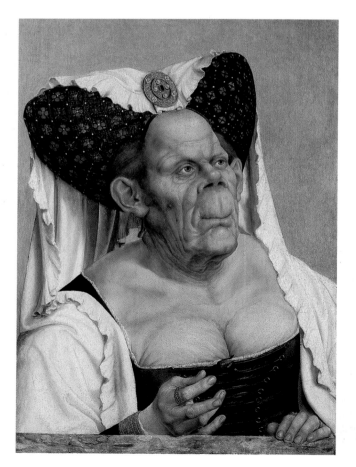

THEO van GOGH

WE THINK OF Theo van Gogh as the sensible one. Mentor and benefactor of his brother, the tormented artist Vincent van Gogh, Theo was nearly everything his brother was not—successful in business, financially solvent, steady and dependable, easy in friendship, a serious family man. Sometimes it is hard to remember that Vincent was the *older* brother, Theo younger by four years. The relationship between them was extraordinary. Without Theo, Vincent van Gogh probably could not have survived as an artist, or survived at all. Without Vincent, Theo probably would have lacked the grand purpose of his life.

Theo was born at the family home in Holland in 1857. When he was a teenager his uncle arranged for him to be apprenticed to a firm of international art dealers, Goupil & Co., as Vincent had been before him. Here the brothers' characters diverged. Vincent soon drifted out of the business. Theo became well established and fairly prosperous, eventually settling in as an art dealer in Paris. From a young age Theo assumed principal responsibility for Vincent's financial support, and he continued in this role through Vincent's life.

The Van Gogh brothers maintained a remarkable intimacy of spirit—surprisingly so, in view of the fact that, except for brief visits, they spent relatively little time in each other's company. They were together in their boyhood, then for two years in Paris, when Vincent stayed with Theo before moving to the south of France. This latter period exhausted Theo; Vincent was never an easy person to live with. Theo described Vincent's presence in the Paris apartment as "unendurable" and was relieved when the artist finally journeyed to Arles.

The thread of Theo and Vincent's connection depended on an immense volume of correspondence. Vincent was compulsive in writing to Theo—his subjects ranging from intensely personal thoughts and emotions through minute descriptions of work in progress. Theo was always there for Vincent. When Vincent finished a series of paintings, he shipped them off to Theo, who did his best to promote and sell the work (with little success). When Vincent was irresponsible, Theo lectured. When Vincent was in financial crisis, Theo sent money. When Vincent was in emotional crisis, Theo arrived to pick up the pieces. Although under no illusion about his brother's difficult temperament, Theo seems to have known from the beginning that Vincent was a brilliant painter and to have considered it his mission to sustain the painter's career.

Theo's marriage to Johanna Bonger in April of 1889 caused a brief strain in the Van Gogh bond. What had been a straight line became a triangle. Vincent suffered over having any of Theo's emotional energy diverted from himself to the new wife. Before long, however, he came to be fond of his sister-in-law and rejoiced in the birth of his nephew.

Vincent shot himself in July of 1890, and Theo was summoned to the deathbed. Three days later Theo wrote to his mother: "One cannot write how grieved one is nor find any solace. . . . Oh, Mother! He was so my own, own brother."[4] Vincent's death left Theo, only thirty-three years old, broken in health and spirits. Within six months he too was dead. The brothers are buried side by side. Afterward, the work of establishing the art of Vincent van Gogh was carried on by Theo's wife and his only child, a son, named Vincent.

Photograph of Theo van Gogh.

2.12 (right) Giovanni Bellini. *Pietà*. c. 1500–05. Oil on wood, 25⅝ × 35⅜″. Gallerie dell'Accademia, Venice.

2.13 (below) W. Eugene Smith. *Loading the Wing Guns of a Curtiss 'Helldiver' with a Belt of 50-Caliber Shells, November 1943.* Collection Center for Creative Photography, The University of Arizona, Tucson.

looking at a woman or at shoes, but at paintings. Are the paintings themselves ugly? If they are beautiful, where does this beauty lie? Can there be a beautiful painting of an unlovely subject? To explore these question we might turn to a work such as Giovanni Bellini's *Pietà* (**2.12**). Italian for "pity," *pietà* is the name for a standard subject in Christian art, that of Mary, the mother of Jesus, holding her Son after he was taken down from the cross on which he suffered death. Viewers who recognize the subject are likely to find the painting beautiful. Viewers who do not are more likely to find it disturbing or even repellent: Who is this woman sitting in a landscape with the near-naked body of a dead man across her lap? Why would anyone interested in making something beautiful paint this?

Some theories link beauty to formal qualities such as symmetry, simple geometrical shapes, and pure colors. Here, for example, the painter has arranged Mary's robes so that they form a symmetrical triangular shape. The white of Christ's loincloth is continued in Mary's head covering. The curve of the head covering is echoed by the curves of the roads in the background. Mary's robes echo the blue of the sky, while the rest of the painting is in subdued but glowing earth colors. When we find the painting beautiful, is it these formal qualities that we are reacting to?

The tension between formal beauty and a disturbing subject arises again in W. Eugene Smith's photograph *Loading the Wing Guns of a Curtiss 'Helldiver' with a Belt of 50-Caliber Shells* (**2.13**). Boldly silhouetted against the sun they block, the dark forms of the men are drawn by the cropped elements of the plane into a central triangle—the same compositional device that Bellini used to structure his *pietà*. The legs of the standing man repeat the triangular shape, while the curve of the other man's back echoes the curve of the plane's nose to the right. Between them a belt of ammunition falls in a swag as graceful as Mary's robes. The date of the photograph, November 1943, places the scene in World War II. This is combat. These men are on an aircraft carrier, preparing for a mission. People will die, perhaps even the men we see here. Is the photographer asking us to find the scene beautiful? In what way? In a famous poem, the Irish poet William Butler Yeats wrote of a "terrible beauty." Could this perhaps be what he meant?

The questions that these artworks bring up are those that philosophers have debated. Can beauty be defined, or must it be apprehended solely by instinct and taste? Is it linked to formal qualities? Are these qualities universally found to be beautiful? Is there perhaps another kind of beauty that is connected to morality or goodness? Is beauty entirely subjective, just a word we use when we personally take pleasure in looking at something? Perhaps in the end one of the functions of an artist is to find new kinds of beauty, to challenge us to go beyond our habits and conventions. "What is beauty?" wrote the American composer John Cage. "Where does it begin and where does it end? Where it ends is where the artist begins."[5]

ART AND APPEARANCES

As discussed in the previous chapter, our habits of perception allow us to recognize a wide variety of images as representing the world around us, even if they do not duplicate the appearances of the world exactly. Yet many people feel that art should aim at representing appearances as faithfully as possible, and that artists who do not do this are not good artists.

The assumption that art should faithfully mirror the visible world is a difficult one to overcome, for it is deeply rooted in Western ideas about art in two ways. First, art has always been linked to the idea of skill. Making lifelike images requires skills that not everyone has (though almost everyone can learn them). Viewers feel that an artist should make images that they cannot, that he or she should be more skilled than they are. Second, the elevation of painting and sculpture to a higher status during the Renaissance went hand in hand with the discovery of new methods for making optically convincing representations. From that time until almost the end of the 19th century, a period of about 500 years, these methods formed the foundation upon which Western art was built.

2.14 (above left) Pablo Picasso. *Portrait of José Ruiz Blasco, the Artist's Father*. 1896. Watercolor on paper, 10 ⅛ × 7″.
Museu Picasso, Barcelona.

2.15 (above right) Pablo Picasso. *Three Women at the Spring*. 1921. Oil on canvas, 6′8¼″ × 5′8 ½″.
The Museum of Modern Art, New York.

2.16 (left) Pablo Picasso. *Three Musicians*. 1921. Oil on canvas, 6′6″ × 7′3¾″.
The Museum of Modern Art, New York.

You may have heard someone say, "That guy's no artist—he can't even draw," as though the ability to draw were a sort of entrance requirement for art. In fact, even though artists during the 20th century came to see that art could be made in other ways, most could draw quite well. A case in point is Pablo Picasso. The son of a painter, Picasso was a precocious talent who mastered traditional Western art techniques at an early age. He was only thirteen years old when he painted the portrait of his father illustrated here (**2.14**). As a mature artist, however, Picasso rarely made use of these particular skills. In *Three Women* (**2.15**), painted when the artist was forty, the faces are drawn with far less finesse and observation. In fact, they all look rather alike. In *Three Musicians* (**2.16**), the faces seem to have been transformed into masks, and the characters look as flat as though they were cut from pieces of colored paper.

REPRESENTATIONAL AND ABSTRACT ART

All three works by Picasso refer to the visible world, yet each has a different relationship to it. *Portrait of José Ruiz Blasco* and *Three Women* are **representational;** that is, they aim to represent the world more or less as our eyes see it. Of these two works, the portrait is much more faithful to visual experience, recording the play of light over the facial features and capturing how the exterior form reflects an inner structure of bone and muscle. We call this approach **naturalistic.** *Three Women*, in contrast, is not naturalistic. The anatomy of the women does not reflect direct, objective observation but instead is **stylized** to conform to an artistic or intellectual idea. For example, the women's profiles all extend in a straight line from the top of the forehead to the tip of the nose. The fingers are stylized into uniform sausage-like shapes, while the idea that the human arm is basically two cylindrical forms hinged at the elbow guides the depiction of the arms. One could imagine a culture in which all artists adopted these "signs" for the human anatomy and passed them down from generation to generation. Artists could learn to draw a woman without ever looking at one, merely by looking at art.

Three Musicians is even farther removed from objective visual experience, although we can still recognize the subject. Picasso takes certain aspects of visual reality, then simplifies and recombines them, a process called **abstraction.** The resulting shapes relate more to each other within the painting than they do to the objects in the real world. For example, the musicians are abstracted into largely rectilinear shapes—shapes made of straight lines—that fit together like a jigsaw puzzle. Their six eyes become six round holes that relate more to the holes of the clarinet and the guitar than they do to a human eye. Little jagged shapes turned one way or another serve for hands.

Naturalism, stylization, and abstraction are like three artistic languages that interpret our visual experience of the world in different ways. Picasso "spoke" all three fluently enough to produce art in them. He painted *Three Women* and *Three Musicians* in the same summer, much as a bilingual writer might write a short story in English and then a poem in Spanish.

Artists in other cultures have also worked in more than one visual language at the same time. In the early African kingdom of Ife, founded by the Yoruba people, rulers were commemorated with naturalistic portraits in brass (**2.17**). Such heads were probably placed on altars dedicated to royal ancestors. The holes around the mouth and along the jawline may have served to attach a veil of beads, much like those the king wore in life (see 18.12). Ife artists also created smaller, abstract heads (**2.18**). The two styles of heads relate to two concepts still current in Yoruba thought: the naturalistic head represents the outer, physical reality that can be perceived by the

2.17 (above, top) *Head of a King*, from Ife. Yoruba, c. 13th century. Brass, life-size. The British Museum, London.

2.18 (above) *Cylindrical Head*, from Ife. Yoruba, c. 13th–14th century. Terracotta, height 6⅜". National Commission for Museums and Monuments, Nigeria.

2.19 (left) Eliot Porter. *Water-Streaked Wall, Warm Spring Canyon, Lake Powell, Utah, 1965*. Dye transfer print, 10³⁄₁₆ × 7⁷⁄₈″. Amon Carter Museum, Fort Worth, Texas.

2.20 (right) Rebecca Purdham. *Chin Up*. 1990. Oil on canvas, 9 × 6′. Courtesy Jack Tilton Gallery.

senses, while the abstract head represents the inner, spiritual reality that can be perceived only by the imagination.

Photography is often thought of as the most objective way yet developed to record appearances, yet it, too, can produce abstract images. Eliot Porter's photograph of a cliff wall at Lake Powell, Utah, is a beautiful example (**2.19**). The image does not include any visual information that would help us understand how tall the wall is, what is above it or next to it, or where on the lake it is. Without the help of the title and the small strip of water visible at the lower edge, we might not be able to make out the subject at all. Like Picasso with his *Three Musicians*, Porter has included just enough clues to let us gradually puzzle out the image and connect it back to reality.

NONREPRESENTATIONAL ART

If you cover up the water at the bottom of Porter's photograph and ignore the title, you might still find it a pleasing arrangement of colors and shapes. You have entered the realm of nonrepresentational art, art that does not refer to the appearances of the visible world. The photograph, of course, remains tied to reality. However, works that resemble it, such as Rebecca Purdham's *Chin Up* (**2.20**), no longer have their beginnings in the natural world of appearances. Nonrepresentational art recognizes that we can have a satisfying aesthetic experience from the elements of art itself such as form, color, line, and shape. Instead of speaking to us by "bouncing off" the appearances of the visible world, nonrepresentational art reaches out to engage our intellect or touch our emotions directly in its own language. Two of Purdham's siblings are mentally handicapped, and she readily admits that this has influenced her ideas about art. "When you have a special person in your family—and I have two—you begin to see that there is a kind of communication that exists way beyond language," she has said. "And when I paint, when I'm really into it, there is a degree of non-verbal communication that becomes everything—it fills me up."[6]

Purdham builds up her images gradually, applying paint directly to the rough canvas with her hands (protected by rubber gloves). The result is intriguingly misty and vague, as though something we could make out were constantly about to take shape, though it never does. The paintings are often very large, filling the viewer's entire field of vision. Paul Klee, in contrast, presents us with clarity and precision in *Monument in Fertile Country* (**2.21**), a small composition of carefully delineated trapezoids filled in with delicate watercolors. The image is nonrepresentational, yet the title encourages us to associate it with aspects of the visible world. For example, we could imagine ourselves in an airplane looking down onto farmland. Or perhaps the yellow shapes are somehow a golden monument standing in the countryside. Or perhaps the painting itself is a monument. There is no single answer. Klee juxtaposes a poetic title with a nonrepresentational image and presents them to us as a sort of plaything for the mind.

The terms *representational*, *abstract*, and *nonrepresentational* categorize art by how it relates to the appearances of the visible world. A work of art, of course, has a place in the visible world itself. It has its own appearance, which is the result of the artist's efforts. A term that helps us categorize art by its own visual characteristics is *style*.

2.21 Paul Klee. *Monument in Fertile Country*. 1929. Watercolor over pencil on paper, mounted on cardboard; 17 7/8 × 12 1/8". Kunstmuseum Bern.

STYLE

Style refers to a characteristic or group of characteristics that we can recognize as constant, recurring, or coherent. If a person we know always wears jeans and cowboy boots, we identify that person with a certain style of dress. If a friend who always wears her long hair in braids gets her hair cut very short, we speak of a change in style. If a family has furnished their home entirely in antiques except for one very modern chair in the living room, we would recognize a mix of styles.

Artistic style is the product of constant, recurring, or coherent visual or conceptual traits. In painting, for example, a style might include characteristic materials, brush strokes, color combinations, subject matter, techniques of representation (stylized versus naturalistic), and so on. Style may be associated with an entire culture (Olmec style in Mesoamerica), with a particular time and place (the early Renaissance style in Rome), with a particular group of artists (Impressionist style), with an individual artist (Van Gogh's style), or with a distinct phase of an individual artist (Picasso's Blue Period style). Some artists develop a style and stick to it; others work in several styles, either simultaneously or sequentially, as we saw above with Picasso and the artists of Ife.

We can see some of these levels of style at work by comparing two paintings with similar subjects (**2.22, 2.23**). Each painting portrays a woman in profile from the waist up. Both were painted during the 18th century, the first in India, the second in England. Most viewers would see immediately that the two paintings differ greatly in style, although they might not be able to articulate those differences.

The Indian painting (2.22) is stylized. Outlines are precise, the jewel-like colors are bright and clear, and no brush strokes are visible. The solid blue background appears flat and does not give any information about where the woman might be. The roundness of the woman's form is suggested but not actually depicted. For example, we know that her left hand is crossing

2.22 (left) *Lady with a Bird,* from Hyderabad, India. c. 1750. Opaque watercolor on paper, 13 × 8½″.
Victoria and Albert Museum, London.

2.23 (right) Joshua Reynolds. *Mrs. Mary Robinson (Perdita).* 1784. Oil on canvas, 30½ × 25″.
The Wallace Collection, London.

in front of her body, but we do not sense how much space there is between them. The hands and body are much smaller than the head would suggest they should be. The pose is formal, and the woman stares off into space with her outsized eye as though unaware that she is showing a small yellow flower to a red bird perched on her hand. A diaphanous muslin blouse reveals her breasts and arms to our gaze, adding an element of sensuality.

The European painting (2.23) is naturalistic. Outlines are often blurred and the colors are muted. The head is carefully painted, while the lower portion of the dress is merely suggested by a flurry of brush strokes that almost take on a life of their own. The dark background sets off the figure, yet it also suggests a deep recession into space, a body of water with the horizon in the distance. Attention to light and shadow makes the roundness of the woman's form clear, as does the slightly tipped head. The pose is informal and invites us to enter the sitter's thoughts—she is pensive, perhaps a little sad.

With more exposure and experience we can begin to see which stylistic traits are common to the culture as a whole, which reflect a particular time and place within the culture, and which point to a particular artist. For example, the flatness of the Indian work and the outsized eye are common to the Hindu painting tradition in India, while the jewel-like colors and detailed finish point to the Islamic tradition. Islamic rulers had been present in India since the 16th century, and the painting here reflects a mingling of the two styles. Turning to the European portrait, we can say that its concern with light, shadow, and deep space is characteristic of European painting beginning with the Renaissance. The woman's hairstyle and costume indicate a date in the late 18th century. The simplicity of the dress and the moody outdoor setting suggest that the work is English. At this point several painters might come to mind, among them Reynolds, who was the greatest portrait painter of his day.

By following stylistic clues such as these, experienced viewers can place a work of art into a larger framework, which often helps understanding and appreciation. Experts can do far more. Many works of art that have come down to us are anonymous, and style is an important factor in determining when, where, and by whom they were created.

ART AND MEANING

"What is the artist trying to say?" is a question many people ask when looking at a work of art, as though the artist were trying to tell us in images what he or she could have said more clearly in a few words. Meaning in art is rarely so simple and straightforward. Rather than a definitive meaning that can be found once and for all, art inspires interpretations that are many and changeable, for images often have multiple or elusive meanings and may speak to individual viewers in different ways. Nevertheless, when we are trying to understand our own experience of a work of art, or to imagine what it meant to the artist or to the artist's intended audience, there are two first steps to take. One is to consider the work's form; the other is to investigate its iconography.

FORM

In the broadest and most basic sense, **form** is the way a work of art looks. Form embraces all the visual aspects that can be isolated and discussed such as size, shape, materials, color, and composition. It is the end result of all the decisions the artist made while translating an idea in the imagination into an object in the world. The next two chapters of this book introduce many individual aspects of form. Here, we look briefly at how form can convey meaning.

WHO IS AN ARTIST?

G AYLEEN AIKEN, whose work is illustrated here, has been making and exhibiting her drawings, paintings, and puppets since she was a young girl. Like many contemporary artists, she draws inspiration from popular culture, comic books, music, and local life—in this case the life of her hometown in Vermont. Aiken is well known, but not simply as an artist. She is known as an outsider artist.

Over the past fifteen years there has been a great deal of interest in outsider art, art by so-called self-taught artists. These artists have little or no formal training in the visual arts and often live far from the urban centers traditionally associated with artistic creativity. With this interest there has been an unprecedented growth in the number of venues that exhibit and sell outsider art. Many outsider artists maintain highly visible careers and have gained impressive followings among collectors and critics. There are even a number of magazines, such as *Raw Vision,* devoted to outsider art.

The term *outsider* has come into common use only recently. *Folk, naive, intuitive, primitive,* and *art brut* (French for "raw art") have also been used over the past century to categorize work by nonprofessional artists. Interest in such work can be traced to the efforts of psychiatrist Hans Prinzhorn, who, from the late 1890s through 1920s, amassed thou-

sands of pieces by schizophrenic patients from psychiatric hospitals around Europe. Prinzhorn's book *Artistry of the Mentally Ill,* published in 1922, greatly inspired many artists and writers. Leading figures of the Surrealist movement, for example, celebrated the art of the "insane," attributing to these artists the most exemplary works of Surrealism. Later some of these same paintings would be used by the Nazis in their infamous Degenerate Art exhibition of 1937 to support their thesis that modern art was "pathological," for it resembled the art of the mentally ill. Many Prinzhorn artists were murdered in Nazi death camps.

Unlike such terms as *Surrealism* or *Impressionism, outsider* does not label a recognizable style or artistic movement. Rather, it attempts to define a group of people and their work as somehow "apart." Questions about what these artists are apart from, where the boundaries are drawn, and what social forces are at work in drawing them have placed outsider art at the center of a hotly contested debate over art's role in reinforcing society's attitudes about such topics as class, race, gender, and human difference. Indeed, the very notion of an artistic "outsider" has been called into question. Since the 19th century at least, critics point out, artists have tended to see themselves as visionaries and outsiders, even as outlaws. Hence, the line between insider and outsider has long been somewhat fuzzy. Paul Gauguin, for example, took great pride in his self-imposed "outsider" status (see 21.9), while the "naive" French painter Henri Rousseau is now considered to have been, with Picasso and Matisse, among the most important artists of the early 20th century (see 3.30).

The popularity of outsider art today is a result of the most progressive aspect of our modernity. The emergence and validation of difference within culture, the collapse of the distinction between "high" and "low," the great proliferation of the popular arts— these are all part of the democratization of culture brought about by modernism.

Gayleen Aiken. *A Beautiful Dream.* 1982. Oil on canvasboard, 12 × 16". Courtesy Grass Roots Art and Community Effort (GRACE), Hardwick, Vermont.

The Norwegian painter Edvard Munch used his art to confront our most basic human experiences: birth, death, fear, loneliness, sexuality, love. The two works here both portray a kiss (**2.24, 2.25**), a subject he treated several times. Yet though the subject is the same, the feeling we get from the two images is very different. In verbalizing what we see, we can better understand why this is and perhaps arrive at some meanings the works might have.

Kiss by the Window (2.24) is painted in soothing blues. It is evening. Lights shine from the shop windows across the street, and small blue forms seem to depict passersby, perhaps hurrying home after work. Inside, the curtain is swept back dramatically. The motion continues with the man's arm as he sweeps the woman into an embrace. The couple's bodies meld together into one mass; we cannot tell where he leaves off and she begins. Their heads alone remain distinct. Munch has divided the scene in two. The left portion of the canvas depicts the realm of public life and society; the right portion depicts the realm of private life and its passions.

The Kiss (2.25) is a much starker image. Sensuous color is sacrificed in favor of severe black and white. Outdoors it is bright daylight. The couple, now naked, embrace directly in front of the window. The curtains sweep back as if to reveal them on a stage. Whereas before their bodies had merged and their heads remained distinct, here the opposite happens: their heads form a single featureless blur, but their bodies are distinct, almost brutally distinct. The balance between private and public realms of *Kiss by the Window* is replaced by extreme tension, as the most private of acts takes place in the most public of ways.

Perhaps *Kiss by the Window* portrays an ideal of romance and *The Kiss,* the reality of lust. One emphasizes a passionate union of two people who yet retain independent identities; the other, all thought overcome by animal urges. One conforms to social guidelines for love; the other confronts society with the reminder that our passions cannot always be predicted or controlled, and that they may well cause chaos in our lives. This interpretation is neither final nor definitive, however. You yourself may interpret the works quite differently as you bring your own experiences, preoccupations, and thoughts to bear on your perception of their form.

2.24 (left) Edvard Munch. *Kiss by the Window*. 1892. Oil on canvas, 28½ × 35¾". Nasjonalgalleriet, Oslo.

2.25 (right) Edvard Munch. *The Kiss*. 1895. Drypoint and aquatint, 13½ × 11". Albertina Collection, Vienna.

ICONOGRAPHY

Earlier in this chapter, while looking at Sir Joshua Reynolds' portrait of *Mrs. Mary Robinson (Perdita)* (see 2.23), you may have wondered who Mrs. Robinson was. If so, you were taking a step toward studying the painting's iconography. **Iconography,** literally "describing images," involves identifying, describing, and interpreting subject matter in art. For example, research would reveal that Mary Robinson was a well-known actress and poet. Her most acclaimed stage role was Perdita, a character in Shakespeare's play *The Winter's Tale.* She became so identified with the role that it served as her nickname for the rest of her life. In the play, Perdita, a princess, is taken across the sea as an infant and abandoned in a foreign land. She is found by a shepherd, who generously raises her as his own daughter. By the play's end, her identity is discovered, she marries a prince, and again crosses the sea to be reunited with her parents. Knowing this, we realize that the sea in the background of the portrait is not there for visual interest alone. It refers to the role that first brought Robinson fame.

Reynolds could safely assume that his audience knew both Mary Robinson and Shakespeare's play. Today, only theater historians and professors of literature would recognize both immediately. The rest of us need to learn again what was once common knowledge. Issues of iconography may arise even more urgently when we look at a work from another culture, such as this statue of *Amida Nyorai* (**2.26**) by the Japanese sculptor Jocho.

Amida Nyorai is a buddha, a fully enlightened being. The historical Buddha was a spiritual leader who lived in India around the turn of the 5th century B.C.E. His insights into the human condition form the basis of

2.26 (left) Jocho. *Amida Nyorai,* in the Hoodo (Phoenix Hall), Byodo-in Temple. c. 1053. Gilded wood, height 9′2″.

2.27 (right) Jan van Eyck. *Arnolfini Double Portrait.* 1434. Oil on wood, 33 × 22 ½″. The National Gallery, London.

2.28 *Arnolfini Double Portrait*, detail.

the Buddhist religion. As Buddhism developed, it occurred to believers that if there had been one fully enlightened being, there must have been others. In Japan, where Buddhism quickly spread, the most popular buddha has been Amida, the Buddha of the Western Paradise.

The iconography of the historical Buddha image was established early on and has remained constant through the centuries. Amida, like most other buddhas, is portrayed following its conventions as well. A buddha wears a monk's robe, a single length of cloth that drapes over his left shoulder and around his body. His ears are elongated, for in his earthly life, before his spiritual awakening, he wore the customary heavy earrings of an Indian prince. The form resembling a bun on the top of his head is a protuberance called *ushnisha* that is symbolic of his enlightenment. Sculptors developed a repertoire of *mudras*, hand gestures, for the Buddha image, and each gesture has its own meaning. Here, Amida's hands form the gesture of meditation and balance, which symbolizes the path toward enlightenment. He sits in the cross-legged position of meditation on a lotus throne. The lotus flower is a symbol of purity. Rising up behind Amida is his halo, radiant spiritual energy envisioned as a screen of stylized flames.

The iconography of the statue is available to us because it forms part of a tradition that has continued unbroken since it first developed almost 2,000 years ago. Often, however, traditions change and meanings are forgotten. We cannot always tell with certainty what images from the past portray, or what they meant to their original viewers. Such is the case with one of the most famous images in Western art, the *Arnolfini Double Portrait* (**2.27**) by Jan van Eyck. Painted with entrancing clarity and mesmerizing detail, the work portrays a man and a woman, their hands joined. He has taken off his shoes, which lie on the floor next to him; hers can be seen on the floor in the background. Seemingly pregnant, she stands next to a bed draped in rich red fabric. Overhead is a chandelier with but one candle. On the floor between the couple stands an alert little dog. A mirror on the far wall (**2.28**) reflects not only the couple but also two men standing in the doorway to the room and looking in—standing, that is, where we are standing as we look at the painting. Over the mirror the painter's signature reads, "Jan van Eyck was here."

By the time the painting ended up in the National Gallery in 1842, it had changed hands so many times that even the identity of the couple had been forgotten. Later in the 19th century, researchers working from old documents identified them tentatively as Giovanni Arnolfini, a rich merchant capitalist, and his wife, Giovanna Cenami, also from a wealthy merchant family of high social standing. But what was the purpose of the painting? What did it depict? During the 20th century, an art historian named Erwin Panofsky came up with an ingenious answer. The painting, he said, recorded a private marriage ceremony. In fact, it served as a sort of marriage certificate, a legal document. The men reflected in the mirror were none other than Van Eyck himself and a friend, who had served as witnesses. Moreover, almost every detail in the painting had a symbolic value: the bride's seemingly pregnant state alluded to fertility, as did the red bed of the nuptial chamber. The single candle signified the presence of God at the ceremony, while the dog was a symbol of marital fidelity and love. The couple had cast off their shoes as a sign that they stood on sacred ground.

Panofsky's theory was so elegant and persuasive that it went almost unquestioned for many years. Recently, however, a number of doubts have been raised. After working patiently through old documents about marriage customs and examining numerous depictions of marriages and interiors, an art historian named Edwin Hall, for example, has concluded that the painting does not depict a marriage, but rather a ceremony of betrothal, an engagement. It commemorates the alliance of two prominent and well-off families. In his view, the objects in the room are probably not symbolic in Panofsky's sense, though many of them indicate the family's affluence. Beds were status symbols at the time and were commonly displayed in the principal room of the house. Candles were enormously expensive, and using one at a time was common thrift. The shoes are of a kind worn by the upper class and were probably taken off routinely upon going indoors. The dog is simply a pet: everyone had dogs.

2.29 Andy Warhol. *Marilyn Diptych*. 1962. Oil, acrylic, and silkscreen on enamel on canvas, 6'8⅞" × 4'9".
Tate Gallery, London.

Does it matter exactly what the painting means? Picasso said famously that "if a work of art cannot live always in the present, then it must not be considered at all."[7] Viewers have been fascinated by the beauty and mystery of the *Arnolfini Double Portrait* for centuries. Today, visitors to the National Gallery commonly linger in front of it for a long time, drinking in the luminous atmosphere and precisely rendered detail. By making the painting a focus of thought and wonder, we continue to ensure that it lives in the present. It is when we stop looking at it or cease caring what it might mean that the painting will fade into the past.

Before leaving this topic, we should consider that our time may leave its own share of mysteries for the future, as the knowledge we take for granted is forgotten. Who, people hundreds of years from now may wonder, was *Marilyn Diptych* (**2.29**)? **Diptych** is not a proper name at all, but a work of art that consists of two parts facing each other like the pages of an open book. Often, though not here, they are hinged to open and close as a book does. As for Marilyn, we recognize her instantly as Marilyn Monroe, a glamorous and tragic movie star whose early death is still shrouded in rumor. Andy Warhol began his series of Marilyn pictures after the star's suicide, and in them he memorialized her as a sort of contemporary goddess. The right panel of the diptych portrays columns of Marilyns in black and white, like lengths of film from an old movie. She comes in and out of focus, as though flickering on the screen of our memory. On the left, colorized versions of her are laid out like endless publicity photos. The color is blatantly artificial and carelessly applied. Is the real Marilyn Monroe anywhere to be found? Was she her image? In an age of mass production, can a person also be a product?

Such questions occur to us naturally as we look at the painting. But how many of these words will need to be explained to future generations: Marilyn, movies, black and white, publicity photographs, Hollywood, newspapers, television, stardom. Will the painting continue to live in the present? We have no way of knowing.

CHAPTER 3

Themes and Purposes of Art

There are several ways to approach the study of art. A popular one is to trace its history chronologically, from the earliest cave paintings of the Stone Age to the art of our own time. This method offers great advantages, because it places works of art in the context of the cultures from which they emerged and allows one to follow the development of art over the centuries. Part Five of this book will present a brief chronological survey of art.

The chronological approach has one drawback, however, in that we may lose sight of the characteristics that works made by different cultures have in common. For instance, a sculpture produced today and one produced ten thousand years ago may seem very different, and a chronological approach emphasizes the differences by focusing on the cultural aspects that influenced each. But suppose the two sculptures are images of political leaders; then we would say they have the same *theme*, so we can make interesting comparisons between them. While it is useful to understand how and why works of art differ, it is also helpful to see how much they are alike, even when thousands of miles and years separate them.

A theme is like a thread running through the entire history of art, and there are many such threads. No doubt every person setting out to name the important themes in art would produce a different list. We have chosen to consider these: arts of daily life, the sacred realm, the social order, storytelling, the here and now, the human experience, invention and fantasy, art and nature, art and art.

The statues of political leaders we imagined earlier would fall under the theme of art and the social order, which is art that reflects ideas about the structure of society. But while the two statues share the same theme, we can easily imagine that they might each have a different purpose. One, for example, could have been commissioned by the government for a public square, where its purpose would be to remind citizens of the leader's benevolence and to support the institution of leadership. The other could have been a satirical portrait of the leader meant to be carried in protest through the streets. Its purpose would be to remind citizens of the leader's flaws, and perhaps even to call for a different form of government altogether.

This chapter examines the nine themes enumerated above, and it looks at some of the purposes for which artists have used them.

ARTS OF DAILY LIFE

In many cultures, art and craft are still one concept, and the artistic impulse is expressed as much through objects created for daily use as it is through images and architecture. Often these objects carry meanings far beyond their practical functions. Among the Pomo Indians of California, for example, the art of basketry is highly valued (**3.1**). Legend tells that when a Pomo ancestor stole the sun from the gods to light the dark earth, he hung it aloft in a basket that he kept moving across the sky. The daily journey of the sun reenacts this original event. Pomo baskets are thus linked to larger ideas about the universe and about the transfer of knowledge from gods to humans at the beginning of the world.

Traditionally a woman's art, basket weaving began with the harvesting of materials. This activity, too, was endowed with ritual significance, for it involved following ancestral paths into the landscape to find the traditional roots, barks, and woods. Here, willow and bracken fern root were used to produce a pattern of alternating lights and darks. Feathers, clam-shell beads, and glass beads procured through trade are woven into the surface. Somewhere in the basket the weaver included a small, barely noticeable imperfection. Called *dau*, it serves as a spirit door, letting benevolent spirits into the basket and allowing evil ones to leave. Feather baskets were produced as gifts for important or honored persons, and they were usually destroyed in mourning when the person died.

In our society, objects of daily life are largely produced by industrial methods, yet someone must still design them. Usually, this person is a specialized artist known as an industrial designer. Architects and sculptors may also see design as an extension of their own concerns. One of the most influential modern sculptors to become involved with design was Isamu Noguchi. Beginning in 1951 and continuing for thirty years, he designed a series of lamps he called *akari*, Japanese for "light as illumination" (**3.2**). The lamps were mass-produced by hand according to traditional Japanese techniques, with handmade mulberry paper covering a bamboo frame.

3.1 (left) Feathered basket. Pomo, c. 1877. Willow, bulrush, fern, feather, shell, glass beads; height 5¹/₂".
Philbrook Museum of Art, Tulsa, Oklahoma.

3.2 (right) Isamu Noguchi. *Akari*. Early 1950s. Paper, bamboo, and metal.
Courtesy The Isamu Noguchi Foundation, Inc.

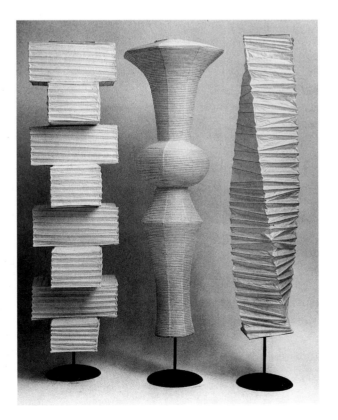

Noguchi viewed his *akari* as sculptures with a double aspect. In daylight, turned off, they can be appreciated for their simple forms and textured surfaces. At night, turned on, their material presence seems to dissolve into weightless forms made of light. Our society does not share a core set of beliefs that would endow such objects with as much meaning as the Pomo give to their baskets. We can take pleasure in their beauty, however, and if occasionally we think of the association of light with the life-giving sun, or of the contrast of material existence with the luminous mind or spirit, then we will have seen them as art for a moment.

THE SACRED REALM

Who made the universe? How did life begin, and what is its purpose? What happens to us after we die? For answers to these and other fundamental questions, people throughout history have turned to a world we cannot see except through faith, the sacred realm of the spirit. Gods and goddesses, spirits of ancestors, spirits of nature, one God and one alone—each society has formed its own view of the sacred realm and how it interacts with our own. Some forms of faith have disappeared into history, others have remained small and local, while still others such as Christianity and Islam have become major religions that draw believers from all over the world. From earliest times art has played an important role in our relationship to the sacred, helping us to envision it, to honor it, and to communicate with it.

Many works of architecture have been created to provide settings for rituals of worship and prayer, rituals that formalize contact between the earthly and divine realms. One such work is the small marvel known as the Sainte-Chapelle, or holy chapel (**3.3**). Located in Paris, the chapel was commissioned in 1239 by the French king Louis IX to house an important collection of relics that he had just acquired, relics he believed to include pieces

3.3 Interior, upper chapel, Sainte-Chapelle, Paris. 1243–48.

of the True Cross, the Crown of Thorns, and other instruments of Christ's Passion. The king's architects created a soaring vertical space whose walls seem to be made of stained glass. Light passing through the glass creates a dazzling effect, transforming the interior into a radiant, otherworldly space in which the glory of heaven seems close at hand.

The Sainte-Chapelle is a relatively intimate space, for it was intended as a private chapel for the king and his court. In contrast, the Great Mosque at Córdoba, Spain, was built to serve the needs of an entire community (**3.4**). A mosque is an Islamic house of worship. Begun during the 8th century, the Great Mosque at Córdoba grew to be the largest place of prayer in western Islam. The interior of the prayer hall is a vast horizontal space measured out by a virtual forest of columns. Daylight enters through doorways placed around the perimeter of the hall. Filtered through the myriad columns and arches, it creates a complex play of shadows that makes the extent and shape of the interior hard to grasp. Alternating red and white sections break up the visual continuity of the arch forms. Oil lamps hanging in front of the focal point of worship would have created still more shadows.

In both the Sainte-Chapelle and the Great Mosque at Córdoba, architects strove to create a place where worshipers might approach the sacred realm. The builders of the Sainte-Chapelle envisioned a radiant vertical space transformed by colored light, while the architects of the Great Mosque at Córdoba envisioned a disorienting horizontal space fractured by columns and shadows. In both buildings, the everyday world is shut out, and light and space are used to create a heightened sense of mystery and wonder.

The sacred realm cannot be seen with human eyes, yet artists throughout the ages have been asked to create images of gods, goddesses, angels, demons, and all manner of spirit beings. Religious images may serve to focus the thoughts of the faithful by giving concrete form to abstract ideas. Often, however, their role has been more complex and mysterious. For example, in some cultures images have been understood as a sort of conduit through which sacred power flows; in others they serve as a dwelling place for a deity, who is called upon through ritual to take up residence within.

3.4 Prayer hall of Abd al-Rahman I, Great Mosque, Córdoba, Spain. Begun 786 C.E.

Our next two images, one Buddhist and one Christian, were made at approximately the same time but some 4,000 miles apart, the Buddhist image in Tibet, the Christian one in Italy. The Buddhist painting portrays Tathagata Amitayus, one of the Five Cosmic Buddhas, seated in a pose of meditation on a stylized lotus throne (**3.5**). His hands support a small vase that holds a single blossom. The Five Cosmic Buddhas are typically portrayed in the bejeweled garb of Indian princes to emphasize their benevolent availability to the human community. Arranged around Amitayus are *bodhisattvas*, also in princely attire. Bodhisattvas are enlightened beings who have deferred their ultimate goal of *nirvana*—freedom from the cycle of birth, death, and rebirth—in order to help others attain that goal. All wear halos signifying their holiness. The buddha, being the most important of the personages depicted, dominates the painting as the largest figure. He faces straight front, in a pose of tranquility, while the others around him stand or sit in relaxed postures.

The second example, painted by the 13th-century Italian master Cimabue, depicts Mary, mother of Christ, with her son (**3.6**). Mary sits tran-

3.5 (left) *A Tathagata Buddha.* Central Tibet, late 12th century. Opaque watercolor and gold on linen, 8′6″ × 5′9″. Los Angeles County Museum of Art.

3.6 (right) Cimabue. *Madonna Enthroned.* c. 1280–90. Tempera on wood, 12′7 1/2″ × 7′4″. Galleria degli Uffizi, Florence.

quilly on her throne, her hand in a classic gesture indicating the Christ child, who is the hope of earth's salvation. On both sides of her are figures of angels, heavenly beings who assist humankind in its quest for Paradise. Again, all these wear halos symbolizing their holiness. Yet again, the Virgin, being the most important figure in this painting, dominates the composition, is the largest, and holds the most serenely frontal posture.

We should not conclude from the remarkable structural similarity of these works that any communication or influence took place between Italy and Central Asia. A safer assumption is that two artists of different faiths independently found a format that satisfied their pictorial needs. Both the Buddha and the Virgin are important, serene holy figures. Bodhisattvas and angels, who are always more active, attend them. Therefore, the artists, from their separate points of view, devised similar compositions.

Art is often the only testimony we have to the beliefs of cultures that have come and gone without leaving written records. An example is this haunting jade figure from the Olmec culture (**3.7**), which flourished from about 1500 to 300 B.C.E. in what is today southern Mexico. The statue seems to portray a shaman, a person who acts as a medium between the human and spirit worlds. Standing in a pose of meditation, the shaman holds up a small creature whose fierce, animated expression contrasts vividly with his own trancelike gaze. The creature's headband, catlike eyes, snub nose, and large downturned mouth identify him as the infant man-jaguar, a supernatural creature mingling animal and human traits. The navels of the creature and the shaman are aligned, as on an axis linking the cosmic and earthly realms. The infant man-jaguar was evidently an important deity in Olmec culture, for it is often depicted in art. We do not know what purpose this figure and others like it served, but we recognize the sculptor's genius in giving visual form to ideas about a shaman's power.

Among the most compelling art forms ever developed to give visual presence to the spirit realm are the masquerades of Africa. The photograph here captures the entry of otherworld spirits into a community of the Bwa people of West Africa (**3.8**). Raffia costumes and carved and painted masks completely disguise the performers' human identities, which are believed to be subsumed into the identities of the spirits. Masks do not appear casually in the human community. Rather, they are called upon during times when the cooperation of the spirits and the natural forces they control are especially needed. For example, masks may appear at festivals surrounding the planting and harvesting of crops, or during the initiation of young people into adulthood, or at funerals, when their help is needed to ensure that the spirit of the deceased leaves the human community and takes its place in the spirit world of ancestors.

The Bwa masks here manifest (make physically present) nature spirits. The tall mask leading the procession is a snake spirit, while the next spirit has taken the form of a buffalo. The final two masks—with their towering plank forms and graphic decoration of Xs, zigzags, circles, and crescents—are spirits that take no known natural form. The snake and buffalo Bwa masks are clearly recognizable abstractions. The two tall plank masks are nonrepresentational. Their markings are symbolic and can be interpreted in many ways.

Like the infant man-jaguar of the Olmec, the abstract and nonrepresentational forms of the Bwa suggest that the spirit world remains fundamentally mysterious and unknowable. We can envision it clothed in the forms of nature, including our human form, but in the end its powers resist such visual limits. Western artists, too, have associated nonrepresentational art with an attempt to go beyond what can be seen. During the early 20th century, many came to view art itself as essentially spiritual in nature. They saw nonrepresentation as a sort of purification process that would let art shed its false nature as a mirror of appearances and reveal its essence as a direct expression of human consciousness. Russian painter Kasimir Malevich, for example, developed an art of simple forms and pure colors that he called Suprematism, which stood for "the supremacy of pure feeling in

3.7 (above, top) Standing figure holding supernatural effigy. Olmec, 800–500 B.C.E. Jade, height 11³/₈". Collection Robert B. Martin, The Guennol Collection, The Brooklyn Museum. Photograph Justin Kerr.

3.8 (above) Bwa masqueraders, Burkina Faso.

3.9 Kasimir Malevich. *Suprematist Composition.* 1915. Oil on canvas, 34⅝ × 27⅝″. Stedelijk Museum, Amsterdam.

creative art." In works such as *Suprematist Composition* (**3.9**) he sought to reveal the timeless and universal beauty that he believed had underlain representational painting all along. Malevich resisted the idea that art should fulfill practical functions such as creating images in the service of established religions. Rather, he felt that art should exist in its own independent realm, reminding us on its own terms that what is immaterial is essential to our well-being.

THE SOCIAL ORDER

Of the many things we create as human beings, the most basic and important may be societies. How can a stable, just, and productive society best be organized? Who will rule, and how? What freedoms will rulers have? What freedoms will citizens have? How is wealth to be distributed? How is authority to be maintained? Many answers to these questions have been posed throughout history, and throughout history the resulting order has been reflected in art.

In many early societies, earthly order and cosmic order were viewed as interrelated and mutually dependent. Such was the case in ancient Egypt, where the pharaoh (king) was viewed as a link between the divine and earthly realms. The pharaoh was considered a "junior god," a personification of the god Horus and the son of the sun god, Ra. As a ruler his role was to maintain the divinely established order of the universe, which included the social order of Egypt. He communed with the gods in temples only he could enter, and he wielded theoretically unlimited power over a country that literally belonged to him.

When a pharaoh died, it was believed that he rejoined the gods and became fully divine. Preparations for this journey began even during his lifetime, as vast tombs were constructed and outfitted with everything he would need in the afterlife. The most famous of these tombs are the three great

pyramids at Giza (**3.10**), which served as the tombs of the pharaohs Menkaure, Khafre, and Khufu. Thousands of years later, the scale of these structures is still awe-inspiring. The largest pyramid, that of Khufu, originally reached a height of about 480 feet, roughly the height of a fifty-story skyscraper. Its base covers over 13 acres. Over two million blocks of stone, each weighing over 2 tons, went into building it. Each block had to be quarried with hand tools, transported to the site, and set in place without mortar. Tens of thousands of workers labored for years to build such a tomb and fill its chambers with treasures.

The pyramids reflect the immense power of the pharaohs who could command such forces, but they also reflect the beliefs underlying the social order that granted its rulers such power in the first place. In the Egyptian view, the well-being of Egypt depended on the goodwill of the gods, whose representative on earth was the pharaoh. His safe passage to the afterlife and his worship thereafter as a god himself were essential for the prosperity of the country and the continuity of the universe. No amount of labor or spending seemed too great to achieve these ends.

Roughly 4,500 years later, another well-known pyramid was erected, this time in Paris (**3.11**). Made of steel and glass, it marks the entry to one of the world's great museums, the Musée du Louvre. The Louvre had originally been built as a royal palace. A portion of it had served as a museum since 1793, after the French Revolution put an end to the monarchy, but it was not until 1981 that the decision was made to turn the entire building over to the museum. The American architect I. M. Pei was engaged to oversee the project. Among his many assignments was the creation of a single entry from which all wings of the vast palace would be accessible.

Pei's solution was to build a complex of spaces under the palace courtyard. The complex includes not only entrances to the three principal wings of the museum but also such amenities as an auditorium, a bookstore, shops, a cafeteria, and a restaurant. Over the entry to the complex, in the middle of the courtyard, Pei erected his transparent pyramid. Entering through the pyramid, visitors descend a spiral staircase to the principal reception area below, for which the pyramid also serves as a skylight. The pyramid complements the architecture of the palace without upstaging it. Its pure geometry contrasts with the palace's highly ornate facade, its transparency with the palace's solidity, and its cool reflective surfaces with the palace's warm ocher stone. Triangular reflecting pools echo the pyramid's shape, and smaller pyramids around it illuminate other underground areas.

3.10 (above) The Great Pyramids, Giza, Egypt. Pyramid of Menkaure (left), c. 2500 B.C.E.; Pyramid of Khafre (center), c. 2530 B.C.E.; Pyramid of Khufu (right), c. 2570 B.C.E.

3.11 (below) Ieoh Ming Pei. Louvre Pyramid, Paris. 1988. Height 65′.

I. M. Pei's name will of course be associated with the pyramid for as long as it stands. But his will not be the only name. The project was the idea of a man named François Mitterrand, who was then president of France. The enlarged Louvre was just one of the many works that Mitterrand commissioned. Through them he left his imprint on Paris and secured a place for himself in the cultural memory of his country.

Mitterrand's works in Paris were largely public monuments for the use and enjoyment of the people of France. Many works of art that we enjoy today in museums, however, were never intended for our eyes but were commissioned by rulers or by members of a social elite for their own private pleasure. Such is the case with the exquisite paintings of the *Akbarnama*, or *Tales of Akbar* (**3.12**). Akbar was a 16th-century monarch of the Mughal empire in India. An excellent administrator and an enthusiastic patron of the arts, he maintained a workshop of Indian and Persian artists at his court. Akbar commissioned a chronicle of his day-to-day activities, and his court artists prepared a lavishly illustrated volume of the resulting tales.

Akbar Hunting with Trained Cheetahs (3.12) shows the emperor at middle right, on a rearing brown horse, watching his cheetah bring down an antelope. The landscape teems with activity. Horses, men, and game rush through the trees and brush, in and around the bulbous, knobby outcroppings of rock. In fact, the trees and rocks themselves seem to be in motion, caught up in the frenzy of the hunt. There is no area of rest for our eyes in this scene. Every inch of the painting is filled with decorative detail and bursting with energy. Akbar must have spent many happy hours poring over the illustrations to his life. Today, we recognize them as among the finest examples of the Mughal style in painting, and through them we remember the name of Akbar, just as he wished.

3.12 (left) Lal and Sanwlah. *Akbar Hunting with Trained Cheetahs,* from the *Akbarnama.* c. 1590. Opaque watercolor on paper, height 15″.
Victoria and Albert Museum, London.

3.13 (right) Akan (Fante) linguists at Enyan Abassa, Nigeria, 1974.

Art forms have served as symbols of rank and signs of status at all levels of society. In our society today, this is not immediately obvious, for we no longer consider many of these tokens as art. For example, if you were to win a swimming meet today, you would be presented with a trophy—a mass-produced, one-size-fits-all figure of a swimmer. However, had you won such a competition in ancient Greece, your reward might have included a small sculpture in bronze, a unique work made by an artist. Even though we no longer consider the mass-produced trophy to be art (although someone certainly designed it), the function of the two works is the same: they are markers of status and achievement within the social order.

In societies where most objects are still handmade, where art has not split off from craft on the one hand and industrial manufacturing on the other, the situation is much clearer. Among the Akan peoples of West Africa, for example, many art forms are associated with leadership and statecraft. Among the most distinctive and well known of these are the staffs carried by linguists (**3.13**). A linguist serves a ruler as translator, spokesperson, adviser, historian, and orator. Every local chief employs at least one linguist, and more powerful chiefs and kings may be attended by many. As a symbol of his office, the linguist carries a staff topped with a small wooden sculpture covered in gold leaf. Each sculptural motif is associated with one or more proverbs, often about the nature of leadership or the just use of power. In the photograph here, for example, the staff at the far left showing two men seated at a table calls forth the proverb, "Food is for its owner, not for the one who is hungry," meaning that the chieftaincy belongs to the man who has the right to it, not just to anyone who wants it.

Commissioned by those in power, art has been used to underscore the legitimacy of the established order and to signal and support distinctions of status within society. Outside of these systems of patronage, however, art has also been used to criticize rulers and speak out against injustices embedded in society. Among the most relentless and skilled of artists ever to turn a cold eye on the social order of his day was the 19th-century Frenchman Honoré Daumier.

Daumier was a painter, but he achieved greater renown as a political cartoonist, and he possessed all the traits necessary for the latter occupation—righteous anger, an eye for the telling detail, and a pen that could strike like a stiletto. In the early 1830s Daumier's harsh political criticism brought him fame but also got him into trouble with the authorities. One image in particular, widely distributed as a print (Chapter 8), caused official wrath, and that was *Murder in the Rue Transnonain* (**3.14**).

3.14 Honoré Daumier. *Murder in the Rue Transnonain*, from *L'Association Mensuelle*. 1834. Lithograph, 11$\frac{1}{4}$ × 17$\frac{3}{8}$". The Metropolitan Museum of Art, New York.

3.15 Robert Frank. *Trolley, New Orleans,* copyright *The Americans,* Robert Frank. 1955–56. Silver gelatin print, 9 × 13″.
Courtesy Pace/MacGill Gallery. Collection The Art Institute of Chicago.

The title of Daumier's work was enough for his contemporary audience to understand the subject. In 1834 France was rocked by a popular uprising against the government of King Louis Philippe. Working-class people who lived on a certain street in Paris, the Rue Transnonain, were suspected of taking part. On April 15 shots were fired from one tenement building, whereupon the civil guard broke in and killed an entire family—without determining their guilt or innocence. Daumier has portrayed the chilling aftermath of that slaughter. The father lies sprawled against a disarrayed bed, nearly covering the body of a dead child. A woman's body, graceless in sudden death, fills the shadows at left, while an old man's blood-spattered head projects into the picture at right.

Daumier's harsh realism gives this image its poignancy. We can't help wondering what these people were doing just a few moments ago, before they were murdered. Were they sleeping? Was the old man sitting in the chair, now overturned? The father's body, bathed in light, has a heroic quality despite the clumsy pose (or perhaps because of it). Daumier's art turned this poor family into martyrs for the cause—as the authorities well knew when they confiscated the artist's original and destroyed most of the copies.

Photography has proved a powerful tool for exposing social injustice. Many photographers have turned their talents to documenting society at large, in the process capturing images that prick at our conscience. In 1955, supported by a grant from the Guggenheim Foundation, the Swiss-born American photographer Robert Frank set out to photograph America. Over the next two years he and his family drove from one end of the country to the other, stopping in rural towns and big cities, observing the well-off and the not so well-off, the right side of the tracks and the other side. Frank took more than 28,000 photographs over the course of the trip. From these, he selected eighty-three for publication in his landmark book *The Americans.*

In *Trolley, New Orleans* (**3.15**), the trolley windows frame a series of individual portraits. We could name them The Mysterious Man, The Suspicious Woman, The Unhappy Children, The Tragic Man, The Smiling Woman. The passengers are all within a few feet of each other, yet they do not interact at all. The photograph is an image of urban isolation, with each person locked up in his or her own world. Yet it is also an image of something else. It is impossible not to notice that the people in the front of the trolley are white. The people in the back of the trolley are black. Here in its casual everyday reality was the great social injustice of segregation. Once seen, it could not be unseen.

Frank's photograph captures a specific instant in time and a visual fragment isolated from the larger flow of events. His art is to capture the most significant moment and the most telling fragment. A painter, on the other hand, can construct a memorable image by compressing many instants and many fragments into a single view. Rarely has anyone ever done this more effectively than Pablo Picasso in *Guernica* (**3.16**). One of the great masterpieces of 20th-century art, *Guernica* was constructed to compress as much horror and outrage into one canvas as possible.

It is necessary to know the story behind *Guernica* to understand its power. In 1937 Europe was moving toward war, and a trial run, so to speak, occurred in Spain, where the forces of General Francisco Franco waged civil war against the established government. Franco willingly accepted aid from Hitler, and in exchange he allowed the Nazis to test their developing air power. On April 28, 1937, the Germans bombed the town of Guernica, the old Basque capital in northern Spain. There was no real military reason for the raid; it was simply an experiment to see whether aerial bombing could wipe out a whole city. Being totally defenseless, Guernica was devastated and its civilian population massacred.

At the time Picasso, himself a Spaniard, was working in Paris and had been commissioned by his government to paint a mural for the Spanish Pavilion of the Paris World's Fair of 1937. For some time he had procrastinated about fulfilling the commission; then, within days after news of the bombing reached Paris, he started *Guernica* and completed it in little over a month. The finished mural shocked those who saw it; it remains today a chillingly dramatic protest against the brutality of war.

At first encounter with *Guernica* the viewer is overwhelmed by its presence. The painting is huge—more than 25 feet long and nearly 12 feet high—and its stark, powerful imagery seems to reach out and engulf the observer. Picasso used no colors; the whole painting is done in white and black and shades of gray, possibly to create a "newsprint" quality in reporting the event. Although the artist's symbolism is very personal (and he declined to explain it in detail), we cannot misunderstand the scenes of extreme pain and anguish throughout the canvas. At far left a shrieking mother holds her dead child, and at far right another woman, in a burning house, screams in agony. The gaping mouths and clenched hands speak of disbelief at such mindless cruelty.

3.16 Pablo Picasso. *Guernica.* 1937. Oil on canvas, 11′5 1/2″ × 25′5 3/4″. Centro de Arte Reina Sofía, Madrid.

Another victim is the dying horse to the left of center, speared from above and just as stunned by the carnage as any of the human sufferers. Various writers have interpreted the bull at upper left in different ways. Picasso drew much of his imagery from the bullfight, an ingrained part of his Spanish heritage. Perhaps the bull symbolizes the brutal victory of the Nazis; perhaps it, like the horse, is also a victim of carnage. There is even more confusion about the symbols of the lamp and the light bulb at top center. These may be indications that light is being cast on the horrors of war, or they may be signals of hope. Picasso did not tell us, so we are free to make our own associations.

A protest against war is a protest against the social order that allows war to happen, for war is an activity that one society wages on another. When war is ended, the victor and the loser must both come to terms with their actions, celebrating and mourning, remembering and questioning. Throughout history, art has played an important role in giving form to these reactions through public monuments raised to commemorate conflicts. By their very nature, such monuments raise the question, "How do we as a society want to remember this event? What is our 'official' memory to be?"

Among our most painful national memories is the Vietnam War, a conflict in which thousands of young men and women gave up their lives, but which divided the country so deeply that returning veterans received virtually no recognition for their sacrifices. It was not until several years after the war's end that a competition to create a memorial was announced.

Today the Vietnam Veterans Memorial in Washington, D.C. (**3.17**), is the most-visited spot in the nation's capital. Completed in 1982, the memorial was designed by Maya Ying Lin, who was just twenty-two years old when her entry was selected from more than 1,400 submitted. When first unveiled to the public, Lin's design was considered highly controversial. It is, after all, nothing more than two long walls of polished black granite, set into the earth so as to form a V, engraved with the names of the missing, the captured, and the dead—column after column of names, almost 58,000 in all. Many viewers felt "the Wall," as it has come to be called, flouted tradition, that it was not sufficiently respectful of those who fought. Many thought a statue of a heroic soldier marching off to battle would be more appropriate.

But public opinion changes. In time the American public came to accept this memorial as a fitting tribute to those who died. Visitors from all over, visitors who had no connection with the war, even young people who cannot remember the war, stand quietly before the roster of names—names on a mass tombstone. Many come to find one name in particular, the name of a relative or friend chiseled forever into the rock and not to be forgotten. They leave flowers and poems, teddy bears and ribbons, photographs and letters, reminders of the past. Mostly they touch the Wall, running their fingers over the carved letters as though to touch once again the life that is gone.

3.17 Maya Ying Lin. Vietnam Veterans Memorial, Washington, D.C. 1982. Black granite, length 492′.

MAYA YING LIN

b. 1959

"EACH OF MY works originates from a simple desire to make people aware of their surroundings, not just the physical world but also the psychological world we live in," Maya Lin has written. "I create places in which to think, without trying to dictate what to think."[1]

The most famous of Maya Lin's places for thought was also her first, the Vietnam Veterans Memorial in Washington, D.C., which she designed while still an undergraduate architecture student at Yale University (see 3.17). Like much of Lin's work, its powerful form was the product of a long period of reading and thinking followed by a moment of intuition. On a trip to Washington to look at the site, she writes, "I had a simple impulse to cut into the earth. I imagined taking a knife and cutting into the earth, opening it up, an initial violence and pain that in time would heal. The grass would grow back, but the initial cut would remain a pure flat surface in the earth with a polished, mirrored surface, much like the surface on

a geode when you cut it and polish the edge." Engraved with the names of the dead, the surface "would be an interface, between our world and the quieter, darker, more peaceful world beyond. . . . I never looked at the memorial as a wall, an object, but as an edge to the earth, an opened side." Back at school, Lin gave her idea form in the university dining hall with two decisive cuts in a mound of mashed potatoes.

Maya Lin was born and grew up in Athens, Ohio. Her father, a ceramist, was chair of the fine arts department at the Ohio University, while her mother, a poet, still teaches in the department of English there. Both parents had immigrated to the United States from China before Maya was born. Lin readily credits the academic atmosphere and her family's everyday involvement with art for the direction her life has taken. Of her father, she writes simply that "his aesthetic sensibility ran throughout our lives." She and her brother spent countless hours after school watching him work with clay in his studio.

Lin admits that it took a long time to put the experience of constructing the Vietnam Veterans Memorial behind her. The prolonged controversy had involved verbal, sometimes racist, attacks on her personally, and they took a toll. For the next several years she worked quietly for an architectural firm before returning to Yale to finish her doctoral studies. Since setting up her studio in 1987, she has created such compelling works as the Civil Rights Memorial in Montgomery, Alabama; *Wave Field*, an earthwork at the University of Michigan in Ann Arbor; and the Langston Hughes Library in Clinton, Tennessee.

Critics are often puzzled about whether to classify Lin as an architect or a sculptor. Lin herself insists that one flows into the other. "The best advice I was given was from Frank Gehry (the only architect who has successfully merged sculpture and architecture), who said I shouldn't worry about the distinctions and just make the work," Lin recalls. That is just what she continues to do.

Maya Lin with a model of the Vietnam Veterans Memorial, 1980.

STORYTELLING

Deeds of heroes, lives of saints, folktales passed down through generations, episodes of television shows that everyone knows by heart—shared stories are one of the ways we create a sense of community. Artists have often turned to stories for subject matter, especially stories whose roots reach deep into their culture's collective memory.

In Christian Europe of the early 15th century, stories of the lives of the saints were a common reference point. One of the best-loved saints was Francis of Assisi, who had lived only about two centuries earlier. The son of a wealthy merchant in the Italian town of Assisi, Francis as a young man renounced his inheritance for a life of extreme poverty in the service of God. He preached to all who would listen (including birds and animals) and cared for the poor and the sick. With the disciples who gathered around him he founded a religious community that was eventually formalized as the Franciscan Order of monks.

The painting here by the 15th-century Italian artist Sassetta illustrates two episodes from Saint Francis' life (**3.18**). To the left, Francis, still a wealthy young man, gives his cloak to a poor man. To the right, Sassetta cleverly uses the house—its front wall made invisible so we can see inside—to create a separate space, a sort of "painting within a painting," for the next part of the story. Here, an angel appears while Francis is sleeping and grants him a dream vision of the Heavenly City of God. The angel's upraised hand leads our eyes to the vision, which is portrayed at the top of the panel.

3.18 Sassetta. *St. Francis Giving His Mantle to a Poor Man and the Vision of the Heavenly City.* c. 1437–44. Oil on panel, 34¼ × 20¾". The National Gallery, London.

These "painting within a painting" areas are called space cells, and artists in many cultures have used them for narration. The Indian painter Sahibdin made ingenious use of space cells to relate a complicated episode from the epic poem *Ramayana*, or Story of Rama (**3.19**). One of the two great founding Indian epics, the *Ramayana* is attributed to the legendary poet Valmiki, and portions of it date as far back as 500 B.C.E. Rama, the hero of the epic, is a prince and an incarnation of the Hindu god Vishnu. He is heir to the throne of an important Indian kingdom, but due to jealous intrigue he is sent into exile before he can be crowned. Soon afterward, his wife, Sita, is carried off by the demon Ravana. The epic chronicles Rama's search for Sita and his long journey back to his rightful position as a ruler.

In the episode depicted here, Rama suffers a setback as he battles Ravana for Sita's release. The story begins in the small, rose-colored space cell to the right, where Ravana, portrayed with twenty heads and a whirl-wind of arms, confers with his son Indrajit on a plan to defeat Rama, who is about to attack the palace. Below, the plan finalized, Indrajit is shown leaving the palace with his warriors. The action now shifts to the left side of the page, where Indrajit, aloft in an airborne chariot, shoots arrows down at Rama and his companion, Lakshmana. The arrows turn into snakes, binding the two heroes. The story continues on the ground, where Indrajit assures the monkey-king Sugriva that Rama and Lakshmana are not dead, but successfully captured. In the yellow cell at the center of the painting, Indrajit stages a triumphal procession back into the palace, where, in the upper right corner, he is joyfully received by Ravana. Meanwhile, Sita, imprisoned in the garden depicted in the yellow space cell immediately below, receives a visit from the demoness Trijata, who takes her in a flying chariot ride (upper left) to witness Rama's defeat. Sahibdin's illustration was made for an audience who knew the epic tale almost by heart and would have delighted in puzzling out the painting's ingenious construction.

History has furnished artists with many stories, for history itself is nothing more than a story we tell ourselves about the past, a story we write and rewrite. In his 1942 painting called *John Brown Going to His Hanging* (**3.20**), Horace Pippin took for his subject an episode from history to which he had a

3.19 Sahibdin and workshop. *Rama and Lakshmana Bound by Arrow-snakes,* from the *Ramayana.* Mewar, c. 1650–52. Opaque watercolor on paper, c. 9 × 15³/₈″. The British Library, London.

3.20 Horace Pippin. *John Brown Going to His Hanging.* 1942. Oil on canvas, 24 1/8 × 30 1/4".
The Pennsylvania Academy of Fine Arts, Philadelphia.

personal connection. During the 1850s the United States was politically and emotionally divided by the conflict between advocates of black slavery and those who deplored the practice of slavery, called abolitionists. Among the most fervent of the abolitionists was a white man named John Brown, whose (sometimes violent) activities in support of freeing the slaves caused him to be arrested and tried for treason in the state of Virginia. Brown was convicted and was hanged on December 2, 1859. The artist Horace Pippin, a descendant of black slaves, was not yet born, but his grandmother was present at the hanging of John Brown, and she pictured the scene, in words, many times. Her grandson later transformed the word-picture into this painting.

We see John Brown at center, silhouetted against the white jailhouse in the background. His arms are bound to his sides, and he is seated on what will be his own coffin. All the occupants of the wagon are dressed in black, but the wagon is drawn by two white horses—surely symbolic of the black-white drama that is being enacted. Directly over Brown's head is a bare tree limb—again, surely symbolic of the tree from which he will soon be hanged. Most of the onlookers are white. They stare at the procession with a kind of morbid fascination, and some chat amiably among themselves. A lone black woman, at far right, turns her back on the scene and stares out fiercely, her arms crossed in anger and accusation. This figure is the artist's grandmother.

THE HERE AND NOW

The social order, the world of the sacred, history and the great stories of the past—all these are very grand and important themes. But art does not always have to reach so high. Sometimes it is enough just to look around ourselves and notice what our life is like here, now, in this place, at this time.

Among the earliest images of daily life to have come down to us are those that survived in the tombs of ancient Egypt. Egyptians imagined the afterlife as resembling earthly life in every detail, except that it continued through eternity. To ensure the prosperity of the deceased in the afterlife, scenes of the pleasures and bounty of life in Egypt were painted or carved on the tomb walls. Sometimes models were substituted for paintings (**3.21**).

3.21 (above) Model depicting the counting of livestock, from the tomb of Meketre, Deir el-Bahri. Dynasty 11, 2134–1991 B.C.E. Painted wood, length 5′8″. Egyptian Museum, Cairo.

3.22 (left) *Court Ladies Preparing Newly Woven Silk*, detail. Attributed to Hui-zong (1082–1135) but probably by a court painter. Handscroll; ink, colors, and gold on silk; height 14 1/2″. Courtesy Museum of Fine Arts, Boston.

This model was one of many found in the tomb of an Egyptian official named Meketre, who died around 1990 B.C.E. Meketre himself is depicted at the center, seated on a chair in the shade of a pavilion. Seated on the floor to his left is his son; to his right are several scribes (professional writers) with their writing materials ready. Overseers of Meketre's estate stand by as herders drive his cattle before the reviewing stand so that the scribes can count them. The herders' gestures are animated as they coax the cattle along with their sticks, and the cattle themselves are beautifully observed in their diverse markings.

Another model from Meketre's tomb depicts women at work spinning and weaving cloth. They would probably have been producing linen, which Egyptians excelled at. In China, the favored material since ancient times has been silk. *Court Ladies Preparing Newly Woven Silk* (**3.22**) is a scene from a long handscroll depicting women weaving, ironing, and folding lengths of silk. The painting is a copy made during the 12th century of a famous 8th-century work, now lost. In this scene, four ladies in their elegant robes stretch a length of silk. The woman facing us irons it with a flat-bottomed pan full of hot coals taken from the brazier visible at the right. A little girl too small to share in the task clowns around for our benefit. If this is a scene from everyday life, it is a very rarefied life indeed. These are ladies of the imperial court, and the painting is just as much an exercise in portraying beautiful women as it is in showing their virtuous sense of domestic duty.

3.23 Georges Seurat. *Bathers at Asnières.* 1883–84. Oil on canvas, 6′10¾″ × 9′10⅛″. The National Gallery, London.

A day off from work altogether is the subject of Georges Seurat's painting *Bathers at Asnières* (**3.23**). Far from the refined atmosphere of the Chinese court, we find ourselves on an unremarkable stretch of river outside Paris, some 1,000 years later and half a world away. In place of the court ladies' sense of community through a shared task, we find a group of young men and boys who seem isolated from each other, alone in their thoughts. They sit at the river's edge or stand in its shallows, their white skin clearly not used to the sun. In the background, a long, low bridge spans the river. Behind it lies a factory with its many tall smokestacks. Industrialization was transforming the countryside during the late 19th century. An issue for artists of the day was how much of this new reality to accept into painting. Even today, many of us seeing such a scene would instinctively aim our cameras elsewhere, trying to preserve the illusion that the river was unspoiled. For Seurat, however, painting the here and now meant finding beauty even in a factory, and dignity in ordinary workers.

THE HUMAN EXPERIENCE

An Egyptian official, a lady of the imperial Chinese court, and a worker in the suburbs of Paris would all have had very different lives. They would have known different stories, worshiped different gods, seen different sights, and had different understandings of the world and their place in it. Yet they also would have shared certain experiences, just by virtue of being human. We are all of us born, we pass through childhood, we mature into sexual beings, we search for love, we grow old, we die. We experience doubt and wonder, happiness and sorrow, loneliness and despair.

Most of us have at one time or another stood in front of a mirror and stared at our reflection, wondering, "Who is that person? Is that what others see? Is that me?" One of the most sustained and moving artistic records of the mystery of identity is the long series of self-portraits painted by the Dutch artist Rembrandt van Rijn (**3.24**). Rembrandt painted himself some fifty times over the course of his adult life, and through the paintings we can witness his progress from youthful high spirits to worldly success to old age and financial ruin.

Rembrandt was fifty-two when he painted the portrait illustrated here. His period of financial success was behind him; two years earlier he had been forced into bankruptcy. He has posed himself in an exotic oriental costume, a heavy cloak about his shoulders. It looks like the type of costume he might have used for an Old Testament patriarch in one of his biblical paintings. The costume seems to weigh as heavily as the years as he pitilessly observes the aging of his own face. Looking out from this part he is playing, his eyes catch himself in the mirror, watching himself watching, watching us watching him. We all play roles, the portrait suggests, but no matter what image we present to the world, it is somehow not really us.

Christian Schumann uses a very different language to explore the puzzle of identity in *Edible* (**3.25**). Born in 1970, the artist was twenty-five when he completed this painting, which brings together images in styles drawn from advertising, comic books, and cartoons to suggest a view from inside, a sort of scrapbook of a self. The head at the center of the top row of images seems to be the hero of the story. The rest of the images suggest his experiences, moods, and shifting self-image. To the left, an unfriendly face is labeled "you." Further on is a pink cartoon figure of can-do optimism. To the right, the hero sees himself as a goony character with a drippy nose. Directly below, the drip is transformed into lights suspended in a retro-sixties interior. The hero sits at a table

3.24 (left) Rembrandt van Rijn. *Self-Portrait.* 1658. Oil on canvas, $52\,^7/_8 \times 40\,^7/_8''$. The Frick Collection, New York.

3.25 (right) Christian Schumann. *Edible.* 1995. Acrylic and mixed media on canvas, $60 \times 40''$. Courtesy Postmasters Gallery, New York.

REMBRANDT
1606–1669

OF THE FEW artists classified as "greatest of the great," Rembrandt seems the most accessible to us. His life encompassed happiness, success, heartbreak, and failure—all on a scale larger than most of us are likely to know. Through his many self-portraits and his portraits of those he loved, we can witness it all.

Born in the Dutch city of Leiden, Rembrandt Harmensz. van Rijn was the son of a miller. At fourteen he began art lessons in Leiden and later studied with a master in Amsterdam. By the age of twenty-two he had pupils of his own. About 1631 he settled permanently in Amsterdam, having by then attracted considerable fame as a portrait painter. Thus began for Rembrandt a decade of professional success and personal happiness—a high point that would never come again in his life.

In 1634 Rembrandt married Saskia van Uijlenburgh, an heiress of good family, thus improving his own social status. The pair must have been rather a dashing couple-about-Amsterdam. The artist's portraits were in demand, his style was fashionable, and he had money enough to indulge himself in material possessions, especially to collect art. One blight on this happy period was the arrival of four children, none of whom survived. But in 1641 Rembrandt's beloved son Titus was born.

Rembrandt's range as an artist was enormous. He was master not only of painting but of drawing and of the demanding technique of etching for prints. (It is said that Rembrandt went out sketching with an etcher's needle as other artists might carry a pencil.) Besides the many portraits, the artist displayed unparalleled genius in other themes, including landscapes and religious scenes.

In 1642 Rembrandt's fortunes again changed, but this time for the worse. Saskia died not long after giving birth to Titus. The artist's financial affairs were in great disarray, no doubt partly because of his self-indulgence in buying art and precious objects. Although he continued to work and to earn money, Rembrandt showed little talent for money management. Ultimately he was forced into bankruptcy and had to sell not only his art collection but even Saskia's burial plot. About 1649 Hendrickje Stoffels came to live with Rembrandt, and she is thought of as his second wife, although they did not marry legally. She joined forces with Titus to form an art dealership in an attempt to protect the artist from his creditors. Capping the long series of tragedies that marked Rembrandt's later life, Hendrickje died in 1663 and Titus in 1668, a year before his father.

Rembrandt's legacy is almost totally a visual one. He does not seem to have written much. Ironically, one of the few recorded comments comes in a letter to a patron, begging for payment—payment for paintings that are now considered priceless and hang in one of the world's great museums. "I pray you my kind lord that my warrant might now be prepared at once so that I may now at last receive my well-earned 1244 guilders and I shall always seek to recompense your lordship for this with reverential service and proof of friendship."[2]

Rembrandt. *Self-Portrait with Saskia in the Parable of the Prodigal Son.* c. 1635–39.
Oil on canvas, 5'3 1/2" × 4'3 1/2".
Staatliche Kunstsammlung, Dresden.

3.26 (left) Auguste Rodin. *The Kiss*. 1886–98. Marble, height 5′11¼″.
Musée Rodin, Paris.

3.27 Janine Antoni. *Gnaw*. 1991. Installation view (above) and details (below).
Courtesy Luhring Augustine Gallery, New York.

in despair. The empty chair opposite and the two glasses of wine on the table suggest that someone has just left—a romantic encounter gone wrong. The lower third of the painting contains images of things that are "under"—an underground cavern, the devil of the underworld, a diver underwater, and emotions kept under as well, like suppressed anger.

Love, as Schumann's painting indicates, is the thing we crave most. *The Kiss*, Rodin's famous sculpture of romantic and sensual love, idealizes one aspect of this form of happiness we seek through others (**3.26**). Carved from cool marble, the figures nevertheless look as though they might be warm to the touch. The roughly carved base contrasts with the couple's smooth and nuanced surfaces. One can almost sense a pulse running under their skin, a pulse that must be racing. The delicacy with which the man poses his hand on the woman's thigh captures the erotic tension of touch, and the space between the twisting bodies is charged with electricity.

Looking at Rodin's *Kiss*, we take what it is made of and how it was made almost for granted. Marble is a standard material for sculpture, and carving is the most typical way of shaping it. With Janine Antoni's *Gnaw*, however, what it is made of and how it was shaped are the first things that grab our attention (**3.27**). *Gnaw* consists of a 600-pound cube of chocolate and a similar one of lard, each gnawed at by the artist herself. The chewed portions of lard were made into lipsticks, while the chocolate was made into heart-shaped, partitioned boxes for fancy gift chocolates. These are displayed in a nearby showcase, as though in an upscale boutique. Chocolate has strong associations with love, both as a token of affection and a substitute for it. Lard summons up obsessions with fat and self-image, which in turn are linked to culturally imposed ideals of female beauty, as is lipstick. *Gnaw* explores the gap between the prettified, commercial world of romance and the private, more desperate cravings it both feeds on and causes.

3.28 Johannes Vermeer. *Woman Holding a Balance.* c. 1664. Oil on canvas, 15⁷/₈ × 14″.
National Gallery of Art, Washington, D.C.

One of the most reticent yet complete evocations of our existence and its fundamental questions is the Dutch painter Johannes Vermeer's quiet masterpiece *Woman Holding a Balance* (**3.28**). Stillness pervades the picture. A gentle half-light filtered through the curtained window reveals a woman contemplating an empty jeweler's balance. She holds the balance and its two glinting trays delicately with her right hand, which falls in the exact center of the composition. The frame of the painting on the wall behind catches the light, drawing our attention. The painting is a depiction of the Last Judgment, when according to Christian belief Christ shall come again to judge, to weigh souls. On the table, the light picks out strands of pearls. Jewels and jewelry often serve as symbols of vanity and the temptations of earthly treasure. Light is reflected too in the surface of the mirror, next to the window. The mirror suggests self-knowledge, and indeed if the woman were to look up, she would be facing directly into it. Scholars have debated whether the woman is pregnant or whether the fashion of the day simply makes her appear so. Either way, we can say that her form evokes pregnancy, the miracle of birth, and the renewal of life.

Birth, death, the decisions we must weigh on our journey through life, the temptations of vanity, the problem of self-knowledge, the question of life after death—all of these issues are gently touched on in this most understated of paintings.

INVENTION AND FANTASY

During the Renaissance, European culture entered a new phase as it began to rediscover and assimilate ideas from the ancient civilizations of Greece and Rome. As a way of absorbing the past into the present, artists began to depict ancient gods and goddesses such as Venus. Of course, since Christianity was held to be the one true faith, a painting of Venus couldn't be considered *true* in the same way that a painting of Jesus was true. A painting of Venus had to be an invention, a fantasy.

Renaissance theorists explained this by likening painting to poetry. With words, a poet could conjure an imaginary world and fill it with people and events. Painting was even better, for it could bring an imaginary world to life before your eyes. Poetry had long been considered an art, and the idea that painting was comparable to it is one of the factors that led to painting's being considered an art as well.

One of the most bizarrely inventive artists ever to wield a brush was the Netherlandish painter Hieronymus Bosch. When we first encounter his *The Garden of Earthly Delights* (**3.29**), we might think we have wandered into a fun house of a particularly macabre kind. Bosch's large **triptych** (a three-section panel, of which we show only the middle portion) is like a peep into Hell—but this is an X-rated earthly Hell. Hundreds of nude human figures cavort in a fantasy landscape peopled also by giant plants, animals both known and unknown, and strange creatures that are part human, part vegetation. Humans ride upon, emerge from, are devoured by, or become part of the plant and animal forms. Bosch has let his imagination and perhaps his dream imagery go wherever it might. He drew upon many sources for his creations, including folklore, literature, astrology, and religious writings, but only his own inventiveness could have constructed such an amazing fantasy land.

3.29 Hieronymus Bosch. *The Garden of Earthly Delights,* center section. c. 1505–10. Oil on panel, 7′2 ⁵/₈″ × 6′4 ³/₄″. Museo del Prado, Madrid.

A far more benign imagination was that of Henri Rousseau. Rousseau worked in France during the late 19th and early 20th centuries. He was acquainted with all the up-and-coming artists of the Parisian scene, and sometimes he exhibited with them. The naiveté of his expression came not so much from ignorance of formal art tradition as from indifference to that tradition. His last work, *The Dream* (**3.30**), combines typical elements: a monumental nude perched on a sofa that has no seat; improbable wild animals and birds that never coexist in nature; lush foliage no botanist ever identified; and a dark-skinned "native" (of where?) playing a musical instrument. Rousseau loved to copy plants and animals from books, to fill in from his imagination, to mix and match in a picture as the inspiration took him. He labored over the meticulous rendering of every leaf and stem, yet the rendering is not lifelike at all, for the landscape does not exist; it is a fantasy land. Rousseau's world—which was apparently very real for him—is the paint on canvas that makes a rich, complex design for the viewer's pleasure.

The idea that a painting may spring from the imagination does not surprise us, for we can all doodle a fantasy image of a creature that doesn't exist. Photography, on the other hand, we associate with facts. We commonly offer photographs as evidence that something really happened or proof that we were really there. Contemporary artist Sandy Skoglund teases our association of photography with reality in works such as *Radioactive Cats* (**3.31**). Dozens of eerily glowing cats run rampant in a gray kitchen where a gray man sits listlessly as his gray wife forages in the gray refrigerator. The couple seem unsurprised by the cats. Perhaps these invasions have been a daily occurrence since the nuclear disaster that left all the cats in the world glowing. Perhaps these are pets who suffered some strange mutation, and the woman is going to feed them.

Skoglund plans each photograph carefully and spends months building the set for it. She made the cats here from chicken wire and plaster and painted them green. She bought the furniture from a junk shop and painted it gray. Another artist who created art from found objects transformed by paint was Louise Nevelson. In sculptures such as *Wedding Chapel IV* (**3.32**) she

3.30 Henri Rousseau. *The Dream.* 1910. Oil on canvas, 6′8 1/2″ × 9′9 1/2″.
The Museum of Modern Art, New York.

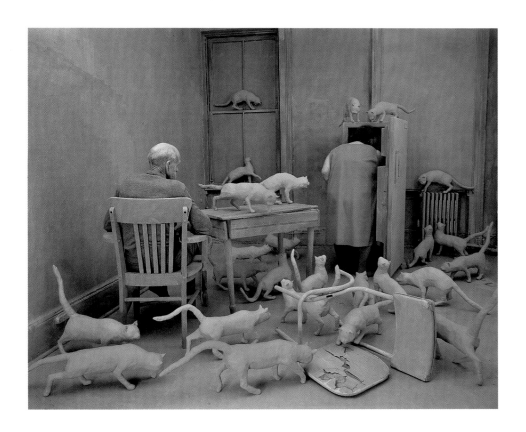

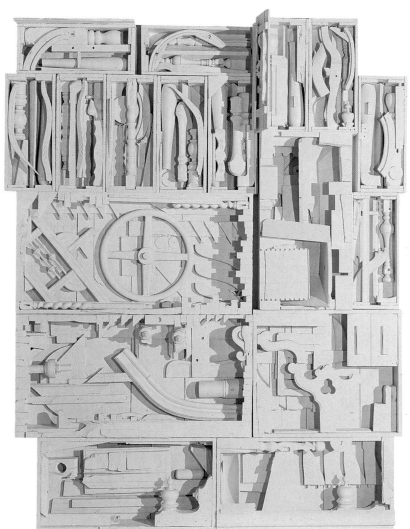

3.31 (above) Sandy Skoglund.
Radioactive Cats. © 1980.
Cibachrome print, 30 × 40″.
Courtesy the artist.

3.32 Louise Nevelson. *Wedding
Chapel IV.* 1960. Painted wood,
height c. 9′.
Private collection.

assembled scraps of wooden crates, dowels, balusters, chair legs, and other worthless odds and ends, then transformed them with white paint so that their individual identities merged into a new whole. Her sculptures are places of mystery, like an unfathomable storage system or an attic full of memories. She offers them not so much as evidence of her own inventiveness, but as places where *our* imaginations can wander and *our* fantasies blossom.

ART AND NATURE

As humans we make our own environment. From the first tools of the earliest hominids to today's towering skyscrapers, we have shaped the world around us to our needs. This manufactured environment, though, has its setting in quite a different environment, that of the natural world. Nature and our relationship to it are themes that have often been addressed through art.

During the 19th century, many painters set out to record the American landscape. For Thomas Cole, who as a young man had emigrated to America from England, the land itself was the new country's greatest heritage, the equal of the ancient architectural wonders of Europe. In *The Oxbow* Cole depicted a curiosity of the New England countryside, the great loop of the Connecticut River as it passes through Northampton, Massachusetts (**3.33**). To the left, a violent thunderstorm passes over a moun-

3.33 Thomas Cole. *The Oxbow (View from Mount Holyoke, Northampton, Massachusetts, After a Thunderstorm).* 1836. Oil on canvas, 4′3½″ × 6′4″.
The Metropolitan Museum of Art, New York.

3.34 Wang Jian. *White Clouds over Xiao and Xiang (after Zhao Mengfu).* 1668. Hanging scroll, ink and color on paper; height 53 1/4″. Freer Gallery of Art, Smithsonian Institution, Washington, D.C.

taintop where gnarled and damaged trees bear witness to the raw power of nature. To the right, emerging into the sunlight after the storm, there extends a broad settled valley. Fields have been cleared for grazing and for crops. Minute plumes of smoke mark scattered farmhouses, and a few boats dot the river. Cole even gives us a role to play: we have accompanied him on his painting expedition and climbed up a little higher for an even better view. On a promontory below us to the right, we see the artist's umbrella and knapsack. A little to the left and down from the umbrella, Thomas Cole himself, seated in front of a painting in progress, looks up at us over his shoulder.

Cole's canvas faithfully records a view he observed. In contrast, Wang Jian's *White Clouds over Xiao and Xiang* (**3.34**), while it is named for an actual place, portrays an imagined landscape, a construct of the mind. Landscape is the most important and honored subject in the Chinese painting tradition, but its purpose was never to record the details of a particular site or view. Rather, painters learned to paint mountains, rocks, trees, and water so that they could construct imaginary landscapes for viewers to wander through in the mind's eye. Here, we might stroll along the narrow footpath by the water's edge to the pavilions that sit out over the lake, visit the rambling house nestled in the hillside, or stand in the pavilion on the overlook higher up, taking in the scenery. While Cole's painting places us on the mountain and depicts what can be seen from a fixed position, Wang Jian's suspends us in midair and depicts a view that we could see only if we were mobile, like a bird.

In addition to their stylistic differences, the two landscapes embody very different attitudes toward nature and our place in it. Thomas Cole's painting draws a sharp distinction between the wild and the tamed. Untamed nature is portrayed as fascinating but dangerous, while the settled plains are calm and good—even the sunlight shines upon them. From our viewpoint on the mountain, we survey the scene with a sense of ownership and pride. In Wang Jian's painting, in contrast, human settlement disturbs nature as little as possible, aiming rather to exist in harmony with it. The distant, aerial viewpoint does not imply ownership but rather reveals to us our small role in the grand scheme of things.

3.35 Stone and gravel garden, Ryoan-ji Temple, Kyoto. Muromachi period, c. 1480.

Nature has been more than a subject for art; it has also served as a material for art. The desire to portray landscapes has been matched by the desire to create them for the pleasure of our eyes. A work such as the famed stone and gravel garden of the Buddhist temple of Ryoan-ji in Kyoto, Japan, seems to occupy a position halfway between sculpture and landscape gardening (**3.35**). Created toward the end of the 15th century and maintained continuously since then, the garden consists solely of five groupings of rocks set in a rectangular expanse of raked white gravel and surrounded by an earthen wall. A simple wooden viewing platform runs along one side. Over time, moss has grown up around the rock groupings, and oil in the clay walls has seeped to the surface, forming patterns that call to mind traditional Japanese ink paintings of landscape.

The garden is a place of meditation, and viewers are invited to find their own meanings in it. We may imagine the rocks as islands in a sea, or as mountain peaks appearing through the clouds. But it is not necessary to transform the rocks into anything other than what they are to appreciate the tranquility and healing beauty of the place.

The simplicity of Ryoan-ji finds an echo in *Spiral Jetty*, an earthwork built by American artist Robert Smithson in 1970 in the Great Salt Lake, Utah (**3.36**). Smithson had become fascinated with the ecology of salt lakes, especially with the microbacteria that tinge their water shades of red. After viewing the Great Salt Lake in Utah, he leased a parcel of land on its shore and began work on this large coil of rock and earth. Smithson was drawn to the idea that an artist could participate in the shaping of landscape almost as a geological force. Like the garden at Ryoan-ji, *Spiral Jetty* continued to change according to natural processes after it was finished. Salt crystals accumulated and sparkled on its edges. Depths of water in and around it showed themselves in different tints of transparent violet, pink, and red.

Spiral Jetty was submerged by the rising waters of the lake soon after it was created. It may soon be restored, but most people know it (and will continue to know it) through photographs. The photograph here was taken by Smithson himself. Interestingly, like Brancusi, whose photograph of his own sculpture opened this book, Smithson chose to portray his work interacting with sunlight, thus emphasizing the shifts in mood and character that reflected its place as part of the natural world.

3.36 Robert Smithson. *Spiral Jetty*. 1970. Rock, salt crystals, earth, algae; coil length 1500′. Great Salt Lake, Utah (now submerged).
Photograph by Robert Smithson, courtesy James Cohan Gallery, New York.

ART AND ART

When asked why he made art, the American painter Barnett Newman is said to have replied, "To have something to look at." There is more than a little truth in his comment. Art is an activity we have come to pursue for its own sake. As such, art can be its own theme, with no other purpose than to give visual pleasure or to pose another answer to the ongoing question, "What is art?"

New materials or techniques can often inspire a creative response. David Hockney, for example, did not have a particular subject in mind when in 1978 he paid a visit to the master printer Kenneth Tyler at his studio in Mount Kisco, New York. He was merely going at Tyler's invitation to see what making paper by hand was all about. Like industrially produced paper, handmade paper is made from vegetable fiber pounded into a pulp with water and then pressed into sheets and dried. The throwaway paper we use for daily needs—newspapers, notebooks, memo pads—is made from tree fiber. Durable paper for art is generally made from cotton or linen rag fiber. At Tyler's workshop, Hockney experimented with using colored pulp to "paint" an image, then pressing it so that paper and image were one. The crude nature of the materials ruled out a lot of precision and detail, and this began to interest Hockney. What were the aesthetic possibilities of this medium? What subject could give play to its strengths while avoiding its limitations?

3.37 David Hockney. *Diving Board with Shadow* (Paper Pool 15). 1978. Pressed paper pulp, 6' × 7'1¹/₂".
Courtesy David Hockney/Tyler Graphics Ltd.

The answer was in the backyard: a swimming pool (**3.37**). Hockney drew a large pool over six sheets of paper. Tyler and his staff then made a mold for each sheet that included removable metal strips to separate basic color areas. Hockney used the molds repeatedly, varying the colors each time. The complex play of light and shadow in moving water came to fascinate him, and he experimented with all manner of techniques and tools to evoke it. Blotches and squiggles were created by dropping the pulp in spoonfuls, squeezing it through a kitchen baster, or manipulating it directly with fingers and hands. For one pool, he worked outside in the rain so that the drops would add their own textural effects. In the end, Hockney stayed much longer than he had originally planned and created a dazzling series of twenty-nine paper pools. Their theme is their own material, and their purpose to give visual pleasure.

Spaces between the six sheets of paper that constitute Hockney's pool suggest a large grid laid over the image. They draw our attention to the contrast between the work's construction in repeated units (the flat sheets of paper) and its portrayal of a unified view in depth (the pool). Grid, repetition, and depth are the entire subject of a much more austere work, Sol LeWitt's *Untitled Cube (6)* (**3.38**). On the floor is a grid that measures out a square. Centered on this square is a grid that measures out a cube. That is all there is to it. LeWitt's cube resembles Hockney's pool with the color and subject matter stripped away. The gridded square on the floor is like the rectangular concrete surface the pool is set in. The gridded cube measures a volume of space; the pool measures cubic volume of water.

Spurning the sensuous appeal of color and the distraction of subject matter was precisely what LeWitt had in mind. LeWitt was one of several artists whose work took a similar direction during the 1960s, a direction that became known as **Minimalism.** Minimalist art favored materials associated more with industry or construction than with art, materials such as brick, plywood, and fluorescent lighting tubes. Often composed of repeated units such as the squares here, the sculptures had an impersonal look, as though they could be designed by the artist and given to others to build. Indeed,

they often were. Most of the artists preferred to call their works "objects" rather than "sculptures," and they placed them on the floor instead of on a pedestal. LeWitt's works in particular often had an intellectual component. Here, viewers eventually realize that the cube and the square contain the same number of line-units. One could take apart the grid and construct the square, or vice versa.

Minimalism was a stage in the ongoing argument about the appropriate purpose, materials, and look of art in an age characterized by mass production and at a time when representational images had been taken over by advertising. If art's job was to tell the truth, Minimalists felt, then it should limit itself to expressing its own materials and its own logic. Anything else was a lie, like advertising, which manipulated images to manipulate people. If art's purpose was to provide an aesthetic experience, how little could provide this experience? Think of the garden at Ryoan-ji (see 3.35), whose fifteen rocks and raked gravel have contented viewers for over 500 years.

For artists who came of age in the 1980s and 1990s, however, Minimalism was no longer part of an argument. They had grown up with it. To them, it was just one more way that art could look. In their hands, minimal forms were flooded with emotion and subject matter—just the things that the original Minimalists thought needed to be expelled.

One artist who uses minimal form for expressive ends is Indian-born Anish Kapoor. On a trip back to his homeland, Kapoor was struck by the beauty of the mounds of intensely colored powders for sale outside of Hindu temples. He translated this vision of pure color and spiritual energy into such works as *At the Hub of Things*, in which powdered blue pigment coats a fiberglass form (**3.39**). *At the Hub of Things* evokes the blue goddess Kali, who is associated with the dark and disturbing side of power. The sculpture stands some 5 feet tall, allowing viewers to lose themselves staring into the velvety depths of its tempting void. Kapoor's sense of what art is was formed by the art he grew up with, and he in turn forms art that will influence the next generation of artists, continuing the cycle.

3.38 (above) Sol LeWitt. *Untitled Cube (6)*. 1968. Painted metal, 15 1/2 × 45 × 45". Whitney Museum of American Art, New York.

3.39 (below) Anish Kapoor. *At the Hub of Things*. 1987. Fiberglass and pigment, height 5'4⅛". Hirshhorn Museum and Sculpture Garden, Smithsonian Institution, Washington, D.C.

PART TWO

THE
VOCABULARY
OF ART

4.1 Henri Matisse. *Interior with an Egyptian Curtain.* 1948.
Oil on canvas, 45 ¼ × 35 ⅛".
The Phillips Collection, Washington, D.C.

The Visual Elements

If somebody asked you what you see in our first illustration (**4.1**), you might say something like "a bowl of fruit on a table in front of a window." This is a form of shorthand that we use all the time when looking at images, for we know of course that it is not a bowl of fruit at all, but a painting of a bowl of fruit, a painting by Matisse. In learning to appreciate art, we want to become as aware of the painting as we are of what it depicts, and to do this we need a vocabulary for talking about what we see.

Earlier chapters have presented some terms that allow us to describe the painting's appearance in general: it is *representational*, but not *naturalistic*. Rather, it is moving toward *abstraction*. *Stylistic* clues suggest that it is a Western work of the 20th century. Viewers who know many of Matisse's paintings would recognize it as an example of his late style.

This chapter continues by introducing the elements from which the painting is constructed. We can see that Matisse used *lines* to define the contours of the fruit and to outline the frame of the window. The curtain marks the foremost point of the picture *space*, which feels shallow and compressed. Matisse uses a shift in *color* to help suggest the *mass* of the table, although he has abstracted the fruit into round *shapes*. He painted a dark shadow around the base of the bowl to imply that *light* is pouring in the window. Outside, a palm tree is rendered as joyously as a display of fireworks, its fronds abstracted into patterns of short repeating strokes that suggest a prickly *texture*. The contrast between the warm, sunny exterior and the cool, dark interior is conveyed by abrupt shifts in *value*, with light rose, blue, and yellow set against black, dark red, and dark green.

These eight things that Matisse used to construct his picture—line, shape, mass, light, value, color, texture, and space—are the ingredients an artist has available in making any work of art. Called the visual elements, they are the elements that we perceive and respond to when we look at a work's form. During the 20th century, time and motion came increasingly to be used as components of art, and we study them in this chapter as well.

LINE

Strictly defined, a line is a path traced by a moving point. You poise your pencil on a sheet of paper and *move* its point along the surface to make a line. When you sit down to write a letter or take out your date book to jot down a note to yourself, you are making lines, lines that are symbols of sounds.

Artists, too, use lines as symbols. Keith Haring relied entirely on lines in the drawings he made on the black paper covering vacant advertising spaces in New York City subway stations during the 1980s (**4.2**). The short curved lines that indicate motion are obviously symbolic: we don't, after all, leave little traces in the air when we move. But in fact *all* the lines in the drawing are symbolic. For example, the person wearing the ferocious animal mask is drawn with a white line, but in reality there is no line separating our body from the air around it. Rather, such lines are symbols of perception. Our mind detaches a figure from its ground by perceiving a boundary between one region (a body) and another (the air). In drawing, we indicate that boundary with a line.

4.2 (below, top) Keith Haring. *Subway Drawing.* c. 1983. Chalk on black paper.

4.3 (below) Judy Pfaff. *cirque, Cirque.* 1992–95. Construction of steel and aluminum tubes, hand-blown glass orbs, and other materials. Permanently installed at Pennsylvania Convention Center, Philadelphia.

Lines can be expressive in themselves. Judy Pfaff's ebullient installation *cirque, Cirque* (**4.3**) is made almost entirely of steel and aluminum tubes that "draw" great looping lines in the air. Pfaff intended the installation to evoke both the thrill of a circus, with its trapeze artists tumbling overhead, and the wonder of the night sky, with its shooting stars and orbiting planets. Following the plainest loop with our eyes, we go on a sort of roller-coaster ride, gliding along the gentle arcs, then speeding up around the tight curves. Following the golden orbit next to it, we spin around and around in a chain of somersaults. Pfaff's installation energizes the vast interior space of the convention center, and suddenly we begin to see lines everywhere—in the girders overhead, in the railings and windowpanes, along the edges of the massive towers.

The ways that Haring and Pfaff use line—to record the borders of form and to convey direction and motion—are the primary functions of line in art. We look more closely at them below.

CONTOUR AND OUTLINE

Strictly speaking, an outline defines a two-dimensional shape. For example, drawing with chalk on a blackboard, you might outline the shape of your home state. On a dress pattern, dotted lines outline the shapes of the various pieces. But if you were to make the dress and then draw someone wearing it, you would be drawing the dress's *contours*. Contours are the boundaries we perceive of three-dimensional forms, and **contour lines** are the lines we draw to record those boundaries. Matisse used pen and ink to make this contour drawing of a model posing for him in front of a mirror (**4.4**). Slender, wiry lines trace the contours of her body so skillfully that they suggest fully rounded forms. Matisse himself appears reflected in the mirror, sketching his model while dressed soberly in a jacket and tie.

4.4 Henri Matisse. *Artist and Model Reflected in the Mirror.* 1937. Pen and ink on paper, 24⅛ × 16″.
The Baltimore Museum of Art.

HENRI MATISSE

1869–1954

H OW IRONIC IT IS that Matisse, of all people, should have provoked a critic to call him a "wild beast," for, while his art may indeed have seemed a bit wild at first, the artist himself could scarcely have been less so. Cautious, reserved, cheerful, hardworking, dedicated to his family, frugal, painstaking—these are the qualities that describe Matisse. His longtime friend and rival Picasso captured more of the headlines, but the steadfast Matisse created art no less innovative and enduring.

Matisse's father intended him to be a lawyer, but a severe bout of appendicitis at the age of twenty-one changed his life—and changed the course of all modern art. Henri's mother bought him a box of paints as a diversion, and, for once, Matisse reacted strongly. Much later he said of this experience, "It was as if I had been called. Henceforth I did not lead my life. It led me."

Matisse enrolled at the Ecole des Beaux-Arts in Paris and studied with the painter Gustave Moreau, a brilliant teacher who is said to have told his young pupil, "You were born to simplify painting." After a period of experimentation in various styles, Matisse exploded onto the Parisian art scene at the Salon d'Automne (autumn salon) in 1905, when he exhib-

ited, along with several younger colleagues, works of such pure, intense, and arbitrary color that a critic labeled the artists *fauves*—wild beasts. In these early years Matisse did not fare much better with the general public. However, he had the good fortune to attract the attention of certain wealthy Americans who have achieved fame as inspired collectors, including the Stein family (Gertrude and her brothers) and the eccentric Cone sisters of Baltimore.

Considering the period in which he lived encompassing two world wars, Matisse kept himself remarkably outside the fray. His art did not touch upon politics or social issues. Throughout his life, his favorite subjects remained the human body (usually a beautiful female body) and the pleasant domestic interior. The joys of home life, of family, of cherished objects dominate his expression. In 1898 Matisse married Amélie Parayre, with whom he maintained a contented relationship for many years. Mme. Matisse was lovely, a willing model, charming and lively, and devoted to her husband's career. Their three children all chose art-related lives, Pierre becoming a prominent art dealer in New York.

We think of Matisse as a painter, but he worked in many fields—sculpture, book illustration, architectural design (of a small, jewel-like chapel near his home), and finally in *découpage*. By the early 1930s Matisse had begun to use cut-up paper as a means of planning his canvases, and a decade later the cut paper had become an end in itself. When he was very old and could no longer stand at his easel, Matisse sat in his wheelchair or in his bed, cutting segments of prepainted paper and arranging them into compositions, some of mural size.

Perhaps it was at the end that he came nearest to his goal: "What I dream of is an art of balance, of purity and serenity, devoid of troubling or depressing subject matter, an art which might be for every mental worker, be he businessman or writer, like an appeasing influence, like a mental soother, something like a good armchair in which to rest from physical fatigue."[1]

Matisse in his studio, 1909 or 1912. Photograph by Henri Monet(?). Pierre Matisse Gallery Archives, The Pierpont Morgan Library, New York.

DIRECTION AND MOVEMENT

In following the looping lines of Judy Pfaff's *cirque, Cirque,* we were doing what comes naturally. Our eyes tend to follow lines to see where they are going, like a train following a track. Artists can use this tendency to direct our eyes around an image and to suggest movement.

Van Gogh used directional lines to disturbing effect in his drawing of the sun rising over a wheat field (**4.5**). Large, round, isolated, and motionless, the sun immediately draws our attention to the right. But just as powerful are the dark converging lines of the wheat field, which pick us up from the chaos of the immediate foreground and rush us off to the left, where a dark wall and a writhing mass of trees block our further progress. Looking at the drawing, the viewer is torn between two conflicting centers of interest, each of which exerts a strong visual pull. By using line to lure our eyes away from the sun, Van Gogh turned a simple landscape into a powerful evocation of a mind in torment.

Directional lines also play an important role in Henri Cartier-Bresson's photograph of a small Italian town (**4.6**). For Cartier-Bresson, the success of a photograph hinged on what he called the "decisive moment." Here, for example, what probably drew his attention was the woman climbing the stairs and balancing a tray of breads on her head. The small loaves resemble the paving stones so closely that it looks as though a piece of the street

4.5 (left) Vincent van Gogh. *Wheat Field with Rising Sun.* 1889. Black chalk, reed pen and brown ink on toned paper; 18 ½ × 24 ¼".
Staatliche Graphische Sammlung, Munich.

4.6 (right) Henri Cartier-Bresson. *Aquila, Abruzzi, Italy, 1951.* Photograph.

were suddenly in motion. Visual coincidences like this delighted Cartier-Bresson, but the decisive moment for the photograph occurred just as the woman was framed by the lines of the iron archway, creating a picture within a picture. Our eyes slide down the line of the steeply pitched railing right to her. Other railing lines carry our eyes into the background, where a cluster of town dwellers stand in the open square. Without the lines of the iron railings, our eyes would not move so efficiently through the picture, and we might miss what Cartier-Bresson wants us to notice.

You may have remarked that the lines our eyes followed most readily in the Van Gogh and Cartier-Bresson illustrations were diagonal lines. Most of us have instinctive reactions to the direction of line, which are related to our experience of gravity. Flat, horizontal lines seem placid, like the horizon line or a body in repose. Vertical lines, like those of an upright body or a skyscraper jutting up from the ground, may have an assertive quality; they defy gravity in their upward thrust. But the most dynamic lines are the diagonals, which almost always imply action. Think of a runner hurtling down the track or a skier down the slope. The body leans forward, so that only the forward motion keeps it from toppling over. Diagonal lines in art have the same effect. We sense motion because the lines seem unstable; we half expect them to topple over.

Thomas Eakins's *The Biglin Brothers Racing* (**4.7**) is stabilized by the long, calm horizontal of the distant shore and its boathouse. The two boats in the foreground are set on the gentlest of diagonals—only a hint, but it is enough to convey their motion. More pronounced diagonals are found in the men's arms and oars. In rowing, arms and oars literally provide the power that sets the boat in motion. In Eakins' painting their diagonals provide the visual power. If you place a ruler over the near oar and then slide it slowly

4.7 Thomas Eakins. *The Biglin Brothers Racing.* 1873–74. Oil on canvas, 24 ⅛ × 36 ⅛".
National Gallery of Art, Washington, D.C.

upward, you will see that the treetops to the left and the clouds in the sky repeat this exact diagonal. It is as if the swing of the oar set the entire painting in motion. The subdued diagonals of Eakins' painting perfectly capture the streamlined quality of sculling, in which slender boats knife smoothly and rapidly through the calm water of a river or lake.

Eakins' painting demonstrates that we experience more than literal drawn lines as lines. In fact, we react to any linear form as a line. For example, we can talk about the line of the men's arms or the line of an oar. Oars and arms are not lines, but they are linear. We also react to lines formed by edges. For example, the white contours of the men's backs contrast strongly with the dark behind them, and we perceive the edges of the backs as lines.

There is a great contrast in linear movement, and thus in emotional effect, between Eakins' work and the next illustration, Théodore Géricault's *The Raft of the Medusa* (**4.8**). Géricault's work is based on an actual event, the wreck of the French government ship *Medusa* off North Africa in 1816. Only a few of those on board survived, some by clinging to a raft. Géricault chose to depict the moment when those on the raft sighted a rescue ship. Virtually all the lines in the composition are diagonal. Like Van Gogh (see 4.5), Géricault uses them to create two conflicting centers of interest, thus increasing the tension of the scene. Picked out by the light, the writhing limbs of the survivors carry our eyes upward to the right, where a dark figure silhouetted dramatically against the sky waves his shirt to attract the rescuers' attention. A lone rope, also silhouetted, carries our eyes leftward to the dark form of the sail, where we realize that the wind is not taking the survivors toward their salvation, but away from it.

4.8 Théodore Géricault. *The Raft of the Medusa.* 1818–19. Oil on canvas, 16′1⅜″ × 23′9″. Musée du Louvre, Paris.

4.9 Jean-Antoine Watteau. *The Pilgrimage to Cythera.* 1717. Oil on canvas, 4′3″ × 6′4½″. Musée du Louvre, Paris.

IMPLIED LINES

In addition to actual lines, linear forms, and lines formed by edges, our eyes also pick up on lines that are only implied. A common example from everyday life is the dotted line, where a series of dots are spaced closely enough that our mind connects them. The 18th-century French painter Jean-Antoine Watteau created a sort of dotted line of amorous couples in *The Pilgrimage to Cythera* (**4.9**). Starting with the seated couple at the right, our eyes trace a line that curves in a gentle *S* and leaves us evaporating into the gauzy air with the infant cupids. Cythera is the mythological island of love. In French, the painting's title is ambiguous, and we do not really know whether these couples are departing *for* the island or *from* it, whether they will be sailing toward their happiness or leaving it behind. Watteau specialized in elegant scenes in which aristocratic men and women gather in a leafy setting to play at love. Often, as here, the scenes are tinged with a gentle melancholy.

In representational art, the same directional cues we follow in life can create implied lines. When a person stops on a street corner and gazes upward, other passersby will also stop and look up, following the "line" of sight. When someone points a finger, we automatically follow the direction of the point. In Raphael's painting *The Madonna of the Meadows* (**4.10**), the three figures are arranged in a triangular composition, with one point of the triangle just above the Madonna's head, another in her extended foot at right, the third beyond the knee of the child at left. Within this greater triangle, however, there is a smaller, implied triangle. Implied lines of sight among the Virgin and the two children help to pull the composition together and

direct the eyes of the viewer to the most important figure in the painting—the child Jesus. The Madonna casts her eyes downward toward John the Baptist, who, in turn, gazes upward at the baby Jesus, establishing a triangular flow. As observers, we instinctively follow these lines of sight around and through the painting, just as we would glance upward if we saw someone in the street staring up.

4.10 Raphael. *The Madonna of the Meadows.* 1505. Oil on panel, 44½ × 34¼".
Kunsthistorisches Museum, Vienna.

SHAPE AND MASS

A **shape** is a two-dimensional form. It occupies an *area* with identifiable boundaries. Boundaries may be created by line (a square outlined in pencil on white paper), a shift in texture (a square of unmowed lawn in the middle of mowed lawn), or a shift in color (blue polka dots on a red shirt). A **mass** is a three-dimensional form that occupies a *volume* of space. We speak of a mass of clay, the mass of a mountain, the masses of a work of architecture.

Because we see the world in images, we may also legitimately talk about the *shape* of a three-dimensional form such as a mountain. In this case, we are emphasizing our awareness of its outline against the sky, as when the sun sets behind it. Images in representational art can occupy the same interesting middle ground. For example, in the painting by Raphael above, the text pointed out that the three figures are grouped in a triangle, a shape.

RAPHAEL
1483–1520

According to the 16th-century biographer Giorgio Vasari, we find in Raphael "an artist as talented as he was gracious," possessed of unbounded "grace, industry, looks, modesty, and excellence of character." Whereas both Michelangelo and Leonardo da Vinci emerge as rather moody, solitary figures, their younger colleague seems to have been the sort of person who charms everybody and to whom success comes as naturally as breathing.

Born in the town of Urbino, Raffaello Sanzio received his first art training from his father, then later became an assistant to the early Renaissance master Pietro Perugino. At twenty-one Raphael struck out on his own, but he continued to study avidly the work of other artists—including Leonardo and Michelangelo, both of whom influenced him greatly. (Vasari claims that Raphael was secretly let into the Sistine Chapel when Michelangelo had temporarily stopped work on the ceiling frescoes so that he could get an advance look at the figures.)

Raphael established his reputation early and throughout his career never lacked for patrons. A major preoccupation was the Madonna-and-child group, of which he made numerous versions. In 1508 Pope Julius II called Raphael to Rome, where the artist began the fresco decoration of four rooms in the Vatican. Among these frescoes was the famous *School of Athens* (7.3).

By his early thirties Raphael had become a busy person indeed, testing his artistic skills in many areas. Increasingly, the work of carrying out his commissions was delegated to assistants. He had been named chief architect of Saint Peter's Basilica in the Vatican and was also director of excavations for ancient Greek and Roman art in and around the city of Rome. On commission from Pope Leo, Julius' successor, Raphael designed ten huge tapestries for the Sistine Chapel and perhaps executed the cartoons (drawings to guide the weavers) himself, although this point is in dispute.

Raphael's private life seems to have been as full and satisfying as his artistic career. At home in any social situation, sought after as a friend, he played as energetically as he worked. He never married—possibly because he hoped to be made a cardinal of the Church—but he lived for many years with the same woman. The biographer Vasari refers to "secret love affairs" and comments that the artist "pursued his pleasures with no sense of moderation." If we are to believe Vasari, Raphael's death at the tragically premature age of thirty-seven came as the aftermath of such lack of moderation, which brought on a "violent fever" made fatal by unwise medical attention.

Among Raphael's great talents was the ability to please his patrons while at the same time fulfilling his own ideals of art. In about 1514 he wrote this to a noble client: "I should consider myself a great master if [a drawing of Galatea] had half the merits you mention in your letter. However, I perceive in your words the love that you bear me; . . . I am making use of a certain idea which comes into my mind. Whether it is possessed of any artistic excellence I do not know. But I do strive to attain it."[2]

Raphael. *Raphael and His Fencing Master.* 1518. Oil on canvas, 39 × 32¾". Musée du Louvre, Paris.

Phrasing the observation this way emphasizes the painting's nature as an arrangement of colored shapes on a flat surface. But it is also true that Raphael's naturalistic approach to painting emphasizes the masses of the forms he depicts—the roundness of the limbs, the voluminous folds of the robe. If we want to talk about what the painting *represents* rather than what it physically *is*, we could also say that Raphael groups his figures in a stable pyramid, a mass.

In Matisse's *The Beasts of the Sea* (**4.11**) there is no such ambiguity. These are shapes. Matisse cut them from sheets of painted paper, pinned them to a wall until he was satisfied with the arrangement, then had them pasted into place on a large white sheet of paper. *The Beasts of the Sea* suggests two translucent pillars of water alive with sleek and spiny creatures and waving plants.

We can divide shapes and masses into two broad categories, geometric and organic. Geometric shapes approximate the regular named shapes of geometry such as square, triangle, hexagon, circle, and so on. Organic shapes are irregular and evoke the living forms of nature. Matisse used both geometric and organic shapes in his cutout, building his aquarium by stacking geometric shapes—largely rectangles—and then filling it with creatures in organic shapes.

In contrast to Matisse's sea creatures, the lovely rounded masses of the Mayan sculpture in our next illustration clearly exist in three dimensions (**4.12**). Of the traditional categories of art, sculpture and architecture deal most directly and literally with mass. In both, to fully appreciate a work, we need to move around it, to view it from every possible vantage point.

4.11 (left) Henri Matisse. *The Beasts of the Sea (Les bêtes de la mer)*. 1950. Gouache on paper, cut and pasted, on white paper; 9'8⅜" × 5'5⅝".
National Gallery of Art, Washington, D.C.

4.12 (right) *Figurine of a Voluptuous Lady*. Maya, Late Classic period, 700–900 C.E. Ceramic with traces of pigment, height 8¾".
The Art Museum, Princeton University.

LIGHT AND VALUE

If you were to close your eyes and pick up the Mayan figurine, your sense of touch could tell you something about its form. Patiently exploring its surfaces with your fingers, you might gradually piece together an image in your mind. Many portions of the figure would remain vague, though, for their details are too fine for fingertips to probe completely. Open your eyes, and the form is instantly much clearer. Rotate the figure slowly, and soon you have a complete grasp of its masses. We rely primarily on our eyes to understand form, and it is light that reveals form to us.

Photography literally means "writing with light." The name makes it clear that in order to record the forms of the world around us, photography records the light that reflects from their surfaces. We understand something of the masses of the Mayan sculpture because the photograph captures the way light and shadow **model** them, or give them a three-dimensional appearance. In Guatemala, where the Mayan civilization once flourished, Mexican photographer Flor Garduño took this photograph of a young girl whose oval face and dignified bearing call to mind the figurine made long ago (**4.13**). Black-and-white film has transposed the many colors of the original scene into their relative **values,** shades of light and dark. Our eyes are more sensitive than film and can distinguish a greater and more subtle range of values. Nevertheless, thanks to black-and-white photography we can readily understand the idea that the world we see in full color can also be expressed in shades of light and dark, and that every color can also be spoken of in terms of its value.

For purposes of analysis, value is usually considered in terms of a scale ranging from white (the lightest) to black (the darkest), with a number of degrees in between (**4.14**). The next section of this chapter will take up value as it applies to color. Here, we will examine how shifts in value provide us with visual clues to form.

4.13 Flor Garduño. *Basket of Light, Sampango, Guatemala, 1989.* Gelatin silver print, 12 × 16".
Courtesy the artist.

IMPLIED LIGHT: MODELING MASS IN TWO DIMENSIONS

We cannot see the source of light in Garduño's photograph (4.13), but we know from the way the shadows fall that it is off to the girl's right and quite strong. The light catches her face on the right side. There her skin tone is at its lightest value. The left side of her face is plunged in medium-value shadow. Within these two broad areas, numerous subtle shifts in value model the planes of her cheeks and forehead. Shadows gauge the depth of the depression between her nose and mouth and the curve of her chin. Light reflected from her blouse defines her left jaw.

Photography easily demonstrates how value models mass for our eyes. But photography was invented only in the mid-19th century. Long before then, European painters had become interested in modeling mass in two dimensions through value. Discovered and perfected by Italian painters during the Renaissance, the technique is called **chiaroscuro,** Italian for light/dark. With chiaroscuro, artists employ values—lights and darks—to record contrasts of light and shadow in the natural world, contrasts that model mass for our eyes. One of the great masters of chiaroscuro was Leonardo da Vinci. His unfinished drawing of *The Virgin and Saint Anne with the Christ Child and John the Baptist* (**4.15**) shows the miraculous effects he could achieve. Working on a middle-value brown paper, Leonardo applied charcoal for a range of darks and white chalk for lighter values. The figures seem to be breathed onto the paper, bathed in a soft, allover light that comes from everywhere and nowhere. The roundness that Leonardo's mastery conveys is immediately evident if we look between the heads of the two children at the raised hand of Saint Anne. Drawn with a contour line but not modeled, it looks jarringly flat, as though it does not yet belong to the rest of the image.

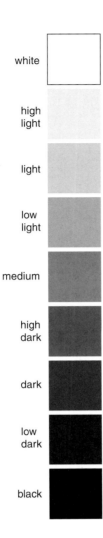

white

high light

light

low light

medium

high dark

dark

low dark

black

4.14 (above) Value scale in gray.

4.15 (left) Leonardo da Vinci. *The Virgin and Saint Anne with the Christ Child and John the Baptist.* Charcoal, black and white chalk on brown paper, 54⅞ × 39⅞". The National Gallery, London.

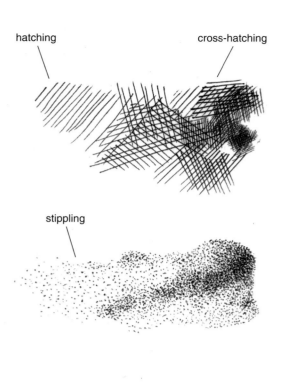

4.16 (left) Albrecht Dürer. *A Goldsmith from Mecheln.* 1520. Brown ink on paper, 6¼ × 4″. Staatliche Museen zu Berlin, Preussischer Kulturbesitz, Kupferstichkabinett.

4.17 (right) Techniques for modeling mass with lines: hatching, cross-hatching, and stippling.

Renaissance artists also perfected a way of indicating values with line alone. The German Renaissance artist Albrecht Dürer relied solely on line in his study of *A Goldsmith from Mecheln* (**4.16**). Taking the white paper as the highest value, Dürer indicated the next step down in value with **hatching,** areas of closely spaced parallel lines. To indicate still darker areas, a second set of lines crosses the first, an effect called **cross-hatching.** Seen from up close the effect seems coarse, but at a certain distance the dark hatch marks seem to average out with the light paper into areas of gray, an effect of vision called optical mixing. Another technique for suggesting value is **stippling,** in which areas of dots suggest value through their density (**4.17**). The more dots crowded into a given area, the darker it appears.

Once artists had mastered the basic techniques of chiaroscuro, they quickly grew to appreciate the dramatic effects that could be achieved through unusual lighting. Painters began to plan their canvases as a theatrical director might plan a moment on the stage, positioning the actors and focusing the lights to direct the audience's attention by picking out some areas and plunging others into darkness. In *A Philosopher Giving a Lecture on the Orrery* (**4.18**), the 18th-century English painter Joseph Wright used lighting to convey the fascination of science, then still in its infancy. An orrery is a model of the solar system. The one here evidently uses a lamp to stand for the sun. Wright uses this "sun" as the sole source of light for his painting. The young boy blocking our view is thrust into shadow, the masses of his body almost completely flattened into shapes. The faces of the children opposite literally light up with interest, while more dramatic lights and darks play over the assembled adults. Light here has a symbolic value as well, for it evokes the illuminating power of scientific knowledge.

ACTUAL LIGHT

Wright closely observed the effects of a low, central light source and probably made numerous value studies before beginning his canvas. But he would have painted the canvas in the even light of day, so that he could watch over and control the effects he was re-creating. In viewing the painting, we too require a steady and even source of light. With sculpture and architecture, on the other hand, we appreciate how shifting conditions of light reveal new aspects of the work. In designing a building, an architect may take into account how light and shadow will play over its masses and interior spaces. In Chapter 3, for example, we compared how architects used light to create mood and heighten awareness in the interiors of the Sainte-Chapelle in Paris and the Great Mosque at Córdoba (see 3.3 and 3.4).

The stained glass of medieval European architecture is one of the inspirations for contemporary artist James Turrell, one of the few artists to take light itself as a primary material for art. Like the medieval craftsmen, Turrell uses light to heighten viewers' awareness and to create a spiritual atmosphere in which the material world seems far away. Works like *Milk Run II* (**4.19**) have no existence but light, in this case fluorescent light projected onto a wall. Seen in person, the light seems to powder off the wall and hang in the air like mist. The wall itself seems to dissolve, for the viewer no longer has any idea of exactly where it is.

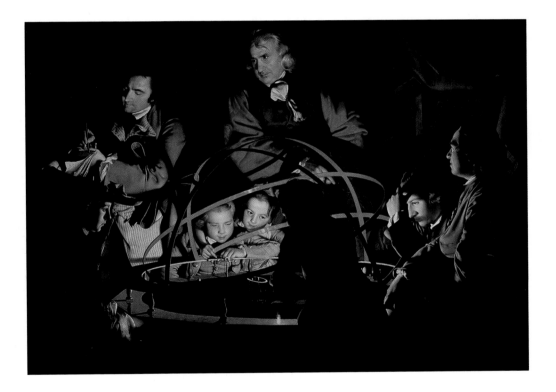

4.18 (above) Joseph Wright. *A Philosopher Giving a Lecture on the Orrery*. 1766. Oil on canvas, 4′10″ × 6′8″.
Derby Museum and Art Gallery, Derby, England.

4.19 (left) James Turrell. *Milk Run II*. 1997. Fluorescent light. Installation at the Kunsthaus Bregenz.
Courtesy Barbara Gladstone Gallery, New York.

COLOR

It is probably safe to say that none of the visual elements gives us so much pleasure as color. Many people have a favorite color that they are drawn to. They will buy a shirt in that color just for the pleasure of clothing themselves in it, or paint the walls of their room that color for the pleasure of being surrounded by it. Various studies have demonstrated that color affects a wide range of psychological and physiological responses. Restaurants often are decorated in red, which is believed to increase appetite and therefore food consumption. Blue surroundings will significantly lower a person's blood pressure, pulse, and respiration rate. In one experiment subjects were asked to identify, by taste, ordinary mashed potatoes colored bright green. Because of the disorienting color cues, they could not say what they were eating. And in one California detention center violent children are routinely placed in an 8-by-4-foot cell painted bubble-gum pink. The children relax, become calmer, and often fall asleep within ten minutes. This color has been dubbed "passive pink." The mechanism involved in these color responses is still unclear, but there can be no doubt that color "works" on the human brain and body in powerful ways.

Color is a function of light. Without light there can be no color. The principles of color theory explain why this effect occurs.

COLOR THEORY

Much of our present-day color theory can be traced back to experiments made by Sir Isaac Newton, who is better known for his work with the laws of gravity. In 1666 Newton passed a ray of sunlight through a prism, a transparent glass form with nonparallel sides. He observed that the ray of sunlight broke up or **refracted** into different colors, which were arranged in the order of the colors of the rainbow (**4.20**). By setting up a second prism Newton found he could recombine the rainbow colors into white light, like the original sunlight. These experiments proved that colors are actually components of light.

In fact, all colors are dependent on light, and no object possesses color intrinsically. You may own a red shirt and a blue pen and a purple chair, but these items have no color in and of themselves. What we perceive as color is reflected light rays. When light strikes the red shirt, for example, the shirt absorbs all the color rays *except* the red ones, which are reflected, so your

4.20 White light separated into its component colors by a prism.

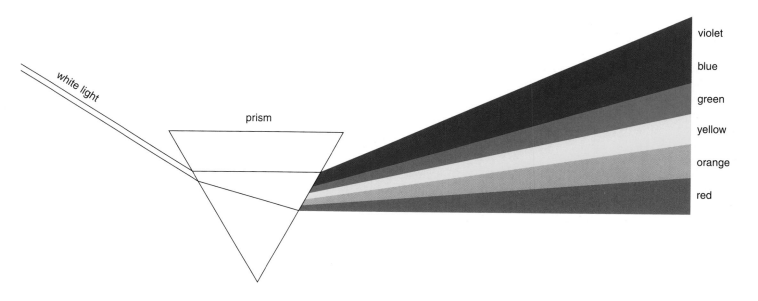

white light

prism

violet
blue
green
yellow
orange
red

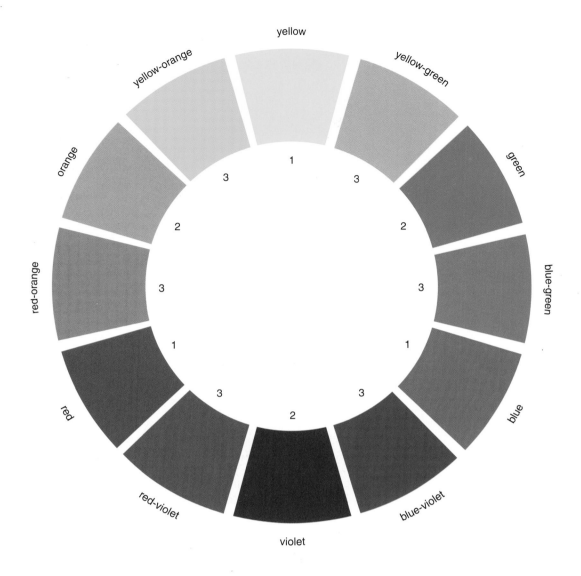

yellow

yellow-orange

yellow-green

orange

green

red-orange

blue-green

red

blue

red-violet

blue-violet

violet

4.21 Color wheel.

eye perceives red. The purple chair reflects the purple rays and absorbs all the others, and so on. Both the physiological activity of the human eye and the science of electromagnetic wavelengths take part in this process.

If we take the colors separated out by Newton's prism—red, orange, yellow, green, blue, and violet—add the transitional color red-violet (which does not exist in the rainbow), and arrange these colors in a circle, we have a **color wheel** (**4.21**). Different theorists have constructed different color wheels, but the one shown here is fairly standard.

Primary colors—red, yellow, and blue—are labeled with the numeral 1 on the color wheel. They are called primary because (theoretically at least) they cannot be made by any mixture of other colors.

Secondary colors—orange, green, and violet—are labeled with the numeral 2. Each is made by combining two primary colors. For most of us this information is not new. Even in kindergarten children working with poster paints learn to make green by mixing yellow and blue.

Tertiary colors, labeled number 3, are the product of a primary color and an adjacent secondary color. For instance, mixing yellow with green yields yellow-green.

Complementary colors are those directly opposite one another on the color wheel. They are assumed to be as different from one another as possible. The relationship between complementary colors, as we shall see, is extremely important in such areas as the optical and emotional effects of color.

COLOR PROPERTIES

Any color has three properties. They are called hue, value, and intensity.

Hue is the name of the color according to the categories of the color wheel—green or red or violet-blue.

Value, again, refers to relative lightness or darkness. Most colors are recognizable in a full range of values; for instance, we identify as "red" everything from palest pink to darkest maroon. In addition, all hues have what is known as a normal value—the value at which we expect to find that hue. We think of yellow as a "light" color and violet as a "dark" color, for example, even though each has a full range of values. The top section of the color chart (**4.22a**) shows the hues on the right side of the color wheel organized according to their normal values in relation to the gray value scale. We could do the same with the left half of the wheel, pairing yellow-orange with light, and so on. The middle section of the color chart (**4.22b**) shows a full range of values, from high light to low dark, for two hues: red and green.

A color lighter than the hue's normal value is known as a **tint;** for example, pink is a tint of red. A color darker than the hue's normal value is called a **shade;** maroon is a shade of red.

Intensity—also called **chroma** or **saturation**—refers to the relative purity of a color. Colors may be pure and saturated, as they appear on the color wheel, or they may be grayed and softened to some degree. The purest colors are said to have high intensity; grayer colors, lower intensity. In the color chart (**4.22c**) we show four intensity gradations of the hue red at normal value. We could construct the same intensity scale for any other hue. To lower the intensity of a color when mixing paints or dyes, the artist may add a combination of black and white (gray) or may add a little of the color's complement.

LIGHT AND PIGMENT

Colors behave differently depending on whether an artist is working with light or pigment. In light, as Newton's experiments showed, white is the sum of all colors. Artists who work directly with light—such as lighting designers who illuminate settings for film, theater, or video productions—learn to mix color by an *additive* process, in which colors of light mix to produce still lighter colors. For example, red and green light mix to produce yellow light. Add blue light to the mix and the result is white (see 4.51). Thus red, green, and blue form the lighting designer's primary triad.

Pigments, like any other object in the world, have to our eyes the color that they reflect. A red pigment, for example, absorbs all the colors in the spectrum except red. When pigments of different hues are mixed, the resulting color is darker and duller, because together they absorb still more colors from the spectrum. Mixing pigments is thus known as a *subtractive* process. The closer two pigments are to being complementary colors on the color wheel, the duller their mixture will appear, for the more they will subtract each other from the mix. For example, while red and green light mix to produce yellow light, red and green pigment mix to produce a grayish brown or brownish gray pigment.

COLOR HARMONIES

A color harmony, sometimes called a color scheme, is the selective use of two or more colors in a single composition. We tend to think of this especially in relation to interior design; you may say, for instance, "The color scheme in my kitchen is blue and green with touches of brown." But color harmonies also apply to the pictorial arts, although they may be more difficult to spot because of differences in value and intensity.

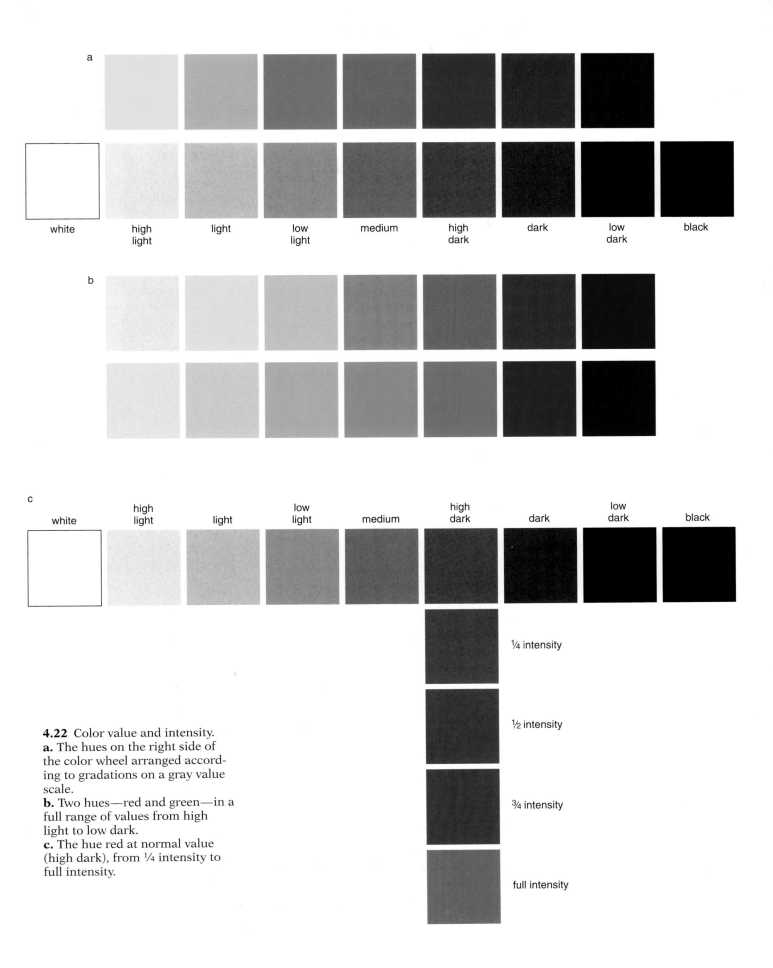

a

white · high light · light · low light · medium · high dark · dark · low dark · black

b

c

white · high light · light · low light · medium · high dark · dark · low dark · black

¼ intensity

½ intensity

¾ intensity

full intensity

4.22 Color value and intensity.
a. The hues on the right side of the color wheel arranged according to gradations on a gray value scale.
b. Two hues—red and green—in a full range of values from high light to low dark.
c. The hue red at normal value (high dark), from ¼ intensity to full intensity.

4.23 (left) Marc Chagall. *The Painter and His Wife.* 1969. Oil on canvas, 36¼ × 28¾".
Private collection, St. Paul de Vence, France.

4.24 (right) Pierre-Auguste Renoir. *Portrait of the Actress Jeanne Samary.* 1878. Oil on canvas, 5′8⅛″ × 3′4½″.
State Hermitage Museum, St. Petersburg, Russia.

Monochromatic harmonies are composed of variations on the same hue, often with differences of value and intensity. A painting all in reds, pinks, and maroons would be considered to have a monochromatic harmony.

Complementary harmonies involve colors directly opposite one another on the color wheel. The most obvious pairings are red and green, violet and yellow, blue and orange. Complementaries "react" with each other more vividly than other colors. They set up a tension, a dynamic bond of opposites, and thereby intensify each other. Marc Chagall's *The Painter and His Wife* (**4.23**) demonstrates just such a forceful complementary scheme. Chagall has divided his canvas into two sections—the "painter" side, represented by a vase of flowers, in an intense green; the "wife" side in saturated red. The two sections vibrate against one another, suggesting a clear duality, and yet they do not appear to be at war. They seem, in fact, to be two halves of the whole.

Analogous harmonies combine colors adjacent to one another on the color wheel, such as red, red-orange, and orange. Pierre-Auguste Renoir used this exact harmony in his lovely portrait of a young actress (**4.24**). With the exception of the white gloves and the gray-green leaves of the potted plant, the painting is composed almost entirely in tints and shades of yellow-orange through red, hues that can all be found on the upper-left third of our color wheel (see 4.21).

Numerous other color harmonies have been identified and named. Artists themselves, however, are more likely to speak generally of working with a **restricted palette** or an **open palette.** Palette is the term for the board on which artists traditionally set out their pigments, but it also refers to the range of pigments they select, either for a particular painting or characteristically. Working with a restricted palette, artists limit themselves to a few pigments and their mixtures, tints, and shades. Renoir's portrait of Jeanne Samary is an example of a restricted palette. With an open palette, artists permit themselves all the colors at their disposal. A stunning example of an open palette is Titian's *Bacchus and Ariadne* (**4.25**). The scene depicts Bacchus, god of wine and fertility, as he arrives with his noisy entourage of revelers on the island of Naxos to marry the princess Ariadne, who had been deserted there by her lover, Theseus. The riot of saturated colors seems appropriate to the magnificent arrival of a god, especially this god of sensuous excess. Titian even invents excuses to include still more colors. The heap of fabric in the foreground, for example, is only an excuse for a patch of yellow.

OPTICAL EFFECTS OF COLOR

Certain uses and combinations of colors can "play tricks" on our eyes or, more accurately, on the way we perceive colors registered by our eyes. For one thing, there is the phenomenon known as **simultaneous contrast.** If you place two complementary colors next to each other, both of them will seem more brilliant: red seems redder, green greener, and so forth. Every painter quickly discovers that color is relative, and that our perception of any one color is influenced by the colors around it. The example here is taken from *The Interaction of Color*, an important text by the artist and teacher Josef Albers (**4.26**). The figure juxtaposes two contrasting rectangular areas of color, one a grayish yellow, the other a violet-tinged gray. The gray of the double *X* that links them falls midway between the two rectangles in value. Seen against the yellowish ground, the *X* darkens until it seems to be the same violet-gray hue as the opposite rectangle. Seen against the violet-gray ground, the *X* takes on a yellow tinge and approaches the yellow rectangle

4.25 (left) Titian. *Bacchus and Ariadne.* 1522. Oil on canvas, 5′8⅞″ × 6′2⅞″. The National Gallery, London.

4.26 (right) Josef Albers. Reversed ground study from *The Interaction of Color.* 1963.

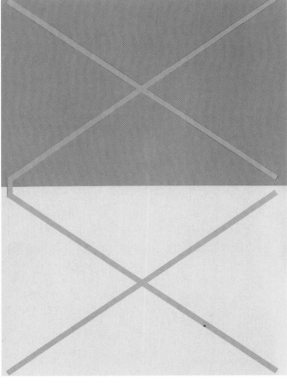

in hue. If you place a finger over the place where the two *X*s join, the effect is even stronger. In fact, you will probably need to remove your finger to convince yourself that the color of the *X* remains constant.

Some colors seem to "advance," others to "recede." Interior designers know that if you place a bright red chair in a room, it will seem larger and farther forward than the same chair upholstered in beige or pale blue. Thus, color can dramatically influence our perceptions of space and size. In general, colors that create the illusion of large size and advancing are those with the warmer hues (red, orange, yellow), high intensity, and dark value; small size and receding are suggested by colors with cooler hues (blue, green), low intensity, and light value.

Colors can be mixed in light or pigment, but they can also be mixed by the eyes. When small patches of different colors are close together, the eye may blend them to produce a new color. This is called **optical color mixture,** and it is an important feature in the painting of Georges Seurat.

Seurat was fascinated by the scientific color theories of his day, and he worked out his canvases with great precision. Most artists blend their colors, either on a palette or on the canvas itself, to produce gradations of hue, but Seurat did not. Instead, he laid down his paints by placing many thousands of tiny dots—or points—of pure color next to each other, a process that came to be called **pointillism.** From a distance of a few inches a Seurat painting looks like a meaningless jumble of color dots (**4.27**). But as the viewer moves back, the dots merge to form a rich texture of subtly varied tones (**4.28**). The painting illustrated here is Seurat's masterpiece, *A Sunday on La Grande Jatte.* Like most of this artist's works, it does not reproduce well in a book, where colors are reduced to ink on paper. Its many verticals of people and trees can make the painting seem static. Seen "in person," however, on the museum wall in Chicago, *La Grande Jatte* sparkles and vibrates with color, comes to life through its myriad little points of light.

EMOTIONAL EFFECTS OF COLOR

Color affects us on such a basic level that few would argue that we have a direct emotional response to it. The problem comes when we try to find universal principles, for we quickly discover that emotional responses to color are both culturally conditioned and intensely personal. Earlier in this chapter, we looked at a painting by Chagall that juxtaposed a large red area with a large green area (see 4.23). By opposing complementary colors, Chagall meant to oppose two different but complementary realms, the green realm of the painter and the red realm of his wife. The painter is present only by his hand, which reaches into the red to present his wife with a green bouquet—a gift of himself and his art. The juxtaposition of the two colors serves as a declaration of mutual affection and support, for red is never so red as when it is next to green, and green is never so green as when it is in the company of red. For most people brought up in America, however, red and green have strong cultural associations with Christmas, and it may be difficult to look at Chagall's painting without that holiday coming to mind. Van Gogh, moreover, once made a painting of a café interior that juxtaposed red and green in order to suggest an environment so tense that men might go mad or be driven to commit a crime.

Most colors could elicit a similar variety of response. For the German painter Franz Marc, blue was the color of male spirituality. As the color of the sky and the ocean, blue is often associated with freedom. It is a "cool" color and has been shown to have a calming effect. In the English language, blue is linked with sadness. In India, blue is the color of the god Vishnu, the god of order and stability, but it is also associated with the dark and disturbing power of the goddess Kali.

4.29 (left) James Abbott McNeill Whistler. *Nocturne in Blue and Gold (Old Battersea Bridge).* c. 1872–75. Oil, 23¾ × 18⅜″. Tate Gallery, London.

4.30 (right) Edvard Munch. *The Scream.* 1893. Tempera and casein on cardboard, 36 × 29″. Nasjonalgalleriet, Oslo.

James Abbott McNeill Whistler certainly had calm in mind when he chose blue for the overall color of his *Nocturne in Blue and Gold* (**4.29**). Except for a distant spangle of fireworks and the reflection of a few lights in the water, the painting is entirely monochromatic, brushed in shades of grayish blue. Blue contributes significantly to the subdued emotional mood of the painting, although it does not create it all alone. The strong, stable vertical lines of the pier, the reassuring horizontals of the bridge and the horizon, the evident tranquility of the scene with its lone boatman silhouetted on the prow of his ship—these elements also play a role in the emotional "temperature" of the work.

Edvard Munch's harrowing painting *The Scream* also depicts a bridge, but the effect is much different (**4.30**). Concerning this work, the Norwegian artist wrote in his diary "I sensed a shriek passing through nature. . . . I painted this picture, painted the clouds as actual blood."[3] Red—which Chagall used to indicate warmth, love, and home—Munch uses to indicate horror, blood, and anguish. But how, outside of his diary, are we to know that Munch did not intend simply to depict a splendid sunset? As in Whistler's nocturne, color does not carry the entire expressive burden by itself. While Whistler's painting is characterized by reassuring vertical and horizontal lines, here unstable diagonals and swirling lines dominate. The horizontal of the horizon is almost obliterated. The figure in the foreground clasps his hands over his ears to block the piercing sound. His head has become a death's head, his body wavers unsteadily. In contrast, the two pedestrians in the background remain unaffected. Evidently they hear nothing out of the ordinary. The scream is a silent one, the interior cry of a soul projected onto nature.

JAPANESE PRINTS

Whistler had fallen under the spell of Japanese prints during his stay in Paris in the late 1850s. He was hardly the only one. Almost all of the Impressionist painters in France collected Japanese prints, and many of the painters of the next generation were influenced by them as well. Why prints, and why then? In 1854, Japan, after being virtually closed to foreigners for over 200 years, had opened itself up to the outside world again. Europe, England, and America were suddenly fascinated by all things Japanese, but it was principally in Paris that artists seriously studied prints, which were the first examples of Japanese art to be imported in quantity. Else-

PAINTINGS SUCH AS *Nocturne in Blue and Gold (Old Battersea Bridge)* (see 4.29) so enraged the English critic John Ruskin that he accused the artist, James Whistler, of flinging a pot of paint in the public's face. The articulate and flamboyant Whistler promptly took Ruskin to court. What angered Ruskin was that the painting didn't really resemble Battersea Bridge at all. "I do not intend it to be a 'correct' portrait of the bridge," Whistler replied. The painting was a moonlit scene, he continued, a reverie, and people could see something in it or not, as they liked.[4]

It is difficult to say whether Whistler would have helped or hurt his case by drawing the judge's attention to his collection of Japanese prints, which included the two works by Hiroshige illustrated here. With its dramatically cropped bridge, lone boatman, and moonlit river, Hiroshige's *Riverside Bamboo Market, Kyobashi* served as the principal model for Whistler's composition, though he imported the idea of fireworks from the Japanese master's *Fireworks at Ryogoku*.

where in this book, their influence can be seen in Mary Cassatt's *The Boating Party* (21.12), Toulouse-Lautrec's *Moulin Rouge: La Goulue* (10.11), and Edgar Degas' *Women at a Café, Evening* (21.7).

Interestingly, one of the factors that allowed Western artists to borrow compositional ideas from Japanese prints so easily was that influence had already flowed in the other direction. The Western system of linear perspective had long been known to Japanese artists. During the 18th century, printmakers even created a special type of print called *uki-e*, "perspective pictures." By Hiroshige's time, printmakers had fully absorbed Western perspective into their own styles, especially in landscape, as the two examples here show so well.

Ando Hiroshige. *Riverside Bamboo Market, Kyobashi* (left) and *Fireworks at Ryogoku* (right), from *One Hundred Famous Views of Edo.* 1857. Honolulu Academy of Arts.

TEXTURE AND PATTERN

Texture refers to surface quality—a perception of smooth or rough, flat or bumpy, fine or coarse. Our world would be bland and uninteresting without contrasts of texture. Most of us, when we encounter a dog or cat, are moved to pet the animal, partly because the animal likes it, but also because we enjoy the feel of the fur's texture against our hands. In planning our clothes we instinctively take texture into account. We might put on a thick, nubby sweater over a smooth cotton shirt and enjoy the contrast. We look for this textural interest in all facets of our environment. Few people can resist running their hands over a smooth chunk of marble or a glossy length of silk or a drape of velvet. This is the outstanding feature of texture: it makes us want to touch it.

ACTUAL TEXTURE

Actual texture is literally *tactile*, a quality we could experience through touch. Texture was an important consideration for the architect Frank O. Gehry in selecting the materials for his recently completed Guggenheim Museum Bilbao (**4.31**). The base is faced in Spanish limestone, smoothed but not polished and pleasantly rough to the touch, like fine sandpaper. The fluid forms above are clad in rectangular panels of titanium. The panels do not lie completely flat, but rather billow gently and unevenly, catching and reflecting the sunlight. From a distance, the titanium surfaces look lightly puckered and uneven, as though the building were made of hammered metal or quilted metallic fabric. Around the entrance itself are the smooth, hard, reflective surfaces of transparent glass. (For more images of the museum, see 4.37, 13.33, and 13.35.)

Like any other visual element, texture can contribute to our understanding and interpretation of a work. In the version here of Brancusi's *Bird in Space* (**4.32**), a roughly carved wooden pedestal supports a smoother

4.31 Frank O. Gehry. Entrance to the Guggenheim Museum Bilbao, Bilbao, Spain. 1997.

limestone element, which in turn serves as a base for the bird. The bird is made of marble, a fine-grained stone that can be polished to a very smooth finish. The progression of textures contributes to our sense of the sculpture's movement. The wooden base exerts a powerful upward thrust, the limestone element acts as a kind of compression zone for gathering energy, then the marble figure makes a final leap into flight. At each step, the texture becomes more refined, less coarse, as though the weight of the material world were falling away.

VISUAL TEXTURE

That we can appreciate the textures of Gehry's architecture or Brancusi's sculpture in a photograph shows that texture has a visual component as well as a tactile one. In fact, even before touching a surface we have formed an idea of its texture by observing the way it reflects light and associating what we see with a sense memory of touch. Brancusi's use of texture can thus be significant for us even though we would certainly not be permitted to touch the sculpture in a museum, and Gehry's use of texture can give us a deeply pleasurable visual experience even if we do not run our hands over it. Naturalistic painting can suggest the texture of objects in the world in the same way that photography does, by faithfully recording their appearances. The surface of a painting has its own actual texture as well, whether smooth as glass or rough with many layers of thickly applied paint.

By visual texture, however, we mean something less literal. We may speak of visual texture in a painting or drawing when markings our eyes associate with texture are there, whether they actually depict texture or not. For example, the many dots and dashes of Seurat's *A Sunday on La Grande Jatte* (see 4.28) seem to weave a tapestry of many colors. Our eyes interpret this woven effect as a sort of allover texture, even though it does not describe any particular object depicted in the painting. Another example is Raoul Dufy's *Regatta at Cowes* (**4.33**). If you were to run your hands over the surface of the painting, you would find it to be smooth. As your eyes run over it, however, they encounter "rough patches" created by the closely spaced forms and small brush strokes, especially in the waves of the sea. The visual texture does not try to depict the texture of the water itself. Rather, it conveys a parallel idea of roughness or choppiness.

4.32 (above) Constantin Brancusi. *Bird in Space.* 1925. White marble, height 5'11⅝", on a base of wood and limestone.
National Gallery of Art, Washington, D.C.

4.33 (left) Raoul Dufy. *Regatta at Cowes.* 1934. Oil on linen, 32⅛ × 39½".
National Gallery of Art, Washington, D.C.

PATTERN

Pattern is any decorative, repetitive motif or design. Pattern can create visual texture, although visual texture may not always be seen as a pattern. The difference between texture and pattern is evident if we compare Dufy's *Regatta at Cowes* (4.33) with a painting from India also set on water (**4.34**). The many boats on Dufy's canvas are certainly repeating motifs, but they repeat with so many variations in size, shape, color, and spacing that we do not perceive them as a pattern. In contrast, the ducks and flowers spread over the water surface of the Indian painting repeat with far fewer variations: their sizes, shapes, colors, and spacing remain constant.

An interesting aspect of pattern is that it tends to flatten our perception of mass and space. In the Indian painting, for example, we understand that the flowers and birds toward the top of the painting are farther away than those at the bottom, but they do not seem to recede in space, for their size is constant. Rather, the pavilion looks as though it were set in front of a backdrop of fabric, just as African photographer Seydou Keïta posed the woman in our next illustration (**4.35**). Keïta's photograph shows well the lush yet flattening effect of piling pattern on pattern. Propped up on a bed in front of a patterned backdrop, the woman wears a patterned dress over a differently patterned skirt. She lies on a checkerboard-patterned rug, which is itself laid over a patterned blanket featuring a stylized crocodile. Everything seems to blend together, clamoring for attention, and we do not have a clear idea of the modeling of the masses of the bed or of the woman's body.

4.34 Page from the Manley *Ragamala*. Rajasthan, c. 1610. Ink and opaque watercolor on paper, 8¼" × 6".
The British Museum, London.

SPACE

The word "space," especially in our technological world, sometimes conveys the idea of nothingness. We think of outer space as a huge void, hostile to human life. A person who is "spaced out" is blank, unfocused, not really "there." But the space in and around a work of art is not a void, and it is very much there. It is a dynamic visual element that interacts with the lines and shapes and colors and textures of a work of art to give them definition. Consider space in this way: How could there be a line if there were not the spaces on either side of it to mark its edges? How could there be a shape without the space around it to set it off?

THREE-DIMENSIONAL SPACE

Sculpture, architecture, and all other forms with mass exist in three-dimensional space—that is, the actual space in which our bodies also stand. These works of art take their character from the ways in which they carve out volumes of space within and around them.

The sculptor Alberto Giacometti was fascinated by how we perceive objects in space. He was intent on finding ways to suggest in his work the space he sensed between himself and his model, and also to situate his own sculptures in space for viewers. In *The Nose* (**4.36**) he went so far as to frame a cube of space around his disturbing sculpture of a head. The image was prompted by a visit Giacometti paid to a friend in the hospital. As Giacometti looked down at his friend's face, gaunt and wasted with illness, it seemed to him that the eyes and cheeks were sinking farther down and that the bony nose was growing longer. He captured that momentary vision of death in this sculpture, which he then suspended in space like a hanged man, or like a shrunken head in an ethnographic museum.

Architecture in particular can be thought of a means of shaping space. Without the walls and roof of a building, the space would be limitless; with

4.35 (above) Seydou Keïta. *Untitled.* 1950s. Photograph. Courtesy Contemporary African Art Collection, Pigozzi Collection, Geneva.

4.36 (below) Alberto Giacometti. *The Nose.* 1947. Bronze, iron, twine, and steel wire, 32 × 28 ½ × 15 ⅜". Hirshhorn Museum and Sculpture Garden, Smithsonian Institution, Washington, D.C.

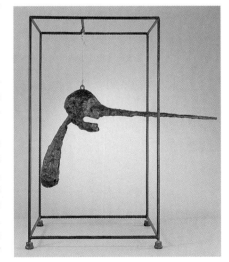

4.37 Frank O. Gehry. Interior of the Guggenheim Museum Bilbao, Bilbao, Spain. 1997.

them, space has boundaries, and therefore has volume. While from the outside we appreciate a work of architecture for its sculptural masses, from the inside we appreciate it as a shaped space or a sequence of shaped spaces. Our experience of architectural space is direct and physical, for we do not look *at* it but rather walk *through* it. When a ceiling is raised or lowered, when walls grow closer together or farther apart, we sense that we have made a transition from one kind of space to another. The photograph here of an exhibition hall from Frank O. Gehry's Guggenheim Museum Bilbao shows the architect's gift for creating fluid and dramatic interior spaces (**4.37**). We can only imagine the effect on someone walking toward us as the intimate area at the far end opens suddenly upward into a light-filled space crossed and recrossed by graceful white forms. (The undulating dark metal surface to the right is part of a sculpture by the artist Richard Serra.)

IMPLIED SPACE: SUGGESTING DEPTH IN TWO DIMENSIONS

Architecture, sculpture, and other art forms that exist in three dimensions work with actual space. When we view the work, we inhabit the same space it does, and we need to walk around it or through it to experience it completely. With painting, drawing, and other two-dimensional art forms, the actual space is the flat surface of the work itself, which we tend to see all at once. Yet on this literal surface, called the **picture plane,** other quantities and dimensions of space can be implied. For example, if you take an ordinary notebook page and draw a tiny dog in the center, the page has suddenly become a large space, a field for the dog to roam about in. If you draw a dog that takes up the entire page, the page has become a much smaller space, just big enough for the dog.

Suppose now that you draw two dogs and perhaps a tree, and you want to show where they are in relation to each other. One dog is behind the tree, say, and the other is running toward it from the distance. These relationships take place in the third dimension, depth. There are many visual cues that we use to perceive spatial relationships in depth. One of the simplest is overlap: we understand that when two forms overlap, the one we perceive as complete is in front of the one we perceive as partial. A second visual cue is position: seated at a desk, for example, we look *down* to see the objects closest to us and raise our head *up* to see objects that are farther away.

Many artistic cultures have relied entirely on these two basic cues to imply depth in two dimensions (**4.38**). In this lively scene of acrobats and musicians performing before an Indian prince, we understand that the performers toward the bottom of the page are nearer to us than ones higher up, and that the overlapping elephants and horses are standing next to each other in a row that recedes away from us. The most important person in the scene is the prince, and the painting makes this clear. Framed by the architectural setting, he sits amid his courtiers and attendants, all of whom are looking at him. The prince, too, is depicted in profile and does not seem to be watching the performance. Yet this seeming inattention is not to be taken literally. The prince would certainly have watched such a wonderful event. Indian artists favored profile views, for they give the least information about depth, and so lend themselves well to the overall flatness of Indian painting.

LINEAR PERSPECTIVE   The sense of space in the Indian painting is *conceptually* convincing, but not *optically* convincing. For example, we *understand* perfectly well that the prince's pavilion is on the distant side of the

4.38 *Maharana Amar Singh II, Prince Sangram Singh, and Courtiers Watch the Performance of an Acrobat and Musicians.* Rajasthan, Mewar, c. 1705–08. Ink, opaque watercolor, and gold on paper; 20½ × 35¾". The Metropolitan Museum of Art, New York.

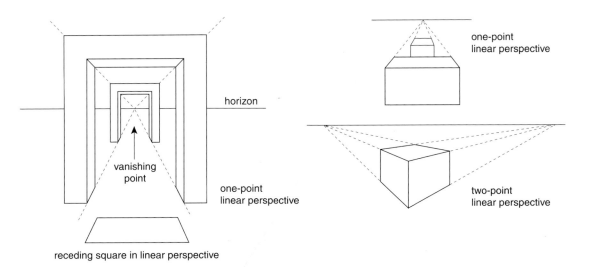

horizon

vanishing
point

one-point
linear perspective

receding square in linear perspective

one-point
linear perspective

two-point
linear perspective

4.39 (above, top) Basic principles of linear perspective.

4.40 (above) Francesco di Giorgio Martini (attr.). *Architectural Perspective.* Late 15th century. Furniture decoration on poplar wood, 4′3⅝″ × 7′7⅝″. Staatliche Museen zu Berlin, Preussischer Kulturbesitz, Gemäldegalerie.

acrobats, but there is actually no evidence to tell our eyes that it is not hovering in the air directly over them. Similarly, we understand that the elephants and horses represent rounded forms even though they appear to our eyes as flat shapes fanned out like a deck of cards on the picture plane. Together, the flatness of Indian painting, the preference for profiles, the use of saturated colors, and the conceptual construction of space make up a coherent system for depicting the world. They work together to give Indian artists tremendous flexibility in assembling complex, vivid, and visually delightful scenes such as this one while preserving narrative clarity.

The chiaroscuro technique developed by Italian artists of the 15th century also forms part of a larger system for depicting the world. Just as Renaissance artists took note of the optical evidence of light and shadow to model rounded forms, they also developed a technique for constructing an optically convincing space to set these forms in. This technique, called linear perspective, is based in the systematic application of two observations:

- Forms seem to diminish in size as they recede from us.
- Parallel lines receding into the distance seem to converge, until they meet at a point on the horizon line where they disappear. This point is known as the vanishing point.

You can visualize this second idea if you remember gazing down a straight highway. As the highway recedes farther from you, the two edges seem to draw closer together, until they disappear at the horizon line (**4.39**).

The development of linear perspective profoundly changed how artists viewed the picture plane. For medieval European artists, as for Indian artists, a painting was primarily a flat surface covered with shapes and colors. For Renaissance artists it became a window onto a scene. The picture plane was reconceived as a sort of windowpane, and the painted view was imagined as receding from it into the distance.

Renaissance artists took up linear perspective with as much delight as a child takes up a new toy. Many paintings were created for no other reason than to show off the possibilities of this new technique (**4.40**). Here, the lines of the stone pavement lay bare the mechanics of linear perspective. We can actually observe the receding lines growing closer, and we can easily continue them in our imagination until they converge at a central point on the horizon, where the sea meets the sky. The rooflines of the various buildings converge at the same point, as do the lines that divide the ceiling of the covered portico in the immediate foreground.

Leonardo da Vinci used linear perspective to construct a very similar space for his portrayal of *The Last Supper* (**4.41**). It was above all the measurable quality of the space created through linear perspective that intrigued Renaissance artists. Here, regular divisions of the ceiling measure out the recession just as the regular divisions of the pavement did in the example above.

Painted on a monastery wall in Milan, *The Last Supper* depicts the final gathering of Jesus Christ with his disciples, the Passover meal they shared before Jesus was brought to trial and crucified. Leonardo captures a particular moment in the story, as related in the Gospel book of Matthew in the Bible. Jesus, shown at the center of the composition, has just said to his followers: "One of you shall betray me." The disciples, Matthew tells us, "were exceeding sorrowful, and began every one of them to say unto him, Lord, is it I?"

In Leonardo's portrayal, each of the disciples reacts differently to the terrible prediction. Some are shocked, some dismayed, some puzzled—but only one, only Judas, knows that indeed, it is he. Falling back from Jesus' words, the traitor Judas, seated fourth from the left with his elbow on the table, clutches a bag containing thirty pieces of silver, his price for handing over his leader to the authorities.

4.41 Leonardo da Vinci. *The Last Supper* (after restoration). c. 1495–97. Fresco, 15′1⅛″ × 28′10½″. Refectory, Santa Maria delle Grazie, Milan.

RESTORATION

Unwise restorations have been the plague of many a great work of art, and there can be no better example than Leonardo da Vinci's *Last Supper* (4.41). Leonardo worked on this masterpiece during the years 1495–97. Always a great one for innovation, he bypassed the established wall painting technique and devised an experimental method for this project. For once Leonardo's genius let him down. What may have been his greatest work soon became a ruin. Within ten years the painting was said to be flaking badly; within about fifty years the biographer Giorgio Vasari (p. 383) wrote that "Nothing is visible but a dazzling mass of blots."

The first major restoration was undertaken in 1726, and five others followed. Each of these restorers did more harm than good. One used a harsh solvent that dissolved Leonardo's colors. Another applied a strong glue that attracted dirt. Yet another restorer managed to give one of the Apostles six fingers on one hand.

To make matters worse, the physical environment of *The Last Supper* could scarcely be more precarious. Sharp variations in heat and humidity all but force the paint off the wall, bringing deep cracks in the surface. Sometime in the 18th century well-meaning friars in the monastery installed a curtain across the mural—which had the effect of trapping moisture on the wall and scraping off yet more paint each time the curtain was drawn back. French soldiers of Napoleon who occupied the monastery in 1796 took turns throwing rocks at the mural and climbing ladders to scratch out the Apostles' eyes. A bomb fell on the monastery during World War II, missing the wall by a yard. It's a miracle that anything is left at all, and little is left.

Finally, nearly five hundred years after Leonardo put down his brushes, sensible measures were taken to save the mural. A Milanese restorer, Dr. Pinan Brambilla Barcilon, began a major restoration in 1977; the project would last more than twenty years. Dr. Brambilla had assets earlier restorers lacked—modern microscopes, chemicals, and measuring devices. Through sensitive probing she could determine what was Leonardo's work and what was somebody else's—and remove the latter. In areas where nothing is left of Leonardo's paint, she did not attempt to reconstruct the imagery, but simply painted in a neutral color.

It has not been easy. Dr. Brambilla's eyesight is permanently altered, and she suffers chronic pain in her shoulders and back. She says, "I often have to clean the same piece a second time, or even a third or fourth. The top section of the painting is impregnated with glue. The middle is filled with wax. There are six different kinds of plaster and several varnishes, lacquers, and gums. What worked on the top section doesn't work in the middle. And what worked in the middle won't work on the bottom. It's enough to make a person want to shoot herself."

Inevitably, Dr. Brambilla will have to cope with people who want to shoot *her*. Every art historian in the world will have an opinion about her restoration, and many of those opinions will be negative, even outraged. Still, she remains philosophical about her project. "I am at peace with what I have done here," she says.[5]

---

left: Dr. Pinan Brambilla Barcilon before a restored portion of Leonardo's *Last Supper.*

right: A portion of the mural before restoration.

To show this fateful moment, Leonardo places the group in a large banquet hall, its architectural space constructed in careful perspective. Cloth hangings on the side walls and panels in the ceiling are drawn so as to recede into space. Their lines converge at a vanishing point behind Jesus' head, at the exact center of the picture. Thus, our attention is directed forcefully toward the most important part of the composition, the face of Jesus. The central opening in the back wall, a rectangular window, also helps to focus our attention on Jesus and creates a "halo" effect around his head.

In the hands of the greatest artists, perspective became a vehicle for meaning, just as any other visual element. Here, for example, it is correct to say that the space is constructed so that the lines converge at a vanishing point in the distance behind Christ's head. But if we view the painting as a flat surface, we see that these lines can also be interpreted as radiating *from* Christ's head, as all of creation radiates from the mind of God. Leonardo has purposefully minimized Christ's shoulders so that his arms, too, take part in the system of radiating lines. Spreading his hands, then, God opens space to this moment, which He had foreseen since the beginning of time.

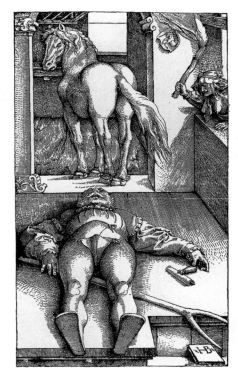

FORESHORTENING In order for pictorial space to be consistent, the logic of linear perspective must apply to every form that recedes into the distance, including objects and human and animal forms. This effect is called foreshortening. You can understand the challenge presented by foreshortening by closing one eye and pointing upward with your index finger in front of your open eye. Gradually shift your hand until your index finger is pointing away from you and you are staring directly down its length and into the distance. You know that your finger has not changed in length, and yet it appears much shorter than it did when it was upright. It appears foreshortened.

Hans Baldung Grien portrays two foreshortened figures in *The Groom and the Witch* (**4.42**). The groom, lying perpendicular to the picture plane, is foreshortened. If we were to shift him so that he lay parallel to the picture plane with his head to the left and his feet to the right, we would have to stretch him back out. The horse, standing at a 45-degree angle to the picture plane, is also foreshortened, with the distance between his rump and his forequarters compressed by the odd angle at which we see him.

Foreshortening presented great difficulties to artists, for the complex, organic masses of a horse or a man do not offer the simple receding lines of architecture. Hans Baldung Grien's teacher, Albrecht Dürer, left us this wonderful image of an artist wrestling logically with a problem of extreme foreshortening (**4.43**). From our point of view, the woman lies parallel to the picture plane. From the point of view of the artist, however, she is directly perpendicular to it. Her knees are closest to him, her head farthest away. He has actually constructed a picture plane in the form of a gridded window

4.42 (above) Hans Baldung Grien. *The Groom and the Witch.* c. 1540. Woodcut, image 13 15/16 × 7 7/8". Staatliche Museen zu Berlin, Preussischer Kulturbesitz, Kupferstichkabinett.

4.43 (below) Albrecht Dürer. *Draftsman Drawing a Reclining Nude,* from *The Art of Measurement.* c. 1527. Woodcut, 3 × 8 1/2".

through which he looks at his model. On the table before him lies a sheet of paper, gridded to match. Standing on the table within the embrace of his arms is an obelisk whose tip just reaches his eye. The obelisk serves to focus his glance, making sure that every time he returns his gaze to the model, it is at the exact same height.

Our artist will work slowly back and forth. Looking across the tip of the obelisk with one eye open, he will observe his model through the grid. Looking down, he will open both eyes and quickly draw from memory what he saw, using the grid lines as reference points. Looking up again, he will refocus one eye on his model over the obelisk and memorize another small bit. Glance by glance, he will complete the drawing.

Dürer's image illustrates well the strengths and drawbacks of linear perspective. It is a scientifically accurate system for rendering space and relationships within space as we perceive them standing in one fixed place, with one eye open, staring at fixed points along one eye level. But in life we have two eyes, not one, and they are always in motion. Nevertheless, the principles of linear perspective dominated Western views of space for almost 500 years, and they continue to influence us through images generated by the camera, which also shows the view seen by one eye (the lens) staring at a point on a fixed level (the center focus).

ATMOSPHERIC PERSPECTIVE   Staring off into a series of hills, you may notice that each succeeding range appears paler, bluer, and less distinct. This is an optical effect caused by the atmosphere that interposes itself between us and the objects we perceive. Particles of moisture and dust suspended in the atmosphere scatter light. Of all the colors of the spectrum, blue scatters the most, hence the sky itself appears to be blue, and things take on a bluish tinge as their distance from us increases. The first European artist to apply this observation systematically was Leonardo da Vinci, who called the effect "aerial perspective." A more common term today is atmospheric perspective.

4.44 Albert Bierstadt. *The Rocky Mountains, Lander's Peak.* 1863. Oil on canvas, 6′1¼″ x 10′3¾″. The Metropolitan Museum of Art, New York.

Atmospheric perspective is the third and final element of the optically based system for representing the world that was developed during the Renaissance. For as long as naturalism remained a goal of Western art, these three techniques—modeling form through value, constructing space with linear perspective, and suggesting receding landscape through atmospheric perspective—remained central to painting.

The German-born American painter Albert Bierstadt used atmospheric perspective to capture the grandeur of the Rocky Mountains (**4.44**). During the 1850s, Bierstadt accompanied a corps of U.S. Army engineers on their expedition to map an overland route from St. Louis to the Pacific Ocean. The sketches he made on the journey later formed the basis for a series of spectacular paintings that gave Americans back East a look at the Western portions of the land, and at the Indian peoples who called them home. In this typically majestic view, Bierstadt uses dramatic lighting and atmospheric perspective to draw our eyes through the Indian encampment on the near shore to a waterfall in the middle distance and then upward to the towering mountain peaks in the far distance.

Chinese and Japanese painters also relied on atmospheric perspective to suggest broad vistas of receding landscape. One of the masterpieces of Chinese landscape painting is *Dwelling in the Fuchun Mountains*, by the 14th-century artist Huang Gongwang (**4.45**). Working in brush and black ink on paper, Huang built up the masses of his mountains with layers of contour strokes. Trees dot the slopes, and houses nestle cozily in the hills. Trees diminish in size and grow fainter as they recede into the distance, and the farthest mountains are rendered as washes of pale gray ink.

Dwelling in the Fuchun Mountains is an example of a handscroll, an intimate format of painting developed in China. Small enough to be held in the hands, as the name indicates, a handscroll was commonly only a foot or so in height, but many feet long. *Dwelling in the Fuchun Mountains*, for example, is about 13 inches in height and over 20 feet long. We illustrate only a small section of it. Handscrolls were not displayed completely unrolled, as today we might see them in museums. Rather, they were kept rolled up and taken out for viewing only occasionally. Viewers would savor the painting slowly, setting it on a table and unrolling a foot or two at a time. Working their way from one end of the scroll to the other, they journeyed through a landscape that commonly alternated stretches of open water and lowlands with hills and mountains. All is painted from a mobile, bird's-eye view, so that as the landscape rolls by us, we can be everywhere and see everything.

4.45 Huang Gongwang. *Dwelling in the Fuchun Mountains,* detail. 1350. Handscroll, ink on paper; 1'7⁄8" × 20'11". National Palace Museum, Taipei.

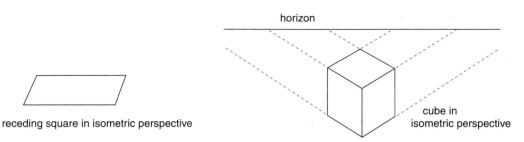

horizon

receding square in isometric perspective

cube in
isometric perspective

4.46 (above, top) Basic principles of isometric perspective.

4.47 (above) *The Night Revels of Han Xizai*, detail. Attributed to Gu Hongzhong, but probably a mid-Song dynasty copy. Handscroll, ink and colors on silk; 11¼″ × 11′. Palace Museum, Beijing.

ISOMETRIC PERSPECTIVE   As we have seen, the converging lines of linear perspective are based on the fixed viewpoint of an earthbound viewer. The viewpoint in Chinese painting, however, is typically mobile and airborne, and so converging lines have no place in their system of representation. To suggest regular forms such as buildings receding from the picture plane, Chinese painters use diagonal lines, but without allowing parallels to converge. This system is known as isometric perspective (**4.46**). The detail here from the long handscroll known as *The Night Revels of Han Xizai* shows isometric treatment of the large seating platform and the low tables, which recede diagonally away from the picture plane without the parallel lines of their forms growing any closer together. Painted during the late 10th century, *The Night Revels of Han Xizai* records the supposedly scandalous and corrupt behavior of a government official. In this scene, Han Xizai and his friends listen to a woman playing the lute in his private chambers. To the right, rumpled bedclothes and the neck of a lute hint at the rest of the story.

TIME AND MOTION

Time and motion have always been linked to art, if only because time is the element in which we live and motion is the very sign of life. It was only during the 20th century, however, that time and motion truly took their places as elements of Western art, and this for the simple reason that due to advances in science and technology, daily life itself became far more dynamic, and the nature of time and its relationship to space and the universe more a matter for thought.

Time became a conscious element of painting with work of the Impressionist painter Claude Monet, whose career began in the 19th century and continued into the first decades of the 20th. Monet's preoccupation with the effects of light led him to realize that each shift in light created a different subject, as though there were no continuing reality but only a collection of moments. He began to paint in series, with each painting catching the subject at a specific moment of time, as defined by light (**4.48**). Here, the simple yet monumental form of a haystack seems to have absorbed the glow of the setting sun. Monet would paint it again at dawn, at noon, in the snow, in the mist. Is there such a thing as a haystack, or are there only glimpses of a haystack in time?

During the first decade of the 20th century, inventions such as the racing automobile and the airplane convinced many artists that the world had changed and that art needed to change with it. Among these were a group of Italian artists who launched an art movement called **Futurism.** The Futurists called for an art that would celebrate motion, speed, energy, and daring. "The gesture which we would reproduce on canvas shall no longer be a fixed *moment* in universal dynamism. It shall simply be the dynamic sensation itself (made eternal)," they wrote in their manifesto of 1910. "A profile is never motionless before our eyes, but it constantly appears and disappears . . . moving objects constantly multiply themselves; their form changes like rapid vibrations . . . a running horse has not four legs, but twenty, and their movements are triangular."[6]

4.48 Claude Monet. *Haystack at Sunset.* 1891. Oil on canvas, 28⅞ × 36½".
Courtesy Museum of Fine Arts, Boston.

4.49 (above) Giacomo Balla. *Dynamism of a Dog on a Leash.* 1912. Oil on canvas, 35⅜ × 43¼″. Albright-Knox Art Gallery, Buffalo, N.Y.

4.50 (right) Alexander Calder. *Lobster Trap and Fish Tail.* 1939. Hanging mobile; painted steel wire and sheet aluminum, about 8′6″ × 9′6″. The Museum of Modern Art, New York.

One of the painters who signed this manifesto was Giacomo Balla. His best-loved painting does not show a running horse, however, but a scurrying little dog (**4.49**). Paws a blur, tail wagging, ears flapping, leash vibrating—everything is dynamic. Today the visual symbols that Balla uses to indicate motion are familiar to us from cartoons, but in Balla's day they were new and radical, for they dissolved moving form into a blur of possibilities.

During the 1930s, the American artist Alexander Calder set sculpture in motion with works that came to be called mobiles (**4.50**). Constructed from abstract forms suspended on slender lengths of wire, they respond by their own weight to the lightest currents of air. Here, a sleek lobster floats over a doodled wire lobster trap and the fanning, petal-like shapes of a swaying fish-tail. The smallest of Calder's mobiles are like delicate, unknown constellations; the largest are motorized and send their forms orbiting majestically through the space they occupy.

Calder's mobiles are examples of **kinetic** art, from the Greek word *kinetos*, moving. The same Greek root also gives us our word *cinema*. Film, which records motion and time, was certainly the most significant new art form of the 20th century. Filmmakers learned to use recorded time as a new sort of raw material that they could cut into lengths and piece together to produce a work of art, a work made of time and motion. With the development of inexpensive video technology during the 1960s, individual artists were also able to experiment with these new possibilities.

The first artist to explore the potential of video technology was Korean-born Nam June Paik. His meditative work *One Candle* uses video to evoke the relationship between life and art and to draw attention to time itself (**4.51**). The work consists of a burning candle, one of the oldest and most pervasive of symbols for the passing of time. A video camera trained on the flame feeds the moving image to three video projectors, one for each of the primaries of light: red, blue, and green. The projectors beam the colored light back onto the wall behind the candle. There, the colors overlap and mix, and the flame is reformed as an image of itself. Viewers play a role in the work as well, for the currents of air they create by their presence cause the flame to flicker.

Steven Pippin is a young British artist whose work often incorporates the element of time. Among his most subtle creations is this pinhole photograph of a street outside of a gallery in New York (**4.52**). To create the photograph, Pippin lined the back wall of the gallery with photosensitive paper. He constructed a partition that blocked out all light between the back wall and the front windows, and in the center of the partition he opened a tiny hole. In essence, the back of the gallery was now a camera. Over the next twenty-four hours, light entering through the hole slowly formed on the photosensitive paper an image of the gallery windows and the street outside. Stationary objects such as trees and the storefronts across the street gradually appeared fully modeled with lights and shadows. Cars that parked for only a few hours registered on top of each other in layers of ghostly blurs. Passing cars left only white lines in the air, traces

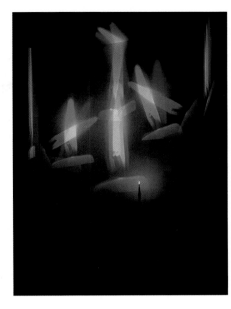

4.51 (above) Nam June Paik. *One Candle.* 1988. Installation: video camera, video projections (and a candle!); 25 × 25′.
Museum für Moderne Kunst, Frankfurt am Main.

4.52 (left) Steven Pippin. *Retrospective.* 1994. Pinhole photograph installation at Gavin Brown Gallery, New York.
Courtesy the artist.

of the sunlight glancing off their surfaces. Pedestrians who stopped to stare did not stay long enough to be recorded, nor did the gallery owner himself, who came and went several times while the photograph was being made. Shown here in the gallery it was created in, the photograph seems formed of traces of time gone by, of time itself, and it invites us to meditate on what is permanent and what is passing.

A fundamental way in which painting, architecture, and sculpture have always incorporated time and motion is in the movement of the viewer. To walk through the interior spaces of a building, to move around a sculpture, to view a painting closer up and farther away—all are processes that take place over time and involve motion. During the 20th century, artists became more conscious of this interactive role of art and viewer. For example, Nam June Paik's *One Candle* responds to the viewers' movements, so that to see the work in person is to affect it.

The late works of Monet are among the earliest paintings that seem to be completed by a moving viewer. A favorite subject of the artist's last years was the surface of the pond that he had had constructed in his garden and planted with water lilies (**4.53**). Floating leaves and blossoms mark the surface of the water, which is otherwise host to dazzling reflections of sky and trees. Underwater plants wave in the transparent depths. Monet placed large canvases end to end to create long, panoramic views, and he painted in brush strokes so large and free that the image seems to be on the verge of dissolving before our eyes into an intoxicating swirl of colors. *Waterlilies at Dusk*, illustrated here, is over 6 feet in height and almost 20 feet long. Viewers drift randomly along its length, drawing closer and then pulling back, losing themselves in one area and then another. They behave, that is, like particles suspended in water, borne by gentle currents and crosscurrents.

Eva Hesse's *Repetition Nineteen III* also takes into account the motion of the viewer, but to much different effect (**4.54**). Its nineteen units sit on the floor. They are vessels of some kind, or receptacles. Irregular and organic, they seem oddly capable of movement, although they don't move. The translucent fiberglass is disturbingly reminiscent of skin. Their openings might be mouths. As we walk around them and crane to see into their depths, we become intensely self-conscious, painfully aware of our height, our awkwardness, our bodies. This uncomfortable self-awareness is part of the effect the artist intended.

The world as we experience it over time and in motion is captured with characteristic ingenuity by David Hockney in his photographic collage of

4.53 Claude Monet. *Waterlilies at Dusk.* c. 1916–22. Oil on canvas, 2 panels, each 6'6¾" × 9'10⅛". Kunsthaus, Zürich.

friends playing a game of Scrabble (**4.55**). Through the assembly of photographs we see before us not only the players' motions and emotions during the game's progress through time but also the moving eye of the spectator, Hockney himself, as he looks from one friend to the other, down at the letters in front of him, or off into the distance. As a final stroke of wit, Hockney lays his photographs down like Scrabble tiles, as though making art about a game were a sort of game itself, or as though we needed as many views to understand a moment as we need letters to make up a word.

Line, shape, mass, light, value, color, texture, pattern, space, time, and motion—these are the raw materials, the elements, of a work of art. In order to introduce them, we have had to look at each one individually, examining its role in various works of art. But in fact we do not perceive the elements one at a time but together, and almost any given work of art is not an example of one element but of many. In the next chapter, we examine how artists organize these elements into art, how this organization structures our experience of looking, and how an understanding of the visual elements and their organization can help us to see more fully.

4.54 (top) Eva Hesse. *Repetition 19, III*. 1968. Nineteen tubular fiberglass units, height of each unit 19–20^{1}/$_{4}$".
The Museum of Modern Art, New York.

4.55 (above) David Hockney. *The Scrabble Game, Jan 1, 1983*. 1983. Photographic collage, edition of 20; 39 × 58".
Courtesy the artist.

CHAPTER 5

Principles of Design

When an artist sets about making any work, he or she is faced with infinite choices. How big or small? What kinds of lines and where should the lines go? What kinds of shapes? How much space between the shapes? How many colors and how much of each one? What amounts of light and dark values? Somehow, the elements discussed in Chapter 4—line, shape, mass, light, value, color, texture, space, and possibly time and motion—must be organized in such a way as to satisfy the artist's expressive intent. In two-dimensional art this organization is often called **composition,** but the more inclusive term, applicable to all kinds of art, is **design.** The task of making the decisions involved in designing a work of art would be paralyzing were it not for certain guidelines that, once understood, become almost instinctive. These guidelines are usually known as the *principles of design.*

All of us have some built-in sense of what looks right or wrong, what "works" or doesn't. Some—including most artists—have a stronger sense of what "works" than others. If two families each decorate a living room, and one room is attractive, welcoming, and pulled together while the other seems drab and uninviting, we might say that the first family has better "taste." Taste is a common term that, in this context, describes how some people make visual selections. What we really mean by "good taste," oftentimes, is that some people have a better grasp of the principles of design and how to apply them in everyday situations.

The principles of design are a natural part of perception. Most of us are not conscious of them in everyday life, but artists usually are very aware of them, because they have trained themselves to be aware. These principles codify, or explain systematically, our sense of "rightness" and help to show why certain designs work better than others. For the artist they offer guidelines for making the most effective choices; for the observer an understanding of the principles of design gives greater insight into works of art.

The principles of design most often identified are unity and variety, balance, emphasis and focal point, proportion and scale, and rhythm. This chapter illustrates some thirty-two works of art that show these principles very clearly. But *any* work of art, regardless of its form or the culture in which it was made, could be discussed in terms of the principles of design, for they are integral to all art.

UNITY AND VARIETY

Unity is a sense of oneness, of things belonging together and making up a coherent whole. Variety is difference, which provides interest. We discuss them together because the two generally coexist in a work of art. A solid wall painted white has unity for sure, but it is not likely to hold your interest for long. Take that same blank wall and ask fifty people each to make a mark on it and you will get plenty of variety, but there probably will be no unity whatever. In fact, there will be so *much* variety that no one can form a meaningful visual impression. Unity and variety exist on a spectrum, with total blandness at one end, total disorder at the other. For most works of art the artist strives to find just the right point on that spectrum—the point at which there is sufficient visual unity enlivened by sufficient variety.

Ben Jones's *Black Face and Arm Unit* (**5.1**) illustrates how unity and variety work together. The work consists of multiple plaster casts of the artist's own head and arms, each painted in a distinctive pattern. Repeating forms and spaces unite the work. Slight variations in the forms—the unpredictable alternation of right and left arms, the various hand positions—provide some variety and impart a subtle sense of movement. Greater variety comes from the bold patterns, no two of which are alike. Set loose on the wall by themselves, these patterns would be merely chaotic. The body parts provide a structure that "tames" them, allowing us to perceive them as purposeful elements in a coherent work of art. *Black Face and Arm Unit* was created at a time when many African American artists were seeking to reclaim African art as part of their own heritage. Here, Ben Jones evokes the African traditions of masking and ritual body painting, as well as the widespread aesthetic preference for pattern.

One way for an artist to achieve unity is by holding some of the visual elements constant and varying others. Henri Matisse used color to unify *The*

5.1 Ben Jones. *Black Face and Arm Unit*. 1971. Painted plaster, twelve life-size plaster casts. New Jersey State Museum, Trenton.

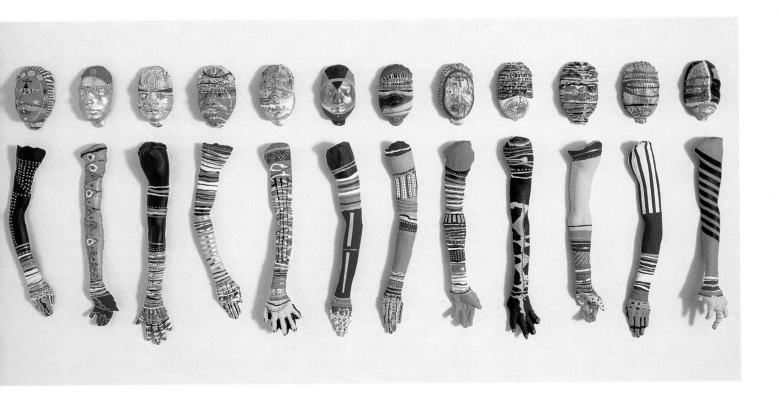

5.2 (left) Henri Matisse. *The Red Studio.* 1911. Oil on canvas, 5'11¼" × 7'2¼".
The Museum of Modern Art, New York.

5.3 (right) Annette Messager. *Mes Voeux.* 1989. Framed photographs and handwritten texts, suspended with twine; 59 × 15¾".
Courtesy Marian Goodman Gallery, Paris.

Red Studio (**5.2**). Walls and floor are saturated with a vivid scarlet, and some of the furniture is drawn as though transparent to let the red show through. By this method Matisse controls the variety of what might be any artist's home studio—paintings displayed and stacked against the wall, a clock and bureau, drawing and eating utensils. Matisse also relies on repeating shapes to hold the work together. A favorite device of his, these repetitions work like visual rhymes. For example, the *S*-curves of the plant tendrils rhyme with the woman drawn on the plate nearby and the openwork chair to the right. The circular form of the plate rhymes with the face of the clock. In fact, the longer we look, the more we realize that Matisse has used red to paint out almost everything *except* things that rhyme visually.

The two works we have just considered demonstrate *visual* unity—unity based in the elements of shape, line, color, and so on. Art can also be unified *conceptually*, that is, through a unity of ideas. Annette Messager relies largely on conceptual unity in her assemblage called *Mes Voeux* (French for "my wishes," **5.3**). If we think about what the photographs have in common, we realize that they all portray isolated body parts—knee, throat, mouth, ear, hand. The framed texts ask not only to be looked at but to be read. Two repeat the word *tenderness* over and over again; another, the word *shame*. Understanding the grouping as a kind of body itself places *consolation* at the head, *tenderness* at the arms, *shame* at the sex, and *luck* at the legs. Repeating shapes and restricted color give visual unity to the work, but it is conceptual unity that asks for our interpretation.

Conceptual unity predominates as well in the works of Joseph Cornell, such as *The Hotel Eden* (**5.4**). Cornell devoted most of his career to making boxlike structures that enclosed many dissimilar but related objects. Contained within the boxes, these objects build their own private worlds. Cornell collected things, odds and ends, wherever he went. His studio held crates of stuff filed according to a personal system. There were even crates labeled "flotsam" and "jetsam." When making his box sculptures, Cornell would select and arrange these objects to create a conceptual unity that was meaningful to him, based on his dreams, nostalgia, and fantasies. By placing such disparate objects and images together in a boxed enclosure with still smaller boxlike divisions within, Cornell imposed a visual unity that asks us to accept them as a coherent whole and to spend some time puzzling out their connections.

The works we have looked at so far strike a balance between unity and variety, and this is most often the artist's goal. Sometimes, however, an artist will aim at extreme unity or extreme variety. In works such as *Convergence*, for example, Jackson Pollock seemed to do away with the traditional concerns of design altogether (**5.5**). Tangles of flung and dripped paint weave a surface that might be characterized as nothing but unity—or perhaps nothing but variety. We have the sense that *Convergence* could extend forever in all directions, and that this is merely a section of it. In fact, this is what Pollock intended. His most important works are large, so large that a viewer standing before them feels engulfed in a vast web of energy—the traces of the painter's gestures and movements.

5.4 (below, top) Joseph Cornell. *The Hotel Eden.* 1945. Assemblage with music box, 15⅛ × 15⅛ × 4¾″.
National Gallery of Canada, Ottawa.

5.5 (below) Jackson Pollock. *Convergence.* 1952. Oil on canvas, 7′11½″ × 12′11″.
Albright-Knox Art Gallery, Buffalo, N.Y.

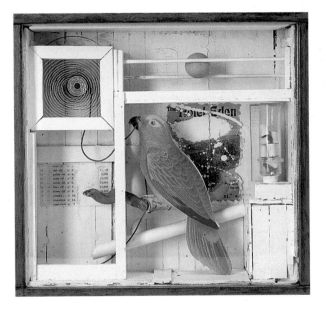

BALANCE

Isamu Noguchi's delightful sculpture *Red Cube* (**5.6**) balances impossibly on one point. Noguchi wittily took the industrial materials and rectangular forms of mid-20th-century architecture and stood them on end, as though the buildings all around were pedestrians and his sculpture a dancer in their midst.

Noguchi's sculpture balances because its weight is distributed evenly around a central axis. The photograph of the sculpture is balanced as well, balanced *visually*. The simple red form set starkly against a dark background draws our attention strongly to the right. The white letters pull our eyes more gently to the left, as do the dark windows and the open hollow of the sculpture itself. Sculpture, hollow, letters, windows—all have a certain visual weight, and together they balance the photograph so that our gaze is never "stuck" in one place but moves freely around the image.

Visual weight refers to the apparent "heaviness" or "lightness" of the forms arranged in a composition, as gauged by how insistently they draw our eyes. When visual weight is equally distributed to either side of a felt or implied center of gravity, we feel that the composition is balanced.

SYMMETRICAL BALANCE

With symmetrical balance, the implied center of gravity is the vertical axis, an imaginary line drawn down the center of the composition. Forms on either side of the axis correspond to one another in size, shape, and placement. Sometimes the symmetry is so perfect that the two sides of a composition are mirror images of one another. More often the correspondence is very close but not exact—a situation sometimes called relieved symmetry.

Georgia O'Keeffe used symmetrical balance in *Deer's Skull with Pedernal* (**5.7**). The skull itself is perfectly symmetrical, and O'Keeffe sets it directly on the vertical axis. She then softens the symmetry with subtle shifts in balance. Toward the top of the image, the dead tree branches off to the right, its branches rhyming with the skull's horns. To the bottom of the image, the trunk swerves off to the right as well, but a pale upward-thrusting branch, a lone cloud, and the distinctive silhouette of Pedernal mountain all add visual weight to the left.

5.6 (left) Isamu Noguchi. *Red Cube.* 1968. Steel painted red. Marine Midland Bank, New York. Photo courtesy The Isamu Noguchi Foundation, Inc.

5.7 (right) Georgia O'Keeffe. *Deer's Skull with Pedernal.* 1936. Oil on canvas, 36 × 30″. Courtesy Museum of Fine Arts, Boston.

GEORGIA O'KEEFFE

1887–1986

European and American painters. He was stunned by O'Keeffe's work. Later that year he included her in a group show at "291," and in 1917 he gave her a solo exhibition. This was the beginning of an extraordinary artistic and personal collaboration that would last until Stieglitz' death in 1946.

O'Keeffe moved to New York. Stieglitz left his wife and lived with her. O'Keeffe painted; Stieglitz exhibited her work and made hundreds of photographs of her. The couple married in 1924, but their union was always an unconventional one. For more than a quarter-century their paths crossed and separated. Stieglitz was most at home in New York City and at his family's summer place at Lake George. O'Keeffe was drawn increasingly to the stark landscapes of Texas and New Mexico. O'Keeffe treasured her husband's presence but could paint at her best only in the Southwest. Stieglitz longed for her company but also wanted her paintings for his gallery.

O'Keeffe gained critical acclaim with her first exhibition, and it never entirely left her. Although major showings of her work were rare after Stieglitz died, no one forgot Georgia O'Keeffe. She was part of no "school" or style. Her work took an exceptionally personal path, as did her life. She dressed almost exclusively in black. She came and went as she pleased and accepted into her world only those people whom she found talented and interesting. More than most, O'Keeffe marched to her own drummer.

After 1949 O'Keeffe lived permanently in New Mexico, the area with which she is most closely associated. In 1972, when she was eighty-four years old, a potter in his twenties, Juan Hamilton, came into her life, and they became close companions. Rumors that they married are probably unfounded, but Hamilton remained with the increasingly feeble, almost-blind artist until her death.

Early on, in her thirties, O'Keeffe had expressed her impatience with other people's standards for life and art: "I decided I was a very stupid fool not to at least paint as I wanted to and say what I wanted to when I painted as that seemed to be the only thing I could do that didn't concern anybody but myself—that was nobody's business but my own."[1]

"At last! A woman on paper!" According to legend, this was the reaction of the famed photographer and art dealer Alfred Stieglitz, in 1916, when he first saw the work of Georgia O'Keeffe. Whether accurate or not, the quote sums up Stieglitz' view of O'Keeffe as the first great artist to bring to her work the true essence and experience of womanhood. Ultimately, much of the critical art world came to share Stieglitz' opinion.

O'Keeffe was born on a farm in Wisconsin. She received a thorough, if conventional, art training at the School of the Art Institute of Chicago and the Art Students League in New York. During the early years she supported herself by teaching art in schools and colleges. By 1912 she was teaching in Amarillo, Texas—the beginning of a lifelong infatuation with the terrain of the Southwest.

In the winter of 1915–16 O'Keeffe sent a number of drawings to a friend in New York, asking her not to show the drawings to anyone. The friend violated this trust—and no doubt helped to set the path for O'Keeffe's entire life and career. She took the drawings to Stieglitz.

By 1916 Stieglitz had gained considerable fame, not only as a photographer but, through his "291" Gallery, as an exhibitor of the most innovative

---

Alfred Stieglitz. *Georgia O'Keeffe*. Gelatin silver print, 9⅓ × 7⅜".
The Metropolitan Museum of Art, New York.

5.8 (left) Edward Weston. *Washbowl*. 1926. Gelatin silver print, 9½ × 7½".
Collection Center for Creative Photography, The University of Arizona, Tucson.

5.9 (right) Tori Busshi. *Shaka Triad*, in the Kondo (Golden Hall), Horyu-ji Temple, Ikaruga, Nara prefecture, Japan. 623. Gilt bronze, height 46".

The central placement of the symmetrical deer skull gives O'Keeffe's painting a forceful, formal presence, as though it were a coat of arms or a symbol on a banner. Edward Weston used this formal quality of symmetrical balance to give surprising dignity to an old washbowl (**5.8**). The play of light on the metal, the slightly irregular mosaics of the floor, and the details of the wall are all that relieve an otherwise perfectly symmetrical composition.

The much used and battered bowl gleams like a halo in the gentle light. Weston probably meant such religious associations to come to mind, for symmetrical composition is often used in religious images that emphasize a central, important being. An example is the *Shaka Triad* (**5.9**), the crowning masterpiece of the 7th-century Japanese sculptor Tori Busshi. Seated in the center in a pose of meditation is the Buddha, dressed in the familiar monk's robes. His gestures promise believers tranquility and a path to salvation. A waterfall of stylized draperies cascades over the platform on which he sits, while behind him rises a halo of stylized flames. Standing to either side of him are two bodhisattvas, slightly less elevated spiritual beings. The reassuring calm and radiant majesty of the statue are due in large measure to the formal order of symmetry.

Paul Gauguin alluded to the association of symmetrical composition and religious imagery in his painting *Day of the Gods* (**5.10**). The prominent statue of a god stands slightly to the left of the vertical axis; directly below it a woman sits at the water's edge, flanked by two curled-up reclining bodies. Together these four figures form the composition's symmetrically balanced center of gravity. Gauguin balanced the rest of the composition, *a*symmetrically around them, with the four attendant women—the two in white to the left of the god and the two in red to the right—serving as a sort of transition between symmetry and asymmetry.

Symmetrical balance served the artist Frida Kahlo with exceptional force in *The Two Fridas* (**5.11**). Kahlo was born in Mexico in 1907, the child of a Hungarian/Jewish father and an Indian/Spanish mother. These two influences—the European and the Mexican—coexisted uneasily in her psyche and her art as long as she lived. *The Two Fridas* shows this graphically. At left is the "European Frida," dressed in an elegant white gown; at right, the "Mexican Frida" wears a costume suited to that country's natives. Both have their hearts exposed in gory anatomical detail, with veins connecting them. The Mexican Frida holds a tiny portrait of the artist Diego Rivera, to whom Kahlo was married. The European Frida snips the vein connected to the portrait, allowing blood to fall on her skirt. This picture's symmetrical format gives a chilling interpretation to the double identity of its maker.

5.10 (above) Paul Gauguin. *Day of the Gods (Mahana No Atua)*. 1894. Oil on canvas, 26⅞ × 36⅛". The Art Institute of Chicago.

5.11 (left) Frida Kahlo. *The Two Fridas*. 1939. Oil on canvas, 5′8½" square.
Museo Nacionale de Arte Moderno, Instituto Nacional de Bellas Artes, Mexico City.

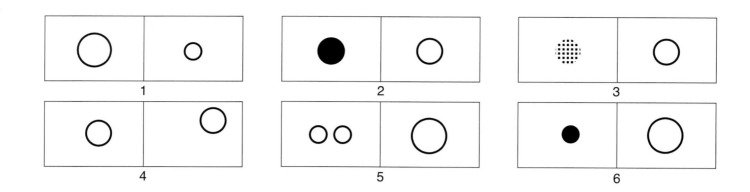

ASYMMETRICAL BALANCE

When you stand with your feet flat on the floor and your arms at your sides, you are in symmetrical balance. But if you thrust an arm out in one direction and a leg out in the other, your balance is asymmetrical (*not* symmetrical). Similarly, an asymmetrical composition has two sides that do not match. If it seems to be balanced, that is because the visual weights in the two halves are very similar. What looks "heavy" and what looks "light"? Unfortunately, there are no mathematical formulas to follow. The drawing (**5.12**) illustrates some very general precepts about asymmetrical or informal balance:

- A large form is visually heavier than a smaller form.
- A dark-value form is visually heavier than a light form of the same size.
- A textured form is visually heavier than a smooth form of the same size.
- A form placed close to the central axis may be visually heavier than a similar form placed near the outer edge of the composition.
- Two or more small forms can balance a larger one.
- A smaller dark form can balance a larger light one.

These are only a few of the possibilities. Keeping them in mind, you may still wonder, but how does an artist actually go about balancing a composition? The answer is unsatisfactory but true: The composition is balanced when it looks balanced. An understanding of visual weights can help the artist achieve balance or see what is wrong when balance is off, but it is no exact science.

5.12 (above) Some principles of visual balance.

5.13 (left) Gustav Klimt. *Death and Life*. Before 1911, finished 1915. 5′10″ × 6′6″. Sammlung Leopold, Vienna.

5.14 (right) Sakai Hoitsu. *Summer Rain,* one of a pair of folding screens. Edo period, late 18th–early 19th century. Color on silver paper, 5′5³/₄″ × 6′3/8″. Tokyo National Museum.

In Gustav Klimt's *Death and Life* (**5.13**), asymmetrical balance dramatizes the opposition between life, envisioned to the right as a billowing form of light-hued patterns and slumbering human figures, and death, a dark skeletal presence at the far left, robed in a chilling pattern of grave markers. The two halves of the painting are linked by the gaze that passes between death and the woman he has come to claim. Klimt has placed her face exactly on the vertical axis of the painting, which here serves as a sort of symbolic border between life and death. The only waking person in the dreaming cloud of life, she smiles awkwardly and gestures as if to say, "Me?" Death leers back, "Yes, you." The intensity of their gaze exerts a strong pull on our attention to the upper left, and Klimt balances this with an equal pull of visual weight to the right and down.

Like many European artists of his day, Klimt's ideas about asymmetrical balance were enriched by a study of Japanese art. Japanese artists had long cultivated dramatic asymmetrical compositions such as this folding screen by Sakai Hoitsu (**5.14**). Like Klimt's painting, Hoitsu's screen balances a simple dark form against a larger and more complex area of lighter values. Small pink flowers serve as visual "stepping-stones" between the stylized blue stream to the upper right and the interwoven arcs of the green grasses. White lilies attract our attention to the lower portion of the composition, where orange flowers draw our eyes to the left. There, a slender, standing, barely visible green plant provides the final counterweight. Isolated, symmetrical, and motionless, it subtly commands our attention.

It would be difficult to imagine a more daring composition than Nonomura Sotatsu's ink painting of *The Zen Priest Choka* (**5.15**). The forms are placed so far to the left as to be barely on the page! Sotatsu relies on an implied line of vision both to balance the composition and to reveal its meaning. We naturally raise our eyes to look at the form of the priest sitting in the tree—that's all there is to look at. We then follow the direction of his gaze down to . . . nothing. Meditation on emptiness is one of the exercises prescribed by Zen Buddhism, and this ingenious painting makes it clear. Our eyes repeatedly seek out the priest, who repeatedly sends us back to focus on nothingness.

For a masterful example of asymmetrical balance as it is more typically found in Western painting, we turn to *The Burning of the Houses of Parliament* by the English painter J. M. Turner (**5.16**). Turner was an eyewitness to the catastrophe, which he watched from a boat on the Thames River in

5.15 (above) Nonomura Sotatsu. *The Zen Priest Choka.* Edo Period, late 16th–early 17th century. Hanging scroll, ink on paper; 37¾ × 14¾". The Cleveland Museum of Art.

5.16 (left) Joseph Mallory Turner. *The Burning of the Houses of Parliament.* c. 1835. Oil on canvas, 36¼ × 48½". Philadelphia Museum of Art.

London. In his painting, he places the viewer on the opposite bank of the river. Our eyes are immediately drawn to the spectacular conflagration in the distance at the left. Turner balances this leftward attraction with the large white form of the bridge to the right, which brings us to the foreground of the painting where a crowd has gathered. A single white street lamp—the lightest value in the painting—draws our eyes to the left, and from there we circle back to the flames, this time allowing the directional lines of the rose and dark smoke to carry our eyes off into the night sky, where a few stars shine.

Turner's composition leads our eyes on a journey around the implied depth of the painting. Depth, or the lack of it, is a fascinating issue in Manet's *A Bar at the Folies-Bergère* (**5.17**). The barmaid seems to stand before a large interior that recedes far back into the distance. Actually she is wedged into a narrow space between the marble bar and a large mirror, which reflects all that she can see but cannot participate in. Her own reflection is displaced to the right, where we see that she is waiting on a man who must be standing where we are standing as we view the painting. Around the central, symmetrical form of the barmaid Manet scatters a dazzling display of visual weights and counterweights. The large dark form of the barmaid's reflection, the bowl of oranges next to the green bottle on the bar, the bottles to either side and their reflections in the mirror, the massive chandeliers and the moonlike white globes in the background, the woman in white who props her elbows on the balcony, even the green-clad feet of the trapeze artist visible at the upper left corner—all have a role to play. Place your finger over any element and you can see the life go out of that part of the painting and the overall balance become destabilized.

5.17 Edouard Manet. *A Bar at the Folies-Bergère.* 1881–82. Oil on canvas, 37¾ × 51¼″.
Courtauld Institute Galleries, Home House Trustees, London.

Balance, then, encourages our active participation in looking. By using balance to lead our eyes around a work, artists structure our experience of it. As an important aspect of form, balance also helps communicate a mood or meaning. The promise of an unchanging, eternal paradise is embodied in the stable, symmetrical balance of Tori Busshi's *Shaka Triad* (see 5.9), just as the dramatic confrontation of life and death is embodied in the dynamic asymmetrical balance of Klimt's *Death and Life* (see 5.13).

EMPHASIS AND SUBORDINATION

Emphasis and subordination are complementary concepts. Emphasis means that our attention is drawn more to certain parts of a composition than to others. If the emphasis is on a relatively small, clearly defined area, we call this a focal point. Subordination means that certain areas of the composition are purposefully made less visually interesting, so that the areas of emphasis stand out.

There are many ways to create emphasis. In *The Banjo Lesson* (**5.18**), Henry Ossawa Tanner used size and placement to emphasize the figures of the old man and young boy. Tanner set the pair in the foreground, and he

5.18 Henry Ossawa Tanner. *The Banjo Lesson.* 1893. Oil on canvas, 49 × 35½".
Hampton University Museum, Hampton, Virginia.

5.19 Paul Cézanne. *The Large Bathers*. 1898–1905. Oil on canvas, 6'10" × 8'3". Philadelphia Museum of Art.

posed them so that their visual weights combine to form a single mass, the largest form in the painting. Strongly contrasting values of dark skin against a pale background add further emphasis. Within this emphasized area, Tanner uses directional lines of sight to create a focal point on the circular body of the banjo and the boy's hand on it. Again contrast plays a role, for the light form of the banjo is set amid darker values, and the boy's hand contrasts dark against light. Tanner has subordinated the background so that it does not interfere, blurring the detail and working in a narrow range of light values. Imagine, for example, if one of the pictures depicted hanging on the far wall were painted in bright colors and minute detail. It would "jump out" of the painting and steal the focus away from what Tanner wants us to notice.

Cézanne uses the lines of tree trunks to narrow the focus of his monumental painting *The Large Bathers* (**5.19**), creating a central, triangular viewing area. He subordinates the upper corners of the painting by limiting visual interest there to brushwork in closely related middle values. The lighter values of the women's bodies draw our attention. Cézanne has massed them into two triangular groupings that echo the shape of the opening. The shared attention of the three women in the foreground links the two groups. Following their gazes and the lines of their arms, we would expect to find a

5.20 Francisco de Goya. *Executions of the Third of May, 1808*. 1814–15. Oil on canvas, 8′9″ × 13′4″. Museo del Prado, Madrid.

focal point, but Cézanne does not give it to us, for it would anchor the painting too firmly in the immediate foreground, and he wants our eyes to travel more freely. Instead, he creates a focal point on the farther shore, where two mysterious figures stand on the bank of the river. Several of the women in the right grouping direct our attention there.

Directional lines and light create the focal point in Francisco de Goya's *Executions of the Third of May, 1808* (**5.20**). The event Goya depicted was the invasion of Spain by Napoleon's armies and their savage execution of Spanish resisters. Our interest is centered on one heroic but doomed Spaniard, his arms raised in a pose of crucifixion. This tragic figure is bathed in light, while most of the rest of the painting remains in shadow. Moreover, the faceless figures of the soldiers point their rifles at him, and even the stance of their bodies focuses our attention on the victim. Goya's sympathies clearly lay with the killed, not the killers. He therefore emphasized the poignant sacrifice of one man, to deemphasize the mechanical slaughter by the others.

SCALE AND PROPORTION

Proportion and scale both have to do with size. **Scale** means size in relation to a standard or "normal" size. Normal size is the size we expect something to be. For example, a model airplane is smaller in scale than a real airplane; a 10-pound prize-winning tomato at the county fair is a tomato on a large

FRANCISCO DE GOYA
1746–1828

W RITERS ON GOYA have long been fascinated by the close friendship between him and the Duchess of Alba, the powerful aristocrat whom many considered the most beautiful woman of her time in Spain. It is a measure of this artist's complexity and uniqueness that the haughty duchess should form a special bond with one who emerged from quite humble origins, whose temperament was often morose and reclusive, and whose imagery could be shockingly gruesome.

Francisco José de Goya y Lucientes was born in a village in the bleak northeast section of Spain. While a young man Goya may have supported himself partially as a bullfighter, but this is one of the many unverifiable stories about his intriguing life. By the age of twenty he was in Madrid.

Goya's earliest commissions were for church murals and tapestry cartoons. In 1783 he was launched in one of the two artistic arenas for which he is best known—portraitist to the nobility. Within a few years he was active at the royal court, and in 1799 he was appointed court painter to Charles IV, King of Spain. Some of Goya's portraits, including two of the

Duchess of Alba, are exquisitely lovely; others have a darker side to them. According to some critics, Goya's pictures of the royal family, while appearing to flatter, were actually subtle revelations of the subjects' stupidity and corruption.

Goya's other major field of expression was prints, of which he was an unexcelled master. Two major series, each having about eighty images constitute the bulk of his work: *Los Caprichos*, in which the many follies of human nature are satirized; and *The Disasters of War*, an often brutally explicit catalogue of the cruelties prevalent in wartime.

Goya achieved both fame and financial success relatively early. While his career prospered, however, his personal life was repeatedly marked by tragedy. His marriage to Josefa Bayeu seems to have been more of a convenience than a passion. She bore him many children—perhaps as many as twenty—but only one survived to maturity. In 1792 the artist was struck by a severe illness that left him almost totally deaf. Another near-fatal illness in 1819 increased his isolation and pessimism; Goya bought a home outside Madrid, known as La Quinta del Sordo ("The House of the Deaf Man"), to which he retired and painted a series of works known as the "Black Paintings," for their dark tonality and aura of despair. After all, the artist's relationship with the Duchess of Alba, whatever it might have been (some maintain that they were lovers), seems to have been one of few bright periods in his life.

Goya's education was sketchy, and as an adult he read and wrote with some difficulty. An announcement for *Los Caprichos* probably was written with the help of a friend, but it captures Goya's attitude toward his art: "Painting, like poetry, selects in the universe whatever she deems most appropriate to her ends. She assembles in a single fantastic personage circumstances and features which nature distributes among many individuals. From this combination, ingeniously composed, results that happy imitation by virtue of which the artist earns the title of inventor and not of servile copyist."[2]

Francisco de Goya. *Self-Portrait in His Studio.*
Real Academia de Bellas Artes de San Fernando, Madrid.

scale. The artist Claes Oldenburg delights in the effects that a radical shift in scale can produce. In *Knife/Ship II* (**5.21**), he created a 40-foot-long pocketknife, outfitted with oars as though it were a royal barge. Motors turn the corkscrew and raise and lower the blades. Shown here in the lobby of the Guggenheim Museum in New York City, *Knife/Ship II* depicts a humble object on a truly heroic scale, and in doing so jars us loose from everyday habits of seeing. "Look at the things around you as though you had never seen them before," the artist is in effect saying, "and notice how wonderful they are."

The scale of a work of art is an important element in our experience of it, an element that is lost in a book, where everything is reduced to more or less the same size. For this reason, it is important to experience as much art as possible at first hand, because its scale in relation to the viewer is part of the effect the artist had in mind.

The Belgian painter René Magritte used many pictorial strategies to suggest that the world around us might not be as rational and ordered as we like to think. One of his favorites was a shift in scale. In *Delusions of Grandeur II* (**5.22**), he invented a sort of telescoping woman, with each section rising out of the one before and continuing on a smaller scale. Transforming one element into another was also a favorite ploy, as when the sky, which looks perfectly normal at the horizon, is revealed farther up to be made of solid blue blocks.

Proportion refers to size relationships between parts of a whole, or between two or more items perceived as a unit. For example, the proportions of each section of the body in the painting by Magritte are naturalistic. The breasts in the top section are in the correct proportion to the size of the neck and arm openings; the navel in the middle section is in the correct proportion to the overall size of the belly.

5.21 (left) Claes Oldenburg and Coosje van Bruggen. *Knife/Ship II*. 1986. Wood, steel, aluminum, painted with polyurethane enamel; dimensions variable, maximum height 31′8″ × 40′5″ × 31′6″. Museum of Contemporary Art, Los Angeles. Installed at the Solomon R. Guggenheim Museum, New York.

5.22 (right) René Magritte. *Delusions of Grandeur II*. 1948. Oil on canvas, 39⅛ × 32⅛″. Hirshhorn Museum and Sculpture Garden, Smithsonian Institution, Washington, D.C.

5.23 (right) Stela of the sculptor Userwer, detail. Egypt, Dynasty 12, 1991–1783 B.C.E. The British Museum, London.

5.24 (below) A royal altar to the hand (*ikegobo*). Benin, 18th century. Brass, height 18″. The British Museum, London.

Many artistic cultures have developed a fixed set of proportions for depicting a "correct" or "perfect" human form. Ancient Egyptian artists, for example, relied on a squared grid to govern the proportions of their figures (**5.23**). Unfinished fragments such as this give us a rare insight into their working methods, for in finished works the grid is no longer evident. Egyptian artists took the palm of the hand as the basic unit of measurement. Looking at the illustration, you can see that each palm (or back) of a hand occupies one square of the grid. A standing figure measures 18 units from the soles of the feet to the hairline, with the knee falling at horizontal 6, the elbow at horizontal 12, the nipple at 14, and so on. The shoulders of a standing male were 6 units wide; the waist about 2½ units.

Artists have often varied human proportions for symbolic or aesthetic purposes, as in this royal altar from the African kingdom of Benin (**5.24**). Cast in brass, the altar is dedicated to the king's hand, a symbol of physical prowess. Hands are depicted around its base, where they alternate with rams' heads. The king is shown seated atop the altar, flanked by attendants in a symmetrical composition. As in the *Shaka Triad* earlier (see 5.9), the composition expresses a hierarchy, though this time a social one. As the most important person, the king is at the center. He is also portrayed on a larger scale than his attendants. The use of scale to indicate relative importance is called **hierarchical scale,** and it is evident in the *Shaka Triad* as well. Proportionally, the king's head takes up a full third of his total height. "Great Head" is one of the terms used in praise of the king, who is felt to rule his subjects as the head, the seat of wisdom and judgment, rules the body. Representations of the king make these ideas manifest through proportion.

The painter El Greco, in contrast, elongated his figures and made their heads proportionally smaller (**5.25**). The twisting, sinuous contours and dramatic, flickering lighting create an effect so extreme and so original that for many generations it was assumed that the painter had some sort of eye trouble that caused him actually to see people this way. In fact, El Greco's treatment of the figure was influenced by contemporary theories that praised a candle flame as ideally beautiful because of its elongated, twisting contours. Here, the spiritual energy released by Christ's triumph over death is imagined as a sort of explosion, and the flamelike figures seem to burn with the intensity of the moment.

5.25 (left) El Greco. *Resurrection.*
c. 1600–05. Oil on canvas, 9′1¼″ × 4′2″.
Museo del Prado, Madrid.

5.26 (below) Leonardo da Vinci. *Study of Human
Proportions according to Vitruvius.* c. 1485–90. Pen
and ink, 13½ × 9¾″.
Gallerie dell'Accademia, Venice.

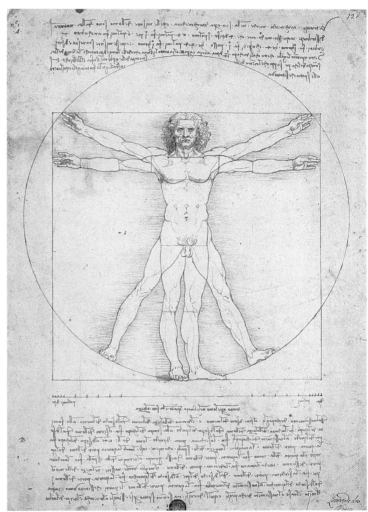

Among the many ideas from ancient Greece and Rome that were
revived during the Renaissance was the notion that numerical relationships
held the key to beauty, and that perfect human proportions reflected a divine
order. Leonardo da Vinci was only one of many artists to become fascinated
with the ideas of Vitruvius, a Roman architect of the first century B.C.E.
whose treatise on architecture, widely read during the Renaissance, related
the perfected male form to the perfect geometry of the square and the circle (**5.26**). Leonardo's figure stands inside a square defined by his height and
the span of his arms, and a circle centered at his navel.

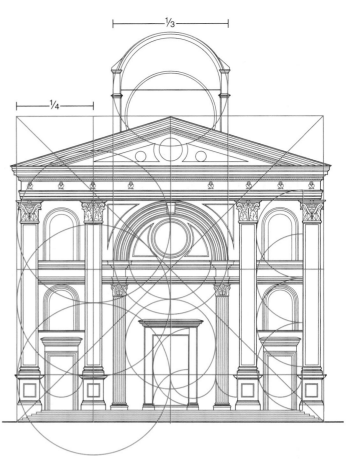

5.27 (left) Leon Battista Alberti. Facade of Sant'Andrea, Mantua. Designed 1470.

5.28 (right) Analysis of the proportions of the facade of Sant'Andrea.

5.29 (below) Proportions of the golden section and golden rectangle.

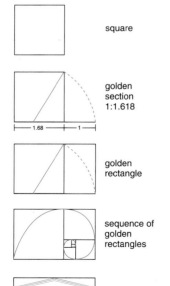

square

golden section 1:1.618

1.68 — 1

golden rectangle

sequence of golden rectangles

proportions of the Parthenon

The Renaissance architect Leon Battista Alberti put these ideas into practice in what is perhaps his greatest work, the church of Sant'Andrea, in Mantua (**5.27**). An analysis of the proportions (**5.28**) reveals that the facade is constructed within a square. The tall pilasters (flat, ornamental columns attached to the surface) are set at one-quarter intervals. The width of the vaulted entryway divides the facade into thirds. The arch over the entryway is a section of a circle that radiates from the exact center of the square. The entryway is as deep as it is wide; that is, its floor area is a square. Alberti uses the dimensions of the entryway square as a basic unit of measure for the interior (see 16.4), so that the facade becomes like a musical overture in which the principal themes to come are announced.

A proportion that has fascinated many artists and architects since its discovery by the ancient Greeks is the ratio known as the golden section. A golden section divides a length into two unequal segments in such a way that the smaller segment has the same ratio to the larger segment as the larger segment has to the whole. The ratio of the two segments works out to 1 to 1.618. The golden section is more easily constructed than it is explained; Figure **5.29** takes you through the steps.

A rectangle constructed using the proportions of the golden section is called a golden rectangle. One of the most interesting characteristics of the golden rectangle, as Figure 5.29 shows, is that when a square is cut off from one end, the remaining shape is also a golden rectangle—a sequence that can be repeated endlessly and relates to such natural phenomena as the spiraling outward growth of a shell. For the Greeks, the intellectual and mathematical interest of the golden rectangle made it beautiful as well, an expression of the mathematical ordering of the universe, and they used it in the design of such structures as the Parthenon (see 14.24), an important and influential building that we will examine later in this book.

Artists and architects have often turned to the golden section when they sought a rational yet subtle organizing principle for their work. During the

20th century, the French architect Le Corbusier related the golden section to human proportions in a tool he called the Modulor (**5.30**). The Modulor is based on two overlapping golden sections. The first extends from the feet to the top of the head, with the section division falling at the navel; the second extends from the navel to the tip of an upraised hand, with the section division falling at the top of the head. Using the height of an average adult, Le Corbusier derived several series of measurements based in the golden section. Le Corbusier used the Modulor to fine-tune the designs of many of his buildings (see 13.28), and he offered it to architects as a tool that could help them arrive at proportions that were both harmonious and practical.

RHYTHM

Rhythm is based in repetition, and it is a basic part of the world we find ourselves in. We speak of the rhythm of the seasons, which recur in the same pattern every year, the rhythm of the cycles of the moon, the rhythm of waves upon the shore. These natural rhythms measure out the passing of time, organizing our experience of it. To the extent that our arts take place in time, they too structure experience through rhythm. Music and dance are the most obvious examples. Poetry, which is recited or read over time, also uses rhythm for structure and expression. Looking at art takes time as well, and rhythm is one of the means that artists use to structure our experience.

Through repetition, any of the visual elements can take on a rhythm within a work. In Edward Hopper's *Early Sunday Morning* (**5.31**), we find several different rhythms moving horizontally across the canvas. At top there is the regular rhythm of the eaves under the roof, and below that the strong rhythmic pulse of the repeating forms of the second-story windows alternating with the wall. Variations in the spacing of the windows and the disposition of shades and curtains relieve the stark repetition and provide a sense of life and movement. At the ground level, storefronts alternate with doorways. As with the windows, the potentially monotonous rhythm is relieved and enlivened by variation.

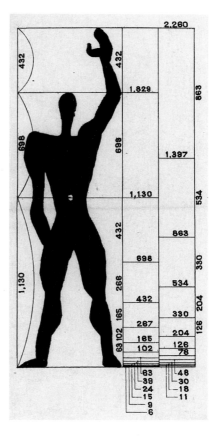

5.30 (above) Le Corbusier. *The Modulor.* 1945.
Courtesy Fondation Le Corbusier.

5.31 (below) Edward Hopper. *Early Sunday Morning.* 1930. Oil on canvas, 2'11" × 5'.
Whitney Museum of American Art, New York.

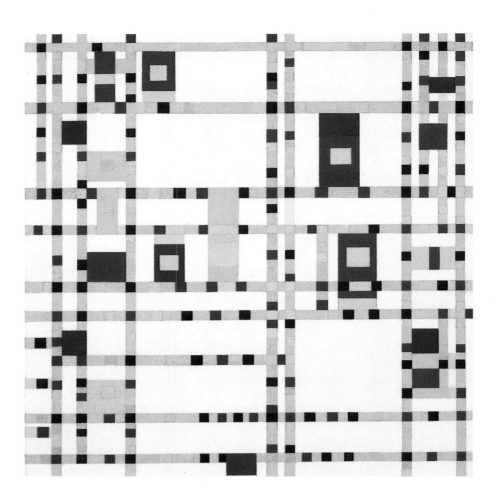

5.32 Piet Mondrian. *Broadway Boogie-Woogie*. 1942–43. Oil on canvas, 50 × 50″.
The Museum of Modern Art, New York.

The rhythms of Piet Mondrian's *Broadway Boogie-Woogie* (**5.32**) are sharp and staccato. Mondrian came to New York from Europe in 1940, toward the end of his life. In Europe, he had largely cultivated an art of tranquility and balance, creating perfectly calibrated compositions based on what he felt to be the basic, universal language of human culture: rectangular forms, horizontal and vertical lines, and primary colors (see 21.29). In New York, the sixty-eight-year-old painter found a rhythm of life that was faster, more energetic, jazzier than he had known. He modified his visual language to capture those rhythms in *Broadway Boogie-Woogie*. We can almost *hear* the painting—the quiet percussion of the little squares and the sudden syncopated shouts of the larger rectangles, like car horns blaring in the busy streets, or like the joyful noise of a boogie-woogie.

The Cuban painter Wifredo Lam used overlapping rhythms to organize *The Jungle* (**5.33**). Vertical rhythms of bamboo and elongated legs predominate, enlivened by cross-rhythms of feet and hands (drawn in much the same way), and of crescent-moon-shaped faces. Human and animal forms mingle in this fascinating work, which contains references to *Santería,* a Caribbean religion that mingles West African and Roman Catholic beliefs. The horse/woman at the far left, for example, refers to the moment in *Santería* ritual practice when a devotee becomes possessed by one of the spirits, called *orisha.* Such believers are said to be mounted by the *orisha,* and hence the image of a horse.

Photographers, too, may use rhythm as an organizational and expressive element in a composition. The difference, of course, is that while painters, sculptors, and architects can create rhythms, photographers must find them. Soviet photographer Georgij Petruscow captured the open, circular rhythms of seated farmworkers to create a picture of communal harmony and collective well-being (**5.34**). Petruscow had been sent into the countryside by his government to document the success of the latest agricultural policies. His

photograph emphasizes not the actual labor of growing food, but its rewards. Petruscow has framed his picture so that only part of each seated group is shown, thus creating a winding path for us to follow into the image and leading our eyes toward the stacks of harvested grain in the distance.

5.33 (left) Wifredo Lam. *The Jungle*. 1943. Gouache on paper mounted on canvas, 7'10¼" × 7'6½".
The Museum of Modern Art, New York.

5.34 (right) Georgij Petruscow. *Midday Break in the Fields*. 1934. Photograph, 15¼" × 10⅞".
Museum Ludwig, Cologne.

ELEMENTS AND PRINCIPLES: A SUMMARY

In the second chapter of this book we examined two paintings by Edvard Munch in order to explore how form could suggest meaning (see 2.24, 2.25). This chapter and the preceding one have introduced the vocabulary of formal analysis, the terms that help us see and describe what we see. In the process, we have examined many artworks, each from a particular formal point of view—as an example of line, value, balance, rhythm, and so on. Before leaving this section, we should analyze one work more fully in order to show how these points of view combine into a more complete way of seeing, and to suggest again how form invites interpretation. The work we will look at is Picasso's *Girl Before a Mirror*.

Painted in 1932, *Girl Before a Mirror* was probably inspired by Marie-Thérèse Walter, Picasso's lover at the time. Iconographically, the motif of a woman looking in a mirror is connected with a subject in European art called the *vanitas*. Latin for "vanity," its themes are the passing of time, the certainty of death, and the futility of piling up earthly treasure. Often, the face the woman sees in the mirror is a death's head. Picasso would have been thoroughly familiar with the *vanitas* tradition, for he was very well versed in art history. Living and working in Paris, Picasso would have known, too, that this particular type of mirror is called in French a *psyché*, after the Greek goddess Psyche. Viewed as the personification of the human soul, she was loved by Eros, the god of love, who forbade her to look on him. This is the background information that Picasso could have expected his viewers to know. Now, what do we see?

Oriented vertically, *Girl Before a Mirror* (**5.35**) is over 5 feet in height. The woman and her reflection occupy almost the entire canvas. Thus she is not miniaturized, as in the illustration here, but portrayed larger than life-size. The scale of the painting and of the woman represented within it makes a powerful impression when seen in person. We confront the work on an equal footing as a presence that rises up before us.

The design is based in symmetrical balance, with the woman on the left and her mirror image on the right. The left post of the mirror falls near the vertical axis, dividing the composition in two. As in Frida Kahlo's double self-portrait (see 5.11), the fundamental symmetry draws our attention to the ways in which the two sides are *not* alike, for it sets them in opposition. Indeed, the reflection of the girl's face in the mirror does not double her exactly. Warm colors are reflected as cool colors, and firm shapes become fluid. This is not the death's head of a traditional *vanitas*, but it is a transformation nevertheless, and it evokes a mysterious, shadowy realm of uncertainty—perhaps the girl's thoughts, perhaps her unconscious, perhaps her soul, perhaps her mortality.

5.35 Pablo Picasso. *Girl Before a Mirror.* 1932. Oil on canvas, 5'4" × 4'3¼".
The Museum of Modern Art, New York.

A composition divided so cleanly in two could easily break apart, and Picasso uses several means to tie the two halves together. The most important is the girl's gesture as she reaches out to the far edge of the mirror, almost in an embrace. The gesture links the girl and her reflection, and it is so important to the composition that Picasso reinforces it with a red-striped shape that begins on the girl's chest and extends to her fingertips. Together, gesture and shape set up a pendulum motion, and as we look at the painting, our eyes swing rhythmically back and forth from one side to the other.

Overall, the unity of the composition rests on the rhythmical curves and repeating circles of the girl and her reflection, culminating in the great oval of the mirror itself. A second unifying device is the lushly painted wallpaper, which extends across the entire canvas. Its diagonal geometric grid acts as a foil for the sweeping organic curves of the girl, and it is almost as important a presence in the painting as she is. Color unifies the composition as well, for while the colors are brilliantly varied, they fall generally in the same range of intensities and values, with the important exception of the girl herself.

And what of the girl? Picasso directs our attention first of all to her face, a natural focal point. He emphasizes it by painting one half bright yellow and by surrounding her head with an oval of white and green that isolates it from the busy pattern of the background and provides enough visual weight to balance the form of the mirror. He also modifies its proportions so that her facial features occupy the entire space of her head. With her yellow hair, circular half-yellow face, and white aura, she is like the sun of the painting, its source of light.

The pale violet portion of her face is depicted in profile, gazing at the mirror. With the addition of the yellow portion she turns her head to look at us—or at Picasso. Cool, pale colors set off by black shapes and lines draw our attention to her body, which is also divided vertically. The left portion is clothed in a striped garment, perhaps a bathing suit; the right portion is nude. The swell of the belly evokes childbearing and the renewal of life. In a remarkable X-ray view, Picasso even paints through her skin to the womb inside, envisioned as another circle. Her biological destiny is emphasized in the mirror image as well, for this part of her body is reflected confidently. Picasso draws our attention to it through an abrupt shift in value—in the dark world of the mirror, the breasts and belly are white.

What is the painting about? It does not have a single meaning, but many layers of meanings and associations. It is about a girl contemplating herself in a mirror, quiet before her own inner mysteries, aware of her life-affirming sexuality and procreative powers. It is about Picasso meditating on women as sensuous symbols of beauty, abundance, and fertility. It is also about Picasso looking with a lover's possessive gaze at Marie-Thérèse Walter, seeing through her clothing to the flesh underneath. Hovering behind the image are the tradition of the *vanitas* and its theme of mortality, and the story of Psyche, a girl who is aware of being loved and being gazed upon, and who turns fatefully to look at her lover.

Picasso did not have a checklist as he worked, dutifully adding the visual elements in the correct proportions of unity, variety, balance, scale, proportion, and rhythm. His student days were far behind him, and such thinking was by now second nature. But as the numerous reworkings evident in the finished painting show, he changed his mind often and made constant adjustments as he worked. Why? Any number of reasons, probably—because the balance was off, because his eye was not traveling freely over the canvas, because there was too much focus here and not enough there, because the mood of the colors was not right. The painting is the end result of all his decisions, a project he stopped at the moment when, as the picture's first viewer, he was content with what he saw. As later viewers, we articulate the elements and principles to make ourselves aware of the dynamic of seeing. With experience, this becomes second nature to us as well.

PART THREE

TWO-DIMENSIONAL MEDIA

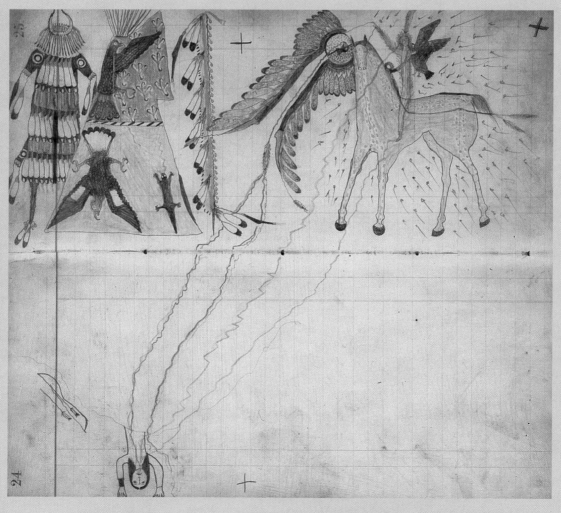

6.1 Henderson Ledger Artist A. *Medicine Vision*. 1882. Pencil, colored pencil, ink on paper; 10⅝ × 11⅞″. Collection Charles and Valerie Diker.

CHAPTER 6

Drawing

Everybody draws. There can scarcely be a person above the age of two who has never made a drawing. Many people take photographs, some paint, a few make sculpture, and a very few may even design a building. But everybody draws. You see a patch of wet sand at the beach, a dusty tabletop, or a blank notepad while you are sitting in class or at a business meeting—and your natural impulse is to draw something.

Children begin to draw long before they begin to write, sometimes before they can talk intelligibly. In drawing far more than in speech, children reveal their fantasies and their fears. Whatever the content, nearly all children draw, which shows how truly universal is this method of expression.

Two qualities often associated with drawing are familiarity and intimacy. Drawing is familiar in that it often uses materials we all are accustomed to—a pencil, a pen, a stick of chalk. There are no mysterious or exotic ingredients. The drawing illustrated on the facing page was done with pencil and colored pencil on the lined paper of an account book (**6.1**), yet these ordinary materials capture an extraordinary event. Drawn by an Arapaho Indian warrior, the drawing records a medicine vision—a mystical experience in which a chosen warrior is visited by a supernatural being. The warrior appears at the bottom of the page, upside down, thrown to the ground by the force of the apparition. Lines edgy with energy connect him to his vision—the Medicine Being who has materialized on horseback to the upper right. Accompanied by an eagle or hawk, the Medicine Being radiates power from his eyes, hands, and feet. He rides a Thunder Horse the color of the sky and spotted with hail, and he offers the warrior a shield trailing feathers. The shield proclaims the warrior's connection to cosmic powers, and it will serve as his insignia in battle.

Drawing seems intimate because it is frequently the artist's private note-taking. Many drawings are not intended for exhibition and therefore are not shown publicly during the artist's lifetime. They may be preliminary sketches for some other work of art or just the artist's refined doodling. We think of such drawings as direct expression—from brain to hand—and they can offer fascinating glimpses into the creative process. Picasso, mindful of his own legacy, began early on to date and save all of his sketches. Thanks to this habit we have almost a complete visual record of his mind at work. Illustrated here is his first sketch for his great antiwar

6.2 (above, top) Pablo Picasso. First composition study for *Guernica*. 1 May 1937. Pencil on blue paper, 8¼ × 10⅝". Museo del Prado, Madrid.

6.3 (above) Frank O. Gehry. Guggenheim Museum Bilbao, west elevation. 1991. Ink on paper, 9 × 12". Courtesy Frank O. Gehry and Associates, Inc.

mural *Guernica* (**6.2**; for the completed mural see 3.16). Much changed between this first rapidly sketched idea and the final painting, but one essential gesture is already in place: the horror will be revealed to us by the light of a lamp held by a figure leaning out of an upper story window.

The architect Frank O. Gehry made a series of similarly loose, gestural sketches as ideas for his Guggenheim Museum Bilbao took shape (**6.3**; for the completed museum see 13.33). We may be surprised that something so massive and complex as a building could begin with no more than a scribble, but Gehry actually kept making drawings long into the design process, even after the first scale models had been built. It is as though he wanted to keep his sense of the building fluid, to prevent his ideas from hardening too soon into precise forms and exact measurements. As in Picasso's sketch, the essential sweep and character of the building are captured in a few lines.

Other factors may contribute to drawing's sense of intimacy. Most drawings are relatively small (compared with paintings), and many are executed quickly. Drawings are often made in great quantities; some artists do hundreds of drawings for every "finished" work. There are exceptions to this generalization, drawings that are large and/or are executed with painstaking attention to detail, including several examples in this chapter. But part of the charm of drawing as a medium must surely be the fact that, even when a work *is* intended for exhibition, it still retains an air of intimacy.

In drawings such as *Dancer Adjusting Her Slipper* (**6.4**), we have the impression of being present at an intimate transaction between artist and model. We can easily imagine Degas adjusting the position of the arm, modifying the contour of the foot, his eyes shifting back and forth between his evolving drawing and the model standing a few feet away. Sketches like this served Degas as a sort of inventory of poses and people—raw materials from which larger compositions could be constructed. The drawing is "squared for transfer," that is, Degas drew a grid over it to make it easier to copy accurately. He used this pose in two finished works, both of dancers in rehearsal.

Artists may draw for no other reason than to understand the world around them, to investigate its forms. There is no better exercise in seeing

6.4 Edgar Degas. *Dancer Adjusting Her Slipper*. 1873. Graphite and charcoal heightened with white chalk on now-faded pink paper, 12⅞ × 9⅝". The Metropolitan Museum of Art, New York.

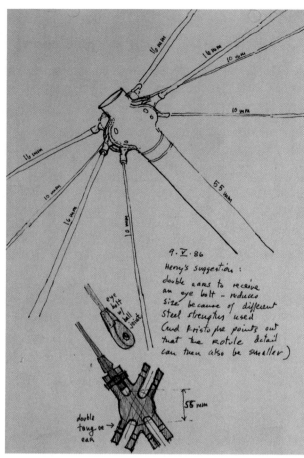

6.5 (left) Leonardo da Vinci. *Star of Bethlehem and Other Plants.* c. 1506–08. Red chalk and pen, 7⅝ × 6⅜″.
The Royal Collection, Windsor Castle, Windsor, England.

6.6 (right) Yann Weymouth. *Ideas for the supporting structure of the Louvre Pyramid.* c. 1986. Ink, colored pencil, and gouache on paper.
Courtesy the artist.

than to take a small part of the natural world and try to draw it in all its detail (**6.5**). Leonardo had the curiosity and the powers of observation of a natural scientist. Some of his sketches served as studies that might find their way into larger compositions, but he also filled notebook after notebook with investigative drawings for their own sake. The drawing here reflects his interest in parallels between the behavior of currents of water and the motions of waving grasses.

Often ideas are more effectively conveyed in images than in words. The annotated drawing in Figure **6.6** is one of many that were made as engineering details were worked out for I. M. Pei's pyramid at the Louvre Museum (see 3.11). The task was to develop a strong yet lightweight metal skeleton that could support the glass pyramid from the inside. Since the skeleton would be visible, it had to be visually compelling as well. The drawing portrays a tentative design for a nodule—a connecting point for the numerous slender steel rods that would make up the skeleton. It was not made to be looked at as art, but there is beauty to be found in its visual economy, sensitive line, and clarity of thought.

The drawings we have been looking at are all on paper, a material we associate closely with drawing. Historically, however, many other surfaces have been used to draw on. The oldest artworks that we know of are the cave drawings in southern France and in Spain (see 1.3). While these images are often referred to as paintings, many have a strong linear quality that would more accurately categorize them as drawings. The artists worked directly on the cave walls, possibly using mats of hair or charred sticks to draw the contours of the many animals they portrayed.

With the development of pottery during the Neolithic era, fired clay became a surface for drawing in many cultures. The durability of fired clay has meant that many examples have survived when works in more perishable materials have not. For example, we know of ancient Greek painting

LEONARDO
1452–1519

N O CLUES ARE OFFERED by the scant knowledge about Leonardo's origins to explain what spawned perhaps the most complex imagination of all time. Leonardo was the illegitimate son of a peasant woman known only as Caterina and a fairly well-to-do notary, Piero da Vinci. He was raised in his father's house at Vinci and, when he was about fifteen, apprenticed to the Florentine artist Andrea del Verrocchio, in whose workshop he remained for ten years. It is said the pupil's talent so impressed his master that Verrocchio gave up painting forever.

In 1482 Leonardo left Florence for Milan, where he became official artist to Lodovico Sforza, duke of that city. There the artist undertook many projects, foremost among them his famous painting of the *Last Supper*. Leonardo remained with Sforza until the latter's fall from power in 1499, after which he returned to Florence.

Sketches and written records indicate that Leonardo worked as a sculptor, but no examples remain. Only about a dozen paintings can be definitely attributed to him, and several of these are unfinished.

There are, however, hundreds of drawings, and the thousands of pages from his detailed notebook testify to the man's extraordinary genius. If Leonardo completed relatively few artistic works, this can only be ascribed to the enormous breadth of his interests, which caused him repeatedly to turn from one subject to another. He was a skilled architect and engineer, engrossed in the problems of city planning, sanitary disposal, military engineering, and even the design of weapons. He made sketches for a crude submarine, a helicopter, and an airplane—with characteristic thoroughness also designing a parachute in case the airplane should fail. He made innovative studies in astronomy, anatomy, botany, geology, optics, and above all mathematics. His contemporaries reported his great talent as a musician—he played and improvised on the lute—as well as his love of inventive practical jokes.

In 1507 Leonardo was appointed court painter to the King of France, Louis XII, who happened to be in Milan at the time. Nine years later the aging artist was named court painter to Louis' successor, Francis I. Francis seems to have revered him for his towering reputation as an artist and his crisp intellect, but to have expected little artistic production from the old man. The king provided comfortable lodgings in the city of Amboise, where Leonardo died.

Solitary all his life, Leonardo did not marry, and he formed very few close attachments. His obsession seems to have been with getting it all down, recording the fertile outpourings of his brain and hand. In his *Treatise on Painting*, assembled from his notebook pages and published after his death, he advised painters to follow his method: "You should often amuse yourself when you take a walk for recreation, in watching and taking note of the attitudes and actions of men as they talk and dispute, or laugh or come to blows with one another . . . noting these down with rapid strokes, in a little pocket-book which you ought always to carry with you . . . for there is such an infinite number of forms and actions of things that the memory is incapable of preserving them."[1]

Leonardo da Vinci. *Self-Portrait*. c. 1512.
Red chalk on paper, 13 × 8¼".
Biblioteca Reale, Turin.

only from literary sources, for not a single example has come down to us. Thanks to the Greek custom of drawing on pottery, however, we have some understanding of what these paintings might have looked like (see 14.22). The Greeks also drew and wrote on papyrus, a paperlike material developed in ancient Egypt that was made from pressed plant stems. Rivaling papyrus was a later invention, parchment. Made from treated animal skins, it was widely used throughout the Roman Empire and continued as the surface of choice in medieval Europe. The ancient Chinese drew on silk, their special material, and many Chinese artists still do. It is the Chinese, too, who are credited with the invention of paper, traditionally said to have been discovered in 105 C.E. From China, paper was introduced into Islamic culture during the 8th century, finally reaching Europe some 600 years later.

Today, artists have a wide array of drawing surfaces and materials to choose from. Some materials have their origins in the distant past, while others depend on space-age technology. In this chapter we examine some of the traditional materials that have been used for drawing and the effects they can produce. Then we look briefly at some recent directions in this oldest of arts.

MATERIALS FOR DRAWING

All drawing media are based on **pigment**—powdered coloring material—mixed with a substance that enables it to adhere to the drawing surface. Drawing materials generally are divided into two categories—dry media and liquid media. The dry media tend to be abrasive. They "scratch" across a paper or some other surface, depositing particles wherever they come in contact with the surface. Liquid media, in contrast, have particles of pigment suspended in fluid, so they flow onto the surface much more freely.

DRY MEDIA

PENCIL The graphite pencil, sometimes called a "lead" pencil, probably has made more drawings than any other medium. Pencils are cheap, readily available, and easy to work with. Mistakes can be erased. If the drawing turns out badly, it can be thrown away at no great expense.

Despite the pencil's humble status, however, some of the most elegant drawings we know have been done with graphite pencil. A master of this technique was Jean-Auguste-Dominique Ingres. In 1819 Ingres used the sharp point of a pencil to create a portrait of his friend, the brilliant Italian violinist Nicolo Paganini (**6.7**). Paganini was a dynamic character, famed equally for his virtuosity on the violin and his vivid personality. The artist captures both of these qualities. Ingres poses his subject standing proudly erect, the violin and bow poised with the absolute assurance of the master musician. Paganini looks us viewers straight in the eye, showing us his intelligence and zest for life—plus more than a trace of arrogance. The lines of the coat suggest a barely restrained energy in the body underneath. We half expect Paganini to break into a smile, thrust his violin under his chin, and play for us.

METALPOINT Metalpoint, the ancestor of the graphite pencil, is an old technique that was especially popular during the Renaissance. Few artists use it now, because it is not very forgiving of mistakes or indecision. Once put down, the lines cannot easily be changed or erased. The drawing medium is a thin wire of metal, often of pure silver (in which case the medium is called **silverpoint**), mounted in some kind of holding device, such as a wooden shaft or a modern mechanical pencil. The drawing surface must be specially coated with poster paint or a similar ground—historically, the coating was bone dust and glue. Silver tarnishes quickly, and while the drawing can be protected to prevent this from happening, the gray tonalities of tarnish are generally desired.

Metalpoint drawings are characterized by a fine, delicate line of uniform width. Perugino drew *A Man in Armor* (**6.8**) with silverpoint on a blue ground, building up the areas of shadow with hatching and cross-hatching. He then painted highlights in white with a very fine brush to suggest the reflective qualities of the polished metal armor. The drawing is unfinished: only the preliminary, tentative contour lines and the white highlight have been sketched in on the shield that the man holds in front of him, propped on the ground.

CHARCOAL   Charcoal's effects are almost the exact opposite of those offered by metalpoint. Where metalpoint produces a thin, delicate line, charcoal's line is dark, sometimes very soft, occasionally harsh. Charcoal is actually burned sticks of wood—the best-quality charcoal coming from special vine wood heated in a kiln until only carbon remains. Charcoal lines can be thin or thick, faint or dark. Elizabeth Murray's *Shake* illustrates well the distinc-

6.7 (left) Jean-Auguste-Dominique Ingres. *Portrait of Nicolo Paganini.* 1819. Graphite pencil, 11¾ × 8⅝″. Musée du Louvre, Paris.

6.8 (right) Perugino. *A Man in Armor.* Late 15th–early 16th century. Metalpoint, heightened with white, on blue ground; 9¾ × 7¼″. The Royal Collection, Windsor Castle, Windsor, England.

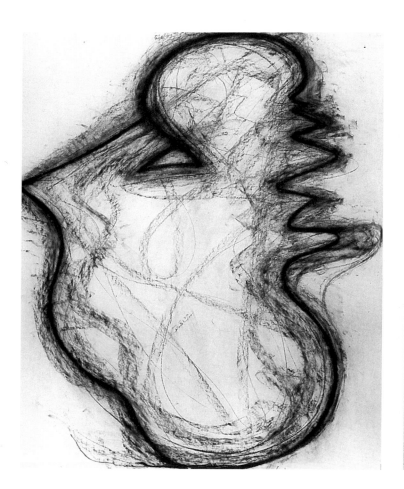

6.9 (left) Elizabeth Murray. *Shake.* 1979. Charcoal on paper, 46½ × 38″.
The Whitney Museum of American Art, New York.

6.10 (right) Georges Seurat. *The Couple,* study for *A Sunday on La Grande Jatte* (4.28). 1884. Conté crayon, 12¼ × 9¼″.
The British Museum, London.

tive qualities of charcoal (**6.9**). The drawing records the process of its own creation, from the first tentative lines as the charcoal was dragged lightly across the paper to the dark, organic form that finally emerged. The velvety blacks created by layer upon layer of strokes are characteristic of charcoal.

CHALK AND CRAYON A wide range of chalks and crayons are available to the artist, and nearly all of them offer color effects. Generally speaking, the main difference between chalks and crayons is the **binder**—the substance that holds particles of pigment together. Chalks have nonfat binders, whereas crayons have a fatty or greasy binder, so there is considerable variation in the way these materials react to contact with paper. If you imagine blackboard chalk and ordinary children's crayons, this difference in effect should be clear.

Chalks, being drier and more crumbly, generally blend well and can be overlaid (two or more colors on top of one another) to produce shaded effects. They respond best to a paper with some tooth, are relatively fragile unless covered by a fixative, and offer a limited range of colors. The greasier crayons adhere well to paper and are more permanent, but they are difficult to blend with one another for subtle tones and gradations. (However, the newer oil-based crayons can be finger-blended almost as easily as oil paints blend.) Crayons usually offer a wider choice of colors than do chalks, and they come in varying degrees of hardness to permit sharp lines or tonal areas.

Crayon can mean anything from the wax crayons used by children through the lithographic crayon meant for drawing on stone in printmaking (Chapter 8). But the commonest drawing material is conté crayon—a fine-textured stick medium available in shades of red, brown, and black.

One artist who comes readily to mind in discussing conté crayon drawings is Georges Seurat. In Chapter 4 we looked at Seurat's painting technique, called pointillism, in which tiny dots of color are massed together to build form. Seurat also did many drawings. By working in conté on rough-textured paper he could approximate the effect of color dots in paint. *The Couple* (**6.10**) is a preliminary study in crayon for Seurat's landmark oil painting, *A Sunday on La Grande Jatte* (see 4.28). It was Seurat's practice to work out his figures very completely as separate units in drawing and then to transfer them to the painted canvas. This drawing is his study for the male and female figures at far right in the painting; it also shows ghost images of the two young women in front of them and the trees in the background.

A chalk technique popular during the 18th century was known simply as "three colors." The colors in question were black, white, and a brownish red called sanguine. A master of this technique was Jean-Antoine Watteau, whose charming *Seated Young Woman* we illustrate here (**6.11**). Watteau used sanguine to suggest warm flesh tones. Black reinforces important contours and serves for basic modeling. White highlights suggest the roundness of a shoulder or the projection of a knee. The tone of the paper itself pulls the three colors together by supplying a middle value against which the white chalk can be seen.

6.11 Jean-Antoine Watteau. *Seated Young Woman.* c. 1717. Red, black, and white chalks on cream-colored paper; 10 × 6¹³⁄₁₆″. The Pierpont Morgan Library, New York.

6.12 (left) Francesco Clemente. *She and she*. Pastel on paper, 24 × 18″. Private Collection.

6.13 (right) Edgar Degas. *The Entrance of the Masked Dancers*. c. 1884. Pastel on paper, 19¼ × 25½″. Sterling and Francine Clark Art Institute, Williamstown, Massachusetts.

The most well known chalk medium is called **pastel.** Available in a full range of colors and several degrees of hardness, pastel is often considered a borderline medium, somewhere between painting and drawing. Artists favor soft pastels for most work, reserving the harder ones for special effects or details. Thanks to their fine texture, pastels can be easily blended by blurring one color into another, obliterating the individual strokes and creating smoothly graduated tones. Francesco Clemente's *She and she* displays this type of blended effect (**6.12**). The faces are those of the artist and his wife, but Clemente has mingled their traits so that they seem to meet on some common ground between genders.

Degas, one of the great masters of pastel in the 19th century, did not generally favor a smoothly blended surface. Instead, he preferred to let individual strokes retain their character, and he often built them up in layers to achieve rich, textured effects. *The Entrance of the Masked Dancers* (**6.13**) shows his pastel technique as well as his fascination with the artifice of the theater. The view is from the wings during a performance. Two exhausted dancers have just come off stage after their portion of the ballet. Wholly concentrated on catching their breath, they do not look at each other or speak. Behind them, the ballet continues as a line of masked dancers sweeps onto the stage. In the background, on the other side of the stage, the black top hat and white tie of one of the producers can be glimpsed amid the scenery.

LIQUID MEDIA

PEN AND INK   Ink flowing onto paper gives a smooth, uninterrupted line. As with other relatively permanent media, there is little possibility for correction once the lines have been inscribed. A major variable in the ink drawing, however, is the relative thickness or thinness of lines, which depends on the pen point used. The lines can be all one width, ranging from fine to heavy, or they can vary. A single line may change, perhaps starting as a fine thread, broadening into thickness, and then tapering down again. Such thick-and-thin lines are referred to as *calligraphic* or *gestural*.

Pen and ink was the favorite sketching medium of one of the greatest draftsmen who ever lived, Rembrandt. Rembrandt made thousands of drawings over the course of his career. Many record ideas for paintings or prints, but many more are simply drawings done for the pleasure of drawing. Among his favorite subjects was the landscape around Amsterdam (**6.14**). The example here shows the "handwriting" of his rapid, sketchy style at its most characteristic. The trees that shade and shelter the farmhouse are drawn in lively, curling pen work that suggests the wind rustling their leaves. The rower and the bushes in the foreground are sketched in at great speed with a bolder, freer line, while the vista that opens up to the left is portrayed with a fine, more controlled line. Rembrandt used a **wash,** ink diluted with water and applied with a brush, to give greater solidity to the farmhouse nestled amid the trees and to suggest the reflective surface of the water.

BRUSH AND INK   The brush has long been the favorite drawing tool of Asian artists. Because in the East the brush is commonly used for writing, its handling seems as natural there as using a pencil does to Westerners. When the brush is manipulated in the Asian way, it is the ideal tool (better than a pen) for producing the calligraphic line—thin at the beginning, broadening along its length, and then tapering again to very thin. The detail here from Yosa Buson's *Narrow Road to the Deep North* (**6.15**) shows how effortlessly writing gives way to drawing in East Asia. One of the most famous of

6.14 (below, top) Rembrandt. *A Man Rowing a Boat on the Bullewyk.* c. 1650. Pen and brown wash and white body color, 5 × 8″. Devonshire Collections, Chatsworth.

6.15 (below) Yosa Buson. *The Narrow Road to the Deep North* (detail). 1778. Handscroll, ink and color on paper; height 11½″. Kyoto National Museum.

6.16 Käthe Kollwitz. *Suicide Victim*. 1928. Brush and ink on paper, 16⁵⁄₁₆ × 15½″. Hamburger Kunsthalle.

Japanese poets, Buson was also a painter and, in fact, may have taken up painting in order to make enough money to support his poetry. The detail here is from a long scroll in which he copied out one of the most beloved works of Japanese literature, a poetic travel diary written by the poet Basho. We can imagine Buson writing out the opening of the book, in which Basho describes taking leave of three loyal friends. Then, pausing only to refresh his brush in the inkwell, he deftly sketches in the friends themselves. One stands silent, another leans on a stick, while the third raises his hand in a gesture of farewell that carries into the eloquent blank space that follows.

Handled somewhat differently, the medium of brush and ink can produce extremely bold effects. Käthe Kollwitz relied largely on thick, aggressive lines of pure black for the powerful image of a *Suicide Victim* (**6.16**). Kollwitz' drawing shows plainly the interaction between drawing medium and imagery. In this case we might suspect that the artist had an image in mind and selected the medium that would best fit that image. Other times the reverse may occur: an artist experiments with a particular medium and thus is inspired with an image idea.

RECENT DIRECTIONS

The prestige of painting within the Western tradition has often relegated drawings to a sort of second-class status as finished artworks. Yet the difference between drawing and painting is not always clear, as we have seen in the works of the cave artists, brush-and-ink drawings, and pastels. Over the past few decades, artists have increasingly questioned such traditional divisions and hierarchies. Many have explored the border between drawing and painting, and others have produced drawings as primary artistic statements. Perhaps drawing—quick, lightweight, improvisatory, adaptable—is

KÄTHE KOLLWITZ
1867–1945

IN A TIME when the word "artist" usually meant a painter or a sculptor, Kollwitz did the bulk of her work in prints and drawings. In a time when vivid, sometimes startling color was preoccupying the art world, Kollwitz concentrated on black and white. And in a time when nearly all artists were men, Kollwitz was—triumphantly—a woman, a woman whose life and art focused on the special concerns of women. This combination of oddities might have doomed a lesser artist to obscurity, but not one of Kollwitz' great gifts and powerful personality.

Käthe Schmidt was born in Königsberg (then in Prussia, now part of Russia), the second child in an intellectually active middle-class family. Her parents were remarkably enlightened in encouraging all their children to take an active part in political and social causes and to develop their talents—in Käthe's case a talent for drawing. Käthe received the best art training then available for a woman, in Berlin and Munich. In 1891, after a seven-year engagement, she married Karl Kollwitz, a physician who seems to have been equally supportive of his wife's career. The couple established themselves in Berlin, where they kept a joint doctor's office and artist's studio for fifty years.

During her student days Kollwitz had gradually focused on line and had come to realize that draftsmanship was her genius. Her conventional artistic training must have intensified the shock when she "suddenly saw that I was not a painter at all."[2] She concentrated then on drawings and prints—etchings and woodcuts early on, lithographs when her eyesight grew weaker.

Five major themes dominate Kollwitz' art: herself, in a great many self-portraits and images for which she served as model; the ties between mothers and their children; the hardships of the working classes, usually interpreted through women's plight; the unspeakable cruelties of war; and death as a force unto itself. As a socialist Kollwitz identified passionately with the sufferings of working people; as a mother she identified with the struggle of women to keep their children safe.

Kollwitz bore two sons—Hans in 1892 and Peter in 1896. The first of many tragedies that marked her later life came in 1914, with the death of Peter in World War I. She lived long enough to see her beloved grandson, also named Peter, killed in World War II. During the almost thirty years between those losses, she continued to work prolifically, but her obsession with death never left her.

Few artists have so touchingly described their attempts to achieve a certain goal, and their continual frustration at falling short. In Kollwitz' case, the artistic goals were generally realized, but the emotional and political goals—never: "While I drew, and wept along with the terrified children I was drawing, I really felt the burden I am bearing. I felt that I have no right to withdraw from the responsibility of being an advocate. It is my duty to voice the sufferings of men, the never-ending sufferings heaped mountain-high. This is my task, but it is not an easy one to fulfill. Work is supposed to relieve you. . . . Did I feel relieved when I made the prints on war and knew that the war would go on raging? Certainly not."[3]

Käthe Kollwitz. *Self-Portrait with Hand on Her Forehead.* 1910. Etching, 6 × 5⅜″. Kupferstich-Kabinett, Staatliche Kunstsammlungen, Dresden.

more suited to our era of technology, virtual reality, and rapid change. Certainly within the West it is less burdened with the weight of tradition and the status of "precious object," and many artists find this liberating. For whatever reason, drawing has come to interest an increasing number of artists. This section concludes with two recent trends in drawing, one that looks forward into the future and another that reaches far back into the past.

DIGITAL REALMS

Programmers began exploring the artistic potential of computer technology almost from the first, but it was only with the development of the personal computer and specialized software programs that artists who were not programmers could explore these possibilities as well. In art as in other applications, computers have proved themselves useful as a tool, enabling some tasks to be performed easily and rapidly that by hand were time-consuming or even impossible. Drawing programs, for example, enable artists to rework endlessly on screen, choose one color and then another, save work in various stages, cut and paste—all before committing themselves to a final output on paper. More interesting to many artists, however, is the digital realm itself and art that is created especially for it.

Jennifer Bartlett was one of several artists invited during the mid-1980s to try a newly developed hardware system called Paintbox, by Quantel (**6.17**). Paintbox features a digitized drawing pad that the artist "draws" on with a special pen-shaped stylus attached to the computer in much the same way that a mouse is. The marks do not appear on the pad, however, but on the screen. A menu allows width, color, texture, and so on, to be selected and changed at will.

Drawing on the computer is essentially drawing with light. As with television or stained glass, the image is made of light that radiates *from* it instead of reflecting *off* it. Bartlett's simple subject takes full advantage of this characteristic, for a transparent glass of water is defined by almost nothing but how it reflects and refracts light. The drawing could, of course, be declared finished and printed at any stage, yet its evolution was also recorded in video. Thanks to recording, all stages of the drawing remain available, instead of each one being covered up by the next. More interestingly, recording suggests that the drawing might *be* its evolution. Instead of reaching a definitive stage and passing onto paper, a drawing might be a process, a series of possibilities that never resolve, an exploration of a subject over time.

6.17 Jennifer Bartlett. *Untitled.* 1986. Frame from videotape.

Elliott Green takes up this idea in the digitally animated loops he calls sketch movies (**6.18**). Each brief movie records the progress of a drawing. We watch as the first lines are laid down, then fleshed into forms, then partially erased, then worked up again. Details fall into place, and the drawing seems to be finished—only to start all over again from the beginning. Green works traditionally in charcoal on paper. He scans his drawing onto the computer at regular intervals, then uses a digital animation program to link the scans in quickened time-lapse sequence, so that we can watch a drawing that may have evolved over days come into being in the space of a minute. He displays his sketch movies on a small computer screen mounted on a wall or set on a pedestal.

6.18 (left) Elliott Green. Frame from *Sketch Movie*. 2000. Charcoal on paper, scanned and digitally animated.
Courtesy Postmasters Gallery, New York.

6.19 (right) Sol LeWitt. *Wall Drawing #912*. 1999. White crayon and black pencil grid on gray walls. First drawn by Sachiko Cho and Emily Ripley, June 1999.
Collection Barbara Gladstone, Sag Harbor, New York.

REACHING FOR THE WALL

In the earliest art we know of, humans reached out to draw images on the expanses of cave walls. Recently, artists have again taken to using the wall itself as a surface for drawing. The large scale of wall drawings broadens our ideas of what a drawing can be, yet for all their impressive size, these drawings are in a sense even more vulnerable than traditional works on paper, for not only are they displayed in the open, without any protective covering, but they are rarely intended to be permanent. Instead they are drawn for a particular exhibition, then painted over when the exhibition ends. Some may later reappear in a varied form in other exhibitions, sort of migratory works that never show themselves in the same place twice. Others exist only once, and then are gone.

One of the first contemporary artists to create wall drawings was Sol LeWitt, whose *Wall Drawing #912* is illustrated here as it was drawn for a private home (**6.19**). LeWitt does not execute his drawings himself. Rather, he creates the instructions for making the drawing and entrusts their execution to others. The subject of the drawing is the instructions for its creation, and LeWitt insists that they be posted nearby. The instructions for *Wall Drawing #912* are: A 12-inch (30.5 cm) grid covering the walls. Within each

12-inch (30.5 cm) square, one arc from the corner or the midpoint of one side. (The direction of the arcs and their placement are determined by the draftsman.)

The drawing here is open, restrained, and elegant, with repeating arcs generating a rhythm like seagulls' wings or rolling waves. The instructions could produce a vast number of other drawings that would look quite different, yet they would all be related because they spring from the same idea. The idea, or concept, is the governing principle and, because of this, the work of LeWitt and other like-minded artists is known as **Conceptual art**.

Like LeWitt's drawing, the wall drawings of Jonathan Borofsky reappear in many variations. Here, however, there is not a single governing *idea*, but a single *source*—the artist's ongoing notebook of sketches. Borofsky was working on other kinds of art when he became intrigued with the small drawings he doodled almost absentmindedly in margins, on scraps of paper, on the backs of envelopes. The drawings were of random images that floated through his mind, especially those from his dreams of the night before. Instead of using these drawings as the basis of more developed works, Borofsky decided to preserve their directness and spontaneity by projecting them onto a wall and tracing over the projection. Given an exhibition space, he covers walls, ceilings, and even floors with enlarged drawings of his thoughts and dreams. For viewers, being in the room is like being inside of someone else's head. Borofsky selects different drawings for each exhibit, but almost always included is *Self Portrait with Big Ears* (**6.20**). The drawing represents "me as a dog or maybe a rabbit and my wanting to hear what they can hear," the artist has said. "They have a special kind of radar. I also see the ears like antennae that send and receive energy."[4]

6.20 Jonathan Borofsky. *Self Portrait with Big Ears (Learning to be Free)*. 1980/1994. Latex on wall, variable dimensions.
Collection The Modern Art Museum of Fort Worth.

In contrast to the drawings of Borofsky and LeWitt, Elise Engler's *Everything They Let Me Draw* (**6.21**) existed only once. Engler was asked by a gallery in New York to participate in an exhibit by drawing the exhibit itself on the wall. Working in colored pencil, Engler drew not only the art but everything in the exhibition space that could be looked at, including lighting fixtures, sockets, water pipes, elevator buttons, wall labels, window shades, and a fire extinguisher. She also broke each work of art down into its components and drew those separately, as though each were a thing worthy of attention in its own right. Everything is drawn roughly the same size, resulting in delightful and disorienting shifts in scale. By refusing to recognize any differences between the many objects that could be seen in the gallery, Engler's witty inventory raised interesting questions about art in a sly and playful way.

The wall drawings of LeWitt, Borofsky, and Engler bring us back full circle to the earliest art of the caves. In bypassing conventional surfaces such as paper, these artists show us that drawing need accept no limits, no restrictive sizes or shapes. Drawing is so much a natural impulse that it can be around us in the most natural way.

6.21 Elise Engler. *Everything They Let Me Draw*. Pencil and colored pencil on wall, 9 × 5'. Art in General, New York, January 29–April 4, 1998.

CHAPTER 7

Painting

In the Western tradition, painting is the queen of the arts. Ask ten people to form a quick mental image of "art," and nine of them are likely to visualize a painting. There are several reasons for the prominence of painting. For one thing, paintings usually are full of color, which is a potent visual stimulus. For another, paintings usually are framed, some quite elaborately, so that one has the impression of a precious object set off from the rest of the world. Even without a frame, a painting may seem a thing apart—a focus of energy and life, a universe unto itself. Whatever the painting shows, it establishes its own visual scope, sets its own rules.

If we consider some of the earliest cave images, especially the more elaborate and colorful ones, to be paintings, then the art has been practiced for at least thirty thousand years. During that long history the styles of painting have changed considerably, as have the media in which paintings are done—the physical substances the painter uses. In the latter case it might be more accurate to say broadened, rather than changed, for few media have been completely abandoned, while many new options have been added to the painter's repertoire.

To begin this discussion of painting, we should define some terms that allow us to understand how, physically, such a work of art is put together. Paint is made of **pigment,** powdered color, compounded with a **medium** or **vehicle,** a liquid that holds the particles of pigment together without dissolving them. The vehicle generally acts as or includes a **binder,** an ingredient that ensures that the paint, even when diluted and spread thinly, will adhere to the surface. Without a binder, pigments would simply powder off as the paint dried.

Artists' paints are generally made to a pastelike consistency and need to be diluted in order to be brushed freely. Aqueous media can be diluted with water. Watercolors are an example of an aqueous medium. Nonaqueous media require some other diluent. Oil paints are an example of a nonaqueous medium; these can be diluted with turpentine or mineral spirits. Paints are applied to a **support,** which is the canvas, paper, wood panel, wall, or other surface on which the artist works. The support may be prepared to receive paint with a **ground** or **primer,** a preliminary coating.

It is impossible to tell which painting medium is the oldest, but we know that ancient peoples mixed their pigments with such things as fat and honey. Two techniques perfected in the ancient world that are still in use today are encaustic and fresco, and we begin our discussion with them.

ENCAUSTIC

Encaustic paints consist of pigment mixed with wax and resin. When the colors are heated, the wax melts and the paint can be brushed easily. When the wax cools, the paint hardens. After the painting is completed, there may be a final "burning in" as a heat source is passed close to the surface of the painting to fuse the colors.

Literary sources tell us that encaustic was an important technique in ancient Greece (the word *encaustic* comes from the Greek for "burning in"). The earliest encaustic paintings to have survived, however, are funeral portraits created during the first centuries of our era in Egypt, which was then under Roman rule (**7.1**). Portraits such as this were set into the casings of mummified bodies to identify and memorialize the dead (see 14.34). The colors of this painting, almost as fresh as the day they were set down, testify to the permanence of encaustic.

The technique of encaustic was forgotten within a few centuries after the fall of the Roman Empire, but it was redeveloped during the 19th century, partly in response to the discovery of the Roman-Egyptian portraits. One of the foremost contemporary artists to experiment with encaustic is Jasper Johns (**7.2**). *Numbers in Color* is painted in encaustic over a collage of paper on canvas. Encaustic allowed Johns to build up a richly textured paint surface (think of candle drippings and you will get the idea). Moreover, wax will not harm the paper over time as oil paint would.

FRESCO

With fresco, pigments are mixed with water and applied to a plaster support, usually a wall or a ceiling coated in plaster. The plaster may be dry, in which case the technique is known as **fresco secco,** Italian for "dry fresco." But most often when speaking about fresco, we mean **buon fresco,** "true fresco," in which paint made simply of pigment and water is applied to wet lime plaster. As the plaster dries, the lime undergoes a chemical transformation and acts as a binder, fusing the pigment with the plaster surface.

Fresco is above all a wall-painting technique, and it has been used for large-scale murals since ancient times. Probably no other painting medium requires such careful planning and such hard physical labor. The plaster can be painted only when it has the proper degree of dampness; therefore, the artist must plan each day's work and spread plaster only in the area that can be painted in one session. (Michelangelo could cover about 1 square yard of wall or ceiling in a day.) Work may be guided by a full-size drawing of the entire project called a **cartoon.** Once the cartoon is finalized, its contour lines are perforated with pinprick-size holes. The drawing is transferred to the prepared surface by placing a portion of the cartoon over the damp plaster and rubbing pigment through the holes. The cartoon is then removed, leaving dotted lines on the plaster surface. With a brush dipped in paint the artist "connects the dots" to re-create the drawing; then the work of painting begins.

There is nothing tentative about fresco. Whereas in some media the artist can experiment, try out forms, and then paint over them to make corrections, every touch of the brush in fresco is a commitment. The only way an artist can correct mistakes or change the forms is to let the plaster dry, chip it away, and start all over again.

Frescoes have survived to the present day from the civilizations of the ancient Mediterranean (see 14.32), from China and India (see 19.6), and from the early civilizations of Mexico. Among the works we consider the greatest of all in Western art are the magnificent frescoes of the Italian Renaissance.

7.1 (above, top) *Young Woman with a Gold Pectoral*, from Fayum. 100–150 C.E. Encaustic on wood, height 12⅝″.
Musée du Louvre, Paris.

7.2 (above) Jasper Johns. *Numbers in Color.* 1958–59. Encaustic and newspaper on canvas, 5′6½″ × 4′1½″.
Collection Albright-Knox Gallery, Buffalo, New York.

While Michelangelo was at work on the frescoes of the Sistine Chapel ceiling (see 16.11, 16.12), Pope Julius II asked Raphael to decorate the walls of several rooms in the Vatican Palace. Raphael's fresco for the end wall of the Stanza della Segnatura, a room that may have been the Pope's library, is considered by many to be the summation of Renaissance art. It is called *The School of Athens* (**7.3**) and depicts the Greek philosophers Plato and Aristotle, centered in the composition and framed by the arch, along with their followers and students. The "school" in question means the two schools of philosophy represented by the two Classical thinkers—Plato's the more abstract and metaphysical, Aristotle's the more earthly and physical.

Everything about Raphael's composition celebrates the Renaissance ideals of perfection, beauty, naturalistic representation, and noble principles. The towering architectural setting is drawn in linear perspective with the vanishing point falling between the two central figures. The figures, perhaps influenced by Michelangelo's figures on the Sistine ceiling, are idealized—more perfect than life, full-bodied and dynamic. *The School of Athens* reflects Raphael's vision of one Golden Age—the Renaissance—and connects it with the Golden Age of Greece two thousand years earlier.

The most celebrated frescoes of the 20th century were created in Mexico, where the revolutionary government that came into power in 1921 after a decade of civil war commissioned artists to create murals about Mexico itself—the glories of its ancient civilizations, its political struggles, its people, and its hopes for the future. *Mixtec Culture* (**7.4**) is one of a series of frescoes painted by Diego Rivera in the National Palace in Mexico City. Mixtec people still live in Mexico, as do descendants of all the early civilizations of the region. The Mixtec kingdoms were known for their arts, and Rivera has portrayed a peaceful community of artists at work. To the left, two men, probably nobles, are

7.3 Raphael. *The School of Athens*. 1510–11. Fresco, 26 × 18′. Stanza della Segnatura, Vatican, Rome.

being fitted with the elaborate ritual headdresses, masks, and capes that were a prominent part of many ancient Mexican cultures (see 20.9, 20.11). To the right, smiths are melting and casting gold. In the foreground are potters, sculptors, feather workers, mask makers, and scribes. In the background, people pan for gold in the stream.

7.4 Diego Rivera. *Mixtec Culture.* 1942. Fresco, 16′1⅝″ × 10′5⅝″ Palacio Nacional, Mexico City.

TEMPERA

Tempera shares qualities with both watercolor and oil paint. Like watercolor, tempera is an aqueous medium. Like oil paint, it dries to a tough, insoluble film. Yet while oil paint tends to yellow and darken with age, tempera colors retain their brilliance and clarity for centuries. Technically, tempera is paint in which the vehicle is an emulsion, which is a stable mixture of an aqueous liquid with an oil, fat, wax, or resin. A familiar example of an emulsion is milk, which consists of minute droplets of fat suspended in liquid. A derivative of milk called casein is one of the many vehicles that can be used to make tempera colors. The most famous tempera vehicle, however, is another naturally occuring emulsion, egg yolk. Tempera dries very quickly, and so colors cannot be blended easily once they are set down. While tempera can be diluted with water and applied in a broad wash, painters who use it most commonly build up forms gradually with fine hatching and cross-hatching strokes, much like a drawing. Traditionally, tempera was used on a wood panel support prepared with a ground of **gesso,** a mixture of white pigment and glue that sealed the wood and could be sanded and rubbed to a smooth, ivorylike finish.

A 20th-century painter who has cultivated a classic tempera technique—although not on panel—is Andrew Wyeth. Wyeth's painting *Braids* (**7.5**) shows the luminous technique at its best. *Braids* is part of a large cache of paintings and drawings that Wyeth had kept secret from most of the art world for fifteen years until a surprise showing in 1986. Nearly all the works depict a woman known as Helga. *Braids* shows Helga's face and upper torso painted in the most painstaking tempera technique. Individual brush strokes highlight single strands of hair, eyelashes, and threads in the sweater, and the face has an almost claylike texture from innumerable tiny strokes of paint.

A different approach to tempera can be seen in the work of Jacob Lawrence. Lawrence said he was drawn to the "raw, sharp, rough" effect of vibrant tempera colors. In this painting from the *Harriet Tubman Series* (**7.6**), Lawrence has thinned his colors and applied them with vigorous brushstrokes in a single translucent layer. Values are keyed high, dramatically setting off the dark skin of his subject. Harriet Tubman was a 19th-century abolitionist who helped hundreds of slaves escape to free states. Lawrence gives her a monumental presence, as though her moral integrity and quiet determination shone through even in the simple act of sawing wood.

7.5 (left) Andrew Wyeth. *Braids.* 1979. Egg tempera on canvas, 16½ × 20½".
Courtesy AM Art, Inc.

7.6 (right) Jacob Lawrence. *Harriet Tubman Series, No. 7.* 1939–40. Casein tempera on hardboard, 17⅛ × 12".
Hampton University Museum, Hampton, Virginia. © Gwendolyn Knight Lawrence, courtesy of the Jacob and Gwendolyn Lawrence Foundation.

JACOB LAWRENCE
1917–2000

T HE NAME "HARLEM" is associated in many people's minds with hardship and poverty. Poverty Harlem has always known, but during the 1920s it experienced a tremendous cultural upsurge that has come to be called the Harlem Renaissance. So many of the greatest names in black culture—musicians, writers, artists, poets, scientists—lived or worked in Harlem at the time, or simply took their inspiration from its intellectual energy. To Harlem, in about 1930, came a young teenager named Jacob Lawrence, relocating from Philadelphia with his mother, brother, and sister. The flowering of the Harlem Renaissance had passed, but there remained enough momentum to help turn the child of a poor family into one of the most distinguished American artists of his generation.

Young Lawrence's home life was not happy, but he had several islands of refuge: the public library, the Harlem Art Workshop, and the Metropolitan Museum of Art. He studied at the Harlem Art Workshop from 1932 to 1934 and received much encouragement from two noted black artists, Charles Alston and Augusta Savage. By the age of twenty Lawrence had begun to exhibit his work. A year later he, like so many others, was being supported by the W.P.A. Art Project, a government-sponsored program to help artists get through the economic void of the Great Depression.

Even this early in his career, Lawrence had established the themes that would dominate his work. The subject matter comes from his own experience, from black experience: the hardships of poor people in the ghettos, the violence that greeted blacks moving from the South to the urban North, the upheaval of the civil rights movement during the 1960s. Nearly always his art has a narrative content or "story," and often the titles are lengthy. Although Lawrence did paint individual pictures, the bulk of his production was in series, such as *The Migration Series* and *Theater*, some of them having as many as sixty images.

The year 1941 was significant for Lawrence's life and career. He married the painter Gwendolyn Knight, and he acquired his first dealer when Edith Halpert of the Downtown Gallery in New York featured him in a major exhibition. The show was successful, and it resulted in the purchase of Lawrence's *Migration* series by two important museums.

From that point Lawrence's career prospered. His paintings were always in demand, and he was sought after as an illustrator of magazine covers, posters, and books. His influence continued through his teaching—first at Black Mountain College in North Carolina, later at Pratt Institute, the Art Students League, and the University of Washington. In 1978 he was elected to the National Council on the Arts.

Many people would call Lawrence's paintings instruments of social protest, but his images, however stark, have more the character of reporting than of protest. It is as though he is telling us, "this is what happened, this is the way it is." What happened, of course, happened to black Americans, and Lawrence the world-famous painter did not seem to lose sight of Lawrence the poor youth in Harlem. As he said, "My belief is that it is most important for an artist to develop an approach and philosophy about life—if he has developed this philosophy he does not put paint on canvas, he puts himself on canvas."[1]

Jacob Lawrence. *Self-Portrait*. 1977.
Gouache on paper, 23 × 31".
National Academy of Design, New York. © Gwendolyn Knight Lawrence, courtesy of the Jacob and Gwendolyn Lawrence Foundation.

OIL

Oil paints consist of pigment compounded with oil, usually linseed oil. The oil acts as a binder, creating as it dries a transparent film in which the pigment is suspended. A popular legend claims that oil painting was invented early in the 15th century by the great Netherlandish artist Jan van Eyck, who experimented with it for this portrait (**7.7**). While we know now that Van Eyck did not actually invent the medium, we still point to him as the first important artist to understand and exploit its possibilities. From that time and for about five hundred years the word "painting" was virtually synonymous with "oil painting." Only since the 1950s, with the introduction of acrylics (discussed later in this chapter), has the supremacy of oil been challenged.

When oil paints were first introduced, most artists, including Jan van Eyck, continued working on wood panels. Gradually, however, artists adopted the more flexible canvas, which offered two great advantages. For one thing, the changing styles favored larger and larger paintings. Whereas wood panels were heavy and liable to crack, the lighter linen canvas could be stretched to almost unlimited size. Second, as artists came to serve distant patrons, their canvases could be rolled up for easy and safe shipment. Canvas was prepared by stretching it over a wooden frame, sizing it with glue to seal the fibers and protect them from the corrosive action of oil paint, and then coating it with a white, oil-base ground.

The outstanding characteristic of oil paint is that it dries very slowly. This creates both advantages and disadvantages for the artist. On the plus side, it means that colors can be blended subtly, layers of paint can be applied

7.7 (left) Jan van Eyck. *Man in a Red Turban (Self-Portrait?)*. 1433. Tempera and oil on panel, 13⅛ × 10⅛".
The National Gallery, London.

7.8 (right) Oskar Kokoschka. *Self-Portrait*. 1917. Oil on canvas, 31⅛ × 24¾".
Van der Heydt Museum, Wuppertal, Germany.

on top of other layers with little danger of separating or cracking, and the artist can rework sections of the painting almost indefinitely. This same asset becomes a liability when the artist is pressed for time—perhaps when an exhibition has been scheduled. Oil paint dries so *very* slowly that it may be weeks or months before the painting has truly "set."

Another great advantage of oil is that it can be worked in an almost infinite range of consistencies, from very thick to very thin. Van Eyck, for example, did much of his painting in **glazes**—thin, translucent veils of color applied over a thicker layer of underpainting. The Austrian-born painter Oskar Kokoschka often used thick oil paints straight from the tube, occasionally squeezing them directly onto the canvas without a brush (**7.8**). He could then mold and shape the thick paint with a palette knife (a spatula-shaped tool) to create actual three-dimensional texture on the canvas. Any thick application of paint is referred to as **impasto,** and Kokoschka's is an extreme version of this. The ability to use paint in this way was important for Kokoschka's expression, because the sinewy coils of paint in the *Self-Portrait* trace the artist's passionate exploration of his inner self. Even his coat seems to writhe and twist around him. A smoother medium could not so define his anguished personality.

The thick, loaded brushwork that oil paint made possible added a new expressive element to painting, and painters were quick to take advantage of it. During the 20th century, this sort of brushwork came to be appreciated for its own sake. The energetic brushwork of Joan Mitchell's *La Grande Vallée XVII, Carl* (**7.9**) is reminiscent of Kokoschka's self-portrait, but here it no longer portrays anything but itself. The title asks us to view the painting as a kind of landscape or interpretation of a landscape. Reflections in a lake, blue shadows of morning, wild flowers, rain, a view through a window—all of these associations may come to mind, though the painting will never limit us to any one of them.

7.9 Joan Mitchell. *La Grande Vallée XVII, Carl.* 1984. Oil on canvas, 9′2¼″ × 8′6⁵⁄₁₆″. FRAC Provence-Alpes—Côte d'Azur.

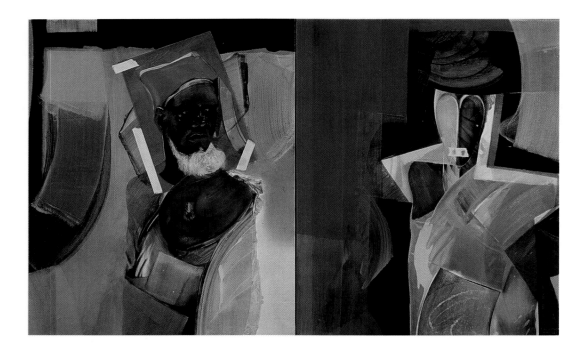

7.10 Fodé Camara. *The Old African, the Medal, and the Statue.* 1988. Collage and oil on canvas, 3′11¼″ × 6′6⅝″. Collection Abdourahim Agne.

Toward the end of the 19th century, oil paint became one of the great artistic exports of European culture, and today it is used by many artists around the world. Contemporary Senegalese artist Fodé Camara used oil paint in his diptych *The Old African, the Medal, and the Statue* (**7.10**). The painting is about the legacy of European colonialism in Africa, and thus the fact that it is in oils is itself significant. To the left is the old African of the title. His head, painted in European style, has been taped over whatever head he used to have. A medal pinned to his chest identifies him as a veteran, one of the thousands of Africans who fought for the French in the days when Senegal was a French colony. The old man gazes to the right at a second figure, a statue whose elegant heart-shaped face resembles the masks carved by the Senufo people of Senegal. The mask, his heritage, could possibly tell the old man something about himself, but its mouth is taped over. It is silent and can offer no help.

WATERCOLOR

Watercolor consists of pigment in a vehicle of water and gum arabic, a sticky plant substance that acts as the binder. As with drawing, the most common support for watercolor is paper. Also like drawing, watercolor is commonly thought of as an intimate art, small in scale and free in execution. Eclipsed for several centuries by the prestige of oil paints, watercolors were in fact often used for small and intimate works. Easy to carry and requiring only a glass of water for use, they could readily be taken on sketching expeditions outdoors and were a favorite medium for amateur artists. Yet watercolors can be large and/or painstakingly executed as well, and we should bear in mind that the entire painting tradition of East Asia, with its monumental landscapes and lengthy scrolls, was created with water-based colors.

The leading characteristic of watercolors is their transparency. They are not applied thickly, like oil paints, but thinly in translucent washes. While opaque white watercolor is available, this is reserved for special uses. More usually, the white of the paper serves for white, and dark areas are built up through several layers of transparent washes, which take on depth without ever becoming completely opaque. Winslow Homer's *Shore and Surf, Nassau* (**7.11**) is a perfect example of what we might think of as "classic" watercolor technique. Controlled and yet spontaneous in feeling, it gives the impression of having been dashed off in a single sitting. The white of the paper serves for the foam of the waves, and even the darks along the shore retain a translucent quality.

For a different approach to watercolor, we turn to Cézanne's *Still Life with Cut Watermelon* (**7.12**). Cézanne took up watercolor only at the end of his life, and in some ways it served him better than oils for recording his scrupulous doubts about what could be portrayed and what could not. Here, as in the painting of China and Japan, the white paper itself is an important element of the composition, and what is left unsaid is as eloquent as what is said. Notice especially how the contours refuse to be fixed, but seem to vibrate. Cézanne was the first Western artist to try to take into account the fact that our eyes are constantly in motion and that forms that curve away from us do not really have edges. He tried to find a way to indicate in paint the experience of seeing, and not just the sight. As such he stands at the beginning of many early-20th-century concerns in art.

7.11 (above) Winslow Homer. *Shore and Surf, Nassau.* 1899. Watercolor on paper, 15 × 21⅜". The Metropolitan Museum of Art, New York.

7.12 (left) Paul Cézanne. *Still Life with Cut Watermelon.* 1902–06. Watercolor and pencil on paper, 12⅜ × 18¾". Ernst Beyeler Collection, Basel.

PAUL CÉZANNE

1839–1906

PAUL CÉZANNE remains one of the most enigmatic figures in modern art history, even though the details of his life are well known. A word often used to describe his personality is "difficult." Clearly, he was a man of intelligence and great sensitivity, yet he could be rude to strangers and boorish with his friends. Although he was acquainted with most of the leading artists then working in Paris, he spent the greater part of his life in isolation in the southern French town of Aix-en-Provence, where he was born.

Cézanne's banker father tried to steer his son into his own profession or the law, but the young man showed so little talent and inclination for either that eventually the father gave up and permitted him to undertake art studies. Cézanne's first attempts at exhibiting his work met with disastrous results; the critics' reactions ranged from ridicule to outrage. Nevertheless, he persevered, struggling on alone to achieve the form in art that was his vision. Cézanne's paintings are difficult to date, because he worked on many canvases at once and often labored over the same painting for several years. So demanding was he with live models that few sitters were willing to pose for him. One who did pose, the art dealer Ambroise Vollard, reported that he was forced to endure 115 sittings, some lasting three hours or more.

In 1869, while visiting Paris, Cézanne met a young woman, Marie-Hortense Fiquet, and they became lovers. Some three years later their son Paul was born. Cézanne went to extraordinary lengths to conceal this liaison from his domineering father, lest his allowance be cut off.

For most of Cézanne's life only the very discerning—and they were few—recognized the genius of his art. After his initial disappointments, the artist stopped exhibiting in Paris for twenty years. Then in 1895 Ambroise Vollard decided to mount a show—Cézanne's first one-man exhibition—and asked the artist to send all available work. Cézanne bundled up 150 canvases and shipped them off to Paris from Aix. The show took Paris completely by surprise and was an immediate sensation. From that time until his death the artist gradually acquired the recognition he deserved; ironically, he had become so embittered by long neglect that the acclaim gave him little pleasure.

While alternately mocked and ignored by critics and the general public, Cézanne never lost faith in himself and his art. In 1874 he wrote this to his mother: "I am beginning to find myself stronger than any of those around me. . . . I must go on working, but not in order to attain a finished perfection, which is so much sought after by imbeciles. And this quality which is commonly so much admired is nothing but the accomplishment of a craftsman, and makes any work produced in that way inartistic and vulgar. I must not try to finish anything except for the pleasure of making it truer and wiser. And you may be sure that there will come a time when I shall come into my own, and that I have admirers who are much more fervent, more steadfast than those who are attracted only by an empty outward appearance."[2]

Paul Cézanne. *Self-Portrait with a Beret.* c. 1906.
Oil on canvas, 25¼ × 21".
Courtesy Museum of Fine Arts, Boston.

GOUACHE

Gouache is watercolor with inert white pigment added. Inert pigment is pigment that becomes colorless or virtually colorless in paint. In gouache, it serves to make the colors opaque, which means that when used at full strength, they can completely hide any ground or other color they are painted over. The poster paints given to children are basically gouache, although not of artist's quality. Like watercolor, gouache can be applied in translucent washes, although that is not its primary use. It dries quickly and uniformly and is especially well suited to large areas of flat, saturated color. For example, Indian paintings such as 2.22 and 4.38 are done in opaque watercolor, although of a formula slightly different than gouache. The opacity of gouache allowed Paul Klee to create his delightful *Landscape with Yellow Birds* (**7.13**). While Klee also used watercolor in the work, that medium alone would never have allowed him to paint such light values—white, yellow, lavender, green—over such a dark ground.

7.13 Paul Klee. *Landscape with Yellow Birds*. 1923. Watercolor and gouache on paper, 13⅞ × 17¼".
Private collection.

ACRYLIC

The enormous developments in chemistry during the early 20th century had an impact in artists' studios. By the 1930s, chemists had learned to make strong, weatherproof, industrial paints using a vehicle of synthetic plastic resins. Artists began to experiment with these paints almost immediately. By the 1950s, chemists had made many advances in the new technology and had also adapted it to artists' requirements for permanence. For the first time since it was developed, oil paint had a challenger as the principal medium for Western painting.

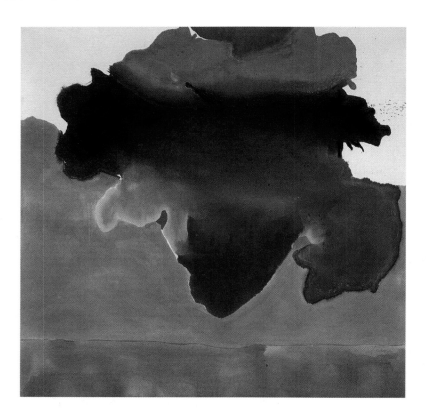

7.14 Helen Frankenthaler. *The Bay*. 1963. Acrylic on canvas, 6′8¼″ × 6′9¾″. Detroit Institute of Arts.

These new synthetic artists' colors are broadly known as acrylics, although a more exact name for them is polymer paints. The vehicle consists of acrylic resin, polymerized (its simple molecules linked into long chains) through emulsion in water. As acrylic paint dries, the resin particles coalesce to form a tough, flexible, and waterproof film.

Depending on how they are used, acrylics can mimic the effects of oil paint, watercolor, gouache, and even tempera. They can be used on both prepared or raw canvas, and also on paper and fabric. They can be layered into a heavy impasto like oils or diluted with water and spread in translucent washes like watercolor. Like tempera, they dry quickly and permanently. (Artists using acrylics usually rest their brushes in water while working, for if the paint dries on the brush, it is extremely difficult to remove.)

Helen Frankenthaler's painting *The Bay* (**7.14**) shows how acrylic can behave when it is thinned to the consistency of a dye or stain and poured onto unprimed cotton canvas, which partially absorbs the color. In this work there is little actual surface texture; any suggestion of pictorial depth comes from the interplay of colors, not from recognizable shapes. The forms are organic, creating a color landscape of their own within the rectangle of the painting, but they make no specific reference to the natural landscape. Free-flowing washes of paint spread and overlap on the canvas in what appears to be an immediate, spontaneous burst of imagery and color. Like Jackson Pollock (see 5.5, 22.1), Frankenthaler often places her canvases flat on the floor, the better to control the flow of paint.

PAINTING-RELATED TECHNIQUES

There are several techniques that might be considered cousins of painting, in that they are used to create designs or pictorial images on a predominantly two-dimensional surface. One is tapestry, a method employing woven threads, which will be considered in Chapter 12. Two others are **collage** and **mosaic.**

COLLAGE

Collage is a French word that means "pasting" or "gluing." In art terms it refers to the practice of attaching objects, such as bits of paper or cloth, to the surface of a canvas or other support, as well as to the resultant artwork. Nowadays we are accustomed to such works, but there was a time when they seemed revolutionary.

During the early part of the 20th century the artists Pablo Picasso and Georges Braque worked together very closely for several years. Their collaboration was fueled by a strong rivalry, with each artist trying to outdo the other in stretching the boundaries of modern art. Apparently it was Braque who first hit upon the idea of pasting real everyday materials onto his canvases, but Picasso wasted no time taking up the challenge.

Guitar, Sheet Music, and Glass (**7.15**) is one of Picasso's earliest collages, perhaps the very first. In the lower left corner he has pasted a bit of the daily newspaper (in French, *Le Journal*), with the headline *"La Bataille s'est engagé"* (the battle is begun). As printed, the headline referred to the current Balkan wars, but what did Picasso mean? Did he go to battle to enrich the possibilities of art by the then-shocking practice of gluing objects to canvas? Or was his battle that of upstaging his ambitious colleague? Probably some of both. Elsewhere Picasso includes a corner torn from sheet music (both artists were absorbed by musical themes), a wood-grain fragment suggesting a guitar, and a sketch of a wine glass. All are pasted onto a patterned paper resembling wallpaper. Despite Picasso's sly allusion to a "battle," we should not read any deep symbolic significance into this collection of items. The artist's main goal was to assemble forms into a visual composition that satisfied him.

7.15 Pablo Picasso. *Guitar, Sheet Music, and Glass.* 1912. Pasted paper, gouache, and charcoal; 18⅞ × 14¾″.
Collection The McNay Art Museum, San Antonio, Texas.

7.16 Romare Bearden. *Mysteries.* 1964. Collage, polymer paint, and pencil on board, 11¼ × 14¼″. Courtesy Museum of Fine Arts, Boston.

After Picasso and Braque, many artists adopted this method of composing a picture by gathering bits and pieces from various sources. An artist who made very personal use of collage was Romare Bearden. Pieced together from bits of photographic magazine illustrations, *Mysteries* (**7.16**) is one of a series of works that evoke the texture of everyday life as Bearden had known it growing up as an African American in rural North Carolina. In Bearden's hands, the technique of collage alludes both to the African American folk tradition of quilting, which also pieces together a whole from many fragments (see 12.16), and to the rhythms and improvisatory nature of jazz, another art form with African roots. The face on the far left includes a portion of an African sculpture (the mouth and nose). In the background appears a photograph of a train. A recurring symbol in Bearden's work, trains stand for the outside world, especially the white world. "A train was always something that could take you away and could also bring you to where you were," the artist explained. "And in the little towns it's the black people who live near the trains."[3]

MOSAIC

The mosaic artist "paints" by assembling small colored stones, bits of glass, or colored clay tiles into a pattern or pictorial image. Usually, mosaic works are set in a wall or ceiling—or even a floor, because the durability of the material allows it to be walked upon.

Mosaic art is commonly associated with the ancient Romans and with the Byzantine Empire in Europe, starting in the 4th century. We see an excellent example of this mosaic art in the portrait panel of *Empress Theodora* (**7.17**), wife of the 6th-century emperor Justinian. The *Theodora* mosaic is especially splendid in its rich, vibrant colors and sumptuous decorative details. The character of Byzantine art is well illustrated by this mosaic. Theodora is meant to be in procession, with her retinue trailing behind her, but we get little sense of this movement. Also, while the artist has used some overlapping, especially in the attendants at right, all the figures appear to be in the same plane, and that plane is identical with the ornately decorated background. But neither motion nor the sense of rounded figures in depth was important to Byzantine artists or the intended audience. Far more compelling was the impression of quiet dignity, the appearance of an empress in majesty accepting the homage of her subjects, and these qualities are conveyed splendidly.

This brief survey should have demonstrated that the various painting media and the artists who use them yield endless possibilities. It would be difficult to say which comes first—that artist's imagery or the material. Did the first cave artist have the impulse to paint something and search about for a material with which to do it? Or did the cave artist find some pigmented material and then speculate about what would happen if the substance were applied to a wall? The answer is not important, but the two aspects—idea and medium—feed upon each other. No visual image could be realized without the medium in which to make it concrete. And no medium would be of any consequence without the artist's idea—and the compelling urge to paint.

7.17 *Empress Theodora and Retinue.* c. 547. Mosaic. San Vitale, Ravenna.

CHAPTER 8

Prints

Ipf you have ever received a handmade greeting card, then you will appreciate the difference between an art print and a mass-produced reproduction. Commercial greeting cards are cranked out by the thousands, even millions, by the major card manufacturers. But many people like to make their own cards with their own original designs. Usually they will *print* the cards by some type of stamping process. The design is carved out on a printing block made of wood, linoleum, or even the cut side of a potato, leaving some areas raised as in a rubber stamp. Then the printing block is coated with ink and pressed carefully onto paper to make the card.

An image made this way is special. For one thing, the design is unique—a personal expression of the individual who conceived it. Also, each card will be slightly different from all the others because of variations in pressure, inking, placement on the paper, and steadiness of the hand. There is a human touch, which we find missing from commercial products. For each separate image, *one* person made it, judged its quality, and was satisfied. All these factors apply equally to art prints.

Prints differ from most other works of art in two important respects. First, they are made by an indirect process. The artist does not draw or paint directly on the work of art but instead creates the surface that *makes* the work of art. (In some cases the artist may add special touches to each print, but this is not the most common practice.) Second, the printing process results in many nearly identical images, which is why it is called an art of multiples. Each image—called an impression—is considered an original work of art. This latter point is crucial to an understanding of art prints, so we need to discuss it more fully.

Before the 1950s there were no strict guidelines for what could genuinely be labeled an "original" print. In the past several decades, however, certain criteria have been established, and the value of contemporary prints has much to do with their adherence to these criteria. The guidelines were set up in an attempt to avoid abuses that had crept into the print market, such as inferior, shoddy, or inauthentic works being passed off as fine art.

Printmaking procedures now are rigidly controlled. The artist works on a plate or stone or some other surface to make the image. Then the image is printed on paper, by hand or by a hand-operated machine, either by the artist or by someone under the artist's immediate supervision. Each print is examined to make sure it meets the artist's standards, and any faulty impressions are destroyed. Usually the artist and printer decide in advance how many impressions will be made—ten, fifty, a hundred or more—and this number is referred to as the **edition.** The size of the edition may be determined by the material used for printing. Hard metal can print many perfect impressions, but a softer material, such as linoleum, will begin to wear down, resulting in a blurred image. Once the planned number of prints has been made, the plate or block is canceled (by scratching cross marks on it) or destroyed so that no more prints can be struck. Finally, the artist signs each print individually and numbers each one. For example, if you buy a print marked 10/100, you will know you have the tenth print made in an edition of one hundred. Prints made earlier in the edition are sometimes considered more valuable.

The type of print we are talking about must be distinguished from posters and other reproductions made by mechanical or photographic processes, such as the illustrations in this book. You can buy a color reproduction of a Rembrandt or Picasso painting, or a poster featuring a rock star or film personality, but these are not prints in the sense that we are discussing in this chapter, not original works of art. The artist who made the images has no supervision over the printing process and may not even know about it. The quality of the reproduction is nowhere near as meticulously controlled as that of an art print. Such reproductions are useful for study purposes, and they often give pleasure, but they have little artistic or monetary value.

Today's art print, above all, is designed to *be* a print. It is not a copy of a work done in some other medium, although it may be adapted from an image in another medium. Some artists, for instance, will take a theme they have used in painting and explore its possibilities in prints, but in this case the artist adjusts the image to fit the physical qualities and expressive potential of the particular print medium chosen.

Like drawings, prints are a great boon to the art lover and the collector. At a time when original paintings by well-known artists are beyond the means of any but the very rich, prints by established artists often can be purchased for just a few hundred dollars. (The most fashionable artists command many thousands of dollars for each print, but this price range is limited to a small group.) Young collectors starting out, and even large corporations with huge resources, have eagerly taken to buying prints. They may be a sound financial investment, but far more important is the fact that they give aesthetic pleasure and the joy of owning original art.

There are four basic methods for making an art print (**8.1**)—relief, intaglio, lithography, and screenprinting. In this chapter we shall look at each in turn and then consider a few advanced and combined techniques.

RELIEF

The term *relief* describes any printing method in which the image to be printed is *raised* from a background (see 8.1). Think of a rubber stamp. When you look at the stamp itself, you may see the words "First Class" or "Special Delivery" standing out from the background in reverse. You press the stamp to an ink pad, then to paper, and the words print right side out—a mirror image of the stamp. All relief processes work according to this general principle.

Any surface from which the background areas can be carved away is suitable for relief printing. Inuit artists in Canada's Northwest Territories work with flat stones, cutting and chipping away the background until only the image areas remain in relief. Then the stone is inked, and paper is laid on top and carefully rubbed by hand to make the print.

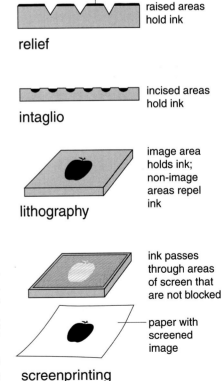

ink

raised areas hold ink

relief

incised areas hold ink

intaglio

image area holds ink; non-image areas repel ink

lithography

ink passes through areas of screen that are not blocked

paper with screened image

screenprinting

8.1 The four basic print methods.

Stone provides an extremely durable printing surface, capable of yielding a virtually endless number of clear impressions. However, the difficulty of carving stone hampers the creation of fine details. Inuit prints are valued for their bold and stylized designs (**8.2**). When printmakers seek greater flexibility in cutting and image-making, they generally turn to the material most commonly associated with relief printing: wood.

WOODCUT

To make a woodcut the artist first draws the desired image on a block of wood. Then all the areas that are not meant to print are cut and gouged out of the wood so that the image stands out in relief. When the block is inked, only the raised areas take the ink. Finally, the block is pressed on paper, or paper is placed on the block and rubbed to transfer the ink and make the print.

The earliest surviving woodcut image was made in China (**8.3**). Dated 868 C.E., this portrayal of the Buddha preaching appears at the beginning of the world's earliest known printed book, a copy of the *Diamond Sutra*, an important Buddhist text. The image probably reproduces an original drawing in brush and ink executed in the slender, even-width lines that Chinese writers likened to iron wire. Although only one copy survives, the edition of the sutra must have been quite large, for a postscript at the end of the 18-foot-long scroll tells us that the project was undertaken at the expense of one Wang Jie, "for universal free distribution." Two great Chinese inventions, paper and printing, are here united.

8.2 (above) Mungituk. *Man Carried to the Moon*. 1959. Stone relief print, 19⅛ × 15″.
The Brooklyn Museum.

8.3 (below) Preface to the *Diamond Sutra*. 868. Woodblock handscroll.
The British Library, London.

8.4 Albrecht Dürer. *Four Horsemen of the Apocalypse,* from the *Apocalypse* series. c. 1497–98. Woodcut, approx. 15⅝ × 11″. The British Museum, London.

In Europe, woodblocks had been used to print patterns on textiles since as early as the 6th century C.E., but it was not until the introduction of paper that printing anything else became practical. Soon after, in the mid-15th century, the invention of the printing press and movable type launched Europe's first great "information revolution." For the first time in the West, information could be widely disseminated.

The printing press, of course, also made it easier to print images in quantity, often as illustrations for books. Albrecht Dürer created this harrowing image of the *Four Horsemen of the Apocalypse* (**8.4**) not long after the printing press was invented. The print was one of fourteen full-page illustrations for Dürer's edition of the biblical Book of Revelation, also known as the Apocalypse. Dürer at the time was a young artist struggling at the start of his career. He had turned to prints in an attempt to increase his income by reaching a larger audience, and indeed prints eventually made both his name and his fortune.

Like the Chinese illustration of the Diamond Sutra, Dürer's woodcut faithfully reproduces a drawing, probably one done in pen and ink. Even the minute hatching and cross-hatching lines used to model mass and suggest tonality have been painstakingly reproduced in wood. As was common practice in his day, Dürer probably did not carve the block himself, but rather employed a skilled carver to carry out his design. And what a design! Spurred on by an angel, the four horsemen ride in a dynamic diagonal, trampling a terrified humanity underfoot. In the lead is Victory with his crown, followed by War with his sword, then Famine with his scales for rationing food, and finally Death by Plague. In the lower left corner yawns the open mouth of the beast of Hell.

ALBRECHT DÜRER
1471–1528

ALBRECHT DÜRER is the first of the northern European artists who seems to us "modern" in his outlook. Unlike most of his colleagues, he had a strong sense of being an *artist*, not a craftsman, and he sought—and received—acceptance in the higher ranks of society. Moreover, Dürer appears to have understood his role in the history of art—sensed that his work would exert great influence on his contemporaries and on artists of the future. This awareness led him to date his works and sign them with the distinctive "AD" (visible in the left background of his self-portrait)—a fairly unusual practice at the time.

Born in the southern German city of Nuremberg, Dürer was the son of a goldsmith, to whom he was apprenticed as a boy. At the age of fifteen young Albrecht was sent to study in the workshop of Michael Wolgemut, then considered a leading painter in Nuremberg. He stayed with Wolgemut for four years, after which he began a four-year period of wandering through northern Europe. In 1494 Dürer's father called him

back to Nuremberg for an arranged marriage. (The marriage seems not to have been a happy one and produced no children.) Soon afterward Dürer established himself as a master and opened his own studio.

Dürer made a great many paintings and drawings, but it is his output in prints (engravings, woodcuts, and etchings) that is truly extraordinary. Many people would argue that he was the greatest printmaker who ever lived. His genius derived partly from an ability to unite the best tendencies in northern and southern European art of that period, for Dürer was a well-traveled man. In 1494 he visited Italy, and he returned in 1505, staying two years in Venice, where he operated a studio. This second trip was a huge success, both artistically and socially. The artist received many commissions and enjoyed the high regard of the Venetian painters as well as of important patrons in the city. Upon his return to Germany Dürer took his place among the leading writers and intellectuals of Nuremberg, who seem to have valued him for his knowledge and wit, as well as for his art. In 1515 he was appointed court painter to the Holy Roman Emperor Maximilian I.

The last years of Dürer's life were devoted largely to work on his books and treatises, through which he hoped to teach a scientific approach to painting and drawing. As a Renaissance artist, he was fascinated by perfection and by an ideal of beauty. He wrote: "What beauty is, I know not, though it adheres to many things. When we wish to bring it into our work we find it very hard. We must gather it together from far and wide, and especially in the case of the human figure throughout all its limbs from before and behind. One may often search through two or three hundred men without finding amongst them more than one or two points of beauty which can be made use of. You, therefore, if you desire to compose a fine figure, must take the head from some, the chest, arm, leg, hand, and foot from others; and likewise, search through all members of every kind. For from many beautiful things something good may be gathered, even as honey is gathered from many flowers."[1]

Albrecht Dürer. *Self-Portrait at Age 28*. 1500.
Oil on wood. $26\frac{5}{16} \times 19\frac{5}{16}$".
Alte Pinakothek, Munich.

By the 14th century, China had advanced to the next step in woodcut by using multiple blocks to print images in full color. A few centuries later, this technique was transmitted to Japan, where during the 18th century it was brought to a level of perfection that has made Japanese prints famous the world over. One of the most justly renowned of all Japanese prints is Katsushika Hokusai's *The Great Wave* (**8.5**), from his series *Thirty-Six Views of Mount Fuji*. The white-capped mountain of the title is far in the distance, symmetrical and serene under the dull sky of winter. In the foreground are whitecaps of a different sort—an angry ocean with claws of foam, about to crash down on three slender fishing boats.

Production of such woodcuts in Japan was a true team effort. The artist was usually engaged by the publisher of the prints, who would eventually sell the edition. It was often the publisher who suggested the subject. The artist executed the design in brush and ink on paper, outlining the forms with slender "iron wire" lines. After his design was approved, it was passed along to the wood carver, who carved a block, called the key block, that reproduced the drawing. A print from the key block was sent to the artist, who approved it and made annotations about color. Guided by the key block, the carver proceeded to carve a series of color blocks, one for each color. For example, one block was carved to print only the light blue areas, another for dark blue. An entire block might need to be carved just to print a small detail in a new color. *The Great Wave* uses few colors—three shades of blue, pale gray, and pale brown—but more elaborate prints often required as many as twenty blocks. The carver was also responsible for the **registration** of the blocks, that is, verifying that they lined up perfectly when printed, with no gaps or overlapping in the colors.

The completed set of blocks was then sent to a third specialist, the printer. Printers received general indications about coloring, but it seems that they had a great deal of leeway in adjusting the color harmonies to their own

8.5 Katsushika Hokusai. *The Great Wave*. c. 1831. Polychrome woodblock print on paper, 9⅞ × 14⅝".
Honolulu Academy of Arts, Honolulu, Hawaii.

KATSUSHIKA HOKUSAI
1760–1849

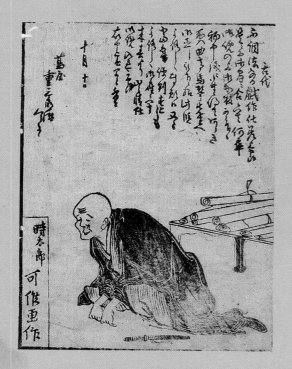

ONE OF THE MOST delightfully eccentric figures in the history of art is the Japanese painter and woodcut designer who has come to be known as Hokusai. During his eighty-nine years Hokusai lived in at least ninety different houses and used some fifty names. The name that stuck for posterity—Hokusai—means "Star of the Northern Constellation."

Hokusai was born in the city of Edo (now Tokyo), the son of a metal engraver. At the age of eighteen he was sent as an apprentice to the print designer Katsukawa Shunsho. So impressed was the master with his pupil's work that he allowed the young man to adopt part of his own name, and for several years Hokusai called himself "Shunro." Later the two quarreled, and Hokusai changed his name.

Even in his early years Hokusai always worked very quickly, producing huge quantities of drawings. As he finished a drawing, he would toss it on the floor, until there were papers scattered all over the studio, making cleaning impossible. When the house got too filthy and disorderly, he would simply move to another, followed by his long-suffering wife.

Hokusai's first book of sketches was published in 1800 and showed various scenes in and around Edo. That same year the artist produced a novel, which he sent off to a publisher accompanied by the self-portrait shown here. (Hokusai's head is shaved in the manner of Japanese artists and writers of that time.) Both books achieved a popular success, but characteristically, Hokusai never bothered to open the packets of money sent by his publisher. If a creditor stopped by, he would hand over a packet or two without counting it. Throughout his life he remained indifferent to money and despite his great accomplishments was usually at the brink of starvation.

As Hokusai's fame spread he was often invited to give public drawing demonstrations. Legends of his virtuosity abound. On one occasion, the story goes, he stood before the assembled crowd outside a temple and drew an immense image of the Buddha, using a brush as big as a broom. Another time he drew birds in flight on a single grain of rice. Hokusai's sense of humor, never far below the surface, came bubbling out when he was asked to perform for the Shogun (the military governor). As onlookers gathered at the palace, Hokusai spread a large piece of paper on the floor, painted blue watercolor waves across it, then took a live rooster, dipped its feet in red paint, and allowed it to run across the painting. Bowing respectfully, he announced to the Shogun that his creation was a picture of red maple leaves floating down the river.[2]

Though well aware of his own skill, Hokusai often amused himself by pretending modesty. In the preface to one of his books he wrote: "From the age of six I had a mania for drawing. At seventy-three I had learned a little . . . in consequence when I am eighty I shall have made still more progress, and when I am a hundred and ten, everything I do . . . will be alive." But the artist did not make it quite that far. As he lay on his deathbed, he cried out: "If Heaven would grant me ten more years!" And then: "If Heaven would grant me *five* more years, I would become a real painter."[3] His grave is marked by a slab on which is carved the last of his names: Gwakio Rojin—Old Man Mad About Drawing.

Katsushika Hokusai. *Kamado Shogun Kanryaku no Maki (Self-Portrait)*, from *The Tactics of General Oven*. 1800. Woodcut, 8⅞ × 5⅞″. The Art Institute of Chicago.

satisfaction. They might sometimes consult about color with the publisher, though, it seems, not with the artist. The key block was printed first, then each color block in turn, following a standard, fixed order. The completed edition was turned over for sale to the publisher, who had been advertising them in the meantime. As in the West, woodcuts in Japan made art available to people who would not have been able to afford unique works such as paintings.

During the latter part of the 19th century, Japanese woodcuts were exported in great quantities to Europe, where many artists fell under the spell of their innovative designs (see 4.29). Fewer artists actually experimented with the technique itself. One who did was the American artist Arthur Wesley Dow. His moody print *Moonrise* (**8.6**) pays homage to the translucent, water-base colors and flat, simplified forms of Japanese prints. Dow, however, eliminated the key block and its dark outline, creating a softer, more atmospheric effect. Dow would have cut the blocks and printed them himself, for this had by now become standard practice for woodcuts in the West.

A radically different approach was pioneered during the early 20th century by German Expressionist artists who found in woodcut a medium uniquely compatible with their style. A splendid example is Emil Nolde's *The Prophet* (**8.7**). Expressionist imagery is stark, sometimes rough, and occasionally shocking. Woodcut readily lends itself to this style by allowing harsh contrasts of black and white as well as broad—even crude—drawing and cutting. Expressionism is just what its name implies—expressive, and also brooding, emotional, uncompromising. Of all the print methods, woodcut offers the greatest possibilities for that expression.

Influenced by the power and sincerity of the German Expressionist style, artists in many parts of the world took up the medium of woodcut, often using it for social and political purposes. Interestingly, one place where

8.6 (above) Arthur Wesley Dow. *Moonrise.* c. 1915. Polychrome woodblock print on paper. Courtesy Hirsch and Adler Galleries.

8.7 (below) Emil Nolde. *The Prophet.* 1912. Woodcut, 12½ × 8¹³⁄₁₆″. National Gallery of Art, Washington, D.C.

8.8 (left) Hu Yichuan. *To the Front!* 1932. Woodcut, 9⅛ × 12″. Lu Xun Memorial, Shanghai.

8.9 (right) Rockwell Kent. *Workers of the World, Unite!* 1937. Wood engraving, 8 × 6″. The Library of Congress, Washington, D.C.

Expressionist woodcuts were admired was China, where woodcut began. In his woodcut *To the Front!* (8.8), Hu Yichuan, then twenty-two years old, employed the crude carving and dramatic immediacy of Expressionism in an attempt to rally the people of China against Japanese invaders. Pressed up against the picture plane in diagonal slashes of black and white, the shouting figure in the foreground conveys a true sense of anguish and emergency.

WOOD ENGRAVING

Created during the same decade as *To the Front!* American artist Rockwell Kent's *Workers of the World, Unite!* also features a dramatic composition with a strong political theme (8.9). But while Hu Yichuan's print gives the impression of having been carved quickly with bold, gashing stokes, Rockwell Kent's image seems to have been created more patiently from innumerable fine white lines on a black ground. These white lines are characteristic of the medium Kent chose, wood engraving.

Wood engraving differs in several aspects from woodcut. For one thing, it is done on the end grain of the wood. If you imagine a board, say a 2-by-4, the long, smooth plank sides would be used for woodcut, but the grainy cut end would be used for wood engraving. The end grain can be cut in any direction without chipping or splintering, unlike the plank sides. The tool used for cutting makes fine, narrow grooves in the wood, and these grooves, which do not take the ink, result in white lines when the inked wood block is pressed to paper.

The 1930s in America were marked by the Great Deression. During this difficult decade, many artists' sympathies lay with industrial workers and their efforts to unionize in order to have a collective voice in their own future. In Kent's image, a lone, heroic worker wields a shovel against the threat of oncoming bayonets. The fire provides a sense of disaster, while in the background can be seen a factory, the source of the worker's livelihood. With its combination

8.10 Pablo Picasso. *Portrait of a Young Girl, after Cranach the Younger, II*. 1958. Linoleum cut, printed in color, 25¹¹⁄₁₆ × 21⁵⁄₁₆". The Museum of Modern Art, New York.

of dramatic nighttime lighting, a common worker, and anonymous bayonets, the composition calls to mind Goya's martyred Spaniards (see 5.20), now fighting back and refusing to die. Rockwell Kent was at the time the most well known and successful graphic artist in the United States, and this print was commissioned from him by the American College Society of Print Collectors.

LINOCUT

A linoleum cut, or linocut, is very similar to a woodcut. The major difference is that the material is much softer than wood, which makes it both easier to carve and less durable in printing multiple impressions, resulting in smaller editions. Linoleum has no grain, so it is possible to make cuts in any direction with equal ease. Some artists dismiss linoleum as being suitable only for schoolchildren (or for greeting cards), but Picasso never let such preconceived ideas interfere with his creativity. His color linocut depicting a *Portrait of a Young Girl, after Cranach the Younger, II* (**8.10**) is an interpretation of a painting by the 16th-century German artist Lucas Cranach, but a more abstract treatment than Cranach could ever have imagined. The splendid colors result from printing with several linoleum blocks, just as is done with color wood blocks. The fluid, curving white lines of the background especially reflect the soft and grainless character of linoleum.

INTAGLIO

The second major category of printmaking techniques is intaglio (from an Italian word meaning "to cut"), which includes several related methods. Intaglio is exactly the reverse of relief, in that the areas meant to print are *below* the surface of the printing plate. The artist uses a sharp tool or acid to make depressions—lines or grooves—in a metal plate. When the plate is inked, the ink sinks

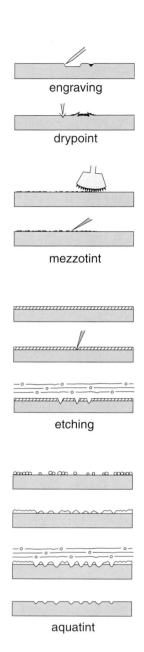

engraving

drypoint

mezzotint

etching

aquatint

into the depressions. Then the surface of the plate is wiped clean. When dampened paper is brought into contact with the plate under pressure, the paper is pushed into the depressions to pick up the image.

There are five basic types of intaglio printing: engraving, drypoint, mezzotint, etching, and aquatint.

ENGRAVING

The oldest of the intaglio techniques, engraving developed from the medieval practice of incising (cutting) linear designs in armor and other metal surfaces. The armorer's art had achieved a high level of expertise, and it was just a short step to realizing that the engraved lines could be filled with ink and the design transferred to paper.

The basic tool of engraving is the burin, a sharp, V-shaped instrument used to cut lines into the metal plate (**8.11**). Shallow cuts produce a light, thin line, while deeper gouges in the metal result in a thicker and darker line. Engraving is closely related to drawing in pen and ink in both technique and the visual effect of the work. Looking at a reproduction it is hard to tell an engraving from a fine pen drawing. As in these drawing media, modeling and shading effects usually are achieved by hatching, cross-hatching, or stippling.

Until the invention of lithography and photography in the 19th century, engravings were the principal way in which works of art were reproduced and disseminated. Professional engravers were extraordinary draftsmen, capable of making extremely accurate copies of drawings, paintings, statues, and architecture. During the Renaissance, the awakening interest in ancient Roman art was fed by engravings, for no sooner was a newly discovered statue unearthed than it was recorded in a drawing, which was then engraved and distributed across Europe.

One of the first artists to create an original composition especially for engraving was Raphael, whose drawing of *The Judgment of Paris* (**8.12**) was entrusted to the engraver Marcantonio Raimondi. The print illustrates a famous episode from Greek mythology in which Paris, son of King Priam of Troy, settled a dispute among three goddesses. He is portrayed here at the

8.11 (above) Plate-making methods for intaglio printing.

8.12 (right) Marcantonio Raimondi, after Raphael. *The Judgment of Paris*. c. 1514–18. Engraving, sheet 11½ × 17". Bibliothèque Nationale, Paris.

left, awarding the golden apple to Aphrodite, the goddess of love. Other gods and goddesses swarm about. In return for a judgment in her favor, Aphrodite had promised Paris the most beautiful woman in the world. She gave him Helen, the wife of a Greek king. Paris abducted Helen to Troy, thus touching off the Trojan War, the prolonged and disastrous conflict that inspired the two Greek epics, the *Iliad* and the *Odyssey*.

Engraved by Raimondi, Raphael's composition achieved immediate fame and was widely imitated. Its influence lasted well into the 19th century, when the three figures in the lower right corner turned up somewhat transformed in a painting that created a scandal (see 21.4). *The Judgment of Paris* shows the clean, sharp line characteristic of engraving, as well as the full range of tonal effects that can be created with fine hatching, cross-hatching, and stippling.

DRYPOINT

Drypoint is similar to engraving, except that the cutting instrument used is a drypoint needle. The artist draws on the plate, usually a copper plate, almost as freely as one can draw on paper with a pencil. As the needle scratches across the plate, it raises a burr, or thin ridge of metal (see 8.11). This burr holds the ink, making a line that is softer and less sharply detailed than an engraved line. If engraving is like fine pen drawing, sharp and distinct, then drypoint is more like drawing in soft pencil or crayon, with slightly blurred edges. This soft, sketchy quality is obvious in Picasso's exuberant drypoint, *At the Circus* (**8.13**).

MEZZOTINT

Mezzotint is a reverse process, in which the artist works from dark to light. To prepare a mezzotint plate, the artist first roughens the entire plate with a sharp tool called a rocker. If the plate were inked and printed after this stage, it would print a sheet of paper entirely black, because each roughened spot would catch and hold the ink. Lighter tones can be created only by smoothing or rubbing out these rough spots so as not to trap the ink. To do this, the artist goes over portions of the plate with a burnisher (a smoothing tool) and/or a scraper to wear down the roughened burrs (see 8.11). Where the burrs are partially removed, the plate will print intermediate values. The lightest values print in areas where the burrs are smoothed away entirely.

The major advantage of mezzotint is that it is capable of subtle gradations from dark to light. Whereas engraving and drypoint are predominantly line techniques, mezzotint is based on values. We see this effect in Peter Pelham's portrait *Cotton Mather* (**8.14**), one of the earliest prints made in the American colonies. So finely modeled is this portrait of the great Puritan leader that, in reproduction, we might almost mistake it for an oil painting in black and white.

ETCHING

Etching is done with acids, which "eat" lines and depressions into a metal plate much as sharp tools cut those depressions in the other methods. To make an etching the artist first coats the entire printing plate with an acid-resistant substance called a **ground,** made from beeswax, asphalt, and other materials. Next, the artist draws on the coated plate with an etching needle. The needle removes the ground, exposing the bare metal in areas meant to print (see 8.11). Then the entire plate is dipped in acid. Only the portions of the plate exposed by the needle are eaten into by the acid, leaving the rest of the plate intact. Finally, the ground is removed, and the plate is inked and printed. Etched lines are not as sharp and precise as those made by the engraver's burin, because the biting action of the acid is slightly irregular.

8.14 Peter Pelham. *Cotton Mather.* 1727. Mezzotint. The Granger Collection, New York.

8.15 Rembrandt. *Christ Preaching.* c. 1652. Etching, 6½ × 8½".
The Pierpont Morgan Library, New York.

Rembrandt, who was a prolific printmaker, made hundreds of etchings. Unfortunately, many of his plates were not canceled or destroyed. Long after his death, and long after the plates had worn down badly, people greedy to produce yet more "Rembrandts" struck impressions from the plates. These later impressions lack detail and give us little idea of what the artist intended. To get a true sense of Rembrandt's genius as an etcher, we must look at prints that are known to be early impressions, such as this impression of *Christ Preaching* (**8.15**). Using only line, Rembrandt gives us a world made of light and shade. He has set his scene in a humble quarter of town, possibly modeled on the Jewish section of the Amsterdam he knew well. Christ, bathed in light and standing barefoot in gentle contrapposto, preaches to the small but curious crowd that has gathered. His attention falls for a moment on the little boy in the foreground, who, too young to understand the importance of what he is hearing, has turned away to doodle with his finger in the dust. Rembrandt's greatness lay in part in his ability to imagine and portray such profoundly human moments.

AQUATINT

A variation on the etching process, aquatint is a way of achieving flat areas of tone—gray values or intermediate values of color. To prepare the plate, the artist first dusts it with finely powdered resin. Several methods are available to control where and how thickly the resin is distributed on the plate. Then the plate is heated, so the resin sticks to it. When the plate is dipped in acid, the acid bites wherever there is no resin, all around the particles (see 8.11). For instance, if the particles are thinly dusted and far apart, the acid will be able to bite into larger areas of the plate, but if the particles are close together, the acid will have limited space to penetrate. Different tones, from light to dark, can be produced depending on the density of the particles, the length of time the plate is held in the acid, or the strength of the acid bath.

Because aquatint does not print lines but only areas of tone, it is nearly always combined with one or more of the other intaglio techniques—drypoint, etching, or engraving. Spanish artist Francisco de Goya combined aquatint with etching in *Hasta la Muerte* (*Until Death*, **8.16**). The black lines of the contours, hair, and facial features were etched, while the grays were produced with aquatint. The grainy quality of the tonal areas is typical of aquatint. *Hasta la Muerte* is from a series of satirical prints called *Los Caprichos*, meaning caprices, whims, eccentricities, freakishness. We see a grotesque old woman primping absurdly for her seventy-fifth birthday party, reflected even

8.16 (left) Francisco de Goya. *Hasta la Muerte (Until Death)*, from *Los Caprichos*. 1797–98. Etching and aquatint, 7½ × 5¼". Galerie P. Proute, Paris.

8.17 (right) Mary Cassatt. *Woman Bathing*. 1891. Drypoint and aquatint, 14⁵⁄₁₆ × 10½". National Gallery of Art, Washington, D.C.

more horribly by her mirror. The look of satisfaction on her face suggests that *she* does not see the ugliness that we and the mocking onlookers see. Goya is poking none-too-gentle fun at her vanity, her girlish costume, her attempt at painting a very faded lily. The message of this print might be: "We do not see ourselves as others see us."

Mary Cassatt employed the more delicate line of drypoint for the contours of her exquisite *Woman Bathing* (**8.17**). The colors were printed in aquatint. Aquatint lends itself beautifully to areas of unmodulated, translucent color, and it allowed Cassatt to transpose the effects of the Japanese woodcuts she admired so much to a European medium.

By combining techniques the intaglio artist can get almost any result he or she wishes. Because the artist can achieve effects ranging from the most precisely drawn lines to the most subtle areas of tone, the possibilities for imagery are much greater than in the relief methods. We turn now, however, to a branch of printmaking that is even more flexible in its effects.

LITHOGRAPHY

All the major printmaking categories except one have origins going far back into history, having developed from other art forms, such as decoration of armor and printing on fabrics. That one exception is lithography. Lithography was invented in a particular place at a particular time by a particular individual—a man named Alois Senefelder.

Senefelder was a young German actor and playwright living in Munich during the 1790s. Frustrated by the expense of publishing his plays, he began experimenting with variations on the etching process as a cheap method of reproducing them. He was too poor to invest much money in copper plates, so he tried working on the smooth Bavarian limestones that lined the streets of Munich, which he excavated from the street and brought to his studio. One day, when he was experimenting with ingredients for drawing on the stone, his laundress appeared unexpectedly, and Senefelder hastily wrote out his laundry list on the stone, using his new combination of materials—wax, soap, and lampblack. Later, he decided to try immersing the stone in acid. To his delight he found that his laundry list appeared in slight relief on the stone. This event paved the way for his development of the lithographic process. While the relief aspect eventually ceased to play a role, the groundwork for lithography had been laid.

Lithography is a **planographic** process, which means that the printing surface is flat—not raised as in relief or depressed as in intaglio. It depends, instead, on the principle that oil and water do not mix. To make a lithographic print the artist first draws the image on the stone with a greasy material—usually a grease-based lithographic crayon or a greasy ink usually known by its German name, *tusche*. The stone is then subjected to a series of procedures, including treatment with an acid solution, that fix the drawing (bind it to the stone so that it will not smudge) and prepare it to be printed. To print the image, the printer dampens the stone with water, which soaks into the areas *not* coated with grease. When the stone is inked, the greasy ink sticks to the greasy image areas and is repelled by the water-soaked background areas. While limestone is still the preferred surface for art prints, lithographs can also be made using zinc or aluminum plates.

For artists, lithography is the most direct and effortless of the print media, for they can draw with a lithographic crayon on stone as freely as with a regular crayon on paper. Preparing the stone for printing and the printing itself are highly specialized skills, however, and artists usually work on their lithographs at a printer's workshop, often directly under the printer's guidance.

8.18 (left) Käthe Kollwitz. *Death and the Mother*. 1934. Lithograph, 20⅛ × 14⅝".
Courtesy The Fogg Art Museum, Harvard University Art Museums, Cambridge, Massachusetts.

8.19 (right) Henri de Toulouse-Lautrec. *The Seated Clowness*, from *Elles*. Color lithograph, 20¾ × 16".
Musée Toulouse-Lautrec, Albi.

Käthe Kollwitz' *Death and the Mother* (**8.18**) illustrates well the direct quality of lithography. If you did not know it was a print, you could easily mistake it for a drawing with crayon or charcoal on paper. *Death and the Mother* depicts three figures locked together in a ghastly embrace. We see only one face—the terrified face of the woman, who clutches her child against her breast as the featureless form of Death claims her from behind. We know the woman already belongs to Death and cannot escape; their union is shockingly intimate. Kollwitz' drawing seems simple, yet its expression is universal: the instinct of all mothers to protect their children and the dread felt by all creatures facing their own mortality.

By using multiple stones, lithography can reproduce images in full color, and during the 19th century it quickly became the preferred method for reproducing art. The artist who more than any other made color lithography a medium for original work was Toulouse-Lautrec. Among his best-known lithographs are the series of posters he designed for the nightclubs and entertainers of his day (see 10.11), but he also created limited editions of lithographs as art prints, among them the wonderful *The Seated Clowness* (**8.19**), from the series *Elles* (those women). The clowness in question is Cha-U-Kao, a famous circus performer of the day. Toulouse-Lautrec has captured her seated inelegantly on a low bench, legs akimbo, giving us a wry look as if to say, "And who are you?" Brushed ink, spattered mists of ink, and crayon were used to create the image, which would have required three stones—one for black, one for yellow, and one for rose.

Modern techniques for transferring photographic imagery to stone or plate have made it possible to print very complex images by the lithographic

8.20 Robert Rauschenberg.
Centennial Certificate, MMA. 1969.
Color lithograph, 35⅞ × 25″.
The Metropolitan Museum of Art,
New York.

process. A good example is Robert Rauschenberg's *Centennial Certificate, MMA* **(8.20).** This print was commissioned of Rauschenberg by the Metropolitan Museum of Art in New York to celebrate its hundredth anniversary, and the museum directors allowed the artist to choose whichever items he wished from the collection to include in the lithograph. Rauschenberg made a collage of reproductions, including Picasso's portrait of Gertrude Stein (second from top at left); a Rembrandt self-portrait (upper right); a study for Ingres's *Odalisque* (bottom right, see 21.1); and a Classical sculpture (lying on its side, above Gertrude Stein). This collage was then transferred photographically to the printing plates. In all, two lithographic stones and two aluminum plates were used to print the image in four colors. One stone carried graph-paper lines and the signatures of museum officials (lower right). At center is a text statement of the museum's goals.

Centennial Certificate, MMA is very much a product of the print medium and equally a product of late-20th-century technology. In effect, Rauschenberg created multiple images (an edition of prints) from his multiple image (the collage). This result would not have been possible without the collaboration of photographic and printmaking processes.

ROBERT RAUSCHENBERG

b. 1925

BORN IN Port Arthur, Texas, Milton Rauschenberg—who later became known as Bob and then Robert—had no exposure to art as such until he was seventeen. His original intention to become a pharmacist faded when he was expelled from the University of Texas within six months, for failure (he claims) to dissect a frog. After three years in the Navy during World War II, Rauschenberg spent a year at the Kansas City Art Institute; then he traveled to Paris for further study. At the Académie Julian in Paris he met the artist Susan Weil, whom he later married.

Upon his return to the United States in 1948, Rauschenberg enrolled in the now-famous art program headed by the painter Josef Albers at Black Mountain College in North Carolina. Many of his long-term attachments and interests developed during this period, including his close working relationship with the avant-garde choreographer Merce Cunningham. In 1950 Rauschenberg moved to New York, where he supported himself partly by doing window displays for the fashionable Fifth Avenue stores Bonwit Teller and Tiffany's.

Rauschenberg's work began to attract critical attention soon after his first one-man exhibition at the Betty Parsons Gallery in New York. The artist reports that, between the time Parsons selected the works to be exhibited and the opening of the show, he had completely reworked everything, and that "Betty was surprised." More surprises were soon to come from this steadily unpredictable artist.

The range of Rauschenberg's work makes him difficult to categorize. In addition to paintings, prints, and combination pieces, he has done extensive set and costume design for dances by Cunningham and others, as well as graphic design for magazines and books. "Happenings" and performance art played a role in his work from the very beginning. In 1952, at Black Mountain College, he participated in *Theater Piece #1*, by the composer John Cage, which included improvised dance, recitations, piano music, the playing of old records, and projected slides of Rauschenberg's paintings. Even the works usually classified as paintings are anything but conventional. One has an actual stuffed bird attached to the front of the canvas. Another consists of a bed, with a quilt on it, hung upright on the wall and splashed with paint. Works that might be called sculptures are primarily assemblage; for example, *Sor Aqua* (1973) is composed of a bathtub (with water) above which a large chunk of metal seems to be flying.

In recent years the artist devoted much of his time to ROCI (pronounced "Rocky"), his Rauschenberg Overseas Culture Interchange, which had as its goal promoting international friendship, understanding, and peace. Through ROCI he brought his work to Mexico, Chile, China, Tibet, Germany, Venezuela, Japan, Cuba, and the former Soviet Union.

We get from Rauschenberg a sense of boundaries being dissolved—boundaries between media, between art and nonart, between art and life. He has said: "The strongest thing about my work . . . is the fact that I chose to ennoble the ordinary."[4]

Robert Rauschenberg at home in Captiva.
Photograph by Ed Chappell,
June 1992.

SCREENPRINTING

To understand the basic principle of screenprinting, you need only picture the lettering stencils used by schoolchildren. The stencil is a piece of cardboard from which the forms of the alphabet letters have been cut out. To trace the letters onto paper, you simply place the stencil over the paper and fill in the holes with pencil or ink.

Today's art screenprinting works much the same way. The screen is a fine mesh of silk or synthetic fiber mounted in a frame, rather like a window screen. (Silk is the traditional material, so the process has often been called **silkscreen** or **serigraphy**—"silk writing.") Working from drawings, the printmaker stops out (blocks) screen areas that are *not* meant to print by plugging up the holes, usually with some kind of glue, so that no ink can pass through. Then the screen is placed over paper, and the ink is forced through the mesh with a tool called a squeegee. Only the areas not stopped out allow the ink to pass through and print on paper (see 8.1).

To make a color screenprint, the artist prepares one screen for each color. On the "blue" screen, for example, all areas not meant to print in blue are stopped out, and so on for each of the other colors. The preparation of multiple color screens is relatively easy and inexpensive. For this reason it is not unusual to see serigraphs printed in ten, twenty, or more colors. This color flexibility would be very difficult to achieve in any of the other methods.

Born in Mexico and living in California, Enrique Chagoya satirizes Mexican American cultural relations in his screenprint *What Appropriation Has Given Me* (**8.21**). In this irreverent image, Mexican painters Diego Rivera (see 7.4) and Frida Kahlo (see 5.11) have been commodified as chips called Dieguitos and Fritas. The unmistakable hand of Mickey Mouse, symbol of American popular culture, offers Dieguitos to the other hands that descend on the food. On the table, in front of an oddly menacing watermelon, the spattered stains of salsa dip look unsettlingly like blood.

8.21 Enrique Chagoya. *What Appropriation Has Given Me*, from *Beyond 1992*. 1992. Serigraph, 30 × 22".
Courtesy Gallery Paule Anglim, San Francisco.

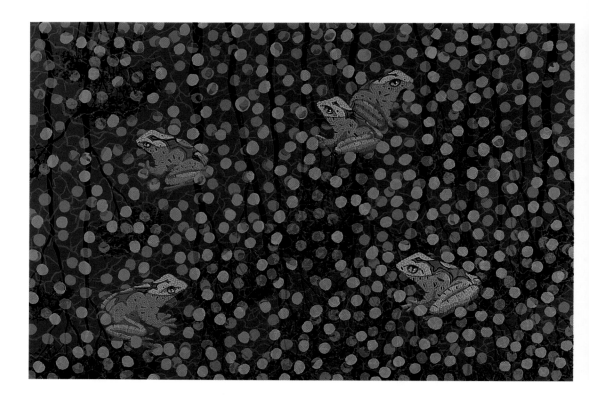

8.22 Lin Onus. *Gumiring Garkman.* 1994. Screenprint, 19⅝ × 29½″. Courtesy the artist.

Chagoya's cartoonlike imagery is well served by the broad, flat areas of color that screenprinting encourages. But the medium lends itself equally to more detailed and realistic approaches, as in Lin Onus's screenprint *Gumiring Garkman* (**8.22**). Here, multiple screens of color laid one over another portray the surface and depths of a pond with almost photographic precision. The exactness of the image suggests that the frogs must be some carefully documented species. In fact, Onus invented the creatures, which bear markings typical of Australian Aboriginal art (see 20.1). Of Aboriginal heritage himself, Lin Onus often incorporated realistically depicted Aboriginal motifs into his work, at once challenging preconceived ideas about what an Aboriginal artist "ought" to paint like and suggesting that Australia itself, its landscape and wildlife, is deeply Aboriginal in ways that later settlers may never fully comprehend.

SPECIAL TECHNIQUES

There is one major exception to the rule, stated at the beginning of this chapter, that prints are an art of multiples. That exception is the **monotype.** Monotypes are made by an indirect process, like any other print, but, as the prefix "mono" implies, only one print results. To make a monotype, the artist draws on a metal plate or some other smooth surface, often with diluted oil paints. Then the plate is run through a press to transfer the image to paper. Or the artist may simply place a sheet of paper on the plate and hand-rub it to transfer the image. Either way, the original is destroyed or so altered that there can be no duplicate impressions. If a series of prints is planned, the artist must do more work on the plate.

Monotype offers several technical advantages. The range of colors is unlimited, as is the potential for lines or tones. No problems arise with cutting against a grain or into resistant metal. One can work as freely as in a direct process like painting or drawing. You may wonder, then, why *not* simply draw or paint? Why bother with the indirect touch of the print? There can be as many reasons as there are monotype artists, but we might list a few. Monotype offers the "accidental" quality of the press as intermediary. Even when the original is finished, one cannot be quite sure how the print will look when it comes through the press. Colors are absorbed into the paper differently, giving a "printed" effect many artists seek. There is the potential for working over the printed image to create a "layered" appearance. Above all, artists love to experiment with techniques that expand their expressive range.

Brush marks are clearly visible in Maurice Prendergast's *Le Quatorze Juillet* (July 14th), which the artist sketched in oil paint on a sheet of glass and then transferred by gentle pressure to paper (**8.23**). July 14th is better known in America as Bastille Day, the day the French set aside as a national holiday to celebrate their revolution. Here, lanterns hung in the trees provide a magical atmosphere as contented citizens promenade along a broad avenue. Born in Boston, Prendergast probably witnessed this festive evening at first hand, for he spent much of his life traveling and painting in Europe. We can imagine him arising the next morning to dash off this postcard-size image, which over a hundred years later retains its power to make us wish we had been there, too.

Until the later 20th century the limitations of printing presses usually restricted an artist to one category of work at a time. A print was either relief *or* intaglio *or* lithography. Now, however, with the increasing sophistication of presses and print workshops, it is possible to combine several print processes in the same image, which broadens the artist's options significantly. Frank Stella's *La penna di hu* (**8.24**), for instance, was made by combining etching, relief, woodcut, screenprint, and other stencil techniques, in twenty-nine colors. Although not actually three-dimensional (unlike many of Stella's works, which have areas projecting forward in depth), *La penna di hu* has an exceptionally rich surface texture and creates a strong sense of visual three-dimensionality.

8.23 (left) Maurice Prendergast. *Le Quatorze Juillet* (Bastille Day). 1892. Monotype in oil colors, image size 6⅞ × 5⅛". The Cleveland Museum of Art.

8.24 (right) Frank Stella. *La penna di hu*. 1988. Relief, etching, woodcut, screenprint, stencil, hand-colored on handmade paper; 4′7½″ × 5′6″. Collection Walker Art Center, Minneapolis.

RECENT DIRECTIONS: THE PHOTO IMAGE AND PRINTMAKING

Ever since its development at the beginning of the 19th century, photography has had a complex relationship with the traditional image-making techniques such as painting and printmaking. As we shall see in the next chapter, early photographers were very much influenced by the vision of the world that had been developed by painting. Influence has since flowed the other way as well, for traditionally trained artists have grown increasingly fascinated with photography as a way to "capture" an image, which can then be used in various ways.

Printmaking and photography have an especially long and close relationship, for printmaking techniques are used on a commercial level to reproduce photographs as illustrations in newspapers, books, and magazines. This book, for example, was printed from metal plates using a mechanical version of lithography called offset lithography. Photographs can also be etched into copper plates for intaglio printing or chemically transferred to screens for screenprinting.

More recently, the computer has given artists still another tool for creating and manipulating images. Now, images can be captured with a camera, transferred to a computer for further work, then printed with traditional printmaking techniques. This was the procedure followed by Victor Burgin in creating the series of prints called *Fiction Film* (**8.25**). In the untitled print illustrated here, an overturned car has burst into flames, and through the smoke appears the face of a beautiful woman. The image pretends to be taken from a film version of a famous French novel called *Nadja*, but in fact such a film never existed. Burgin asks us to imagine that a film of *Nadja* was made and then lost. Only these few still pictures survive. Burgin created the prints using actual stills from old French movies and video footage he himself took in France. He fed the images into a computer, where he could combine and manipulate them freely. He then printed the results as a series of two-tone screenprints, which he varnished to give them the glossy finish of photographs. Burgin here plays games with illusion and reality, creating photographs that aren't photographs of a film that was never a film.

One of the oldest photographic techniques is the photogram, in which an object is laid directly on top of a sheet of photosensitive paper or other material, which is then exposed to light. The parts of the paper shaded by the object remain white, while the exposed portions darken. Swiss artist Markus Raetz used this process in *Shadows* (**8.26**), a print that toys with perception and the nature of images. The series of sinuous, looping forms was formed of a single piece of plastic-covered electric wire, which the artist twisted and placed on a series of six photogravure plates, photosensitized metal plates used to create an intaglio printing plate from a photographic negative.

As each plate was exposed to the light, the wire loop cast a shadow, which registered on the photosensitive surface. The plates were then bathed in acid, which ate into the recorded shadows to create an intaglio printing plate. As in any other intaglio process, the bitten areas hold ink, so that the shadows of the wire finally print in subtle grays. The lighter portions were overprinted with aquatint in a delicate, pale blue. The result is a series of wispy loops that seem to twist in space, finally resolving into the image of a pipe. They can also be seen as a pipe with a series of smoke rings floating upward, or as frames from a film of a single smoke ring shifting in shape as it rises.

8.25 Victor Burgin. *Untitled,* from *Fiction Film,* 1991. Computer-manipulated image printed as a photoscreenprint, varnished, on white paper; sheet 30⅞ × 37½″. Courtesy the artist.

The darkest portions of the print were formed by the parts of the wire that were in direct contact with the plate, while the lighter parts are shadows cast from farther away. Since the image of the pipe at the bottom varies considerably from dark to light, we understand that the wire was not twisted into a pipe shape, exactly. Rather, it was twisted into a shape that projected a *shadow* that looked like a pipe. Raetz's perception puzzle has still another level of wit to it, for the pipe itself refers to a famous painting by René Magritte, a painting of a similar pipe inscribed with the words "This is not a pipe." (It is a painting of a pipe, just as here it is a pipelike shadow cast by a simple piece of twisted wire.)

If you had any doubt at the beginning of this chapter that printmaking is a lively art, chances are you have changed your mind by now. In some ways it is an art ideally suited to our lifestyle. The painter, the sculptor, the architect—all these make *one* work of art at a time, that will reside in one place. People who want to see the original must journey to do so. But the print made in an edition of a hundred will reside in a hundred different places and be enjoyed by thousands of people. Truly, the print allows nearly anyone to corner a small piece of the world of art.

8.26 Markus Raetz. *Shadows.* 1991. Photogram/photogravure and aquatint, printed from eight plates on one sheet of paper; image 9 × 12⅜″ (each plate); sheet 5′9½″ × 2′2½″. Courtesy the artist and Crown Point Press.

CHAPTER 9

The Camera Arts

Photography, Film, and Video

A room with a view. This phrase may make you think of real estate or of a classic novel, but we may borrow it here, because it describes the essence of a camera. *Camera* is the Latin word for "room," and it is not farfetched to think of any camera as being a little room with a view—real or imaginary—of the outside world.

The desire to record and preserve images is probably as old as civilization. In the 4th century B.C.E. the Greek philosopher Aristotle understood the most basic principle of the camera, for he noted the ability of light, under controlled circumstances, to duplicate an image. Not until the 16th century, however, did anyone manage to construct a practical device that could harness the image-transferring property of light. That device came to be known as the camera obscura.

You can make a camera obscura yourself. Find a light-tight room, even a closet or a very large cardboard box. Arrange for a small hole, no bigger than the diameter of a pencil, in one wall of the room to admit light. Inside, hold a sheet of white paper a few inches from the hole. You will see an image of the scene outside the room projected on the paper—upside-down and rather blurry, but recognizable. That is the principle of the camera obscura, which simply means "dark room."

Our illustration (9.1) shows a portable shack serving as a camera obscura sketched in cutaway, with one wall and the roof removed for illustration purposes. Artists of the Renaissance had welcomed the camera obscura with enthusiasm, because it aided them in achieving a major goal—to reproduce the natural world as accurately as possible, with correct proportions and perspective. By the 16th century the mechanism had come into use as a drawing tool. Once an image had been captured in the camera obscura, the artist could trace over it, thus ensuring an accurate rendering of the scene.

Today we have come a long way from the camera obscura, but its principles remain intact. The modern camera is still dependent on controlled light, and it is still a room with a view. That view may be anything the artist chooses to make it, from a straightforward recording of the natural scene to the most elaborate special effects the mind can conceive. Let us now consider the camera arts—photography, film, and video—and their unique view of the world.

PHOTOGRAPHY

Photography is the art form that best demonstrates a basic truth: Artistry resides not in the hands but in the head. People who cannot draw well sometimes think painters have some unusual skill in their hands, just as a singer may have an exceptional voice. But while some art forms do demand manual skill, the difference between a merely competent mechanical performance and a great work of art lies not in the artist's hands but in the brain—in the artistic inspiration that tells the hands what to do.

It is this confusion between mechanical skill and inspiration that has caused some people to question photography as an art form. After all, painters and sculptors *create* forms; photographers only *find and record* forms. Nevertheless, just as the painter's brain tells the hands what marks to make on canvas, so the photographer's brain interprets what is seen by the eyes and tells the camera what to do. Whereas the average person walks through the world seeing trees and buildings and people, the creative photographer walks through the world seeing compositions—possible photographs. We might almost say that the photographer has an invisible frame somewhere behind the eyes—a frame that is constantly composing pictures.

Two photographs of the same subject reveal how the camera can respond to an artist's creative vision. John Sexton (9.2) and Eliot Porter (9.3) were both attracted to the natural beauty of trees bordering running water, yet the ways they have chosen to translate their experience into a photograph are quite different.

9.1 *Camera Obscura*, in cutaway view. 1646. Engraving. International Museum of Photography at George Eastman House, Rochester, N.Y.

John Sexton chose black-and-white film for *Merced River and Forest, Yosemite Valley, California* (**9.2**). This fundamental decision meant that in order to compose a photograph he had to imagine how the scene in front of his eyes would translate into values on a gray scale. He selected an area along the bank opposite a young tree whose pale foliage contrasts with the darker values of the forest in general, providing an intriguing center of interest. He then framed his view to divide the composition roughly in half horizontally, with the lower half devoted to the river and the upper half to the forest. The pale tree stands just to the left of the vertical axis, its leftward pull on our eyes subtly balanced by the pale linear branches of the dark-trunked tree to the right. Sexton used a slow shutter speed so that the swiftly flowing water registered as a blur, its foaming detail fused together in a ghostly white mist through which dark, shining rocks protrude like strange aquatic creatures.

Sexton's many decisions created an image of contrasts and comparisons. The upper portion emphasizes minute detail; the lower portion emphasizes large abstract forms. The upper portion is still; the lower portion is all motion. The upper portion captures a pale tree against a darker ground; the lower portion captures dark rocks against a pale ground. The rhythms of the trees in the upper portion are vertical; the flow of the water in the lower portion is horizontal. The similarity in values encourages us to connect the pale tree on the opposite bank with the water in some way, seeing it perhaps as a spray of foam frozen in time. However we see it, it is a presence that draws our eye, but that the intervening river will always prevent us from reaching.

Eliot Porter, in contrast, worked with color film for his *Pool in a Brook, Pond Brook, New Hampshire* (**9.3**). This fundamental decision meant that while values would play a role, color harmonies could also be taken into account. In fact, color is the dominant element in the photograph. Porter chose a clear autumn day, when the orange and yellow-orange foliage of the trees and the blue and blue-violet of the sky intensify each other, as complementary colors do. However, he did not photograph this motif directly, but rather indirectly, as it was reflected in the surface of a pool. The moving water interrupts and blurs the reflection, making us less aware of trees and sky and more aware of the play of pure, saturated color. The composi-

tion is punctuated by a few floating leaves. Captured in sharp focus, they bring us back to the surface of the otherwise abstract image and help us understand what exactly it is that we are looking at.

Porter and Sexton searched through similar scenery looking for a subject for their work, for raw material that they could transform through photography into an image that would reward our attention. The subjects they found and the way they treated them reflect their personal preoccupations and artistic concerns. The resulting images reflect as well their awareness of and control over the numerous variables in the photographic process. In their hands, a camera is as subtle and versatile a tool for image-making as a pencil in the hands of a traditionally trained artist.

THE STILL CAMERA AND ITS BEGINNINGS

Despite the amazing sophistication of modern photographic equipment, the basic mechanism of the camera is simple, and it is no different in theory from that of the camera obscura. A camera is a light-tight box (**9.4**) with an opening at one end to admit light, a lens to focus and refract the light, and a light-sensitive surface (today it is usually film) to receive the light-image and hold it. The last of these—the holding of the image—was the major drawback of the camera obscura. It could capture an image—and later versions of the camera obscura had a lens to focus the image and make it sharp—but there was no way to preserve the image, much less walk away with it in your hand. It was to this end that a number of people in the 19th century directed their attention.

One of them was Joseph Nicéphore Niépce, a French inventor. Working with a specially coated pewter plate in the camera obscura, Niépce managed, in 1826, to record a fuzzy version of the view from his window after an exposure of eight hours. Although we may now consider Niépce's "heliograph" (or sun-writing), as he called it, to be the first permanent photograph, the method was not really practical.

9.3 (above) Eliot Porter. *Pool in a Brook, Pond Brook, New Hampshire*, 1953. Dye transfer print. Amon Carter Museum, Fort Worth, Texas.

9.4 (below) The basic parts of a camera.

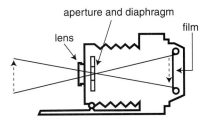

Niépce was corresponding with another Frenchman, Louis Jacques Mandé Daguerre, who was also experimenting with methods to fix the photographic image. The two men worked separately and communicated in code to keep their progress from prying eyes. When Niépce died in 1833, his son Isidore continued the experiments. It was Daguerre, however, who in 1837 made the breakthrough, recording an image in his studio that was clear and sharp, by methods that others could duplicate easily. Daguerre's light-sensitive surface was a copper plate coated with silver iodide, and he named his invention the **daguerreotype.**

Daguerre made the image illustrated here in 1839, the year the French government announced his discovery to the world (**9.5**). In the entrancing detail characteristic of daguerreotypes, it records a seemingly deserted boulevard in Paris. In fact, the boulevard was a bustling thoroughfare. In order to record an image, Daguerre's plate needed to be exposed to sunlight for ten or even twenty minutes! The only person to stand still long enough to be recorded was a man who had stopped to have his shoes shined. Visible at the lower left, he is one of the first people ever to appear in a photograph, and certainly the first to have his image taken without knowing it.

Within two years after Daguerre's discovery was made public, dramatic improvements were made. From England came a better method for fixing the final image so that it didn't continue to change in the light, and also a more light-sensitive coating for the plate that reduced exposure time. From Vienna came an improved lens that gathered sixteen times as much light as previous lenses, further reducing exposure time to around thirty seconds. While still a far cry from the split-second exposures that later technology would make possible, the daguerreotype was now poised to become the first commercially viable method for making permanent images from reflected light.

EARLY SUBJECT MATTER

PORTRAITS Daguerre's invention caused great excitement throughout Europe and North America. Entrepreneurs and the general public alike were quick to see the potential of photography, especially for portraits. It is hard to realize now, but until photography came along only the rich could afford to have their likenesses made, by sitting for a portrait painter. Within three years after Daguerre made his first plate, a "daguerreotype gallery for portraits" had opened in New York, and such galleries soon proliferated.

9.5 Louis Jacques Mandé Daguerre. *Le Boulevard du Temple.* 1839. Daguerreotype. Bayerisches National Museum, Munich.

9.6 Mathew Brady. *Lincoln "Cooper Union" Portrait.* 1860. Photograph.
Library of Congress, Washington, D.C.

Yet for all its early success, the daguerreotype was ultimately a blind alley for photography. The process produces a *positive* image, an image in which light and dark values appear correctly. This image is unique and cannot be reproduced. The plate *is* the photograph. The future of photography instead lay with technology that produced a *negative* image, one in which light and dark values were reversed. This negative could be used again and again to create multiple positive images on light-sensitive paper. Instead of a single precious and delicate object, photography found its essence as an art of potentially unlimited, low-cost multiples. An early version of the negative/positive print process was the calotype, which used a paper negative. Toward the middle of the 19th century, the vastly superior collodion process was developed, which produced a negative on glass.

The possibility of unlimited multiples touched off a craze for *cartes de visite*, French for "visiting card"—a photograph of yourself, roughly the size of a playing card, that you could hand out as a sort of introduction or souvenir. In 1860, a young presidential hopeful named Abraham Lincoln dropped by the New York City studio of Mathew Brady to pose for a *carte de visite* (**9.6**). Lincoln was in town to make a speech at a college called Cooper Union. Brady was then the most renowned and successful portrait photographer in the United States. In 1844, at the age of twenty-one, he had opened a daguerreotype studio in New York. Later there was a studio in Washington and more studios in New York. From these bases he set out to photograph all the illustrious people of the time, and he very nearly succeeded. He employed many assistant photographers, called "operators," including Timothy O'Sullivan, whose work we shall see later in the chapter (see 9.9). In many cases it is impossible to tell which pictures Brady himself took, because his name appears on all products of his studios.

The photograph shown here, however, almost certainly came from Brady's own camera. Brady shows us a young Lincoln, clean-shaven, not yet torn by the heartache of war, fresh out of the back country of Illinois. His suit is obviously new, bought for the occasion, with the shirt cuff hanging down awkwardly from the jacket sleeve. Lincoln's facial expression is stern

9.7 (left) Julia Margaret Cameron. *Charles Darwin.* 1868. Carbon print, 10½ × 8¼″. The Museum of Modern Art, New York.

9.8 (right) Manuel Alvarez-Bravo. *Frida Kahlo in Manuel Alvarez-Bravo's Studio.* 1930s. Gelatin silver print, 9⅝ × 7¼″. Museum of Fine Arts, Houston.

and dignified, but we also sense a bit of apprehension—perhaps caused by the leap into national politics, perhaps caused by the novel experience of having his portrait done.

Lincoln's Cooper Union speech was a success. Brady's photograph was in great demand, and thousands of copies were sold. After the election, Lincoln said, "Brady and the Cooper Union speech made me President."

Another famous portraitist of the 19th century, and an equally fascinating personality, was Julia Margaret Cameron, who, without benefit of multiple assistants, was fully as prolific as Brady. Cameron worked in England in the 1860s and 1870s. She had a wide circle of prominent friends and, by virtue of her strong personality, was able to cajole (or bully) most of them into posing for her. Cameron's photographs have given us likenesses of the great English poet Alfred, Lord Tennyson; the American poet Henry Wadsworth Longfellow; naturalist Charles Darwin, who developed the theory of evolution; and a great many others. The portrait of Darwin (**9.7**) illustrates many elements of Cameron's unique style: a strong contrast of dark and light, emphasis on the head and face, a soft—faintly blurred—focus, and fondness for the profile view. Over and over Cameron searched out the deepest character of her sitters, and then held that character at a slight distance from us through the soft focus of her lens. Cameron's studies show real people transformed into a photographic ideal.

The desire to record what people look like remains an important function of photography for professionals and amateurs alike. Some of the most fascinating portraits result when both photographer and sitter have strong artistic identities. An example is the portrait of the painter Frida Kahlo by Mexican photographer Manuel Alvarez-Bravo (**9.8**). One of the great photographers of the 20th century, Alvarez-Bravo was born in 1902. Brought up in a highly cultivated family, he studied music, painting, and literature as a young man before turning finally to photography. Like Frida Kahlo herself, Alvarez-Bravo came of age during the Mexican Revolution, and he was part

JULIA MARGARET CAMERON
1815–1879

IN A LARGE family of colorful individuals, Julia Margaret Cameron was the standout. Her great-niece, the writer Virginia Woolf (no stranger herself to unconventional conduct), wrote with a kind of fond awe that Julia Cameron "had a gift of ardent speech and picturesque behaviour." Woolf continues: "There was no eccentricity that she would not have dared. . . ."[1]

Child of a Scottish father and a French mother, Julia Margaret Pattle was born in India, then educated in France and England. Of the seven Pattle sisters, only Julia was plain; the rest were exceptionally lovely. Julia Margaret, however, was not one to allow a lack of physical beauty to cramp her style. Possessed of an exuberant spirit and a zest for life, she set out to *make* beauty wherever she could. At twenty-three she married Charles Hay Cameron, a well-to-do scholar and legal reformer. Their marriage was to be a happy one. The couple settled in England, where they raised eleven children—six of their own and five adopted— while conducting an astonishingly active social life.

Stories abound of Mrs. Cameron's generosity, enthusiasm, energy, and strong will. She maintained a vast correspondence, averaging three hundred letters a month. She collected interesting and talented friends by the score, charming them with her wit and creative escapades, overwhelming them with gifts and favors. Her circle included poets, novelists, scientists, actors, politicians, diplomats—the cream of Britain's intellectual and artistic crop.

In 1863, when Julia Cameron was forty-eight, her daughter bought her a special present: a large wooden box camera and darkroom equipment. From that moment Cameron's life changed, for her energies were channeled into a new passion. A chicken coop on the Camerons' property was converted into a "glass house," or photographic studio. Servants, friends, and relatives were recruited as models, and her demands on them became the talk of the countryside.

Cameron favored long exposure times, so a sitter might be forced to maintain some horribly uncomfortable pose, without moving, for up to ten minutes. If that picture didn't turn out well, there must be another and another, hours of posing without rest, until the model staggered exhausted out of Cameron's "glass house." Virginia Woolf tells us that "boatmen were turned into King Arthur; village girls into Queen Guenevere. Tennyson was wrapped in rugs; Sir Henry Taylor was crowned with tinsel. . . . She cared nothing for the miseries of her sitters nor for their rank."[2]

Cameron's images mounted to the hundreds, eventually thousands, but she continued to think of herself as an amateur photographer. Although she exhibited her work and had several one-artist shows, she did not sell her photographs. Instead, she gave them away in great bunches to friends, or to whoever took her fancy. Only near the end of her life did Cameron offer for sale a series of photographs, beautifully bound and copyrighted in her name.

In 1865 the Camerons left England and settled in Ceylon (now Sri Lanka), the island nation off the coast of India, where Julia continued to pursue her art in her customary manner. One visitor, a Miss North, complained that "she made me stand with spiky coconut branches running into my head . . . and told me to look perfectly natural."[3] At the age of sixty-three Julia Cameron caught a bad chill and died. She left behind an unfinished memoir entitled "Annals of My Glass House," in which she wrote: "From the first moment I handled my lens with a tender ardour, and it has become to be as a living thing, with voice and memory and creative vigour."[4]

Henry Herschel Hay Cameron. *Julia Margaret Cameron.* 1870. Silver print, 9¾ × 8½".
Gernsheim Collection, Harry Ranson Humanities Research Center, The University of Texas at Austin.

9.9 Timothy O'Sullivan. *Sand Springs, Nevada.* 1867. Photograph.
Library of Congress, Washington, D.C.

of the extraordinary group of artists, writers, and intellectuals who set out to give voice and identity to the newly independent country. By photographing Kahlo seated and by opening up the space around her, Alvarez-Bravo captures at once her diminutive stature and her regal beauty. Seen through his eyes, she appears proud, temperamental, and sure of her talent.

LANDSCAPE From the first, landscape has been a popular subject for photographers, whether the natural beauty of the countryside or the constructed landscape of the city. Some early photographers, like Timothy O'Sullivan, went to great extremes to capture nature's forms. Hauling what was then very cumbersome photographic equipment through mountains and desert presented a real challenge, but the results were well worth the effort.

In 1867 O'Sullivan signed on as official photographer to an expedition commissioned by the federal government to explore the territories of Nevada and Colorado. One of his most dramatic photos from this trip (**9.9**) shows the mule-drawn ambulance O'Sullivan had hired to carry water for his traveling darkroom. Tiny and stark against the vast shifting dunes, the vehicle looks like a toy. We can easily imagine that all traces of its passing were erased by the wind soon after.

The acknowledged master of 20th-century landscape photography was Ansel Adams. Our illustration (**9.10**) shows one of his most famous pictures, *Moon and Half Dome*. Although the scene that Adams chose to photograph is undeniably dramatic, that alone does not account for the artistry of this picture. Adams had "set up" the shot by choosing a precise vantage point; by *framing* the photo precisely (that is, including just the portion of landscape he wanted and no more); and by waiting until the moon, light, and shadows seemed just right. The composition is perfectly balanced, with the dark foreground rock at left and the dark shadow at right framing the lighted expanse of the rock known as Half Dome. The brilliant moon at top not only completes the balance of the picture but is its major focal point. Light is used to define natural forms, to create contrast, to pick out textures and details; indeed, light structures the entire photograph. Adams demonstrates that the successful landscape photo, far from being a happy accident, is a demanding art.

The urban landscape was a favorite theme with Berenice Abbott, who did her most concentrated work during the 1930s. *Nightview, New York* (**9.11**) shows the city as a gleaming expanse of lights, pulsating with energy, yet clean and pure. No poor people huddle in the streets of this city—although they surely would have done so in this Depression year. No dirty papers collect in the gutters, no taxis blare their horns impatiently, no danger lurks in the dark side streets. To its four edges, this picture is filled with glittering light. Abbott shows us not the harsh reality of the city, but the magic we all hope to find in the metropolis.

THE HERE AND NOW The long exposure time and bulky equipment of early photography meant that a photograph was still a special occasion, an occasion for standing still. By the 1880s, however, technical advances had reduced exposure time to a fraction of a second, allowing the cameras to capture life as it happened, without asking it to pose. Then, in 1888, an American named George Eastman developed a camera called the Kodak that changed photography forever. Unlike earlier cameras, the Kodak was lightweight and handheld, which meant it could be taken anywhere. Sold with the slogan "You press the button, we do the rest," the camera came loaded with film for one hundred photographs. Users simply took the pictures (which quickly became known as "snapshots") and sent the camera back to the company. Their developed and printed photographs were returned to them along with their camera, reloaded with film.

The Kodak and cameras like it opened photography up to middle-class amateurs, and it quickly became a popular hobby. While serious photographers continued (and still continue) to oversee the development and printing of their own work, they, too, benefited from the portable, lightweight technology. Almost anywhere a person could go, a camera could now go; almost anything a person could see, a camera could record. Daily life, the life we live now, became photography's newest and perhaps most profound subject.

9.10 (left) Ansel Adams. *Moon and Half Dome.* 1966. Photograph. Courtesy The Ansel Adams Publishing Rights Trust/CORBIS.

9.11 (right) Berenice Abbott. *Nightview, New York.* 1932. Gelatin silver print. © Berenice Abbott/Commerce Graphics Ltd., Inc.

Taken in 1910, *Crow Camp* (**9.12**) records a moment in the life of a Crow Indian family. A man stands in front of a dwelling, a tipi. In his arms he gently cradles a child. His wife and family look on from the foreground. The photograph may record a naming ceremony, a Crow tradition that continues to this day. Many fascinating photographs of American Indians have been preserved from the early decades of photography, most taken by European Americans determined to document what they saw as an exotic, sometimes noble, sometimes savage, but certainly vanishing way of life. What is remarkable about this photograph, however, is precisely that it is unremarkable, an ordinary human moment of family affection and intimacy. Not incidently, the photographer, Richard Throssel, was an American Indian himself, born a Cree and later adopted by the Crow people. The view is a view from inside, not "this is how we see you" but "this is how we see *ourselves*, this is what is important to *us*."

Contemporary photographer Raghubir Singh celebrated the realities of the here and now in India, and in doing so he gave the world a clear-eyed view of modern life in a country that many think of as exotic or picturesque, the land of the Taj Mahal, silks and spices, and jewel-toned miniature paintings. *Through a Jewelry Store, Bombay* (**9.13**) presents a view of a busy urban scene made magical by the reflections of lights that seem to dance over the heads of the pedestrians, as though a parallel universe were suddenly visible for a moment.

PHOTOGRAPHY IN PRINT: PHOTOJOURNALISM

Newspapers during the 19th century were illustrated with wood engravings or lithographs. Honoré Daumier, for example, drew his powerful lithograph *Murder in the Rue Transnonain* (see 3.14) for a newspaper. Winslow Homer, whose watercolor of the Bahamas we looked at in Chapter 7 (see 7.11), earned his living for many years as a freelance illustrator, supplying drawings and paintings that were translated into wood engravings or lithographs.

The most important event that Homer covered as a visual reporter was the American Civil War. Mathew Brady and other photographers also went to the war, which became the first major conflict to be documented in photographs. Yet Brady's photographs also had to be translated into wood engravings to appear in the news, for the technology did not yet exist to print photographs

9.12 Richard Throssel. *Crow Camp, 1910.*
Modern print from a negative in the Lorenzo Creel Collection, Special Collections, University of Nevada, Reno Library.

commercially on ordinary paper. Then, around 1900, the first process for photomechanical reproduction—high-speed printing of photographs along with type—came into being.

Today nearly every event that might remotely be considered newsworthy is covered by photojournalists, from the carnage of war to the escape of a pet snake in a residential neighborhood. News photographers must depend to a certain extent on luck. Their best pictures result when they are in the right place at the right time, when some extraordinary event occurs. Nevertheless, it is the photographer's skill that turns a record of an event into a great picture.

Photojournalism quickly became about more than just getting a photograph to illustrate an article. While a single photograph may be all the general public sees at the time, photojournalists often create a significant body of work around an event, place, or culture. A historical episode that brought out the best in many of the finest photographers of the day was the Great Depression in the United States. The Great Depression, which began in 1929 and lasted until the onset of World War II, caused hardships for photographers as well as for the population as a whole. To ease the first problem and document the second, the Farm Security Administration (FSA) of the U.S. Department of Agriculture subsidized photographers and sent them out to record conditions across the nation. One of these was Dorothea Lange.

Dorothea Lange's travels for the FSA took her to nearly every part of the country. In one summer alone she logged 17,000 miles in her car. Lange devoted her attention to the migrants who had been uprooted from their farms by the combined effects of Depression and drought. *Heading West, Tulare Lake, California* (**9.14**) shows a mother and her two children, dirty and disheveled, in a battered truck. Despair is written on all three faces, as the eyes stare off at some distant point that may offer no relief from misery. Lange's masterful composition gives an importance, a universal quality, to the tragedy of one family. The picture's basic structure is a triangle, with the boy's head at the apex, one side running down through his leg, the other diagonal through the mother's head and the younger child, and the base resting on the bottom of the photo. FSA photos like this one were offered free to newspapers and magazines.

9.13 (left) Raghubir Singh.
Through a Jewelry Store, Bombay.
1997.
Courtesy the artist.

9.14 (right) Dorothea Lange.
Heading West, Tulare Lake, California. 1939. Photograph.
Library of Congress, Washington, D.C.

9.15 Sebastião Salgado. *Gold Miners at Serra Palada, Para, Brazil, 1987.*

During the 1950s and 1960s, a series of popular, large-format periodicals brought photojournalism to a broad public. Editors, art directors, writers, and photographers collaborated closely on stories that were told equally through photographs and words. The rise of television put an end to these magazines, and today, while photojournalists still provide images for news stories, they rely principally on museums, galleries, and books to reach the public with a more extended body of work.

One of the most widely respected photojournalists working today is Brazilian-born Sebastião Salgado. His photograph of gold miners illustrated here (**9.15**) is from his book *Workers: An Archaeology of the Industrial Age.* In *Workers,* Salgado explores and exposes the persistence of hard physical labor in an age when the machine is thought largely to have made such grueling work obsolete. The photographs are at once a tribute to the workers themselves and an exposé of the often harsh conditions of their lives. "I don't want anyone to appreciate the light or the palette of tones," the photographer has said. "I want my pictures to inform, to provoke discussion—and to raise money."[5] The formal beauty of Salgado's photographs is undeniable, however, and it raises a central paradox of art, and especially of photojournalism: Would the images hold our attention and speak to us so urgently if they were not also beautiful?

PHOTOGRAPHY AND ART

The development of photography has been seen as freeing painting and sculpture from practical tasks such as recording appearances and events, and it is certainly true that Western artists began to explore the potential of abstraction and nonrepresentation only after photography was well established. Ironically, to many people's way of thinking, these older forms took the definition of "art" with them, leaving photography to assume many of the traditional functions of art with none of the rewards.

Yet from the beginning there were photographers and critics who insisted that photography could also be practiced as an art. Today, over 150 years later, photography is fully integrated into the art world of museums and galleries, and many artists who are not primarily photographers work with photographic images. This brief section looks at how photography found its way both *as* an art and *into* art.

The existing art that photography resembled most was painting. In practicing photography as an art, many early photographers naturally turned to painting as a model. A wonderful example is Henry Peach Robinson's *Fading Away* (**9.16**). The English public of the day reveled in paintings that told a story, preferably a sentimental one. Robinson created his photograph with this audience in mind. We see a young woman on her deathbed. For all that she is about to expire, she looks remarkably beautiful and remarkably healthy. Her grieving relatives hover at the bedside (one turns toward the window in despair), as our heroine prepares to expel her last shuddering breath. But this scene is not real. It was posed; in fact, it was made as a composite image from five separate negatives. The people are actors, and they were carefully arranged in this stagy episode.

One aspect of photography that some felt stood in the way of making art was its detailed objectivity, which seemed more suited to science. In a movement called pictorialism, photographers used a variety of techniques to undercut the objectivity of the camera, producing gauzy, atmospheric images that seemed more painterly, and thus more like art. An important American pictorialist was the photographer Alfred Stieglitz. Stieglitz, however, grew dissatisfied with pictorialism. He came to the conclusion that for photography to be an art, it must be true to its own nature; it should not try to be painting.

9.16 Henry Peach Robinson. *Fading Away.* 1858. Albumen composite print, 9⅝ × 15⅜". The Royal Photographic Society, Bath.

ALFRED STIEGLITZ
1864–1946

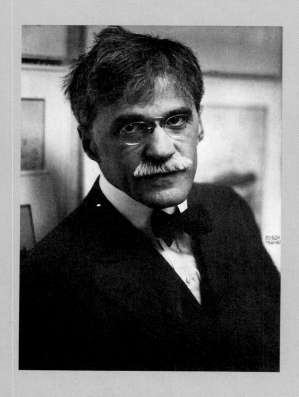

IF ONE HAD to choose the individual most responsible for establishing photography as an art form, the strongest candidate probably would be Alfred Stieglitz. Born in Hoboken, New Jersey, Stieglitz was the eldest child of German parents. His youth was spent in travel between Europe and the United States, and he studied at both the City College of New York and the University of Berlin. In 1883, at the age of nineteen, Stieglitz bought his first camera in Berlin; thereafter his life's work seems never to have been in doubt.

Stieglitz settled more or less permanently in New York in 1890, although he continued to travel widely. The first of his major efforts to promote photography as an art form came in 1896, when he was instrumental in founding the Camera Club of New York. The following year he became editor of its quarterly publication, *Camera Notes*. But the group most closely associated with his name was the "Photo-Secession," founded in 1902. A loosely structured national organization of photographers, the Photo-Secession was devoted to promoting exhibitions of photographers, later of contemporary painters and sculptors as well.

Stieglitz served as editor of its quarterly, *Camera Work*, which maintained extremely high standards for photographs published and reproduction quality.

As a photographer, Stieglitz dedicated his talents to demonstrating that the medium was accessible to anyone, even those with unsophisticated equipment and little training. He often worked with the simplest cameras, had his photographs printed commercially, and delighted in shooting under difficult conditions—in rain, fog, and darkness. His pictures were exhibited widely and were collected by major museums.

In 1905 Stieglitz, along with photographer Edward Steichen—whose portrait of Stieglitz is shown here—opened the Little Galleries of the Photo-Secession at 291 Fifth Avenue in New York, usually called "291." There the American public viewed the work of "art" photographers and also had its first opportunity to see the paintings of Picasso, Matisse, Cézanne, and other avant-garde European artists, as well as the most innovative Americans. Through his gallery Stieglitz had great influence on the spread of modern art.

Among the artists showing at 291 was the painter Georgia O'Keeffe. In 1918 Stieglitz left his first wife and moved in with O'Keeffe, whom he married after his divorce became final. His photographic portraits of O'Keeffe, including many close-up studies of her hands, are among his most sensitive and striking images. Although Stieglitz and O'Keeffe were frequently apart, often at different parts of the globe (their chronology for the next twenty years or so reads like a travelogue), they remained married until his death at eighty-two.

Stieglitz wrote extensively about his work, but perhaps the most characteristic statement can be found in the catalogue notes he prepared for an exhibition of his photographs in 1921: "My teachers have been life—work—continuous experiment. Incidentally a great deal of hard thinking. Any one can build on this experience with means available to all.... I was born in Hoboken. I am an American. Photography is my passion. The search for Truth my obsession."[6]

Edward Steichen. *Alfred Stieglitz at "291."* 1915.
Gray pigment gum-bichromate over platinum or gelatin silver, 11⅜ × 9⁹⁄₁₆".
The Metropolitan Museum of Art, New York.

The photograph that has become most closely associated with Stieglitz's revolutionary idea is *The Steerage* (**9.17**). The story of how *The Steerage* was made illustrates our point about photographers moving through the world with an invisible frame behind their eyes. In 1907 Stieglitz was aboard ship on his way to Europe, traveling first class. One day as he was walking the deck, he happened to look down into the lowest-class section, called steerage. Before him he saw a perfectly composed photograph—the smokestack leaning to the left at one end, the iron stairway leaning to the right at the other, the chained drawbridge cutting across, even such details as the round straw hat on the man looking down and the grouping of women and children below. Stieglitz knew he had only one unexposed plate left (the equivalent of one exposure at the end of a roll of film). He raced to his cabin to get his camera. When he returned, the scene was exactly the same; no one had moved. That one plate became *The Steerage*.

The type of photography that Stieglitz championed came to be known as "pure" or "straight" photography. Practitioners of "pure" photography consider it a point of honor not to crop or manipulate their photographs in any way. The composition is entirely visualized in advance, framed with the viewfinder, then photographed and printed. We might ask what difference there is between this kind of photography and photojournalism. The answer must lie in the intentions of the artist, and not the photograph itself. The photojournalist Salgado, for example, took his photograph of Brazilian gold miners primarily to draw our attention to their working conditions (see 9.15), while Stieglitz took his photograph of passengers primarily to record a chance alignment of formal elements. Yet Salgado's photograph is just as carefully composed as Stieglitz', while Stieglitz' photograph does, in fact, show something of the conditions of the poor immigrants in steerage.

At the same time that early-20th-century painters were experimenting with abstraction by simplifying forms and reducing them to their most characteristic aspects, photographers discovered that a camera, too, could produce abstract images. In *Abstraction* (**9.18**), Paul Strand used a close-up view to

9.17 (left) Alfred Stieglitz. *The Steerage*. 1907. Chloride print, 13¹/₈ × 10⁷/₁₆".
The Art Institute of Chicago.

9.18 (right) Paul Strand. *Abstraction*. 1915. Photogravure, 8¹⁵/₁₆ × 6⁹/₁₆".
The Museum of Modern Art, New York.

9.19 Hannah Höch. *Cut with the Kitchen Knife Dada through Germany's Last Weimar Beer Belly Cultural Epoch.* 1919. Collage, 44⅞ × 35⅜".
Staatliche Museen zu Berlin, Preussischer Kulturbesitz, Nationalgalerie.

obscure the literal subject of his photograph, creating instead an abstract composition of repeating curves. Used in this way, photography turned out to be not only a new way of recording reality but also a new way of seeing it.

With the development of photomechanical reproduction—which brought photographs into newspapers, periodicals, posters, and advertising—everyday life was suddenly flooded with photographic images. Artists were quick to recognize that this constant flow of secondhand reality constituted a new kind of experience, and that life had fundamentally changed. Artists such as Hannah Höch used these "found" images as a new kind of raw material for art.

Höch's *Cut with the Kitchen Knife* (**9.19**) combines images and letters from printed sources to portray the overwhelming experience of a modern city with its masses of people and machines. The word *dada* that appears in several places refers to the art movement that Höch belonged to. **Dada** was formed in 1916 as a reaction to the unprecedented slaughter of World War I, which was then being fought. The word *dada* itself has no meaning, for, faced with the horror of mechanized killing and the corruption of the societies that allowed it, Dada refused to make sense in traditional ways. A Dada manifesto written in 1918, the year the war ended, called for an art "which has been visibly shattered by the explosions of the last week, which is forever trying to collect its limbs after yesterday's crash. The best and most extraordinary artists will be those who every hour snatch the tatters of their bodies out of the frenzied cataract of life."[7] Höch, for her part, spent her life snatching bits and pieces from the frenzied cataract of images.

Another artistic movement that arose after World War I was **Surrealism.** Surrealist artists were fascinated by the unconscious, and they looked for the intrusion of strange, dreamlike moments into ordinary, everyday life. Photography turned out to be an excellent Surrealist medium, for nothing could be more matter-of-fact than a photograph, and yet by taking a moment

from the flow of time and freezing it for our inspection, it often revealed something strange. Henri Cartier-Bresson's *Valencia, 1933* (**9.20**) illustrates this well. Here, a straightforward "pure" photograph looks almost like a collage, so ambiguous are the spatial relationships. Like a dream, it seems full of mysterious signs that must have a meaning, if only we could understand them—the number 7, the half circle, the reflecting eyeglass lens, the face in the rectangle, the blurred man at the left who turns to us. In life, this moment would soon give way to another, and we could never have appreciated all of its details. Only photography could freeze it when, just for this fraction of a second, everything came together.

"Pure" photography is a judgmental name, for it implies that other ways of making a picture are "impure." However, artists have always been ready to experiment with new technology. If we think of the camera as a tool for making images instead of as a tool for recording the world, then there are no "right" or "wrong" ways to use it, only choices, discoveries, and experiments.

The Surrealist artist Man Ray experimented with several unusual photographic techniques in the 1920s and 1930s. One of them was solarization, a process by which an exposed negative is briefly reexposed to light during development. This causes chemical changes in the photographic emulsion—the light-sensitive coating on film. Actually, although Man Ray's name is usually associated with solarization, it may have been his companion at the time, photographer Lee Miller, who discovered the effect—albeit accidentally. She has written:

> Something crawled across my foot in the darkroom and I let out a yell and turned on the light. I never did find out what it was, a mouse or what. Then I realized that the film was totally exposed: there in the development tanks, ready to be taken out, were a dozen practically fully developed negatives of a nude against a black background. Man Ray grabbed them, put them in the [fixer solution] and looked at them.[8]

Miller's own portrait of a woman shows the effect that can be produced when the "accident" is controlled (**9.21**). This image combines the visual appearance of a photographic negative *and* a positive print. The ghostly dark shadows around the hand and parts of the face give the woman's portrait an otherworldly quality.

9.20 (above) Henri Cartier-Bresson. *Valencia, 1933*. Gelatin silver print, 12^{15}/$_{16}$ × 19 ^{7}/$_{16}$″. Museum of Modern Art, New York.

9.21 (below) Lee Miller. *Solarized Portrait of an Unknown Woman*. 1930. Gelatin silver print, 9½ × 7½″. Lee Miller Archives, Chiddingly.

Like Alfred Stieglitz and Paul Strand, whose works we looked at earlier (9.17, 9.18), Miller uses formal elements to insist that her image is as much about being a photograph as it is about what it depicts. Other artists have continued along the path pioneered by Hannah Höch (see 9.19) and draw attention to the role of photography in our society and the assumptions we make about it. Duane Michals, for example, uses straightforward but effective means to explore the limits of photography to document our own lives in *This Photograph Is My Proof* (**9.22**). "She did love me. Look, see for yourself," the text urges. And we do look, but what we see is that the photograph does not prove what he so desperately wants it to. No photograph could. We can take all the pictures we want, but we can never know what someone else is really thinking, and in love that is all that matters.

Cindy Sherman uses photography to create images of herself as someone else, often a woman she has invented or a woman who appears in a famous work of art. *Untitled Film Still* (**9.23**) is from a series of photographs

9.22 (below, top) Duane Michals. *This Photograph Is My Proof.* 1967, 1974. Gelatin silver print with hand-applied text, 8 × 13″. Courtesy Pace/MacGill Gallery, New York.

9.23 (below) Cindy Sherman. *Untitled Film Still.* 1978. Black-and-white photograph, 8 × 10″.

that pretend to be stills from grade-B Hollywood movies of the 1940s and 1950s. The moments Sherman chose to invent constitute a virtual catalogue of stereotypical roles for young women of the time. Here, Sherman plays the plucky young girl who has come to the big city. She works as a secretary, perhaps. She is apprehensive—the city can be an intimidating place at first!—but determined and resourceful.

Photography's ability to capture detail is exploited to haunting effect in Andres Serrano's *Black Supper (II)* (**9.24**). Serrano took a small plaster souvenir sculpture of Leonardo's famous mural (see 4.41), painted it black, and immersed it in water. Gradually the air trapped inside the plaster emerged, covering the sculpture with minuscule bubbles. The result, captured in photography and enlarged to a height of 5 feet, is a strange unearthly beauty. The figures seem to be molded out of the night itself, covered in globes of silver or mercury and set with stars. Serrano's goal was to restore an aura of mystery and wonder to religious images that had become overly familiar, and also to explore his unresolved feelings about the Catholicism of his childhood. A kind of mystical dream vision, *Black Supper (II)* shows the continuing influence of Surrealism in the 20th century, as well as the ability of photography to transform its subject, not just record it.

The computer has been welcomed by many artists who work with photography as a natural extension of the medium. Recently developed digital cameras use no film at all, but instead store photographs as data on disk. A

9.24 Andres Serrano. *Black Supper (II)*. 1990. Cibachrome print, 60 × 40″. Courtesy Paula Cooper Gallery, New York.

CENSORSHIP: ROBERT MAPPLETHORPE

THE PHOTOGRAPH BY Andres Serrano called *Black Supper II* (see 9.24) was one of a series of works in which the artist photographed religious icons through various fluids, especially bodily fluids. Another work in the series was *Piss Christ,* a photograph of 1987 showing a crucifix immersed in a radiantly lit, yellowish liquid that turned out to be the artist's own urine. Despite the strange beauty of the image and Serrano's many interesting statements about his intentions, the description of the work together with its provocative title caused a furor among conservative social organizations.

Serrano was one of several artists whose work enraged conservatives during the late 1980s. The situation came to a head over a group of photographs called the "X Portfolio," by the photographer Robert Mapplethorpe. Starting in 1976, with his first solo exhibition, Mapplethorpe gained considerable fame, but the fame acquired a troublesome edge when the public at large became aware of his "X Portfolio," for that series of photographs contains images of sadomasochism and homoeroticism, images so frank as

to be profoundly disturbing to many (even most) viewers.

Mapplethorpe died of AIDS in the spring of 1989. Soon after, an exhibition of his work was organized, including several examples from the "X Portfolio." The show was planned to tour the United States. Here the saga begins, and it probably will be discussed and debated in art circles for many years to come.

The Mapplethorpe show was scheduled to open at Washington's Corcoran Gallery of Art, a public museum, in the summer of 1989. Before the opening, however, it came to the attention of Senator Jesse Helms, Republican of North Carolina, who denounced the photographs as obscene. Senator Helms' chief objection was that part of the funding for the exhibition had come from the National Endowment for the Arts—in other words, from American taxpayers. His attempt to persuade Congress to prohibit funding for work he considered obscene caused a furor, with intense argument on both sides. In the heat of this controversy, the Corcoran canceled, but the show later opened, to general acclaim, at Washington's Project for the Arts.

After Washington, the Mapplethorpe show moved to Hartford, Connecticut, and Berkeley, California; in both places it ran without major incident or protest. Next on the itinerary, however, was a city well known for its strict opposition to pornography: Cincinnati. And in Cincinnati the controversy became an uproar. No longer was the issue merely public funding. Now it became: Should these photographs be shown at all?

On opening day in Cincinnati, police closed the Contemporary Arts Center while they videotaped the exhibition for evidence. Then the exhibition was reopened, and it played to huge crowds for the duration of its stay. But a grand jury indicted both the gallery and its director on obscenity charges. If convicted, the gallery's director could serve up to a year in jail.

Before discussing the outcome of the trial, it might be well to pause and consider some of the issues involved. Is the Mapplethorpe case really a matter of censorship, and what, in fact, is censorship?

For our purposes here, we will define censorship as the supervision by one individual or group over the artistic expression of another individual or group. This definition assumes that person or group A has the power to control the expression of person or group B. Usually, the power is exerted for political, religious, or moral reasons. In other words, A can prevent B from making or showing work that conflicts with A's political, religious, or moral point of view.

We expect to find censorship in totalitarian societies, and we are seldom disappointed. Absolute rule survives only *because* it is absolute, so it cannot tolerate other points of view. But in the United States today censorship for political reasons is far less an issue than is censorship concerning religious or moral standards.

We have a pluralistic society, representing many religions, many moral points of view. People of goodwill and thoughtful convictions disagree about what is "right" or "wrong," what should be allowed or not allowed. One of the most explosive areas of disagreement concerns the issue of free expression, specifically as it pertains to the arts. Should artists, writers, and performers be allowed to express whatever they wish? Or should there be limits on that expression to control material that large segments of society consider morally wrong?

Proponents of free expression cite the First Amendment to the Constitution, which states in part: "Congress shall make no law . . . abridging the freedom of speech." Yet that amendment does *not* give you the right to say anything you please. You cannot, for example, deliberately tell a lie about another person, either verbally (slander) or in print (libel). Such lies are prohibited, and the other person could sue you.

In a classic example from the early part of this century, Supreme Court Justice Oliver Wendell Holmes, Jr., said, "No one has a right falsely to shout 'fire' in a crowded theatre." So freedom of speech is *not* absolute; it has limits. Moreover, the Supreme Court historically has held that it is permissible to ban obscene speech, obscene writing, obscene imagery. The problem lies in deciding just *what* is obscene.

As of this writing the Supreme Court standard for obscenity comes from a 1973 case called *Miller v. California*, which held that something is obscene if the "average person applying contemporary community standards" would find it so, and if "the work taken as a whole lacks serious literary, artistic, political or scientific value." Obviously, this judgment raises more questions than it answers. Who is the average person? Which community? Who decides whether the artistic value is serious?

Further complicating the problem is the issue of public funding for the arts. Many people feel that tax-payers' money should not be used to support the arts at all. Others think the government should finance the arts, but not "obscene" art—whatever that is. Those who oppose limits on spending fear that such limits would lead to a situation like the one that has existed in totalitarian societies, where government controls the arts rigidly.

In our system we pay our taxes and allow our elected representatives to decide how the money should be spent. And in 1965 Congress passed the National Foundation on the Arts and Humanities Act, whose declaration of purpose includes this statement: "It is necessary and appropriate for the Federal Government to help create and sustain not only a climate encouraging freedom of thought, imagination and inquiry, but also the material conditions facilitating the release of this creative talent."

Again as of this writing, funding for the National Endowment for the Arts has been sharply curtailed but will continue. Grants to individual artists have been eliminated. Only organizations and institutions may now apply. The question of funding for "obscene" art—and the method of determining what is "obscene"—remains vague. Of course, there will *never* be absolute answers to any of these questions, answers acceptable to everyone. Readers of this book must make up their own minds, as the courts continue to grapple with these complex issues. That brings us back to the Mapplethorpe case.

Six months after the Cincinnati gallery and its director were indicted on obscenity charges, a jury of local citizens found them not guilty. The jurors were not art experts; most of them had never been in an art museum, knew nothing about art, and cared little about it. Yet they were willing to be guided by opinions of people who were presented to them as experts, art professionals brought in by the defense. As one juror said afterward, "We had to go with what we were told. It's like Picasso. Picasso from what everybody tells me was an artist. It's not my cup of tea. I don't understand it. But if people say it's art, then I have to go along with it."

The Mapplethorpe jurors were "average persons" who, even when applying the standards of a rather conservative "community," found that the works in question *did* have "serious artistic value." That was the resolution of one case, but there will be many cases, and the question of censorship can never have a definite answer.

printing process has also been developed to print images directly from a computer onto standard photography paper. For photojournalists, digital cameras allow images to be transmitted back to a newspaper over telephone lines, like e-mail. For artists, the new technology allows them to gather photographic images, feed them into a computer, work with them, and print the end product as a photograph.

With photographs such as Mariko Mori's *Empty Dream* (**9.25**), we have come full circle back to the Victorian work that opened this section (see 9.16). Like Robinson's *Fading Away*, Mori's image is pieced together, but this time on a computer. The scene is completely and deliriously artificial, including Mori's own multiple appearances as a fetching mermaid and a sky that seems to be printed on a giant screen. We aren't expected to believe it for a moment. We are only expected to enjoy how photography can make the impossible seem real in the same way that dreams seem real.

The ability of photography to bear witness to a vanished past underlies the power of Christian Boltanski's *Altar to the Chases High School* (**9.26**). Chases was a private Jewish high school in Vienna. Boltanski began with a photograph that he found of the graduating class of 1931. Eighteen years old in the photograph, the students would have been twenty-seven when Austria was annexed by Germany at the start of World War II. Most probably perished in the death camps, victims of the Nazi program to exterminate the Jews of Europe. Boltanski rephotographed each face, then enlarged the results into a series of blurry portraits. The effect is as though someone long gone were calling out to us; we try to recognize them, but cannot quite. Our task is made even more difficult by the lights blocking their faces, lights that serve as halos on the one hand, but also remind us of interrogation lamps. We wonder, too, what the stacked tin boxes might hold. Ashes? Possessions? Documents? They have no labels, just as the blurred faces have almost no identities.

The first audiences for photography were both fascinated and disturbed by the new technology, and advances in photographic technologies still have the power both to intrigue us and to make us uneasy. Daniel Canogar explores this dual reaction in *Alien Memory* (**9.27**), which consists of photographs of body parts projected onto the walls of a room through a tangle of fiber optic cables. Fiber optic technology is used in medicine for endoscopy, a procedure that sends tiny exploratory lenses into the body to transmit back images of, for example, the inside of the stomach. The photographs here are mostly of orifices, openings in the body through which we are vulnerable to such invasions. Some orifices are open, while others are being covered up. "There is

9.25 Mariko Mori. *Empty Dream*. 1995. Cibachrome print, aluminum frame; 9′ × 24′ × 3″. Courtesy Deitch Projects, New York.

an innate curiosity to see inside the body, accompanied by a sense of horror at being invaded by alien technology," says the artist. "The work attempts to address this ambiguity by simultaneously opening and closing up, exposing and protecting."[9] Viewers must move through the room to experience *Alien Memory*, and as they do, they become part of it, for the images project onto their bodies, and their bodies cast shadows on the walls.

9.26 (left) Christian Boltanski. *Altar to the Chases High School.* 1987. Photographs, tin frames, metal lamps. Museum of Contemporary Art, Los Angeles.

9.27 (below) Daniel Canogar. *Alien Memory.* 1998. Fiber-optic cables, slides, light generator projected photographs; dimensions variable. Courtesy Galeria Helga de Alvear, Madrid.

PHOTOGRAPHY AND MOTION

Throughout history artists have tried to create the illusion of motion in a still image. Painters have drawn galloping horses, running people, action of all kinds—never being sure that their depictions of the movement were "correct" and lifelike. To draw a running horse with absolute realism, for instance, the artist would have to freeze the horse in one moment of the run, but because the motion is too quick for the eye to follow, the artist had no assurance a running horse ever does take a particular pose. In 1878 a man named Eadweard Muybridge addressed this problem, and the story behind his solution is a classic in the history of photography.

Leland Stanford, a former governor of California, had bet a friend twenty-five thousand dollars that a horse at full gallop sometimes has all four feet off the ground. Since observation by the naked eye could not settle the bet one way or the other, Stanford hired Muybridge, known as a photographer of landscapes, to photograph one of the governor's racehorses. Muybridge devised an ingenious method to take the pictures. He set up 24 cameras, each connected to a black thread stretched across the racecourse. As Stanford's mare ran down the track, she snapped the threads that triggered the cameras' shutters—and proved conclusively that a running horse does gather all four feet off the ground at certain times (**9.28**). Stanford won the bet, and Muybridge went on to more ambitious studies of motion. In 1887, he published *Animal Locomotion*, his most important work. With 781 plates of people and animals in sequential motion, *Animal Locomotion* allowed the world to see for the first time what positions living creatures really assume when they move.

The decades following Muybridge's experiments saw increasing sophistication in photographic equipment. As both films and cameras became faster, photographers discovered the ability to *stop* motion to the split second.

9.28 Eadweard Muybridge. *Horse Galloping.* 1878. Collotype, 9³⁄₁₆ × 12″. Courtesy George Eastman House, Rochester, New York.

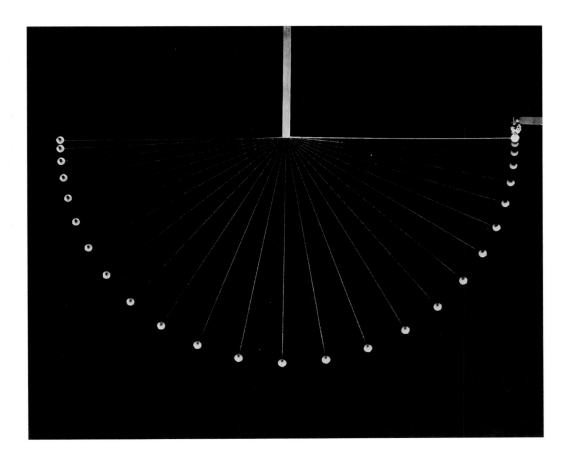

In the late 1950s, Berenice Abbott, whose photograph of New York at night we looked at earlier (see 9.11), took this multiple stop-action photograph of the swing of a pendulum (**9.29**). Abbott had long been fascinated by science, and she was convinced that photography could build a bridge between science and the public. Her opportunity finally came in 1957, when, faced with superior Soviet achievements in space, the Physical Science Study Committee at the Massachusetts Institute of Technology began to develop a new and more rigorous science curriculum for American high schools. The committee was looking for a photographer to illustrate a projected textbook, and Abbott eagerly applied for the job. "I was never good at selling myself," she later recalled, "but this one time!"[10] Hired on the spot, Abbott spent the next two years creating innovative and elegant photographs illustrating scientific principles and, less happily, weathering the resentment of her usually younger, usually male colleagues.

Eadweard Muybridge's experiments in the 1880s had two direct descendants. One was stop-motion photography, such as we have seen in the last example. The other was *continuous*-motion photography. Undoubtedly, Muybridge had whetted the public's appetite to see *real* motion captured on film. The little room with a view had glimpsed a different world, a world that does not stand still but spins and moves and dances, and the public wanted more of this. The public did not have long to wait.

9.29 Berenice Abbott. *Pendulum Motion and Galileo* (also known as *The Transformation of Energy*). 1958–60. Gelatin silver print on mount board trimmed flush, $6 \times 7\frac{5}{8}''$.
© Berenice Abbott/Commerce Graphics Ltd., Inc.

FILM

On the night of December 28, 1895, a small audience gathered in the basement of a Paris café, which was to become the first commercial movie theater in history. The audience viewed several very short films, including one of a baby being fed its dinner, another of a gardener being doused by a hose. One film in particular caused a strong reaction. *L'Arrivée d'un train en gare (The Arrival of a Train at the Station)* set the audience to screaming, ducking for cover, and jumping from their seats, because it featured a train hurtling directly toward the viewers. Never before, except in real life, had people seen anything of the kind, and they responded automatically. From the beginning, motion pictures could make an image on a screen seem real indeed.

THE ORIGINS OF MOTION PICTURES

Film depends on a phenomenon called persistence of vision. The human brain retains a visual image for a fraction of a second longer than the eye actually records it. If this were not true, your visual perception of the world would be continually interrupted by blinks of your eyes. Instead, your brain "carries over" the visual image during the split second while the eyes are closed. Similarly, the brain carries over when still images are flashed before the eyes with only the briefest space between them. Motion-picture film is not real motion but a series of still images projected at a speed of 24 frames per second, which makes the action seem continuous.

Interest in moving pictures really predates the development of the still camera. As early as 1832 a toy was patented in Europe in which a series of drawn images, each slightly different from the next, was made to spin in a revolving wheel so that the image appeared to move. Eadweard Muybridge later applied this principle to his multiple photographic images, spinning them in a wheel he called the zoopraxiscope.

Commercial applications of the motion picture, however, awaited three major developments. In 1888 the American George Eastman introduced celluloid film, which made it possible to string images together. Another big step was taken by Thomas Edison, the famous American inventor. It was in Edison's laboratory, in 1894, that technicians created what was apparently the first genuine motion picture. Lasting only a few seconds, the film was made on celluloid. Its "star" was one of Edison's mechanics, a man who could sneeze amusingly on command. Its title: *Fred Ott's Sneeze*.

One major problem remained. There was no satisfactory method for projecting the films to an audience. Here the challenge was taken up by two Frenchmen, brothers appropriately named Lumière (*lumière* means "light"), who in 1895 succeeded in building a workable film projector. The films shown in that Paris café were made by the brothers Lumière. From that point the motion-picture industry was off and running.

The fabulous era of silent films began with the Lumières' movie snippets, and it lasted for just over thirty years. During that time a wholly new creature—the movie star—came into being. Silent-film stars filled a gap in the American consciousness, for they lived and behaved like royalty. Some would have long careers in the cinema. Others fell victim to the next major breakthrough in film technology. Sound film was introduced in 1927, and not all stars of the silent era could make the transition, for their voices did not match their physical attributes. Quite a few virile leading men and sultry leading ladies were discovered to have squeaky little voices.

By the late 1920s the camera—the little room with a view—had come of age. Soon it would see things undreamed of before. Filmmaking of the twenties and thirties seems amazing in at least three respects: the tiny budgets; the rapid production times—perhaps just two or three weeks of shooting; and the small number of people involved. Today a major film may cost tens of millions, be in production for a year or more, and involve hundreds of people. But from the beginning of motion-picture history the greatest films, the classic films, have often been the product of one creative imagination. Usually, though not always, the creative force behind an important film is its director. Let us turn now to a brief survey of classic films and the creative artists who made them.

FILMS AND FILMMAKERS

The word "epic," in films, suggests a picture that is long, crowded, and grand. Usually, an epic film has a story taken from some significant point in history, or perhaps from the Bible. It will employ many actors—the proverbial "cast of thousands"—in climactic scenes with considerable action, such as battles, riots, or natural disasters. Often, the epic film has a moral to preach to its audience. Through the history of film there have been many epics, but the pioneer of the form was a man named David Wark Griffith.

D. W. Griffith began his movie career in 1908 as a director of very short (ten-minute) silent films cranked out at the rate of two a week. This apprenticeship taught him much about the mechanics of filmmaking, so that by the time Griffith had attained greater creative independence, he was ready for it. In 1914 the producer-director shot his first feature-length picture, and even its title proclaims an epic: *The Birth of a Nation* (**9.30**). Griffith took his story from a contemporary novel. *The Birth of a Nation* is set in the American South before, during, and after the Civil War. In a now-familiar device, it interweaves the histories of two families—one northern, one southern—whose paths cross and whose members fall in love with one another. The plot allowed for many battle scenes and a particularly effective staging of President Lincoln's assassination. We must remember that this was a *silent* film. All action, all plot, all emotions had to be conveyed by visual images only, without dialogue or sound effects. (There was usually live musical accompaniment in the early movie theaters.)

Most viewers today would find it difficult to sit through *The Birth of a Nation*, for when it is not exaggerated in style it is offensive in its racial prejudice and simplistic morality. Even in its day some audiences reacted strenuously to these aspects of the movie. Reviewing the film on March 4, 1915, *The New York Times* complained about "melodramatic and inflammatory material." The *Times*, however, went on to evaluate "the film as a film" and deemed it "an impressive new illustration of the scope of the motion picture camera."[11] So it was, for Griffith had revolutionized the mechanics of filmmaking.

9.30 Scene from *Birth of a Nation*, directed by D. W. Griffith. Released 1915.

9.31 Charles Chaplin as "Charlie," the Little Tramp, in a scene from *Modern Times*, directed by Charles Chaplin. 1936.

Each unbroken sequence of movie frames, with the camera rolling, is called a shot. Before Griffith, the standard in the films had been the full shot, showing actors from head to toe. Griffith preferred to experiment with a range of shots for dramatic effect: the medium shot (from the waist up), the close-up (head and shoulders), the extreme close-up (part of a face), and the long shot (seen from the distance). Dissatisfied with the camera as immobile observer of a scene, Griffith developed the pan shot (camera moving from side to side) and the traveling shot (camera moving from back to front on a track). He also perfected the technique of cross-cutting, in which two or more scenes are alternated to advance the action of the film. For example, he might film scenes of a heroine in distress and her hero rushing to save her, then cut back and forth rapidly between the two in order to build suspense.

This last shows Griffith's mastery of film editing, or assembling the film creatively after all scenes have been photographed. In *The Birth of a Nation* Griffith also made effective use of the iris shot (see 9.30), in which the edges of the film are blacked out to create a circle of interest. *The Birth of a Nation* even has flashbacks, or cuts to episodes that are supposed to have taken place before the main action of the film. To sum up, Griffith had virtually written a menu of possibilities for future filmmakers.

The mechanics of filmmaking being in place, other creative movie people could focus on story line. The next great genius of the film was a man who tapped the endlessly entertaining possibilities of the human condition— of laughing at oneself and the ridiculous situations one encounters in daily life. His name was Charles Chaplin.

Chaplin began his career as an actor. Sometime in the years 1913–14 he began to develop the character of "Charlie," the Little Tramp, whom he played in most of his films. Physically, Charlie was what today we might call a "wimp"—undersized, clumsy, comical in appearance, wearing shoes and trousers far too big for him, sporting an absurd derby hat and a cane. Charlie was inevitably the one who got the pie in the face, the splash of slush from a passing streetcar, the foot caught in a goldfish bowl. He was the perennial outsider, always looking in wistfully at people who were rich, graceful, beautiful, and successful. But Charlie had courage, and he had a heart of gold.

He would rush to save a maiden in trouble, only to lose her affections to the handsome leading man. Charlie was Everyman adrift in a world where anything could go wrong, anybody could trip him up.

Through many silent films Chaplin refined the character of Charlie and also honed his skills as a filmmaker. Soon he was not only acting but writing, directing, and producing as well. By the 1930s Chaplin was at the top of his form. *Modern Times* (**9.31**) is considered by many to be his greatest film. In this movie Chaplin pits himself against the modern assembly line and, predictably, loses the contest. Chaplin's inventive genius goes into high gear as Charlie struggles against the machine and the machine fights back. *Modern Times* continues the battle of the odd little hero against adversity, but now his opponents are mechanical, not human. As with all his films, Chaplin concealed a message in *Modern Times*—that our fast-paced world is hard on innocent nonconformists—but the message is presented with side-splitting humor.

Color photography for films was feasible in the early 1930s. By the end of that decade it had been perfected sufficiently to be available to master producer David O. Selznick when he set out to film *Gone with the Wind*, Margaret Mitchell's best-selling novel of the Civil War. Filming *Gone with the Wind* presented a special problem. Mitchell's book had so thoroughly captivated the imaginations of millions of readers that a potential audience *knew* exactly what the movie should look like. Selznick took full charge of the project, overwhelming writers and directors, and he delivered. The movie of *Gone with the Wind* was, and remains, a tremendous success with audiences.

The color effects in *Gone with the Wind* are always vivid (**9.32**). For the most intense scenes, such as the burning of Atlanta, Selznick poured on a saturated red. Red worked for Selznick and the film on different levels. It is associated with the clayey soil of Georgia, where the story takes place. It is inherently dramatic. It often symbolizes passion, in this case the passions of war and the passion between those two lovers, Scarlett O'Hara and Rhett Butler. To our eyes now, accustomed to color films, the "scorched" effects of *Gone with the Wind* may seem a little exaggerated, but for that time and that movie they were exactly right.

9.32 "The Burning of Atlanta," scene from *Gone with the Wind*, produced by David O. Selznick. 1939.

Selznick's control of *Gone with the Wind* was considerable, but it may seem modest compared with the creative involvement by the next filmmaker we shall study. In 1941 R.K.O. released a film created almost single-handed by a twenty-six-year-old "boy genius" who played the starring role, produced and directed the film, co-authored the screenplay, supervised the editing and set design, and, it is said, even sewed some of the costumes himself. The film was not a success with contemporary audiences or critics. Today, however, when movie people compile lists of the "ten best" filmmakers and films, we are sure to find the names of Orson Welles and his masterpiece, *Citizen Kane* (**9.33**).

Welles based his story, loosely, on the life of the newspaper publisher William Randolph Hearst, here renamed Charles Foster Kane (played by Welles). What could have been a simple biography of a powerful man was turned by Welles into a startling cinematic achievement. *Citizen Kane* was innovative on a number of levels. Its structure, at first glance an ordinary flashback, begins with Kane's death, then traces his life from childhood and youth up through old age and back to his death again. But the actual telling of the story is far more complex than that. Kane's life on film is divided into five sections—the first played out in blaring newsreel films, the other four narrated in turn from the points of view of four people involved with Kane. Welles begins with a superficial outside view of the brash, successful young Kane, then gradually probes deeper and deeper into Kane's psychic center, as that center slowly disintegrates into lonely, bitter old age.

Cinematically, the movie opens the filmmaker's grab bag of tricks—all meant to highlight Kane's personality. There are low-angle shots (to show a towering Kane), dramatic long shots, and many traveling shots intended to convey physical and emotional separation. For instance, as Kane's relationship with his first wife becomes cooler, the camera shows the couple farther and farther apart at the ends of an ever-lengthening dinner table. Welles calculated every shot to convey the mood, the emotional symbols, the portrait of a character he intended. *Citizen Kane* could not be a stage play. It is too dependent on film techniques for its impact. More than any filmmaker before him, Welles had shown what the camera, used imaginatively, could do.

9.33 Orson Welles as Charles Foster Kane and Ruth Warrick as his first wife in a scene from *Citizen Kane,* produced and directed by Orson Welles. 1941.

With a few exceptions, American filmmakers dominated the industry in the early days, but by the 1950s and 1960s critical attention began to focus on European directors with serious aims. Two of these—one Swedish, one Italian—attracted special attention in the United States: Ingmar Bergman and Federico Fellini.

Ingmar Bergman's first internationally successful film, and some would say his greatest, was *The Seventh Seal*, made in 1957. *The Seventh Seal* is an allegory, a story filled with religious and macabre symbolism, set in the 14th century apparently in Sweden. As it begins, a knight returning from the Crusades is met on the beach by the figure of Death, who announces that the knight's time has come. Stalling for time, the knight challenges Death to a game of chess, and they agree that Death will not claim him until the game is over (**9.34**). The knight hopes to use this borrowed time to find some meaning in life, to accomplish some deed that he cannot name. As the game goes on intermittently, the knight and his squire, with other characters they meet, journey toward the knight's castle. Along the way they encounter a young couple, Jof (Joseph) and Mia (Mary) and their baby son—undoubtedly symbolic of the Christ child and his parents. In the end Death wins the chess game and calls the knight and his party to darkness, but the knight tricks Death into sparing the innocent couple and their baby.

Bergman, who both wrote and directed *The Seventh Seal*, was able to put an unusually personal stamp on this and all his films, because over the years he developed a close-knit repertory company of actors and supporting crew, accustomed to him and to one another. Both he and Welles are examples of what is called an **auteur.** The French word *auteur* translates literally as "author," but in relation to films it implies a great deal more. A cinematic *auteur* has maximum control over a film's production and imparts an individual style to a film or series of films. He or she often writes the screenplay—or closely supervises its writing—and may draw upon personal imagery, dreams, obsessions, fears, memories, beliefs, or loves as subject matter. This was certainly true of Ingmar Bergman, and it was equally true of his counterpart in Italy, Federico Fellini.

9.34 Death and the knight playing chess, from *The Seventh Seal*, directed by Ingmar Bergman. 1957.

Where Bergman is somber and melancholy, Fellini is flamboyant. His films may at first seem lighthearted, but there is a darker quality beneath the surface. A good example of this complexity is found in one of Fellini's best-known films, *La Dolce Vita*. The title, translated as "the sweet life," surely is ironic, for Fellini's camera zeroes in on people for whom life has become a series of superficial, momentary pleasures, carried to the extreme of depravity. Contrasts are made throughout the film between the old, stable values and society's new focus on instant sensual gratification. Fellini establishes this in his opening sequence, when a huge Christ figure is carried dangling from a helicopter over the city of Rome (**9.35**). A number of young women in bikinis, sunbathing on a rooftop, rise to wave at it. The symbolism is apt. Rome is, after all, a city of many churches, the seat of the Roman Catholic Church. But the Romans caught by Fellini's camera are more interested in indulgences of the flesh. They are rich, privileged, idle, and dissolute. Major events in the film include a suicide and an orgy. Fellini's message seems to be that this "sweet life" is not sweet at all, but poisonous; its participants not alive, but acting out a living death.

Despite the prominence of European filmmakers, Hollywood still could support a serious filmmaker, indeed an *auteur*, and it found its own in the person of a transplanted English director named Alfred Hitchcock. We might describe Hitchcock as the "purest" of filmmakers in the sense that his fascination lay almost entirely with the techniques of the camera. Hitchcock had limited interest in story line, even less in dialogue, and he did not much care to direct his performers in interpreting their lines. Actually, by the time the cameras were ready to roll and the actors were in position, most of his creative work was over—a remarkable stance for a director. For Hitchcock, by then, would have plotted every shot to the last detail, established the camera angles and cuts, visualized the completed film. No editor could tamper with his work afterward, because, contrary to the usual practice, he did not shoot several versions of each scene. He shot only what he wanted in the film, what he had determined beforehand.

We see Hitchcock's masterful control of visual imagery in a classic scene from his thriller *North by Northwest*, released in 1959 (**9.36**). The hero, played by Cary Grant, has been duped into riding a bus to an isolated spot in the middle of a cornfield. There he stands, waiting for a supposed meeting with a man he does not know (and who, it turns out, does not exist). As

9.35 Opening sequence of *La Dolce Vita*, directed by Federico Fellini. 1959.

9.36 Cary Grant in a scene from *North by Northwest*, directed by Alfred Hitchcock. 1959.

Grant waits in the hot sun, there is no sound but the scrunch of his feet on the ground. Hitchcock gives no "meaningful" background music. Then a small airplane appears in the distance, flies closer, and heads directly for Grant. We realize the plane is trying to mow him down. Again, there is no sound but the airplane's engine and Grant's breathing as he runs this way and that, trying to elude the plane. The scene is eerily terrifying, not least because viewers are unprepared for the spectacle of a man in a business suit, stranded in flat country, trying to escape death from a dive-bombing airplane.

Considered logically, this scene is absurd; businessmen do not get attacked by murderous airplanes. Considered cinematically, it is a triumph—a life-and-death struggle of man against anonymous machine. Hitchcock spoke of how he planned this scene to be the *opposite* of what normally we would expect to be a menacing situation. Most filmmakers, setting up danger, would show darkness, looming buildings, mysterious figures peering from windows. Not Hitchcock. He gave us: "Just nothing. Just bright sunshine and a blank, open countryside with barely a house or tree in which any lurking menaces could hide."[12] That is the genius of Hitchcock's technique. Menace drops out of the sky into ordinary life.

In today's world of dazzlingly high-budget films, with their consequent monetary risk, it is unusual for a filmmaker to have the kind of absolute creative freedom that Hitchcock did. One filmmaker who has managed to maintain the position of *auteur* right up to the present is Woody Allen. Allen, who began his career as a stand-up comic and gag writer, began making films in 1969 and has averaged one a year since then. He first achieved both critical and commercial success with *Annie Hall* in 1977, and since then his reputation as a "genius" filmmaker has grown steadily. Legends gain special privileges, and Allen is aware of his extraordinary position when he says, "I have control of everything, and I mean everything. I can make any film I want to make. Any subject—comic, serious. I can cast who I want to cast."

And Allen *does* make any film he wants to make. Hating to repeat himself, he has experimented with various genres—comedies, dramas, fantasies, a mystery, even a musical. Nearly always, however, there is an aura of glamour, of sophistication, a "sheen" on his films that sets them apart from everyday life. He says: "I've never felt Truth was Beauty. Never. I've always felt that people can't take too much reality. . . . You spend your whole life searching for a way out."[13]

9.37 (left) Jeff Daniels and Mia Farrow in a scene from *The Purple Rose of Cairo,* directed by Woody Allen. 1984.
Orion (courtesy Kobal).

9.38 (right) Scene from *King Kong.* 1932.

One of Allen's favorite films—and the public's—is *The Purple Rose of Cairo,* released in 1984 (**9.37**). In the film a young woman (Mia Farrow), whose life is drab and humdrum, escapes to the movie theater, where, sitting rapt in the dark, she can lose herself in the romantic scenes being played out on the screen. When a movie called "The Purple Rose of Cairo" is playing, she sees it over and over, and falls swooningly in love with its hero (Jeff Daniels). Then an amazing thing happens. While the movie is playing, the hero suddenly steps right off the screen, walks down the theater aisle, and approaches the young woman. He enters her world, and eventually draws her into his fantasy world. In other words, her workaday Truth interacts and collides with his fantasy Beauty. The ensuing developments are both comic and poignant.

Like most of the films we have considered, *The Purple Rose of Cairo* is basically "straight." Its view is of a world that *could* be real, even if it isn't exactly real. Before closing our brief discussion of the film, we should look at another kind of world that is often captured in the camera—a world in which dogs talk, giant apes climb on buildings, creatures from other planets land in the suburbs of California, and galaxies go to war with one another. This is the world of special effects and animation.

SPECIAL EFFECTS AND ANIMATION

King Kong was not the first film to employ special effects, but it was certainly one of the more memorable. Made in 1932, *King Kong* is an adventure story concerning a giant gorilla, some 50 feet tall, which is captured in Africa and somehow transported to New York for display as a curiosity. Also, the film is an odd kind of love story, because when Kong inevitably escapes from his captors, he falls in love with a normal-sized woman and carries her around with him. Mostly, though, *King Kong* was an opportunity to try some of the most imaginative and startling visual effects yet attempted on film.

The model of Kong used for filming was about 18 inches tall. Through trick photography the figure was transformed into a monster capable of climbing the Empire State Building and grabbing at the airplanes that try to shoot him down (**9.38**). Effects like these were achieved because filmmakers had become more comfortable with the potential of the camera. No longer need anyone's imagination be limited by physical constraints. A filmmaker could daydream, "What if a giant ape climbed the Empire State Building?" and then proceed to make it happen on film. In life or on the stage, such a feat would present staggering difficulties. In film, anything is possible.

Animation is another tool that expands the filmmaker's range of possibilities. The word *animation* means "bringing to life," and that is precisely what the filmic animator does with drawings of people, animals, and inanimate objects. Animated films are, in principle, little more than sophisticated versions of Muybridge's sequential photographs (see 9.28) made to spin in a wheel. They involve a series of drawings or cartoons, each slightly different from the next, arranged on film and projected at a speed that makes the drawn figures seem to move. The classic method of animation was perfected by Walt Disney Studios in the late 1920s. You can appreciate how time-consuming this was if you realize how much your body moves just in walking two steps, and consider how many drawings it would take to capture that movement. If the motion is not to seem jerky and unnatural, every shift of position by the merest fraction of an inch requires a new drawing. The smoothest animation, therefore, demanded about 24 different drawings per *second* or some 130,000 drawings for a feature-length film. In its heyday, the 1930s and 1940s, Disney Studios employed armies of illustrators.

Today the mechanics of animation have been simplified by computers. Modern animation is accomplished directly at the computer terminal, using light rather than paint. The artist draws an original picture on the display screen and then programs the computer to "draw" the changing images that simulate action. Images and colors can be varied at will, live action can be combined with animation—the possibilities are literally endless.

One of the most critically acclaimed animated films is Walt Disney's *Beauty and the Beast* (**9.39**), released in 1991. Although some think it is meant for children, the film offers much to engage and delight adults. Through sophisticated animation, all sorts of objects come to life and sing and dance—a teapot, a clock, a feather duster, a footstool, an entire set of silverware. In a sly tribute to the pioneers of film, *Beauty*'s animated candelabrum is named "Lumière"—a double play on words indicating its light-giving nature.

The possibilities for visual expression in film have expanded tremendously since the brothers Lumière set up their little projector barely a hundred years ago. But another medium, also based on the camera, has come farther and faster in half the time. The video arts—of which television is most prominent—probably touch more people more significantly than all the other media discussed in this book put together.

9.39 Belle and the Beast, in a scene from the animated film *Beauty and the Beast*. 1991. © The Walt Disney Company.

VIDEO

All art is about communication, but the video arts in particular are about *mass* communication. No other medium even approaches television in its potential for presenting to millions of people the same visual experience at the same moment. A national or international event—such as a grand wedding in the British royal family or the Olympic Games—is telecast simultaneously into homes around the globe, complete with the graphics and other visual trappings devised by the networks to capture our attention. Viewers can, if they wish, compare their responses to an identical visual stimulus. This holds true not only for dramatic one-of-a-kind events, but also for the recurring fare of television. In offices, in supermarkets, in schools across the United States, conversations start with, "Did you see [name a popular show] last night?" For anyone alive now this is normal, but for all the billions of people who populated the earth before the 1950s it would be almost incomprehensible. Thanks to television, living with art has acquired another dimension: It is a mass visual experience.

The first official television broadcast in the United States took place in 1939, in connection with the opening of the New York World's Fair. Few people noticed, however, because there were practically no television receivers to accept the transmission. Not until about 1950 did the television set become an expected fixture in American homes. Now, of course, more homes around the globe have television than have indoor plumbing.

Readers of this book are intimately familiar with commercial television, so there is no need for discussion of its myriad offerings. Less well known, perhaps, is the work of serious video artists, who took up the medium almost from its beginning. In one form of video art the image is actually created on the television screen by manipulating dials, selecting colors, combining figures and other elements. Many artists believe this type of expression to be the most valid for our electronic age.

9.40 Nam June Paik. *Fin de Siècle*. 1989. Video installation: 280 television sets, 7-channel laser disk.
Courtesy Holly Solomon Gallery, New York.

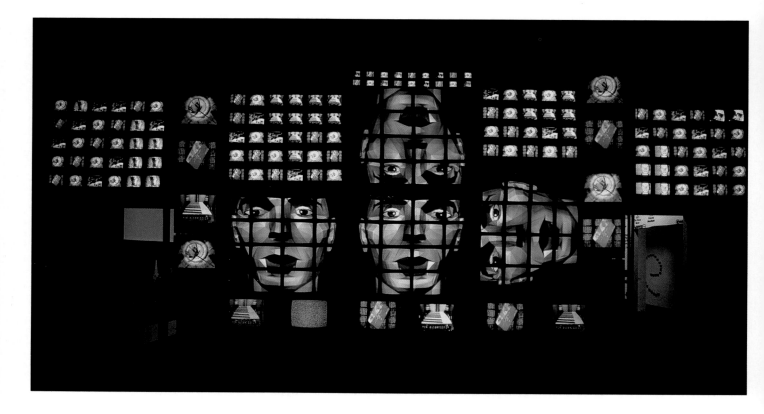

9.41 Peter Campus. *Three Transitions*. 1973. Video. Electronic Arts Intermix, New York.

Foremost among video artists working in this realm is Korean-born, New York-based Nam June Paik. Paik envisioned a new art of video technology as early as 1960. He does not *reproduce* images electronically, as network television might show an image of a painting by Picasso or Renoir. Rather, the image is *produced* and controlled by means of the electronic equipment itself (**9.40**). What is especially exciting about this approach is its immediacy, its "aliveness." According to Paik, "Most paintings reflect light. So when it's white paint, for example, you see the white light. Whereas television pictures are glowing light. Light is coming out, sprouting out. So it is much more intense physically. . . ."[14] Paik's video installations are expensive and take up space; they are not the sort of art that most collectors could expect to have in their homes. Still, they draw large crowds at museum exhibitions. We have grown accustomed to television. The fascination of transitory images is inherent in our world. Click—the art is there; click—it's gone; click—it's back again.

Another type of video art is related to filmmaking in the sense that it creates a visual continuum, perhaps even a story. What sets it apart from film is the possibility for electronic manipulation of the imagery, the greater freedom to "play" offered by the video camera. Peter Campus's *Three Transitions* (**9.41**), a classic work in video art, is a very brief (less than five-minute) exercise in electronic displacement of the artist's own face and body. In the first "transition," Campus seems to stab himself in the back, climb out through the wound, then emerge intact on the other side. In the second he wipes away his face with his hand, revealing another same face underneath. And in the last Campus appears to burn his living face as though it were a photograph. These operations are made visually possible—even believable—through sophisticated video technology.

Peter Campus's *Three Transitions* was made to be shown on a television monitor, and it could be broadcast just like a commercial television program to reach people around the world. Campus also created video environments—rooms in which video was projected onto walls or other surfaces, just as Daniel Canogar did with photographs in *Alien Memory* (see 9.27). The idea of involving the viewer more actively in the experience of video has appealed to many artists. Viewers of Bill Viola's *The Crossing* (**9.42**) enter a darkened room containing a large, double-sided projection screen. On one side of the screen, they can watch the distant figure of a man approaching from far away through a darkened space. When he is so close that his body almost fills the screen, he stops and stares directly ahead. A small votive candle appears at his feet. Suddenly, flames shoot upward from it, leaping higher and higher. Soon his entire body is engulfed and a roaring sound fills the room. When the flames die down, the man has disappeared. The screen darkens; then the cycle starts again. On the other side of the screen, another video is projected. Again a man approaches from the distance and stops. This time, however, it is water that annihilates him, falling first in droplets, then raging into a roaring deluge. The two videos are in perfect synchronization, with the appearance of the man, his drawing near, and the crescendos of fire and water happening at the same time.

Like much of Viola's art, *The Crossing* attempts to find a new visual language for religious experience. "The two traditional natural elements of fire and water appear here not only in their destructive aspects, but manifest their cathartic, purifying, transformative, and regenerative capacities as well," the artist has written. "In this way self-annihilation becomes a necessary means to transcendence and liberation."[14] While in this book we illustrate frames from both videos side by side, viewers in person were not able to see both at the same time, and this experience, however they chose to structure it and reflect on it, was part of the work.

Iranian-born Shirin Neshat has also used simultaneous projections to involve viewers more actively in her work. In *Rapture* (**9.43**), two videos are projected simultaneously onto opposite walls, placing viewers literally in the middle, forced to turn from one to the other in trying to experience the whole

9.42 Bill Viola. *The Crossing.* 1996. Video/sound installation.

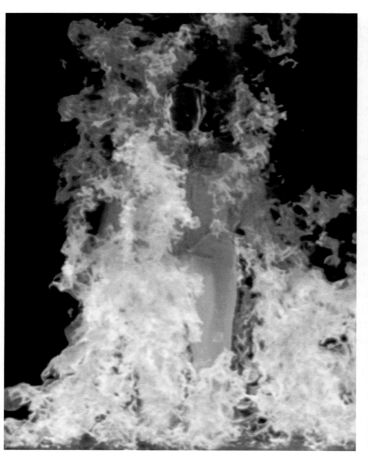

9.43 Shirin Neshat. *Rapture.*
1999. Production stills.
Courtesy Barbara Gladstone.

of the story. In one video, a group of men enter a fortified hilltop castle. In the other, a group of women approach the castle from a vast distance across a windy desert. The men take little notice of the women, but instead engage in ritualized activities that seem important to them, though trivial to us. The women observe, shut out. Suddenly, they shriek in unison. The men stop, and both groups look at each other. The women turn their backs and continue across the barren landscape toward the sea, laboriously dragging a heavy boat through the sand. The men return to their important activities. At the water's edge, six of the women climb into the boat and set out to sea with neither oars nor sails, trusting to the current, yet free. The men, who have gathered on the ramparts of the castle—or is it now a prison?—wave.

Neshat's immediate subject is the situation of women in contemporary Islamic societies, yet her work goes beyond the specifics of Islam to address men and women in general, gender and society, outcasts and power, freedom and bondage, and perhaps as well two ways of being in the world. It is a fable that seems timeless and universal, where every action is symbolic, but where no fixed interpretation is offered.

A room with a view—the camera. What do we see through the peephole of the room? Images from the past, images of the present, images of a possible future. Our fondest memories and our most horrifying nightmares. Colors and shapes known or imaginary. The artistry of those who direct the camera's view need accept no limitations, for the view outside grows bigger all the time.

CHAPTER 10

Graphic Design and Illustration

All art has to do with communication, but this is uniquely true of graphic design. Graphic design has as its goal the communication of some *specific* message to a group of people, and the success of a design is measured by how well that message is conveyed. The message might be "This is a good product to buy," or "This way to the elevators (or rest rooms or library)," or any of countless others. If it can be demonstrated that the public received the intended message—because the product sold well or the traveler found the right services—then the design has worked.

Not all graphic design has to do with selling, but much of it does, and so for a long time it was known as "commercial art." The term "graphic design" is more inclusive and describes more accurately what artists in this field really do: They attend to the visual presentation of information as it is embodied in words and/or images. Books, book jackets, newspapers, magazines, advertisements, packaging, websites, CD covers, television and film credits, road signs, and corporate logos are among the many items that must be designed before they can be printed or produced.

Graphic design is as old as civilization itself. The development of written languages, for example, entailed a lengthy process of graphic design, as scribes gradually agreed that certain symbols would represent specific words or sounds. Over the centuries, these symbols were refined, clarified, simplified, and standardized—generation after generation of anonymous design work. The field as we know it today, however, has its roots in two more recent developments: the invention of the printing press in the 15th century and the Industrial Revolution of the 18th and 19th centuries.

Anyone can write up a notice to be posted on a door. The printing press made it possible to devise a notice that could be reproduced hundreds of times and distributed widely. Someone, however, had to decide exactly how the notice would look; they had to design it. How would the words be placed on the page? Which words should be in large type, which small? Should there be a border around them? An image to accompany them?

The Industrial Revolution, for its part, dramatically increased the commercial applications of graphic design. Before the Industrial Revolution, most products were grown or produced locally to serve a local population. A person who wanted a new pair of shoes, say, could walk down the road to the village cobbler, or perhaps wait for the monthly fair at which several cobblers from neighboring towns might appear. With the advent of machines, huge quantities of goods were produced in centralized factories for wide distribution. For manufacturers to succeed in this newly competitive and anonymous environment, they had to market both themselves and their wares through advertising, distinctive packaging, and other graphic means. At the same time, the invention of faster presses, automated typesetting, lithography, and photography expanded designers' capabilities, and the growth of newspapers and magazines expanded their reach.

Today, international commerce, communications, and travel continue to feed the need for graphic design; and technological developments, most notably the computer, continue to broaden its possibilities.

SIGNS AND SYMBOLS

On the most basic level, we communicate through symbols. The sound of the syllable *dog*, for example, has no direct relation to the animal it stands for. In Spanish, after all, the syllables *perro* indicate the same animal. Each word is part of a larger symbolic system, a language. Visual communication is also symbolic. Letters are symbols that represent sounds; the lines that we use to draw representational images are symbols for perception.

Symbols convey information or embody ideas. Some are so common that we find it difficult to believe they didn't always exist. Who, for example, first used arrows to indicate directions? →↑↓↖↗↙↘. We follow them instinctively now, but at some point they were new and had to be explained. Other symbols embody more complex ideas and associations. Two well-known and ancient symbols are the yin-yang symbol and the swastika (**10.1**).

The yin-yang symbol, also known as the *taiji* (or *tai chi*) diagram, embodies the worldview expressed in ancient Chinese philosophy. It gives elegant visual form to ideas about the dynamic balance of opposites that are believed to make up the universe and explain existence: male (yang) and female (yin), being and nonbeing, light and dark, action and inaction, and so on. The symbol makes it clear that these opposites are mutually interdependent, that as one increases the other decreases, that a portion of each is in the other, that they are defined by each other, that both are necessary to make the whole, and many other ideas. It is a model of successful graphic design.

The swastika has an important lesson to teach about symbols, which is that they have no meaning in themselves but are given a meaning by a society or culture. The swastika was first used as a symbol in India and Central Asia, possibly as early as 3000 B.C.E. It takes its name from the Sanskrit word *svastika*, meaning "good luck" or "good fortune." (Sanskrit was the most

10.1 Yin-yang symbol (left) and swastika (right).

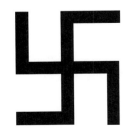

10.2 (left) Roger Cook and Don Shanosky. Poster introducing the signage symbol system developed for the U.S. Department of Transportation. 1974.

10.3 (right) Paul Rand. Logos for IBM (1956), Westinghouse (1960), UPS (1961), and ABC (1962).

important language of ancient India.) In Asia, the swastika is still widely used as an auspicious symbol, even on commercial products. Until the 1930s, the swastika was a popular good-luck symbol in the West as well. Today, however, it is so thoroughly associated with the Nazis, who adopted it as their emblem, that it has become for us a symbol of fascism, racial hatred, and the unspeakable atrocities of the concentration camps. Our instinctive recoil from the swastika underscores not only the power of symbols to serve as repositories for ideas and associations, but also the ability of those ideas and associations to change, sometimes radically.

Graphic designers are often asked to create visual symbols. In 1974, the U.S. Department of Transportation commissioned the American Institute of Graphic Arts to develop a set of symbols that could communicate essential information across language barriers to international travelers (**10.2**). Designers selected by the institute researched symbols then in use in transportation centers around the world, evaluating them for clarity and effectiveness. The final set of symbols were drawn up by the design firm of Cook and Shanosky Associates and introduced in this poster, which explains their meanings. Today, the symbols are a familiar part of signs in airports and train stations, where they help direct travelers to bus and taxi stands, telephones, hotel information, rest rooms, and other key facilities.

Among the most pervasive symbols in our visual environment today are logos and trademarks, which are symbols of an organization or product. An impressive number of these are the work of Paul Rand, one of the most influential of all American graphic designers (**10.3**). Simple, clear, distinctive, and memorable, each of these corporate logos has become familiar to millions of people around the world, instantly calling to mind the company and its products or services. As with any symbol, a logo means nothing in itself. It is up to an organization to make its logo familiar and to convince people through sound business practices to associate it with such virtues as service, quality, and dependability. Because symbols serve as focal points for associations of ideas and emotions, one of the most effective ways for a company to change its image is to redo its logo.

A logo is often the first and key element in a complete corporate identity program, which extends a unified design concept to advertising, posters, packaging, stationery, folders, business cards, and other printed matter. Using design to send a consistent message was considered so important at companies such as IBM that even Paul Rand had trouble getting his now-famous *Eye, Bee, M* poster approved (**10.4**). Although the poster was initially created for an in-house event, and not for the public, executives of the company were wary of tampering with their corporate identity in such a frivolous way.

By the 1980s, corporate logos had become such a familiar part of the visual landscape that one of the most powerful symbols of the decade consciously appropriated their authority (**10.5**). Developed by an artists' collective called the Silence=Death Project, the Silence=Death logo was developed to operate just as a corporate logo does: it would appear everywhere, on everything, gradually penetrating the public consciousness, in this case with a message about AIDS—that the disease existed, that people were dying, that they weren't going to go quietly, and that something needed to be done. Like the swastika, the pink triangle had been used by the Nazis, in this case to distinguish homosexual prisoners from other undesirables such as Jews and Gypsies. Gay activists had taken over the symbol during the 1970s, turning it into a badge of courage. The Silence=Death logo vividly rekindled the link with death, in this case from a disease that was viewed initially by many segments of the public as specifically targeting gay people.

10.4 (left) Paul Rand. *Eye, Bee, M.* 1981. Poster.

10.5 (right) *Silence=Death* button. Logo designed by the Silence= Death Project, New York. 1986.

TYPOGRAPHY AND LAYOUT

Part of the power of the Silence=Death logo is in its **typography,** the arrangement and appearance of the letters. The stark, no-nonsense letterforms convey a mood of seriousness and urgency. The carnival mood of *silence=death*, for example, would have had a completely different and inappropriate visual impact.

Cultures throughout history have appreciated the visual aspects of their written language. In China, Japan, and Islamic cultures, calligraphy is considered an art. While personal writing in the West has never been granted that status, letters for public architectural inscriptions have been carefully designed since the time of the ancient Romans, whose alphabet we have inherited. With the invention of movable type around 1450, the alphabet again drew the attention of designers. Someone had to decide on the exact form of each letter, creating a visually unified alphabet that could be mass-produced as a **typeface,** a style of type. No less an artist than Albrecht Dürer turned his attention to the design of well-balanced letterforms (**10.6**). Constructing each letter within a square, Dürer paid special attention to the balance of thick and thin lines and to the visual weight of the serifs, the short cross lines that finish the principal strokes (at the base of the *A*s, for example).

The letters Dürer designed would have been laboriously carved in wood or cast in metal, and they would have been set (placed in position) by hand prior to printing. Today, type is created and set by computer and photographic methods. The design of typefaces continues to be an important and often highly specialized field, and graphic designers have literally hundreds of styles to choose from. The text of this book, for example, is set in New Aster, which is popular for books since it is easy to read, legible in fairly small sizes, and not tiring to the eyes. The chapter titles, in contrast, are set in a sans-serif face, a face without finishing lines on the strokes, called Stone Sans.

Despite these myriad available typefaces, special letterforms may still be created by hand. In the poster illustrated here advertising an exhibit of design from Spain (**10.7**), the *o* and *s* in *Diseño* (design) were set from a standard typeface. The rest of the letters in the word were drawn especially for this project. Evenly spaced, vertical red bars were modified with

10.6 (left) Albrecht Dürer. Letters, from *Treatise on Measurement.* 1525.

10.7 (right) Ott & Stein. Poster for an exhibit of Catalan design. 1989.

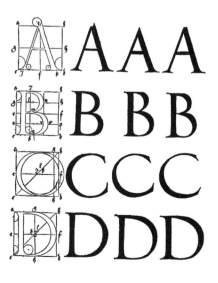

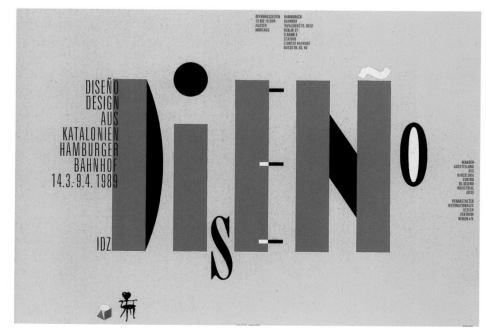

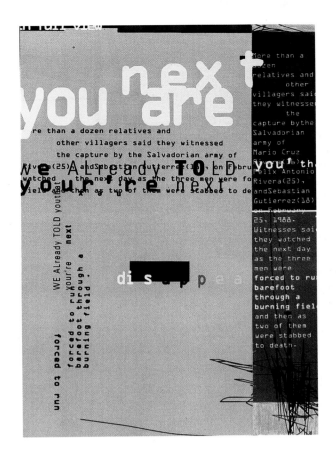

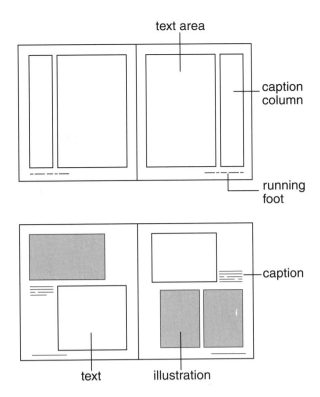

geometric additions in black and white, turning the word *design* into the principal visual focus of the poster, which was printed in the dramatic colors of the Spanish flag.

Joan Dobkin combined commercial typefaces and handmade letterforms in her informational leaflet for Amnesty International, an organization that monitors human rights around the world (**10.8**). Menacing phrases jump out at us from a disorienting tangle of words: *You are next* and *Already told you*. The word *disappear* itself disappears. Dobkin took the texts from first-person accounts of political terror in El Salvador. By fragmenting and layering their words, she communicates the helplessness and terror felt by the victims in order to provoke a direct, emotional response from the pamphlet's target audience: potential supporters of Amnesty International.

A layout is a designer's blueprint for an extended work in print such as a book or a magazine. It includes such specifications as the dimensions of the page, the width of the margins, the sizes and styles of type for text and headings, the style and placement of running heads or feet (lines at the top or bottom of the page that commonly give the chapter or part title and page number), and many other elements. The layout of this book, for example, places a single column of text asymmetrically on the page, leaving a slender outer column (for captions) and a narrow inner margin (**10.9**, top). Each spread (two facing pages) is thus fundamentally symmetrical, with left and right pages in mirror image. Illustrations are placed to relieve and even disguise this symmetry, and the page makeup artists took pains to arrange each spread in a pleasing asymmetrical composition (**10.9**, bottom).

Beginning in the 1980s, a number of designers began to experiment with more radical approaches that sacrificed easy legibility for visual appeal. Among the most controversial of these designers is David Carson. In magazines such as *Beach Culture* and *Ray Gun,* Carson rarely used a consistent layout, preferring to create each spread as a new composition. Text might be scattered, run upside down or on an angle, printed over itself, or made to disappear into a photograph. One spread often continued over the page turn into the next, creating a free-flowing, cinematic feel.

10.8 (left) Joan Dobkin. Informational leaflet for Amnesty International. 1991.

10.9 (right) Layout for *Living with Art* (top) and a sample spread (bottom).

10.10 David Carson, art director, and Chris Cuffaro, photographer. "Morrissey the Loneliest Monk," *Ray Gun,* 1994.

The spread illustrated here opened a 1994 *Ray Gun* article on musician Morrissey (**10.10**), and it shows how David Carson turned traditional graphic design principles on their heads. The title of the article would normally be considered the most important typographic element, but Carson splits it up and sets it in small type, part vertically (mor- rissey) and part on a diagonal (the loneliest monk). A quote from the musician, also fragmented and scattered, serves as the principal typographic focus. The photograph of the star, conventionally as important as the title, is cropped to hide half of his face and seems to be fading into invisibility. To detractors who claim that his work is chaotic and illegible, Carson points out that legibility and communication are not the same thing. Communication begins by attracting and engaging the viewer's attention. Readers attracted to the mood of the design will be willing to make an effort to decipher its message.

WORD AND IMAGE: POSTERS AND OTHER ADVERTISEMENTS

Among the services offered by early printers in the 15th century was the design and printing of single sheets called broadsides. Handed out to town dwellers and posted in public spaces, broadsides argued political or religious causes, told of recent events, advertised upcoming festivals and fairs, or circulated woodcut portraits of civic and religious leaders. They were the direct ancestors not only of advertising and posters but also of leaflets, brochures, newspapers, and magazines.

With the development of color lithography in the 19th century, posters came into their own as the most eye-catching form of advertising, for color printing was not yet practical in magazines or newspapers, and television was still a hundred years away. Among the most famous of all 19th-century posters are those created by Toulouse-Lautrec for the cabarets and dance halls of Paris (**10.11**). In this poster for a famous dance hall called the Moulin Rouge, the star performer, La Goulue, is shown dancing the cancan, while in the foreground rises the wispy silhouette of another star attraction, Valentin, known as "the boneless one." The flattened, simplified forms and the dramatically cropped composition show the influence of Japanese prints, then so popular in Europe. Lautrec's posters were immediately recognized as collectors' items, and instructions circulated secretly for detaching them from the kiosks on which they were pasted.

An extraordinary flowering of graphic design occurred during the decade following the Russian Revolution of 1917, when an art movement called **Constructivism** called on artists to be actively involved in creating the new society for which all had such high hopes. Constructivists believed that instead of making paintings and sculpture for an elite audience, artists should apply their skills to designing posters, magazines, theatrical productions, industrial products, and other useful objects. Naturally, they believed that a new and advanced society could only be brought about by the newest and most advanced art, and so the radical art trends of the day were suddenly applied to everyday concerns, as in this bold film poster designed by the brothers Vladimir and Georgii Stenberg, who had originally been trained as sculptors (**10.12**). Such artistic freedom and optimism were not to last, however. During the 1930s, the Soviet government came to view advanced art with distrust. Independent artists' groups were abolished, and the government decreed that all artists must now work in a clear, easy-to-understand, realistic style. Those suspected of resisting risked imprisonment and death.

10.11 (left) Henri de Toulouse-Lautrec. *La Goulue at the Moulin Rouge*. 1891. Poster, lithograph printed in four colors; 6'2⅘" × 3'9¹³⁄₁₆".
The Metropolitan Museum of Art, New York.

10.12 (right) Vladimir and Georgii Stenberg. Poster for *Nepobedimye (The Unvanquished)*. 1928. Offset lithography, 39⅜ × 28⅜".
The Museum of Modern Art, New York.

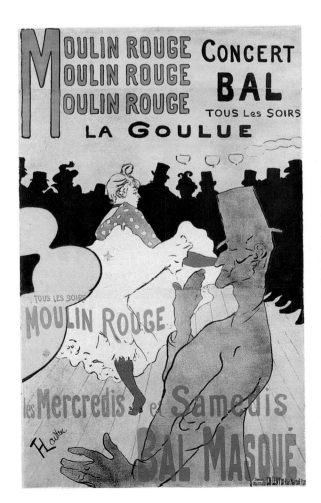

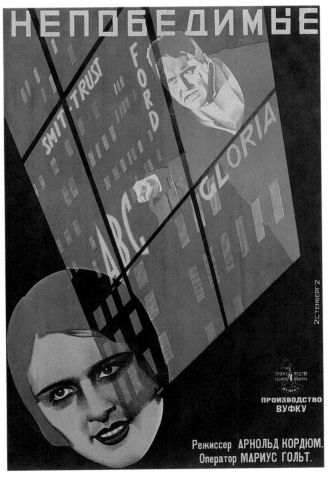

The work of Toulouse-Lautrec and the Stenberg brothers demonstrates the close links that often exist between graphic design and current developments in art. A contemporary example is this poster by the American graphic designer Milton Glaser (**10.13**). Like many successful designers, Glaser has a remarkable ability to reinvent himself, exploring new styles that always seem in step with the times. The colorful, hand-drawn images that first made him famous epitomized the mood of the 1960s and had strong links to Pop Art (see 22.11). Here, thirty years later, Glaser draws on the continuing influence of Conceptualism and the increasing role of photography in recent art. The design contrasts an image of a hat with the word *hat*, which Glaser finds hidden in the word *whatever*. Conceptual Art has often explored images and words as alternate symbolic systems of representation (see 22.16). The hat itself is a tribute to Surrealist painter René Magritte, many of whose paintings featured anonymous-looking men in bowler hats.

ILLUSTRATION

10.13 (left) Milton Glaser. *Art is . . .* Poster. 1996.

10.14 (right) Norman Rockwell. *The Tom Boy*, cover for *The Saturday Evening Post*, May 23, 1953. Courtesy the Curtis Publishing Company.

An illustration is an image created to accompany words. It may help readers imagine what the words are describing, or it may simply provide visual interest and appeal. Many of the works of art included in this book were created as illustrations. Examples include Sahibdin's intricate imagining of an episode from the Hindu epic the *Ramayana* (3.19) and the Limbourg brothers' exquisite winter scene from *Les Très Riches Heures* (16.20). As we saw in

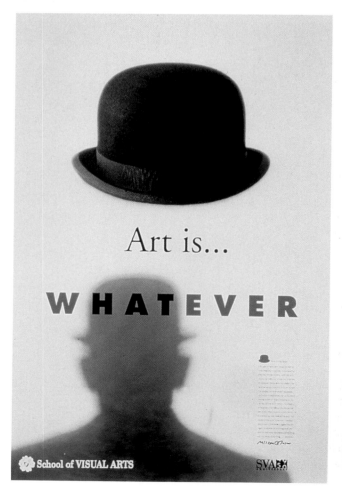

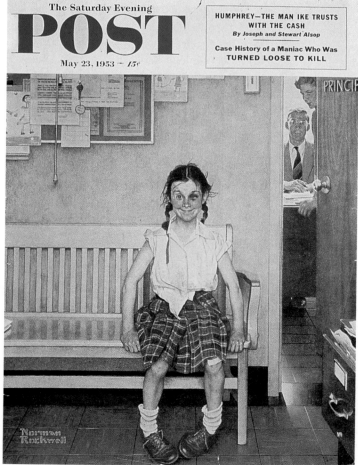

10.15 Gene Greif. Illustration to "The Chef: Tadashi Ono," *The New York Times*, January 12, 2000. Courtesy the artist.

Chapter 8, the earliest extant printed book, a 9th-century copy of the Diamond Sutra, opens with a woodblock illustration (8.3), and Albrecht Dürer issued his *Apocalypse* prints as illustrations to the biblical text (8.4).

One of the most famous American illustrators of the 20th century was Norman Rockwell, whose work appeared regularly on the cover of a popular weekly magazine called *The Saturday Evening Post* (**10.14**). Rockwell was just twenty-two years old when, in 1916, he presented himself at the Philadelphia offices of the magazine. He carried two paintings meant as potential *Post* covers and a sketch for a third. The *Post's* art director was impressed and immediately bought the young artist's illustrations, requesting more. Rockwell's first *Post* cover appeared in May of that year, and his covers continued to appear regularly until 1963, when the artist branched out to other magazines. His last *Post* cover was a portrait of President John F. Kennedy, used as a memorial on the December 14 issue—three weeks after the president's assassination. During those forty-seven years Rockwell averaged about six covers each year—an amazing feat when one considers that each of the illustrations was a fully developed painting, often including many characters. Every Rockwell cover was greeted with delight by *Post* readers and guaranteed an increase in sales.

The tight deadlines and throwaway nature of daily newspapers provide a different kind of environment for illustrators. To labor over a time-consuming oil painting is out of the question, but a resourceful and imaginative artist can create an eye-catching image through less labor-intensive means (**10.15**). Gene Greif used collage to create this lighthearted and witty accompaniment to a newspaper article featuring a Japanese chef's recipe for shrimp. The wave, of course, is clipped from Hokusai's famous *The Great Wave* (see 8.5), and it immediately sets us in Japan. The chili, salt shaker, and frying pan were taken from other sources, including early-20th-century advertising images. A shrimp and a shower of salt, sketched in by hand, pull the composition together by echoing the curve of the great wave itself, with the salt cleverly substituting for the snowy sky of Hokusai's original. Greif mixed visual ingredients into a composition the way a cook might toss edible ingredients into a pan.

ILLUSTRATION • 251

THE DIGITAL REALM

Much of the freedom that today's designers enjoy is the result of the computer, which enables them to explore multiple approaches quickly and easily. With advanced graphics programs, type can be manipulated almost as a plastic substance—stretched, molded, turned in space, enlarged, reduced, colored and recolored. Images too can be enlarged, reduced, cropped, placed, and moved. A design can be completely worked out on the computer and transmitted in digital form to the printer. More often, the computer is used as simply another tool, although a powerful one, in a design process that also includes traditional studio methods and darkroom techniques.

With the dramatic expansion of the World Wide Web and the increasing popularity of CD-ROM technology, the computer has also become an exciting new *place* for design. Design for the Web draws on such traditional models as posters, magazine layout, and advertising. To these it adds the potential for motion and interactivity—reactions to choices made by a visitor to the site.

Light radiates from a computer screen as it does from a television, allowing a deeper and more luminous sense of space than traditional print media. Brothers and design partners Christopher and Matthew Pacetti exploit this sense of space beautifully in their elegant design for a website for Polygram records (**10.16**). The layered background, whose repeating curves imply the motion of a spinning CD, subtly includes the word *Poly-Gram*, which also appears in violet to the left. The saturated, jewel-like colors radiate like stained glass. Against this layered ground, the navigation choices are clearly listed in white type with corresponding symbols, which also carry through to later pages.

An influential voice in the forefront of graphic design by and for the computer is John Maeda, head of the Media Laboratory at the Massachusetts Institute of Technology. As the director of the Aesthetics and Computation Group there, Maeda works to bridge the gap between engineers and artists. He believes that artists interested in using the computer must master the language of the computer itself, which is programming. To rely on

10.16 Christopher Pacetti, Matthew Pacetti. Website design for Polygram records. 1997.

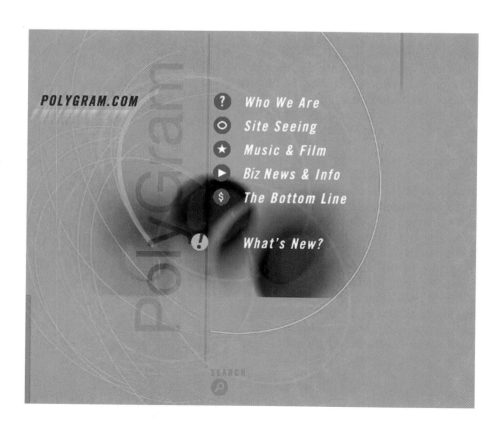

POLYGRAM.COM

? Who We Are

○ Site Seeing

★ Music & Film

▶ Biz News & Info

$ The Bottom Line

! What's New?

SEARCH

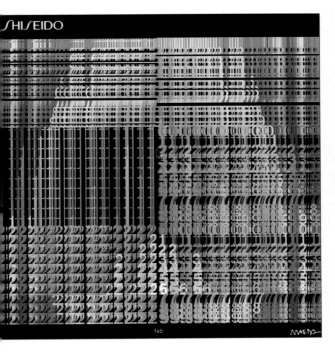

10.17 (left) John Maeda, Maeda Studio. September/October, from the Shiseido JAVA Calendar. 1997. Courtesy Maeda Studio.

10.18 (right) *Shakespeare Project*, ® 1997 MIT. David Small, developer; John Maeda, project director.

off-the-shelf design software, he points out, is to accept the limits of someone else's imagination. To help artists understand the basics of computer design, Maeda published *Design by Numbers*, a book that introduces a simple programming language he developed. The book, Maeda says, is "an attempt to demystify the technology behind computer art, to show how simple it is, and that people can do it."[1]

Maeda's own work includes an interactive online calendar created for Shiseido, a Japanese cosmetics company (**10.17**). The calendar divides the year into six, two-month segments, with each segment programmed for a specific design theme. The July/August segment, for example, allows the user's mouse to coax the numbers of the days into animated fireworks displays. For September/October, illustrated here, users can trigger shimmering patterns in blue, recalling the heat of summer and ocean waves.

Many websites take the form of succeeding "pages." This way of presenting information is deeply rooted in our way of thinking, for we have been storing information on pages in books for almost 2,000 years. Yet the computer also permits a more fluid, cinematic sense of space whose graphic possibilities are only beginning to be explored. David Small's experimental *Shakespeare Project* (**10.18**) may give us an idea of developments to come. A member of Maeda's Aesthetics and Computation Group, Small focuses on typographic displays that move away from the idea of a flat page toward three-dimensional "information environments." Here, the text of a play by Shakespeare is set in a single long column. Annotations, traditionally positioned as footnotes at the bottom of a page, are set at the same level as the lines they relate to, but at a 90-degree angle. Small developed a variety of intuitive interface devices that allow users to navigate the space freely, positioning themselves anywhere in the text, moving smoothly between detailed views and overviews, angling the columns to read now the text, now the annotations.

Although they are working with the most advanced technology of the day, designers such as Small and Maeda are actually quite conservative, for their work embraces the principles of visual elegance and communicative clarity that have been at the core of graphic design since anonymous scribes first developed writing.

PART FOUR

THREE-DIMENSIONAL MEDIA

11.1 Deborah Butterfield. *Vermillion*. 1989. Painted welded steel, height 6′3″.
The Metropolitan Museum of Art, New York.

CHAPTER 11

Sculpture

The study of sculpture confronts us with the third dimension, with the concept of *depth*. This seems like an easy and obvious point, but there is more to it than you might imagine. Our everyday lives are so flooded with images from the media that we have grown used to adjusting our perceptions of depth to compensate. We see images of people on the movie screen or on television, photographs of people in newspapers and magazines. Even though these are, in reality, two-dimensional images, we understand the people to be full-bodied and three-dimensional. This correction for depth becomes automatic, and we don't have to think about it.

As we approach sculpture, however, we might suspend this visual habit and train ourselves to be more *actively* aware of depth, for a heightened perception of the third dimension is essential to our full appreciation of sculpture. The experience of looking at a flat painting on a wall—or a photograph in an art book—is quite unlike the experience of walking up to a freestanding sculpture, circling it, observing it from various viewpoints. As an exercise, you might pick up a nearby object. It almost doesn't matter what it is—a desk lamp, stapler, telephone, alarm clock—all will do. Rotate it slowly in a complete 360-degree turn, watching the forms shift. From some angles it probably looks quite foreign. From others, it looks more characteristic. But notice that only when you integrate many visual perceptions can you begin to understand the form as a whole.

Sculpture has one of the longest histories of any art, and yet it is especially exciting today. A major reason for the vitality of contemporary sculpture is the use of materials, techniques, and concepts that were unheard of just a century ago. Deborah Butterfield, for example, created her sculpture *Vermillion* from scrap metal (**11.1**). The Bible speaks of hammering swords into plowshares as a metaphor for turning the tools of war into the tools of peace. Butterfield accomplishes a similar transformation, hammering (and cutting and welding and bending) old, sometimes rusted bodies of tractors, automobiles, and other industrial-age scrap metal into horses. Instead of being melted down and reformed, the metal retains traces of its previous use, and this history adds another layer of meaning to the sculpture: a horse, our ancient form of transportation, rises like a ghost from the scraps of our modern one.

We begin this chapter by looking at sculptors' methods and materials, for Butterfield's technique is only one of the many ways that sculpture can be made.

METHODS AND MATERIALS OF SCULPTURE

There are four basic methods for making a sculpture: modeling, casting, carving, and assembling. **Modeling** and **assembling** are considered additive processes. The sculptor begins with a simple framework or core or nothing at all and *adds* material until the sculpture is finished. Carving is a subtractive process in which one starts with a mass of material larger than the planned sculpture and *subtracts*, or takes away, material until only the desired form remains. **Casting** involves a mold of some kind, into which liquid or semiliquid material is poured and allowed to harden.

Let us consider each of these methods in more detail and look as well at some of the materials they are used with.

MODELING

Modeling is familiar to most of us from childhood. As children we experimented with play dough or clay to construct lopsided figures of people and animals. For sculpture, the most common modeling material is clay, an earth substance found in most parts of the world. Wet clay is wonderfully pliable; few can resist the temptation to squeeze and shape it. As long as clay remains wet, the sculptor can do almost anything with it—add on more and more clay to build up the form, gouge away sections, pinch it outward, scratch into it with a sharp tool, smooth it with the hands. But when a clay form has dried and been fired (heated to a very high temperature), it becomes hard. Fired clay, sometimes called by the Italian name *terra cotta*, is surprisingly durable. Much of the ancient art that has survived was formed from this material.

A female figure made in Cyprus more than three thousand years ago (**11.2**) is typical of the fertility images found in most early cultures. The artist who created this little statue had learned to exploit many of the possibilities of clay. After the overall form had been shaped by the fingers, delicate lines defining the form were incised with a sharp tool. The arms and "earrings" were shaped of separate pieces of clay and then added to the main piece.

Clay can also be modeled with great subtlety and detail. This small sculpture by the 18th-century French artist Clodion illustrates well the rough warmth and sensual appeal of terra cotta (**11.3**). Bacchantes were female followers of Bacchus, the ancient Roman god of wine and fertility. Satyrs were mythological beings, half goat and half man, whose behavior was notoriously unbridled. In its playful depiction of lighthearted love with no commitments and no consequences, this elegant sculpture is typical of the 18th-century style known as **Rococo** (see Chapter 20).

In some ways modeling is the most direct of sculpture methods. The workable material responds to every touch, light or heavy, of the sculptor's fingers. Sculptors often use clay modeling in the same way that painters traditionally have used drawing, to test ideas before committing themselves to the finished work. As long as the clay is kept damp, it can be worked and reworked almost indefinitely. Even the terminology is the same; we sometimes call a clay test piece a "sketch."

CASTING

In contrast to modeling, casting seems like a very *indirect* method of creating a sculpture. Sometimes the sculptor never touches the final piece at all. Metal, and specifically bronze, is the material we think of most readily in relation to casting. Bronze can be superheated until it flows, will

11.2 Female figure, from Cyprus. c. 1500–1200 B.C.E. Terra cotta, height 6⅛".
The Metropolitan Museum of Art, New York.

pour freely into the tiniest crevices and forms, and then hardens to extreme durability. Even for a thin little projection, like a finger, there is no fear of it breaking off. Also through casting, the sculptor can achieve smooth rounded shapes and a glowing, reflective surface, such as we see in this Indian sculpture of the bodhisattva Avalokiteshvara (11.4). Cast in bronze and then gilded (covered with a thin layer of gold), the smooth, gleaming surfaces of the body contrast with the minutely detailed jewelry, hairstyle, and flowers, demonstrating the ability of metal to capture a full range of effects. In Buddhism, bodhisattvas are those spiritually advanced beings who have chosen to delay their own buddhahood in order to help others. Avalokiteshvara is the most popular and beloved of these saintly presences. He is depicted here in princely garb, his hair piled high, seated in a relaxed and sinuous pose on a stylized lotus throne. Lotus blossoms, symbols of purity, twine upward beside him.

11.3 (left) Clodion (Claude Michel). *Satyr and Bacchante.* c. 1775. Terracotta, height 23¼″. The Metropolitan Museum of Art, New York.

11.4 (below) *The Bodhisattva Avalokiteshvara*, from Kurkihar, Bihar, Central India. Pala Dynasty, 12th century. Gilt bronze, height 10″. Patna Museum, Patna.

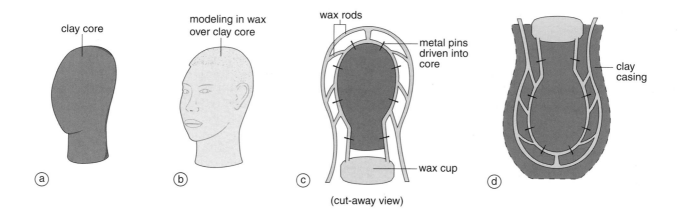

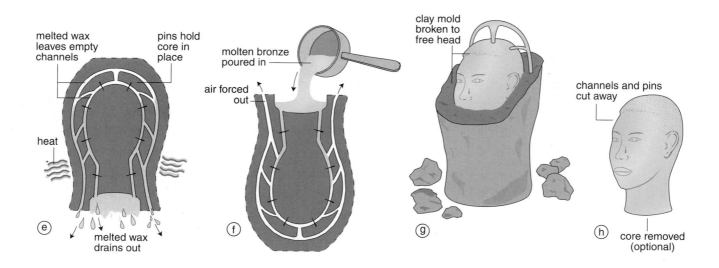

11.5 The lost-wax casting process.

The most common method for casting metal is called the **lost-wax** process, sometimes known by its French name, *cire perdue*. Dating back to the third millennium B.C.E., the basic concept is simple and ingenious. We describe it here as it was practiced by the African sculptors of ancient Ife to create heads such as the one illustrated in Chapter 2 (**11.5;** see 2.17).

First, a core is built up of specially prepared clay (a). Over this core, the sculptor models the finished head in a layer of wax (b). When the sculpture is complete, wax rods and a wax cup are attached to it to form a sort of "arterial system," and metal pins are driven through the wax sculpture to the core inside (c). The whole is encased in specially prepared clay (d). When the clay has dried, it is heated so that the wax melts and runs out (hence "lost wax") and the clay hardens (e). The lost wax leaves a head-shaped void inside the block. Where the wax rods and block were, channels and a depression called a pouring cup remain. The pins hold the core in place, preserving the space where the wax was. Next, the mold is righted, and molten metal is poured into the pouring cup. The metal enters the mold through the channels, driving the air before it (f). When the metal bubbles up through the air channels, it is a sign that the mold is probably filled. Metal, therefore, has *replaced* the wax, which is why casting is known as a replacement method. When the metal has cooled, the mold is broken apart, freeing the head (g). The channels, now cast in metal as well, are cut away, the clay core is removed (if desired), holes or other flaws are patched or repaired, and the head is ready for smoothing and polishing (h).

A sculpture cast in this way is unique, for the wax original is destroyed in the process. Standard practice today is a variation called indirect or investment casting, which allows multiples to be made. In this method, the artist finishes the sculpture completely in clay, plaster, or other material. A mold is formed around the solid sculpture (today's foundries use synthetic rubber for this mold). The mold is removed from the sculpture in sections, then reassembled. Melted wax is painted or "slushed" inside the mold to build up an inner layer about 3/16″ thick. After it has hardened, this wax casting is removed from the mold and checked against the original sculpture for accuracy: it should be an exact duplicate, but hollow. The wax casting is fitted with wax rods, pierced with pins, then encased in solid plaster, which both fills and surrounds it, just as in 11.5d. This plaster is called the investment. From this point on, the process is the same: the investment is heated so that the wax melts and runs out, metal is poured into the resulting void, and the investment is broken away to free the casting. The key difference is that the mold that makes the wax casting is reusable, thus multiple wax versions of an original can be prepared and multiple bronzes of a sculpture cast. All but the simplest sculptures are cast in sections, which are then welded together. (Imagine two halves of an eggshell being cast separately in metal, then welded together to form a hollow metal egg.) As with prints (see Chapter 8), each casting is considered an original work of art, and a limited edition may be declared and controlled.

While today artists bring their sculptures to specialists to be cast, earlier sculptors often cast their own work. In his enormously entertaining *Autobiography*, Renaissance sculptor Benvenuto Cellini left us a vivid description of the drama and danger that attended the casting of his statue of *Perseus and Medusa* (**11.6**).

The tale begins with a challenge: Cellini's patron, Duke Cosimo I de' Medici, visits the artist's studio to view the final wax version of the statue (probably a layer of wax over a clay core). It is too complicated to cast, the duke says. It cannot be done. Cellini insists that he has devised a way, but the duke thinks he is merely bragging. The two quarrel, and the duke leaves. Cellini sets to work. He attaches a system of wax rods to the figure, encases the whole in specially prepared clay, then heats it to draw out the wax, thus creating a mold. Leaving the mold standing, he and his assistants build a brick furnace up around it. For two days and nights, a slow fire burns in the furnace, baking the mold to hardness. Next, using a system of ropes and pulleys, they lift the mold out of the furnace and lower it upright into a deep pit they have dug in the earth. They pack earth around the mold to hold it firm, so that molten metal can be poured into it.

The furnace is newly stoked with wood and filled with metal scraps to be melted. But now things start to go wrong. In the intense heat, the workshop catches fire. Wind and rain sweeping in threaten to cool the furnace, but the process cannot be stopped now. Cellini, suddenly ill, takes to his bed, raving with fever and convinced he is dying. Two hours later an assistant comes to tell him all is lost: the metal is curdling and won't continue to melt. Suspecting sabotage, Cellini rushes back to the studio and, with tremendous effort and skill, gets the metal melting again. What a scene it is! Cellini is everywhere at once, stoking the furnace, sending workmen up to the roof to fight the fire, commandeering carpets and hangings to block the wind and

11.6 Benvenuto Cellini. *Perseus and Medusa.* 1545–54. Bronze, height 18′.
Loggia dei Lanzi, Piazza della Signoria, Florence.

rain. The project seems saved, when all at once there is a thunderous explosion and a great flash of fire: the furnace has cracked open, and the bronze is leaking out!

Cellini rushes to open the mouths to the channels of the mold, and the metal begins pouring into it. But there isn't enough! He sends for his pewter plates and bowls: every piece he owns is thrown into the furnace and melted down. The day is saved; the metal is flowing freely. "And then in an instant my mold was filled," he writes. "So I knelt down and thanked God with all my heart."[1]

When it was all over, Cellini relates, he sent for earthenware plates to replace the pewter he had sacrificed, and everyone feasted together. Two days later, he began to uncover the mold and break it open. The statue was perfect but for a small, easily repaired flaw in one foot, just as he had predicted to the duke. While casting today is rarely so dramatic, an element of uncertainty still remains, for it is impossible to see what is happening inside the mold.

CARVING

Carving is more aggressive than modeling, more direct than casting. In this process the sculptor begins with a block of material and cuts, chips, and gouges away until the form of the sculpture emerges. Wood and stone are the principal materials for carving, and both tend to resist the sculptor's tools. When approaching the block to be carved, the sculptor must study the grain of the material—its fibrous or crystalline structure—so as to work *with* that material. Any attempt to violate the grain could result in a failed sculpture.

A poem sung in West Africa about the Yoruba sculptor Olowe of Ise praises him for carving the hardest wood as though it were as soft as melon, and looking at the spectacular bowl illustrated here, we can sense the justice of the compliment (**11.7**). The lid of the bowl, crowned by four dancing women with towering crested hairstyles, is carved from a single piece of wood. Even more astonishing, the base—including the bowl, the tall kneeling woman presenting it, and the numerous shorter supporting figures—is also carved from a single piece. As though that were not impressive enough, Olowe permitted himself a further bravura touch by carving a freely rolling head *inside* the cage formed by the supporting figures beneath the bowl.

Types of wood and stone vary considerably in their suitability for carving. Jade, for example, is too hard to be carved at all and can be shaped only through abrasion—patient rubbing with an even harder stone such as quartzite or diamond. Artists throughout history have learned to work with the natural properties of available materials and to master the capabilities of available tools. The ancient Olmec sculptors of Mesoamerica understood well the properties of the local basalt that they favored for monumental works (**11.8**). A volcanic stone, fine-grained but exceedingly hard, basalt does not lend itself to highly detailed work. Olmec sculptors instead devised a broad style of plain surfaces and subtle modeling. Using stone tools—probably quartz blades—they carved numerous colossal heads such as this one. Among the most famous works of Mesoamerican art, the heads are thought to be portraits of rulers.

ASSEMBLING

Assembling is a process by which individual pieces or segments or objects are brought together to form a sculpture. Some writers make a distinction between assembling, in which parts of the sculpture are simply placed on or near each other, and constructing, in which the parts are actually joined together through welding, nailing, or a similar procedure. This book uses the term *assemblage* for both types of work.

11.7 (above, top) Olowe of Ise. *Bowl with Figures.* Early 20th century. Wood, pigment; height 25″. National Museum of African Art. Smithsonian Institution, Washington, D.C.

11.8 (above) *Colossal Head.* Olmec, 1500–300 B.C.E. Basalt, height c. 8′. Museo de Antropología, Veracruz.

OLOWE OF ISE

18??–1938

OLOWE OF ISE was born in the Nigerian town of Efon Alaye, less than fifty miles from Ife, the holy city of the Yoruba. We do not know the date of Olowe's birth; since he was a respected elder at his death in 1938, he was probably born between 1850 and 1880. We also know little about his training as an artist, although we assume that he apprenticed to an older sculptor before establishing himself as a master.

By the end of the 19th century, Olowe had moved to the royal city of Ise, where he became an emissary to the king. As an artist who was given commissions by kings and religious groups throughout the easternmost Yoruba lands, Olowe was well qualified for the position. Olowe also acted as court sculptor for the king of Ise, and he supervised a workshop in the palace which employed a dozen assistants.

During his lifetime, Olowe of Ise's work was known in England as well as in Nigeria. One of his elaborate wooden bowls with figures (similar to Figure 11.7) was brought back to England by a British visitor around 1900. In 1924, a pair of doors sculpted by Olowe and belonging to the king of Ikere were displayed at the British Empire Exhibition in London. They depicted the king receiving the British colonial officer who was helping to impose British rule over the formerly independent Yoruba kingdoms. The king was persuaded to donate the doors to the British Museum, receiving in exchange an elaborate English chair he could use as a throne. He commissioned a new pair of doors from Olowe to replace them. Strange as it seems today, no one at the museum asked the king for the name of the artist who had carved the doors, and for the next twenty years they were attributed to an "unknown" Yoruba artist. Many

European collectors of African art even assumed the Yoruba artists worked in complete anonymity. Such notions were not challenged until Olowe of Ise was interviewed by a British researcher shortly before his death.

Like many prosperous Yoruba men of his generation, Olowe of Ise married several wives and had many children. His fourth wife, Oloju-ifun Olowe, was interviewed more than fifty years after his death. She was able to recite a praise poem, or *oriki*, in his honor. It includes the following lines:

> Olowe, my excellent husband . . .
> One who carves the hard wood of
>   the *iroko* tree as though it
>   were soft as a calabash.
> One who achieves fame with the
>   proceeds of his carving . . .
> My lord, I bow down to you.
> Leader of all carvers . . .

There are no surviving photographs of Olowe of Ise, and no painted or sculpted artworks capture his physical likeness. Instead, the carved roof support illustrated here can be seen as revealing the basic character of this artist. Although it was once owned by a king, it is a metaphorical self-portrait of the artist as well as the patron, the visual and tactile equivalent of these descriptive lines from the *oriki* of Olowe of Ise:

> Outstanding leader in war.
> Emissary of the king.
> One with a mighty sword.
> Handsome among his peers.

Olowe of Ise. *Veranda Post with Mounted Hunter.* Before 1938. Wood, pigment; height 7′. Staatliches Museum für Völkerkunde, Munich.

The 20th-century American sculptor David Smith came to assemblage in an unusual way. While trying to establish himself as an artist, Smith worked as a welder. Later, when he began to concentrate on sculpture, he adapted his welding skills to a different purpose. His mature works broke new ground in both materials and forms (**11.9**). Sculptures like *Cubi IX* are of steel, which eventually became Smith's favorite material. Steel had long been used for the framework of cars, of refrigerators, of locomotives, but Smith explored its aesthetic potential. He polished the surfaces so they would shine in the sunlight when exhibited outdoors. The form of these works is also daring—block piled upon block, the parts joined at seemingly precarious angles. Steel, with its great strength, makes possible the dynamic balance of *Cubi IX*, and assemblage makes possible the soaring composition.

Like Smith's *Cubi IX*, Nancy Graves' *Extend-Expand* (**11.10**) interacts with space in a free-flowing, give-and-take way. But whereas *Cubi IX* is based in geometric forms, *Extend-Expand* is based in organic forms—literally. Using a process called **direct casting,** Graves made bronze casts of leaves, vines, seed pods, and other organic matter. In direct casting, there is no wax intermediary. Instead, the object itself, such as a leaf, is fitted with wax rods and encased in plaster. When molten metal is poured in, the heat is so intense that it vaporizes the leaf on contact, replacing it with a bronze replica. Graves kept a large inventory of bronze forms on hand as building blocks for her sculpture—some cast directly from organic matter, others cast from such found objects as discarded wheels, musical instruments, or furniture parts. She assembled them into ingenious balancing acts such as this one, then welding them together and painting them in bright-hued enamels.

The austere geometric forms of David Smith and the colorful playfulness of Nancy Graves both owe a great deal to the example of Alexander Calder. For Calder, art was a kind of serious play for adults, and coming upon one of his sculptures can provoke in us an adult version of a child's sudden delight in a new toy. We looked at one of his mobiles in Chapter 4 (see 4.50). Calder also made stabiles—sculptures that did not move, but sat still on the

11.9 (left) David Smith. *Cubi IX.* 1961. Stainless steel, 8′9¾″ × 4′10⅝″ × 3′7⅞″. Collection Walker Art Center, Minneapolis.

11.10 (right) Nancy Graves. *Extend-Expand.* 1983. Bronze with polychromed patina, 7′1″ × 4′3″. Museum of Modern Art, New York.

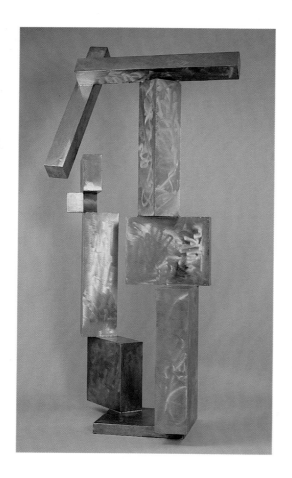

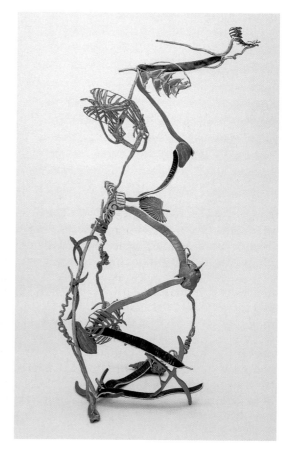

ground like everyone else's. Here, he created a hybrid (**11.11**): a stable form that serves as a base for mobile elements. Set outdoors, its bright geometric forms shifting in the wind, it looks like a friendly though completely incomprehensible traffic signal, or a manic weather instrument.

Alice Aycock uses assemblage to create complex sculptures that fulfill her own spiritual and mystical ideals. According to one art critic, her *Fantasy Sculpture I* (**11.12**) looks like "a kind of combination Ferris wheel and merry-go-round," but this is only the initial view. As we approach the large work, we are inevitably drawn into Aycock's world of magic, personal symbolism, and cosmic mysteries. We puzzle over the unexpected combinations of forms, the cryptic words stenciled onto the raw wood of the understructure. Aycock's work has specific and very rich content. It "tells a story," and even if the story isn't fully accessible to us, we are intrigued by it.

11.11 (above, top) Alexander Calder. *Ordinary*. 1969. Painted steel, 19′ × 19′8³⁄₁₆″ × 19′. Private collection.

11.12 (above) Alice Aycock. *Fantasy Sculpture I*. 1990. Wood, steel, stone, copper, lucite, moving parts, plants; 20′6″ × 18′ × 33′. Lent by the artist for a 1990 installation at Storm King Art Center, Mountainville, N.Y.

SCULPTURE AND THE THIRD DIMENSION

Most of the sculptures we have looked at are in the round, or freestanding and completely finished on all sides. There is another category of sculpture, however, called **relief** sculpture, which is meant to be viewed from one side only. Relief sculptures have three-dimensional depth, but they do not occupy space as independently as sculptures in the round. Often they are used to decorate architecture or functional objects.

If you have a nickel in your pocket, take it out and look at it. On the face you'll see a profile of Thomas Jefferson and on the back an image of his home, Monticello. Both images are in **low relief,** sometimes called by the French name **bas-relief.** The subjects project very slightly from their background. Many kinds of flat surfaces serve as fields for low-relief sculpture—coins, tombstones, walls, decorative plates, book covers. The illustration here (**11.13**) is the lid of the sarcophagus of Pacal, a Mayan ruler who died in 683 C.E. Carved in low relief on a slab of limestone, the scene depicts the exact moment of the ruler's death as it was understood in Mayan belief. We easily recognize Pacal himself near the center. Knees drawn up, head tilted back, he is falling from life to death. The rest of the motifs, which at first glance seem merely decorative, are actually highly stylized representations of deities and cosmic symbols. They make it clear that Pacal is dying as a god and will rise as one after his death.

When a sculpture projects more boldly from the background, we call it **high relief** (or **haut-relief**). To fit this category, the sculptured elements should project by at least half their depth, and parts of the figures may be in the round, unattached to the background as in this 7th-century monumental relief panel from a temple in Mamallapuram, India (**11.14**). The panel depicts a battle between the goddess Durga and the buffalo demon. To the left, eight-armed Durga, mounted on a lion, rushes forward with her victorious army. To the right, the buffalo demon and his supporters flee in defeat. The figures in this dynamic composition are all carved well away from the background, some considerably more than half-round. The panel belongs to

11.13 (above) Sarcophagus lid, from the Temple of Inscriptions, Palenque, Chiapas, Mexico. Maya, late Classic period, 684 C.E. Limestone, 12'2³/₈" × 7'1³/₈".

11.14 (right) *Durga Fighting the Buffalo Demon*, Mahishamardini Cave, Mamallapuram, Tamil Nadu, India. c. 670–700 C.E.

11.15 (left) Auguste Rodin. *The Burghers of Calais.* 1884–85. Bronze, 6'10½" × 7'11" × 6'6".

11.16 (below) Stephen Haweis and Henry Coles. Two views of *The Burghers of Calais.* c. 1905–10. Gum bichromate prints. Musée Rodin, Paris.

an extraordinary Indian tradition in which entire temples were cut directly into cliffsides or carved from gigantic boulders. Interior and exterior—columns, doorways, arched ceilings, statues, and reliefs—were hewn from living rock, making of the temple itself a gigantic piece of walk-in sculpture.

Although we have already looked at several examples of sculpture in the round, it will be useful here to consider one work primarily from the standpoint of its complex interaction with space. Sculpture in the round exists wholly in our world. We can walk around it and see it from every angle. This is a terrific challenge to the sculptor's compositional ability, since every viewpoint must be under control. Even when there is a definite front and back, as there usually is in figurative sculpture, all viewpoints should be interesting. And the fact that the work looks different from every angle makes the observer's experience much richer.

An excellent example of sculpture in the round is Rodin's *The Burghers of Calais* (**11.15**). Rodin made this sculpture for public display in the city of Calais, in France, and it depicts an episode from the town's medieval history. Six men have offered to give their lives to ransom their city from the English, who hold it captive. Each of them faces certain death, but they confront their sacrifice in different ways. One is angry, one sorrowful, one merely resigned, and so on—but each is unique, facing a personal tragedy amid shared crisis. We can read the men's emotions from their various postures, facial expressions, and gestures. The six hostages march in an irregular circle, some determinedly erect, others drooping in despair. And the viewer must also walk in a circle, because there is no angle from which all faces are visible. Rodin's message is complex, so he expressed it in the complex form of sculpture in the round.

While he seems never to have taken a photograph himself, Rodin was one of the first artists to integrate photography into his studio practice. Among the photographers he allowed to take pictures of his work were the English-speaking partners Stephen Haweis and Henry Coles, whose images of the *The Burghers of Calais* illustrated here allow us to see the grouping from other angles (**11.16**). The photographs are of a plaster cast of the work that Rodin kept in his studio after a bronze cast had been made for the city of Calais. Interestingly, while the technology existed for clear, detailed photographs, Rodin evidently preferred the moody, impressionistic images of Haweis and Coles, for he signed a contract allowing them to sell their photographs of his work to the public.

THE HUMAN FIGURE IN SCULPTURE

A basic subject for sculpture, one that cuts across time and cultures, is the human figure. If you look back through this chapter, you will notice that almost all the representational works portray people. One reason, certainly, must be the relative permanence of the common materials of sculpture. Our life is short, and the desire to leave some trace of ourselves for future generations is great. Metal, terra cotta, stone—these are materials for the ages, materials mined from the earth itself. Even wood may endure long after we are gone.

From earliest times, rulers powerful enough to maintain a workshop of artists have left images of themselves and their deeds. The royal tombs of ancient Egypt, for example, included statues such as the one illustrated here of the pharaoh Menkaure and Khamerernebty, his Great Royal Wife (**11.17**). Portrayed with idealized, youthful bodies and similar facial features, the couple stand proudly erect, facing straight ahead. Although each has the left foot planted slightly forward, there is no suggestion of walking, for their shoulders and hips are level. Menkaure's arms are frozen at his sides, while his wife touches him in a formalized gesture of "belonging together." This formal pose is meant to convey not only the power of the rulers but also their serene, eternal existence. The pharaoh, after all, ruled as a "junior god" on earth and, at death, would rejoin the gods in immortality. Egyptian rulers must have been pleased with this pose, for their artists repeated it again and again over the next two thousand years.

A second reason for the many human forms portrayed in sculpture is a little more mysterious. We might call it "presence." Sculpture, as pointed out earlier in this chapter, exists wholly in our world, in three dimensions. To portray a being in sculpture is to bring it into the world, to give it a presence that is close to life itself. In the ancient world, statues were often

11.17 (left) *Menkaure and Khamerernebty.* Egypt. c. 2460 B.C.E. Slate, height 4′6½″. Courtesy Museum of Fine Arts, Boston.

11.18 (right) Tilman Riemenschneider. *Virgin and Child on the Crescent Moon.* c. 1495. Lime wood, height 34⅛″. Museum für Angewandte Kunst, Cologne.

believed to have an ambiguous, porous relationship to life. In Egypt, for example, the Opening of the Mouth ceremony that was believed to help a dead person reawaken in the afterlife was performed not only on his or her mummified body but also on his or her statue. In China, the tomb of the first emperor was "protected" by a vast army of terra cotta soldiers, buried standing in formation (see 19.14). A famous Greek myth tells of the sculptor Pygmalion, who fell so in love with a statue that it came to life.

Among the human images that artists are most often asked to make present in the world through sculpture are those connected with religion and the spirit realm. A lovely example is this figure of the *Virgin and Child on the Crescent Moon* (**11.18**), carved of lime wood by Tilman Riemenschneider, one of the foremost German sculptors of the late Middle Ages. Mary stands in a gentle, informal S-curve, as though she might move at any moment. The infant Jesus is even more animated, and his body twists in a spiral motion. Like many artists of his time, Riemenschneider depicted Jesus unclothed and in motion in order to emphasize the completeness of His incarnation as a man. Just as the formal pose of the Egyptian rulers emphasizes their godly status, the informal pose of Mary and Jesus emphasizes their connection to humanity.

A similar contrast between the meanings of formal and informal poses can be seen in the art of Buddhism. As a perfected being, Buddha has liberated himself from the repeating cycle of life and time and exists in an eternal, unchanging realm. The formal symmetry of his typical seated pose reflects this idea well (see 2.26, 5.9). Bodhisattvas, on the other hand, are more directly available to the human world and are commonly shown in a relaxed, informal pose (see 11.4). Buddhist priests, saints, and other role models of the past are also often brought into the world through statues. A touching example is this wooden statue of *Kuya Preaching* (**11.19**), by the Japanese sculptor Kosho. Kuya was a Buddhist monk who lived during the 10th century. He devoted his life to roaming the countryside and teaching people to chant the simple phrase *Namu Amida Butsu* (Hail to Amida Buddha). Kosho beautifully captures the monk's endearing humility, but his stroke of artistic genius lies in the six small buddhas that issue from Kuya's mouth, one for each voiced syllable of the chant he taught to help people enter paradise: *na-mu-a-mi-da-bu-(tsu)*.

The human figure is also the most common subject of traditional African sculpture, yet in fact the sculptures rarely represent humans. Instead, they generally represent spirits of various kinds. This masterful carving by a Baule sculptor of a seated woman carrying a child on her back depicts a spirit spouse (**11.20**). Once again, a formal pose and an impassive face are used to express the dignity of an otherworldly being. Baule belief holds that each person has, in addition to their earthly spouse, a spirit spouse in the Other World. If this spirit spouse is happy, all is well. But an unhappy or jealous spirit spouse may cause trouble in one's life. A remedy is to give the spirit spouse a presence in this world by commissioning a statue (called a "person of wood"). The statue is made as beautiful as possible in order to encourage the spirit to take up residence within it, and it is placed in a household shrine and tended to with gifts and small offerings.

11.19 (right, top) Kosho. *Kuya Preaching*. Kamakura period, before 1207. Wood, with paint and inlaid eyes; height 46½".
Rokuhara Mitsu-ji Temple, Kyoto.

11.20 (right, bottom) *Spirit Spouse*, from Ivory Coast. Baule, early 20th century. Wood, height 17⅛".
University of Pennsylvania Museum, Philadelphia.

PRIMITIVISM

Looking back years later, the artists themselves disagreed on who was the first. Historians may never fully sort the matter out, but all agree that around 1906, in Paris, advanced young artists began to take an interest in African carvings. One of the first was the Fauve painter André Derain. Matisse and Picasso quickly followed suit, along with Brancusi and many others. The artists purchased their first examples of African sculpture in flea markets and antique shops. European colonial rule over Africa, consolidated at the turn of the 20th century, resulted in hundreds of carvings being imported as "curiosities." When the artists wanted to see more, they went to the museum. Not an art museum, for African carvings were not then considered to be art, but to a museum of ethnography, where sculptures, masks, utensils, weapons, ornaments, and other artifacts were jumbled together in dusty display cases. And yet, the young artists insisted, these carvings *were* art, and art of a very high order.

The "discovery" of African art was the culmination of several decades of interest in cultures outside of the European mainstream, beginning with the Impressionists' fascination with Japanese prints in the 1860s. (See Crossing Cultures: Japanese Prints, page 101.) More recently, exhibitions had been held in Paris of Islamic art (1904) and ancient Iberian art (1906)—art from the region of present-day Spain from the 5th and 6th centuries B.C.E. The decorative patterns of Islamic art had a lasting influence on Matisse, while Picasso went through a brief "Iberian" phase. African art was the next step, the latest and most radical reach outside of the West.

For artists seeking ways to break free of the tradition of European naturalism, African sculpture offered a seemingly limitless supply of ingenious solutions for abstracting the human face and form. Fascination with the beauty and power of African art quickly extended beyond Paris into advanced artistic circles across Europe, and it lasted for most of the first half of the 20th century. The interest in African art was more than formal, however. It was part of a larger, more complex, and more troubling phenomenon called primitivism. The word primitive refers to something that is less complex, less sophisticated, or less advanced than what it is being compared to—an earlier stage of it. Designating a culture as "primitive" excused European domination of it. Yet artists, at odds with the larger culture, admired all things primitive. Hoping to renew art by taking it back to its infancy, they looked to the "primitive" arts of Africa and Oceania, which they believed to be instinctive, unchanging, and primordial.

In *Kneeling Mother and Child*, Paula Modersohn-Becker portrays woman in her aspect of life-giver and nurturer, a basic force of nature itself. African sculptures often emphasize these female roles. The woman's monumentalized naked form has an earthbound, sculptural presence. The face especially is "primitivized"—painted in a purposefully unsophisticated, unbeautiful way.

The legacy of primitivism is complicated. Artists were instrumental in drawing serious attention to African and Oceanic art, yet they were completely wrong in thinking of it as primitive. Almost a century later, we are still struggling to see African art on its own terms.

Paula Modersohn Becker. *Kneeling Mother with a Child at Her Breast*. 1907. Oil on canvas, $44^{1}/_{2} \times 29^{1}/_{8}$". Staatliche Museen zu Berlin, Preussischer Kulturbesitz, Nationalgalerie.

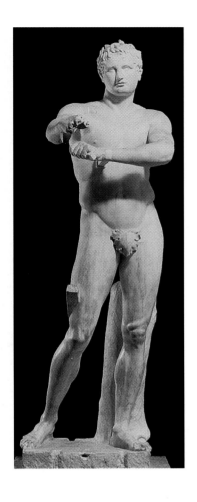

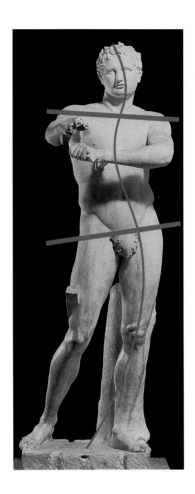

Portrayals of rulers, heroes and heroines, and religious or spirit figures unite the many sculptural traditions of the world. Western culture, however, is marked as well by a tradition of sculpting the human figure for its own sake and of finding the body to be a worthy subject for art. This we owe ultimately to the ancient Greeks. Cultivating the body through gymnastics and sport was an important part of Greek culture, and they admired their athletes greatly. (The Olympics, after all, were a Greek invention.) Not surprisingly, perhaps, they came to believe that the body itself was beautiful. From the many athletic bodies on view, sculptors derived an ideally beautiful body type, governed by harmonious proportions. They gave these idealized, perfected bodies to images of gods and mythological heroes, who were usually depicted nude, and also to images of male athletes, who actually did train and compete unclothed. Finally, Greek artists developed a distinctive stance for their standing figures. Called **contrapposto,** it can be seen here in this statue of an athlete scraping himself off after a workout (**11.21a**).

Contrapposto, meaning "counterpoise" or "counterbalance," sets the body in a gentle *S*-shaped curve through a play of opposites (**11.21b**). Here, the athlete's weight rests on his left foot, so that his left hip is raised and his right leg is bent and relaxed. To counterbalance this, his right shoulder is raised. By portraying the dynamic interplay of a standing body at rest, contrapposto implies the potential for motion inherent in a living being. We can easily imagine that a moment earlier the athlete's weight was arranged differently, and that it will shift again a moment from now.

During the Renaissance, the study of Greek and Roman achievement brought the expressive, idealized body and the contrapposto stance back into Western art. We can see this clearly in such works as Michelangelo's *The Dying Slave* (**11.22**). The sculpture is one of a series of works that

11.21a (left) *Apoxyomenos (Scraper).* Roman copy of a bronze original by Lysippos, c. 320 B.C.E. Marble, height 6′8¾″. Musei Vaticani, Museo Pio Clementino, Rome.

11.21b (center) The dynamics of contrapposto.

11.22 (right) Michelangelo. *The Dying Slave.* 1513–16. Marble, height 7′6″. Musée du Louvre, Paris.

Michelangelo planned for the tomb of Pope Julius II, a project he never completed. We do not know what the figure represents: *The Dying Slave* is simply a name that has become attached to it over the centuries. A companion work depicting a muscular nude struggling against his bonds is known as *The Rebellious Slave*. The two statues may represent the arts in bondage after the death of Pope Julius, one of their great patrons. Less literally, they may also represent two reactions to the bondage of the soul, which longs for release from its earthly prison, the body. What is clear is that the figures are not meant to represent a specific person such as a saint or a martyr, but rather to express an idea or emotion through the body.

Since the Renaissance, the body has continued to serve as a subject through which sculptors express feelings and ideas about the human experience. One 20th-century sculptor who devoted most of his career to the human form was Henry Moore (**11.23**). Moore's particular fascination lay in abstracting the body to explore its visual harmonies with landscape, especially with the sea-smoothed rock formations of his native English coast. The reclining female figure here seems to be sheathed in some kind of close-fitting, elastic covering that she has "sculpted" from within by movements of her limbs. Her alert, vertical torso and head express the idea of consciousness rising out of the natural forms of the earth.

In contrast to Moore's soothing vision of our harmony with natural creation, the works of Polish sculptor Magdalena Abakanowicz suggest a more troubling view of humanity. Many of Abakanowicz' sculptures consist of body parts, repeated over and over, acquiring power and intensity—even menace—by their very repetition. A well-known piece from the late 1970s consisted of eighty headless human torsos, seated and viewed from behind, called *Backs*. A more recent work, *Infantes* (*Children*, **11.24**), presents a long, curving row of paired legs attached to headless, armless torsos. Made of burlap, as are many of Abakanowicz' sculptures, these forms have the texture of skin that is old and wrinkled, possibly burned. One critic has written that the forms suggest victims of a firing squad,[2] and we can readily imagine that some brutal force has hacked at these bodies, leaving them, inexplicably, standing. The

11.23 Henry Moore. *Reclining Figure: Hand.* 1979. Bronze, length 7'3".
The Henry Moore Foundation, Perry Green, England.

sculptor's title is mysterious. If these are children, are they children of war and violence or perhaps children in a harsh school or prison? Whatever the case, these half-bodies, shorn of their heads and features, acquire tremendous dignity. They reproach us, though we are not sure what we have done to harm them.

For Kiki Smith, who came of age artistically during the decade around 1990, the body is a subject that connects the universal and the personal in a unique way. "I think I chose the body as a subject, not consciously, but because it is the one form that we all share," she has said. "It's something that everybody has their own authentic experience with."[3] *Honeywax* (**11.25**) depicts a woman, her knees and right hand drawn up to her chest, her left arm relaxed at her side, her eyes closed. It is hard to say whether she is retreating from the world or about to be born into it. Though Smith set the work on the floor, the figure's pose is that of a person suspended—in air, in fluid, in a dream. Translucent and easily injured, the wax surface suggests human skin, vulnerability, and impermanence. Within the history of sculpture, wax is the material of lost-wax casting, the material that will be discarded to make way for something else, something durable. "I feel I'm making physical manifestations of psychic and spiritual dilemmas," Smith has said. "Spiritual dilemmas are being played out physically."[4] Her words might just as easily have been spoken by Michelangelo about his *Dying Slave* (11.22), and they demonstrate the continuing vitality of the human body as a vehicle for expressing the human experience.

11.24 (above, top) Magdalena Abakanowicz. *Infantes.* 1992. Burlap and resin; 33 figures, height of each c. 4′7″.
Courtesy Marlborough Gallery, New York.

11.25 (above) Kiki Smith. *Honeywax.* 1995. Beeswax, 15½ × 36 × 20″.
Milwaukee Art Museum.

SCULPTURE AND THE ENVIRONMENT

11.26 (left) Red Grooms. *Philadelphia Cornucopia*, detail. 1982. Mixed media. Installed at Institute of Contemporary Art, University of Pennsylvania, Philadelphia.

11.27 (right) Coulibaly Siaka Paul, Emile Guebehi, and Koffi Kouakou, sculptors, with photographs by Malick Sidibé. *The Clubs of Bamako*, as installed at Deitch Projects, New York, 1999.

The term "environmental sculpture" may be used in several ways. First, it can refer to sculptures that are large enough for viewers to enter and move about in, sculptures that create their own environments. Second, it can mean large sculptures designed for display in the outdoor environment, such as a sculpture commissioned for a city square. And third, it can be sculptures that are actually a part of the natural environment, such as the presidents' heads carved out of the natural rock of Mount Rushmore. We will look at one or two examples of each type.

Red Grooms has made a kind of specialty of the huge-scale, zany, colorful sculptured environment depicting a place or event. His constructions—always witty and entertaining, always crammed with people, buildings, and things—resemble a cross between an amusement-park funhouse and a comic strip come to three dimensions. In 1975 Grooms lampooned New York City,

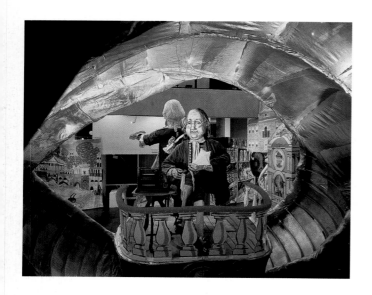

with comic depictions of a subway car, the Brooklyn Bridge, and other landmarks. In 1982 the city of Philadelphia requested the same madcap treatment, in honor of its three-hundredth birthday. The result was *Philadelphia Cornucopia* (**11.26**), a 2,500-square-foot environment installed at the Institute of Contemporary Art. Inspired by the history, romance, and glorious tradition of the city, Red Grooms really went to town. His centerpiece is an 11-foot-tall figure of George Washington, proudly standing at the helm of a "ship of state" whose figurehead is an image of Martha Washington. Many other ghosts from Philadelphia's past rise up in colorful caricature, including Benjamin Franklin (shown here), Thomas Jefferson, and Betsy Ross.

Grooms' constructions are built of any material at hand—wire, cloth, wood, plastic, metal. And they are painted, but not with naturalistic skin tones. Grooms paints his figures the way a clown puts on makeup—the broader, the more exaggerated, the better. *Philadelphia Cornucopia* demonstrates Grooms' desire for active audience participation in large-scale works of art. Viewers are allowed to walk among the structures and interact with the outlandish creatures who dwell there. To enter this environment is to suspend judgments about reality and let the magic take over.

Magic and also music took over in a sculptural environment created recently by a group of African artists (**11.27**). The occasion was a 1999 exhibit of photographs by the Malian photographer Malick Sidibé. Taken during the 1950s and 1960s, the decades in which much of Africa gained its freedom from colonial rule, the photographs capture the vibrant club scene that flourished in the city of Bamako, in Mali, where young people danced every weekend to a mix of European, American, and African hits.

For this exhibit, Coulibaly Siaka Paul, a sculptor from Ivory Coast, was commissioned to carve life-size figures of some of the dancers from the photographs. He in turn invited three colleagues to help him meet the tight deadline. Carved from wood in the naturalistic style favored by many contemporary African sculptors, the wonderfully gyrating figures are painted with glossy enamel paint in flesh tones, shades and tints of gray, and pale yellow, situating them somewhere between the black-and-white world of the photographs and the full spectrum of life itself. Dance music from the period filled the gallery, and few viewers could suppress a smile when they found themselves wandering amid the joyful sights and sounds of Bamako in the 1960s.

Richard Hunt's large work *Jacob's Ladder* (**11.28**) is an example of a sculpture designed both physically and iconographically to fit a particular space. Created for the atrium of Chicago's Carter Woodson Library, the sculpture relates, in abstract terms, the story of the biblical patriarch Jacob. While traveling in the desert, Jacob fell asleep one night and dreamed of a ladder reaching from the earth to Heaven. Angels were moving up and down the ladder, and God appeared at the top, speaking to Jacob. "Jacob's ladder" thus becomes a metaphor for the gateway to Heaven.

In Hunt's interpretation, two giant bronze arms reach down from the skylight (symbolically Heaven), and one holds a curving ladder. On the floor below is a bronze sculpture representing an altar in the desert, with Jacob just waking from his sleep. This metaphor, however, has another layer of meaning. The Carter Woodson Library is located in a predominantly black section of Chicago and is staffed and used mostly by blacks. Richard Hunt, who himself is black, intends his "Jacob's ladder" to represent learning, knowledge, literacy—all of which can be acquired in the library—as the gateway to the "heaven" of equality.

Environmental sculpture on a grand scale occurs when an artist sets out to sculpt the earth itself. The idea is an old one—much older, in fact, than recorded history. Some three thousand years ago, highly organized cultures became established in the Ohio River Valley of what is now the United States. People of the Adena and Hopewell cultures, known collectively as the Mound Builders, constructed giant earthworks, often used as burial mounds and sometimes taking the shapes of animals or birds. The most

11.28 Richard Hunt. *Jacob's Ladder*. 1977. Bronze, overall height of space 18′. Installed at the Carter G. Woodson Regional Library, Chicago.

PUBLIC ART

RARELY HAS THE question "What is art?" caused such a public uproar as in a controversy that erupted in New York City in the early 1980s. At the center of the drama was a monumental sculpture by Richard Serra, entitled *Tilted Arc*, a 12-foot-high, 120-foot-long steel wall installed in a plaza fronting a government building in lower Manhattan.

Commissioned by the Art-in-Architecture division of the General Services Administration, *Tilted Arc* was part of a program that allocates 0.5 percent of the cost of federal buildings to the purchase and installation of public art. Soon after the sculpture's installation, however, the public for whom it was intended spoke out, and their message was a resounding *"That's not art!"* More than 7,000 workers in surrounding buildings signed petitions demanding the sculpture's removal. Opponents of the work had numerous complaints. *Tilted Arc*, they maintained, was ugly, rusty, and a target for graffiti. It blocked the view. It disrupted

pedestrian traffic, since one had to walk all the way around it rather than straight across the plaza. It ruined the plaza for concerts and outdoor ceremonies. At a public hearing, one man summed up the opposition view: "I am here today to recommend its relocation to a better site—a metal salvage yard."[5]

Artists, dealers, and critics rushed to the sculpture's defense. The sculptor himself argued vehemently against any attempt to move *Tilted Arc*, maintaining that it had been commissioned specifically for that site and any new location would destroy its artistic integrity.

The battle raged for many months, and, while there were dissenting voices from all sides, it shaped up principally as a struggle between the art establishment (pro) and the general public (con). At last, in an unusual editorial, *The New York Times*—a newspaper that heavily supports the arts—took a stand. "One cannot choose to see or ignore 'Tilted Arc,' as if it were in a museum or a less conspicuous public place. To the complaining workers in Federal Plaza, it is, quite simply, unavoidable. . . . The public has to live with 'Tilted Arc'; therefore the public has a right to say no, not here."[6]

This time the public won, and the question "What is art?" was answered by a kind of popular referendum, a majority decision. *Tilted Arc* was dismantled and removed in March of 1989.

Does this outcome mean that *Tilted Arc* is not art, or that it isn't good art? No, it does not mean either of those things. It means simply that, in this particular circumstance, the people for whom the art was intended chose to reject the art. And similar circumstances have, very likely, occurred since the earliest artists of prehistory began painting on the walls of their caves.

Richard Serra. *Tilted Arc*. 1981. Cor-Ten steel, 12′ × 120′ × 2½″. Installed at Federal Plaza, New York; Collection General Services Administration (destroyed 1989).

famous of these is the Serpent Mound near Locust Grove, Ohio (**11.29**). No one has yet dated this mound precisely, but it was made at least a thousand years ago. Uncoiled, it would measure a quarter mile in length. From the serpent's head, the body curves back and forth along the crest of a hill, then ends in a spiral tail. Just as we do not know the mound's exact age, we do not know how or why it was built. But this splendid creation fascinates us simply because it survives, long after its makers have vanished from the earth they marked.

Our last two works in this section have something in common that we rarely associate with sculpture: impermanence. Much like the wall drawings we examined at the end of Chapter 6 (see 6.19, 6.20, 6.21), they were created to exist for a brief time only. The idea of impermanent sculpture may surprise us at first, but in fact most of us not only are familiar with it but have made it. An outdoor figure modeled in snow on a cold winter afternoon is destined to melt before spring, but we take pleasure in sculpting it anyway. Castles and mermaids modeled in wet sand by the shore will be washed away when the tide comes in, but we still put great energy and inventiveness into creating them. For festivals and carnivals the world over, weeks and even months are spent creating elaborate figures and floats, all for the sake of a single day's event.

Since the 1960s, many artists have been intrigued by these kinds of events and activities—by the way they bring people together, focus their energy, and intensify life for a moment before disappearing. In their different ways, festivals and sandcastles suggested answers to such questions as how to bring art closer to daily life, and how to make art without making an object that could be sold and owned.

Among the most famous artists to work with these ideas are the husband and wife team of Christo and Jeanne-Claude. For over three decades they have planned and carried out vast art projects involving the cooperation of hundreds of people. A recent work was the wrapping of the Reichstag, a famous building in Berlin and the seat of the German government (**11.30**). Completed on the 24th of June 1995, the wrapping was the result of 25 years of planning and negotiations—not to mention over 60 tons of fabric, 10 miles of blue rope, and the labor of 90 climbers and 120 installation workers! For two weeks, the dark, heavy, ornate building was transformed into a light, shimmering, silvery presence that delighted millions of viewers. Then the wrapping was taken down. The materials were recycled, and the site was left pristine. Christo and Jeanne-Claude accept no funding

11.29 (left) Serpent Mound, near Locust Grove, Ohio. c. 1000 C.E. or earlier. Overall length (uncoiled) c. 1300'.

11.30 (right) Christo and Jeanne-Claude. *Wrapped Reichstag*. Berlin. 1971–1995.
Photo Wolfgang Volz, Christo.

CHRISTO AND JEANNE-CLAUDE

Many artists over time have worked on a grand scale, but none have done so as consistently and as spectacularly as Christo and Jeanne-Claude. Their body of work consists of "projects," most of which have been colossal. Often they wrap things—*large* things—like giant gift packages. They have wrapped a whole section of the Australian coast, cliffs and all, in woven erosion-control fabric. They have wrapped a historic bridge in Paris with 10 acres of silky champagne-colored fabric. In 1995 they wrapped the Reichstag, the German Parliament building in Berlin, with more than a million square feet of shiny aluminum-hued cloth. No passerby could possibly miss these "projects" or ignore them.

Christo and Jeanne-Claude's art is very public, very much out in the open, but the artists themselves remain something of a mystery. According to the brief and rather formal biography they release, Christo Javacheff was born in 1935 in Bulgaria, in eastern Europe. He studied at the Fine Arts Academy in Sofia, then traveled by way of Prague and Vienna to Paris. It was in Paris, in 1958, that Christo began wrapping, at first on a modest scale. As he tells it, he began with small objects, such as chairs and tables and bottles. In Paris, too, Christo met

Jeanne-Claude de Guillebon, born in Casablanca, Morocco, who became his partner.

The first of the large-scale wrapped projects was made in Cologne, Germany, in 1961, when Christo and Jeanne-Claude allowed their own art exhibition to spill outside a gallery beside the Rhine harbor onto the docks. A stack of barrels and other paraphernalia, plus rolls of industrial paper, became the *Dockside Packages.* Other ambitious wrappings followed, but the two artists had yet grander plans. The project that established their international reputation was not, strictly speaking, a wrapping. It was actually more of a *draping.* In 1972 Christo and Jeanne-Claude strung a 4-ton orange nylon curtain between two mountains in Colorado, an arrangement that held intact only long enough to be photographed. They called it *Valley Curtain.*

Two projects in particular transformed Christo and Jeanne-Claude into media celebrities. The first was *Running Fence,* in the mid-1970s, which set up a white nylon barrier 24½ miles long over the hills of northern California. The other was *Surrounded Islands,* in the early 1980s, for which eleven little islands in Florida's Biscayne Bay were circled with pink polypropylene cloth. Earlier projects had been remarkable, daring, extravagant—but these two were lovely. Even people who had objected to such manipulations of the landscape came to admire them. People had to admire quickly, though, for Christo and Jeanne-Claude's structures are meant to stand physically for only a few days or weeks. After a predetermined period, workers remove them, leaving no trace. The projects live on afterward in preparatory sketches, photographs, books, and films.

Some observers have criticized the artists for the transitory nature of their works, but Christo has a ready reply: "I am an artist, and I have to have courage.... Do you know that I don't have any artworks that exist? They all go away when they're finished. Only the sketches are left, giving my works an almost legendary character. I think it takes much greater courage to create things to be gone than to create things that will remain."[7]

Christo and Jeanne-Claude on the roof of the Reichstag, 1995.
Photo by Wolfgang Volz.

from outside sources for such projects, preferring instead to raise the money themselves by selling drawings, collages, and other artwork generated during the planning stages. They are careful to emphasize that their art is not just the end result, but the entire process from planning through dismantling, including the way it energizes people and creates relationships.

Wrapped Reichstag existed only once. In contrast, Jeff Koons' *Puppy* (**11.31**) has already made four appearances in the world and may well make more. One of the most talked-about sculptures of the 1990s, *Puppy* is a 43-foot-tall West Highland terrier made of marigolds, begonias, impatiens, petunias, and other flowering plants set into a steel framework. Koons created *Puppy* for a temporary exhibit in Germany in 1992. In the years since, it has appeared in Sydney, Australia; at the new Guggenheim Museum Bilbao in Spain; and, most recently, at Rockefeller Center in New York, where the photograph shown here was taken. *Puppy* is strictly a warm-weather sculpture. Over the months, his trim green silhouette grows shaggy as he blossoms more and more profusely (an interior irrigation system keeps *Puppy* watered). After a few months, *Puppy* is taken down—possibly to be reerected somewhere else in the world.

Like much of Koons' work, *Puppy* explores issues of taste. It takes its inspiration from objects that people who learn to admire "high art" are traditionally taught to look down on—sentimental paintings of big-eyed dogs on velvet, or little porcelain figurines of adorable animals in pastel colors. Koons enlarges the idea to monumental proportions, covers it in flowers, and dares us not to like it. But it's impossible not to like *Puppy*, a joyful work that wants nothing but to make us happy and to gain our affection.

Apart from its sheer charm, *Puppy* makes an important point about the nature of sculpture: We cannot evaluate sculptures according to how long they last. Classical civilizations made sculptures to survive for all eternity, but they will not. Wood sculptures may burn; stone sculptures are eaten away by acid rain and industrial pollution. In times of war metal sculptures have sometimes been melted down to be turned into bullets. What is important is the sculptor's expression and the experience of the viewer—even if it lasts only for a moment.

11.31 Jeff Koons. *Puppy*. Installation at Rockefeller Center, New York (Summer 2000). Live flowering plants, earth, geotextile, and internal irrigation system; 39′4″ × 16′5″ × 21′4″.
Courtesy the artist.

CHAPTER 12

Crafts

The works of art considered in this chapter have certain things in common with one another, but they also share traits with other media, such as sculpture. Most of them have roots in the traditional trades of the European Middle Ages—potter, glassblower, blacksmith, woodworker, weaver. It is from this background that the word "craft" derives, referring to expert work done by hand. We still describe as "well-crafted" anything finely made, including a chair, an automobile, a house, even sometimes a painting or sculpture. The specific connotation of craft, however, is an object made by hand, not by machine, and this is true of all the works shown in this chapter.

As we discussed in Chapter 2, "craft" and "art" originally shared the same meaning. It was only during the Renaissance that painting, sculpture, and architecture began to be seen as different kinds of activities from carving a chair or forging a wrought iron gate. Indeed, as you read the chapters in the next part of this book, which examine art in a historical context, you will find that art history prior to the Renaissance includes many objects that we might consider crafts, such as Greek vases or medieval European stained glass.

Exploring artistic traditions beyond the West often challenges our categories of art and craft. Many cultures, for example, attribute the kind of meanings that we associate with art to objects we think of as crafts, such as textiles or basketry (see, for example, the Pomo basket, 3.1). Others may value painting as highly as we do, but give equal status to media that we do not, such as ceramics. One common assumption that people make is that craft objects are functional, while art objects are not. Yet in many cultures art objects are quite functional (see, for example, the Baule spirit spouse sculpture, 11.20, which was carved to help solve its owner's personal problems, and which functioned as a dwelling for a spirit).

What, then, separates the craft object from the art object? There is no definite line, nor should there be one. Labels are a convenience for talking about art, but they should not force artworks into cubbyholes. What *may* help to distinguish the crafts from the other arts is their emphasis on particular materials. The traditional materials of the crafts are clay, glass, metal, wood, and fiber. To these we might add jade and lacquer, two materials with important traditions outside the West. Most craft artists concentrate on one material only and have learned to realize its potential for many different kinds of expression. Each of these materials has its own capabilities and limitations, and each lends itself to certain kinds of structural and decorative possibilities. We begin by considering each of these materials in turn.

CLAY

The craft of **ceramics** involves making objects from clay, a naturally occurring earth substance. When dry, clay has a powdery consistency; mixed with water it becomes **plastic**—that is, moldable and cohesive. In this form it can be modeled, pinched, rolled, or shaped between the hands. Once a clay form has been built and permitted to dry, it will hold its shape, but it is very fragile. To ensure permanence the form must be fired in a kiln, at temperatures ranging between about 1,200 and 2,700 degrees Fahrenheit, or higher. Firing changes the chemical composition of the clay so that it can never again be made plastic.

Nearly every culture we know of has practiced the craft of ceramics, and civilizations in the Middle East understood the basic techniques by as early as 5000 B.C.E. A major requirement for most ceramic objects is that they be hollow, that they have thin walls around a hollow core. There are two reasons for this. First, many ceramic wares are meant to contain things—food or liquids, for instance. Second, a solid clay piece is difficult to fire and may very well explode in the kiln. To meet this need for hollowness, ceramists over the ages have developed specialized forming techniques.

One such technique is called slab construction. The ceramist rolls out the clay into a sheet, very much as a baker would roll out a pie crust, and then allows the sheet to dry slightly. The sheet, or slab, can then be handled in many ways. It can be cut into pieces for assembly into a box form, curled into a cylinder, draped over a mold to make a bowl, or shaped into free-form sculptural configurations.

Slab construction was used to create the little horse shown here (**12.1**). This charming figure is an example of *haniwa*—clay figures placed around Japanese burial mounds between the 3rd and the 6th centuries. *Haniwa* were made to represent many subjects—horses, warriors, birds, and elegant costumed ladies. They were rendered in simple, tubular forms—the word *haniwa* means "circle of clay." This figure intentionally looks more like a toy horse than a real one. The slab construction lends itself readily to the creation of these basic sculptural forms.

12.1 *Haniwa* figure of a horse. Japan, 5th–6th century C.E. Terra cotta, height 23″. The Cleveland Museum of Art.

12.2 (left) María and Julián Martínez. Jar. Matte black on polished black earthenware.

12.3 (right) Stem cup with three fruits. China, Ming dynasty, c. 1430. Porcelain painted in underglaze red, height 4″.
National Palace Museum, Taipei.

Coiling is another technique for making a thin, hollow form. The ceramist rolls out ropelike strands of clay, then coils them upon one another and joins them together. A vessel made from coils attached one atop the other will have a ridged surface, but the coils can be smoothed completely to produce a uniform, flat wall. The native peoples of the southwestern United States made extraordinarily large, finely shaped pots by coiling. In this century their craft has been revived by a few supremely talented individuals, including the famous Pueblo potter María Martínez (**12.2**).

By far the fastest method of creating a hollow, rounded form is by means of the potter's wheel. Egyptian potters were using the wheel by about 4000 B.C.E. Despite some modern improvements and the addition of electricity, the basic principle of wheel construction remains the same as it was in ancient times. The wheel is a flat disk mounted on a vertical shaft, which can be made to turn rapidly either by electricity or by foot power. The ceramist centers a mound of clay on the wheel and, as the wheel turns, uses the hands to shape, "open," and lift the clay form—a procedure known as throwing. Throwing on the wheel always produces a rounded or cylindrical form, although the thrown pieces can later be reshaped, cut apart, or otherwise altered. Two or more thrown forms can also be joined together, as was done with this elegant Chinese cup (**12.3**). The cup is made of a special clay mixture, which, when fired at very high temperatures, becomes a translucent, white, glasslike ceramic called **porcelain.** The secret of porcelain was discovered and perfected in China, and for hundreds of years potters elsewhere tried without success to duplicate it. European potters finally stumbled onto the secret in 1710, but even today our word for the finest pottery is the same as the name of the country that invented it, china.

Porcelain is made of a mixture of a fine white clay called kaolin and a feldspar quartz called petuntse. Other types and mixtures of clay result in other types of ceramic, each with its own characteristics. Stoneware clays, which fire at medium temperatures, are generally brown or grayish. Much commercial dinnerware is made of stoneware, and these clays have been popular among artist-potters. Earthenware clays, generally red or brown, fire at lower temperatures. Fired earthenware is often called by its Italian name, terra cotta. Flowerpots are a good example of terra cotta in everday use.

If you've ever watered a plant in a terra-cotta pot, you know that earthenware is porous and soaks up water. To make it watertight, it must be

MARÍA MARTÍNEZ
1881(?)–1980

IT IS A long way in miles and in time between the tiny pueblo of San Ildefonso in New Mexico and the White House in Washington, D.C. But the extraordinary ceramic artist María Martínez made that journey, and many others, in a long lifetime devoted to the craft of pottery making. María—as she signed herself and is known professionally—began her career as a folk potter and ended it six decades later as a first-ranked potter of international reputation.

A daughter of Pueblo people, María most likely was born in 1881, but there are no records. As a child she learned to make pottery, using the coil method, by watching her aunt and other women in the community. Part of her youth was spent at St. Catherine's Indian School in Santa Fe, where María became friends with Julián Martínez. The couple married in 1904.

Although the husband worked at other jobs, the two Martínezes early formed a partnership for making pottery—she doing the building, he the decorating. Between 1907 and 1910 he was employed as a laborer on an archaeological site near the pueblo, under the direction of Dr. Edgar L. Hewett. The amazing career of María Martínez was launched in a simple way; Dr. Hewett gave her a broken piece of pottery from the site and asked her to reconstruct a whole pot in that style using the traditional blackware techniques.

About 1919 the Martínezes developed the special black-on-black pottery that was to make them and the pueblo of San Ildefonso famous. The shiny blackware—created from red clay by a process of smothering the dung-fueled bonfire used for firing—was decorated with matte-black designs. This black-on-black ware was commercially quite successful. María Martínez and her husband became wealthy by the standards of the pueblo and, as was customary, shared that wealth with the entire community.

María bore four sons who survived. Eventually they and their wives and children and grandchildren became partners in her enterprise. One shadow on her domestic life was her husband's serious alcoholism, which began early in their marriage and contributed to his death in 1943. After he was gone, María's daughter-in-law Santana took over much of the decorating of pots, later to be followed by María's son Poponi Da.

As María's fame spread, she traveled widely, giving demonstrations at many world's fairs. Among the awards she received were an honorary doctorate from the University of Colorado and the American Ceramic Society's highest honor for a lifetime of devotion to clay. Her visit to Washington during the 1930s was a highlight. President Franklin D. Roosevelt was not at home, but Mrs. Eleanor Roosevelt was, and she told María, "You are one of the important ones. We have a piece of your pottery here in the White House, and we treasure it and show it to visitors from overseas."

Undoubtedly, María's greatest achievement was in reviving and popularizing the traditions of fine pottery making among the Pueblo people. Not long before her death, according to her great-granddaughter, she said: "When I am gone, essentially other people have my pots. But to you I leave my greatest achievement, which is the ability to do it."[1]

Photograph of María Martínez.

12.4 George Ohr. High glaze free-form bowl. Height 3½". The Ohr-O'Keefe Museum of Art, Biloxi, Mississippi.

coated with glaze. A **glaze** is a glasslike material applied to the surface of an already fired ceramic piece. The piece is then fired a second time to fuse the glaze with the clay body. While there are clear glazes, most glazes have color, and this is a major reason for their application. There is virtually no limit to the different effects that can be produced by combination of glazes or by the various methods of applying them. The red pomegranate that seems to have breathed itself onto the side of the Chinese porcelain cup, for example, was produced with an underglazing technique. The persimmon was painted directly onto the fired body of the cup; then the white glaze was applied over it. During firing, the white glaze becomes transparent, and the red (the underglaze) shows through.

A more informal approach to glazing can be seen in this free-form bowl by George Ohr (**12.4**). One of the true eccentrics of American art, Ohr dubbed himself "the mad potter of Biloxi," after his hometown in Mississippi. Using local clays he dug himself, he could throw as perfectly formed a pot as any potter who ever lived, but his most famous pieces use the thrown form simply as a starting point. While the clay was still pliable, Ohr would take the newly formed pot and start to play with it, bending, pinching, tearing, and folding it into a unique sculptural form such as the one here. While the rich colors of his glazes brought him fame, Ohr himself insisted that color was a distraction, although admittedly a seductive one, from the all-important form. He intentionally left many of his later works unglazed, and he wrote in anger to a critic, "Colors and Quality counts *nothing* in my creations . . . God put no color or quality in souls."[2]

GLASS

If clay is one of the most versatile of the craft materials, glass is perhaps the most fascinating. Few people, when presented with a beautiful glass form, can resist holding it up to the light, watching how light changes its appearance from different angles.

While there are thousands of formulas for glass, its principal ingredient is usually silica, or sand. The addition of other materials can affect color, melting point, strength, and so on. When heated, glass becomes molten, and in that state it can be shaped by several different methods. Unlike clay, glass never changes chemically as it moves from a soft, workable state to a hard, rigid one. As glass cools it hardens, but it can then be reheated and rendered molten again for further working.

Glass as a material holds many risks, both during the creative process and afterward. The shaping of a glass object demands split-second timing—quick decisions and quick handwork—while the glass remains hot. What's more, a finished glass piece is the most fragile of all craft wares. One swift blow can shatter it irreparably. There is something almost heroic about an artist who would spend days, weeks, even months making an object that is so vulnerable.

A special branch of glass craft, **stained glass** is a technique used for windows, lampshades, and similar structures that permit light to pass through. Stained glass is made by cutting sheets of glass in various colors into small pieces, then fitting the pieces together to form a pattern. Often the segments are joined by strips of lead, hence the term *leaded* stained glass. The 12th and 13th centuries in Europe were a golden age for stained glass. In the religious philosophy that guided the building of the great cathedrals of that time, light was viewed as a spiritually transforming substance. The soaring interiors of the new cathedrals were illuminated by hundreds of jewel-like windows such as the one illustrated here from the Cathedral of Notre Dame at Chartres, France (**12.5**). The central motif is a branching tree that portrays the royal lineage of Mary, mother of Jesus. The tree springs from the loins of the biblical patriarch Jesse, depicted asleep at the base of the window. Growing upward, it enthrones in turn four kings of Judaea, then Mary, then Jesus himself.

Glass is commonly shaped by blowing, a technique that dates from Roman times. To blow glass, the artist dips up a portion of molten glass at the end of a long pipe. By blowing through the opposite end of the pipe he or she produces a glass bubble that can be shaped or cut by various methods while it is still hot. Contemporary glass artists often strive for a balance of form and decoration. Dale Chihuly's designs are exuberant and deliberately sculptural (**12.6**). Their decoration seems to evolve from the form itself, rather than being applied to an existing structure. Chihuly's blown-glass works are very thin and translucent; they have an organic quality that is reminiscent of shapes in the natural world.

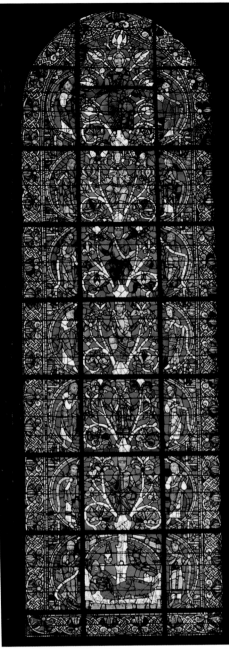

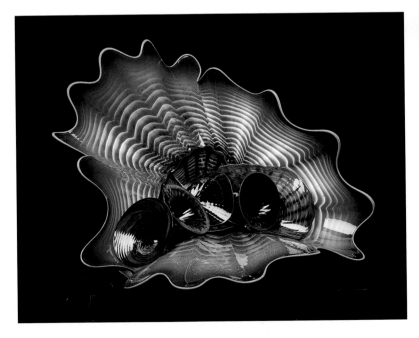

12.5 (above) *Tree of Jesse*, west facade, Chartres Cathedral, France. c. 1150–70. Stained glass.

12.6 (left) Dale Chihuly. *Violet and Green Persian Set*. 1990. Blown glass, 18 × 32 × 32". Courtesy the artist.

METAL

From the most fragile craft material we turn to the most indestructible. Metals rust and corrode under some circumstances, but they do not shatter, chip, or rot away. Ever since humans learned to work metals, they have made splendid art, as well as functional tools, from this versatile family of materials. One distinctive aspect of metal is that it is equally at home in the mundane and the sublime—the bridge that spans a river or the precious ring on a finger; the plow that turns up the earth or the crown on a princess' head. Whatever the application, the basic composition of the material is the same, and the methods of working it are similar.

As discussed in Chapter 11, metal can be shaped by heating it to a liquid state and pouring it into a mold, a process known as casting (see 11.5). Another ancient technique is **forging**—the art of the blacksmith. Forging involves heating a chunk of metal over a fire until it is red-hot, then beating and shaping it with hammers. This is how horseshoes traditionally were made, and it is also the method of making wrought iron, as for balconies and railings.

Some metals, such as gold and silver, are soft enough to be worked cold—cut and hammered into shape without heating. The silver gilt covering for this 10th-century Byzantine reliquary (**12.7**) was hammered in a thin sheet over a wooden core—a technique known as *repoussé*—then set with precious stones and enameled gold panels. Enamel is a mixture of pigment and powdered glass, melted and fused to a metal surface at high heat. Here it was applied using the *cloisonné* technique, a Byzantine specialty in which color areas are first outlined with thin metal bands (known by their French name, *cloisons*) and the enamels are poured into the resulting compartments.

12.7 Lid of the Limburg Staurotheca. Byzantine, 968–985 C.E. Hammered gilt metal, enamels, gems, on a wooden core; 19 × 13¾".
Diocesan Museum, Limburg an der Lahn.

A reliquary is a container for sacred remains, in this case for slivers of wood believed to have come from the cross on which Christ was crucified. The radiant exterior was thus intended as an outward sign of the precious nature of its contents. An inscription around the border tells us that this reliquary, one of the most important surviving examples of Byzantine metalwork, was commissioned by an official named Basil, the illegitimate son of a Byzantine emperor and an important patron of the arts.

Every bit as expert as the Christian artists of medieval Byzantium were their neighbors, the artists of the Islamic empires that then stretched from southern Spain across North Africa and east to the borders of India. The richly decorated basin illustrated here (12.8) was made for al-Nasir Muhammad ibn Qala'un a 14th-century sultan of the Mamluk dynasty, which ruled from Cairo, in Egypt. Fashioned of hammered brass and decorated with gold and silver inlay, such basins were among the most coveted products of Islamic metalworkers. The principal decoration is a flowing calligraphic inscription in praise of the sultan himself. The roundels (circular areas) are filled with a design of lotus flowers and were probably inspired by imported Chinese textiles.

One of the oldest uses of metal as an expressive medium is for jewelry. This has been true since prehistoric times. Early cultures believed that wearing special stones or special metals could ward off disease and evil spirits—a practice continued today in the wearing of copper bracelets for therapeutic purposes. Apart from its supposed magical powers, metal has great symbolic value. People wear jewelry to symbolize wealth and status. They also wear jewelry to symbolize belonging—to a person (a wedding ring), to an institution (a school ring), to a group (a club or fraternity or religious ring).

In many parts of the world, jewelry and other forms of dress may also signal ethnicity and social standing. In the bustling African trading towns along the southern fringes of the Sahara desert, you might encounter merchants and customers from numerous regional peoples. But if you saw a woman wearing earrings like the ones illustrated here (12.9), you would know immediately that she was Fulani. Made of beaten gold and varying in size from discreet to shoulder-grazing, these distinctive four-lobed earrings are a traditional Fulani design. In a culture that emphasizes physical beauty and display, such jewelry serves at once as a personal ornament, a sign of ethnic identity, and an investment: a woman literally wears her family's wealth.

12.8 (above) Basin made for Sultan al-Nasir Muhammad ibn Qala'un. Cairo or Damascus, c. 1320–41. Brass, gold, silver; height 9″; diameter 21¼″. The British Museum, London.

12.9 (below) Pair of earrings. Fulani. Hammered gold. Private collection.

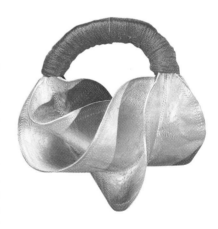

WOOD

There are two reasons for the great popularity of wood as a craft material. One is that it is relatively easy to work. The simplest tools will shape it, and there is no need for extreme heat, as with clay, glass, or metal. The second reason is that wood is so widely available. In most inhabited areas of the globe, wood is abundant and easy to obtain. These two qualities would make wood the ideal material were it not for certain drawbacks. Because of its organic nature, wood is not very durable. Cold and heat distort it, water rots it, and insects can eat it away. We must assume that only a tiny fraction of the wood objects made over the centuries have survived.

Woods vary in hue from rich black through creamy off-white. Renaissance crafts workers made ingenious use of this natural palette in a technique called **intarsia,** in which woods were painstakingly cut and inlaid to form mosaic images such as the one illustrated here (**12.10**). This latticed cupboard, its doors open to reveal books and other possessions, is a detail from the intarsia murals covering the walls of a private study built in 1480 for an Italian nobleman named Federico da Montefeltro, Duke of Urbino. The duke was a learned man, a patron of scholars and artists, and the cabinets depicted in his study are filled with objects that point to his interests and duties—books, scientific and musical instruments, armor, honors, and insignia. All are depicted according to the newly discovered principles of linear perspective and chiaroscuro: even the cast shadows are painstakingly pieced in wood.

A far more common product of the woodworker's art is furniture. The basic forms of furniture are surprisingly ancient. The chair, for example, seems to have been developed in Egypt around 2600 B.C.E. Massive thrones for rulers and humble stools for ordinary people had existed earlier, but the idea of a portable seat with a back and armrests was an innovation (**12.11**). Miraculously preserved by the dry desert climate of Egypt, this chair, one of the oldest known, shows that artistic attention was lavished on furniture

12.10 *Cabinet with Books and Order of the Garter,* detail of the *Gubbio Studiolo.* c. 1480. Intarsia. The Metropolitan Museum of Art, New York.

from the very beginning. The chair's legs are carved as the legs and paws of a lion, an emblem of royal power. Within the open frames of the armrests are carved bouquets of papyrus flowers, a symbol of Lower (northern) Egypt.

Any symbolism in Klindt Houlberg's *Phantasy Plenishing* (**12.12**) must be purely personal, but it certainly would be interesting to know what it is! *Phantasy Plenishing* looks like a normal, well-crafted bed frame—up to about a foot from the floor. Above that the artist's imagination runs wild. One bedpost is a nude female figure, another a fantasy tree with a bird perched on top, and so on. Houlberg's work makes us realize how rich our environment could be if more everyday objects were treated with this kind of creative expressiveness.

12.11 (left) Chair of Hetepheres. Egypt, Dynasty 4, reign of Sneferu, 2575–2551 B.C.E. Wood and gold leaf.
Egyptian Museum, Cairo.

12.12 (right) Klindt Houlberg. *Phantasy Plenishing.* 1980. Wood, height 6′8″.
Courtesy the artist.

FIBER

The design possibilities for works of fiber are enormous. By fiber we mean a narrow strand of vegetable or animal material (cotton, linen, wool, silk) or the modern-day synthetic equivalents. Like wood, fiber is widely available and quite perishable, but the construction methods used for fiber are unique to this pliable medium.

For centuries the most common method of working with fiber has been weaving. Weaving involves placing two sets of parallel fibers at right angles to one another and interlacing one set through the other in an up-and-down movement, generally on a loom or frame. One set of fibers is held taut; this is called the warp. The other set, known as the weft or woof, is interwoven through the warp to make a textile. Nearly all textiles, including those used for our clothing, are made by some variation of this process.

The ancient Incas, whose civilization flourished in the mountains of Peru during the 15th century, held textiles in such high regard that they draped gold and silver statues of their deities with fine cloth offerings. Textiles were also accepted as payment for taxes, for they were considered a form of wealth. Standardized patterns and colors on Incan tunics instantly signaled the wearer's ethnicity and social status in much the same manner

12.13 (left) Tunic, from Peru. Inca, c. 1500. Wool and cotton, 35⅞ × 30″.
Dumbarton Oaks Research Library and Collections, Washington, D.C.

12.14 (right) *The Unicorn in Captivity* from *The Hunt of the Unicorn*. Franco-Flemish, c. 1500. Wool, silk, and silver and silver-gilt threads; 12′ × 8′3″.
The Metropolitan Museum of Art, New York.

as the Fulani earrings we examined earlier (see 12.9). Woven around 1500, the fascinating royal tunic illustrated here (**12.13**) is a virtual catalogue of such patterns, although scholars have not yet succeeded in identifying them all. The black-and-white checkerboard pattern, for example, represents the Inca military uniform in miniature. By wearing this tunic, the king visually declared his dominance over all of Incan society.

Tapestry is a special type of weaving in which the weft yarns are manipulated freely to form a pattern or design on the front of the fabric. Often the weft yarns are of several colors, and the weaver can use the different-colored yarns almost as flexibly as a painter uses pigment on canvas. Tapestry weaving experienced a golden age in Europe from the late 14th through the 17th centuries. For those who could afford it, tapestry was the art of choice. In place of the paintings we would expect to see now, the castles and great houses of Europe were hung with finely woven cloths, often with elaborate pictorial images.

Among the best-known and most admired of these works is *The Hunt of the Unicorn*, a series of seven panels depicting a popular medieval story. According to legend, the unicorn, a wild and fleet one-horned beast, could be tamed only by a virgin. Early panels in the series show the unicorn being hunted by a band of men. When it lays its head in a virgin's lap, it is captured and killed, then brought back to the castle. Finally, the unicorn is restored to life. The final tapestry shows *The Unicorn in Captivity* (**12.14**), seemingly content in its wooden pen. Medieval European art and storytelling often mix mythological and religious themes, and *The Hunt of the Unicorn* provides an excellent example. The unicorn legend is intended as a parallel to the Passion of Christ, who assumed a human nature through being born of the Virgin Mary, was killed, and then was resurrected. Yet another layer of meaning shows in the last panel, for the abundant foliage surrounding the captive unicorn was associated with love and fertility, suggesting that these tapestries were woven to celebrate a marriage.

Islamic cultures, in contrast, do not have a history of tapestries, but instead have focused a great deal of aesthetic attention on carpets and rugs. Among the most famous Islamic textiles is the pair of immense rugs known as the Ardabil carpets, of which we illustrate the one in the collection of London's Victoria and Albert Museum (**12.15**). Like most Islamic carpets, they were created by knotting individual tufts of wool onto a woven ground. The labor was minute and time-consuming: the London Ardabil carpet has forty-six knots per square inch, or over twelve million knots in all!

The design features a central sunburst medallion with sixteen radiating pendants. Two mosque lamps, one larger than the other, extend from the medallion as well. Quarter segments of the medallion design appear in the corners of the rug. These elements seem to float over a deep blue ground densely patterned with flowers, making of the carpet a sort of stylized garden. (In a similar figure of speech, we talk of a field in springtime as being "carpeted in flowers.") Paradise in Islam is imagined as a garden, and such flower-strewn carpets represent a luxurious, domesticated reminder of this ideal world to come. Underscoring the religious associations of the design is a couplet from the 14th-century Persian poet Hafiz, woven into a square at one end of the carpet: "I have no refuge in the world other than thy threshold; / My head has no resting-place other than this doorway."

In the United States, one of the most popular textile arts is quilting. Quilting has a strong social component, for it has often furnished a regular occasion for women to spend an evening together, sewing, telling stories, sharing their lives. Quilting also has a special relationship to the African American community, for examples survive made by slaves and former slaves during the 19th century. One of the most famous of these is the *Bible Quilt* by Harriet Powers (**12.16**). Unlike many quilts, this was not a group effort but represents Powers' own unique artistic vision. Using a technique called appliqué, in which pieces of colored fabric are cut and sewn to a fabric ground to create a design, she illustrated a series of scenes drawn from the Bible as well as moments from local lore that were believed to show God's working in the world. The scene at the very center, for example, depicts a meteor show that was witnessed over Georgia in November 1833. It was interpreted as a sign that the world was coming to an end, Powers later explained, until God's hand stayed the falling stars. Two squares to the left is a depiction of Jonah being swallowed by a great fish, as related in the Bible.

12.15 (above) Ardabil carpet. Persia (Tabriz?). 1539–40. Wool pile on undyed silk warps, length 34'5¾".
Victoria and Albert Museum, London.

12.16 (left) Harriet Powers. *Bible Quilt.* c. 1898. Pieced, appliquéd, and printed cotton embroidered with plain and metallic yarns. 5'8⅞" × 8'9⅛".
Courtesy Museum of Fine Arts, Boston.

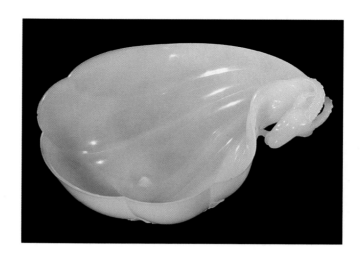

JADE AND LACQUER

12.17 (above) *The Shah Jahan Cup*. Mughal, 17th century. Jade, length 7⅜".
Victoria and Albert Museum, London.

12.18 (below) Jitoku Akazuka. Writing box entitled *Dancing Cranes*. 1921. Lacquer, gold, and mother-of-pearl on wood, 8¾ × 10 × 2⅛".
The National Museum of Modern Art, Kyoto.

Jade and lacquer have long histories as craft media, although not in the West. Jade is a common name for two minerals, nephrite and jadeite. Ranging in color from white through shades of brown and green, the two stones are found principally in East and Central Asia and Central America. While their underlying structures differ, both share the extreme hardness, the ice-cold touch, and the mesmerizing, translucent beauty that have caused jade to be treasured in cultures lucky enough to have access to it.

The ancient Olmecs, whose jade figure of a shaman we looked at in Chapter 3 (see 3.7), prized green jade. They associated its color with plant life—especially with corn, their most important crop—and its translucence with rainwater, on which agricultural bounty depended. In China, jade of all colors has been prized and carved for some 6,000 years. In early Chinese belief, the stone was credited with magical properties.

Eastern Islamic rulers also developed a taste for jade, which they procured from their lands in Central Asia. During the 17th century, jade from this region was made available to Shah Jahan, a ruler of the Mughal empire, an Islamic kingdom in India. Among the objects that issued from the royal workshops was this wine cup, made for Shah Jahan himself (**12.17**). Carved of translucent white jade, the cup takes the form of a gourd that swirls gently into a handle carved in the form of an ibex head. On the underside, not visible here, is a small pedestal carved as an overturned lotus blossom. A more exquisite vessel has never been imagined.

Lacquer is a material specific to East Asia, for it is made of the sap of a tree that originally grew only in China. Harvested, purified, colored with dyes, and brushed in thin coats over wood, the sap hardens into a smooth, glasslike coating. The technique demands great patience, for up to thirty coats of lacquer are needed to build up a substantial layer, and each must dry thoroughly before the next can be applied. Ancient Chinese artisans used lacquer to create trays, bowls, storage jars, and other wares that were lightweight and delicate-looking yet water-resistant and airtight. Exported along with other luxury goods over the long overland trade route known as the Silk Road, Chinese lacquerware was admired as far away as the Roman Empire.

The technique of lacquer spread early from China to Korea and Japan, as did cultivation of the sap-producing tree. A 20th-century example of lacquerware is this box for writing materials by the Japanese lacquer artist Jitoku Akazuka (**12.18**). Built up over a thin wooden core, the black lacquer surface is subtly textured to suggest flowing water. Cranes created with mother-of-pearl inlay and sprinkled gold powder wheel gracefully over the lacquer waves. An auspicious symbol of longevity, cranes are a popular decorative motif in East Asia.

BLURRING THE BOUNDARIES: ARTISTS AND CRAFTS

Most people are surprised to learn that Leonardo da Vinci, in addition to painting, designed costumes and scenery for elaborate theatrical productions. Another Renaissance artist, Raphael, drew designs for tapestries. Benvenuto Cellini, whose sculpture of Perseus we looked at in the previous chapter (see 11.6), was by training a goldsmith, and his most famous work is a gold saltcellar (a serving bowl for salt) created for King Francis I of France. During the 20th century, Picasso designed and decorated pottery, the sculptor Alexander Calder made jewelry, and Matisse designed stained glass windows and rugs.

Artists have often reached out to apply their talents for visual expression and organization to crafts. Beginning in the 1970s, however, some artists also began bringing the materials and techniques of crafts into art. An important force behind this blurring of the boundaries was the first wave of feminism. Angered by a gallery and museum system that overwhelmingly favored male artists and by a standard account of art history in which women artists played virtually no role, early feminist artists sought to create art that was specifically female, art rooted in the biological, psychological, social, and historical experience of women.

Judy Chicago's *The Dinner Party* (**12.19**) is perhaps the most important and influential work from this time. A collaborative work, *The Dinner Party* was executed with the help of hundreds of women and several men. Arranged around a triangular table are thirty-nine place settings, each one created in honor of an influential woman such as the Egyptian ruler Hatshepsut and

12.19 Judy Chicago. *The Dinner Party*. 1979. Mixed media, each side 48′.

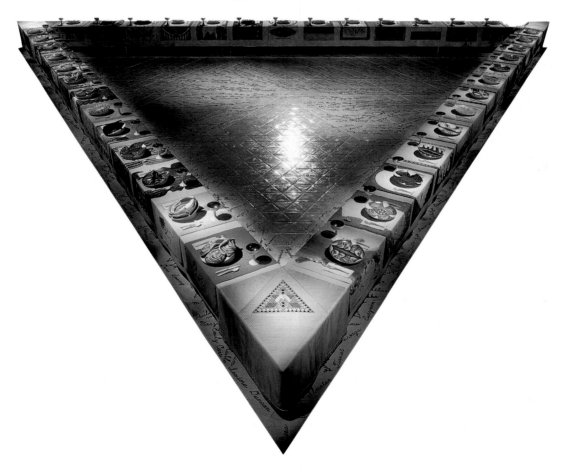

the novelist Virginia Woolf. The names of an additional 999 important women are written on the tile floor. By using such craft techniques as ceramics, weaving, needlepoint, and embroidery, Chicago demanded artistic equality for occupations that had long been considered "women's work." Confined to the domestic sphere, the vast majority of women throughout history had been limited to these expressive outlets—including the expressive outlet of setting and decorating a table—and *The Dinner Party* honors them. The thirteen places on each side of the triangle intentionally evoke the seating arrangement of Leonardo's *Last Supper* (see 4.41), a central work in the history of Western art, and one that depicts an all-male gathering.

Another artist who draws on the historical role of crafts in women's lives is Faith Ringgold, whose *The Purple Quilt* (**12.20**) is painted in acrylic on a ground created of tie-dyed and printed fabric, pieced together and quilted. One of a series of "painted story quilts," *The Purple Quilt* is a tribute to Alice Walker's novel *The Color Purple*. It is meant to celebrate not only women's experience but also black experience, and it draws on the tradition of such works as Harriet Powers' *Bible Quilt*, which we looked at earlier in this chapter (see 12.16).

Thanks in part to the pioneering efforts of artists such as Judy Chicago and Faith Ringgold, artists have become increasingly sensitive to the expressive possibilities of crafts. Kiki Smith, for example, employed glassblowers to execute the weighted, droplike forms of *Shed* (**12.21**), which she then arranged across the floor in a gentle arc. This "shedding" could be of any red substance, but the one that comes to mind, correctly, is blood. In Chapter 11 we looked at Smith's wax figure of a woman as a recent example of the human figure in sculpture (see 11.25). *Shed* demonstrates how the artist's

12.20 (left) Faith Ringgold. *The Purple Quilt*. 1986. Acrylic on cotton canvas, tie-dyed, printed, and pieced fabrics; 7'7" × 6'. Private collection.

12.21 (right) Kiki Smith. *Shed*. 1996. Glass, forty-three units, height 2¹/₂–10¹/₂"; dimensions variable with installation. Courtesy Shoshana Wayne Gallery, Santa Monica.

investigation of our physical nature begins with more basic questions: What is a body, and what is it to have one? Encased in a fragile and permeable skin, the body is full of organs we would rather not think about and fluids we are taught not to mention. Over the years, Smith has given them sculptural presence. Tears and sperm, blood and urine, uterus and rib cage—all of these have appeared in her art, translated into such diverse craft materials as glass, silver, and ceramic.

The body is present by its absence in Oliver Herring's *Castle*, from the series *A Flower for Ethyl Eichelberger* (**12.22**). Ethyl Eichelberger was the stage name of a performance artist who committed suicide while dying of AIDS. Shortly afterward, in 1991, Herring began an extended memorial project, knitting a series of garments in Mylar, a flimsy, shiny plastic material with no "art pedigree." Knitting is a traditionally feminine craft, and Herring chose it deliberately as a tribute to Eichelberger's gender-bending stage persona. Monotonous and repetitive, knitting is also a way of marking time. Looking at the light-filled, almost ghostlike coat, we sense time's slow passing as stitch by stitch, row by row, the minutes, hours, and weeks of grief pass by for the survivor. Both the open coat and the bed it lies on point to the person who is absent, whose body will no longer fill the coat, no longer rest in the bed.

Herring could have carved his tribute in marble or cast it in bronze, but the ordinary, everyday materials and techniques of craft add a layer of poignancy that these more majestic and durable materials could not offer. Like *Castle*, much recent art formed of craft materials speaks of intimate or deeply personal concerns, reminding us that while spectacular craft objects may often have been made for the rich and powerful, the roots of craft are in our daily lives.

12.22 Oliver Herring. *Castle*, from *A Flower for Ethyl Eichelberger*. 1994. Knitted transparent Mylar, 9 × 47 × 65".
Courtesy Max Protech Gallery, New York.

CHAPTER 13

Architecture

Architecture satisfies a basic, universal human need for a roof over one's head. More than walls, more than a chair to sit on or a soft bed upon which to lie, a roof is the classic symbol of protection and security. We've all heard the expression "I have a roof over my head," but it would be unusual to hear someone say, "I'm all right because I have walls around me." Of course, in purely practical terms a roof does keep out the worst of the elements, snow and rain, and in warm climates a roof may be sufficient to keep people dry and comfortable. The roof seems to be symbolic of the nature of architecture.

More than any of the other arts, architecture demands structural stability. Every one of us daily moves in and out of buildings—schools, houses, offices, stores, churches, bus stations, banks, and movie theaters—and we take for granted, usually without thinking about it, that they will not collapse on top of us. That they do not is a tribute to their engineering; if a building is physically stable, this means it adheres faithfully to the principles of the particular *structural system* on which its architecture is based.

STRUCTURAL SYSTEMS IN ARCHITECTURE

Any building is a defiance of gravity. Since earliest times architects have tackled the challenge of erecting a roof over empty space, setting walls upright, and having the whole stand secure. Their solutions have depended upon the materials they had available, for, as we shall see, certain materials are better suited than others to a particular structural system. There are two basic families of structural systems: the shell system and the skeleton-and-skin system.

In the shell system one building material provides both structural support and sheathing (outside covering). Buildings made of brick or stone or adobe fall into this category, and so do older (pre-19th-century) wood buildings constructed of heavy timbers, the most obvious example being the log cabin. The structural material comprises the walls and roof, marks the boundary between inside and outside, and is visible as the exterior surface. Shell construction prevailed until the 19th century, when it began to fall out of favor. Today, however, the development of strong cast materials, including many plastics, has brought renewed interest in shell structures.

The skeleton-and-skin system might be compared to the human body, which has a rigid bony skeleton to support its basic frame and a more fragile skin for sheathing. We find it in modern skyscrapers, with their steel frames (skeletons) supporting the structure and a sheathing (skin) of glass or some other light material. Also, most houses today—at least in the United States—are built with a skeleton of wood beams nailed together, topped with a sheathing of light wood boards, shingles, aluminum siding, or the like. Skeleton-and-skin construction is largely a product of the Industrial Revolution; not until the mid-19th century could steel for beams or metal nails be manufactured in practical quantities.

Two factors that must be considered in any structural system are weight and tensile strength. Walls must support the weight of the roof, and lower stories must support the weight of upper stories. In other words, all the weight of the building must somehow be carried safely to the ground. You can get a sense of this if you imagine your own body as a structural member. Suppose you are lying flat on your back, your body held rigid. You are going to be lifted high in the air, to become a "roof." First you are lifted by four people: One supports you under the shoulders, one under the buttocks, one holds your arms extended above your head, another holds your feet. Your weight is therefore channeled down through four vertical people to the ground, and so you can hold yourself horizontally with some ease. Next you are lifted by two people, one holding your shoulders, another your feet. A lot of your weight is concentrated in the center of your body, which is unsupported, so eventually you sag in the middle and fall to the floor. Then you are lifted by one person, who holds you at the center of your back. The weight at both ends of your body has nowhere to go, nothing to carry it to the ground, and you sag at both ends.

Tensile strength, as applied to architecture, is the ability of a material to span horizontal distances with minimum support from underneath. Returning to the analogy of the body, imagine you are made not of flesh and blood but of strong plastic or metal. Regardless of how you are held up in the air, you can stay rigid and horizontal, because you have great tensile strength.

If you keep these images in mind, you may find it easier to understand the various structural systems we shall consider below. They are introduced here in roughly the chronological order in which they were developed. As was mentioned earlier, all will be of the shell type until the 19th century.

LOAD-BEARING CONSTRUCTION

Another term for load-bearing construction is "stacking and piling." This is the simplest method of making a building, and it is suitable for brick, stone, adobe, ice blocks, and certain modern materials. Essentially, the builder constructs the walls by piling layer upon layer, starting thick at the bottom, getting thinner as the structure rises, and usually tapering inward near the highest point. The whole may then be topped by a lightweight roof, perhaps of thatch or wood. This construction is stable, because its greatest weight is concentrated at the bottom and weight diminishes gradually as the walls grow higher.

Load-bearing structures tend to have few and small openings (if any) in the walls, because the method does not readily allow for support of material above a void, such as a window opening. Yet it would be a mistake to think that such basic methods must produce basic results. The Great Friday Mosque at Djenne, in Mali, is a spectacular example of monumental archi-

post-and-lintel

tecture created from simple techniques and materials (**13.1**). Constructed of **adobe** (sun-dried brick) and coated with mud plaster, the imposing walls of this mosque have a plastic, sculptural quality. The photograph shows well the gentle tapering of the walls imposed by the construction technique as well as the small size of the windows that illuminate the covered prayer hall inside. The protruding wooden poles serve to anchor the scaffolding that is erected every few years so that workers can restore the mosque's smooth coating of mud plaster.

POST-AND-LINTEL

After stacking and piling, post-and-lintel construction is the most elementary structural method, based on two uprights (the posts) supporting a horizontal crosspiece (the lintel, or beam). This configuration can be continued indefinitely, so that there may be one very long horizontal supported at critical points along the way by vertical posts to carry its weight to the ground. The most common materials for post-and-lintel construction are stone and wood. Since neither has great tensile strength, these materials will yield and cave in when forced to span long distances, so the architect must provide supporting posts at close intervals.

Post-and-lintel construction has been, for at least four thousand years, a favorite method of architects for raising a roof and providing for open space underneath. The ruins of a portion of the ancient Egyptian temple of Amon-Mut-Khonsu illustrate the majesty and also the limits of post-and-lintel construction in stone (**13.2**). Carved as bundles of stems capped by stylized papyrus-flower buds, the stone columns support rows of heavy stone lintels, with each lintel spanning two columns. The lintels would in turn have supported wooden roof beams and roofing. Because stone does not have great tensile strength, the supporting columns must be closely spaced. A large hall erected in post-and-lintel construction was thus a virtual forest

13.1 (below) Great Friday Mosque, Djenne, Mali. Rebuilt 1907 in the style of a 13th-century original.

13.2 (opposite page, top) View of the hypostyle from the courtyard temple of Amon-Mut-Khonsu, Luxor. Begun c. 1390 B.C.E. Height of columns 30′.
Photo by Wim Swaan. Library, Getty Research Institute, Los Angeles, Wim Swaan Photograph Collection, 96.P.21.

of columns inside. We call such spaces **hypostyle** halls, from the Greek for "beneath columns." Ancient Egyptians associated hypostyle halls with the primal swamp of creation, where, according to Egyptian belief, the first mound of dry land arose at the dawn of the world. They designed their columns as stylized versions of plants that grew in the marshes of the Nile to make this connection clear. Surrounded by load-bearing walls pierced high up by small windows, the hypostyle halls of Egyptian temples were dark and mysterious places.

In ancient Greece, the design of post-and-lintel buildings, especially temples, became standardized in certain features. Greek architects developed and codified three major architectural styles, roughly in sequence. We know them as the Greek **orders.** The most distinctive feature of each was the design of the column (**13.3**). By the 7th century B.C.E. the **Doric** style had been introduced. A Doric column has no base, nothing separating it from the floor below; its **capital,** the topmost part between the shaft of the column and the roof or lintel, is a plain stone slab above a rounded stone. The **Ionic** style was developed in the 6th century B.C.E. and gradually replaced the Doric. An Ionic column has a stepped base and a carved capital in the form of two graceful spirals known as volutes. The **Corinthian** style, which appeared in the 4th century B.C.E., is yet more elaborate, having a more detailed base and a capital carved as a stylized bouquet of acanthus leaves.

The most famous and influential work of Greek architecture is certainly the Parthenon, a Doric temple that we will examine in Chapter 14 (see 14.24).

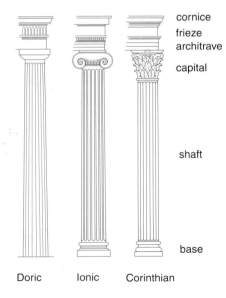

cornice
frieze
architrave

capital

shaft

base

Doric   Ionic   Corinthian

13.3 Column styles of the Greek orders.

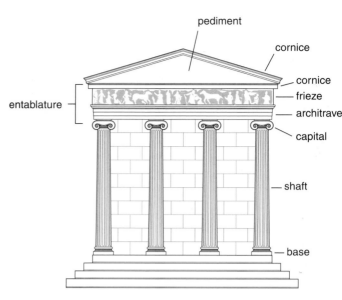

13.4 (left) Kallikrates. Temple of Athena Nike, from the east, Acropolis, Athens. 427–424 B.C.E. Pentelic marble.

13.5 (right) Elevation, Temple of Athena Nike.

Here we look at the smaller Temple of Athena Nike (**13.4**), which stands nearby on the hilltop site in Athens known as the Acropolis. With their stepped bases and volute capitals, the columns indicate that this is an Ionic temple. The columns support a structure whose remains, reconstructed here in a line drawing (**13.5**), display other important elements of Greek architecture. The plain, horizontal stone lintels of Egypt are here elaborated into a compound structure called an **entablature.** The entablature consists of three basic elements. The simple, unadorned band of lintels immediately over the columns is the **architrave.** The area above the architrave is the **frieze,** here ornamented with sculpture in relief. The frieze is capped by a shelflike projection called a **cornice.** The entablature in turn supports a triangular element called a **pediment,** which is itself crowned by its own cornice. Like the frieze, the pediment would have been ornamented with sculpture in relief. If these elements look familiar to you, it is because they have passed into the vocabulary of Western architecture and form part of the basis of the style we refer to broadly as classical. For centuries, banks, museums, universities, government buildings, and churches have been built using the elements first codified and named by the Greeks, then adapted and modified by the Romans.

Many of the great architectural traditions of the world are based in post-and-lintel construction. The architectural style developed in China provides a good contrast to that of Greece, for while its principles were developed around the same time, the standard material is not stone, but wood. We know from terra-cotta models found in tombs that the basic elements of Chinese architecture were in place by the second century B.C.E. During the 6th century C.E., this architectural vocabulary was adopted by Japan along with other elements of Chinese culture. We illustrate it here with a Japanese building, the incomparable Byodo-in (**13.6**).

Built as a palace, Byodo-in was converted to a Buddhist shrine after the death of the original owner in 1052 C.E. Among the works of art it houses is Jocho's sculpture of Amida Buddha, discussed in Chapter 2 (see 2.26). Our first impression is of a weighty and elaborate superstructure of gracefully curved roofs resting—lightly, somehow—on slender wooden columns. The effect is miraculous, for the building seems to float; but how can all of that weight rest on such slender supports? The answer lies in the cluster of interlocking wooden brackets and arms that crowns each column (**13.7**). Called bracket sets, they distribute the weight of the roof and its large, overhanging eaves evenly onto the wooden columns, allowing each column to bear up to five times the weight it could support directly. Chinese and Japanese architects developed many variations on the bracket set over the centuries, making them larger or smaller, more elaborate or simpler, more prominent or more subtle.

The distinctive curving profile of East Asian roofs is made possible by a stepped truss system (**13.8**). (Western roofs, in contrast, are usually supported by a rigid triangular truss, as in the Greek pediment.) By varying the height of each level of the truss, builders could control the pitch and curve of the roof. Taste in roof styles varied over time and from region to region. Some roofs are steeply pitched and fall in a fancifully exaggerated curve, almost like a ski jump; while others are gentler, with a subtle, barely noticeable curve.

The post-and-lintel system, then, offers potential for both structural soundness and grandeur. When applied to wood or stone, however, it leaves one problem unsolved, and that is the spanning of relatively large open spaces. The first attempt at solving this problem was the invention of the round arch.

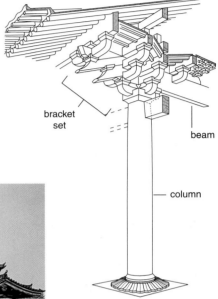

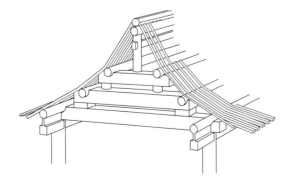

13.6 (center) Hoodo (Phoenix Hall), Byodo-in Temple, Uji, Kyoto Prefecture, Japan. Heian period, c. 1053.

13.7 (above, right) Bracket system.

13.8 (left) Stepped truss roof structure.

ROUND ARCH AND VAULT

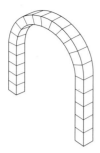

round arch

Although the round arch was used by the ancient
several centuries before our common era (see 14.9),
oped by the Romans, who perfected the form in the
get a sense of how the arch works, we might go back
body. Imagine that, instead of lying flat on your back,
ward into a curve, and again you will be lifted into the
support your hands, another your feet. As long as yo
proper arc—that is, your two supporters stand the corre
you can maintain the pose for some time. If they stand
you start to topple first one way and then the other; if t
apart, you have insufficient support in the middle and plu
An arch incorporates more complex forces of tension (pulli
compression (pushing together), but the general idea is the san

The arch has many virtues. In addition to being an attracti
enables the architect to open up fairly large spaces in a wall withou
the building's structural soundness. These spaces admit light, redu
weight of the walls, and decrease the amount of material needed. As utu
by the Romans, the arch is a perfect semicircle, although it may seem elon
gated if it rests on columns. It is constructed from wedge-shaped pieces of
stone that meet at an angle always perpendicular to the curve of the arch.
Because of tensions and compressions inherent in the form, the arch is stable only when it is complete, when the topmost stone, the **keystone,** has
been set in place. For this reason an arch under construction must be supported from below, usually by a wooden framework.

Among the most elegant and enduring of Roman structures based on
the arch is the Pont du Gard at Nîmes, France (**13.9**), built about 15 C.E.
when the empire was nearing its farthest expansion (see map, p. 355). At
this time industry, commerce, and agriculture were at their peak. Roman
engineering was applied to an ambitious system of public-works projects,
not just in Italy but in the outlying areas as well. The Pont du Gard functioned as an aqueduct, a structure meant to transport water, and its lower
level served as a footbridge across the river. That it stands today virtually
intact after nearly two thousand years (and is crossed by cyclists on the
route of the famous Tour de France bicycle race) testifies to the Romans'
brilliant engineering skills. Visually, the Pont du Gard exemplifies the best
qualities of arch construction. Solid and heavy, obviously durable, it is shot
through with open spaces that make it seem light and its weight-bearing
capabilities effortless.

13.9 Pont du Gard, Nîmes,
France. Early 1st century C.E.
Length 902′.

barrel vault

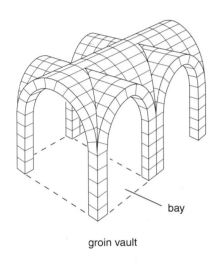

bay

groin vault

13.10 Interior, Sainte-Foy, Conques, France. c. 1050–1120.

When the arch is extended in depth—when it is, in reality, many arches placed flush one behind the other—the result is called a **barrel vault.** This vault construction makes it possible to create large interior spaces. The Romans made great use of the barrel vault, but for its finest expression we look many hundreds of years later, to the churches of the Middle Ages.

The church of Sainte-Foy (**13.10**), in the French city of Conques, is an example of the style prevalent throughout Western Europe from about 1050 to 1200—a style known as **Romanesque.** Romanesque builders adopted the old Roman forms of round arch and barrel vault so as to add height to their churches. Until this period most churches had beamed wooden roofs, which not only posed a threat of fire but also limited the height to which architects could aspire. With the stone barrel vault, they could achieve the soaring, majestic space we see in the **nave** (the long central area) of Sainte-Foy.

On the side aisles of Sainte-Foy (not visible in the photograph) the builders employed a series of **groin vaults.** A groin vault results when two barrel vaults are crossed at right angles to each other, thus directing the weights and stresses down into the four corners. By dividing up a space into square segments known as **bays,** each of which contains one groin vault, the architects could cover a long span safely and economically. The repetition of bays also creates a satisfying rhythmic pattern.

POINTED ARCH AND VAULT

While the round arch and vault of the Romanesque era solved many problems and made many things possible, they nevertheless had certain drawbacks. For one thing, a round arch, to be stable, must be a semicircle; therefore, the height of the arch is limited by its width. Two other difficulties were weight and darkness. Barrel vaults are both literally and visually heavy, calling for huge masses of stone to maintain their structural stability. Also, the builders who constructed them dared not make light-admitting openings in or around them, for fear the arches and vaults would collapse, and so the interiors of Romanesque buildings tend to be dark. The **Gothic** period in Europe, which followed the Romanesque, solved these problems with the pointed arch.

13.11 Nave, Reims Cathedral, France. 1211–c. 1290. Height 125′.

pier flying
buttress

pointed
arches

Elements of Gothic architecture

The pointed arch, while seemingly not very different from the round one, offers many advantages. Because the sides arc up to a point, weight is channeled down to the ground at a steeper angle, and therefore the arch can be taller. The vault constructed from such an arch also can be much taller than a barrel vault. Architects of the Gothic period found they did not need heavy masses of material throughout the curve of the vault, as long as the major points of intersection were reinforced. These reinforcements, called ribs, are visible in the nave ceiling of Reims Cathedral (**13.11**).

The light captured streaming into the nave of Reims Cathedral in the photograph vividly illustrates another important feature of Gothic church architecture: windows. While Romanesque cathedrals tended to be dark inside, with few and small window openings, Gothic builders strove to open up their walls for large stained glass windows such as the two radiant round windows, called rose windows, visible in the photograph. (Most of the stained glass windows in Reims Cathedral have suffered damage and been replaced with clear glass, which is why the light is so evident in the photograph.) Fearing that the numerous window openings could disastrously weaken walls that were already under pressure from the outward thrust of arches, Gothic builders reinforced their walls from the outside with supports called **buttresses, piers,** and **flying buttresses.** The principles are easy to understand if you imagine yourself using your own weight to prop up a wall. If you stand next to a wall and press the entire length of your body against it, you are a buttress. If you stand away from the wall and press against it with outstretched arms, your body is a pier, and your arms are flying buttresses. The illustration here (**13.12**) of the exterior of the Cathedral of Le Mans, in France, shows the Gothic system of buttresses, piers, and flying buttresses, as well as the numerous windows that made them necessary.

13.12 Exterior of the Cathedral of Le Mans, France, showing buttresses, piers, and flying buttresses. 1217–54.

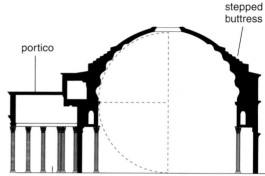

portico

stepped buttress

13.13 (left) Pantheon, Rome. 118–125 C.E.

13.14 (right) Section drawing of the Pantheon.

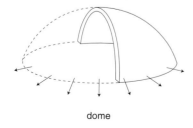

dome

DOME

A dome is an architectural structure generally in the shape of a hemisphere, or half globe. One customary definition of the dome is an arch rotated 360 degrees on its axis, and this is really more accurate, because, for example, the dome based on a pointed arch will be pointed at the top, not perfectly hemispherical. The stresses in a dome are much like those of an arch, except that they are spread in a circle around the dome's perimeter. Unless the dome is buttressed—supported from the outside—from all sides, there is a tendency for it to "explode," for the stones to pop outward in all directions, causing the dome to collapse.

Like so many other architectural structures, the dome was perfected under the incomparable engineering genius of the Romans, and one of the finest domed buildings ever erected dates from the early 2nd century. It is called the Pantheon (**13.13, 13.14**), which means a temple dedicated to "all the gods"—or, at least, all the gods who were venerated in ancient Rome. We reproduce here an 18th-century painting of the interior (**13.15**) because the circular building is so vast that it is impossible to find a camera angle to convey adequately its shape and scale.

As seen from the inside, the Pantheon has a perfect hemispherical dome soaring 142 feet above the floor, resting upon a cylinder almost exactly the same in diameter—140 feet. The ceiling is **coffered**—ornamented with recessed rectangles, coffers, which lessen its weight. At the very top of the dome is an opening 29 feet in diameter called an **oculus,** or eye, thought to be symbolic of the "eye of Heaven." This opening provides the sole (and plentiful) illumination for the building. In its conception, then, the Pantheon is amazingly simple, equal in height and width, symmetrical in its structure, round form set upon round form. Yet because of its scale and its satisfying proportions, the effect is overwhelming.

The combined structural possibilities of the dome and the vault enabled the Romans to open up huge spaces such as the Pantheon without interior supports. Another important factor that allowed them to build on such a scale was their use of concrete. While Greek and Egyptian buildings had been made of solid stone, monumental Roman buildings were made of concrete, poured into hollow walls of concrete brick as though into a mold, then faced with stone veneer to look as though they were made of solid stone. An important technological breakthrough, the use of concrete cut costs, sped construction, and enabled building on a grand scale.

Visitors enter the Pantheon through the rectangular **portico,** or porch, that is joined somewhat incongruously to it. Here we recognize the characteristic form of the Greek temple as inherited by the Romans: post-and-lintel construction, Corinthian order, entablature, and pediment. Faced in plain brick, the outside of the domed chamber is drab and uninteresting by comparison. In fact, visitors were not supposed to be too aware of it. In Roman times, an approach to the building was built that led to the portico while obscuring the rest of the temple. Thinking that they were entering a standard post-and-lintel temple, visitors must have been stunned to see the enormous round space open up before their eyes. Tourists today experience the same theatrical surprise.

13.15 Giovanni Paolo Panini. *Interior of the Pantheon.* c. 1740. Oil on canvas, 4'2½" × 3'3". National Gallery of Art, Washington, D.C.

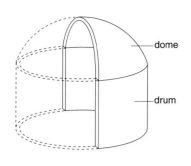

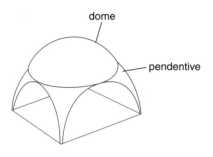

13.16 (below, left) Interior, Hagia Sophia, Istanbul. 532–37. Height of dome 183'.

13.17 (below, right) Hagia Sophia, Istanbul. 532–37.

The Pantheon is a **rotunda,** a round building, and its dome sits naturally on the circular **drum** of the base. Often, however, architects wish to set a dome over a square building. In this case, a transitional element is required between the circle (at the dome's base) and the square (of the building's top). An elegant solution can be found in Hagia Sophia (the Church of the Holy Wisdom) in Istanbul (**13.16, 13.17**). Designed by two mathematicians, Anthemius of Tralles and Isidorus of Miletus, Hagia Sophia was built as a church during the 6th century, when Istanbul, then called Constantinople, was the capital of the Byzantine Empire (p. 364). When the Turks conquered the city in the 15th century, Hagia Sophia was converted for use as a mosque. It was at this time that the four slender towers, **minarets,** were added. The building is now preserved as a museum. In sheer size and perfection of form it was the architectural triumph of its time and has seldom been matched since then.

The dome of Hagia Sophia rises 183 feet above the floor, with its weight carried to the ground by heavy stone piers—in this case, squared columns— at the four corners of the immense nave. Around the base of the dome is a row of closely spaced arched windows, which make the heavy dome seem to "float" upward. (The exterior view makes it clear that these windows are situated between buttresses that ring the base of the dome, containing its outward thrust and compensating for any structural weakening caused by the window openings.) Each of the four sides of the building consists of a monumental round arch, and between the arches and the dome are curved triangular sections known as **pendentives.** It is the function of the pendentives to make a smooth transition between rectangle and dome.

The domes of the Pantheon and the Hagia Sophia serve primarily to open up vast interior spaces. Seen from the outside, their hemispherical form is obscured by the buttressing needed to contain their powerful outward thrust. Yet the dome is such an inherently pleasing form that architects often

used it for purely decorative purposes, as an exterior ornament to crown a building. In this case, it is often set high on a drum, a circular base, so that it can be seen from the ground. A famous example of a building crowned by an ornamental dome is the Taj Mahal, in Agra, India (**13.18**).

The Taj Mahal was built in the mid-17th century by the Muslim emperor of India, Shah Jahan, as a tomb for his beloved wife, Arjummand Banu. Although the Taj is nearly as large as Hagia Sophia and possessed of a dome rising some 30 feet higher, it seems comparatively fragile and weightless. Nearly all its exterior lines reach upward, from the graceful pointed arches, to the pointed dome, to the four slender minarets poised at the outside corners. The Taj Mahal, constructed entirely of pure white marble, appears almost as a shimmering mirage which has come to rest for a moment beside the peaceful reflecting pool.

The section drawing (**13.19**) clarifies how the dome is constructed. Over the underground burial chambers of Shah Jahan and his wife, the large central room of the tomb rises to a domed ceiling. Over this, on the roof of the building, sits a tall drum crowned by a pointed dome. A small entryway gives access to the inside for maintenance purposes, but it is not meant to be visited. The exterior is shaped in a graceful, bulging *s*-curve silhouette that obscures the actual drum-and-dome structure evident in the cutaway view.

13.18 (top) Taj Mahal, Agra, India. 1632–53.

13.19 (above) Section, Taj Mahal.

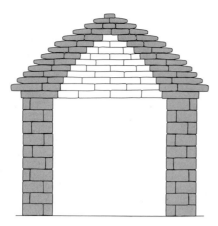

corbelled dome

CORBELLED ARCH AND DOME

Islamic architects knew the use of the arch and the dome because Islam came of age in a part of the world that had belonged first to the Roman and then to the Byzantine empires. When Islamic rulers settled in India, their architects brought these construction techniques with them, resulting in such buildings as the Taj Mahal. Indigenous Indian architecture, in contrast, does not make use of the arch or dome, but is based on post-and-lintel construction. To create arch- and dome-like forms, Indian architects used a technique called corbelling. In a corbelled arch, each course (row) of stones extends slightly beyond the one below, until eventually the opening is bridged.

Just as a round Roman arch can be rotated 360 degrees to create a dome, corbelling can also be used to create a dome form, as in this temple interior (**13.20**). Ornamented by band upon band of ornate carving and set with figures of the sixteen celestial nymphs, the corbelled dome rests on an octagon of lintels supported by eight columns. Pairs of stone brackets between each column provide additional support. The elaborate, filigreed carving that decorates every available surface testifies to the virtuosity of Indian stoneworkers, in whose skillful hands stone was made to seem as light as lace.

While to the naked eye a corbelled arch may be indistinguishable from the round arch described above, it does not function structurally as a round arch does, channeling weight outward and downward, and so does not enable the construction of large, unobstructed interior spaces.

CAST-IRON CONSTRUCTION

With the perfection of the post-and-lintel, the arch, and the dome, construction in wood, stone, and brick had gone just about as far as it could go.

13.20 (left) Interior of the Jain temple of Dilwara, Vimala temple, Mount Abu, South Rajasthan, India. Completed 1032.

13.21 (right) Joseph Paxton. Crystal Palace, Hyde Park, London. 1851, destroyed by fire 1936. Contemporary lithograph by Joseph Nash. Guildhall Library, London.

Not until the introduction of a new building material did the next major breakthrough in structural systems take place. Iron had been known for thousands of years and had been used for tools and objects of all kinds, but only in the 19th century did architects realize that its great strength offered promise for structural support. This principle was demonstrated brilliantly in a project that few contemporary observers took seriously.

In 1851 the city of London was planning a great exhibition, under the sponsorship of Prince Albert, husband of Queen Victoria. The challenge was to house under one roof the "Works of Industry of All Nations," and the commission for erecting a suitable structure fell to Joseph Paxton, a designer of greenhouses. Paxton raised in Hyde Park a wondrous building framed in cast iron and sheathed in glass—probably the first modern skeleton-and-skin construction ever designed (**13.21**). The Crystal Palace, as Paxton's creation came to be known, covered more than 17 acres and reached a height of 108 feet. Because of an ingenious system of prefabrication, the whole structure was erected in just sixteen weeks.

Visitors to the exhibition considered the Crystal Palace a curiosity—a marvelous one, to be sure, but still an oddity outside the realm of architecture. They could not have foreseen that Paxton's design, solid iron framework clothed in a glass skin, would pave the way for 20th-century architecture. In fact, Paxton had taken a giant step in demonstrating that as long as a building's skeleton held firm, its skin could be light and non-load-bearing. Several intermediary steps would be required before this principle could be translated into today's architecture.

Another bold experiment in iron construction came a few decades later just across the English Channel, in France, and involved a plan that many considered to be foolhardy, if not downright insane. Gustave Eiffel, a French engineer, proposed to build in the center of Paris a skeleton iron tower, nearly a thousand feet tall, to act as a centerpiece for the Paris World's Fair of 1889. Nothing of the sort had ever been suggested, much less built. In spite of loud protests, the Eiffel Tower (**13.22**) was constructed, at a cost of about a million dollars—an unheard-of sum for those times. It rises on four arched columns, which curve inward until they meet in a single tower thrusting up boldly above the cityscape of Paris. (The writer Guy de Maupassant claimed that he lunched in a restaurant on the tower as often as possible, because "it's the only place in Paris where I don't have to see it."[1])

The importance of this singular, remarkable structure for the future of architecture rests on the fact that it *was* a skeleton that proudly showed itself without benefit of any cosmetic embellishment. No marble, no glass, no tiles, no skin of any kind—just the clean lines drawn in an industrial-age product. Two concepts emerged from this daring construction. First, metal in and of itself can make beautiful architecture. Second, metal can provide a solid framework for a very large structure, self-sustaining and permanent. Today the Eiffel Tower is the ultimate symbol of Paris, and no tourist would pass up a visit. From folly to landmark in a century—such is the course of innovative architecture.

Iron for structural members was not the only breakthrough of the mid-19th century. The Industrial Revolution also introduced a new construction material that was much humbler but equally significant in its implications for architecture: the nail. And for want of that simple little nail, most of the houses we live in today could not have been built.

13.22 Alexandre Gustave Eiffel. Eiffel Tower, Paris. 1889. Iron, height 934′.

BALLOON-FRAME CONSTRUCTION

So far in this chapter the illustrations have concentrated on grand and public buildings—churches, temples, monuments. These are the glories of architecture, the buildings we admire and travel great distances to see. We should not forget, however, that the overwhelming majority of structures in the world have been houses for people to live in, or domestic architecture.

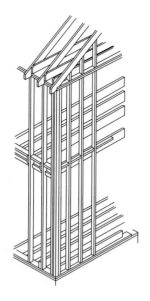

balloon-frame construction

Until the mid-19th century houses were of shell construction. They were made of brick or stone (and, in warmer climates, of such materials as reeds and bamboo) with load-bearing construction, or else they were post-and-lintel structures in which heavy timbers were assembled by complicated notching and joinery, sometimes with wooden pegs. Nails, if any, had to be fabricated by hand and were very expensive.

About 1833, in Chicago, the technique of balloon-frame construction was introduced. Balloon-frame construction is a true skeleton-and-skin method. It developed from two innovations: improved methods for milling lumber and mass-produced nails. In this system, the builder first erects a framework or skeleton by nailing together sturdy but lightweight boards (the familiar 2-by-4 "stud"), then adds a roof and sheathes the walls in clapboard, shingles, stucco, or whatever the homeowner wishes. Glass for windows can be used lavishly, as long as it does not interrupt the underlying wood structure, since the sheathing plays little part in holding the building together.

When houses of this type were introduced, the term "balloon framing" was meant to be sarcastic. Skeptics thought the buildings would soon fall down, or burst just like balloons. But some of the earliest balloon-frame houses stand firm today, and this method is still the most popular for new house construction in Western countries.

The balloon frame, of course, has its limitations. Wood beams 2 by 4 inches thick cannot support a skyscraper ten or fifty stories high, and that was the very sort of building architects had begun to dream of late in the 19th century. For such soaring ambitions, a new material was needed, and it was found. The material was steel.

STEEL-FRAME CONSTRUCTION

Although multistory buildings have been with us since the Roman Empire, the development of the skyscraper, as we know it, required two late-19th-century innovations: the elevator and steel-frame construction. Steel-frame construction, like balloon framing, is a true skeleton-and-skin arrangement. Rather than piling floor upon floor, with each of the lower stories supporting those above it, the builders first erect a steel "cage" that is capable of sustaining the entire weight of the building; then they apply a skin of some other material. But if one is going to erect a building of great height, one cannot expect people to walk up ten or more flights of stairs to get to the top floors. Hence, the elevator made its appearance.

What many consider to be the first genuinely modern building was designed by Louis Sullivan and built between 1890 and 1891 in St. Louis. Known as the Wainwright Building (**13.23**), it employed a steel framework sheathed in masonry. Other architects had experimented with steel support but had carefully covered their structures in heavy stone so as to reflect traditional architectural forms and make the construction seem reliably sturdy. Centuries of precedent had prepared the public to expect bigness to go hand in hand with heaviness. Sullivan broke new ground by making his sheathing light, letting the skin of his building echo, even celebrate, the steel framing underneath. Regular bays of windows on the seven office floors are separated by strong vertical lines, and the four corners of the building are emphasized by vertical piers. The Wainwright Building's message is subtle, but we cannot mistake it: the nation had stopped growing outward and started growing *up*.

Sullivan's design looks forward to the 20th century, but it nevertheless clings to certain architectural details rooted in classical history, most notably the heavy cornice (the projecting roof ornament) that terminates upward movement at the top of the building. In a very few decades even these backward glances into the architectural past would become rare.

Toward the middle of the 20th century skyscrapers began to take over the downtown areas of major cities, and city planners had to grapple with

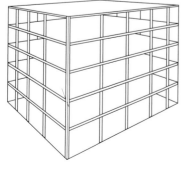

steel-frame construction

unprecedented problems. How high is too high? How much air space should a building consume? What provision, if any, should be made to prevent tall buildings from completely blocking out the sunlight from the streets below? In New York and certain other cities ordinances were passed that resulted in a number of look-alike and architecturally undistinguished buildings. The laws required that if a building filled the ground space of a city block right up to the sidewalk, it could rise for only a certain number of feet or stories before being "stepped back," or narrowed; then it could rise for only a specified number of additional feet before being stepped back again. The resultant structures came to be known as "wedding-cake" buildings. A few architects, however, found more creative ways of meeting the air space requirement. Those working in the **International** (in fact, European) style designed some of the most admired American skyscrapers during the 1950s and 1960s. International style architecture emphasized clean lines, geometric (usually rectilinear) form, and an avoidance of superficial decoration. The "bones" of a building were supposed to show and to be the only ornament necessary. A classic example of this pure style is Lever House.

Lever House in New York (**13.24**), designed by the architectural firm of Skidmore, Owings, and Merrill and built in 1952, was heralded as a breath of fresh air in the smog of look-alike structures. Its sleek understated form was widely copied but never equaled. Lever House might be compared to two shimmering glass dominoes, one resting horizontally on freestanding supports, the other balanced upright and off-center on the first. At a time when most architects of office buildings strove to fill every square inch of air space to which they were entitled—both vertically and horizontally—the

13.23 (left) Louis Sullivan. Wainwright Building, St. Louis. 1890–91.

13.24 (right) Gordon Bunshaft of Skidmore, Owings, and Merrill. Lever House, New York. 1952.

13.25 Golden Gate Bridge, San Francisco. 1937. Joseph B. Strauss, chief engineer; O. H. Ammann, Charles Derleth, Jr., and Leon S. Moisseiff, consulting engineers; Irving F. Morrow, consulting architect.

elegant Lever House drew back and raised its slender rectangle aloof from its neighbors, surrounded by free space. Even its base does not rest on the ground but rides on thin supports to allow for open plazas and passageways beneath the building. Practically no other system of construction except steel frame could have made possible this graceful form.

SUSPENSION

Also made feasible by steel, suspension is the structural method we associate primarily with bridges, although it has been employed for some buildings as well. The concept of suspension was developed for bridges late in the 19th century. In essence, the weight of the structure is suspended from steel cables supported on vertical pylons, driven into the ground. A long bridge, such as the Golden Gate Bridge in San Francisco (**13.25**), may have only two sets of pylons planted in the riverbed, but the steel cables suspended under tension from their towers are strong enough to support a span between them almost four-fifths of a mile long. With their long sweeping curves and slender lines, suspension structures are among the most graceful in architecture.

REINFORCED CONCRETE

Concrete is an old material that was known and used by the Romans. A mixture of cement, gravel, and water, concrete can be poured, will assume the shape of any mold, and then will set to hardness. Its major problem is that it tends to be brittle and has low tensile strength. This problem is often observed in the thin concrete slabs used for sidewalks and patios, which may crack and split apart as a result of weight and weather. Late in the 19th century, however, a method was developed for reinforcing concrete forms by imbedding iron rods inside the concrete before it hardened. The iron contributes tensile strength, while the concrete provides shape and surface. In the 20th century reinforced concrete, also known as **ferroconcrete,** has been used in a wide variety of structures, often in those with free-form, organic shapes. While it may seem at first to be a skeleton-and-skin construction,

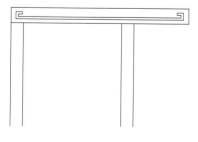

reinforced concrete

ferroconcrete actually works more like a shell, because the iron rods (or sometimes a steel mesh) and concrete are bonded permanently and can form structures that are self-sustaining, even when very thin.

A special kind of ferroconcrete construction—precast reinforced sections—was used to create the soaring shell-like forms of the Sydney Opera House in Australia (**13.26**). The Opera House, which is really an all-around entertainment complex, is almost as famous for its construction difficulties as it is for its extraordinary design. So daring was its concept that the necessary technology virtually had to be invented as the project went along. Planned as a symbol of the great port city in whose harbor it stands, the Opera House gives the impression of a wonderful clipper ship at full sail. Three sets of pointed shells, oriented in different directions, turn the building into a giant sculpture in which walls and roof are one. Reinforced concrete is the sort of material that allows the builder to experiment and try new techniques, that allows the architect to dream impossible dreams.

13.26 Joern Utzon. Sydney Opera House, Australia. 1959–72. Reinforced concrete, height of highest shell 200′.

GEODESIC DOMES

Of all the structural systems, probably the only one that can be attributed to a single individual is the geodesic dome, which was developed by the American architectural engineer R. Buckminster Fuller. Fuller's dome is essentially a bubble, formed by a network of metal rods arranged in triangles and further organized into tetrahedrons. (A tetrahedron is a three-dimensional geometric figure having four faces.) This metal framework can be sheathed in any of several lightweight materials, including wood, glass, and plastic.

The geodesic dome offers a combination of advantages never before available in architecture. Although very light in weight in relation to size, it is amazingly strong, because its structure rests on a mathematically sophisticated use of the triangle. It requires no interior support, and so all the space encompassed by the dome can be used with total freedom. A geodesic dome can be built in any size. In theory, at least, a structurally sound geodesic dome 2 miles across could be built, although nothing of this scope has ever

geodesic dome

13.27 R. Buckminster Fuller. U.S. Pavilion, Expo 67, Montreal. 1967. Geodesic dome, diameter 250′.

been attempted. Perhaps most important for modern building techniques, Fuller's dome is based on a modular system of construction. Individual segments—modules—can be prefabricated to allow for extremely quick assembly of even a large dome. And finally, because of the flexibility in choice of sheathing materials, there are virtually endless options for climate and light control.

Fuller patented the geodesic dome in 1947, but it was not until twenty years later, when his design served as the U.S. Pavilion at the Montreal World's Fair, that the public's attention was awakened to its possibilities. The dome at Expo 67 (**13.27**) astonished the architectural world and fair-goers alike. It was 250 feet in diameter (about the size of a football field rounded off) and, being sheathed in translucent material, lighted up the sky at night like a giant spaceship set down on earth.

After Expo 67 some predicted that before long all houses and public buildings would be geodesic domes. This dream has faded considerably, but Fuller's dome has proved exceptionally well suited for government and scientific operations in arctic climates. To build a habitable structure in the freezing wastes of Antarctica, for example, one needs a lightweight material that can be shipped and assembled easily, great strength to withstand below-freezing temperatures and high winds, and control of the interior environment. The geodesic dome meets all these requirements.

In this brief survey of the major structural systems we have seen that the form of architecture and its method of construction are largely determined by the materials available. Wood readily lends itself to post-and-lintel construction and balloon-frame construction; stone works for post-and-lintel also, as well as for the arch and dome; metal allows for steel-frame construction, suspension, or reinforced concrete; and so on. But there is another factor—often a more important one—that affects the shape of architecture, and that is the purpose a building will serve.

R. BUCKMINSTER FULLER
1895–1983

THE TERM "ECCENTRIC GENIUS" might have been coined to describe the 20th-century architect/-engineer/inventor/philosopher R. Buckminster Fuller, known to his friends as "Bucky." Whether history will characterize him as more of an eccentric or more of a genius remains to be seen.

Born in a suburb of Boston, Fuller was the black sheep of a distinguished New England family. He attended Harvard University for a short time, but, as he explained afterward, "I cut classes and went out quite deliberately to get into trouble, and so naturally I got kicked out." There followed a variety of odd jobs and a stint in the Navy. After he married Anne Hewlett in 1917, Fuller went into partnership with his father-in-law, an architect, in a building-block company. The year 1922 marked a crisis in his life. The business did not prosper, and the Fullers' daughter Alexandra died on her fourth birthday. Fuller sank into a terrible depression—working all day and drinking all night. At the lowest ebb he seriously considered suicide. Then in 1927, for some reason, he reached a critical turning point. One night, he later recalled, he found himself saying, "You do not have the right to eliminate yourself. You do not belong to you. You belong to the universe." From that moment he dedicated his life to discovering "the principles operative in the universe and [turning] them over to my fellow men."

The theory Fuller eventually formulated was both simple and extraordinarily grandiose: any problem in the world can be solved by design and technology. He believed wholeheartedly that "there is absolutely nothing that cannot be done." Fuller liked to talk about our planet as "Spaceship Earth" and felt that it should be designed as efficiently as any space vehicle; one of his twenty-five books is entitled *Operating Manual for Spaceship Earth*.

The first practical application of Fuller's theories was the Dymaxion House, patented in 1927. This experimental dwelling had glass walls, rooms hung from a central mast, and such energy-efficient devices as an automatic vacuum-cleaning system. Next came the Dymaxion automobile, a three-wheeled vehicle capable of speeds up to 120 m.p.h. Neither invention achieved any popular success, but in 1947 Fuller patented the design for which he is most famous—the geodesic dome. Based on a system of triangles arranged into four-planed figures, or tetrahedrons, the geodesic dome could enclose a huge amount of space without interior support and allow for total climate control. Thousands of Fuller's domes have been built around the world. One of his most ambitious projects, however—the complete enclosure of midtown Manhattan in a dome 3 miles across—was (understandably) considered impractical.

Fuller remained active almost until the day he died, at the age of eighty-seven. He traveled widely, lecturing about his theories, and particularly enjoyed speaking to college audiences, among whom he attracted rather a cult following. Education was one of his many interests, for, he said: "Every child is born a genius. It is my conviction, from having watched a great many babies grow up, that all of humanity is born a genius and then becomes degeniused very rapidly by unfavorable circumstances and by the frustration of all their extraordinary built-in capabilities."[2]

Photograph of R. Buckminster Fuller.

PURPOSES OF
ARCHITECTURE

Architecture is seldom miscellaneous. Nearly every structure is designed to serve a specific function, and we evaluate a structure according to the way in which it fulfills its purpose. Although architecture through the ages has been enormously diverse, almost every structure fits into one of just a few major categories: government buildings; other public buildings, such as libraries or museums; commercial buildings, including offices, banks, and shops; buildings for transportation—airline terminals, train stations, and the like; religious buildings; and, of course, residences.

Beyond function, every structure has a particular character or style. It creates a certain environment within its walls and projects a certain image to the broader environment outside. A bank, for instance, may seem grand and imposing, or small-town and friendly, or modern and high-tech. By choosing a style of architecture, the bankers tell us about their self-image and about the customers they hope to attract. Similar effects are evident with other types of structures.

This section looks briefly at function and style in architecture. We begin by comparing individual buildings that serve the same function, examining in turn examples of houses of worship, museums, office buildings, and dwellings. We then enlarge our view to look at how architecture has been used to create environments in which each individual building plays a role in a larger ensemble.

TWO HOUSES OF WORSHIP

Earlier in this chapter we discussed two medieval houses of worship—the church of Sainte-Foy and Reims Cathedral (see 13.10, 13.11). These are enormous structures, capable of enclosing hundreds of worshipers. Here we turn our attention to two much smaller, more intimate religious buildings. Both are considered "pilgrimage churches," in that they are meant to offer spiritual and physical refreshment to travelers, and each will hold about three hundred people. In their styles, however, the two buildings could hardly be more different.

Notre-Dame-du-Haut at Ronchamp, in France, is the masterpiece of the French architect Charles-Édouard Jeanneret, known as Le Corbusier. Its site is a high, windswept hill in extreme eastern France, near Switzerland, at a spot believed to have been used for religious gatherings since pre-Christian times. Le Corbusier was commissioned to design the chapel to replace a building destroyed in World War II, and his plan was utterly different from its predecessor and unique in all the world.

The exterior of Notre-Dame-du-Haut (roughly, Our Lady of the high place; **13.28**) cannot be understood from one photograph, since the chapel is different from every angle, but this southeast view hints at the massiveness of the stuccoed, rubble-filled walls pierced by irregular, small openings. The soaring roof of reinforced concrete does not rest on the walls but rides on vertical supports inside them. This arrangement leaves a 4-inch space between the roof and walls to create a floating-roof effect and admit some light to the interior. Le Corbusier claimed the roof shape was inspired by a crab shell he'd picked up on a beach, but the visitor is just as likely to envision a giant sail poised to catch the wind and fly the little church away.

The interior of Notre-Dame-du-Haut has the mystery and solidity of a cave, a shelter in which one can find both safety and privacy. Like the outside, it is unpredictable. No one vantage point gives visitors a sense of the whole, so one must explore as one would explore a cave, trying to under-

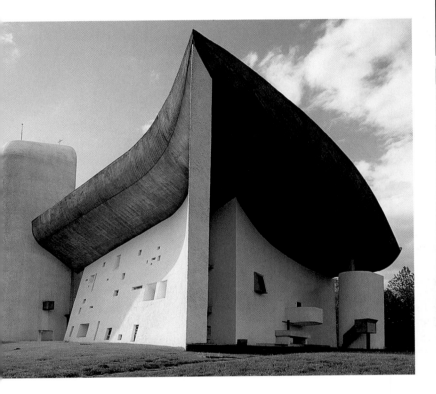

stand the unusual sight lines of seating to altar to side chapels. The changing light admitted by small, deep-set windows and the floating roof contributes to Ronchamp's secretive quality.

Another architect's masterpiece provides just about as strong a contrast to Notre-Dame-du-Haut as one could ask for. Thorncrown, a nondenominational chapel in Eureka Springs, Arkansas (**13.29**), is the award-winning creation of Fay Jones, an Arkansas native. The walls are glass, supported by a forest of wood beams, and natural light floods the interior from all directions. If Ronchamp is a cave, Thorncrown is a tree house, which was the effect Jones intended. It occupies a heavily wooded site, and the architect chose his materials carefully, so builders could carry them along a narrow path and not disturb existing trees. As Ronchamp is complex and unpredictable, Thorncrown is brilliantly simple—a glass shed with clear sight lines. Pilgrims at Thorncrown can be sheltered from the elements, but they are visually, perhaps spiritually, at one with the natural world.

13.28 (left) Le Corbusier. Notre-Dame-du-Haut, Ronchamp, France. Exterior view from southeast. 1950–55.

13.29 (right) Fay Jones and Associates. Thorncrown Chapel, Eureka Springs, Arkansas. 1980. Overall dimensions 60 × 24', height 48'.

TWO MUSEUMS

Museums make an interesting study in architectural design, because they are works of art meant to display other works of art or history. How they go about fulfilling this purpose tells us much about the nature of architecture.

The National Gallery of Art in Washington, D.C., houses one of the finest collections of Western art in the world (**13.30, 13.31**). Built between 1937 and 1941, the museum was a gift to the nation from the banker and industrialist Andrew Mellon, who not only engaged the architect and funded construction but also donated his own personal art collection to the museum and encouraged his friends to do likewise. The architect Mellon selected was John Russell Pope, a master of the neoclassical ("new classical") style, which is a style based on the vocabulary of ancient Greek and Roman architecture. Pope had already designed two important buildings in the capital, Constitution Hall and the National Archives, as well as the Baltimore Museum of Art and numerous private residences.

The focal point at the center of Pope's symmetrical building is a temple facade leading to a domed rotunda, a combination clearly derived from the Pantheon in Rome (see 13.13, 13.15). To either side of the rotunda, great barrel-vaulted corridors provide access to suites of skylit galleries. For Pope,

13.30 (below, top) John Russell Pope. The National Gallery (now known as the West Building), Washington, D.C.

13.31 (below) General view, National Gallery, Washington, D.C.

13.32 Ieoh Ming (I. M.) Pei. National Gallery, East Building, Washington, D.C. 1978.

the Pantheon was not merely a great building from the distant past but also one with distinctly American overtones. In founding the United States as a republic, the framers of the Constitution had looked to the example of the Republic of Rome. Thomas Jefferson, seeking to link the young country to the heritage of Greece and Rome, had designed a domed rotunda for his home, Monticello, and another as part of the campus of the University of Virginia (see 13.42). In fact, Pope paid a final tribute to Jefferson with still another rotunda, the Jefferson Memorial, also in Washington, which he created at the same time as the National Gallery.

Sadly, neither Pope nor Mellon lived to see the museum dedicated by President Franklin D. Roosevelt in 1941. Although it was an instant hit with the public, the building was not well received by critics and younger architects, who found its conservative design both bombastic and boring. Defenders have since pointed out that the building is very well suited to the art it was meant to house, which is art from the heart of the Western tradition as it defined itself from the Renaissance through the 19th century. Today, the initial controversy having long ago died away, Pope's building looks timeless and confident, and its generous spaces provide a deeply pleasurable environment for looking at art.

In 1978, Andrew Mellon's children, Paul Mellon and Ailsa Mellon Bruce, presented to the nation a newly completed addition to the National Gallery, the East Building (**13.31, 13.32**). Designed by the American architect I. M. Pei, whose pyramidal entry to the Louvre Museum we looked at in Chapter 3 (see 3.11), the East Building houses an ever-growing collection of 20th-century art as well as temporary exhibition spaces and administrative and research facilities. In designing the new building, Pei was faced with both aesthetic and practical challenges: how to design a modernist building that would be compatible with Pope's classical one, and how to deal with an awkward trapezoidal site created by intersecting avenues.

Pei's fascinating solution was at once boldly innovative and respectful of his predecessor. And it came to him in an airplane. "I was returning to New York after a gallery meeting in 1968, trying to find a solution to that difficult site," he later recalled. "I sketched a trapezoid on the back of an envelope. I drew a diagonal line across the trapezoid and produced two triangles: one for the museum, the other for the study center. This was the beginning."[3]

Distinguished by the three tower galleries at its corners, the museum portion of Pei's East Building takes the form of an isosceles triangle (two sides of equal length); the study center attached to it takes the form of a right triangle. The museum's street-level entrance faces Pope's West Building, establishing a conceptual link across the intervening street. An underground passageway links the buildings physically, so visitors can easily pass from one to the other. The double-triangle solution not only complemented the regular geometry of Pope's architecture but also allowed Pei to continue the strong east-west axis of Pope's building through his own, further cementing their connection: an imaginary line drawn down the center of the West Building can be extended straight to the apex of the isosceles triangle of the East Building. Finally, Pei sheathed his building in marble from the same Tennessee quarry that had furnished the stone for the West Building.

Pei has said that if he had been commissioned to design an independent museum for the site, his solution would have been much different. His task instead was to make a bold new statement that also respected the past. The architect Frank O. Gehry had no such restrictions when it came to designing a new museum in Bilbao, in the Basque region of northern Spain (**13.33**). Gehry had originally been asked to evaluate the possibility of converting a huge abandoned warehouse in Bilbao into a museum, preserving the industrial exterior and redesigning the interior. However, it quickly became clear to all concerned that the warehouse was not workable (Gehry suggested that it might be better converted into a hotel with places to shop), and that a much more exciting site could be found by the river that flowed through the town, an area which the city was trying to revitalize. Instead of preserving an old building, Gehry would create a new one.

In Chapter 6 we looked at one of the gestural drawings that Gehry made while working out his ideas for the museum (see 6.3), and in Chapter 4 we

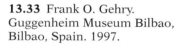

13.33 Frank O. Gehry. Guggenheim Museum Bilbao, Bilbao, Spain. 1997.

saw views of the museum's entryway and dramatic interior spaces (see 4.31 and 4.37). Here we have a view of the museum as a whole, set in its water garden by the river. In Gehry's words, its titanium-clad forms unfold like a great "metal flower." Others have seen in their fluid curves the forms of boats or fish.

The organic forms of Gehry's building have an intuitive, almost improvisational quality, as though they might be assembled differently tomorrow or grow and shift on their own as the "flower" unfolds. This is an illusion, of course, for in order to be constructed the forms had to be drawn and measured with great precision. This overwhelming task was helped enormously by a computer program called Catia. Originally developed for the French aerospace industry, Catia generated renderings of the museum (**13.34**) by digitally mapping a working model constructed of wood and paper (**13.35**). The program enabled Gehry's team to work within the construction budget by allowing them to follow every design decision through to its practical consequences in terms of construction methods and exact quantities of materials. In essence, the program built and rebuilt a virtual museum many times before the actual museum was begun.

THREE OFFICE BUILDINGS

The architecture of commerce, like that of government, often has strong symbolic value. Its primary purpose is to house offices, but a secondary one may be to make a statement about the firm that owns the building. When a company decides to erect a new office building, its leaders give serious thought to the images that will be projected by that building and lodged in the minds of the public. Unlike the government structure, however, the office building rarely seeks a model in traditional architecture, but rather attempts to convey the impression of dynamic modernism—of a company forging ahead to the future. The office building of the 20th century has therefore tended to be a creature of fashion, taking its design from the trend of the times. Three examples spanning sixty years will illustrate this.

The Chrysler Building in New York, indisputably the gem of early skyscrapers, was completed in 1930 and was the first office building to rise above

13.34 (above) Catia rendering of the Guggenheim Museum Bilbao.

13.35 (below) Design model of the Guggenheim Museum Bilbao. Basswood and paper. Fall 1992 to December 1993.

1,000 feet. Its slender, elegantly pointed spire (**13.36**) changed the skyline of New York dramatically and still remains distinctive, in spite of later, taller buildings around it. We might list three elements that contributed to this splendid building: the great success of the automobile industry, which enabled Walter Percy Chrysler to erect a monument to his name; the relative cheapness of fine building materials and labor; and the prevalence of the style known as **Art Deco.**

Art Deco, then at the height of fashion, was marked by geometric patterns and a rich display of surface decoration. (The term "deco" came from the Exposition des Arts Décoratifs, held in Paris in 1925, where the style first appeared as a significant force.) Art Deco was definitely a product of the machine age, for its favorite materials were chrome and steel and glass and aluminum—modern materials that glitter and sparkle, preferably in elaborate combinations to dazzle the eye. Its symbolism, unquestionably, is razzle-

13.36 (left) William Van Alen. Chrysler Building, New York. Completed 1930.

13.37 (right) Ludwig Mies van der Rohe and Philip Johnson. Seagram Building, New York. 1958.

13.38 (bottom) Arata Isozaki & Associates. Team Disney Building, Orlando, Florida. Completed 1991.

dazzle, and it celebrates the speed of the automobile and the airplane, people on the move. The top of the Chrysler Building is layered in an overlapping sunburst pattern pierced with triangular windows—a streamlined, geometric sculpture cutting through the sky.

The patterned forms of Art Deco gave way in the 1940s to the pared-down, austere design aesthetic of the International style. In a sense the roots of the International style might be traced back to Louis Sullivan (see 13.23), who insisted that "form follows function." In other words, the form of a building or any other object should be expressive of what it is supposed to do, not overlaid with arbitrary decoration. This theme was taken up by two European architects, Le Corbusier and Ludwig Mies van der Rohe, and translated into a style that dominated American architecture through the 1970s. Le Corbusier would eventually discard the geometric simplicity of the International style in favor of more organic expressions like the Ronchamp chapel (see 13.28), but Mies van der Rohe added another catchphrase to the history of art when he made his often-quoted statement: "Less is more." By this he meant that architects (and other designers) must strip their forms to the barest essentials, the parts necessary to the work's function, so as to achieve a more honest, satisfying design.

As mentioned earlier, the International style was introduced to the United States by such buildings as Lever House (see 13.24). Diagonally across the street from Lever House is a building many consider to be the quintessence of that style. The Seagram Building (**13.37**), designed by Mies van der Rohe and Philip Johnson, is almost the direct opposite of the Chrysler Building in its design aesthetic. A stark vertical slab resting on stilts, the Seagram Building rises abruptly from the base and terminates abruptly at the top, with no attempt at accent or decoration. Its form is the extended cube, and much of its visual appeal comes from the combination of bronze-colored steel and amber glass sheathing.

For more than twenty years after the Seagram Building was completed, through the 1970s, the International style held sway as the most luxurious and sophisticated style for skyscraper architecture. Across the United States towers of steel and glass vied with one another for height and simplicity of design. By about 1980 it became clear that some change was due, that the business firm of the 1980s and 1990s would be looking for an image quite different from "the old company that lived in a box." Architects too were ready for change, and so the Postmodern style came to corporate America. Not surprisingly, one of the companies that would most ardently embrace Postmodernism was the Disney organization.

The Team Disney Building near Orlando, Florida (**13.38**), captures the style at its most inventive, being complex, irregular, exuberant, and colorful. The building *does* have cubes, but they are not always vertical, not always parallel to one another, and certainly not a uniform, muted color. Disney's architect, Arata Isozaki, splashed a palette of pink and green and blue and red and yellow over the building's facade, and designed the side wings (which are much longer than this photo shows) to look rather like plaid. The huge central funnel introduces a curving form to play against the square shapes. It is actually a working sundial, the world's largest, inside which Isozaki constructed a Japanese garden of river-washed stones. Above the main entrance projects a stylized, elegant version of—yes—*mouse ears*. This may be an office building where serious business takes place, but it is, after all, an office building at Walt Disney World.

The commercial building, by its design, not only sends a message to the outside world about the image a given company wishes to project. It also sends a message to the people who work inside the building: This is who we want you to be. In the case of Team Disney, we must assume the company wants its employees to be creative, colorful—and a bit outside the traditional mold.

THREE DWELLINGS

Ever since humans came down from the trees or out of their caves, most of the architecture built has been in the form of dwellings. Needless to say, dwellings from different times and places have displayed enormous variety. Each of the three examples considered here reflects a special point of view about what it means to dwell within a building—that is, what kind of roof one should have over one's head.

A type of dwelling that has been with us at least since the times of the ancient Romans is the apartment house, and as space on our planet gets tighter and tighter, such dwellings will no doubt become even more common. Except that their height was limited to five stories, Roman apartment houses resembled most apartment houses today—a more or less massive building, subdivided inside into individual "cookie-cutter" dwellings all more or less the same. In most modern apartment buildings, the most coveted apartments are those at the very top, the penthouses, which offer amenities most apartment dwellers must do without, including light and air on all sides and a private outdoor area.

One of the most famous experiments in apartment design attempted to bring these luxuries to everyone. Habitat in Montreal (**13.39**), designed by Moshe Safdie, was intended as an experiment in the housing of the future, in both form and construction. Like Fuller's dome (see 13.27), it was unveiled at Expo 67, the Montreal World's Fair. The complex consists of 354 prefabricated concrete boxes, stacked one on top of another to form 158 apartments, some on one level, others constructed as duplexes. Although the boxes are of uniform size, they were ingeniously designed for varied uses and floor plans. One box could be a living-dining area with kitchen, another two bedrooms and a bath; some boxes are self-contained units of living room, kitchen, bedroom, and bath. Through this modular system, almost any family size can be accommodated. Each apartment has a private entrance, windows on all sides, and a terrace—the flat roof of one dwelling providing the garden terrace for its neighbor above. In effect, every family lives in a penthouse.

When it first opened, Habitat was considered exciting as a concept but rather sterile as a living environment. But Habitat has aged quite well in the three decades since, as residents have impressed their human stamp on technology. Some families have added sun porches, some skylights; everywhere there are trees, plants, and flowers. All these touches have turned the apartment house of the future into a sought-after home for the present.

Architects usually make their reputations on the "big" commissions—the office buildings, museums, airport terminals, hotels—and only incidentally design private houses. But for the man whom many consider to have been America's greatest architect, the reverse is true. Although he did design important public buildings, Frank Lloyd Wright will always be remembered as a builder of houses.

Wright's approach to domestic architecture was characterized by two related principles: first, a house should blend with its environment; second, the interior and exterior of a house should be visually and physically integrated. Together, these principles comprised Wright's theory of "organic" architecture. The Kaufmann House in Bear Run, Pennsylvania, usually known as "Fallingwater," is considered to be his masterpiece (**13.40**).

Kaufmann house was designed for a wooded site beside a stream with a little waterfall. Much of the house is built of stone quarried from the immediate area, creating a conceptual as well as a visual relationship to the surroundings. Three terraces project outward from the house, two of them cantilevered over the waterfall. A **cantilever** is a horizontal form supported at one end and jutting out into space at the other. Reinforced concrete, with its high tensile strength, makes such a construction possible. Wright was among the first to use the cantilever for domestic architecture. Here, the cantilevered terraces echo the shape of the stone ledge at the head of the waterfall, further linking the house visually to the site.

The interior of "Fallingwater" consists mainly of one large room opening out to the terraces, providing an "organic" flow of spaces with no disruptive partitions. Wright believed that a hearth is the core of a home, so his plans included a massive stone fireplace, the chimney of which is visible in this photograph. As was his custom in private commissions, the architect also designed much of the furniture, building it into the structure so the owners could not tamper with his overall scheme.

The third dwelling we take up here makes a fundamental but often overlooked point: architecture is for everybody. Everyone deserves a comfortable dwelling. This is the philosophy behind Rural Studio, a program for architecture students directed by architect Samuel Mockbee at Auburn University in Alabama. For the duration of the three-month-long course, the students live together in an old abandoned house in distant, rural Greensboro. There

13.39 (below) Moshe Safdie. Habitat, Montreal. 1967.

13.40 (bottom) Frank Lloyd Wright. Fallingwater, Bear Run, Pennsylvania. 1936.

FRANK LLOYD WRIGHT

1867–1959

MANY CRITICS CONSIDER Frank Lloyd Wright to have been the greatest American architect of his time; certainly few would dispute the claim that he was the greatest designer of residential architecture. To see a Wright-designed building dating from the first decade of the 20th century is to be shocked by how remarkably modern it seems.

Wright had very little formal education. He attended high school in Madison, Wisconsin, but apparently did not graduate. Later, he completed the equivalent of about one year's course work in civil engineering at the University of Wisconsin, while holding down a job as a draftsman. In 1887 he moved to Chicago and eventually found work in the architectural firm headed by Louis Sullivan, the great designer of early office buildings. Before long Wright had assumed responsibility for fulfilling most of the residential commissions that came into the company, and in 1893 he opened a firm of his own.

During the next two decades Wright refined the principles of the "Prairie houses" that are his trademark. Most are in the Midwest, and they echo that flat expanse of the Great Plains—predominantly horizontal, stretching out over considerable ground area but usually in one story. All expressed Wright's special interest in textures and materials; he liked whenever possible to build with materials native to the immediate surroundings, so that the houses blend with their environments. Interiors were designed in an open plan, with rooms flowing into one another (an unusual practice for the time), and the inside and outside of the house were also well integrated. These ingredients added up to what Wright always referred to as "organic" architecture.

For most of his long life Wright's personal situation was far from tranquil. His parents seem to have had a bitterly unhappy marriage, and they divorced in 1885, when Wright was seventeen—an extraordinary event for that era. Wright himself had a troubled marital history. His first marriage ended when he eloped to Europe with Mamah Brothwick, the wife of a former client, leaving his own wife and six children behind. Five years later, back in Wisconsin, Brothwick was brutally murdered by a deranged servant while Wright was out of the house. This tragedy sent the architect off on a period of wandering through faraway parts of the world. A final marriage in the late 1920s lasted out his lifetime and appears to have given him his first real happiness.

Although he is best known for his domestic architecture, Wright also designed many large-scale commercial and public buildings, including the Solomon R. Guggenheim Museum in New York. His innovative design for the Imperial Hotel in Tokyo, planned to be stable in an area plagued by earthquakes, proved successful when the hotel survived without damage a devastating quake just a year after it was completed.

Wright was the author of several books on his theories of architecture, and always he focused on the organic nature of his work and on his own individuality. "Beautiful buildings are more than scientific. They are true organisms, spiritually conceived, works of art, using the best technology by inspiration rather than the idiosyncrasies of mere taste or any averaging by the committee mind."[4]

Photograph of Frank Lloyd Wright.

they design a project and then build it with their own hands, using whatever materials they can find and whatever money is available. Their clients are local county people, usually poor, who could never hire an architect on their own.

Rural Studio's first full-scale residential project was Bryant House (**13.41**). It was built for Shephard and Alberta Bryant, an aging couple who had made do for most of their lives with a leaky, patchwork shed. Reviving an ancient practice, the students constructed the walls from bales of hay, a material that is inexpensive, easy to work with, and a natural insulator. Stucco plastering inside and out gives the walls a smooth, weatherproof coating. Across the front of the house, in keeping with southern tradition, is a long and hospitable porch whose inexpensive acrylic sun-visor roof is poised on colorful yellow pillars. Inside the house, a hearth with a wood-burning stove provides heat in the winter, and cozy sleeping niches set in a wall await visiting grandchildren. The entire house, including plumbing and kitchen fixtures, cost only $16,500 to build, a sum covered by grants and gifts from local merchants.

After the house was completed, one student returned to build an outbuilding, a small smokehouse where Mr. Bryant, an avid fisherman, could cure his catch. Visible to the right in the photograph, it was constructed almost entirely of found materials. The walls, made of fragments of concrete curbstones, are inset with colored glass bottles that admit light. The gently twisting tin roof is supported by salvaged timbers. Inside, the ceiling is lined with old street signs. Total cost of materials, $40.

Rural Studio helps students bridge a gap between theory and practice, between learning about architecture and hands-on experience, while also benefiting the local community. It reminds us that architecture is fundamentally about how we live. Through architecture, we build our own human environment within the natural world. We turn next to a larger sense of what it means to design our own surroundings.

BEYOND THE BUILDING: ENVIRONMENTAL DESIGN

Environmental design can be defined as large-scale planning to improve the aesthetic and functional qualities of the surroundings in which we live, to make them more habitable. The target environment could be huge or small, anything from a whole city to a little playground or park. This type of design may involve architects, urban planners, landscape designers, and even psychologists and sociologists.

Today's environmental design is as varied as the populations it intends to serve. At its best, it asks many questions before attempting to provide answers. Where is this environment—city, suburbs, or country? What are its geographical location and climate? Who lives in the environment—children, teenagers, young adults, middle-aged adults, elderly people, or a mixed group? How do they move about—on foot, on bicycle, by car, or by mass transit? What do they do in the environment—eat, sleep, work, study, play, or some combination of these? How do the people who plan it, and those who will use it, feel about themselves, and what do they want to show to the world?

To see how designers have grappled with these questions, we will look at a few environmental designs. Some should be familiar to readers of this book.

DESIGN FOR LEARNING:
THREE COLLEGE CAMPUSES

Thomas Jefferson referred to the college campus as an "academical village." This term is apt, because a campus typically possesses most of the characteristics we would find in a traditional village. It is self-contained. It provides nearly all the essentials for daily life—sleeping and eating facilities, work spaces, health care, supplies of goods and services, places for social gathering. Its inhabitants interact closely with one another and have common interests and goals.

The stereotypical view of a college campus evokes the "halls of ivy"—that is, imposing monumental buildings, perhaps in the Gothic style, possibly with ivy growing thickly up the walls. As a matter of fact, some campuses do look like this, at least in their older sections. But campus design is just as diversified as any other. The personality of each college is unique.

There could hardly be a more challenging or interesting task for the environmental designer than planning a college campus. After all, it is much like designing a city from the ground up, and few people in history have had the opportunity to do that. The campus will, presumably, endure for many hundreds of years. It will serve as a working environment and home away from home for a constantly changing population of students and professors. It must be comfortable and efficient, but above all it must express the special personality of the college. It must say through its design: This is who we are. Let us see how three designers tackled this challenge.

Jefferson was not trained as an architect, much less as an environmental designer—if such a term could have existed in the early 19th century. In his day, however, the educated person was expected to be informed on many subjects. Honored now as drafter of the Declaration of Independence and third president of the United States, Jefferson drew more satisfaction from being a cultivated student of the arts and sciences. His great pride was the college he established and whose architecture and overall layout he designed—the University of Virginia (**13.42**).

Jefferson's plan for the University of Virginia combined the qualities we admire in the man himself: idealism and practicality. Idealism was embodied in the veneration of knowledge; practicality in the belief that one's surroundings when pursuing knowledge should be comfortable and conducive to study. The university is organized around a rectangle, with a large, grassy lawn at its center. Its focus is the Rotunda, the library, which is modeled after the Pantheon in Rome (see 13.13), for Jefferson's ideals were rooted in the traditions of ancient Greece and Rome. Strung out along the two sides of the lawn are ten "pavilions," each meant to house the professor of one branch of learning and his college of students. This situation was intended to provide natural and spirited communication between teacher and pupils.

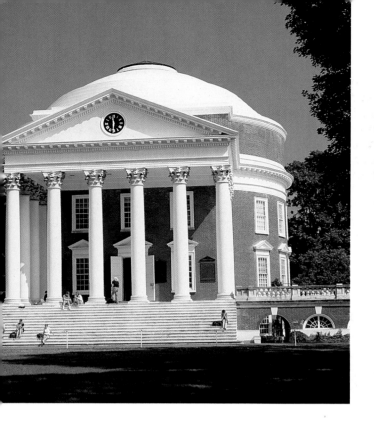

(In Jefferson's time education was based on the tutorial system. Each subject had one distinguished professor, around whom students grouped.)

The pavilions are not identical, but each is based on a specific classical prototype, some in the Doric style, some the Ionic. Joined to one another by roofed colonnades, the pavilions are planned for an elegant balance between ready access and studious seclusion. Behind the pavilions are formal gardens, then another range of buildings on each side, including "hotels" meant as dining rooms. Overall, Jefferson's design expresses magnificently his concept of "who we are." The "we" in this case—the students and faculty of the University of Virginia—are rational, orderly, and dedicated to learning; they are the enlightened heirs to the great legacy of Greece and Rome.

Just over half a century later, and a continent apart from Virginia, another great university, a very different one, was established and designed. Its patron was Leland Stanford, once governor of California, who endowed the university in memory of his dead son. (We met Governor Stanford earlier in this book, in connection with a bet on his racehorse that inspired Eadweard Muybridge's serial photographs, fig. 9.28).

In contrast to the University of Virginia, Stanford University is not classical in its design aesthetic. Rather, it draws its inspiration from the Romanesque monastery cloister, but even more specifically from California history. During the 18th and early 19th centuries Spanish Franciscan priests had established a series of mission churches up and down the coast of California. It is this "mission-style" architecture, with its low buildings and red-tiled roofs, that Stanford University emulates (**13.43**). Seen from a distance, the university looks rather like a Mediterranean village, growing naturally from the landscape. Its basic motif is not the square post-and-lintel of Jefferson's design, but the graceful arch. For Stanford University, "who we are" is identified with the West, with California, with the legacy of Spanish colonists.

13.42 Thomas Jefferson. Rotunda, University of Virginia, Charlottesville. 1817–26.

13.43 Charles A. Coolidge. Stanford University, Palo Alto, California. Begun 1886.

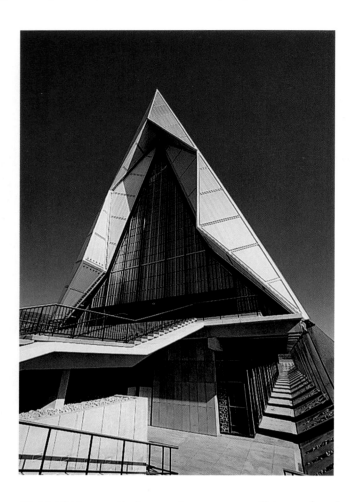

13.44 Skidmore, Owings and Merrill. United States Air Force Academy, Colorado Springs, Colo. 1956–63.

Yet another half century or so brings us to our third campus design—in this instance a design rooted in time and technology rather than place. The U.S. Air Force was organized as an independent branch of the military in 1947, and in 1954 it established its own service academy (**13.44**). Rejecting the architectural examples of its kin—the army academy at West Point (Gothic) and the naval academy at Annapolis (Classical)—the U.S. Air Force Academy sought an environment that would speak to the present and the future. The architectural firm of Skidmore, Owings and Merrill designed for the Colorado Springs site a campus that is consciously modern, sleek as an airplane, boasting of speed, progress, and technological power. For the students and faculty of the Air Force Academy, obviously, "who we are" is a people meant to fly, to be the wave of the future.

Design of the "academical village" is not static. Over the years needs change, student populations grow, buildings must be added. Even Jefferson foresaw this, leaving the grassy central rectangle at the University of Virginia open on one end for possible future expansion. Nevertheless, design of the campus does afford the rare opportunity for total, harmonious environmental planning. And so—to say the very least—does our next design category.

DESIGN FOR SHOPPING: THE MALL

The visionary architect R. Buckminster Fuller (p. 315) once proposed to build a 3-mile-wide geodesic dome over the whole midtown area of Manhattan Island. Fuller probably realized his idea would never be put into practice. In the abstract, however, the dome concept had its attractions. Think of it: The business district of New York City no longer would be plagued by the stifling heat of August or the cold and slush of January. Individual buildings would not need to be heated or cooled; the entire atmosphere under the dome would be climatically ideal year-round. Air pollution, too, would become obsolete. Workers returning from their weekends would be greeted by a light (artificially lighted, if necessary), cheerful environment. Perhaps depressions would lift and crime rates plummet.

In effect, what Fuller dreamed of was turning midtown Manhattan into one giant mall. He was indeed a visionary and well ahead of his time, for, having died in 1983, he had never seen a phenomenon that is now part of our contemporary culture—the MEGAMALL.

The mall has become the equivalent of the old-time village green, a gathering place as comprehensive as the medieval cathedral. Nearly all the social activities one could want are satisfied within the enclosed environment of the mall—sports and entertainment, music and dramatic performances, socializing with friends, having a meal or a snack, and, of course, buying or simply admiring an endless array of consumer goods. The people of medieval Europe walked, so their obvious gathering place was the cathedral in the center of town. The people of suburban North America drive cars; their obvious gathering place is the mall.

A recent entry in the "build-the-megamall" competition is the Mall of America in Bloomington, Minnesota (**13.45**). Mall of America is *big*—78 acres, to be exact, or about the size of 88 football fields housed under one roof. For your shopping pleasure there are several department stores and more than 350 shops. If you are hungry, you can choose from among some 40 restaurants. But if you want entertainment, there is always Camp Snoopy, the world's largest indoor amusement park, which features a full-size roller coaster and a four-story waterfall. Movies? Certainly. A 14-screen theater gives you plenty of choice. No matter what the weather outside—and Minnesota has a brutal winter climate—you can pursue whatever activities you fancy under the roof. One can't help but think Buckminster Fuller would have loved it. The mall is, after all, one version of life inside the dome.

Architecture and environmental design touch us more directly than any of the other arts. As we move through our everyday lives, we are influenced profoundly by the structures and environments we enter, leave, or pass by.

In years to come these design disciplines will change rapidly, because our lives are changing rapidly. We don't know what factors will influence human life fifty or a hundred years hence, or what functions will need to be served. To be sure, certain conditions are predictable. Population will increase, and there will be a greater need for housing. Industrial pollution must be eliminated or counteracted. But how will the dominance of the computer affect our buildings and our environments? How will space travel influence coming generations?

Whatever forms architecture and environmental design may take in the future, certain characteristics will remain essential to our buildings and our little worlds: They will still tell us who we are. They will still show us the face we want to present to the world.

13.45 The Mall of America, Bloomington, Minnesota. Opened 1992.

PART FIVE

ARTS IN TIME

14.1 *Horse and Geometric Symbol.* Cave painting, Lascaux, France. c. 13,000 B.C.E.

CHAPTER 14

Ancient Mediterranean Worlds

An important factor in understanding and appreciating any work of art is some knowledge of its place in time. When and where was it made? What traditions was the artist building on or rebelling against? What did society at that time expect of its artists? What sort of tasks did it give them?

For this reason, the last part of this book is devoted to a brief survey of art as it has unfolded in time. As elsewhere, we focus mainly on the Western tradition, but we also examine briefly the development of art in the cultures of Islam and Africa; of India, China, and Japan; and of Oceania, Australia, and the early Americas. Not only are these non-Western artistic traditions fascinating in their own right, but they also introduce us to other ways of thinking about art, other roles that art can play in society, and other formal directions that art can take. Many Western artists today draw as deeply on non-Western traditions as they do on Western ones, just as many contemporary artists beyond the West have been profoundly influenced by Western developments. More than at any other time in history, the entire range of humankind's artistic past nourishes its present.

THE OLDEST ART

The title of this chapter narrows our focus from the entire globe to the region around the Mediterranean Sea. It is here—in Africa, the Near East, and Europe—that the story of Western art begins. In these lands, beginning around 3000 B.C.E., numerous ancient civilizations arose, overlapped and interacted; learned from each other and conquered each other; and finally faded into the world we know today.

These civilizations—the "worlds" of our title—were preceded by far older human societies about which we know very little. Scattered evidence of their existence reaches us over a vast distance of tens of thousands of years, fascinating, mysterious, and mute. In Chapter 1, we looked at a detail from the wall paintings in the Chauvet cave in present-day France (see 1.3). Dating from later in the Upper Paleolithic Period are the paintings of the caves at Lascaux, also in France (**14.1**). Until the discovery of the Chauvet

1.3 Lion panel, Chauvet cave

The Ancient
Mediterranean

RELATED WORKS

1.4 Stonehenge

cave in 1996, the images at Lascaux were the oldest known paintings in Europe. The horse illustrated here has fascinated scholars because of its seemingly pregnant condition, the feathery forms near its forelegs, and the mysterious geometric symbol depicted above it. The paintings at Chauvet are even more finely executed, and they must surely be the result of a long tradition whose origins go back even further in time.

As at Chauvet, the paintings at Lascaux are almost all of animals. Experts agree that the images are meaningful, although what their exact meaning is remains obscure. The once-popular theory that they were made as a form of magic to ensure success in the hunt no longer seems credible. Recent theories have focused on the arrangement of the animals by species or gender, or on their distribution through the various chambers of the caves. Perhaps certain animals are symbolic. Perhaps others represent mythical spirits or spirit "contacts" in the other world. Perhaps some images track migration patterns. Artifacts and traces of human footprints suggest that many painted chambers served as gathering places, perhaps for ritual occasions. Do the images relate to these gatherings? Perhaps.

The question of why a work of art was made arises also with ancient sculptures. Nearly as old as the Chauvet cave paintings is a little female statuette that often serves as an emblem of art history's beginnings. She is made of stone, was formed about 25,000 years ago, and was found near a town in present-day Austria. Most people call her the *Venus of Willendorf* (**14.2**).

The title "Venus" may seem strange, given our usual image of the goddess of love. The name, of course, was applied by modern scholars, possibly supposing that people many thousands of years ago considered this sort of figure a sexual ideal. It seems clear that the statuette was a fertility image, possibly meant to be carried around as an amulet, or good-luck charm (the *Venus* is less than 5 inches tall). Only the features associated with child-bearing have been stressed—the belly, breasts, and pubic area. Venus' face is obscured. Her arms, crossed above the breasts, are barely defined, and her legs taper off to nothing. If we take this figure literally, she could not see or speak or walk or carry. What she could do was bear and nurture children.

How difficult it is for us living now to imagine what childbirth meant all those millennia ago. On the one hand it must have been a pressing necessity. Children were needed to help in the task of survival, and there may also have been an instinct to continue life through future generations. On the other hand, however, the process by which children are conceived and born was a mystery to these early peoples. No wonder elements of magic and ritual became associated with childbirth. Many scholars assume that fertility figures like the *Venus of Willendorf*, which are extremely common in early art, were meant to play a cause-and-effect role. The sculptor would form an image of a woman with exaggerated reproductive features, and this figure would *result* in a child being born. (It would be fascinating to know whether this figure was carved by a woman or a man.) Much prehistoric art seems to have been created for this purpose—to make sense out of the universe and to exert some control over the forces of nature.

Beginning around 9000 B.C.E. and continuing over the next 4,000 years, the Paleolithic Period, or Old Stone Age, gradually gave way to the Neolithic, or New Stone Age. The Neolithic is named for new types of stone tools that were developed, but these tools were only one aspect of what in fact was a completely new way of life. Instead of gathering wild crops as they could find them, Neolithic people learned to cultivate fruits and grains. Farming was born. Instead of following migrating herds to hunt, Neolithic people learned to domesticate animals. Dogs, cattle, goats, and other animals served variously for help, labor, meat, milk, leather, and so on. Dugout boats, the bow and arrow, and the technology of pottery—clay hardened by heat— vastly improved the standard of living. Settled communities grew up, and with them, architecture of stone and wood. The most famous work of Neolithic architecture in Europe is the monument known as Stonehenge, in England, which we discussed in Chapter 1 (see 1.4).

Tantalizing glimpses of daily life in the Neolithic Period survive in the rock paintings of the Tassili n'Ajjer region of Algeria, in northern Africa (**14.3**). Today, Tassili n'Ajjer is part of the Sahara, the world's largest desert. But at the time these images were painted, roughly between 5000 and 2000 B.C.E., the desert had not yet emerged. Instead, the region was a vast

14.2 (below) *Venus of Willendorf*. c. 23,000 B.C.E. Limestone, height 4⅜". Naturhistorisches Museum, Vienna.

14.3 (bottom) *Women and Cattle*. Rock painting at Tassili n'Ajjer, Algeria. Pastoralist style, after 5000 B.C.E.

grassland, home to animals, plants, and the people we see depicted here—five women, gathered near their cattle. Other images painted on the rock walls at Tassili n'Ajjer depict women harvesting grain or occupied with children, men herding cattle, and enclosures that may represent dwellings.

The art that has come down to us from the Stone Age is fragmentary and isolated. Ancient cave paintings. A small statue of a woman. A circular stone monument. Paintings on rock walls in the desert. Our examples are separated from one another by thousands of years and thousands of miles. Each one must have been part of a long local artistic tradition that stretched back in history and continued for many millennia afterward. Yet for each one, we are faced with questions: "What came before, what came after, and where is it?"

In studying art of the past, it is important to keep in mind that the cultures we examine most fully are not necessarily those in which the *most* art was made or the *best* art was made. They are, rather, the cultures whose art *has been found or preserved*. Art has been produced at all times and in all places and by all peoples. But in order for it to be available to future generations for study, it must survive—possibly even after the culture that produced it has disappeared. Certain conditions foster the preservation of art, and the ancient cultures that we are able to study in depth across time fulfill most of them.

First, the artists worked in durable materials such as stone, metal, and fired clay. Second, the local environment is not destructive to artworks; for instance, the hot, dry climate of Egypt provides an excellent milieu for preservation. Third, the culture was highly organized, with stable population centers. Great cities normally house the richest troves of artwork in any culture, for they are where rulers dwell, wealth is accumulated, and artists congregate. Fourth, the culture had a tradition of caching its artworks in places of limited or no accessibility. A huge portion of the ancient art that has survived comes from tombs or underground caves.

The first cultures of the ancient Mediterranean world to meet most of these conditions arose in Mesopotamia—a region in the Near East—and in Egypt, in northeastern Africa. Here, for the first time, we find a coherent, reasonably intact artistic production about which we have come to know a good deal. It is no accident that the civilizations of both Mesopotamia and Egypt developed along the banks of mighty rivers—the Tigris and Euphrates in Mesopotamia and the Nile in Egypt. Rivers provided both a means of transportation and a source of water. Water enabled irrigation, which in turn allowed for vaster and more reliable farming, which in turn supported larger and denser populations. Cities developed, and with them social stratification (the division of society into classes such as rulers, priests, nobles, commoners, and slaves), the standardization of religions and rituals, the creation of monumental architecture, and the specialization that allowed some people to farm, some to be merchants, and others to make art.

Our study of ancient Mediterranean worlds properly begins here, in the lands along the great rivers.

MESOPOTAMIA

The region known to the ancient world as Mesopotamia occupied a large area roughly equivalent to the present-day nation of Iraq. Fertile soil watered by the Tigris and Euphrates rivers made Mesopotamia highly desirable, yet a lack of natural boundaries made it easy to invade and difficult to defend. Successive waves of people conquered the region in ancient times, yet each new ruling group built on the cultural achievements of its predecessors, and so we can speak with some justice of a continuing Mesopotamian culture.

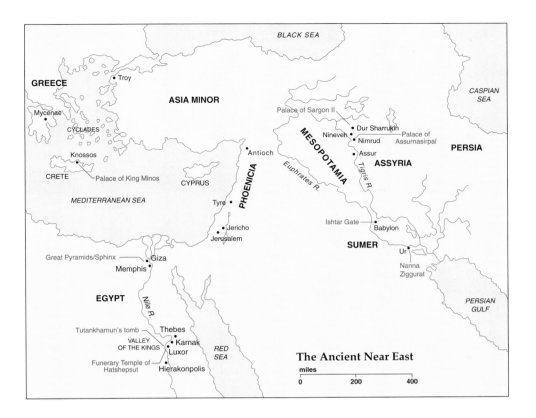

The first cities of Mesopotamia arose in the southernmost area, a region called Sumer. By about 3400 B.C.E. some dozen Sumerian city-states—cities that ruled over their surrounding territories—had emerged. The Sumerians were the first people to leave behind them not just artifacts but words: the wedge-shaped marks that they pressed into damp clay to keep track of inventories and accounts developed over time into a writing system capable of recording language. Called cuneiform (Latin for "wedge-shaped"), it served as the writing system of Mesopotamia for the next 3,000 years.

Lacking stone, the Sumerians built their cities of sun-dried brick. The largest structure of a Sumerian city was the **ziggurat**, a temple or shrine raised on a monumental stepped base (**14.4**). The example illustrated here, partially restored but still missing its temple, was dedicated to the moon god Nanna, the protective deity of the Sumerian city of Ur. In the flat land of Sumer, ziggurats were visible for miles around. They elevated the temple to a symbolic mountain top, a meeting place for heaven and earth, where priests and priestesses communicated with the gods.

14.4 Nanna Ziggurat, Ur (present-day Maqaiyir, Iraq). c. 2100–2050 B.C.E.

14.5 (top) *Ram in Thicket,* from Ur. c. 2600 B.C.E. Wood, gold foil, lapis lazuli; height 10″.
The University of Pennsylvania Museum, Philadelphia.

14.6 (above) Head of an Akkadian ruler (Sargon 1?), from Nineveh, Iraq. c. 2250 B.C.E. Bronze, height 12″.
Museum of Antiquities, Baghdad.

14.7 (right) *Human-Headed Winged Lion.* Assyrian, from Nimrud. 883–859 B.C.E. Limestone, height 10′2½″.
The Metropolitan Museum of Art, New York.

The refined and luxurious aspect of Sumerian art is evident in this small figure of a goat standing with its forelegs propped on a flowering tree (**14.5**). Crafted over a wooden core (now lost) of gold, silver, and a precious stone called lapis lazuli, the delicate figure probably served to support a small tray or tabletop.

By 2300 B.C.E., the Sumerian city-states had been conquered by their neighbors to the north, the Akkadians. Under their ruler Sargon I, the Akkadians established the region's first empire. Though it crumbled quickly, the empire seems to have extended all the way from the shores of the Mediterranean to the Persian Gulf. Sargon himself may be portrayed in the splendid Akkadian sculpture illustrated here (**14.6**). Certainly the expensive material (copper) and the fine workmanship suggest that it represents a ruler of some kind. The lifelike features—heavy-lidded eyes, strong nose, and sensitive mouth—argue that this is a naturalistic portrait of a real person and not a generic or idealized head. Such naturalism is extremely rare in early art.

A more stable and long-lived Mesopotamian empire was established by the Amorites, who consolidated their rule over the region by about 1830 B.C.E. and established a capital at Babylon. The most important legacy of the Babylonian empire is not artistic but legal: a set of edicts and laws compiled under the ruler Hammurabi (ruled c. 1792–1750 B.C.E.). Known as Hammurabi's Code, it is the only complete legal code to survive from the ancient world, and it has provided historians with valuable insights into the structure and concerns of Mesopotamian society.

Mesopotamia's history was marked by almost continual warfare and conquest, and a major goal of architecture was the erection of mighty citadels to ensure the safety of temples and palaces. Such a citadel was that of the Assyrian ruler Assurnasirpal II, built at Nimrud in the 9th century B.C.E. Based in northern Mesopotamia, the Assyrians had been gathering power and territory since before 1100 B.C.E. Their military strength increased greatly under Assurnasirpal II, and within a few centuries they would amass the largest empire the region had yet seen. Assurnasirpal's palace had gates fronted by monumental stone slabs carved into enormous human-headed winged beasts, a bull and a lion. The lion (**14.7**) wears a horned cap indicating divine status. Its body has five legs, so that from the front it appears motionless but from the side it is understood to be walking. Visitors to the citadel were meant to be impressed—and no doubt intimidated—by these majestic creatures.

The walls of the palace were lined with alabaster reliefs depicting Assyrian triumphs and royal power. A popular subject is the lion hunt (**14.8**), in which the king is depicted slaying the most powerful of beasts. The ceremonial hunt was probably carried out as it is pictured here, with armed guards releasing captive animals into an enclosure for the king to kill from his chariot. Slaying lions was viewed as a fitting demonstration of kingly power. The lions' anatomy is beautifully observed, and the many overlapping figures show the sculptor's confidence in suggesting three-dimensional space.

When the Babylonians again came to power in Mesopotamia, late in the 7th century B.C.E., they formed a kingdom we call Neo-Babylonian. These "new" Babylonians surely must be ranked among the great architects of the ancient world. They developed a true arch before the Romans did and were masters of decorative design for architecture. Moreover, like their forebears, they had a formidable leader in the person of Nebuchadnezzar, an enthusiastic patron of the arts and architecture who built a dazzling capital city at Babylon.

14.8 *Lion Hunt,* from the palace complex of Assurnasirpal II, Kalhu (present-day Nimrud, Iraq). c. 850 B.C.E. Alabaster, height 39″. The British Museum, London.

14.9 Ishtar Gate (restored), from Babylon. c. 575 B.C.E. Glazed brick, height 48′9″.
Staatliche Museen zu Berlin, Preussischer Kulturbesitz, Vorderasiatisches Museum.

A genuine planned city, Babylon was constructed as a square, bisected by the Euphrates River, with streets and broad avenues crossing at right angles. Stone is scarce in this region of Mesopotamia, and so the architects made liberal use of glazed ceramic bricks. Babylon must have been a city of brilliant color. Its main thoroughfare was the Processional Way, at one end of which stood the Ishtar Gate (**14.9**), built about 575 B.C.E. and now restored in a German museum. The gate consists of thousands of glazed mud bricks, with two massive towers flanking a central arch. On ceremonial occasions Nebuchadnezzar would sit under the arch in majesty to receive his subjects. The walls of the gate are embellished with more glazed ceramic animals, probably meant as spirit-guardians.

The history of Mesopotamia parallels in time that of its neighbor to the southwest, the kingdom of Egypt, with which it had regular contacts. In Egypt, however, we will find considerably less political turmoil. Protected to the south by a series of cataracts (rocky, unnavigable stretches of the Nile) and to the east and west by vast deserts, Egypt during much of its long history was spared the waves of immigration and invasion that continually transformed Mesopotamia.

EGYPT

The principal message of Egyptian art is continuity—a seamless span of time reaching back into history and forward into the future. The Greek philosopher Plato wrote that Egyptian art did not change for ten thousand years; while this is an exaggeration, there were many features that remained stable over long periods of time. The Sphinx (**14.10**), the symbol of this most important characteristic of Egyptian art, is the essence of stability, order, and endurance. Built about 2530 B.C.E. and towering to a height of 65 feet, it faces into the rising sun, seeming to cast its immobile gaze down the centuries for all eternity. The Sphinx has the body of a reclining lion and the head of a man, thought to be the pharaoh Khafre, whose pyramid tomb is nearby. Egyptian kings ruled absolutely and enjoyed a semidivine status, taking their authority from the sun-god, Ra, from whom they were assumed to be descended. Power and continuity both are embodied in this splendid monument.

An even earlier relic from Egyptian culture, the so-called *Palette of Narmer* (**14.11**), illustrates many characteristics of Egyptian art. The palette (so named because it takes the form of a slab for mixing cosmetics) portrays a victory by the forces of Upper (southern) Egypt, led by Narmer, over those of Lower (northern) Egypt. Narmer is the largest figure and is positioned near the center of the palette to indicate this high status. He holds a fallen enemy by the hair and is about to deliver the death blow. In the lowest sector of the tablet are two more defeated enemies. At upper right is a falcon representing Horus, the god of Upper Egypt. In its organization of images the palette is strikingly logical and balanced. The central section has Narmer's figure just to left of the middle, with his upraised arm and the form of a servant filling the space, while the falcon and the victim complete the right-hand side of the composition.

Narmer's pose is typical of Egyptian art. When depicting an important personage, the Egyptian artist strove to show each part of the body to best advantage, so it could be "read" clearly by the viewer. Thus, Narmer's lower body is seen in profile, his torso full front, his head in profile, but his eye front again. This same pose recurs throughout most two-dimensional art in Egypt. It is believed that the priests, who had much control over the art, established this figure type and decreed that it be maintained for the sake of continuity. Obviously, it is not a posture that suggests much motion, apart from a stylized gesture like that of Narmer's upraised arm. But action was not important to Egyptian art. Order and stability were its primary characteristics, as they were the goals of Egyptian society. We see this in official sculptures, such as the double portrait of Menkaure and Khamerernebty in Chapter 11 (see 11.17), and also in less formal works.

14.10 (left) *The Great Sphinx*, Giza. c. 2500 B.C.E. Limestone rock, height 66'.

14.11 (right) *Palette of Narmer*, from Hierakonpolis. c. 3100 B.C.E. Slate, height 25". Egyptian Museum, Cairo.

14.12 (left) *Seated Scribe*, from Saqqara. c. 2450 B.C.E. Painted limestone, height 21″. Musée du Louvre, Paris.

14.13 (right) Funerary temple of Hatshepsut, Deir el-Bahri. c. 2009–1997 B.C.E.

RELATED WORKS

11.17 Menkaure and Khamerernebty

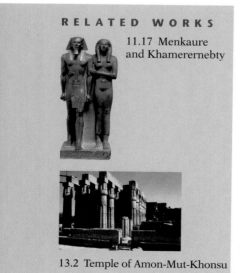

13.2 Temple of Amon-Mut-Khonsu

A common sculpture type from the same period as the Menkaure figure is the *Seated Scribe* (**14.12**), depicting a high court official whose position might be explained as "professional writer." In an era when literacy was rare, the scribe played a vital role in copying important documents and sacred texts, and his work commanded much respect. This sculpture, while somewhat more relaxed than standing pharaoh portraits, is still symmetrical and reserved. The scribe's face shows intelligence and dignity, and his body is depicted realistically as thickening and rather flabby, no doubt a sign of his age and sedentary occupation, perhaps also an indicator of wisdom.

The most famous architectural creation of Egypt is the pyramid (see 3.10), but Egyptian architects also built homes, palaces, temples, shrines, and other structures. A pyramid, in fact, was only one element of a royal funerary complex, which also included a temple for the worship of the deceased ruler, who had rejoined the gods in immortality. One of the best-preserved and most innovative funerary temples is that of Hatshepsut, one of the few female rulers in Egypt's history (**14.13**). Planned by the architect Senenmut, it rises in a series of three broad terraces and then continues *into* the steep cliffs behind it, from which an inner sanctuary was hollowed out. Over 200 statues of Hatshepsut once populated the vast complex, which contained shrines to several Egyptian deities as well as to Hatshepsut and her father, the ruler Tuthmose I.

Egyptian painting reveals the same clear visual design and illustrative skill as the works in stone. A wall painting from Thebes (**14.14**), depicting a hunting scene, poses the main figure very much like the figure of Narmer, although the two works are separated in time by some 1,650 years. Again the hunter's body is stylized: his head, eyes, torso, and legs are each shown from the most advantageous viewpoint. In keeping with the Egyptians' love of exact detail, this painter draws the birds and other creatures with almost biological precision. If we recognize the species, we can identify them. Even the fish are rendered meticulously; we don't see them as we would through a blur of water, but rather as we *know* the fish to look.

We know other things as well. The use of hierarchical scale tells us that the hunter, probably a nobleman, is the most important figure in the composition, because he is the biggest. Apart from clues provided by clothing, we know that he is a man and the figure at right is a woman. By convention, regardless of race or complexion, the Egyptians painted men darker (reddish) and women lighter (yellowish).

Typical of Egyptian art, the image has many layers of meaning. The man is depicted young and in the prime of life, the form he hopes to have in eternity. His victorious pose proclaims his ability to triumph in the journey to the afterlife, which was thought to be fraught with peril. The marsh setting is also significant. It was in a marsh that the Egyptian goddess Isis prepared her husband Osiris for resurrection, and that life itself began at the time of creation. A marsh is thus a site where life renews itself, just as the man will renew himself by rising from death.

One brief period in the history of Egyptian culture stands apart from the rest and therefore has fascinated scholars and art lovers alike. This was the reign of pharaoh Amenhotep IV, who came to power about 1353 B.C.E. For a civilization that prized continuity above all else, Amenhotep was a true revolutionary. He changed his name to Akhenaten and attempted to establish monotheism (belief in one god) among a people who had traditionally worshiped many gods. He built a new capital at what is now called Tell el-Amarna, so historians refer to his reign as the Amarna period. Akhenaten was apparently quite active in creating a new style of art for his reign, and under his direction the age-old, rigid postures of Egyptian art gave way to more relaxed, naturalistic, and even intimate portrayals.

Nowhere is this more apparent than in the famous portrait bust of his queen, Nefertiti (**14.15**). While enchanted by Nefertiti's beauty, the modern viewer is perhaps even more taken by how contemporary she seems, how she appears to bridge the gap of more than three thousand years to our own world. With her regal headdress and elongated neck, Nefertiti presents a standard of elegance that is timeless.

RELATED WORKS

3.21 Model from the tomb of Meketre

14.14 (left) Fragment of a wall painting from the tomb of Nebamun, Thebes. c. 1450 B.C.E. Paint on plaster, height 32″. The British Museum, London.

14.15 (right) *Queen Nefertiti*. c. 1345 B.C.E. Painted limestone, height 20″. Staatliche Museen zu Berlin, Preussischer Kulturbesitz, Ägyptisches Museum.

14.16 (left) *Akhenaten and His Family,* from Akhetaten (modern Tell el-Amarna). c. 1345 B.C.E. Painted limestone relief, 12¼ × 15¼″. Staatliche Museen zu Berlin, Preussischer Kulturbesitz, Ägyptisches Museum.

14.17 (right) Burial mask of Tutankhamun. c. 1325 B.C.E. Gold, inlaid with blue glass and semiprecious stones; height 21¼″. Egyptian Museum, Cairo.

Even more intimate is the charming domestic scene depicted in this limestone relief (**14.16**). Akhenaten and Nefertiti sit facing each other on cushioned thrones. Akhenaten tenderly holds one of their three daughters, who gestures toward her mother and sisters. Seated on Nefertiti's lap, the older daughter looks up at her mother as she points across to her father; the youngest daughter tries to get her mother's attention by caressing her cheek. Above, Akhenaten's god, Aten, the sun-disk, shines his life-giving rays upon them. The sculpture is an example of **sunken relief.** In this technique, the figures do not project upward from the surface. Instead, outlines are carved deep into the surface, and the figures are modeled within them, from the surface down.

Akhenaten's reforms did not last. After his death, temples to the old gods were restored and temples that had been built to Aten were dismantled. The city of el-Amarna was abandoned, and the traditional Egyptian styles of representation were reimposed. Thus it is that the immobile mask of eternity greets us again in the stunning gold burial mask of Akhenaten's son-in-law and successor, the young Tutankhamun (**14.17**).

From earliest times, Egyptians had buried their most lavish art in royal tombs. Rulers were sent into eternity outfitted with everything they would need to continue life in the sumptuous style they had known on earth—furniture, jewelry, chariots, clothing, and artifacts of all kinds. From earliest times as well, grave robbers have coveted that buried treasure—and not for its artistic merits. Most of the royal tombs that have been discovered in modern times have been empty, their fabulous contents looted long ago. It was not until 1922 that modern eyes could assess the full splendor of ancient Egypt. In that year, the English archaeologist Howard Carter discovered the tomb of Tutankhamun, its treasures virtually intact after 3,000 years.

Whose Grave Is This Anyway?

W HEN HOWARD CARTER and his party opened the tomb of the Egyptian king Tutankhamun in 1922, there was rejoicing around the world. The tomb was largely intact, not seriously pillaged by ancient grave robbers, so it still contained the wonderful artifacts that had been buried with the young king more than three millennia earlier. Over the next several years Carter and his team systematically photographed and catalogued the objects from the tomb, then transported them to the Cairo Museum.

There is a certain irony in this story that raises complex ethical questions. Why are Carter and his party not called grave robbers? Why are their actions in stripping the tomb acceptable—even praiseworthy—when similar behavior by common thieves would be deplored? No matter who opens a tomb and takes away its contents, that person is violating the intentions of those who sealed the tomb originally. No matter what the motivation, a human body that was meant to rest in peace for all time has been disturbed. Should this not make us feel uncomfortable?

From the beginning some were uneasy about the propriety of unearthing Tutankhamun's remains. When Lord Carnarvon, Carter's sponsor, died suddenly from a mosquito bite, and several others connected with the project experienced tragedies, rumors arose about the "curse of King Tut." But Carter himself died peacefully many years later, and the talk subsided.

Perhaps it is the passage of time that transforms grave robbing into archaeology. Carter would no doubt have been outraged if, say, his grandmother's coffin had been dug up to strip the body of its jewelry. But after three thousand years Tutankhamun has no relatives still around to protest.

Perhaps it is a question of the words we use to describe such ancient finds. We speak of Tutankhamun's "mummy," and mummy is a clean, historical-sounding word. Parents bring their children to museums to see the mummies and mummy cases. We can almost forget that a mummy is the embalmed body of a dead human being pulled out of its coffin so that we can marvel at the coffin and sometimes the body itself.

Or, perhaps the difference between grave robbing and archaeology lies in the motives of the perpetrators. Common thieves are motivated by greed, by their quest for money to be made by selling stolen objects. Carter and his team did not sell the treasures from Tutankhamun's tomb but stored them safely in the Cairo Museum, where art lovers from around the world can see them. They were, in effect, making a glorious gift to the people of our century and centuries to come (while at the same time, one must point out, acquiring significant glory for themselves).

The basic issue is a clash of cultural values. To the Egyptians, it was normal and correct to bury their finest artworks with the exalted dead. To us, the idea of all that beauty being locked away in the dark forever seems an appalling waste. We want to bring it into the light, to have it as part of our precious artistic heritage. Almost no one, having seen these magnificent treasures, would seriously propose they be put back in the tomb and sealed up.

In the end, inevitably, our cultural values will prevail, simply because we are still here and the ancient Egyptians are not. After three thousand years, Tutankhamun's grave really isn't his anymore. Whether rightly or wrongly, it belongs to us.

Howard Carter and an assistant unwrapping the innermost of Tutankhamun's three nested coffins. The third coffin is solid gold and contained the king's mummified body.

Tutankhamun—quickly dubbed "King Tut" by the 1922 newspapers—was a relatively minor ruler. The tombs of the great would have been far more lavish. Yet even Tutankhamun's tomb was a virtual warehouse of priceless objects superbly crafted of alabaster, precious stones, and above all gold—gold in unimaginable quantities. Gold in Egyptian thought signified more than mere wealth. It was associated with the life-giving rays of the sun and with eternity itself. The flesh of the gods was believed to be gold, which would never decay. Tutankhamun's solid gold coffin, and the solid gold face mask (14.17) that rested on the head and shoulders of his mummified body inside, were meant to confer immortality. Projecting over the young king's forehead are the alert heads of a cobra and a vulture, symbols of the ancient protective goddesses of Lower and Upper Egypt.

When Tutankhamun died, around 1323 B.C.E., Egyptian civilization was already ancient—a continuous culture that looked back confidently on some 1,700 years of achievement and power. Egypt would continue for another 1,300 years into the future, yet its years of supremacy were waning. Other, younger cultures were gathering force elsewhere around the Mediterranean. Two of these upstarts, Greece and Rome, would eventually conquer Egypt. We turn our attention to Greece next, after a brief look at some of the cultures that preceded it on the islands of the Aegean Sea.

THE AEGEAN

Between the Greek peninsula and the continent of Asia Minor (modern-day Turkey) is an arm of the Mediterranean Sea known as the Aegean (see map, p. 348). Greek culture arose on the lands bordering this small "sea within a sea," but the Greeks were preceded in the region by several fascinating cultures that thrived on the islands that are so plentiful there.

The artistic cultures of the Aegean parallel in time those of Egypt and Mesopotamia, for the earliest begins about 3000 B.C.E. There were three major Aegean cultures: the Cycladic, centered on a group of small islands in

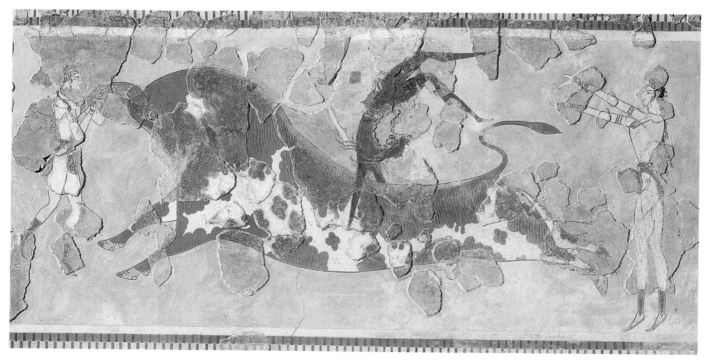

the Aegean; the Minoan, based on the island of Crete at the southern end of the Aegean; and the Mycenaean, on the mainland of Greece.

Cycladic art is a puzzle, because we know almost nothing about the people who made it. Nearly all consists of nude female figures like the one illustrated here (**14.18**)—simplified, abstract, composed of geometric lines and shapes and projections. The figures vary in size from the roughly 2-foot height of our example to approximately life-size, but they are much alike in style. Presumably they were meant as fertility images, although they are a far cry from the fleshier "Venuses" found earlier in the north. To modern eyes the Cycladic figurines seem astonishingly sophisticated in their sleek abstraction of the human figure. Indeed, 20th-century artists such as Alberto Giacometti (see 4.36) studied Cycladic art when they were forging their own abstract styles.

The Minoan culture on Crete can be traced to about 2000 B.C.E. and centers around the great city of Knossos. We take the name from a legendary king called Minos, who supposedly ruled at Knossos and whose queen gave birth to the dreaded creature, half-human, half-bull, known as the Minotaur. Numerous frescoes survive at Knossos—some fragmentary, some restored— and from these we have formed an impression of a lighthearted, cheerful people devoted to games and sport. Among the finest wall paintings is a work known as the *Toreador Fresco* (**14.19**), featuring the Minoans' special animal, the bull. This modern title suggests the Spanish sport of bullfighting (a *toreador* being a bullfighter), but we can see that the Minoans' game was unique to them. A young male acrobat vaults over the back of the racing bull; he will be caught in the waiting arms of the young woman at right. Another female player, at left, grasps the bull's horns; perhaps she is ready to take her turn somersaulting over the animal. Most striking here is the contrast between the hefty, charging bull and the lithe, playful flip of the acrobat. The composition is marvelously balanced, with the women at both sides serving as anchors, the tumbling male figure and the curving tail counterweighing the massive bull's head. Many graceful curves—of the bull's back, the bull's underbelly, the tumbler's arched body—reinforce our experience of motion, captured to the split second.

Mycenaean culture, so called because it formed around the city of Mycenae, flourished on the south coast of the Greek mainland from about 1600 to 1100 B.C.E. Like the Minoans, the Mycenaeans built palaces and temples, but they are also noted for their elaborate burial customs and tombs— a taste apparently acquired from the Egyptians, with whom they had contact. It seems probable that Egypt or Nubia was also the source of the Mycenaeans' great supplies of gold, for they alone among the Aegean cultures were master goldsmiths. Burial places in and around Mycenae have yielded large quantities of exquisite gold objects, such as the *rhyton*, or drinking cup, in the shape of a lion's head (**14.20**). The craftsmanship of this vessel is wonderful, contrasting smooth planar sections on the sides of the face with the more detailed snout and mane. The Mycenaeans also used gold for masks, jewelry, and weapons.

When we use the word "Classical" in connection with Western civilization, we are referring to the two cultures discussed next in this chapter— ancient Greece and ancient Rome. The term itself indicates an aesthetic bias, for anything "classic" is supposed to embody the highest possible standard of quality, to be the very best of its kind. If true, this would mean that Western art reached a pinnacle in the few hundred years surrounding the start of our common era and has not been equaled in the millennium and a half since then. This is a controversial idea that many would dispute vehemently. Few can deny, however, that the ancient Greeks and Romans *intended* to achieve the highest standards. Art and architecture were matters of public policy, and it was accepted that there could be an objective, shared standard for the best, the purest, the most beautiful.

14.20 Rhyton in the shape of a lion's head, from Mycenae. c. 1550 B.C.E. Gold, height 8″. National Museum, Athens.

GREECE

No doubt a major reason we so respect the ancient Greeks is that they excelled in many different fields. Their political ideals serve as a model for contemporary democracy. Their poetry and drama and philosophy survive as living classics, familiar to every serious scholar. Their architecture and sculpture have influenced most later periods in the history of Western art.

It is assumed the Greeks' genius shone equally in painting, but we know very little about this because most painted works have been lost. We would know even less were it not for the large number of painted clay vases that were produced from about the 8th century B.C.E. Terra cotta (baked clay) is an extremely durable material; it can shatter but will not disintegrate, and so the pieces can be reassembled. For this reason a large quantity of Greek art has survived to our day.

Few cultures can match the Greeks in the elaborate painting of vases, which represent a major part of their artistic output. These terra cotta vessels served as grave monuments, storage urns for wine or oil, drinking cups, and so forth. An early example is the so-called *Dipylon Vase* (**14.21**), named for the cemetery in Athens where it was found. Made in the 8th century B.C.E., the *Dipylon Vase* offers a superb example of the geometric style of vase painting, the first clearly defined Greek style we know. Much of the vase's decoration consists of geometric lines and patterns, including the "meander" pattern that runs around the top just under the rim. Images of people are little more than stick figures wonderfully integrated in the overall geometric design.

The *Dipylon Vase* provides an interesting commentary on the burial customs of the Greeks, especially as contrasted with the Egyptians. The pharaoh Tutankhamun's tomb was elaborately fitted out for a prestigious afterlife, since that is what the Egyptians expected. The Greeks were not so optimistic. To them, life beyond the grave was a gray and shadowy place of little interest. A funerary urn like the *Dipylon Vase* was placed above the burial spot to receive liquid offerings and was intended to show the respect of the deceased's relatives. A funeral procession is painted on the vase. But there is no provision for enjoyment of the next world, only recognition of the one left behind.

Greece in the Age of Perikles
c. 440 B.C.E.

Through later centuries Greek vase painting prospered. Our next illustration (**14.22**) shows detail from the interior of a kylix (a drinking cup) representing *Eos and Memnon*. The painting is in the red-figure style, which developed late in the 6th century B.C.E. A background of black was created from the glaze, leaving the figures in the natural red color of the clay. Despite this technically difficult technique, the painting is remarkably fine. Eos, the goddess of dawn, holds the body of her dead son, Memnon, who has been killed by the hero Achilles. There is a suggestion of depth in the overlapping of Memnon's body in front of Eos and in the crossed legs; the dangling arms of the body visually balance Eos' half-spread wings. Finely drawn textures of gown, hair, and wings reveal the skill of the painter's brush. As a mark of the esteem in which vase painters were held, and their pride in the work, this kylix is signed by the painter, Douris.

While all Greek and Roman art is broadly termed Classical, one particular Greek era, the 5th and 4th centuries B.C.E., is known as the Classical period. At that time Greece consisted of several independent city-states, often at war among themselves. Chief among the city-states—from an artistic and cultural point of view, if not always a military one—was Athens.

Like many Greek cities, Athens had been built around a high hill, or acropolis. Ancient temples on the Acropolis had crumbled or been destroyed in the wars. About 449 B.C.E. Athens' great general Perikles came to power as head of state and set about rebuilding. He soon embarked on a massive construction program, meant not only to restore the past glory of Athens but to raise it to a previously undreamed-of splendor.

Perikles' friend, the sculptor Phidias, was given the job of overseeing all architectural and sculptural projects on the Acropolis. The work would continue for several decades, but it took an amazingly short time given the ambitious nature of the scheme. By the end of the century the Acropolis

14.21 (left) *Dipylon Vase.* Athens, 8th century B.C.E. Terra cotta, height 42⅝".
The Metropolitan Museum of Art, New York.

14.22 (right) Douris. *Eos and Memnon,* interior of a kylix by Kalliades. c. 490–480 B.C.E. Terra cotta, diameter 10½".
Musée du Louvre, Paris.

Perikles

H IS ENEMIES CALLED him "onionhead." Contemporary writers tell us that Perikles had an unusually high, sloping brow reaching up to a domed crown of the head, and that he is always portrayed wearing a helmet to cover this supposed deformity. For modern students, however, the term "onionhead" may take on another meaning. We peel away layer after layer, yet we never fully understand this complex man who is so admired 2,400 years after his death.

Perikles was born about 495 B.C.E., son of the Athenian general Xanthippus. Being of a noble family, he received a thorough education, first from Damon, the master of music—"music" in those times being understood to include reading, writing, mathematics, singing, and poetry. Later he studied with the philosopher Anaxagoras. Under these teachers Perikles developed habits of independent thought, enormous self-discipline, and (even his rivals admitted) unblemished integrity. After an early military career, he became active in the government of Athens. About 449 B.C.E. Perikles was elected head of state, a post he held until his death.

An arranged marriage to a cousin produced two sons but little domestic happiness. All sources agree that the companion of Perikles' heart was the beautiful and brilliant Aspasia, a *hetaera*, or upper-class courtesan, with whom he lived openly for many years. Aspasia was possessed of wit and charm that drew to her side (and therefore to Perikles' side) the great artists and thinkers of the day, even Socrates himself. She seems also to have been a clever political adviser.

According to the ancient biographer Plutarch, Perikles excelled not only as a general and statesman but also as an orator, whose "tongue was armed with thunder and lightning." But for our purposes in this book another trait stands out: Perikles had both the means and the vision to become an incomparable patron of the arts.

Soon after assuming power in Athens, Perikles gave his friend, the sculptor Phidias, the task of rebuilding the temples on the Acropolis—but rebuilding them on a far more elaborate scale. Under Perikles' sponsorship, Plutarch remarks, "many edifices, each of which would seem to have required the labor of several successive ages, were finished during the administration of one prosperous man."[1] The jewel of these was, of course, the Parthenon, built with hand labor and embellished with many sculptures in just fifteen years.

Perikles took a lively interest in the other arts as well. The theater, offering both dramas and comedies, prospered in that time, and Perikles saw to it that all citizens received free tickets. He built a music hall, the Odeum, and personally judged the musical contests held each year. This exhilarating climate for the arts continued until a plague swept Athens in 430 B.C.E. Although Perikles recovered from the disease, he was weakened and died the next year.

We who so highly value the Parthenon, even in its ruined state, cannot imagine it not existing, yet Perikles' building program was not universally popular. Critics charged he had emptied the treasury to serve his own ambitions. But Perikles' ambitions were not for himself. They were for Athens, for her glory in those times and her glory down through the ages. He spoke of it this way: "What I would prefer is that you should fix your eyes every day on the greatness of Athens as she really is, and should fall in love with her."[2]

Perikles. Roman copy after a Greek original of c. 429 B.C.E, probably by Kresilas. Marble. Vatican Museums, Rome.

probably looked much like the reconstruction shown here (**14.23**). The large columned building at lower right in the photo is the Propylaea, the ceremonial gateway to the Acropolis through which processions winding up the hill would pass. At left in the photo, the building with columned porches is the Erechtheum, placed where Erechtheus, legendary founder of the city, supposedly lived.

But the crowning glory of the Acropolis was and is the Parthenon (**14.24**). Dedicated to the goddess Athena *parthenos*, or Athena the warrior maiden, the Parthenon is a Doric-style temple with columns all around the exterior and an inner row of columns on each of the short walls. The roof originally rose to a peak, leaving a pediment (visible in the reconstruction) at each end. The pediments were decorated with sculptures, as was the frieze. (To review the vocabulary of Classical architecture, see p. 297.) In the manner of Greek temples, the Parthenon was painted in vivid colors, principally red and blue. The architects Iktinos and Kallikrates, directed by Phidias, completed the structure in just fifteen years.

The Parthenon has been studied in greater detail than perhaps any other building in the Western tradition, for it served generations of European architects as a model of perfection. Research has discovered numerous painstaking refinements that contribute to the temple's pleasing effect. First, as mentioned in Chapter 5, the ratio of length to height of the facade reproduces the proportion known as the golden section (see 5.29), which the Greeks found intellectually and aesthetically pleasing. Legend claims there are no straight lines in the Parthenon, but this is probably a romantic exaggeration. Many of the lines we expect to be straight, however, are not. Instead, the builders adjusted the physical lines of the temple so they would *appear* to be straight. For example, tall columns that are absolutely straight may appear to bend inward at the center, like an hourglass, so the columns

13.4 Temple of Athena Nike

14.23 (below) Model reconstruction of the Acropolis, Athens, viewed from the northwest. Courtesy Royal Ontario Museum, Toronto.

14.24 (bottom) Iktinos and Kallikrates. Parthenon, Athens. 447–432 B.C.E.

14.25 *Three Goddesses*, from the east pediment of the Parthenon. c. 438–432 B.C.E. Marble, over life-size.
The British Museum, London.

on the Parthenon have been given a slight bulge, known as **entasis,** to compensate for the visual effect. Also, a long horizontal, such as the Parthenon's porch steps, may appear to sag in the middle; to correct for this optical illusion, the level has been adjusted, rising about 2½ inches to form an arc higher at the center. A large building rising perpendicular to the ground may loom over the visitor and seem to be leaning forward; to avoid this impression, the architects of the Parthenon tilted the whole facade back slightly. Corner columns, seen against the sky, would have seemed thinner than inside columns, which have the building as a backdrop; therefore, the outside columns were made slightly heavier than all the others.

The inner chamber of the Parthenon once housed a monumental statue of the goddess Athena, made by Phidias himself of gold and ivory and standing 30 feet tall atop its pedestal. Contemporary sources tell us Phidias was an artist of unsurpassed genius, but we must take their word for it, since neither the Athena nor any of his other sculptures are known to survive. Other sculptures from the Parthenon have been preserved, however, and these were probably made by Phidias' students, under his supervision.

One existing sculpture group, now in the British Museum, depicts *Three Goddesses* (**14.25**). In Perikles' time this group stood near the far right side of the pediment; if you imagine the figures with their heads intact, you can see how they fit into the angle of the triangle. Carved from marble and now headless, these goddesses still seem to breathe and be capable of movement, so convincing is their roundness. The draperies flow and ripple naturally over the bodies, apparently responding to living flesh underneath.

The Parthenon sculptures represent a high point in the long period of Greek experimentation with carving in marble. We can trace this evolution from the 6th to the 2nd century by comparing three treatments of a favorite Greek sculpture type—the nude male figure. While many marble statues were of females, the most typical Greek figure is male, a nude proportioned to indicate an ideal of physical perfection.

The Greeks' approach to sculpture was a radical departure from artistic precedents in other parts of the Mediterranean world. Egyptian sculptures more often were attached to a support; Greek figures generally are free-standing, in the round. Egyptian figures usually were clothed; the Greeks introduced total nudity in the male figure and in later centuries moved toward increasing nudity in female statues (see 2.4). Most of the Egyptian sculptures we know are of pharaohs, their queens, their children, and other members of the court. The Greeks seem to have been far more interested in physical beauty than in high status. To be sure, some of their finest sculptures represent gods, but they are gods in human form—magnificent human form. And many are depictions of anonymous young men, to whom scholars have given the name **kouros,** meaning "youth" or "boy."

The reasons for this new approach to sculpture are clear from Greek philosophy and literature. Whereas the Egyptians emphasized continuity of the state, the Greeks sought perfection of the state *through* perfection of the individual. The ideal human body symbolized an ideal divine soul, dedicated to the highest principles. If perfection could be chiseled into marble, then perhaps the sought-after perfection in human affairs could be attained.

Three figures, made over a period of about 150 years, will show the enormous progress of Greek sculptors in striving toward an ideal of naturalism and physical perfection. The first is a *kouros* that dates from the early Archaic period, around 600 B.C.E. (**14.26**). The debt to Egypt is clear. Not only does the work reproduce the characteristic Egyptian pose—one leg forward, arms at the sides, hands clenched (see 11.17)—but it even follows the Egyptian grid system of proportions (see 5.23). We can almost envision the cube of marble the sculptor began with from the square appearance of the form. Although more than 6 feet tall, the figure seems puny and underdeveloped, its torso too small and slender, its shoulders too narrow. The hair is a stylized braid, the eyes blank and staring, the feet featureless slabs with rigid cylinders for toes. Nevertheless, this sculptor has made great strides toward a natural approach. The musculature of arms and legs has been studied carefully, the legs separated from one another, the arms separated from the body, the body fully released from the block of stone.

Another *kouros*, carved some seventy-five years later but still in the Archaic period (**14.27**), shows considerable progress toward naturalism. This body is far better proportioned, the hips and torso broader, the arms and legs well-developed. We can easily believe a human body might be shaped like this, which is hard to imagine of the earlier *kouros*. In spite of these advances, however, the sculpture retains a blocklike quality, is still imprisoned in the cube of stone. The left foot is set slightly forward to suggest motion, but we do not really believe in that motion because the hips and shoulders are level and the arms held rigidly at the sides. If you try to assume this pose, you will find it almost impossible, for when you take a step forward with one foot, the opposing hip and shoulder go up, and your arms move in counterbalance. There is no indication of this in the statue. On the *kouros'* face is an expression that has been dubbed the "archaic smile"—a grimace apparently meant to convey animation.

Now let us compare the *Spear Bearer* by the great sculptor Polyclitus (**14.28**), made yet another seventy-five years or so later, in the Classical

14.26 (left) *Kouros*. c. 580 B.C.E. Marble, height 6'4". The Metropolitan Museum of Art, New York.

14.27 (center) *Kroisos (Kuros from Anavysos)*. c. 525 B.C.E. Marble, height 6'4". National Archaeological Museum, Athens.

14.28 (right) *Doryphorus (Spear Bearer)*. Roman copy after a bronze original of c. 450–440 B.C.E. by Polykleitos. Marble, height 6'6". Museo Nazionale Archeologico, Naples.

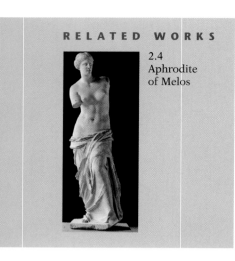

2.4
Aphrodite
of Melos

period of the 5th century B.C.E. (Like so many Greek statues, the original bronze of the *Spear Bearer* has been lost and is known to us only through later, and probably inferior, Roman copies in marble.) Here we find the *contrapposto* of a figure capable of motion. (To review contrapposto, see p. 269.) With the weight on the right foot, the left knee is bent, the right hip and left shoulder rise, the arms reach outward from the body, and the whole form stands in a relaxed *S*-curve. The musculature of a well-developed body has been carefully observed and recorded. Gone is the archaic smile, to be replaced by a natural, pensive expression.

The last phase of Greek art is known as **Hellenistic**—a term that refers to the spread of Greek culture eastward through Asia Minor, Egypt, and Mesopotamia—lands that had been conquered by the Macedonian Greek ruler Alexander the Great. The beginning of the Hellenistic era is usually dated to Alexander's death in 323 B.C.E. Hellenistic sculpture tends to be more dynamic and emotional than that of the Classical 5th century. One of the best-known examples of this style in the *Laocoön Group* (**14.29**), which we know from what is probably a Roman copy of a Greek bronze of the 2nd century B.C.E.

Laocoön was a priest of the sun-god, Apollo, and his story involves one of the most famous events in Greek mythology. In the last year of the war between the Greeks and the Trojans, the Greeks devised a fabulous ruse to overrun the city of Troy. They built a giant wooden horse, concealed inside it a large number of Greek soldiers, and wheeled it up to the gates of Troy, claiming it was an offering for the goddess Athena. While the people of Troy were trying to decide whether to admit the horse, their priest, Laocoön, suspected a trick and urged the Trojans to keep the gates locked. This angered the sea-god, Poseidon, who held bitter feelings toward Troy, and he sent two

14.29 *Laocoön Group*. Roman copy, late 1st century B.C.E.–early 1st century C.E., of a Greek bronze(?) original, possibly by Agesander, Athenodorus, and Polydorus of Rhodes. Marble, height 8′.
Musei Vaticani, Rome.

dreadful serpents to strangle Laocoön and his sons. The sculpture depicts the priest and his children in their death throes, entwined by the deadly snakes.

Compared with statues from the Classical period, such as the *Spear Bearer*, the *Laocoön Group* seems theatrical. Its subject matter, filled with drama and tension, would have been unthinkable three centuries earlier. The Classical sculptor wanted to convey an outward serenity, and thus showed the hero in perfection but not in action, outside of time, not throwing the spear but merely holding it. Hellenistic sculptors were far more interested than their predecessors in how their subjects reacted to events. Laocoön's reaction is a violent, anguished one, and the outlines of the sculpture reflect this. The three figures writhe in agony, thrusting their bodies outward in different directions, pushing into space. Unlike earlier figures, with their dignified reserve, this sculpture projects a complicated and intense movement.

ROME

The year 510 B.C.E. is usually cited as the beginning of the Roman era, for it was then, according to ancient historians, that the Roman Republic was founded. There followed a long period of expansion and consolidation of territories brought under Roman rule. Roman legions swept eastward through Greece into Mesopotamia, west and north as far as Britain, across the sea to Egypt, throughout the rim of northern Africa. In 27 B.C.E., when Augustus took the title of "caesar," Rome officially became an empire.

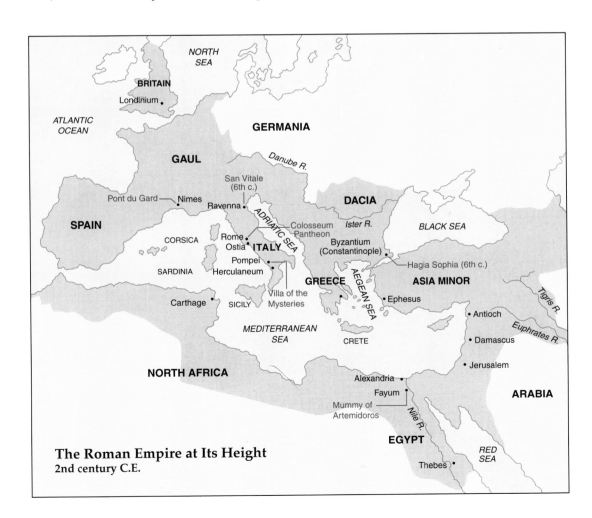

The Roman Empire at Its Height
2nd century C.E.

Rome came of age during the Hellenistic period, when the prestige of Greek culture was at its height in the ancient Mediterranean world. The Romans were great admirers of Greek achievements in the arts. Many works were taken from Greece and brought to Rome. Statues and paintings were commissioned from Greek artists, and copies were made in marble of Greek bronze originals, such as the *Spear Bearer* of Polykleitos (14.28) and the *Laocoön Group* (14.29) illustrated above. As these two examples suggest, much of our knowledge of Greek art is through Roman copies, for most bronze originals were melted down and their metal recycled, often by the Romans themselves.

One aspect of Hellenistic art was a tendency toward realistic portrayals of individuals, as opposed to idealized portrayals of *types* of people. No longer forever young and perfect, an athlete such as a boxer might be portrayed as the survivor of years of physically punishing bouts, his face lined, his body thickening with the onset of middle age. Roman sculptors excelled at this realism in their portrait busts of ordinary citizens.

One such example (**14.30**) is a portrait of a Roman husband and wife who are fully realized as individuals. Obviously, we cannot know what these people actually looked like, but it is safe to assume the sculptor made a good likeness, with a minimum of idealizing. The husband is old, the creases in his face well defined, his expression patient; we might read from his image a long experience in the trials of the world and gentle resignation to those trials. His wife seems stronger, less marked by pain, and her supportive clasp of the husband's hand is touching. Scholars have read into this pose the highly esteemed Roman virtues of *fides* (faith or fidelity) and *concordia* (harmony). Whereas the Greek sculptures and many of the Roman ones seem to

14.30 (left) *Double Portrait of Gratidia M.L. Chrite and M. Gratidius Libanus.* Late 1st century B.C.E. White marble with traces of color, height 23¾″.
Museo Pio Clementino, Musei Vaticani, Rome.

14.31 (right) Equestrian statue of Marcus Aurelius (before restoration). 164–166 C.E. Bronze, height 11′ 6″.
Piazza del Campidoglio, Rome.

14.32 Wall painting, from Villa of the Mysteries, Pompeii. c. 50 B.C.E. Fresco.

exist in a world apart, these portrait busts are wonderfully accessible. They allow us to identify with people who have been dead for two thousand years.

One highly influential invention of Roman sculptors was the equestrian portrait—the portrayal of an admired leader on horseback. The sole Roman example that has survived into modern times is the bronze statue illustrated here of the emperor Marcus Aurelius (**14.31**). Seated on his mount, he extends his arm in an oratorical gesture, as if delivering a speech. His calm in victory contrasts with the spirited motions of his horse, which was originally shown raising its hoof over a fallen enemy, now lost. The equestrian statues that ornament our cities—monuments to leaders of the American Revolution, the Civil War, and other conflicts—are the direct descendants of this fine Roman work, which has inspired imitations ever since it was rediscovered during the Renaissance.

The Romans were equally masterful at painting, but were it not for a tragedy that occurred in 79 C.E., we would know little more about Roman painting than we do about the Greek. In that year Mt. Vesuvius, an active volcano, erupted and buried the town of Pompeii, about a hundred miles south of Rome, along with the neighboring town of Herculaneum. The resulting lava and ashes spread a blanket over the region, and this blanket acted as a kind of time capsule. Pompeii lay undisturbed, immune to further ravages of nature, for more than sixteen centuries. Then in 1748 excavations were undertaken, and their findings were made public by the famous German archaeologist Joachim Winckelmann. Within the precincts of Pompeii the diggers found marvelous frescoes that were exceptionally well preserved. Pompeii was not an important city, so we cannot assume that the most talented artists of the period worked there. In fact, there is some evidence to suggest that the fresco painters were not Roman at all, but immigrant Greeks. Nevertheless, these wall paintings do give some indication of the styles of art practiced within the empire at the time.

One fresco, from a house known as the Villa of the Mysteries (**14.32**), shows a scene believed to represent secret cult rituals associated with the wine god Dionysus. The figures stand as though on a ledge, in shallow but convincing space, interacting only slightly with one another. Although the artist has segmented the mural into panels separated by black bands, the figures overlap these panels so freely that there is no strong sense of individual episodes or compartments. Rather, the artist has established two rhythms—one of the figures and another of the dividing bands—giving a strong design unity.

RELATED WORKS

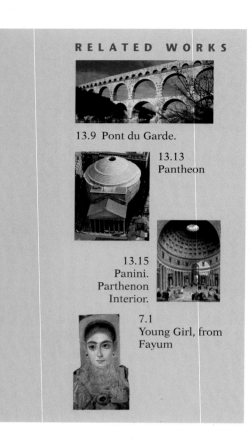

13.9 Pont du Garde.

13.13
Pantheon

13.15
Panini.
Parthenon
Interior.

7.1
Young Girl, from
Fayum

For all their production in sculpture and painting, the Romans are best known for their architecture and engineering. We saw two of their masterpieces, the Pont du Gard and the Pantheon, in Chapter 13 (see 13.9, 13.13, 13.15). But the most familiar monument—indeed, for many travelers the very symbol of Rome—is the Colosseum (**14.33**).

The Colosseum was planned under the Emperor Vespasian and dedicated in 80 C.E. as an amphitheater for gladiatorial games and public entertainments. A large oval covering 6 acres, the Colosseum could accommodate some fifty thousand spectators—about the same number as most major-league baseball stadiums today. Few of the games played inside, however, were as tame as baseball. Gladiators vied with one another and with wild animals in bloody and gruesome contests. On special occasions the whole structure could be filled with water for realistic naval battles.

Even in its ruined state this structure displays the genius of the Romans as builders. The Colosseum rises on three tiers of arches, each of the levels distinguished from the next by a different style of column between the arches—Doric on the lowest level, Ionic on the second, and Corinthian on the third. Around the base are eighty arched openings for entry and exit; it is said that the entire building could be emptied in a matter of minutes. Above all, the structure is logical and coherent. Roman architects tell us in visual detail exactly how the building is organized—which parts are separate from other parts, where to enter, where to go, and so on. The exterior view gives us a clear sense of the inside, the walkways, the scheme as a whole.

By the year 100 of our era, the Roman Empire ringed the entire Mediterranean Sea. It extended eastward through Asia Minor and into Mesopotamia, westward through Spain, northward into England, and south across North Africa and Egypt. Yet the many cultures that came under Roman rule did not cease to be themselves and suddenly become Roman. Instead, the empire extended its umbrella over a vast array of cultures, languages, and religions, all of which now mingled freely thanks to Roman rule and Roman roads.

14.33 Colosseum, Rome. 72–80 C.E.

Our last illustration gives us a glimpse of the multicultural world of late Rome (**14.34**). The illustration shows the mummy of a young man named Artemidoros, from Fayum, in Egypt. It dates from sometime in the 2nd century of our era. Egypt was then part of the Roman Empire, and Artemidoros was a Roman subject. Artemidoros, however, is a Greek name, and it is written in Greek letters on his mummy. Why a Greek in Egypt? Alexander the Great had conquered Egypt in 323 B.C.E. For the next 300 years, Egypt was ruled by a Greek dynasty, the Ptolomies. Greeks constituted an elite part of the population, but while they preserved their own language, they adopted the Egyptian religion, with its comforting belief in an eternal afterlife. Thus the body of Artemidoros, an Egyptian of Greek ancestry and identity, was mummified for burial, and on his mummy are depicted ancient Egyptian gods, including Anubis, the jackal-headed god of the dead, visible at the center just under Artemidoros' name.

Rome conquered Egypt from the last of the Ptolomies, the celebrated queen Cleopatra, in 31 B.C.E. Greek remained the principal administrative language of Egypt, even under Roman rule. Roman customs and fashions, however, were widely imitated by Egyptians who wanted to appear "up to date." One such custom was the funeral portrait, a commemorative painting of a recently deceased person. Thus Artemidoros' mummy includes a funeral portrait, painted in encaustic on wood in a Greek-Roman style. (To review the technique of encaustic, see page 163.) What are we to call Artemidoros? Roman-Greek-Egyptian? After thousands of years of history, cultural identities could have many layers in the ancient Mediterranean world.

Influence flowed from Rome's conquests to Rome as well. Like the Greeks before them, the Romans were fascinated by Egyptian culture, which was so much older than their own. They imported many Egyptian statues to Rome, and Roman artists worked to satisfy a craze for new sculptures in the Egyptian style. While Roman gods and goddesses remained the "official" deities of Rome, the worship of the Egyptian goddess Isis spread through the empire as far away as Spain and England. So did Mithraism, the worship of the sun-god of the Persians, some of whose ancient territories also fell under Roman rule.

In these heady if sometimes perplexing times, who could have foreseen that the future would belong to a completely new religion that had only recently arisen in the eastern part of the vast empire? Based in the teachings of an obscure Jewish preacher named Jesus, it was called Christianity.

14.34 Mummy case of Artemidoros, from Fayum. 100–200 C.E. Stucco casing with portrait in encaustic on limewood with added gold leaf, height 67¼".
The British Museum, London.

CHAPTER 15

Christianity and the Formation of Europe

According to tradition, Jesus, known as the Christ or "anointed one," was born in Bethlehem during the reign of Emperor Augustus. In time his followers would become so influential in world affairs that our common calendar takes as its starting point the presumed date of Jesus' birth, calling it "year 1." As a matter of fact, the 6th-century calendar makers who devised this plan were wrong in their calculations. Jesus probably was born between four and six years earlier than they had supposed, but the calendar has nevertheless become standard.

The faith preached by the followers of Jesus spread with remarkable speed through the Roman Empire, yet that empire itself was about to undergo a profound transformation. Overextended, internally weakened, and increasingly invaded, it would soon disintegrate. The western portion would eventually reemerge as western Europe—a collection of independent, often warring kingdoms united by a common religious culture of Christianity. The eastern portion would survive for a time as the Byzantine Empire, a Christianized continuation of a much-diminished Roman Empire. The Near East, Egypt, North Africa, and most of Spain, meanwhile, would become the heartlands of yet another new religious culture, Islam.

We will discuss the arts of Islam in Chapter 18. This chapter continues the story of the Western tradition with the rise of Christianity, the arts of Byzantium, and the formation of western Europe.

THE RISE OF CHRISTIANITY

Christianity was but one of numerous religions in the late Roman Empire, but it quickly became one of the most popular and well organized. Rome's attitude toward this new cultural force within its borders varied. Often, the faith was tolerated, especially since it came to attract an increasing number of wealthy and influential people. At other times, Christians were persecuted, sometimes officially and sometimes by mobs. One reason for the persecutions was that Christians refused to worship the gods and goddesses of the state religion, including the emperor himself, in addition to their own god. Clearly such people were a threat to the political stability and well-being of the empire.

Little art that is specifically Christian survives from these first centuries. Gathering places for the faithful were probably built in some of the major centers of the empire, but none survive. Most early worship took place in private homes, although only one such early house-church has been discovered. Some of the earliest Christian art has been preserved in underground burial chambers that were later forgotten. The portion of a mosaic illustrated here is from the vault of an underground necropolis (from the Greek for "city of the dead") in Rome (15.1). The mosaic was created around the same time as the mummy of Artemidoros discussed in Chapter 14 (see 14.34), and it offers a similarly fascinating mixture of imagery.

In depicting Christ in triumph, the artist has borrowed the iconography of the Greek and Roman god Apollo, who was often portrayed riding his chariot across the sky as the sun god. Rays of light emanating from the head of this Christ-Apollo are modified to suggest a cross. The grape leaves of the surrounding pattern were associated with the Greek god Dionysus, known to the Romans as Bacchus, the god of fertility and wine (see 4.25, 11.3). Christians appropriated the grape leaf as a symbol, for Christ had spoken of himself as the true vine, whose branches (the faithful) would bear fruit (the kingdom of God on earth). The benefit for artists was that the grape-leaf patterns they had learned as apprentices could serve for Christian clients as well as pagan ones.

Christianity's situation changed abruptly in the year 313, when the Roman emperor Constantine issued an edict of tolerance for all religions. Not only were all faiths now free to practice openly, but Constantine himself patronized Christianity, for he attributed his success in a key battle to the Christian god. Under his imperial sponsorship, architects raised a series of large and opulent churches at key locations in the empire. One of these was

15.1 *Christ as the Sun*, detail of a mosaic under Saint Peter's necropolis, Rome. Mid-3rd century.

15.2 (left) Reconstruction of Old St. Peter's, Rome. Begun c. 320.

15.3 (right) St. Paul's Outside the Walls, Rome. Begun c. 385. Interior. Engraving by Piranesi.

Old St. Peter's, built on the spot in Rome where it was believed that Peter, Jesus' first apostle, had been buried. This structure was demolished in 1506 to erect the "new" St. Peter's now in Rome (see 16.13), but contemporary descriptions and drawings have enabled scholars to make informed guesses about its design (**15.2**). A similar church built some sixty years later, St. Paul's Outside the Walls, stood intact until the 19th century, and an artist's rendering gives testimony to its grandeur (**15.3**).

What should a church look like? Most Roman, Greek, and even Egyptian and Mesopotamian temples had essentially been conceived as dwelling places for the gods they were dedicated to. Priests might enter to perform rites of sacrifice and worship, but groups of ordinary people viewed these rites from outside, if they viewed them at all. Christianity from the beginning emphasized congregational worship, and so a fundamentally different kind of building was needed, one that could contain a lot of people. Roman architects already had such a structure in their repertoire of standard building types, a multipurpose meeting hall called a **basilica** (**15.4**, top).

As the plan shows, a basilica was basically a long rectangular hall. Entrances might be on the long or short sides (here, they are on the long side). At one or both ends (both, in this example) might be a curved section called an **apse.** In order to admit light, the open center space, called the **nave,** extended up higher than the surrounding **aisles.** This upward extension was called the **clerestory,** and it was pierced with windows called clerestory windows. If you look back at the drawing of Old St. Peter's (15.2), you can now clearly see the central nave with its clerestory windows and the lower side aisles that buttress it. In the distance, at the far end of the nave, is an apse.

A plan of Old St. Peter's (**15.4**, bottom) makes this clear and also shows an additional element. The basilica form is turned so that entry is through one of the short sides. Inside we find the wide central nave flanked by narrower aisles. At the far end is the apse. A natural focal point for anyone entering the church, the apse provides a setting for the altar, the focal point of Christian worship. In addition, this far wall is extended slightly to each side of the building. The extensions create a lengthwise section perpendicular to the nave called a **transept.** Together, nave and transept form a cross, a fundamental Christian symbol. Preceding the church was an atrium. An open courtyard surrounded by a covered walkway, the atrium was a standard element of Roman domestic architecture. The arm of the walkway directly in front of the church served as an entry porch called a **narthex.** The elements here—nave, aisles, clerestory, apse, transept, and narthex—formed the basic vocabulary of church architecture in the West for many centuries. We will use them often in this chapter.

In 324, Constantine made another decision with far-reaching consequences: judging that the empire could be more securely ruled from the East, he ordered his architects and engineers to transform the ancient Greek colony of Byzantio, known in Latin as Byzantium, into a new capital city called Constantinople (present-day Istanbul, in Turkey). Six years later, he moved his administration there. As a symbol of his continuing presence in Rome, Constantine commissioned a 30-foot-tall statue of himself, portrayed seated in majesty, and had it installed in an apse added especially for that purpose to a prominent Roman basilica. Fragments of the statue have survived, including the massive head (**15.5**). The prominent nose and chin undoubtedly reproduce Constantine's distinctive features. But the overall style of the image is far from the idealized naturalism of Greece and the realism of earlier Rome. Instead, exaggerated, stylized eyes stare out from geometric, semicircular sockets under an abstracted representation of hair. The stage is set for the art of Byzantium.

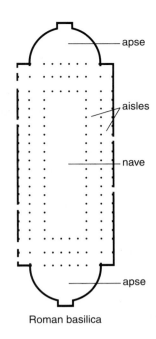

Roman basilica

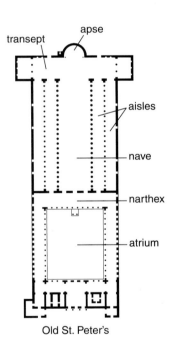

Old St. Peter's

15.4 Plan of a Roman basilica (above, top) and plan of Old St. Peter's (above).

15.5 (left) *Constantine the Great.* 325–26 C.E. Marble, height of head 8′6″.
Palazzo dei Conservatori, Rome.

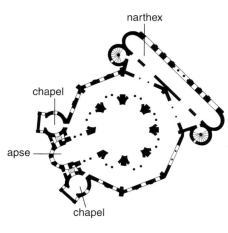

BYZANTIUM

15.6 (left) San Vitale, Ravenna.
c. 527–47.

15.7 (right) Plan of San Vitale.

7.17 Empress Theodora
Mosaic

13.16
Interior,
Hagia
Sophia

13.17 Exterior, Hagia
Sophia

The actual territory ruled from Constantinople varied greatly over the centuries. At first, it was the entire Roman Empire. By the time the city was conquered by Islamic forces in 1453, it was a much-reduced area. But no matter the actual extent of their dominion, the title that Byzantine rulers inherited was "emperor of all the Romans." They viewed themselves as the legitimate continuation of the ancient Roman Empire, with one important difference: Byzantium was Christian. While Constantine had extended his protection and patronage to Christianity, his successors went one step further: they made Christianity the official state religion. Church and state were intertwined in Byzantium, and its art marries the luxurious splendor of a powerful earthly kingdom—its gold and silver and jewels—with images that focus on an eternal, heavenly one.

The great masterpiece of early Byzantine architecture is the Hagia Sophia, which we examined in Chapter 13 (see 13.16, 13.17). A smaller gem of the early Byzantine style is San Vitale, built during the 6th century in Ravenna, Italy, which was then under Byzantine control (**15.6, 15.7**). San Vitale does not follow the cross plan that became standard for Western churches, but instead uses a central plan favored in the East. Central plan churches are most often square with a central dome, as in the Hagia Sophia. San Vitale, however, takes the unusual form of an octagon. While an apse protrudes from one wall and a narthex is attached to two others, the fundamental focus of the building is at its center, over which rises a large dome. The major axis of a central-plan church is thus vertical, from floor to dome, or symbolically from earth to the vault of heaven.

The interior of San Vitale is decorated in glittering mosaics, including the panel we looked at in Chapter 7 depicting the empress Theodora and her retinue (see 7.17). Mosaic continued as a favored Byzantine technique, resulting in such masterpieces as the interior of the Abbey Church of Monreale, a 12th-century Byzantine church in Sicily (**15.8**). Set in the half-dome crowning the apse illustrated here is a large figure of Christ as *Pantokrator,* Greek for "Ruler of All." A standard element of later Byzantine iconography, the *Pantokrator* image emphasizes the divine, awe-inspiring, even terrifying majesty of Christ as opposed to his gentle, approachable, human incarnation as Jesus. Directly below Christ is Mary, the mother of Jesus, enthroned with the Christ child on her lap. She is flanked by angels and saints.

We can see here how Byzantine artists had moved away from the naturalism and realism of classical Greece and Rome toward a flattened, abstracted style. Like the artists of ancient Egypt, Byzantine artists strove to portray often complex religious doctrines and beliefs, not scenes from daily life. Their subject was not the impermanent earthly world of the flesh, but the eternal and sacred world of the spirit. By de-emphasizing the roundness, the weight, the "hereness" of human bodies in this world, they emphasize that what we are looking at is not in fact *here*, but *there*. The glittering gold background of the mosaics is typical, and it sets the figures in a Byzantine vision of heavenly splendor.

A characteristic Byzantine art form is the **icon,** a picture of a sacred subject painted on a wooden panel (**15.9**). The example here shows the crucified Christ flanked by his mother, Mary, and his disciple John. Above the arms of the cross, two angels representing all of heaven lament. Again the elongated, weightless figures stand not in an earthly landscape but in the gold realm of heaven, for this is a painting about ideas, not an attempt to envision the actual event. Mary's head is lowered in mourning and reflection. With her gesture she directs our attention to the pitiable sight of Jesus on the cross. The gesture is also directed at Jesus himself, asking him to explain the contradiction between his eternal existence as God and his human suffering and death. John is there as a witness, but also because Christian scripture relates that Christ during his final agonies offered John as a son to Mary, and Mary to John as a mother. This gesture was interpreted symbolically as designating Mary as a new Eve, mother of all the faithful. John thus stands for all Christians. The artist has taken pains to depict Christ as dead and yet alive, a central miracle of Christianity. Struggling for words to express this difficult concept, medieval writers sometimes spoke of Christ as "asleep" on the cross, and that is the effect here. Framing this central grouping are painted medallions of saints, angels, and important men and women of the early Church.

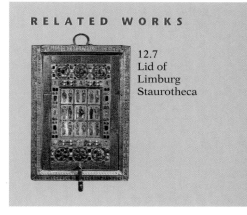
15.8 (left) *Pantokrator*, from the abbey church of Monreale, Palermo. Before 1183. Mosaic.

15.9 (right) *Icon with the Crucifixion*. Byzantine, c. 1100. Tempera on wood, 11⅛ × 8½". The Holy Monastery of Saint Catherine, Sinai, Egypt.

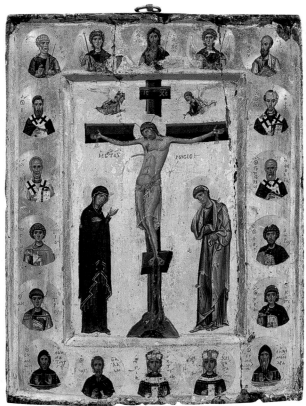

By the time this icon was painted, around 1100 C.E., vast changes had occurred in the territories that Constantinople was built to rule. Constantine's vision of a unified Roman Empire did not prevail: the territory was simply too vast. His successors partitioned the empire into eastern and western halves, each with its own emperor. Within 150 years, the western empire had fallen, overwhelmed by a massive influx of Germanic peoples arriving from the north and east. Constantinople claimed authority over the entire empire again, but could not enforce it. The western Church, based in Rome, preserved its imperial organization and religious authority, but true political and military power had passed to the local leaders of the newcomers, who settled throughout the lands of western Europe. It is to these peoples and their art that we now turn our attention.

THE MIDDLE AGES IN EUROPE

The Middle Ages is the name that historians long ago gave to the period in Europe between the defeat of the last western Roman emperor in 476 and the beginnings of the Renaissance in the 15th century. To these early historians, the period was a dark one of ignorance and decline, an embarrassing "middle" time between one impressive civilization and another. Today, we view the Middle Ages as a complex and fascinating period worthy of study in its own right. During these centuries, Europe was formed, and a distinctive Christian culture flowered within it. Far from ignorant, it was a time of immense achievement.

THE EARLY MIDDLE AGES

The kingdoms of the early Middle Ages in Europe were inhabited by descendants of migratory tribes that had traveled southward and westward on the continent during the 4th and 5th centuries. Ethnically Germanic, these peoples emerged, for the most part, from the north-central part of Europe, or what today we would call northern Germany and Scandinavia. The Romans referred to them as "barbarians" (meaning "foreigners") and considered them crude—with some justification, for, being nomadic, they had a considerably lower level of culture than did the settled citizens of the empire. Moreover, it was continual invasion by the "barbarians" that brought about the empire's ultimate collapse, near the end of the 5th century.

By the year 600 the migrations were essentially over, and kingdoms whose area roughly approximated the nations of modern Europe had taken form. Their inhabitants had steadily been converted to Christianity. For purposes of this discussion, we will focus initially on the people who settled in two areas—the Angles and Saxons in Britain, and the Franks in Gaul (modern France).

On the island of Britain north of London (then Londinium) was Sutton Hoo, where the grave of an unknown 7th-century East Anglian king has been found. Objects discovered at the burial site include a superb gold and enamel purse cover (**15.10**), with delicately made designs. The motifs are typical of the **animal style** prevalent in the art of northwestern Europe at that time—a legacy, very likely, from the migratory herdsmen who were these people's ancestors. Animal-style images were often accompanied by **interlace,** patterns formed by intricately interwoven ribbons and bands. We can see interlace clearly in the upper-center medallion of the Sutton Hoo purse cover, where it is combined with abstracted animals.

Among the most important artistic products of the early Middle Ages were copies of Christian scriptures. In these days before the printing press, each book had to be copied by hand. During the early Middle Ages, this copying was carried out in monasteries, for monks, educated by the Church, were the only literate segment of the population. Monks not only copied texts but also **illuminated** them—furnished them with illustrations and decorations. The full-page illumination here (**15.11**) was probably made by Irish monks working in Scotland. It announces the beginning of the Gospel of Mark—one of the four accounts in the Bible of the life and works of Jesus—and it shows how the monks adapted animal style and interlace to a Christian setting. At the center of the page is St. Mark's symbolic animal, the lion. Monks in Scotland could never have seen a lion, of course, and the fanciful creature they have come up with closely resembles the beasts on the cover of the Sutton Hoo purse. The borders of the illumination display the intricate interlace patterns that became a specialty of Irish illuminators.

In France a different style of art was taking root, called **Carolingian** after the emperor Charlemagne. Charlemagne, or Charles the Great, was a powerful Frankish king whose military conquests eventually gave him control over most of western Europe. On Christmas Day of the year 800 the Pope crowned Charlemagne Holy Roman Emperor—making him the first of many rulers to bear that title. The title is significant because it united two major forces. Charlemagne was *Roman* in that he thought of himself as inheriting the legacy of the old Roman Empire. He was called *holy* for being a Christian king, the dominant Christian king.

Charlemagne seems to have been much aware of the past glories of the old Roman Empire, and he wished to imitate or surpass them in his own reign, his own empire. Following the example of Roman emperors before him, he took an active interest in artistic and cultural matters. At his capital, Aachen,

15.10 (left) Purse cover, from the Sutton Hoo ship burial. 625–33. Gold with garnets and enamels, length 7½″.
The British Museum, London.

15.11 (right) Page with *Lion*, from the *Gospel Book of Durrow*. Scotland(?), c. 675. Ink and tempera on parchment, 9⅝ × 5¹¹/₁₆″.
The Board of Trinity College, Dublin.

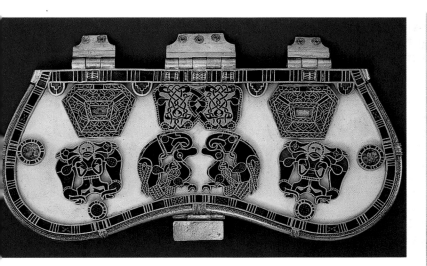

Europe
in the Age of
Charlemagne
c.800 C.E.

15.12 Interior, Palace Chapel of Charlemagne, Aachen. 792–805.

Charlemagne ordered built a splendid Palace Chapel to be his personal place of worship (**15.12**). The architecture of the chapel gives several clues to his ambitions. Its basic design is modeled after San Vitale in Ravenna (see 15.6), which Charlemagne apparently had seen and admired. Very likely he wished to copy the perfection of that octagonal church, to match the architectural ideals of Byzantium. At the same time, however, the details of the Palace Chapel are much heavier, more massive, more *Roman*, especially the robust Roman arches. Charlemagne—the Frankish king from the north—intended to be a Roman emperor, even to the design of his holy place.

Some writers consider Charlemagne's coronation day to be the end of the early Middle Ages. The emperor was crowned not by his own people but rather by the Pope, the leader of the Christian religion, and he was crowned *Holy* Roman Emperor. For the first time a political ruler had the sanction of the Church of Rome, and this opened a new chapter in European history.

THE HIGH MIDDLE AGES

The Middle Ages was a time of intense religious preoccupation in Europe. It was during this era that most of the great cathedrals were built. Also, a major portion of the art that has come down to us is associated with monasteries, churches, and cathedrals.

Historians generally divide the art and architecture of the high Middle Ages into two periods: the Romanesque, from about 1050 to 1200, based on southern styles from the old Roman Empire; and the Gothic, from about 1200 into the 15th century, which has more of a northern flavor. (The term "Gothic" derives from the Goths, who were among the many nomadic tribes sweeping through Europe during the 4th and 5th centuries. It was applied to this style by later critics in the Renaissance, who considered the art and architecture of their immediate predecessors to be vulgar and "barbarian.")

The Romanesque period was marked by a building boom. Contemporary commentators were thrilled at the beautiful churches that seemed to be springing up everywhere. Later art historians called the style of these buildings Romanesque, for despite their great variety they shared certain features reminiscent of ancient Roman architecture, including an overall massiveness, thick stone walls, round arches, and barrel-vaulted stone ceilings.

One reason for the sudden burst of building was the popularity of pilgrimages. In the newly prosperous and stable times of the 11th and 12th centuries, people could once again travel safely. While some made the trip all the way to Jerusalem, in the Holy Land, most confined their pilgrimages to sites associated with Christian saints in Europe. Churches—and also lodgings and other services—arose along the most popular pilgrimage routes as way stations for these large groups of travelers.

The earliest Romanesque pilgrimage church still standing is the Abbey Church of Sainte-Foy, in France (**15.13, 15.14**). This aerial photograph makes clear the church's cross-form plan. Even from the exterior we can distinguish the nave, the slightly less tall aisles, and the transept. Two square towers flank the entry portal, and an octagonal tower marks the intersection of the transept and the nave. The round arches of the windows are continued in the interior, which has a barrel-vaulted nave and groin-vaulted aisles. The interior of Sainte-Foy is illustrated in Chapter 13 (see fig. 13.10).

The plan (15.14) shows how Romanesque architects modified church design in order to accommodate large crowds of pilgrims. Aisles now line the transept as well as the nave and continue in a semicircle around the back of the apse, allowing visitors to circulate freely. The aisle around the apse is called an **ambulatory,** Latin for walkway. Small chapels radiate from the ambulatory. The apse itself is now preceded by an area called the choir. Together, apse and choir served as a small "church within a church," allowing monks to perform their rites even as pilgrims visited.

Pilgrims stopping at Sainte-Foy would have come to see the relics of Saint Foy herself, which were kept there in a bejeweled statue (**15.15**). Like the Byzantine reliquary we looked at in Chapter 12 (see 12.7), it is made of gold over a wooden core and set with gems. Saint Foy, known in English as Saint Faith, was supposed to have been put to death as a young girl, possibly in the 3rd century, for refusing to worship pagan gods.

The reliquary statue of Saint Foy is a fine example of the treasures that were offered to and displayed in medieval churches. Another famous work

15.13 (bottom left) Aerial view of Sainte-Foy, Conques, Auvergne, France. c. 1050–1120.

15.14 (bottom right) Plan of Sainte-Foy.

15.15 (below) Reliquary statue of Sainte Foy. Late 10th–early 11th century. Gold and gemstones over a wooden core, height 33½". Cathedral Treasury, Conques, France.

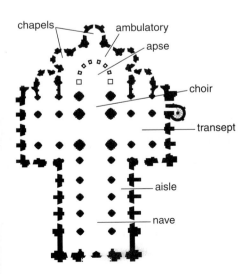

369

Hildegard of Bingen

In summer of the year 1098, in the German town of Bermersheim, a knight called Hildebert and his lady Mechthilde welcomed their tenth and last child, a daughter, whom they named Hildegard. The little girl was frail in health, but from early childhood she showed unusual spirituality. At about age five, as she would tell it much later, young Hildegard experienced a mystical vision of brilliant light, accompanied by images from Heaven. It was this combination of fragility and religious devotion, apparently, that caused her parents to place Hildegard in a convent at the age of seven or eight.

At the convent Hildegard was tutored in Latin, music, the scriptures, and religious studies. She took her vows as a nun when she was about eighteen. Little is known of her life for the next twenty years, until 1136. In that year Hildegard, at age thirty-eight, was elected abbess of the convent.

Perhaps her new status gave Hildegard the courage to confide in others, to reveal the secret she had kept for so long—that she was subject to visions of God, Christ, the cosmos, biblical events, and religious symbols. In any case, she did so, and she was taken seriously. Encouraged by her churchly mentors, Hildegard began to write.

Her first major work, started in 1142, was called *Scivias*, which translates from the Latin as *Know the Ways (of the Lord)*. In this book, a ten-year project, Hildegard tells of her visions, describing them in exact detail and illustrating them with painted illuminations that are startlingly modern in their simplicity. Some believe she made the paintings herself, but it is more likely they were done by others under her close supervision.

Vision two, shown here, is a portrait of Hildegard at the moment of her spiritual awakening. Seated in a small room, dressed in the robes of a courtly woman, Hildegard is struck by heavenly tongues of fire, which engulf her head. She is poised ready to record the event, as is her secretary, Volmar, standing awestruck at right. Symbolically, the spiritual flames will unloose Hildegard's own tongue, inspiring her to speak of God's ways.

Mystical though she may have been, Hildegard was no stranger to worldly concerns. She seems to have been an exceptionally good administrator, strong-willed and skillful at getting her own way. For long years her nuns had occupied the tiny women's quarters of a monastery, forced to endure domination and crowding by the monks. When she proposed to leave and establish a separate convent, she met bitter opposition from the men, who would thus lose the considerable wealth the nuns had brought to the community. Hildegard was undeterred. Taking care to enlist the protection of highly placed clergy and nobility, she departed with her nuns, about 1150, for a new convent site at Rupertsberg, near the town of Bingen.

Hildegard's last decades were extremely productive. Several other books followed the *Scivias*, including a medical text and a nine-book treatise on botany, biology, geology, and astronomy. She wrote the music and text for some sixty-three hymns and also a miracle play, which was performed as an opera. All the while she maintained a vast correspondence, exchanging letters with monarchs and church leaders, scholars and ordinary people. In her last years she traveled rather widely, and she was called to preach in the great cathedrals. Her services were much in demand as an exorcist, capable of driving out evil spirits.

Many contemporary accounts about Hildegard report her recurring, serious illnesses, but we do not know how she died. We have only the date. The extraordinary life of Hildegard of Bingen, spanning eighty-one years, came to an end on September 17, 1179.

Hildegard of Bingen Recording Her Visions, from a facsimile of a 12th-century manuscript of *Scivias* in the Codex Rupertsberg.

of Romanesque art originally commissioned for display in a church is the *Bayeux Tapestry* (**15.16**)—misnamed, because it is actually a work of embroidery. (In the past, large-scale fabrics, especially those hung in buildings, often were loosely called "tapestries," regardless of the construction method.) **Embroidery** is a technique in which colored yarns are sewn to an existing woven background; frequently the sewing takes the form of decorative motifs or images, as here. The *Bayeux Tapestry* is like a long picture book—20 inches high and 231 feet long—telling the story of the conquest of England by William of Normandy in 1066. The scene illustrated, one of seventy-two separate episodes reading from left to right, shows the Norman boats setting sail to wage war on Saxon England. The fabric's pictorial design is simple and flat. The smaller boat is meant to be seen as farther away than the two large ones, though it almost seems to be floating in the air. Despite the charming naïveté of these images, however, scholars have learned more about the events surrounding the Norman Conquest from the *Bayeux Tapestry* than they have from any of the literature of the time.

We rarely know exactly where and how architectural styles started. Who "invented" the Romanesque style? Where did it first appear? With the Gothic style that followed it, however, we are in the unusual position of knowing where, when, and how it came about. A powerful French abbot named Suger wanted to enlarge and remodel his church, the Abbey Church of Saint-Denis, near Paris. Inspired by early Christian writings, he came to believe that an ideal church should have certain characteristics: it should appear to reach up to heaven, it should have harmonious proportions, and it should be filled with light. To this his architects responded with pointed arches, ribbed vaulting, flying buttresses, and stained glass windows so large they seemed like translucent walls. (To review these architectural terms, see Chapter 13, pp. 302–303.) Finished in two stages in 1140 and 1144, the graceful, light-filled interior of Saint-Denis immediately attracted attention and imitation. Gothic style was born, the creation of a brilliant architect whose name the good abbot did not bother to record.

15.16 *Norman Fleet Sailing to England,* detail of the *Bayeux Tapestry.* c. 1073–88. Wool embroidery on linen; height 20″, overall length 231′. Town Hall, Bayeux, reproduced with special authorization of the City of Bayeux.

15.17 (bottom left) Chartres Cathedral, France. Begun 1134, completed c. 1260.

15.18 (bottom right) West facade, Chartres Cathedral.

15.19 (below) Plan of Chartres cathedral.

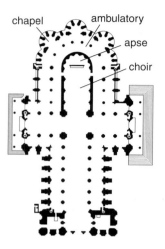

The cathedral at Chartres, in France, shows the soaring quality of Gothic architecture (**15.17**). Here, the unadorned, earthbound masses of the Romanesque have given way to ornate, linear, vertical elements that direct the eye upward. Clearly visible are the flying buttresses that line the nave and apse to contain the outward thrust of the walls. Because portions of Chartres were built at different times, the cathedral also allows us to see something of the evolution of Gothic style. For example, the first thing most people notice about the facade of the cathedral (**15.18**) are the mismatched corner towers and spires. The north (left) tower was built first, between 1134 and 1150. Its plain, unadorned surfaces and solid masses are still fundamentally Romanesque. The south (right) tower and its spire were completed next, between 1142 and 1160. Designed in the very earliest Gothic style, they are conceived so that each level grows out of the one before, and all the elements work together to lead the eye upward.

The towers, south spire, and facade had originally been built as additions to an older Romanesque church that stood on the site. When a fire in 1194 burned this church to the ground, it was rebuilt over the course of the next sixty years in the Gothic style we see today. The plan (**15.19**) shows the familiar cross form, but the choir and ambulatory have taken on much larger proportions compared with those at Sainte-Foy. The soaring, open spaces of the interior were created with ribbed vaulting and pointed arches much like those we saw in Chapter 13 in the cathedral at Reims, built around the same time (see 13.11). The final addition to Chartres was the north (left) spire of the facade. Built in the early 16th century, it illustrates the last phase of Gothic style—a slender, elongated, and highly ornamental style called Flamboyant, French for "flamelike."

Sculpture in the Middle Ages was often created to embellish architecture. Over two thousand carved figures decorate the exterior of the Chartres Cathedral. Concentrated especially around principal entryways, they serve as a transition between the everyday world of the town and the sacred space within, forming a sort of "welcoming committee" for the faithful as they enter. Like the architecture itself, the sculptures were created at different times, and in them, too, we can appreciate the transition from Romanesque to Gothic.

Romanesque style can be seen in the elongated and flattened bodies of these 12th-century carvings from the principal entry of the cathedral (**15.20**). In fact, it is difficult to believe that there are actual bodies under the draperies at all. The linear folds of the draperies are not so much sculpted as incised—drawn into the stone with a chisel. We can think of them as a sculptural equivalent of the garments in the Byzantine mosaic we looked at earlier (see 15.8), created around the same time.

Carved a mere hundred years later, this second group of figures (**15.21**) displays the mature Gothic style. While the bodies of the earlier statues took the form of the columns they adorned, the bodies here are more fully rounded and have begun to detach themselves from their architectural supports. The three saints on the right still seem to float somewhat, as though suspended in midair, but the figure of Saint Theodore at the far left truly stands, his weight on his feet. A sense of underlying musculature is evident in armor covering his arms, and his garment, while not yet fully naturalistic, is carved with an awareness of a body underneath. It will remain for another era to conceive of the body *first,* and then figure out how clothing would drape over it.

15.20 (left) Door jamb statues, west facade, Chartres Cathedral. c. 1145–70.

15.21 (right) *Saints Theodore, Stephen, Clement, and Lawrence,* door jamb, south transept, Chartres Cathedral. 13th century.

15.22 (left) Rose window and lancets, north transept, Chartres Cathedral. 13th century. Diameter of rose window, 42′.

15.23 (right) Page with *Louis IX and Queen Blanche of Castile,* Moralized Bible, from Paris. 1226–34. Ink, tempera, and gold leaf on vellum, 15 × 10½″. The Pierpont Morgan Library, New York.

RELATED WORKS

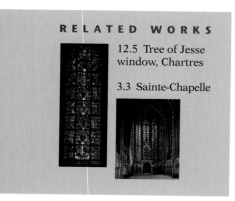

12.5 Tree of Jesse window, Chartres

3.3 Sainte-Chapelle

The glory of Gothic cathedrals is their magnificent stained glass. Chartres contains over 150 stained glass windows. Their motifs include stories from the Bible, lives of the saints, signs of the zodiac, and donors from every level of society, from knights and nobles to tradespeople such as butchers and bakers. Among the most resplendent medieval windows are the great, radiating, circular groupings called rose windows (**15.22**). This rose window, one of three at Chartres, is dedicated to Mary, the mother of Jesus. She is depicted at its center enthroned as the Queen of Heaven. Radiating from her are windows portraying doves and angels, Biblical kings, symbols of French royalty, and prophets. Like the gold of Byzantine mosaics, the gemlike colors of stained glass represent a medieval vision of heavenly splendor.

Gothic style became known in the rest of Europe as "French style," after the country where it originated. France was equally famous as a center for the production of luxuriously illuminated books. This page from a manuscript produced in Paris in the early 13th century shows the influence of stained glass on manuscript illumination (**15.23**). On a radiant ground of gold, subtly embossed, four figures sit in their individual compartments, set off like four medallions in a stained glass window. The upper two figures represent Louis IX, then king of France, and his mother, Blanche of Castile, who had ruled until he came of age. Still a young man here, Louis will later commission the Sainte-Chapelle, which we looked at in Chapter 3 (see 3.3). Beneath the royal pair sits a monk reading a text to a scribe, who dutifully writes it all down. The circles on the page the scribe is busy with define areas that will be filled in with illuminations later.

TOWARD THE RENAISSANCE

The Gothic style lasted in northern Europe into the early 16th century. By this time, however, it was overlapping with far different ideas about art that had their origins in the south, in Italy. Living in the heart of what was the ancient Roman Empire, Italians were surrounded with the ruins of the classical world. More treasures lay buried in the earth, awaiting excavation. All that was needed was an intellectual climate that encouraged an interest in such things. This climate eventually arose, and we call it the Renaissance. But the Renaissance did not happen all at once. Many developments prepared the way, some in scholarship, some in political thought, others in art.

The last two artists in this chapter were influential in making the shift from art styles of the Middle Ages to the quite different styles of the Renaissance. Duccio was an artist of Siena, in Italy. His masterpiece was the *Maestà Altar*, a multisection panel meant to be displayed on the altar of a church, of which we illustrate the part showing *Christ Entering Jerusalem* (**15.24**). What is most interesting about this painting is Duccio's attempt to create believable space in a large outdoor scene—a concern that would absorb painters of the next century. Christ's entry into the city, celebrated now on Palm Sunday, was thought of as a triumphal procession, and Duccio has labored to convey the sense of movement and parade. A strong diagonal thrust beginning at the left with Christ and his disciples cuts across the picture to the middle right, then shifts abruptly to carry our attention to the upper left corner of the painting—a church tower that is Christ's presumed goal. The architecture plays an important role in defining space and directing movement. This was Duccio's novel, almost unprecedented, contribution to the art of the period, the use of architecture to demarcate space rather than to act as a simple backdrop.

15.24 Duccio. *Christ Entering Jerusalem*, detail of *Maestà Altar*. 1308–11. Tempera on panel, 40 × 21". Museo dell'Opera, Siena.

15.25 Giotto. *The Lamentation.* 1305–06. 7'7" × 7'9". Arena Chapel, Padua.

Duccio's contemporary, a Florentine artist named Giotto, made an even more remarkable break with art traditions of the Middle Ages. Most of Giotto's best work was in fresco, and the most notable examples are in a small church in Padua called the Arena Chapel. *The Lamentation* (**15.25**), a work depicting Mary, St. John, and others mourning the dead Christ, illustrates Giotto's highly original use of space in painting. The scene has been composed as though it were on a stage and we the viewers are an audience participating in the drama. In other words, space going back from the picture plane seems to be continuous with space in front of the picture plane, the space in which we stand. Accustomed as we are now to this "window" effect in painting, it is difficult to imagine how revolutionary it was to medieval eyes, used to predominantly flat, decorative space in painting. Moreover, Giotto seems to have developed this concept of space largely on his own, with little artistic precedent. The figures in *The Lamentation* are round and full-bodied, clustered low in the composition to enhance the effect of an event taking place just out of our reach.

Giotto's grouping of the figures is unusual and daring, with Christ's body half-hidden by a figure with its back turned. This arrangement seems casual and almost random, until we notice the slope of the hill directing attention to Christ's and the Virgin's heads, which are the focal point. Yet another innovation—perhaps Giotto's most important one—was his interest in depicting the psychological and emotional reactions of his subjects. The characters in *The Lamentation* interact in a natural, human way that gives this and the artist's other religious scenes a special warmth.

Neither Duccio nor Giotto had an especially long career. Each did his most significant work in the first decade of the 14th century. Yet in that short time the course of Western art history changed dramatically. Both artists had sought a new direction for painting—a more naturalistic, more human, more engaging representation of the physical world—and both had taken giant steps in that direction. Their experiments paved the way for a flowering of all the arts that would come in the next century.

CHAPTER 16

The Renaissance

Throughout the Middle Ages, painters were considered skilled crafts workers on a level with goldsmiths, carpenters, and other tradespeople. By the mid-16th century, in contrast, Michelangelo could claim that "in Italy great princes as such are not held in honor or renown; it is a painter that they call divine."[1] From anonymous crafts workers to divinely talented individuals more honored and renowned than princes—what had happened?

The simplest answer is that Michelangelo lived and worked during the time that we call the Renaissance. Covering the period roughly from 1400 to 1600, the Renaissance brought vast changes to the world of art. The way art looked, the subjects it treated, the way it was thought about, the position of the artist in society, the identities and influence of patrons, the cultures that served as points of reference—all of these things changed. We might even say that the Renaissance was the time when the concept of "art" arose, for it was during these centuries that painting, sculpture, and architecture began to earn their privileged positions in Western thought.

The word *renaissance* means "rebirth," and it refers to the revival of interest in ancient Greek and Roman culture that is one of the key characteristics of the period. Scholars of the day worked to recover and study as many Greek and Latin texts as possible. Referring to themselves as humanists, they believed that a sound education should include not only the teachings of the Church and the study of early Christian writers but also the study of the liberal arts—grammar, rhetoric, poetry, history, politics, and moral philosophy—about which the pre-Christian world had much to teach.

Renaissance humanists believed in the pursuit of knowledge for its own sake. Above all, they held that humankind was not worthless in the eyes of God, as the Church had taught during the Middle Ages. Rather, humankind was God's finest and most perfect creation. Reason and creativity were God's gifts, proof of humankind's inherent dignity. People's obligation to God was thus not to tremble and submit but rather to soar, striving to realize their full intellectual and creative potential.

The implications of these ideas for art were tremendous. Artists became newly interested in observing the natural world, and they worked to reproduce it as accurately as possible. Studying the effects of light, they developed the technique of chiaroscuro; noting that distant objects appeared smaller

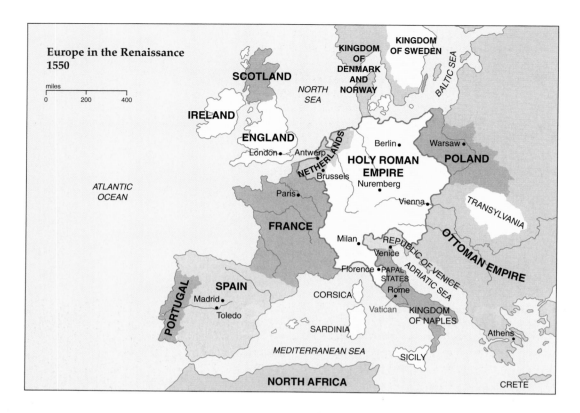

Europe in the Renaissance
1550

miles
0   200   400

SCOTLAND
IRELAND
ENGLAND
  London• Antwerp•
  NETHERLANDS
  Brussels•
  Paris•
FRANCE
ATLANTIC
OCEAN
PORTUGAL
  Madrid•
  Toledo•
SPAIN
CORSICA
SARDINIA
  Milan•
  Venice•
  Florence•
  PAPAL STATES
  Rome•
  Vatican
REPUBLIC OF VENICE
KINGDOM OF NAPLES
SICILY
MEDITERRANEAN SEA
NORTH AFRICA
NORTH SEA
KINGDOM OF DENMARK AND NORWAY
KINGDOM OF SWEDEN
BALTIC SEA
  Berlin•
HOLY ROMAN EMPIRE
  Nuremberg•
  Vienna•
  Warsaw•
POLAND
TRANSYLVANIA
OTTOMAN EMPIRE
ADRIATIC SEA
  Athens•
CRETE

than near ones, they developed the system of linear perspective; seeing how detail and color blurred with distance, they developed the principles of atmospheric perspective.

The nude reappeared in art, for the body was held to be the noblest of God's creations. "Who is so barbarous as not to understand that the foot of a man is nobler than his shoe," said Michelangelo, "and his skin nobler than that of the sheep with which he is clothed?"[2] To portray the body with understanding, artists studied anatomy, even going so far as to dissect cadavers.

Under the influence of the ancient Greek philosopher Plato, whose works were newly available, beauty became equated with moral goodness. Renaissance artists sought an idealized beauty, one they created by taking the most beautiful features of numerous examples and combining them. "Be on the watch to take the best parts of many individual faces," wrote Leonardo da Vinci.[3] And the German Renaissance painter Dürer advised the same: "You, therefore, if you desire to compose a fine figure, must take the head from some, the chest, arm, leg, hand, and foot from others. . . . For from many beautiful things something good may be gathered, even as honey is gathered from many flowers."[4]

The ten-volume treatise on architecture by the Roman writer Vitruvius was read avidly in an attempt to understand classical thought and practice, including ideas about beauty and harmonious proportions. Greek and Roman ruins still standing were studied in detail—described, measured, analyzed, and drawn. Excavations revealed still more examples, along with astonishing statues such as the *Laocoön Group* (see 14.29), which served as an inspiration and ideal for Renaissance artists.

Perspective and chiaroscuro, close observation of nature, the study of anatomy, theories of beauty and proportion—these established painting, sculpture, and architecture as intellectual activities allied with mathematics, science, and poetry. Artists were no longer mere crafts workers, but learned persons whose creative powers were viewed as almost miraculous. The greatest artists were considered a breed apart, comprising a class of their own that transcended the social class determined by birth—not nobility, not bourgeoisie, not clergy, but a separate and elite category of people respected not because of who they were, but because of what they could *do*. They lived in the courts of the nobles and popes, they moved freely in good society, their company was sought after, their services in demand.

The character of art patronage reflected the changing times. Before the Renaissance only two groups of people could afford to be art patrons—the nobility and the clergy. Both continued to be active sponsors of art, but they were joined in the 15th century by a new class of merchant-rulers, very rich, socially ambitious, fully able to support extravagant spending on art. The climate could not have been more fertile for a flowering of art: the best artists were available, and virtually unlimited funds existed to support them. With this preamble, then, let us look at the artists of the Renaissance.

THE EARLY AND HIGH RENAISSANCE IN ITALY

Why did the Renaissance begin in Italy and not elsewhere? Scholars have offered many reasons. First, Italy had been among the first areas to recover economically from the chaos of the early Middle Ages. Powerful city-states engaged in extensive trade and banking had developed. Wealthy, independent, and fiercely competitive, the city-states would vie with each other to engage the finest artists, as would the merchant-princes whose fortunes sustained them. The Church, also an important patron of the arts, was centered in Italy as well. Humanism arose first in Italy, and it was in Italy that the first university position in Greek studies was established. Finally, Italians had long lived amid the ruins of ancient Rome, and they viewed themselves as the direct descendants of the citizens of the earlier civilization. If anyone could bring back its glories, surely it was they.

Among the first generation of Renaissance artists, the finest sculptor by far was Donatello. His statue of *Saint Mark* (**16.1**), an early work, shows the characteristics of this new era, especially if we compare it to the statue of Saint Theodore from Chartres Cathedral, carved during the High Middle Ages (see 15.21). Whereas Gothic sculptors carved what they observed from the surface—face, clothing, limbs—Donatello thought methodically in the new way: the body provides the framework on which the fabric drapes, and therefore it must be considered first. Renaissance sculptors often created a full-scale model of a nude figure in clay, then draped clay-soaked linen about it to create garments, arranging the folds before the fabric dried. This model was then copied in marble. Scholars believe that Donatello was one of the first sculptors to use this method.

The statue is placed in a niche, but unlike most architectural sculptures from the Middle Ages, it does not depend on this framework for support. Rather, the fully rounded figure stands independently in true contrapposto, the weight on the right leg, left leg bent. The shoulders compensate: right shoulder lower, left shoulder higher. The clothing responds to the form underneath. Where the left knee bends outward, the robe falls back; where the right arm is pressed to the body, the sleeve wrinkles. We sense that if St. Mark moved, the garments would move with him. The figure is as naturalistic as any ancient Greek statue, yet there is a stamp of individual personality in both face and body that may have come from Donatello's reading of Mark's Gospel.

Donatello's teacher was an artist named Lorenzo Ghiberti, who had established his reputation in 1401 by winning a competition to design a set of bronze relief sculptures for the doors of the baptistry of the Cathedral in his native town of Florence. In 1425, a second set of doors was commissioned from Ghiberti. In between these two dates, the system of linear perspective had been discovered, described, and published. Ghiberti took full

16.1 Donatello. *St. Mark.* 1411–13. Marble, height 7'9". Or San Michele, Florence.

advantage of the possibilities opened up by the new discovery, as we can see in *The Story of Jacob and Esau*
(**16.2**), one of the ten panels he executed for this second set of doors. The graceful, rounded figures in the
foreground stand on a pavement whose converging
lines begin a recession in space that is carried systematically through the architectural setting sculpted in low
relief in the background. Renaissance artists used this
new, rationally conceived space to bring clarity and
order to their compositions, two qualities that Greek
philosophy associated with beauty.

Artists had long used architectural settings to structure their compositions. Ghiberti's great innovation was
to conceive of the architecture and the figures on the
same scale instead of relying on the miniaturized, symbolic architecture of earlier artists such as Duccio (see
15.24). Ghiberti quite rightly boasted of this in his *Com-
mentaries.* "I executed this work with the most painstaking and loving care," he wrote, ". . . with the buildings
drawn with the same proportions as they would appear
to the eye and so true that, if you stand far off, they
appear to be in relief. Actually they are in very low relief.
The figures in the foreground look larger and those in the
distance smaller, just as they do in reality."[5]

The youth of the great innovators of the Renaissance can sometimes astonish us. Donatello was
twenty-five when he began work on *St. Mark;* Ghiberti
was twenty-three when he won the competition for the
baptistry doors. Our next artist, Masaccio, transformed
the art of painting at age twenty-four with his fresco
*Trinity with the Virgin, St. John the Evangelist, and
Donors* (**16.3**) in the church of Santa Maria Novella in
Florence. Masaccio does here for painting what Ghi-

16.2 (left) Lorenzo Ghiberti. *The
Story of Jacob and Esau,* from *The
Gates of Paradise.* c. 1435. Gilt
bronze, 31¼″ square.
Museo dell'Opera del Duomo, Flo-
rence.

16.3 (right) Masaccio. *Trinity
with the Virgin, St. John the Evangelist, and Donors.* 1425. Fresco.
21′9″ × 9′4″.
Santa Maria Novella, Florence.

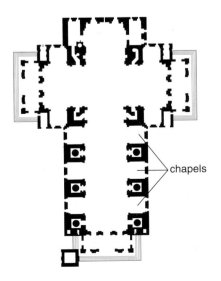

16.4 (left) Leon Battista Alberti. Interior of Sant'Andrea, Mantua. 1470–1493.

16.5 (below) Plan of Sant'Andrea.

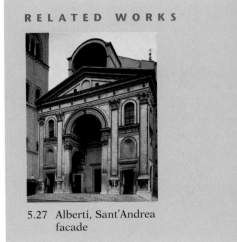

RELATED WORKS

5.27 Alberti, Sant'Andrea facade

berti did for sculpture in relief, using the new technique of linear perspective to construct a deep, convincing architectural space as a setting for his figures. Comparing this painting to the Byzantine icon we looked at in Chapter 15 (see 15.9), we can see both the continuity of the iconography (the two works depict the same subject) and the profound stylistic changes of the Renaissance.

Masaccio has arranged the figures in a stable triangle that extends from the head of God the Father, who stands over the dead Christ, through the two donors who kneel to either side of the holy grouping and outside their sacred space. Triangular (or pyramidal) organization would remain a favorite device of Italian Renaissance artists. Earlier in this book, we noticed it in Raphael's *The Madonna of the Meadows* (see 4.10). Masaccio's composition is organized by a vanishing point located directly under the cross, at the midpoint of the ledge on which the donors kneel. Five feet above the floor, it is at the eye level of an average viewer. The painting thus is designed to present as convincing an illusion as possible to visitors to the church that the sacred scene is really present before them.

Even the architectural setting that Masaccio has painted is in the new Renaissance style. We can see the sort of interior that inspired him in the church of Sant'Andrea in Mantua (**16.4, 16.5**), by the architect Leon Battista Alberti. In Chapter 5 we examined the proportions of the facade of this church (see 5.27, 5.28). The photograph here is taken looking up the nave toward the apse; the light in the middle distance is entering through the dome that rises over the intersection of the transept and the nave.

Sant'Andrea was Alberti's last work. Construction began in 1472, the year of his death, and was completed two decades later. Though marred by some changes carried out during the 18th century, the interior still allows us to see how Alberti developed the themes and elements announced by his facade. As in the facade, the square, arch, and circle dominate. The aisles of the standard basilica plan have given way to a procession of square, barrel-vaulted chapels along a majestic barrel-vaulted nave. This sequence of barrel-vaulted spaces placed at right angles to each other carries through the

chapels

GIORGIO VASARI

A BIOGRAPHER IS BY nature a gossip. We value the art of biography because it enables us to better understand the work of noted individuals through knowing their histories. At a more basic level, however, nearly all of us love to learn the details of other people's lives—in other words, gossip. And one of the most delightful gossips in history was Giorgio Vasari.

Vasari was a painter and architect of considerable skill. Born in Arezzo, in the Italian province of Tuscany, in 1511, he pursued the career of artist throughout his life. Many of his paintings still exist, and his major work as an architect, the Uffizi Palace in Florence, is now an important museum. But for two facts, Vasari might today be known as a prominent artist of the Renaissance. The facts are these: Vasari was inevitably overshadowed by the giants of the previous generation, notably Leonardo da Vinci, Michelangelo, and Raphael. And Vasari's artistic production was overshadowed by his own brilliant literary endeavor—a comprehensive biography of the outstanding Renaissance artists.

The first edition of his masterwork, *Lives of the*

Most Excellent Architects, Painters, and Sculptors, was published in 1550, after seven years of hard work. (A revised and expanded edition of the book was published in 1568.) Although other biographies had been written, nothing on this scale had ever been completed. Reading the *Lives* today, we may find the style a trifle precious, but at the time Vasari's approach was considered natural and conversational. For his research, Vasari traveled constantly (on horseback, over bad roads), spoke with anyone he could, viewed works of art whenever possible. Some of his subjects, including Raphael, were long dead when he began the *Lives,* so he depended on secondhand sources. Others, like Michelangelo, were close and respected friends. It is on Michelangelo that Vasari pours out the flowery extremes of his admiration.

Everyone seems to have liked Vasari. He had a vast network of friends, a huge correspondence, a long list of patrons. His genial temperament gave him access to information about all the leading artists. In the *Lives,* Vasari's style is so charming, so enthusiastic, so *cheerful,* that reading him now, more than four hundred years later—we like him too.

Against his extremely busy public life, Vasari's personal life was uneventful. Under pressure from one of his patrons, a cardinal of the Church, he "resolved to do something, which hitherto I had not wished to do, that is to take a wife." In 1550 he married Niccolosa Bacci, always called Cosina, for whom he seems to have had a rather absent-minded affection but little passion. The couple had no children.

As historian and biographer, Vasari must be taken with a grain of salt. His grasp of dates is particularly casual. We should remember, however, that Vasari was breaking new ground. In his day there were no reference books to check facts, no encyclopedias, no public libraries. Under the circumstances, the *Lives* must be viewed as a staggering achievement, giving us a picture of Renaissance artists that is true in its quality if shaky in some specifics. For without Vasari, we would have had little picture at all.

Giorgio Vasari. *Self-Portrait.* c. 1571.
Galleria degli Uffizi, Florence.

theme announced in the entryway while also preparing us for the grander right-angle crossing of the transept. The roundel (circular area) set in the pediment of the facade and again over its doors is repeated on the walls of the nave between the chapels and culminates with the great circular opening of the dome. The vast interior space composed of geometric volumes harks back to Roman examples such as the Pantheon (see 13.15).

In addition to Christian themes, Renaissance artists also turned to stories of Greek and Roman gods and goddesses for subject matter, as did many Renaissance poets. An example is *The Birth of Venus* (**16.6**), by Sandro Botticelli. Born in 1445, Botticelli belonged to the third generation of Renaissance artists. Early in his career, he had the great fortune to enjoy the patronage of the Medici, the ruling merchant family of Florence, who probably commissioned this painting. The Medici sponsored an Academy—a sort of discussion group—where humanist scholars and artists met to discuss Classical culture and its relationship to Christianity. The reconciliation of these two systems of thought gave rise to a philosophy known as Neo-Platonism, after the Greek philosopher Plato.

Venus was the Roman goddess of love and beauty. According to legend, she was born from the sea, and so Botticelli depicts her floating upward on a shell. The wind god Zephyr and his wife blow her gently toward the shore, where a figure representing spring waits ready to clothe Venus in a flowing garment. Botticelli paints the goddess in the nude, with strategically placed hands and a tress of hair the only concessions to modesty. Such a large-scale depiction of the female nude in art had been virtually unknown since Classical times. Venus' pose is modeled after a Roman sculpture of the goddess, which Botticelli had studied in the Medici collection, but her lightness, her fragile quality, her delicate beauty and billowing hair—these are Botticelli's own.

16.6 Sandro Botticelli. *The Birth of Venus.* c. 1480. Tempera on canvas, 6′ 7″ × 9′ 2″. Galleria degli Uffizi, Florence.

While Botticelli's unusual linear style and shallow modeling was an exception to Renaissance norms, it was highly appreciated by the Medici circle. Venus, for example, looks as though she might be modeled in high relief, but not fully rounded. The implied space is shallow, with the sea and receding shoreline serving almost as a flat backdrop, as in a theatrical production. Medici intimates would also have understood the subtle Neo-Platonic overtones of the scene. In Neo-Platonic thought, Venus was identified with both Eve and the Virgin Mary; her birth from the water was related to the baptism of Christ by John the Baptist. Botticelli's work displays the rarefied and learned side of Renaissance art. It was not painted for a large public, but for a cultivated audience of initiates.

Botticelli painted in tempera. The favorite medium of medieval and early Renaissance artists, tempera was about to be eclipsed by oil paint, which had recently been developed in northern Europe. An early master of the new medium was the Venetian painter Giovanni Bellini. While the artists of Florence and Rome emphasized sound drawing above all other artistic virtues, the painters of Venice became known for their interest in color and light. Oil paint lent itself especially well to their concerns, as we can see in Bellini's *St. Francis in the Desert* (**16.7**).

Francis was a holy man, a monk and preacher, born in the Italian town of Assisi in the late 12th century. According to legend, he was able to converse with the birds and animals, in a language both man and creatures understood freely. Francis' goodness was so profound that God bestowed upon him the stigmata—marks or wounds upon his hands and feet like those Christ had suffered when he was nailed to the cross at his Crucifixion. The artist Bellini has chosen to capture the moment when Francis received the stigmata, a moment of intense pain and great joy. A brilliant golden light bathes the scene, presumably the light of God shining down on the holy man. Francis stands in awe of the light, his arms outstretched, his gaze cast upward, welcoming this sign of God's favor.

Bellini frames the saint in a protective craggy foreground landscape as solidly constructed as a work of architecture. The middle ground is defined by a grassy knoll on which a donkey stands. In the distance is a town at the foot of a hill; still farther is a hilltop fortress, and in the farthest blue-tinted distance a mountain. Unlike the setting for Botticelli's *Venus,* Bellini's magnificent landscape recedes convincingly into deep space. The recession is not smooth and continuous, however. Rather, it proceeds step by step by giving us something to look at in each new area. Our eyes follow a series of focal points into the distance, ignoring the gaps between them. (For example, there is no transition between the rocky foreground and the grassy knoll. One stops, then the other begins.) To create a continuous recession into deep space in a landscape is quite difficult. More progress would be made by the painters of the next generation, many of whom would be indebted to Bellini's explorations of color, light, and atmosphere.

We come now to a period known as the High Renaissance—a brief but glorious time in the history of art. In barely twenty-five years, from shortly before 1500 to about 1525, some of the most celebrated works of Western art were produced. Many artists participated in this brilliant creative endeavor, but the outstanding figures among them were unquestionably Leonardo da Vinci and Michelangelo.

The term "Renaissance man" is applied to someone who is very well informed about, or very good at doing, many different, often quite unrelated, things. It originated in the fact that several of the leading figures of the Renaissance were artistic jacks-of-all-trades. Michelangelo was a painter, sculptor, poet, architect—incomparably gifted at all. Leonardo was a painter, inventor, sculptor, architect, engineer, scientist, musician, and all-around intellectual. In our age of specialization these accomplishments seem staggering, but during the heady years of the Renaissance nothing was impossible.

2.12 Bellini, *Pietà*

Leonardo is the artist who most embodies the term "Renaissance man"; many people consider him to have been the greatest genius who ever lived. Leonardo was possessed of a brilliant and inquiring mind that accepted no limits. Throughout his long life he remained absorbed by the problem of how things work, and how they might work. A typical example of his investigations is the well-known *Study of Human Proportions* (see 5.26), in which the artist sought to establish ideal proportions for the human body by relating it to the square and the circle. Above and below the figure is Leonardo's eccentric mirror writing, which he used in his notes and journals.

Leonardo's interest in mathematics is also evident from his careful rendering of perspective. In Chapter 4 we examined his masterpiece *The Last Supper* (see 4.41), which uses one-point linear perspective to organize the many figures in the composition and set them into deep space. Yet another interest, experimental painting techniques, served the artist less well in *The Last Supper*. Rather than employing the established fresco method, Leonardo worked in a medium he devised for the *Last Supper* project, thus dooming his work to centuries of restoration (p. 110).

In spite of his vast accomplishments, Leonardo often had difficulty completing specific projects. Many of his most ambitious works were left

16.7 Giovanni Bellini. *St. Francis in the Desert*. c. 1485. Oil on panel, 4′1½″ × 4′7″.
The Frick Collection, New York.

16.8 Leonardo da Vinci. *Mona Lisa*. c. 1503–05. Oil on panel, 30¼ × 21″.
Musée du Louvre, Paris.

RELATED WORKS

4.15 Leonardo, *Virgin and St. Anne*

4.41 Leonardo, *The Last Supper*

5.26 Leonardo, *Study of Human Proportions*

unfinished, possibly including his best-known painting, the *Mona Lisa* (**16.8**). *Mona Lisa* has been the object of special fascination ever since it was painted. Leonardo himself seems to have been especially attached to the painting, for he kept it with him. The sitter has been identified as Lisa Gherardini del Giocondo, wife of a Florentine merchant. Leonardo has posed her half-length figure in a stable pyramidal form. She was originally framed by columns that rose from the low wall behind her. These were cut away at some point during the painting's long history, but a glimpse of their bases can still be seen at the left and right edges of the canvas. The columns would have made it clearer that she sits on a balcony overlooking a mysterious landscape of rock and water. A small bridge over the river to the right and a twisting path to the left are the only indications of a human presence.

Leonardo was especially fond of evening light, and he thought that people looked their most beautiful in its mellow glow. Though there is no specific time of day suggested in the portrait (another of its mysterious qualities), Leonardo suggests a hushed light similar to evening with a technique called **sfumato** (derived from the Italian for "smoke"), in which layer upon layer of translucent glazes produce a hazy atmosphere, softened contours, and velvety shadows. *Sfumato* leaves unresolved the corners of the sitter's eyes and mouth, and so her expression, with its hint of a smile, seems to shift in mood as we look. Sad, kind, haughty, flirtatious, amused, skeptical, confident, vulnerable, warm, distant—she seems made of opposites, and perhaps it is our desire to resolve them that gives this painting its special magic.

VINCENZO PERUGIA

At 7:20 on the morning of August 21, 1911, three members of the maintenance staff at the Louvre paused briefly in front of the *Mona Lisa*. The chief of maintenance remarked to his workers, "This is the most valuable picture in the world." Just over an hour later the three men again passed through the Salon Carré, where Leonardo's masterpiece hung, and saw that the painting was no longer in its place. The maintenance chief joked that museum officials had removed the picture for fear he and his crew would steal it. That joke soon proved to be an uncomfortably hollow one. *Mona Lisa* was gone.

Thus begins the story of the most famous art theft in history, of the most famous painting in the world, and of the man who would inevitably become the most famous art thief of all time: Vincenzo Perugia.

French newspapers announced the catastrophe under the banner headline "Unimaginable!" All during the weeks that followed, rumors abounded. A man carrying a blanket-covered parcel had been seen jumping onto the train for Bordeaux. A mysterious draped package had been spotted on a ship to New York, a ship to South America, a ship to Italy. The painting had been scarred with acid, had been dumped in the sea. All clues, however far-fetched, were followed up, but no trace of *Mona Lisa* could be found.

More than two years would pass before the thief surfaced. Then, in November of 1913, an art dealer in Italy received a letter from a man who signed himself "Leonard." Would the dealer like to have the *Mona Lisa*? Would he. Of course it was a joke. But was it? The dealer arranged to meet "Leonard" in a hotel room in Florence. "Leonard" produced a wooden box filled with junk. The junk was removed, a false bottom came out of the box, and there, wrapped in red silk and perfectly preserved, was the smiling face of *Mona Lisa*. The dealer swallowed his shock and phoned for the police.

"Leonard" was actually an Italian named Vincenzo Perugia—a house painter who had once done some contract work in the Louvre. As he told the story of the theft, it was amazingly simple. On the morning in question Perugia, dressed in a workman's smock, walked into the museum, nodded to several of the other workers, and chose a moment when no one else was in the Salon Carré to unhook the painting from the wall. Then he slipped into a stairwell, removed the picture from its frame, stuck it under his smock, and walked out. Stories that Perugia had accomplices have never been proved.

What were the thief's motives? And why, after pulling off what can only be described as the heist of the century, did he so naively offer the painting to the Italian dealer? Perugia claimed he was motivated by patriotism. *Mona Lisa* was an Italian painting by an Italian artist. Believing (mistakenly) that it had been stolen by Napoleon to hang in France, he wanted to restore it to its rightful home. At the same time, however, he expected to be "rewarded" by the Italian government for his heroic act and thought $100,000 would be a good amount. No one shared this point of view.

Perugia was tried, convicted, and sentenced to a year in prison. After his release he served in the army, married, settled in Paris, and operated a paint store. Soon Perugia, who had so briefly captured the world's headlines, settled back into the obscurity from which he had emerged.

And *Mona Lisa*? After a triumphal tour of several Italian museums, she was returned to France. She hangs—at least as of this writing—safely in the Louvre. Romantics say her smile is even more enigmatic than before.

"Mug shot" of Vincenzo Perugia (with the name misspelled) after his arrest in 1913.

16.9 (left) Michelangelo. *David.* 1501–04. Marble, height 18′. Galleria dell'Accademia, Florence.

16.10 (right) Interior, Sistine Chapel, Vatican, Rome. 1473–80.

During the years when Leonardo was painting the *Mona Lisa*, Michelangelo, a quarter-century younger, also was in Florence, at work on one of the projects for which he is best known. Michelangelo had established his reputation as a sculptor by the age of twenty-five. A year later he received the commission for a colossal image of the biblical hero David (**16.9**), the young Hebrew shepherd who killed the giant Goliath with a single stone from his slingshot. The *David* statue reveals Michelangelo's debt to Classical sculptures; we might compare it to the Roman copy of the Greek *Spear Bearer* (see 14.28). *David* is not, however, a simple restatement of Greek art. The Greeks knew how bodies looked on the outside. Michelangelo knew how they looked on the inside, how they worked, because he had studied human anatomy and had dissected corpses. He translated this knowledge into a figure that seems made of muscle and flesh and bone, though all in marble.

There are other characteristics that make *David* a Renaissance sculpture, not a copy of a Greek one. For one thing, it has a tension and energy that are missing from Greek art. Hellenistic works such as the *Laocoön Group* (see 14.29) expressed these qualities through physical contortions, but to have this energy coiled within a figure standing quietly was new. David is not so much standing in repose as standing in readiness. Another Renaissance quality is the expression on David's face. Classical Greek statues tended to have calm and even vacant expressions. But David is young and vibrant—and angry, angry at the forces of evil represented by the giant Goliath. Contemporary Florentines found David a fitting emblem for their small but proud city, which had recently battled giants by expelling the ruling Medici family to found a republic. They placed the statue in the city square in front of the seat of the new government. (It has since been moved indoors.)

Not long after completing the *David*, Michelangelo embarked on the masterpiece which has become his best-known work, the ceiling frescoes of the Sistine Chapel in the Vatican, in Rome (**16.10**). He had been called to Rome by Pope Julius II, who wanted the artist to design his tomb, a large

MICHELANGELO
1475–1564

HE IS BEYOND legend. His name means "archangel Michael," and to his contemporaries and those who came after, his stature is scarcely less than that of a heavenly being. He began serious work as an artist at the age of thirteen and did not stop until death claimed him seventy-six years later. His equal may never be seen again, for only a particular time and place could have bred the genius of Michelangelo.

Michelangelo Buonarroti was born in the Tuscan town of Caprese. According to his devoted biographer and friend, Giorgio Vasari, the young Michelangelo often was scolded and beaten by his father for spending too much time drawing. Eventually, however, seeing his son's talent, the father relented and apprenticed him to the painter Domenico Ghirlandaio. At the age of fourteen Michelangelo was welcomed into the household of the wealthy banker Lorenzo de' Medici, who operated a private sculpture academy for promising young students. There he remained until Lorenzo's death, after which Michelangelo, just seventeen years old, struck out permanently on his own.

He traveled to Venice and Bologna, to Florence, then finally to Rome, where he attracted the first of what would become a long list of patrons among the clergy. A *Pietà* (Virgin mourning the dead Christ)

made in 1500 and now in St. Peter's established his reputation as a sculptor. Within a dozen years after that he had completed the two works most closely associated with his name: the *David* statue and the ceiling frescoes in the Sistine Chapel.

From his teen years until his death Michelangelo never lacked for highly placed patrons. He served—and survived—six popes, and in between accepted commissions from two emperors, a king, and numerous members of the nobility. All his life he struggled to keep a balance between the work he wanted to do and the work demanded of him by his benefactors. His relationships with these powerful figures were often stormy, marked by squabbles about payment, insults given and forgiven, flight from the scene followed by penitent return.

Michelangelo served these masters, at various times, as painter and architect, but he considered himself above all to be a sculptor. Much of his time was spent supervising the quarrying of superior stones for sculptural projects. His greatest genius lay in depictions of the human figure, whether in marble or in paint. Vasari writes that "this extraordinary man chose always to refuse to paint anything save the human body in its most beautifully proportioned and perfect forms." To this end Michelangelo made extensive anatomical studies and dissected corpses to better understand the inner workings of the body.

Michelangelo formed a number of passionate attachments during his life. These inspired the artist, always a sensitive and gifted poet, to write numerous sonnets. One of his most poignant verses, however, was written as a commentary on his labors up on the scaffold under the Sistine Chapel ceiling. We might find it amusing if it were not so heartfelt:

> I've grown a goiter by dwelling in this den—
>   As cats from stagnant streams in Lombardy,
>   Or in what other land they hap to be—
>   Which drives the belly close beneath the chin;
> My beard turns up to heaven; my nape falls in,
>   Fixed on my spine; my breast-bone visibly
>   Grows like a harp: a rich embroidery
>   Bedews my face from brush-drops thick and
>   thin. . . .[6]

---

monument with numerous sculptures. Michelangelo set to work, but a year later Julius abandoned this project and proposed instead to use the artist's skills as a painter. Michelangelo, whose distaste for painting is well documented, resisted the plan, but in the end he was forced to capitulate. For the next four years, he would spend most of his waking hours on a scaffold 68 feet above the floor.

The Sistine Chapel, named after an earlier pope called Sixtus, has a high vaulted ceiling 128 feet long and 44 feet wide. Julius required that Michelangelo cover this entire expanse, 700 square yards, with a painted decoration based on religious themes. Fresco was the only practical medium, and the difficulties of this technique are considerable (Chapter 7). Paint must be applied to fresh plaster just when it has the proper degree of dampness; only a small area can be covered at a time; and the painting must be done directly, with no allowance for correction of mistakes. For this project the artist had to work in a cramped position, with paint and plaster continually dripping in his face. So situated, he was only inches away from the working

16.11 Michelangelo. Ceiling, Sistine Chapel. 1508–12. Fresco, 44 × 128′. Vatican, Rome.

surface, yet the paintings had to be readable and compelling to a viewer standing on the floor, nearly 70 feet below.

Even more overwhelming than the physical constraints was the challenge of making a coherent composition in such a huge area. Michelangelo organized the ceiling into a painted architectural framework of squares, rectangles, and triangles (**16.11**). These segments depict Old Testament stories of the creation of the world, the creation of Adam and Eve, the Fall of Man, and other biblical events. Some figures on the ceiling are from Greek and Roman mythology, for Michelangelo meant to connect the older Classical cultures with Christian theology of his own time.

Each of the segments is self-contained, yet the panels flow gracefully from one to the next, thanks to the artist's placement of overlapping *ignudi* (nude youths) in the spaces between them. The iconographic identity of the *ignudi* is unknown. Some historians have suggested they may represent angels. Throughout the composition Michelangelo's painted figures have the same anatomical fullness and muscular energy as his sculptures.

16.12 Michelangelo. *Creation of Adam,* detail of Sistine Chapel ceiling. 1511.

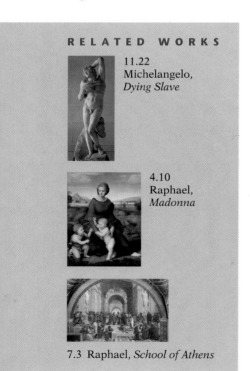
The *Creation of Adam* (**16.12**) is the most familiar of the ceiling images. Based on the biblical book of Genesis, this scene shows Adam, the first man, reclining on a rock. He is well-formed but listless; the spirit of life—the soul— has not yet been breathed into him. At right the dynamic figure of God sweeps toward Adam, wrapped in a symbolic cloak of Heaven. God's left arm embraces a woman thought to represent Eve, the first woman, who at this point in the story is still an idea in God's mind. His left forefinger points to a child, probably meant to be the Christ child, who will come much later to redeem the world. The focal point of this composition is the two hands, stretching toward one another. In a split second they will meet, and the long history of humankind will begin. Michelangelo's genius is nowhere clearer. He does not show us the consummation. He shows us, rather, the thrilling potential.

The ceiling frescoes were an immediate success, and Michelangelo continued as a papal favorite, although his commissions were not always in his preferred line. Just as Pope Julius had urged the sculptor to work as a painter, one of Julius' successors, Pope Paul III, encouraged the sculptor to work as an architect. In 1546 Paul named Michelangelo the official architect of the new St. Peter's, the ceremonial cathedral that is the "headquarters" of the Roman Catholic Church. This structure would be erected on the site of *old* St. Peter's (see 15.2), dating from the Early Christian era in the 4th century. By the time he began work on the project, Michelangelo was an old man, well into his seventies and physically tired, but his creative vigor was undiminished.

Construction on the new church had already begun, based on a plan by an architect named Bramante, who had died in 1514. Michelangelo revised Bramante's plan, gathering its elaborate fussiness into a bold and harmonious design (**16.13, 16.14**). Central and cross plans here merge in a new idea that relates the powerfully symbolic cross to the geometric forms that Renaissance artists loved, the square and the circle. Michelangelo did not live to see his church finished. The magnificent central dome was completed after his death by another architect, who modified its silhouette. During the 17th century, the nave was lengthened and the facade remodeled. The photograph illustrated here, however, was taken from the rear of the church and shows the building that Michelangelo conceived. An organic whole with pulsating contours and a powerful upward thrust, it is the architectural equivalent of his muscular nudes.

The concentration of artistic energy in Rome during the Renaissance was such that while Michelangelo was working on the Sistine ceiling, his slightly younger rival Raphael was only a few steps away, painting his fresco *The School of Athens* (see 7.3) in the private library of the same pope, Julius II. In 1513, Julius was succeeded as pope by Giovanni de' Medici, whose family was now back in power in Florence. Raphael was increasingly in demand as a portraitist, and Giovanni de' Medici, now Pope Leo X, commissioned a likeness from him (**16.15**). Leo X was a passionate collector of books and manuscripts, and he eventually amassed a fine library. Raphael portrays him seated before one of his prized illuminated manuscripts, a magnifying glass in his left hand. Standing beside him are two nephews he had elevated to the office of cardinal (church officials next in rank to the pope). The rich fabrics, sumptuously painted, tell of the worldly splendor of the Church in Rome, while the keenly observed faces convey without flattery the aura of power and ambition that drove Leo X and his family.

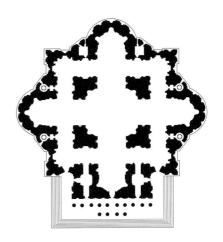

16.13 (left) Michelangelo. Saint Peter's Basilica, Vatican. c. 1546–64 (dome completed 1590 by Giacomo della Porta).

16.14 (above) Plan of St. Peter's.

16.15 (below) Raphael. *Pope Leo X with Two Cardinals*. c. 1518. Oil on wood, 5'3⅜" × 3'8⅞". Galleria degli Ufizzi, Florence.

After Rome and Florence, the third great artistic center of Italy was Venice, where Giovanni Bellini worked and taught (see 16.7). Bellini's two finest students, Giorgione and Titian, went on to become the greatest Venetian painters of the High Renaissance.

The iconography of Giorgione's painting *The Tempest* (**16.16**) is unknown. Even the artist's contemporaries seem not to have known what story he was depicting or to have been able to identify the nude woman nursing a child at right and the soldier (or shepherd) at left. But regardless of the meaning of its subject, *The Tempest* makes an important contribution to Renaissance art in the way it is composed. Artists of earlier generations would compose a scene by concentrating on the figures and painting the landscape as a kind of backdrop. Giorgione, however, has started by constructing a landscape and then placing his figures in it. This approach paved the way for the great landscape paintings of the centuries to follow.

In *The Tempest*, as the title implies, the subject is really the approaching storm, which closes in dramatically over the city while the two foreground figures are still bathed in sunlight. The artist's debt to his teacher, Bellini, will be obvious if you compare this work with the older master's *St. Francis in the Desert* (see 16.7), which also shows a highlighted foreground figure and a distant landscape. Giorgione, however, is less concerned with the human experience. His principal interest seems to have been the contrast of bucolic foreground against the city rendered in careful

16.16 Giorgione. *The Tempest.* c. 1505. Oil on canvas, 32¼ × 28¾".
Gallerie dell'Accademia, Venice.

perspective, with the two drawn together by the violent effects of nature. The storm and the lush vegetation create a world in which nature dominates, not people, and the painting evokes a powerful, compelling mood of apprehension and anticipation.

Giorgione died in his early thirties, and so we will never know what other wonders he might have accomplished. Titian, however, lived a long and productive life, and his career, like that of Michelangelo, allows us to witness the full arc of a great artist from youth through maturity to old age. Like many other Venetian painters, Titian absorbed the lessons of Giorgione's poetic style. In fact, an early work of Titian's known as *Fête Champêtre* (**16.17,** also known as *Pastoral Concert* or *Pastoral Scene*) was attributed to Giorgione until quite recently. Like *The Tempest*, it places figures in a landscape that evokes a mood. It is a poetic reverie, not a depiction of an actual event or mythological scene.

Fête Champêtre stands near the beginning of a long tradition of painting that looks back to the Classical Roman writer Virgil, whose poems called eclogues celebrated the pleasures of the country as appreciated by sophisticated urban dwellers. The group here are evidently from the town depicted in the background. The young men may be poets and the unclad women their muses. The well-dressed, aristocratic youth recites his verses to the accompaniment of a lute, a courtly instrument. In contrast, an untutored shepherd in the distance plays the rustic bagpipes.

The poetic landscape pioneered by Giovanni Bellini and Giorgione remained an important element of Titian's art. In Chapter 4, we saw a later example in his *Bacchus and Ariadne* (see 4.25). The clean contours, saturated hues, and symphonic color harmonies of that painting are typical of Titian's first mature style. The work also shows Titian to have been well versed in the mythological subjects that Renaissance painters were expected to illustrate for their educated patrons.

Titian became the most sought after portraitist of his day. Scholars, philosophers, and friends sat for him, as did popes, emperors, and Venetian rulers, but he never painted a more engaging portrait than the one here

16.17 Titian. *Fête Champêtre.* 1511. Oil on canvas, 43⁵⁄₁₆ × 51⅛″. Musée du Louvre, Paris.

RELATED WORKS

4.25 Titian, *Bacchus and Ariadne*

16.18 (left) Titian. *Portrait of Ranuccio Farnese.* 1542. Oil on canvas, 35¼ × 29″.
National Gallery of Art, Washington, D.C.

16.19 (right) Titian. *The Annunciation.* c. 1560. Oil on canvas, 13′2⅝″ × 7′8½″.
Chiesa di San Salvador, Venice.

of a twelve-year-old boy named Ranuccio Farnese (**16.18**). The grandson of Pope Paul III, Ranuccio Farnese was pursuing his studies in nearby Padua at the time that Titian painted him. The painting shows well the sympathetic insight that Titian could bring to his portraits. It shows us, too, something of what it meant to grow up within a powerful Renaissance family. Ranuccio's endearing, shy expression undercuts the worldly confidence his silk clothing tries to project, and the sword and cloak of the military-religious order of the Knights of Malta, recently conferred upon him, weigh heavily—perhaps too heavily—on his young frame. He would be made a cardinal at the age of fifteen.

As Titian aged, his brushwork became freer and his colors grew more subdued and burnished. Contemporaries marveled that his paintings, seen up close, seemed nothing but a senseless frenzy of brush strokes. Yet as the viewer stepped back, there came into focus an image of unparalleled richness. An example is *The Annunciation* (**16.19**), painted when the artist was seventy-five. The subject is the moment when an angel appears to Mary to tell her that she has been chosen to bear the Son of God. In Titian's imagining of the event, Mary turns quietly from her prayers and lifts her veil to look at her visitor. The angel arrives as though in a hurry, his cheeks still flush with the excitement of the news he brings. Mary does not see that behind her the air itself has opened with the force of an explosion, and from the golden light formed of endless cherubim descends the dove of the Holy Spirit. In this work, Titian produced a vision of heavenly glory as rhapsodic as the gold realm of Byzantium or the stained glass of the Middle Ages.

THE RENAISSANCE IN THE NORTH

In the northern countries of western Europe—Switzerland, Germany, northern France, and the Netherlands—the Renaissance did not happen with the sudden drama that it did in Italy, nor were its concerns quite the same. Northern artists did not live among the ruins of Rome, nor did they share the Italians' sense of a personal link to the creators of the Classical past. Instead of the exciting series of discoveries that make the Italian Renaissance such a good story, the Northern Renaissance style evolved gradually out of the late Middle Ages, as artists became increasingly entranced with the myriad details of the visible world and better and better at capturing them.

We can see this fondness for detail in one of the most famous works of the late Middle Ages, the illuminated prayer book known as *Les Très Riches Heures* ("the very rich hours"). The book was created at the beginning of the 15th century by three artist brothers, the Limbourgs, for the duke of Berry, brother to the king of France.

Meant for daily religious devotion, the *Très Riches Heures* contains a calendar, with each month's painting featuring a typical seasonal activity of either the peasantry or the nobility. Our illustration shows the *February* page (**16.20**). At top in the lunette (half-moon shape) the chariot of the Sun is shown making its progress through the months and signs of the zodiac. Below, the Limbourgs depict their notion of lower-class life in the year's coldest month.

16.20 Limbourg Brothers. *February*, from *Les Très Riches Heures du Duc de Berry*. 1416. Illumination, 8⅞ × 5⅜″. Musée Condé, Chantilly.

This view of everyday life focuses on a small peasant hut with its occupants clustered around the fire, their garments pulled back to get maximum benefit from the warmth. With a touch of artistic license, the Limbourgs have removed the front wall of the hut so we can look in. Outside the cozy hut we see what may be the earliest snow-covered landscape ever painted. Sheep cluster in their enclosure, a peasant comes rushing across the barnyard pulling his cloak about his face to keep in the warm breath. From there the movement progresses diagonally up the slope to a man chopping firewood, another urging a donkey uphill, and finally the church at the top.

One should bear in mind this is a miniature, only 9 inches high, to appreciate the richness of details. So acute is the Limbourgs' observation, on so tiny a scale, that we understand the condition of each player—the exertion of the woodcutter, the chill of the running figure, the nonchalant poses of the couple in the hut, and the demure modesty of the lady in blue.

The Limbourgs' manuscript marks a high point in a medieval tradition dating back hundreds of years (see 15.11). Within a few decades, however, the printing press would be invented, and the practice of copying and illustrating books by hand would gradually die out. In the meantime, an increasing number of Northern artists were turning to painting on panel with the newly developed medium of oil paint. An early master of the medium was Robert Campin, a prominent artist in the Flemish city of Tournai, in present-day Belgium. The subject of his *Mérode Altarpiece* (**16.21**) is the Annunciation, the same event we saw depicted by Titian earlier in this chapter (see 16.19). Campin painted this work in 1426, right around the time that the principles of linear perspective were discovered in Italy. The Italian system would not make its way north for another seventy-five years. Campin relies instead on intuitive perspective, in which receding parallel lines converge unsystematically. He uses it here with charming inconsistency, tilting the tabletops toward us, for example, so we can get a look at everything that sits on them.

The Annunciation setting is replete with symbols, most of them referring to Mary's purity: the lilies on the table, the just-extinguished candle, the white linen, among others. At upper left, between two round windows, the tiny figure of a child carrying a cross flies down a light ray toward Mary's ear, signifying that the infant Jesus will enter Mary's womb through God's will, not through human impregnation. The right wing of the altarpiece shows Joseph, who will become Mary's husband, at work in his carpenter shop. By tradition,

16.21 Robert Campin. *Mérode Altarpiece.* c. 1426. Oil on panel, 25³⁄₁₆ × 24⁷⁄₈″ (center), 25³⁄₈ × 10³⁄₄″ (each wing).
The Metropolitan Museum of Art, New York.

Joseph is making a mousetrap, symbolic of the soon-to-come Jesus' "trapping" the Devil, bringing good to banish evil. In the left wing the donors, who commissioned the painting, kneel to witness the holy scene.

No recitation of this picture's details should overshadow its sheer beauty. Mary's face, modest above her crimson gown, is among the loveliest in all Renaissance art. The angel, with his luminous face and brilliant gold wings, displays an unearthly radiance. Both central figures wear robes that flow into rivers of sculptural folds. The *Mérode Altarpiece* is only about 2 feet in height. Its exquisitely rendered details, its clear colors, and the artist's skillful placement of light and shadow combine to give it a jewel-like quality.

Northern artists' preoccupation with decoration and surface and *things* derives naturally from their heritage. The North had a long tradition of painted miniatures, manuscript illuminations, stained glass, and tapestries—all decorative arts with a great deal of surface detail. Whereas the Italian masters were obsessed with structure—accurate perspective and the underlying musculature of the body—Northern artists perfected their skill at rendering the precise outer appearance of their subjects. They were unsurpassed at capturing in paint the textures of satin or velvet, the sheen of silver and gold, the quality of skin to its last pore and wrinkle.

In a fundamental way, Northern paintings are about *looking*. An apt example is Rogier van der Weyden's *St. Luke Drawing the Virgin* (**16.22**). At left is the Virgin Mary nursing the infant Jesus. At right is St. Luke, author of one of the four Gospels in the Bible and patron saint of artists, drawing the mother and child in silverpoint. The two larger figures are carefully balanced in an architectural setting, behind which, through a window, we glimpse a landscape in depth. Typical Northern touches include Rogier's minute attention to detail in the room—woodwork, tiles, canopy, window panes; wonderfully lavish drapery in the garments; rich colors; and faces so finely modeled and human we can think of them as portraits. There is great emotional warmth in this picture. The Virgin and Child exchange tender

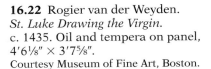
16.22 Rogier van der Weyden.
St. Luke Drawing the Virgin.
c. 1435. Oil and tempera on panel,
4′6⅛″ × 3′7⅝″.
Courtesy Museum of Fine Art, Boston.

3.29 Bosch, *Garden of Earthly Delights*

glances, while St. Luke, in his effort to capture their likeness, seems almost overcome with reverence and love. Everyone in the painting is caught up in looking, including the distant couple gazing out at the horizon.

While Rogier's painting is gentle, religious art of the Northern Renaissance could also be harsh in its emotionalism—far harsher than that of Italy. Northern art abounds in truly grim Crucifixions, gory martyrdoms of saints, and inventive punishments for sinners. Italian artists did sometimes undertake these subjects, but they never dwelt so fondly on the particulars.

Matthias Grünewald, a German artist active in the early 16th century, painted the Crucifixion of Christ as the center of his great masterpiece, the *Isenheim Altarpiece* (**16.23**). Originally, the altarpiece reposed in the chapel of a hospital devoted to the treatment of illnesses afflicting the skin, including syphilis. This helps to explain the horrible appearance of Christ's body on the cross—pockmarked, bleeding from numberless wounds, tortured beyond endurance. Without question the patients in the hospital could identify with Christ's sufferings and thus increase their faith.

In Grünewald's version of the Crucifixion, the twists and lacerations of the body speak of unendurable pain, but the real anguish is conveyed by the feet and hands. Christ's fingers splay out, clutching at the air but helpless to relieve the pain. His feet bend inward in a futile attempt to alleviate the pressure of his hanging body. To the left of the Cross the Virgin Mary falls in a faint, supported by St. John, and Mary Magdalene weeps in an agony that mirrors Christ's own. To the right John the Baptist offers the only sign of hope. He points calmly at the dying Savior in a gesture that foreshadows Christ's Resurrection. Grünewald's interpretation of the Crucifixion is in keeping with a stark Northern tradition in which depictions of extreme physical agony were commonplace.

It was Albrecht Dürer (see 4.16 and 8.4) who more than any other artist attempted to fuse Italian ideas and discoveries with the Northern love of meticulous observation. Dürer had visited Italy as a young artist in 1494 and returned for a longer stay in 1505. He came to share the Italian preoccupation with problems of perspective, ideal beauty, and harmony. In Dürer's view, Northern art had relied too heavily on instinct and lacked a firm grounding in theory and science. Toward the end of his life he summarized his philos-

16.23 Matthias Grünewald. *Isenheim Altarpiece* (exterior). 1515. Panel, 8′10″ × 10′1″. Musée d'Unterlinden, Colmar.

ophy of art by writing and illustrating two important works, *Treatise on Measurement* and *Four Books on Human Proportions*.

An artist who matured in the climate of thought that Dürer had created was the German painter Hans Holbein. While not as intellectual as Dürer, Holbein recognized the need to grapple with the issues that Dürer had introduced. He mastered perspective and studied Italian paintings. Under their influence his modeling softened and his compositions grew more monumental. He did not lose the great Northern gift for detail, however, as his masterpiece known as *The Ambassadors* makes clear (**16.24**).

Holbein painted *The Ambassadors* in England, where his skills as a portraitist earned him the position of court painter to King Henry VIII. The painting was commissioned by the man on the left, Jean de Dinteville, the French ambassador to England. To the right is his friend Georges de Selve, a French bishop who also served as an ambassador. They look out at us from either side of a table richly laden with objects symbolizing the four humanist sciences—music, arithmetic, geometry, and astronomy. The imported Islamic rug speaks of contacts with the wider world, and the globe placed on the lower shelf reminds us that the Renaissance was also the age of European exploration and discovery. Close inspection reveals that the lute resting on the lower shelf has a broken string and that the book before it is open to a hymn by Martin Luther. The broken string symbolizes discord: Europe was no longer in harmony because of the difficult issues raised by Martin Luther's recent accusations against the Church in Rome. The movement Luther started, known as the Reformation, would very soon see Europe permanently divided into Protestant countries and Catholic countries. The religious unity that had characterized the Middle Ages would be gone forever.

The strangest element in the painting is the amorphous diagonal shape that seems to float in the foreground. Dinteville's personal motto was *memento mori*, Latin for "remember you must die." Holbein acknowledged

16.24 Hans Holbein the Younger. *The Ambassadors*. 1533. Oil on panel, 6′9½″ × 6′10½″. The National Gallery, London.

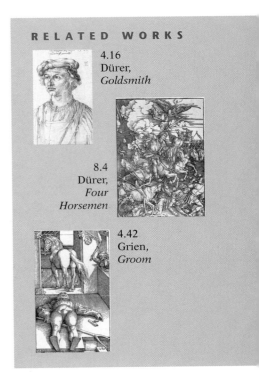

RELATED WORKS

4.16 Dürer, *Goldsmith*

8.4 Dürer, *Four Horsemen*

4.42 Grien, *Groom*

16.25 Pieter Bruegel the Elder. *The Harvesters*. 1565. Oil on panel, 46½ × 63¼". The Metropolitan Museum of Art, New York.

this with a human skull, stretched as though made of rubber. The skull is painted to come into focus when the painting is viewed up close and at an angle. Death thus cuts across life and shows itself by surprise. Holbein's painting celebrates worldly splendor and human achievement even as it reminds us that death will eventually triumph. It stands as a portrait of two men, a portrait of a friendship, and a portrait of an era.

Protestant reforms of the 16th century included an attitude toward religious images that ranged from wariness to outright hostility. Images of saints and other figures, reformers felt, had all too often been thought to possess sacred powers themselves. In their view the Church in Rome had encouraged these beliefs, which amounted to idol worship. The walls of Protestant churches were bare: "The kingdom of God is a kingdom of hearing, not of seeing," said Martin Luther.[7] One result was that Northern artists turned increasingly to the everyday world around them for subject matter, and one of the most fruitful subjects they began to explore was landscape.

We opened this brief survey of Northern Renaissance art with a manuscript page by the Limbourg brothers depicting a peasant household with a winter landscape in the background (see 16.20). *The Harvesters* (**16.25**), by the 16th-century Netherlandish painter Pieter Bruegel the Elder, advances the season to late summer and shows us how far painting has come in 150 years. Like the February page from the *Très Riches Heures*, *The Harvesters* formed part of a cycle depicting the months of the year. In the foreground, a group of peasants have paused for their midday meal in the shade of a slender tree. No doubt they have been working in the fields since dawn. The little group sits, chatting and eating. One man has loosened his breeches and stretched out for a nap. In the middle ground, the still unmowed portion of the field stretches out like a golden carpet. Some people are still at work, the men mowing with their scythes, the women stooping to gather the wheat into sheaves. Beyond there opens a vast panorama, a peaceful, domesticated landscape stretching as far as the eye can see. Landscape, which served the Limbourg brothers as a backdrop, has here become the principal theme, a grand setting in which humans take their appointed place, the rhythm of their work and lives falling in with the rhythm of the seasons and of creation.

THE LATE RENAISSANCE
IN ITALY

Scholars generally date the end of the High Renaissance in Italy to the death of Raphael in 1520. The next generation of artists came of age in the shadow of this great period and with two of its most intimidating artists, Titian and Michelangelo, still going strong. Of the various artistic trends that emerged, the one that has interested art historians most is known as Mannerism.

The word Mannerism comes from the Italian *maniera*, meaning "style" or "stylishness," and it was originally used to suggest that these painters practiced an art of grace and sophistication. Later critics characterized Mannerism as a decadent reaction against the order and balance of the High Renaissance. Today, however, most scholars agree that Mannerism actually grew out of possibilities suggested by the work of High Renaissance artists, especially Michelangelo, whose influence on the next generation was enormous.

Agnolo Bronzino's bizarre *Allegory* (**16.26**) illustrates some of the fascinating and unsettling characteristics of Mannerism. The painting seems to have been commissioned by Cosimo de' Medici as a gift for Francis I, the king of France. The subject is clearly allegorical; that is, all of the figures and objects also stand for ideas or concepts, and we should be able to "decode" their interaction, perhaps to draw a moral lesson. But the allegory is so obscure that scholars have yet to reconstruct it. This fondness for elaborate or obscure subject matter is typical of Mannerist artists and the highly cultivated audience they painted for. Also typical is the "forbidden" erotic undercurrent. We recognize Venus and Cupid in the foreground. They are mother and son, but their interaction hints at a different sort of relationship, and

16.26 Agnolo Bronzino. *Allegory* (*"Venus, Cupid, Folly, and Time"*). c. 1545. Oil on wood, 5'1" × 4'8¾".
The National Gallery, London.

both are clearly arranged for our erotic appraisal as well. The elongated figures and twisting S-shaped poses are part of the Mannerist repertoire, as is the illogical picture space—a shallow, compressed zone filled with an impossible number of people.

Bronzino's painting is an extreme example of the highly artificial and self-conscious aspects of Mannerist art. But Mannerist elements can also be seen in less exotic works such as Sofonisba Anguissola's lovely group portrait *The Chess Game* (**16.27**). The first woman artist known to have achieved celebrity among her contemporaries, Anguissola was born about 1535 in Cremona, the eldest of six sisters. She was well educated and was trained in painting; by about age twenty-two she had attracted the admiring attention of Michelangelo.

The Chess Game dates from 1555, when the artist was about twenty. It portrays two of her sisters engaged in a playful game outdoors on a balmy afternoon, while another sister and their maidservant look on. A misty landscape is seen in the distance. At left is Lucia, who gazes toward us serenely as she makes her move, to the apparent consternation of Minerva, at right. In the center little Europa displays her impish amusement at her older sister's downfall on the chess board. To understand Anguissola's originality, we might compare *The Chess Game* with Raphael's *Pope Leo X* (see 16.15). Raphael poses his three subjects formally, with no interaction among them. By contrast, Anguissola, while giving us fully realized portraits of her sisters, also sets them in motion, gives them something to do, shows us their relationships and their feelings. The modeling of the faces and the misty background landscape owe something to the example of Leonardo da Vinci, but the crowding of the figures into a compressed foreground space is characteristic of Mannerism.

The Protestant Reformation in northern Europe drew large numbers of people away from the Roman Catholic Church. Deeply wounded, the Church of Rome regrouped itself and struck back. The Catholic Counter-Reformation, begun in the second half of the 16th century and continuing into the 17th, aimed at preserving what strength the Church still had in the southern countries and perhaps recovering some lost ground in the North. The concerns of the reformers extended to art, which they recognized as one of their strongest weapons. They insisted that all representations of sacred subjects

16.27 Sofonisba Anguissola. *The Chess Game.* 1555. Oil on canvas, 23³/₈″ × 38¹/₈″. Narodowe Museum, Poznan, Poland.

conform strictly to the teachings of the Church and that artists arrange their compositions to make these teachings evident. They also understood and encouraged art's ability to appeal to the emotions, to engage the hearts of the faithful as well as their intellects.

The Last Supper (**16.28**) by the Venetian painter Tintoretto is an excellent example of the art encouraged by the Counter-Reformation. The greatest painter of the generation after Titian, Tintoretto developed his style from the virtuosic brushwork and dramatic lighting effects of Titian's late works (see 16.19). Tintoretto has chosen to portray the central theological moment of the Last Supper, when Christ breaks bread and gives it to his disciples to eat—the basis for the Christian sacrament of communion. The dramatic diagonal of the table sweeps our eyes into the picture and toward the figure of Christ, who stands near the very center of the canvas. His potentially obscure position in the distance is compensated for by the light that radiates from his head. Lesser glows of saintliness shine from the heads of his apostles, who sense the importance of the moment. Only Judas, who will soon betray Christ, does not emit the light of understanding. He is seated close to Jesus, but alone on the opposite side of the table, a symbolic placement that is both obvious and effective. Witnesses from heaven crowd into the scene from above, swirling in excitement. Though unseen by the servants, who go about their business, they are visible to us, who are left in no doubt that a miracle is taking place.

Comparing Tintoretto's version of *The Last Supper* to Leonardo's High Renaissance fresco of the event (see 4.41), we can see that what was internalized, subtle, and intellectual has here become externalized, exaggerated, and emotional. Tintoretto's work prepares us well for the next era in art, for key elements of his *Last Supper*—the dramatic use of light, the theatricality, the heightened emotionalism, and even the diagonal composition—will play prominent roles in a style soon to be taken up across all of Europe, the Baroque.

16.28 Tintoretto. *The Last Supper.* 1592–94. Oil on canvas, 12′ × 18′8″. San Giorgio Maggiore, Venice.

RELATED WORKS

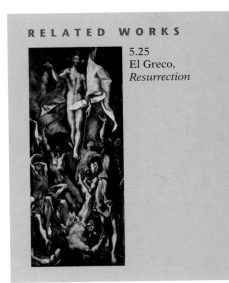

5.25 El Greco, *Resurrection*

CHAPTER 17

The 17th and 18th Centuries

The period encompassing the 17th and 18th centuries in Europe has often been called "The Age of Kings." Some of the most powerful rulers in history occupied the thrones of various countries during this time: Frederick the Great of Prussia, Maria Theresa of Austria, Peter the Great and Catherine the Great of Russia, and a succession of grand kings named Louis in France, to name but a few. These monarchs governed as virtual dictators, and their influence dominated social and cultural affairs of the time as well as political matters.

This same period could equally be called "The Age of Colonial Settlement." By the early 17th century the Dutch, the English, and the French had established permanent settlements in North America. (Spain and Portugal had earlier laid claim to much of Central and South America.) The first successful English colony was at Jamestown, in Virginia, where a party led by John Smith arrived in 1607. Thirteen years later the plucky little ship *Mayflower* made landing in what is now Massachusetts. The settlers endured many hardships as they struggled through their first winters in the New World. At Jamestown the colonists went through a period still known as the "starving time." Ironically, the "starving time" in North America coincided exactly with a European style so opulent that its name is now synonymous with extravagance: the Baroque.

THE BAROQUE STYLE IN EUROPE

Baroque art differs from that of the Renaissance in several important respects. Whereas Renaissance art stressed the calm of reason, Baroque art is full of emotion, energy, and movement. Colors are more vivid in Baroque art than in Renaissance, with greater contrast between colors and between light and dark. In architecture and sculpture, where the Renaissance sought a classic simplicity, the Baroque favored ornamentation, as rich and complex as possible. Baroque art has been called dynamic, sometimes even theatrical. This theatricality is clearly evident in the work of the Baroque's leading interpreter, the artist Gianlorenzo Bernini.

Bernini would have been a fascinating character in any age, but if ever an artist and a style were perfectly suited for one another, this was true of Bernini and the Baroque. Largely for his own pleasure, he was a painter, dramatist, and composer. In architecture and sculpture, however, his gifts rose to the level of genius. Bernini's talents are on full display in the Cornaro Chapel in the church of Santa Maria della Vittoria in Rome (**17.1**). In this small alcove, the funeral chapel of Cardinal Federigo Cornaro, Bernini integrated architecture, painting, sculpture, and lighting into a brilliant ensemble. On the ceiling is painted a vision of heaven, with angels and billowing clouds. At either side of the chapel sit sculptured figures of the Cornaro family, donors of the chapel, in animated conversation, watching the drama before them as though from opera boxes. The whole arrangement is lighted dramatically by sunlight streaming through a yellow-glass window.

The centerpiece of the chapel is Bernini's sculptured group known as *St. Teresa in Ecstasy* (**17.2**). Teresa was a Spanish mystic, founder of a strict order of nuns, and an important figure in the Counter-Reformation. She claimed to be subject for many years to religious trances, in which she saw visions of Heaven and Hell and was visited by angels. It is in the throes of such a vision that Bernini has portrayed her. Teresa wrote:

> Beside me, on the left hand, appeared an angel in bodily form, such as I am not in the habit of seeing except very rarely. . . . He was not tall but short, and very beautiful; and his face was so aflame that he appeared to be one of the

17.1 (left) Gianlorenzo Bernini. Cornaro Chapel, Santa Maria della Vittoria, Rome. 1642–52.

17.2 (right) Gianlorenzo Bernini. *St. Teresa in Ecstasy*, from the Cornaro Chapel. 1645–52. Marble and gilt bronze, lifesize.

GIANLORENZO BERNINI
1598–1680

GIANLORENZO BERNINI falls into a category we find fascinating in all the arts—the youthful prodigy. Born in Naples, he trained with his father, Pietro, a talented sculptor, and by the age of seventeen he had received a commission from the pope. Too late in history to be a man of the Renaissance, Bernini was nonetheless a Renaissance man—sculptor, painter, architect, stage designer, playwright, composer of music, and, by all accounts, a great wit. He lived into his eighties and displayed throughout his life enough energy and enthusiasm and inventiveness for a dozen ordinary people.

Nearly all of Bernini's life was spent in Rome, and he outdid even his great predecessor Michelangelo in papal patronage, serving seven popes over a period of half a century. Master always of the grand design, he executed many huge projects, including the Cornaro Chapel group with *St. Teresa in Ecstasy* and the piazza and colonnade of St. Peter's. Several outdoor fountains in Rome—elaborate figural sculptures—are also of his design. This last is typical of Bernini, for, grand showman that he was, he loved to incorporate such effects as light, smoke, or in this case water in his creations. Often he was called upon to plan important public events, such as state funerals or celebrations in honor of the saints.

As a sculptor, Bernini excelled at the portrait bust—the head-and-shoulders likeness in marble of an individual. One of the loveliest of these depicts Costanza Bonarelli, the wife of Bernini's assistant who was also Bernini's mistress. Sometime in the mid-1630s the current pope, Urban VIII, urged the artist to terminate this relationship and take a wife. So in 1639 Bernini, then forty-one years old, married a young woman half his age, Caterina Tezio. The story is told that Bernini felt compelled to give away the portrait bust of Costanza Bonarelli, which until then he had kept in his home. The artist's wife eventually bore him eleven children, nine of whom survived to maturity.

Bernini's fame as an architect and sculptor spread throughout Europe. In 1665 Louis XIV, king of France, summoned the artist to Paris to work on a new design for the Louvre palace. The trip was not a success. Bernini's plan for the Louvre was rejected, and the artist alienated his hosts by expressing his preference for Italian art and contempt for French art. He returned to Rome, where he remained until his death.

One major work did result from Bernini's sojourn in Paris—a splendid portrait bust of Louis carved after Bernini had made numerous sketches of the king going about his daily activities. It was in Paris, too, that the artist reportedly explained the problems of portrait sculpture: "If a man whitened his hair, beard, eyebrows and—were it possible—his eyeballs and lips, and presented himself in this state to those very persons that see him every day, he would hardly be recognized by them. . . . Hence you can understand how difficult it is to make a portrait, which is all of one color, resemble the sitter."[1]

Gianlorenzo Bernini. *Self-Portrait.* c. 1625, Oil on canvas. Galleria Borghese, Rome.

highest rank of angels, who seem to be all on fire. . . . In his hands I saw a great golden spear, and at the iron tip there appeared to be a point of fire. This he plunged into my heart several times so that it penetrated to my entrails. When he pulled it out, I felt that he took them with it, and left me utterly consumed by the great love of God. The pain was so severe that it made me utter several moans. The sweetness caused by this intense pain is so extreme that one cannot possibly wish it to cease. . . . This is not a physical, but a spiritual pain, though the body has some share in it—even a considerable share.

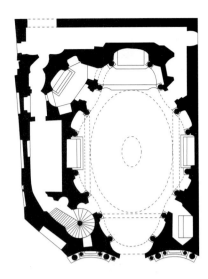

Just as Bernini transformed the chapel itself into a sort of theater complete with sculpted spectators, he has set the drama of Saint Teresa as if on a stage. We can imagine that the curtains have just parted, revealing Teresa in a swoon, ready for another thrust of the angel's spear. She falls backward, yet is lifted up on a cloud, the extreme turbulence of her garments revealing her emotional frenzy. The angel, wielding his spear, has an expression on his face of tenderness and love; in other contexts he might be mistaken for a Cupid. Master of illusions, Bernini has anchored the massive blocks of marble into the wall with iron bars so that the scene appears to float. The gilt bronze rods depicting heavenly rays of light are themselves lit from above by a hidden window: this little stage set has its own lighting. The deeply cut folds of the swirling garments create abrupt contrasts of light and shadow, dissolving solid forms into flamelike flickerings. Standing before the chapel, our experience is also theatrical, for we can both watch the ecstasy and watch people watching the ecstasy; we are both caught up in the performance and aware of it *as* a performance.

One of the great projects of Baroque Rome was the completion of St. Peter's, which had been designed by Michelangelo (see 16.13, 16.14). During the early 17th century, an architect named Carlo Maderno lengthened the nave and created a new facade. Upon Maderno's death, Bernini continued the redecoration of the interior and designed a spectacular colonnade (row of columns) to enclose the vast square in front of the church. Interestingly, Bernini's architecture was more conservative than his sculpture. To fully appreciate the innovative daring of Italian Baroque architecture we do better to turn to his principal rival, Carlo Maderno's nephew Francesco Borromini.

Like the architects of the Renaissance, Borromini worked his designs out logically so that every least detail reflected a guiding idea. But instead of basing his work in the square and the circle, he favored more subtle and dynamic forms such as the oval. Borromini's most influential building is a small church called San Carlo alle Quattro Fontane ("Saint Charles at the Four Fountains"). The domed interior, designed first, takes the form of an oval gently indented to suggest a cross (**17.3**). The resulting walls alternate between convex and concave curves, creating a softly undulating motion and an organic, almost pulsating space. The church became instantly famous, and requests for the plans flooded in from all over Catholic Europe.

The facade (**17.4**), designed twenty-five years later and completed after Borromini's death, carries the logic through to the exterior. Alternating convex and concave elements dominate, their curves describing sections of ovals. The interplay of surfaces is complex. Notice, for example, how the central portion of the facade is convex at the street level but becomes a concave setting for convex elements above, culminating in a framed oval held aloft by two angels that seem to hover in front of the building. The protrusion of the facade forward into the viewer's space is typical of Baroque architecture, as is the buildup of interest in the central portion and the overall sense of plasticity—the sense that a building can be modeled and sculpted almost like clay.

Unlike architecture or sculpture, a painting cannot literally project its figures into the viewer's space. Baroque artists, however, learned to create a similar effect by lighting their figures dramatically and plunging the back-

17.3 (above, top) Plan of San Carlo alle Quattro Fontane.

17.4 (above) Francesco Borromini. Facade of San Carlo alle Quattro Fontane, Rome. 1665–7.

17.5 Artemisia Gentileschi. *Judith and Maidservant with the Head of Holofernes.* c. 1625. Oil on canvas, 6'1½" × 4'7¾".
The Detroit Institute of the Arts.

grounds into shadow. Artemisia Gentileschi used this technique effectively in *Judith and Maidservant with the Head of Holofernes* (**17.5**). The artist took her subject from the biblical story of Judith. According to the scripture, Judith, a pious and beautiful Israelite widow, volunteered to rescue her people from the invading armies of the Assyrian general Holofernes. Judith charmed the general, accepted his invitation to a banquet, waited until he drank himself into a stupor, then calmly beheaded him, wrapped up his head in a sack, and escaped.

Other of Gentileschi's paintings show the decapitation in progress. Here she focuses on the moments after the gory deed is done. She poses Judith tensely, caught in the wavering light from a single candle, one hand still clutching the bloody sword, the other poised in a gesture of silence. These Baroque devices heighten the sense of danger, the urgency of deeds committed in the dark of night.

Gentileschi's dramatic way with light and dark was the influential invention of a painter named Caravaggio. His magnificent *Entombment of Christ* (**17.6**) is an example of the kind of painting that inspired Gentileschi and many other artists. The *Entombment* depicts the crucified Christ being lowered into an open grave. The body is held by two of Christ's followers—his disciple St. John and the Jewish ruler Nicodemus, to whom Christ had counseled that a man must be "born again" to enter Heaven. The group also includes the three Marys—Christ's mother, the Virgin Mary, at left; Mary Magdalene, center; and Mary Cleophas, at right—who look on in despair. Caravaggio's structure is a strong diagonal leading from the upraised hand at top right down through the cluster of figures to Christ's face. The light source seems to be coming from somewhere outside the top left edge of the picture. Light falls on the participants in different ways, but always enhances the sense of drama. Mary Magdalene's face, for example, is almost totally in shadow, but a bright light illuminates her shoulder to create a contrast with the bowed head. Light also catches the pathetic outstretched hand of the Virgin. Christ's body is the only figure lit in its entirety; the others stand in partial darkness.

The perspective of the painting places the viewer's eye level at the slab the grouping stands on. Set on a diagonal, the slab seems to project forward from the picture plane and into our space, involving us in the action. We may imagine ourselves standing in the grave that is about to receive Christ: perhaps this is why Nicodemus looks at us. Caravaggio painted this work to hang over an altar, and the head of a priest standing at the altar would have been at the ideal viewing level, the level of the slab. During the most solemn moment of the mass, the priest holds the communion bread aloft and repeats the words Christ spoke at the Last Supper, "This is my body." The raised bread would have been visibly juxtaposed with the body in the painting, restoring to the words an intense emotional impact.

We might compare Caravaggio's *Entombment* with a work painted just a few years later, *The Raising of the Cross* (**17.7**) by the Flemish artist Peter Paul Rubens. Although he spent most of his life in Antwerp (in modern Belgium), Rubens had traveled to Italy and studied the works of Italian masters, including Caravaggio. There are similarities between these two paintings—in the sharply diagonal composition and dramatic lighting—but we

17.6 (left) Caravaggio. *Entombment of Christ*. 1604. Oil on canvas, 9′9⅛″ × 6′7¾″. Musei Vaticani, Pinacoteca, Rome.

17.7 (right) Peter Paul Rubens. *The Raising of the Cross*. 1609–10. Oil on canvas, 15′2″ × 11′2″. Antwerp Cathedral.

PETER PAUL RUBENS
1577–1640

IN ALL THE history of art, one of the most civilized figures was the Flemish painter Peter Paul Rubens. Rubens was born in the German town of Siegen, but he returned with his mother at the age of ten to her native Antwerp (then in the Spanish-controlled Netherlands, now a city of Belgium) after the death of his father. There he was placed as a page in a wealthy home—a post that seems to have taught him the tact and courtly manners that would serve him well in the years to come. Coupled with these was an innate intelligence and pleasant disposition, all of which contributed to an enormously productive, rewarding life.

Rubens began his art studies in Antwerp. At the age of twenty-two, however, he set out for Italy, where he was to remain for eight years. During this time he traveled widely through all the major cities, studied the works of the great Italian masters, and was employed as court painter by the Duke of Mantua.

When the final illness of Rubens' mother called him home in 1608, the artist fully expected to return to Italy. But several inducements persuaded him to remain in Antwerp, which became his base for the rest of his life. For one thing, he was immediately successful as an artist and found many lucrative commissions. For another, the political and intellectual climate satisfied him. Perhaps most important, Rubens met, fell in love with, and married a young woman of Antwerp, Isabella Brant. This union lasted for seventeen years, produced three children, and was an extremely happy one. Rubens painted their wedding portrait, shown here.

In an atmosphere of domestic fulfillment, Rubens settled down to work. He became court painter to the Archduke Albert and his wife (also named Isabella), who were at the time rulers of the Netherlands. Over many years he also served them as political emissary and diplomat to foreign courts, often being entrusted with the most secret of negotiations. Artistic commissions poured in from all parts of Europe. Rubens was able to fulfill them mainly because he had a well-organized studio and many assistants. For certain large works, Rubens would make preliminary drawings, assistants would execute routine parts of the canvas, and then the master would make corrections and provide finishing touches.

Rubens' personal life took a stunning blow in 1626, when his wife died suddenly. Four years later, however, the artist remarried. His second wife was Hélène Fourment, and at the time of their marriage she was sixteen, Rubens fifty-three. This marriage, too, seems to have been a most successful one and produced five children. It was cut short by the artist's death, at sixty-three, from heart failure caused by gout.

The workshop approach perfected by Rubens occasionally got him into trouble. In 1621 he was forced to write this letter to a dissatisfied client: "I am quite willing that the picture painted for My Lord Ambassador Carleton be returned to me and that I should paint another . . . making rebate as is reasonable for the amount already paid, and the new picture to be entirely by my own hand without admixture of the work of anyone else, which on the word of a gentleman I will carry out."[2]

Peter Paul Rubens. *Self-Portrait with Isabella Brandt.* c. 1609. Oil on canvas, 5'10½" × 4'5½". Alte Pinakothek, Munich.

also find several differences in the two masters' styles. Caravaggio's figures seem almost frozen in a moment of anguish, but Rubens' painting teems with movement and energy, each of the participants balanced precariously and straining at his task. While the Caravaggio group projects from the picture plane, its action is contained on four sides within the frame of the canvas. But Rubens' figures burst outside the picture in several directions, suggesting that the action continues beyond the painting. Rubens' heroic treatment of musculature recalls Michelangelo's paintings on the Sistine Chapel ceiling (see 16.11), but the writhing *S*-curve of Christ's body is typically Baroque.

While Baroque artistic principles were taken up across Europe, each country developed them in its own way. France, for example, favored a more restrained, "classical" version of Baroque style in which the order and balance of the Renaissance were retained, though infused with a new theatricality and grandeur.

Foremost among French painters of the 17th century was Nicolas Poussin, who actually spent most of his career in Rome. Steeped in the philosophy and history of the Classical past, he came to believe that art's highest purpose was to represent noble and serious human actions. An example is his painting *The Ashes of Phokion* (**17.8**). Phokion was a famous Athenian general of the 4th century B.C.E. In his old age, he was unjustly accused of treason, tried, and sentenced to death. The cremation or burial of his remains was outlawed. His friends and supporters dared not defy the court to accord him an honorable funeral. Only his widow did not desert him, arranging for cremation and performing the rites herself. She is shown here gathering up her husband's ashes outside of the city walls. Her virtuous act was much admired by the ancient Roman Stoic philosophers, who taught that virtue was the only good, vice the only evil, and that the triumphs and sufferings of life were to be accepted calmly and without passion.

Poussin's visual response to this story and its Stoic setting inspired a composition that is far removed from the emotionalism of Caravaggio or the energy of Rubens. In place of their active diagonals, calm verticals and hor-

17.8 Nicolas Poussin. *The Ashes of Phokion.* 1648. Oil on canvas, 3′9¾″ × 5′9¼″
Walker Art Gallery, Liverpool.

izontals dominate. Only the manipulation of light marks the painting as Baroque. Zones of light and shadow alternate across the canvas, and the white of the widow's clothing is lit as if with a spotlight, drawing our attention to the principal actor on this vast stage. In the foreground, wind-tossed trees watch over Phokion's widow and her anxious servant. The trees are linked by visual rhymes to the mountain and clouds in the distance, emphasizing that her courageous act answers to a higher law than that of the city: the natural law of instinct.

To grasp fully the flavor of the Baroque in France, we should look at a king who for all time exemplifies the term "absolute monarch"—Louis XIV. Louis ascended the throne of France in 1643, at the age of four. He assumed total control of the government in 1661 and reigned, in all, for seventy-two years. During that time he made France the artistic and literary center of Europe, as well as a political force to be reckoned with. Showing the unerring instincts of a master actor, he created an aura around his own person that bolstered the impression of divinity. Each day, for example, two ceremonies took place. In the morning half the court would file into Louis' chambers, in full pageantry, to participate in the king's *lever*—the king's "getting up." At night the same cast of characters arrived to play ritual roles in the king's *coucher*—his "going to bed."

A life in which the simple act of climbing in and out of bed required elaborate ceremony surely also needed an appropriate setting, and Louis did not neglect this matter. He summoned Bernini from Rome to Paris to work on completion of the Louvre palace (although the final design of the building was the work of others). But Louis' real love was the Palace of Versailles, in a suburb of the capital, which he substantially rebuilt and to which he moved his court in 1682. It was from this remarkable structure that the power of kingship flowed forth.

17.9 Louis Le Vau and Jules Hardouin Mansart. Central portion of the garden (west) facade, Palace of Versailles. 1669–85.

In all, Versailles occupies an area of about 200 acres, including the extensive formal gardens and several grand châteaux. The palace itself, redesigned and enlarged during Louis' reign, is an immense structure, more than a quarter of a mile wide (**17.9**). The illustration here shows the central portion of the west facade, which overlooks the gardens and houses the royal apartments. Baroque style is evident in the way the facade occasionally breaks forward and in the way interest gathers toward its center, but these effects are realized in a very understated way.

If the exterior of the palace reflects the continuing classical tendencies of France, the interior revels in full Baroque splendor. As in Bernini's Cornaro Chapel, though on a much grander scale, architecture, sculpture, and painting are united, creating a series of lavish settings for the pageantry of Louis XIV and his court. Of the countless rooms inside, the most famous is the Hall of Mirrors (**17.10**), 240 feet long and lined with large reflective glasses. In Louis' time the Hall of Mirrors was used for the most elaborate state occasions, and even in our own century it has served as the backdrop for momentous events. The treaty ending World War I was signed in the Hall of Mirrors.

The French court clearly was a model of pomp and pageantry, and the Spanish court to the south was eager to emulate that model. King Philip IV of Spain reigned for a shorter time than his French counterpart and could not begin to match Louis in either power or ability. Philip had one asset, however, that Louis never quite managed to acquire—a court painter of the first rank. That painter was one of the geniuses of Spanish art—Diego Velázquez.

17.10 Jules Hardouin Mansart and Charles Le Brun. Hall of Mirrors, Palace of Versailles. c. 1680.

In his capacity as court painter Velázquez created his masterpiece, *Las Meninas (The Maids of Honor)* (**17.11**). At left we see the artist, working on a very large canvas, but we can only guess at the subject he is painting. Perhaps it is the young princess, the *infanta*, who stands regally at center surrounded by her attendants *(meninas)*, one of whom is a dwarf. Or perhaps Velázquez is actually painting the king and queen, whom we see reflected in a mirror on the far wall. Their participation is clear, but where are they standing? Possibly they are outside the picture, standing next to us, the observers. This ambiguity is part of the picture's fascination, as is the dual nature of the scene. Although it shows a formal occasion, the painting of an official portrait, Velázquez has given the scene a warm, "everyday" quality.

Like Caravaggio, Velázquez uses light to create drama and emphasis, but light also serves here to organize and unify a complex space. The major light source comes from outside the top right corner of the painting, falling most brilliantly on the *infanta*, leaving the others in various degrees of shadow. Another light source illuminates the mysterious figure in the open doorway at back. Velázquez may have put him there to direct attention to the reflected images of the king and queen. Light also strikes the artist's face and the mirror reflection. What could have been a very disorderly scene has been pulled together by the device of spotlighting, much as a designer of stage lighting would control what the audience sees. The theatricality of the Baroque is more subtle in Velázquez than in Bernini, but it is no less skillful.

To end this discussion of 17th-century art, we move north, to the Netherlands. The Dutch Baroque, sometimes called the "bourgeois Baroque," is quite different from Baroque movements in France, Spain, and Italy. In the North, Protestantism was the dominant religion, and the outward symbols of faith—imagery, ornate churches, and clerical pageantry—were far

17.11 Diego Velázquez. *Las Meninas (The Maids of Honor)*. 1656. Oil on canvas, 10'5¼" × 9'¾". Museo del Prado, Madrid.

less important. Dutch society, and particularly the wealthy merchant class, centered not on the church but instead on the home and family, business and social organizations, the community. We see this focus in the work of two Dutch artists with very different styles—Rembrandt and Judith Leyster.

Rembrandt's principal teacher, a painter named Lastman, had traveled in his youth to Italy, where he had come under the influence of Caravaggio. Returning to the Netherlands to establish his career, he brought with him the new kind of dramatic lighting that Caravaggio had invented. We can see how Rembrandt incorporated this lighting into his own personal style in the famous group portrait *Sortie of Captain Banning Cocq's Company of the Civic Guard* (**17.12**).

The painting portrays a kind of private elite militia. Such groups had played a prominent role in defending the city during the recent wars against Spanish domination, and while by Rembrandt's time their function was largely ceremonial, they were still widely respected, and all the most important men of the town belonged to one. Dutch civic organizations often commissioned group portraits, and painters usually responded by portraying the members seated around a table or lined up for the 17th-century equivalent of a class photograph. Rembrandt's innovation was to paint individual portraits within the context of a larger activity, a call to arms. He groups the figures naturally, in deep space, with Captain Cocq, resplendent in a red sash, at the center. The composition builds on a series of broad *V*-shapes, pointing upward and outward. The nested *V*-shapes make the picture seem to burst out from its core—and may have made its subjects feel they were charging off heroically in all directions, into battle. Lest this geometric structure seem rigid, Rembrandt has "sculpted" it into greater naturalness through his dramatic lighting of the scene. Light picks out certain individuals: Cap-

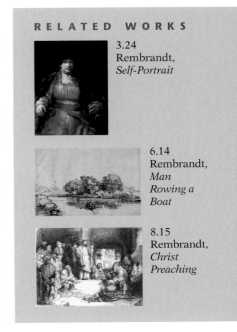

3.24
Rembrandt,
Self-Portrait

6.14
Rembrandt,
*Man
Rowing a
Boat*

8.15
Rembrandt,
*Christ
Preaching*

17.12 Rembrandt. *Sortie of Captain Banning Cocq's Company of the Civic Guard (The Night Watch).* 1642. Oil on canvas, 12′2″ × 17′7″. Rijksmuseum, Amsterdam.

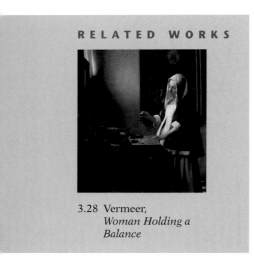

3.28 Vermeer,
*Woman Holding a
Balance*

tain Cocq himself; the drummer at far right; the lieutenant at Cocq's side, awaiting orders; and especially the little girl in a golden dress, whose identity and role in the picture remain a mystery.

For many years Rembrandt's painting was known as *The Night Watch*, and it is still informally called by that name. The reason has nothing to do with the artist's intent. A heavy layer of varnish on top of the oil paint combined with smoke from a nearby fireplace had gradually darkened the picture's surface until it seemed to portray a nighttime scene. No one alive could remember it any differently. It was only when the work was cleaned in the mid-20th century that the light-filled painting we know today reemerged. Even now, though, some members of the group can be seen more clearly than others, and viewers have often wondered how this could have been acceptable to the militia. Documents have revealed that each member contributed to the commission according to how prominently he would appear in the finished painting, and history records no complaints about the results.

Baroque light is also a prominent feature in works by Rembrandt's contemporary Judith Leyster. The 17th century was the great age of Dutch **genre** painting—painting that focused on scenes of everyday life—and during her lifetime Leyster was highly regarded as a genre painter. After her death, however, she was virtually forgotten. Paintings from her hand made their way into important collections and museums, but many seem to have been attributed to another (in our time, far better known) Dutch painter, Frans Hals. Leyster's disappearance from art history prevailed for some two centuries. Then, in 1893, a Dutch art historian who had just sold a "Hals" to the Louvre museum in Paris discovered Leyster's distinctive monogram on the canvas. Since then, other works by "Hals" have been reattributed to Leyster.

17.13 Judith Leyster. *The Proposition*. 1631. Oil on canvas, 11⅞ × 9½″.
Mauritshuis, The Hague.

17.14 Jacob van Ruisdael. *View of Ootmarsum.* 1628/29–82. Oil on canvas, 23¼ × 28⅞". Alte Pinakothek, Munich.

The Proposition (**17.13**), a genre painting from 1631, shows Leyster's mature style at its best. A young woman sits quietly, intent on her sewing. Behind her shoulder looms a crude, rough-looking man who offers her gold coins to buy her sexual favors. The man's left hand rests possessively on the woman's arm, but she does not look up from her work. One can almost hear her thinking, "If I ignore him, he will go away. *Please* go away!" Typically, the artist has placed a candle in a strategic position to light this scene. Light shines on the woman's face and casts a sheen on her smooth forehead. Her white blouse, surely a symbol of purity and virginity, is brightly illuminated. The lustful man, however, lurks in the gloom outside the candle's glow, and his shadow is thrown menacingly on the wall behind him. For this painting, then, Leyster manipulates light to show the sharpest of polarities: good versus evil.

The 17th century was also a great period for landscape painting in the Netherlands. Typical of Dutch landscape painting was the work of Jacob van Ruisdael. Van Ruisdael's *Extensive Landscape with a View of the Town of Ootmarsum* (**17.14**) shows not only the famed flatness of the Dutch landscape, but also the artist's reaction to that flatness as an expression of the immense, limitless grandeur of nature. The artist makes a contrast between the land—where human order has been established in the form of buildings and cultivation—and the sky, with its billowing clouds, yielding to the wind, which mere people can never tame. The horizon line is set quite low, and, significantly, only the church steeple rises up in silhouette against the sky, perhaps symbolizing that humankind's one connection with the majesty of nature is through the church.

Despite this emphasis on the church building, Van Ruisdael's art is essentially secular, as is that of Leyster and Rembrandt. Although religious subjects continued to appear in art—and do so even now—never again would religious art dominate as it did in the Renaissance and Italian Baroque periods. No doubt this is largely because of the change in sponsorship; popes and cardinals became less important as patrons, while kings, wealthy merchants, and the bourgeoisie became more so. We can follow this increasing secularization of art as we move out of the 17th century into the 18th.

RELATED WORKS

4.9 Watteau, *Pilgrimage to Cythera*

11.3 Clodion, *Satyr and Bacchante*

THE 18TH CENTURY

The first half to three-quarters of the 18th century is often thought of as the age of **Rococo**—a development and extension of the Baroque style. The term "rococo" was a play on the word "baroque," but it also refers to the French words for "rocks" and "shells," forms that appeared as decorative motifs in architecture, furniture, and occasionally in painting. Like the Baroque, Rococo is an extravagant, ornate style, but there are several points of contrast. Baroque, especially in the South, was an art of cathedrals and palaces; Rococo is more intimate, suitable for the aristocratic home and the drawing room. Baroque colors are intense; Rococo leans more toward the gentle pastels. Baroque is large in scale, massive, dramatic; Rococo has a smaller scale and a lighthearted, playful quality.

The Rococo style of architecture originated in France but was soon exported. We find some of the most developed examples in Germany, especially in Bavaria. The Mirror Room of the Amalienburg, a little house in Nymphenburg Park near Munich (**17.15**), demonstrates amply why the word "rococo" has come to mean "elaborate and profuse." Designed by a Frenchman, François Cuvillies the Elder, the Mirror Room is a perfect riot of sinuous, twisting, almost visibly *growing* decorative forms. The line between walls and ceiling has been obscured deliberately to create the illusion of "sky" above the room. Large arched mirrors multiply the effect of playful design everywhere the eye might focus. Rococo was above all a sophisticated style, and the Amalienburg shows us the height of that sophistication.

Sophistication was paramount in painting as well. In Chapter 4 we looked at *Pilgrimage to Cythera* by Jean-Antoine Watteau (see 4.9). Painted in 1717, it stands at the very beginning of the Rococo style. The dreamlike world Watteau invented must have appealed to French aristocrats weary of the formal grandeur of Versailles and the ceremonial character of daily life there. Even the new king, Louis XV, seems to have found his role exhausting, for he created within the palace a modest apartment that he could escape to and live, if only for a few hours, like a simple (if rather well off) gentleman.

Just over half a century later, the aging king's mistress, the Countess du Barry, commissioned one of the last masterpieces of Rococo art, a set of four large paintings by Jean-Honoré Fragonard called *The Progress of Love*, of which we illustrate *The Pursuit* (**17.16**). Through a lushly overgrown garden on the grounds of some imaginary estate, an ardent youth chases after the girl who has captured his heart. He holds out to her a single flower, plucked from the abundance that surrounds them. She, surprised while sitting with her friends, flees, but so prettily that we know it is all a game. She will surely

17.16 Jean-Honoré Fragonard. *The Pursuit*, from *The Progress of Love*. 1771–73, 1790–91. Oil on canvas, height approx. 10′5″. The Frick Collection, New York.

not run *too* fast. Above, a statue of two cupids seems to participate, watching over this latest demonstration of their powers to see how it will all turn out.

Madame du Barry had commissioned the paintings to decorate a new pavilion she had just had built on her estate. But while Fragonard never painted a lovelier set of works, his patron rejected them. She considered them too old fashioned and sentimental. Rococo taste had run its course. Seriousness was now in vogue, together with an artistic style called Neoclassicism ("new classicism"). Since 1748, excavations at the Roman sites of Pompeii and Herculaneum in Italy had been uncovering wonders such as the wall paintings we looked at in Chapter 14 (see 14.32). Patrons and artists across Europe were newly fascinated by the Classical past, and their interest was encouraged by rulers and social thinkers hoping to foster civic virtues such as patriotism, stoicism, self-sacrifice, and frugality—virtues they associated with the Roman Republic.

Among the many young artists who flocked to Italy to absorb the influence at first hand was a young painter named Jacques-Louis David. Upon his return to France, David quickly established himself as an artist of great potential, and it was none other than the new king, Louis XVI, who commissioned his first resounding critical success, *The Oath of the Horatii* (**17.17**).

17.17 Jacques-Louis David. *The Oath of the Horatii.* 1784–5. Oil on canvas, approx 11 × 14'. Musée du Louvre, Paris.

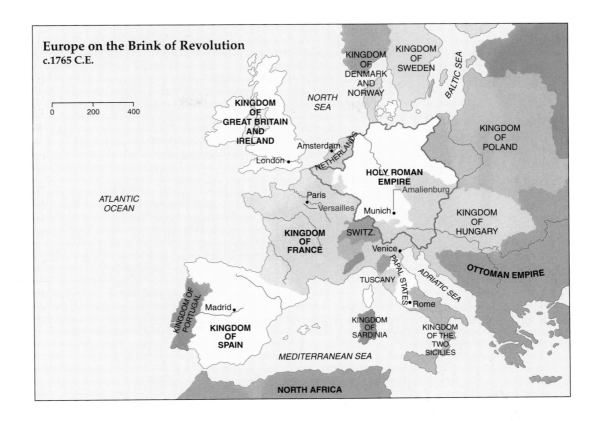

Europe on the Brink of Revolution
c.1765 C.E.

The painting depicts the stirring moment when three Roman brothers, the Horatii of the painting's title, swear before their father to fight to the death three brothers from the enemy camp, the Curiatii, thus sacrificing themselves to spare their fellow citizens an all-out war. The subject combines great patriotism with great pathos, for as David's audience would have known, one of the Horatii was married to a sister of the Curiatii, and one of the Curiatii was engaged to a sister of the Horatii. David paints these two women at the right. They are overcome with emotion, knowing that tragedy is the only possible outcome. In fact, of the six brothers, only one, one of the Horatii, will survive the bloody combat. Arriving home, he finds his sister in mourning for her slain fiancé. Outraged at her sorrow, he kills her.

Gone are the lush gardens and pastel colors of the Rococo. In their place, David has conceived an austere architectural setting beyond which there is merely darkness. Spread across the shallow foreground space, the dramatically lit figures are portrayed in profile as though carved in relief. The creamy brush strokes and hazy atmosphere of Fragonard have given way to a smooth finish and a cool, clear light. Colors are muted except for the father's tunic, which flows like a river of blood next to the three gleaming swords.

Along with the stern "Roman family values" promoted by Neoclassicism, the late 18th century was under the spell of a new taste for simplicity and naturalness. One of the people most taken by the new informality was Louis XVI's queen, Marie-Antoinette. Another advocate of all that was unaffected was the queen's favorite portrait painter, Elisabeth Vigée-Lebrun. Inspired in part by the spareness of classical costume (note the women in David's painting) and in part by an ideal of the "innocent country girl," Vigée-Lebrun coaxed her highborn models into posing in airy white muslin dresses, their hair falling loosely about their shoulders, a straw bonnet tied with a satin ribbon on their head, and a flower or two in their hands.

The image confirmed the public's worst suspicions: their queen was frivolous and flirtatious. In an attempt to repair the queen's reputation, Vigée-Lebrun was asked to paint a different sort of portrait, *Marie-Antoinette and*

17.18 Elisabeth Vigée-Lebrun. *Marie-Antoinette and Her Children.* 1787. Oil on canvas, 8'8" × 6'10". Palace of Versailles, France.

Her Children (**17.18**). Here, Marie-Antoinette is portrayed as a devoted and beloved mother. She is a woman who knows that her place is in the home, not meddling in politics or advertising her charms. In a gesture meant to tug at viewers' heartstrings, her elder son, the heir to the throne, draws our attention to an empty cradle; his youngest sibling had recently died in infancy. The queen's formal velvet gown and the glimpse of the fabled Hall of Mirrors in the background are meant to convey that she is aware of the seriousness of her position and fully capable of the quiet dignity needed to fulfill it.

It was too late. Far too much damage had already been done for a single painting to repair. The nation was teetering on the brink of financial disaster. Popular opinion blamed the deficit on the queen's extravagant ways and suspected her as well of shocking personal vices. Vigée-Lebrun herself tells us that when the large canvas was carried into the palace, she heard angry voices crying, "There is the deficit."

Although Vigée-Lebrun later made several copies of her own portraits of the queen, she never again painted Marie-Antoinette from life. Within two years revolution had swept the country, ultimately destroying the monarchy and the aristocracy. The artist fled and took refuge outside France. The queen died by the guillotine.

ELISABETH VIGÉE-LEBRUN
1755–1842

F ROM HER SELF-PORTRAIT she gazes directly at us, her viewers—calm, self-possessed, sure of her talent, sure of her place in the world. Her brush is poised over the canvas; we have momentarily interrupted her work on a portrait of her great patron, the Queen of France. She will not be interrupted for long. Throughout her remarkable life, Elisabeth Vigée-Lebrun knew where she was going and remained steadfast on that path.

Born in Paris, the daughter of a portrait painter, Elisabeth Vigée was convent-educated and encouraged from an early age to draw and paint. At eleven she began serious art studies. After her father's untimely death, Elisabeth resolved to work as a painter, and by age fifteen she was her family's chief financial support. Patrons flocked to her studio, eager to have their portraits done by the young artist, and her fees multiplied.

One dark spot was her mother's remarriage, to a man who seems mainly to have coveted his stepdaughter's income. Because of this unpleasant circumstance, Elisabeth made the one real mistake of her life. Although she "felt no manner of inclination for matrimony," she succumbed to her mother's urgings and accepted the proposal of Jean-Baptiste-Pierre Lebrun, hoping "to escape from the torture of living with my stepfather." Alas for the twenty-year-old artist, she had merely "exchanged present troubles for others." Lebrun was "quite an agreeable person," but, his wife soon discovered, "his furious passion for gambling was at the bottom of the ruin of his fortune and my own." The happiest result of the union was Vigée-Lebrun's only child, her daughter Julie.

Neither marriage nor motherhood interfered with the artist's burgeoning career and social life. By all evidence she was lovely, witty, charming, and perfectly at home in any company. Quite independent of her husband, she entertained a growing circle of aristocratic friends, many of whom commissioned portraits. In 1779 a summons came from the Palace of Versailles. Marie-Antoinette sought her services, and Vigée-Lebrun made the first of some twenty portraits of the queen. The two women became friends—a splendid advantage for the artist initially, but a dangerous liability as resentment of the monarchy grew. When revolution came in 1789, Vigée-Lebrun fled the country, taking Julie with her. Lebrun was left behind forever.

Then commenced Vigée-Lebrun's twelve years of "exile" from France. And what an exile it was! She traveled first to Rome and Vienna, then to St. Petersburg and Moscow, spending six years altogether in czarist Russia. Wherever she went she was treated like visiting royalty, entertained lavishly, invited to join the local painters' Academy. Wherever she went she was overwhelmed with portrait commissions. Kings and queens, princesses, counts, duchesses—she painted them all, in between the elaborate dinners and balls to which they invited her. In her memoirs she tells us she missed painting Catherine the Great because the empress died just before the first scheduled sitting.

In 1801, the furies of the revolution having abated, Vigée-Lebrun returned to Paris. She had not, however, quite satisfied her urge to travel. Only after a three-year stay in London and two visits to Switzerland did she finally settle down to write her memoirs and paint the survivors of the French nobility. She died in her eighty-seventh year, having painted more than 660 portraits. Her memoirs conclude with these words: "I hope to end peacefully a wandering and even a laborious but honest life."[3] And she did.

Elisabeth Vigée-Lebrun, *Self-Portrait at the Easel*. c. 1789. Oil on canvas. Galleria degli Uffizi, Florence.

REVOLUTION

The leaders of the French Revolution continued to evoke the example of Rome and to admire Roman civic virtues. Neoclassicism became the official style of the Revolution and Jacques-Louis David its official artist. David served the Revolution as propaganda minister and director of festivals. As a deputy to the Convention of 1792 he was among those who voted to send his former patron Louis XVI to the guillotine. One of the events orchestrated by David was the funeral of the revolutionary leader Jean-Paul Marat. David staged the exhibition of Marat's embalmed cadaver to the public, and he memorialized the leader's death in what has become his most famous painting, *The Death of Marat* (**17.19**).

A major figure in the Revolution, Jean-Paul Marat pursued the goal of wiping out France's greedy and corrupt aristocracy. He was responsible for the execution by guillotine of hundreds of people. Because of a painful skin ailment Marat spent his days in the bathtub, which was fitted out with a writing desk so he could work, and there he received callers. A woman named Charlotte Corday, incensed by Marat's excesses with the guillotine, gained entry to his apartment and stabbed him to death.

In lesser hands Marat's demise could have been laughable—a naked man murdered in his tub by a furious woman caller. But David has invested the event with all the pathos and dignity of Christ being lowered into his

17.19 (left) Jacques-Louis David. *The Death of Marat.* 1793. Oil on canvas, 5′5″ × 4′2½″. Musée Royaux des Beaux-Arts de Belgique, Brussels.

17.20 (right) John Singleton Copley. *Paul Revere.* 1768–70. Oil on canvas, 35 × 28½″. Courtesy Museum of Fine Arts, Boston.

tomb. (Compare Caravaggio's *Entombment*, 17.6.) Marat is shown, in effect, as a kind of secular Christ martyred for the Revolution. All the forms are concentrated in the lower half of the composition, and light bathes the fallen leader in an unearthly glow, both of these devices contributing to the sense of tragedy. Marat's face and body could be those of a fallen Greek warrior, sculpted in marble by an ancient master. David's purpose in this work was to transform a man whom many considered Satan himself into a sainted hero. He projected the image the leaders of the Revolution wished to have of themselves, just as Vigée-Lebrun's art had projected the image desired by the French monarchs.

Two other revolutions occurred at more or less the same time as that in France. One was the American Revolution, preceding the French by thirteen years. During the relatively brief period covered by this chapter, the American colonists had progressed from the "starving time" of Jamestown to a nation of people capable of independence and self-government. During that time also the area that was to become the United States had developed its own artistic styles. And by the eve of the Revolution the colonies had their own master artist, born on home soil—John Singleton Copley.

Born in Boston, Copley grew up in the home of his stepfather, the artist Peter Pelham, whose portrait of *Cotton Mather* we saw in Chapter 8 (see 8.14). Copley would paint many people who later became heroes of the Revolution, including *Paul Revere* (**17.20**). Legend and poetry have preserved the image of Paul Revere taking his "midnight ride" on horseback, from Boston to Concord, to warn his fellow colonists that "the British are coming!" In his day, however, Revere was better known as a silversmith. The artist poses him with a silver teapot in one hand, the tools of his trade scattered elegantly on the table.

Copley's portrait is in much the same Neoclassical style as David's tribute to Marat. The subject sits quietly behind his table, gazing straight toward us. We as viewers might be seated just opposite him. Although he is dressed informally, Revere shows great dignity and an obvious pride in his work. Copley has rendered his subject's features, the garments, and the polished tabletop with wonderful fidelity. We sense fullness, a three-dimensional volume, in the body and especially in the hand clasping the teapot.

The third revolution of this time was not a political uprising but an economic and social upheaval. Many would argue that the Industrial Revolution, which began slowly in the last half of the 18th century, is still going on.

It is difficult to overestimate the impact—social, economic, and ultimately political—of the change from labor done by hand to labor done by machine. Within the space of a few decades the machine drastically altered a way of life that had prevailed for millennia. People who had formerly worked in their homes or on farms suddenly were herded together in factories, creating a new social class—the industrial worker. Fortunes were made virtually overnight by members of another new class—the manufacturers. Naturally, all this upheaval was reflected in art. At the beginning of the 19th century, then, Western civilization faced a totally new world.

CHAPTER 18

Arts of Islam and of Africa

The ancient civilizations discussed in Chapter 14 culminated with the growth of the Roman Empire, which by 100 C.E. encompassed the entire Mediterranean region. Chapter 15 saw the empire divided into eastern and western halves after the death of the emperor Constantine. The eastern portion continued for a time as Byzantium. The western portion, after an unstable period, emerged as Europe, which we left in the last chapter on the brink of our own modern age. But what of the Roman lands along the southern shores of the Mediterranean, the lands of North Africa, Egypt, the Near East, and Mesopotamia? The answer is the religious culture of Islam, and thus it is with Islam that our brief exploration of artistic traditions beyond the West begins. (The story of Western art resumes with Chapter 21.)

ARTS OF ISLAM

Islam arose during the early 7th century C.E. on the Arabian Peninsula. There, according to Islamic belief, God—who had spoken through such prophets as Abraham, Moses, and Jesus—spoke directly to humanity for the last time. Through the angel Gabriel, He revealed His word to the Prophet Muhammad. Stunned by the revelations, Muhammad began to preach. At the heart of his message was *islam*, Arabic for "submission," meaning submission to God. Those who accepted Muhammad's teachings were called Muslims, "those who submit." Collected and set in order after his death, the revelations Muhammad recited make up the Qur'an ("recitation"), the holy book of Islam.

In 622, Muhammad emigrated from the city of Mecca northward to the city of Medina. Known as the *hijra*, this move marks the year 1 in the Islamic calendar, the beginning of a new era. Muhammad became a political leader in Medina as well as a spiritual one, and much of the Arabian Peninsula was brought into the Islamic community. After Muhammad's death in 632, his successors led Arab armies to victory after victory, and by the middle of the 8th century, Islamic rule extended from Spain and Morocco in the west to the borders of India in the east.

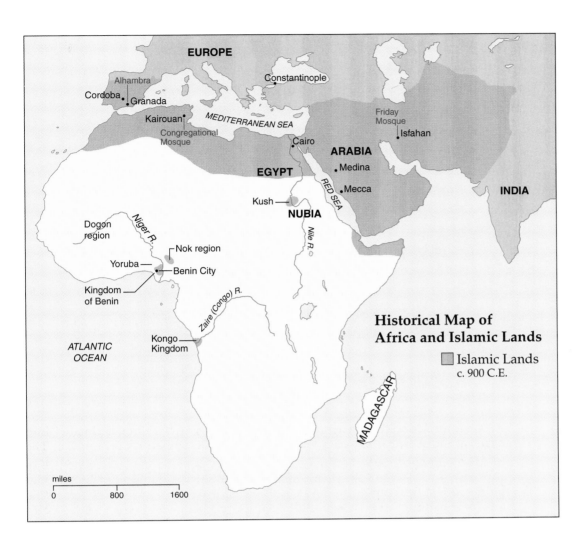

Historical Map of Africa and Islamic Lands

Islamic Lands
c. 900 C.E.

Islam transformed the Arab peoples from a collection of warring tribes with a largely oral culture to a people united by faith, anchored by the written word, and sovereign over vast territories. These new conditions nurtured the growth of a new artistic culture. The need for places to worship and palaces for rulers inspired works of monumental architecture; the establishment of princely courts supported the production of luxury arts such as fine textiles and ceramics; and the centrality of the Qur'an led to a flowering of book arts, including calligraphy and illustration. Wherever Islam extended its influence, local artistic traditions were transformed by Islamic patronage. At the same time, converts from many lands transformed Islam itself into a true world religion. From its beginnings as an Arab faith, Islam became a spiritual and intellectual environment in which many cultures have thrived.

ARCHITECTURE: MOSQUES AND PALACES

One of the first requirements of Islamic rulers in new lands was a suitable place for congregational prayer, a mosque (from the Arabic *masjid*, "place for bowing down"). Early Islamic architects drew their inspiration from descriptions of the Prophet's house in Medina. Like most houses in Arabia, Muhammad's residence was built of sun-dried brick around a central courtyard. An open porch made of palm trunks supporting a roof of palm fronds ran along one wall, providing shade and shelter. There the Prophet had preached to the gathered faithful.

18.1 Congregational Mosque, Kairouan. 836 and later.

The Congregational Mosque at Kairouan, in Tunisia, shows how these elements were translated into monumental form (**18.1**). The shaded porch of Muhammad's house became a large prayer hall (the covered structure to the left). Just as the roof of Muhammad's porch was supported by rows of palm trunks, the roof of the hall is supported inside by rows of columns. The courtyard before the prayer hall is lined with covered arcades (rows of arches). Over the entry to the courtyard rises a large, square tower called a minaret. From its height a crier calls the faithful to prayer five times a day.

Two domes visible on the roof mark the prayer hall's center aisle. A worshiper entering from the courtyard and walking up this aisle would be walking toward the *mihrab*, an empty niche set into the far wall. This is the *qibla* wall, which indicates the direction of Mecca. Muhammad told his followers to face Mecca during prayer, and all mosques, no matter where in the world, are oriented toward that city. Inside every mosque, a *mihrab* marks the *qibla* wall, the wall Muslims face during prayer.

The minaret of the Kairouan Mosque was modeled on a Roman lighthouse, and the mosque's vocabulary of column, arch, and dome is based in Roman and Byzantine architecture. Cultural exchange between Islam and Byzantium can be seen again in the Great Mosque at Córdoba, in Spain. We looked at the interior of the prayer hall of this mosque in Chapter 3 (see 3.4). The illustration here shows the dome before the *mihrab* (**18.2**). Eight intersecting arches rising from an octagonal base lift a fluted, melon-shaped dome over the hall below. Light entering through windows opened up by the arches plays over the glittering gold mosaics that cover the interior. Gold mosaics may remind you of Byzantine churches (see 15.8). In fact, the 10th-century ruler who commissioned the mosaics sent an ambassador to the Byzantine emperor requesting a master artisan to oversee the work. The emperor reportedly sent him not only the artisan but also a gift of 35,000 pounds of mosaic cubes.

Whereas the mosaics in a Byzantine church might depict Jesus, Mary, and saints, the mosaics here do not portray any people, much less God Himself. The Qur'an contains a stern warning against the worship of idols, and in time this led to a doctrine forbidding images of animate beings in religious contexts. As a result, artists working for Islamic patrons poured their genius into decorative geometric patterns and stylized plant forms—curving tendrils, stems, foliage, and flowers. Arabic script, too, became an important element of decoration. A passage from the Qur'an appears here in an octagonal band over the arches.

To the east, Islamic civilization was colored by the culture of Persia (present-day Iran), which had been Byzantium's great rival before its empire fell to Arab armies. During the 12th century, Persian architecture inspired a new form of mosque, illustrated here by one of the earliest and most influential examples, the Friday Mosque at Isfahan, in Iran (**18.3**). The photograph shows the view from the entrance to the courtyard. Directly ahead is a large vaulted chamber whose pointed-arch opening is set in a rectangular frame. This is an *iwan*, a form that served to mark the entry to a royal reception hall in Persian palaces.

Each side of the mosque's courtyard is set with an *iwan*. This four-*iwan* plan became standard in Persia, and its influence extended west to Egypt and east into Central Asia and India. The Taj Mahal in India, for example, is based in Persian architectural forms, and each of its four facades is set with an *iwan* (see 13.18). Our photograph of the Friday Mosque at Isfahan was taken from the shade of the entry *iwan*, whose great pointed arch frames the view. Across the courtyard is the *qibla iwan*, oriented toward Mecca. Two slender minarets rise over its corners. The *qibla iwan* serves as a prayer hall, while the other three *iwans* are used as places for study, rest, or schooling. In back of the *qibla iwan* is a large domed chamber. Constructed for the private prayers of the ruler and his court, the domed chamber contains the *mihrab*.

The interior of the *qibla iwan* seems to be formed of triangular scoops as though it had been hollowed out by a giant spoon. Added during the 14th century, these niche-like scoops, *muqarnas*, are one of the most characteristic of Islamic architectural ornaments. They appear in more typical form in the stunning entryway to the 17th-century Shah Mosque, also in Isfahan

RELATED WORKS

3.4
Interior,
Great
Mosque,
Córdoba

18.2 (left) Dome in front of the *mihrab*, Great Mosque, Córdoba. c. 965. Mosaic.

18.3 (right) *Qibla iwan*, Friday Mosque, Isfahan. Rebuilt after 1121–22 (with later work).

18.4 (left) Entry portal, Shah Mosque, Isfahan. 1611–66.

18.5 (right) Court of the Lions, Alhambra palace, Granada. Mid-14th century.

(**18.4**). Cascading downward from a sunburst motif at the top of the pointed arch, the tiers of clustered *muqarnas* seem to multiply into infinity, like honeycomb or stalactites.

The blue glazed tile mosaic that blankets every surface of the entryway was a specialty of Persian artists. Glazed tile had been used to decorate buildings in the region since the ancient civilizations of Mesopotamia (see 14.9). An inscription flows around the perimeter of the frame, brilliant white on a deep blue ground; another band of calligraphy appears beneath the *muqarnas*. The rest is patterned in stylized flowering plants. Like the *muqarnas*, the patterns seem to multiply into infinity, as though a garden with blossoms as numerous as the stars had spread itself like a carpet over the building.

After roughly a century of unity under Arab leadership, Islamic lands were ruled by regional dynasties, and Arab dynasties took their place alongside dynasties founded by African, Persian, Turkish, and Central Asian groups. Little survives of the sumptuous palaces built for these rulers, for palaces were commonly destroyed or abandoned when a dynasty fell from power. A rare exception is the Alhambra, in Granada, Spain. Constructed largely during the 14th century under the Nasrid dynasty, the Alhambra was a royal city of gardens, palaces, mosques, baths, and quarters for artisans, all built within the protective walls of an older hilltop fortress. From the outside, the Alhambra looks every inch the forbidding fortress it began as. Once inside, however, visitors find themselves in a sheltered world of surpassing delicacy and refinement (**18.5**).

The Court of the Lions, shown here, takes its name from the stone lions supporting the fountain at its center. Water brought from a distant hill flows through the Alhambra in hidden channels, surfacing in fountains and pools. Indoor and outdoor spaces also flow into each other through open entryways, porches, and pavilions. Here, stucco screens carved in lacy openwork patterns and "fringed" with *muqarnas* are poised on slender columns, allowing light and air to filter through. The Nasrids were to be the last Islamic dynasty in Spain. Christian kings had already reclaimed most of the peninsula, and in 1492 Granada fell to Christian armies as well, ending almost 800 years of Islamic presence in western Europe.

BOOK ARTS

Writing out the Qur'an—which Islamic scholars commonly memorize—is viewed as an act of prayer. Calligraphy thus became the most highly regarded art in Islamic lands, and great calligraphers achieved the renown Europeans accorded to painters and sculptors. As a religious text, the Qur'an was never illustrated with images of animate beings. Instead, artists ornamented manuscripts with geometric patterns and stylized plant forms, just as they did mosques. An example is this left portion of a double frontispiece (pair of facing pages before the first page of text) from a seven-volume copy of the Qur'an produced in Cairo in the early 14th century (**18.6**). The number of the volume is written in white on a blue starburst medallion created by an ingeniously interlocking gold lattice pattern. Sinuous plant forms fill the medallion and ornament the carpet-like ground beneath the lattice's gold frame. Inside the book, the text is written in gold, with each letter outlined in a hair-thin black line.

While the Qur'an could not be illustrated with images, other books could. Books were the major artistic outlet for painters in Islamic culture. Working with the finest pigments and brushes that tapered to a single hair, artists created scenes of entrancing detail such as *Bahram Gur and the Princess in the Black Pavilion* (**18.7**). Bahram Gur was a pre-Islamic Persian king whose legendary exploits were often recounted in poetry. *Haft Manzar* ("seven portraits"), by the 16th-century Persian poet Hatifi, tells of Bahram Gur's infatuation with the portraits of seven princesses. He eventually wins them all and builds for each a pavilion decorated in a different color. The Russian princess is housed in a red pavilion, the Greek princess in a white one. Here, Bahram Gur visits the Indian princess in her black pavilion.

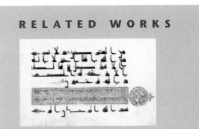
18.6 (left) Left half of a frontispiece of a manuscript of the Qur'an. Cairo, 1304–6. 18½ × 12⅝".
The British Library, London.

18.7 (right) *Bahram Gur and the Princess in the Black Pavilion*, from a manuscript of Hatifi's *Haft Manzar*. Bukhara, 1538.
Freer Gallery of Art, Washington, D.C.

18.8 Underglaze-painted mosque lamp from the Dome of the Rock in Jerusalem. Isnik, 1549. Height 15⅛″.
The British Museum, London.

RELATED WORKS

12.8 Brass basin

12.15 Ardabil carpet

12.17 Shah Jahan cup

The complex, flattened architectural setting and strong colors mark the style of the artist Shaykhazada, whose work this probably is. Floor coverings piled pattern on pattern are tilted toward the picture plane, while the brass vessels set on them are seen in perspective. The king and his princess sit demurely on their individual carpets before a wall ornamented with glazed tile. The setting above resembles the square frame and arched opening of an *iwan*, the pervasive Persian architectural form that might well have graced a pavilion built for an Indian princess.

DECORATIVE ARTS

Western thinking about art has tended to relegate decorative art such as rugs and ceramics to "minor" status. In Islamic cultures, however, these arts are to be savored as equals. Carpets and other textiles, for example, are an important facet of Islamic art. We saw one of the most famous of all Persian textiles in Chapter 12, the Ardabil carpet (see 12.15). Metalwork was highly prized in such works as the brass basin made in Cairo for Sultan al-Nasir Muyammad ibn Qalawun (see 12.8), and jade from Central Asia resulted in such masterpieces as the Shah Jahan cup (see 12.17), made for a ruler of the Mughal Empire in India.

We end this look at Islamic arts with an example of ceramic art, a mosque lamp made during the 16th century in the Ottoman Empire (**18.8**). Based in Turkey, the Ottoman dynasty came to power in 1281. In 1453, Ottoman armies took Constantinople, putting an end to the Byzantine Empire. Constantinople, later called Istanbul, served as the Ottoman capital until the creation of the present-day nation of Turkey in the 20th century. The lamp was found in the Dome of the Rock, a 7th-century building in Jerusalem that is often called the first work of Islamic architecture. Ottoman rulers sponsored a renovation of that monument, and this lamp may have been made for it. Modeled after similar hanging lamps of glass, it probably served a symbolic function, for it would not have shed any light. The palette of blue, turquoise, and white, familiar from mosques at Isfahan (see 18.3, 18.4), points to the presence of Persian potters at the Ottoman court. The mixture of decorative motifs includes elements derived from Chinese ceramics, which were collected and admired in eastern Islamic lands. Finally, we see again the proud verticals and swirling ribbons of the Arabic script, writing made beautiful enough to carry God's word.

ARTS OF AFRICA

When Arab armies invaded Africa in the 7th century C.E., their first conquest was the Byzantine province of Egypt, the site of Africa's best-known early civilization. Chapter 14 introduced ancient Egypt in the context of the Mediterranean world, for its interactions with Mesopotamia, Greece, and Rome are an important part of Western art history. But it is useful to remember that Egyptian culture arose in Africa and was the creation of African peoples.

The Nile that nourished Egypt also supported kingdoms farther to the south, in a region called Nubia. Nubia was linked by trade networks to African lands south of the Sahara, and it was through Nubia that the rich resources of Africa—ebony, ivory, gold, incense, and leopard skins—flowed into Egypt. The most famous Nubian kingdom was Kush, which rose to prominence during the 10th century B.C.E. and lasted for over 1,400 years. The gold ornament illustrated here comes from a Kushan royal tomb, the pyramid of Queen Amanishakhetro (**18.9**). A sensitively modeled ram's head protrudes from the center of the ornament, a symbol in Kush, as in Egypt, of the solar deity Amun. Over the ram's head, the disk of the sun rises before a faithful representation of an entryway to a Kushan temple.

Carrying their conquests farther west across the Mediterranean coast of Africa, Arab armies quickly routed Byzantine forces from the Roman coastal cities. Far more difficult to subdue were the African people known as Berbers. Berber kingdoms were well known to the ancient Mediterranean world. In the days of the Roman Empire, Berbers mingled with the Roman population in Africa and occasionally rose to high rank in the Roman army. One Berber general became a Roman emperor. After the Islamic conquests, Berbers gradually converted to Islam, and Islamic Berber dynasties held sway in Morocco, Algeria, and Spain. Berber groups were also involved in the long-distance trade across the Sahara that linked the Mediterranean coast with the rest of the continent to the south. Along these ancient trade routes, Islam spread peacefully through much of West Africa, eventually resulting in such African Islamic art as the mosque at Djenne, in Mali (see 13.1).

The Africa that Islamic travelers found south of the Sahara was and is home to literally hundreds of cultures, each with its own distinctive art forms. More than any other artistic tradition, the arts of Africa challenge us to expand our ideas about what art is, what forms it can take, what impulses it springs from, and what purposes it serves. Much of the history of these arts is lost to us, in part for the simple reason that most art in Africa has been made of perishable materials such as wood. Nevertheless, excavations during the 20th century have revealed many fascinating works in stone, metal, and terra cotta, including sculptures such as this terra-cotta head (**18.10**).

The smooth surfaces and *D*-shaped eyes are characteristic of works from the culture known as Nok, named after the town in Nigeria where the first examples of its art were found. Scientific testing suggests that most Nok works were made between 500 B.C.E. and 200 C.E., or around the time of ancient Greece and Rome. Broken off at the neck, the life-size head here probably formed part of a complete figure. Judging by the few complete figures that have been recovered, its elaborate, sculptural hairstyle would have been complemented by lavish quantities of jewelry and other ornaments.

18.9 (left) Ornament from the tomb of Queen Amanishakheto. Kush, Meroitic period, 50–1 B.C.E. Gold with glass inlay, height 2½″. Staatliche Sammlung Ägyptischer Kunst, Munich.

18.10 (right) Head, fragment of a larger figure. Nok culture, 500 B.C.E.– 200 C.E. Terra cotta, height 14³⁄₁₆″. The National Commission for Museums and Monuments, Lagos.

RELATED WORKS

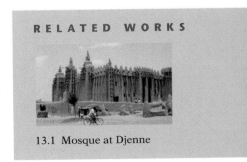

13.1 Mosque at Djenne

5.24
Royal altar,
Benin

3.13 Asante linguists

It seems likely that Nok culture influenced later cultures in the region, although we cannot say for sure. What is certain is that two of the most sustained art-producing cultures of Africa arose some centuries later not far from the Nok region. One is the kingdom of Benin, which began to take shape during the 13th century. Located in a region of Nigeria south of the Nok sites, Benin continues to the present day under a dynasty of rulers that dates back to the first century of its existence.

Like the rulers of ancient Egypt, the kings of Benin are viewed as sacred beings. Sacred kingship is common to many African societies, and art is often used to dramatize and support it. In Chapter 5, we looked at a brass altar to the Benin king's hand (see 5.24). The altar conveyed the king's centrality through symmetrical composition, his importance through hierarchical scale (he is larger than his attendants), and the symbolic role of his head through proportion (the head takes up one-third of his total height).

These elements can be seen again in the royal altars of the palace compound (18.11). Traditionally, each king upon assuming office commissioned and dedicated an altar to his father. The altar illustrated here is dedicated to Ovonramwen, who ruled toward the close of the 19th century. At the center of the altar is a brass statue depicting a standing king flanked by two attendants. As in the small altar to the hand, hierarchical proportion underscores the king's importance. This symmetrical composition stands at the center of a still larger symmetrical composition, the assemblage of the altar itself. Around the perimeter of the platform, ceremonial brass bells are displayed, three to the left, three to the right. Four large brass sculptures depicting heads of rulers are also set out symmetrically, each capped by an elephant tusk carved in relief with dozens of royal motifs.

In 1897, British forces attacked the Benin palace and took much of the art it contained—works in brass, ivory, terra cotta, and wood produced over a period of about 400 years. As a result, objects like the ones shown in the photograph here can be found in museums around the world. Examining a brass head or a carved tusk from Benin is a rewarding experience, yet these objects were not meant to be seen in isolation, much less in a museum. Rather, they were intended to take their place as elements in a larger, composite work of art—the assemblage of a sacred altar.

18.11 The palace altar to King Ovonramwen (r. 1888–97), Benin, Nigeria.

AFRICA LOOKS BACK

AFRICAN MASQUERADES RANGE from sacred and secret performances before a small group of initiates to public spectacles that verge on secular entertainment, though no masquerade is ever entirely secular. The largest masquerades may be performed in stages over many days and feature dozens of masks. Spirits of nature and natural forces; spirits of ancestors and of the recent dead; spirits of human types or social roles such as young maidens, blacksmiths, and farmers; spirits of abstract ideas such as beauty or fertility or wisdom—all may put in an appearance. Our knowledge of this rich and varied art form comes largely from Western researchers such as anthropologists and art historians, who over the past century have spent time "in the field"—that is, in various African communities, where they observe, photograph, and document the performances. Yet the nature of masquerades is such that often the observers have found themselves to be the observed.

The masker illustrated here was photographed during a masquerade performed in an Igbo community.

He is *onyeocha*, "white man." With his pith helmet, notepad, and pen, he may be a scholar who has come to do important research on these interesting Africans. While the other maskers in his troupe danced, he did not. Instead, he haughtily observed the goings on and took notes. Europeans, it is well known, are obsessed with writing everything down. But what can they hope to understand that way?

White-man masks depicting European government officers began to appear during the early 20th century, when colonial rule was imposed over the continent. Today, when tourism helps support many public masquerades, masks depicting tourists often appear. Armed with a carved wooden "camera," they elbow their way through the crowd, angling for a good view. One European couple portrayed in a Yoruba masquerade actually danced, but what a dance! They began with a waltz, then switched to a disco number that got them so overheated they ended up writhing on the ground making love! To the Yoruba, the public displays of affection that Europeans commonly indulge in are shocking. Indeed, the European couple was followed in the performance by maskers portraying a dignified, well-behaved Yoruba couple for contrast. In a masquerade performed by the Dogon people, a white-man mask sat at a table and asked silly questions. He was an anthropologist, of course!

Europeans are not the only outsiders to have been incorporated into masquerades. Masks of Muslim scholars have appeared, as have masks portraying irksome neighboring peoples. Most outside characters are portrayed satirically, often providing comic relief in a masquerade where genuinely powerful and sacred masks will also dance. The new masks demonstrate the vitality of this living art form, which easily absorbs new powers and presences into its view of the world. Yet the masks also bring us up short by questioning the limits of our ability to "study" another culture while it "holds still." "You do not stand in one place to watch a masquerade" goes an Igbo saying. Indeed, all cultures are always in motion, affecting each other through contact, both the observer and the observed.

Onyeocha ("white man") at an Igbo masquerade, Amagu Izzi, Nigeria, 1983.

18.12 Airowayoye I, ruler of Orangun-Ila, seated in state, 1977.

RELATED WORKS

2.17 Yoruba brass head

2.18 Yoruba terra-cotta head

According to oral tradition, the current dynasty of Benin rulers was founded by a prince from the Yoruba city of Ife to the northwest. Yoruba rulers, too, were considered sacred, and artists sculpted portrait heads in their honor. We saw two of these sculptures in Chapter 2: a naturalistic work from the 13th century representing the ruler's outer, physical head and an abstract work representing his inner, spiritual head (see 2.17, 2.18). While Yoruba artists no longer make such works, Yoruba kings are still regarded as sacred, and art still serves to dramatize their exceptional nature.

Taken in 1977, the photograph here shows the Yoruba ruler Airowayoye I seated in his regal robes (**18.12**). His right hand grasps a beaded staff, and on his head is a cone-shaped beaded crown. Abstracted faces of the king's ancestors stare out from the crown; their dark, white-rimmed eyes are easily discernible. At the pinnacle of the crown is a beaded bird, and numerous bird heads protrude from the cone. The birds refer to the female ancestors whose powers the king must draw on. Known as Our Mothers, they are believed able to transform themselves into night birds. A beaded veil obscures the ruler's face, for his subjects are not allowed to gaze directly on a sacred being. The crown gives form to the idea that the living king is one with his godly ancestors, for in wearing it his head merges with theirs, and their many eyes look out.

Similar ideas are conveyed by a spectacular beaded display piece commissioned by a Yoruba king in the early 20th century (**18.13**). The base of the piece resembles the conical royal crown. As on the crown, faces of ancestors stare out from the front and back (not visible here). Over this base rises the figure of a royal wife with a magnificent crested hairstyle and a child on her back. It is as though the bird at the pinnacle of Airowayoye's crown had turned back into one of the female ancestors who guarantees his power. The woman carries an offering bowl with a small bird on its lid. Female attendants flock around her body, while four protective male figures with guns ring the crown at the base. Male power is here seen as based in strength, while female power, greater and more mysterious, generates ritual (the offering) and new life (the child).

Complementary gender roles are also the subject of this elegant sculpture by an artist of the Dogon people, who live in present-day Mali (**18.14**). The sculpture portrays a couple seated side by side, rendered in a highly conventionalized, abstract manner. The stool they share links them physically and symbolically, as does the man's arm placed around the woman's shoulder. With their tilted heads, tubular torsos, angular limbs, horseshoe-shaped hips, and evenly spaced legs, the two bodies are almost mirror images of each other. Yet within this fundamental unity, differences appear. The man, slightly larger, speaks for the couple through his gestures, while the woman is quiet. His right hand touches her breast, suggesting her role as a nurturer. His left hand rests above his own genitals, signaling the idea of procreation. On her back, not visible here, she carries a child; on his back he carries a quiver. As often in African sculpture, abstraction is a clue here that the work does not represent specific people but spirits or ideas. He is the begetter, hunter, warrior, and protector; she is the life-bearer, mother, and nurturer. Together with their child they form a family, the basic unit of a Dogon community. The four small figures beneath the stool may refer to the support they receive from ancestors or other spirits. The carving probably would have been kept in a shrine, where it served as a kind of altar—a site for communication between this world and the world of spirits, including spirits of ancestors.

In many African cultures, men's and women's organizations play important roles. Such associations may be in charge of initiations, preparing young boys and girls for their adult roles. Others help govern their communities or provide spiritual services and counseling. The dignified figure here belonged to a Gwan or Jo society (**18.15**). Formed among the Bamana, who live in Mali to the southwest of the Dogon, these associations help women generally, especially those who have had trouble conceiving, bearing, or rearing children. With her regal bearing and downcast eyes, the seated figure seems to summon up strength from within herself. On her head is a cap hung with amulets. The cap marks her as an exceptional woman, for such caps are usually worn only by powerful male hunters or sorcerers. On her lap she holds a baby, carved so that it melts into her form; perhaps it is being formed *from* her. Above the child's upraised arms, full breasts promise nourishing milk. Displayed in annual festivals, the statue embodies the central wish of those who come to Gwan or Jo for help.

Art in Africa often serves as an agent in order to bring about some desired state of affairs, usually through contact with spirit powers. Among the most well known and visually compelling works of spiritual agency are the power figures, *minkisi* (singular *nkisi*, "medicine"), of the Kongo and

18.13 (below, left) Display piece. Yoruba. Early 20th century. Cloth, basketry, beads, fiber; height 41¾".
The British Museum, London.

18.14 (left) *Seated Couple*. Dogon. Wood and metal, height 29".
The Metropolitan Museum of Art, New York.

18.15 (above) *Gwandusu* (mother-and-child) display figure. Bamana. 13th–15th century. Wood, height 48⅝".
The Metropolitan Museum of Art, New York.

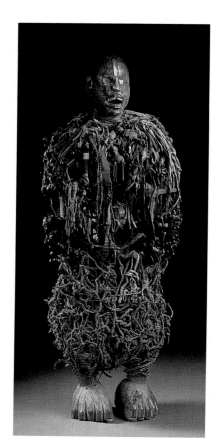

neighboring peoples of central Africa (**18.16**). *Minkisi* are containers. They hold materials that allow a ritual specialist to harness the powers of the dead in the service of the living. Almost any container can be a *nkisi*, but the most famous *minkisi* outside of Africa are statues of ferocious hunters such as the one here. Called *minkondi* (singular *nkondi*), they hunt down and punish witches and wrongdoers.

A *nkondi* begins its life as a plain carved figure, commissioned from a sculptor like any other. To empower it, the ritual specialist adds packets of materials to its surface, materials linked to the dead and to the dire punishments the *nkondi* will be asked to inflict. Other materials may be added as well. Hunting nets tangled around the legs of the *nkondi* here remind him of his purpose, while mirrors in his eyes enable him to see approaching witches. Working on behalf of a client who has sought his help, or even a whole community, the specialist invokes and enrages the *nkondi* into action, particularly by driving iron nails or blades violently into it. Over the years, nails and other materials accumulate, offering visual testimony to the *nkondi*'s fearsome prowess.

The great African art of spiritual agency, and perhaps the greatest of African arts, is the masquerade. Involving sculpture, costume, music, and movement, a masquerade does not merely contact spirit powers to effect change; it brings the spirits themselves into the community. In Western museums, African masks are commonly exhibited and admired as sculpture. But in Africa a mask is never displayed in public as an isolated, inert object. It appears only in motion, only as the head or face of a spirit being that has appeared in the human community.

The mask photographed here is *nowo* (**18.17**), the guiding spirit of a Temne women's organization called Bondo, which regulates female affairs. Bondo prepares young girls for initiation into adult status and afterward presents them to the community as fully mature women. As in many African societies, young people deemed ready for initiation are taken from their

18.16 (above) *Nkondi* figure. Lower Congo. Before 1878. Royal Museum of Central Africa, Tervuren.

18.17 (right) Temne *nowo* masquerade with attendants, Sierra Leone, 1976.

RELATED WORKS

11.20 Spirit spouse (Baule)

18.18 *Ijele* masquerade at an Igbo second burial ceremony, Achalla, Nigeria, 1983.

families. Isolated together away from the community, they learn the secrets of adulthood and undergo physical ordeals. During this time, they are considered to be in a vulnerable "in between" condition, neither children nor adults. They need the protection, guidance, and sponsorship of spirits to make the transition successfully from one stage of life to the next.

Nowo appears here accompanied by several attendants as part of a Bondo ceremony. The lustrous black mask represents a Temne ideal of feminine beauty and modesty. The rings around the base are compared to the chrysalis of a moth: just as the caterpillar emerges from its chrysalis transformed, so girls emerge from Bondo as women. The rings are also seen as ripples of water, for *nowo* is said to have risen out of the depths of a pool or river, where female spirits dwell. The white scarf tied to *nowo*'s elaborate hairstyle indicates her empathy for the initiates under her care, whose bodies are painted white during their isolation as a sign of their "in between" state.

Even our preconceived ideas of what a mask *is* must be discarded when faced with the extraordinary spectacle of *ijele* (**18.18**). The most honored mask of the Igbo people of Nigeria, *ijele* appears at the funeral of an especially important man, welcoming his spirit to the other world and easing his transition from one stage of being to the next. The meanings of *ijele* are fluid and layered. In its towering aspect, *ijele* resembles an anthill—structures that in Africa may reach a height of 8 feet and which the Igbo regard as porches to the spirit world. *Ijele* is also a venerable tree, the symbol of life beneath whose branches wise elders meet to discuss weighty matters. Amid the tassels, mirrors, and flowers on *ijele*'s "branches" are numerous sculpted figures of people, animals, and other masks—a virtual catalogue of the Igbo and their world. Multiple large eyes suggest the watchfulness of the ever-present (though usually invisible) community of spirits. Majestic in appearance, *ijele* nevertheless moves with great energy, dipping, whirling, shaking, and turning. It is the great tree of meaning—of life itself—appearing briefly in the human community.

RELATED WORKS

3.8 Bwa masquerade

CHAPTER 19

Arts of East Asia: India, China, and Japan

The previous chapter took us from the Mediterranean world into Asia with the spread of Islam to the east. This chapter continues our eastward journey with a brief look at three of the most influential civilizations of East Asia: India, China, and Japan.

In truth, these civilizations have already appeared "behind the scenes" in this story of art many times. Chapter 14, for example, pointed out that the regions of Mesopotamia and Egypt were in contact with each other from early on. But Mesopotamia was also in contact with India to the east, where an impressive civilization had arisen in the Indus River Valley. Akkadian writings from around 2300 B.C.E. mention the presence of Indus merchants and ships in Mesopotamia, along with their valuable goods of copper, gold, ivory, and pearls. Later, during the days of the Roman Empire, a long network of trade routes called the Silk Road allowed the citizens of Rome to enjoy the lacquerware and silk textiles of China. Rome had only the vaguest idea about where these exquisite products came from. China, more curious, avidly collected information about Rome and other Western lands. Still later, during the Renaissance, European explorers stumbled on the island nation of Japan. Japanese artists of the time delighted in recording the appearance of these exotic visitors from the West, whose customs were so strange.

Closer and more influential, however, were the contacts between these three Asian cultures themselves. China's greatest exports were writing, urban planning, administration, and philosophy, all of which it transmitted to Japan, together with styles of painting and architecture. India's greatest export was the religion of Buddhism, which travelers and missionaries brought over the Silk Road to China, and which then passed from China to Japan. With these paths of contact in mind, we begin our look at the arts of East Asia.

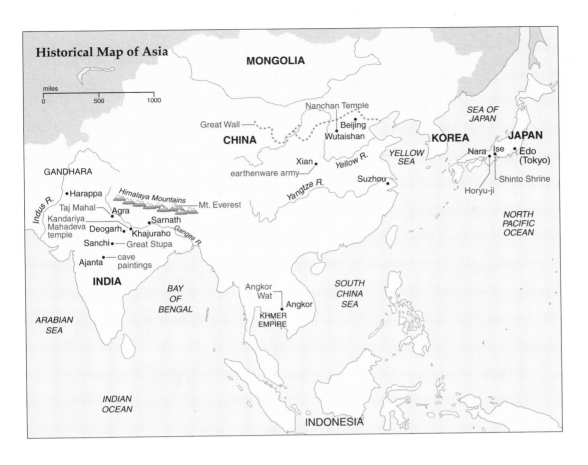

Historical Map of Asia

ARTS OF INDIA

The area of India's historical territories is so large and distinct that it is often referred to as a subcontinent. Another name for it is South Asia. Jutting out in a great triangle from the Asian landmass, South Asia is bordered along most of its northern frontier by the Himalaya Mountains, the tallest mountain range in the world. To the northwest, the mountain range known as the Hindu Kush gradually descends to the fertile valley of the Indus River, in present-day Pakistan.

INDUS VALLEY CIVILIZATION

Like the Tigris and Euphrates in Mesopotamia and the Nile in Egypt, the Indus River provided water for irrigation and a central artery for transportation and travel. Cities arose along its length around 2600 B.C.E., or roughly the same time as Sumerian civilization developed in Mesopotamia. The engineering skills of the Indus architects were quite advanced. The most famous Indus city, Mohenjo-Daro, was built on stone foundations, with straight, stone-paved streets laid out in a grid pattern. Houses constructed of fired brick were connected to a citywide drainage system.

The Indus people did not bury their dead with troves of precious objects, and thus we do not have an extensive record of their art. One of the most intriguing sculptures to have been found is this small sandstone torso (**19.1**). The softly modeled, rounded forms contrast dramatically with the armor-like musculature of ancient Mediterranean sculpture, reflecting a different way of thinking about the body. Later Indian sculpture will continue in this same vein. Scholars have interpreted the relaxed abdomen as a sign

19.1 Torso, from Harappa. Indus Valley civilization, c. 2000 B.C.E. Red sandstone, height 3¾". National Museum, New Delhi.

that the Indus people practiced the breathing exercises we know from later Indian culture as a component of yoga, the system of physical self-mastery that can be used to lead to spiritual insights.

A meditating yogi certainly seems to be the subject of this small, slightly damaged seal (**19.2**). Thousands of such seals have been found. Carved of steatite stone, they served to stamp an impression in wax or clay. At the top of the seal is an inscription. Scholars have not been able to decipher the Indus writing system, and anything it has to tell us about Indus culture must remain a mystery. The yogi sits in the classic Indian pose of meditation familiar from later images of the Buddha, his knees outspread, his feet tucked back and crossed. Other aspects of the image—the headdress with its curved horns and the small animals in the background—suggest the later Hindu god Shiva. We saw Shiva in his guise as Nataraja in Chapter 1 (see 1.9), but in another guise he is known as Lord of Beasts.

Indus culture began to disintegrate around 1900 B.C.E. Until recently, scholars believed that the cities were conquered by invaders entering the subcontinent from the northwest, a nomadic people who called themselves Aryas, "noble ones." New findings have overturned the idea of conquest, suggesting instead that Mohenjo-Daro was abandoned after the Indus River changed its course and that other cities were ruined when a parallel river ran dry. During these same centuries, the Aryas began to arrive.

BUDDHISM AND ITS ART

Beginning around 800 B.C.E., urban centers again arose in northern India, and by the 6th century B.C.E. numerous principalities had taken shape. During this time, Aryan religious practice became increasingly complex. The priestly class of Aryan society, brahmins, grew powerful, for only they understood the complicated sacrificial rituals that were now required. Brahmins also began to impose rigid ideas about social order derived from the Vedas, their sacred texts. Disturbed by these developments, many sages and philosophers of the day sought a different path, preaching social equality and a more direct and personal access to the spiritual realm. Of these numerous leaders, the one who has had the most lasting impact on the world was Siddhartha Gautama, later known as the Buddha.

Gautama was born a prince of the Shaka clan in northern India, near present-day Nepal. His dates are traditionally given as 563–483 B.C.E., although recent research suggests that he lived slightly later, dying around 400 B.C.E. According to tradition, his life was transformed when a series of

19.2 (above) "Yogi" seal, from Mohenjodaro. Indus Valley civilization, 2300–1750 B.C.E. Steatite.
National Museum, New Delhi.

19.3 (below) Great Stupa, Sanchi, India. Sunga and early Andhra periods, 3rd century B.C.E.–1st century C.E.

19.4 Detail of east gate with *yakshi*. Great Stupa, Sanchi. Early Andhra period, 1st century B.C.E. Sandstone, height of figure c. 5′.

chance encounters brought him face to face with suffering, sickness, and mortality. This, he realized, was our common fate. What is to be done? Renouncing his princely comforts, he studied with the spiritual masters of the day and tried every accepted path to understanding, but to no avail. He withdrew into meditation until one day, finally, everything became clear. He was *buddha,* "awakened."

Buddha accepted the belief, current in the India of his day, that time is cyclical and that all beings, even gods and demons, are condemned to suffer an endless series of lives unless they can gain release from the cycle. His insight was that we are kept chained to the world by desire. His solution was to extinguish desire by cultivating nonattachment, and to this end he proposed an eightfold path of moral and ethical behavior. By following this path we too may awake, see through the veil of illusion to the true nature of the world, and free ourselves from the cycle of life, death, and rebirth.

Buddha attracted followers from all walks of life, from beggars to kings, both men and women. After his death, his cremated remains were distributed among eight memorial mounds called stupas. During the 3rd century B.C.E., a Buddhist king named Ashoka called for these remains to be redistributed among a much larger number of stupas, including this one at Sanchi (**19.3**). A stupa is a solid earthen mound faced with stone. Over it rises a stylized parasol that symbolically shelters and honors the relics buried inside. Pilgrims come to be near the energy that is believed to emanate from the Buddha's remains. They visit the stupa by ritually walking around it. The two stone fences evident in the photograph, one at ground level and one higher up, enclose paths for circling the stupa.

Four gateways erected late in the 1st century B.C.E. punctuate the outer enclosure at Sanchi. Their crossbars are carved in relief with stories from the Buddha's life. Numerous figures ornament the gateways, including this voluptuous female (**19.4**). This is probably a *yakshi,* a nature spirit embodying ideas of fertility and abundance. The *yakshi* is not part of the Buddhist faith but belongs to older and more widespread Indian beliefs. The female form was considered auspicious in Indian thought. It was even held that women were able to cause trees to blossom or bear fruit. The *yakshi* here enlaces her arms in a mango tree, which has blossomed at the sound of her laughter. Together with her numerous companions on the other gateways, she showers blessings of abundance on the site and all who enter it.

Interestingly, the reliefs at Sanchi that narrate the story of the Buddha do so without showing the Buddha himself. Early Buddhist art avoided depicting the Buddha directly. Instead, sculptors indicated his presence through symbols. A pair of footprints, for example, indicated the ground where he walked; a parasol indicated space he occupied. Nevertheless, the Buddhist community must eventually have felt the need for an image to focus their thoughts, for toward the end of the 1st century C.E. these began to appear.

Several artistic centers in India were famous for images of the Buddha, and their styles are quite distinct. The statue here was carved in the 5th century C.E. in the workshops at Sarnath, in northern India (**19.5**). Typical of Sarnath style, the robe the Buddha wears molds itself discretely to the smooth, perfected surfaces of his body. The neckline and the hanging sleeves are almost the only signs that he is wearing a robe at all. Seated in the pose of meditation, the Buddha forms the *mudras* (hand gesture) that indicates preaching. He is understood to be preaching his first sermon, known as the Sermon at Deer Park (note the two deer carved in relief to either side of him).

The workshops at Sarnath were patronized by the Gupta dynasty. Based in central India, these rulers had brought many of the regional kingdoms of the subcontinent into an empire. The Gupta period, which lasted from around 320 to 647 C.E., is regarded as a high point in Indian culture. During this time, Buddhism attained its greatest influence and often benefited from royal patronage, which enabled larger and more expensive projects to be undertaken. One of the most extraordinary projects was realized at Ajanta, in central India, where a series of halls, shrines, and residences for monks were hollowed out from an exposed cliff face. Murals ornamenting the walls

19.5 *Buddha Preaching the First Sermon,* from Sarnath. c. 465–85 C.E. Sandstone, height 5′3″. Archaeological Museum, Sarnath.

THE EARLY BUDDHA IMAGE

THE EARLY ART of Buddhism did not include an image of its founder. Instead, in such works as the relief carvings at Sanchi (see 19.3, 19.4), the Buddha was represented by symbolic traces of his presence. Thus, an empty chair represented his seated presence, and a pathway represented him walking. That artists should have avoided depicting the Buddha directly is not so surprising. After all, the entire point of his teaching was that he was in his last earthly life. Henceforth, he would have no bodily form. Besides, the Buddha had lived 550 lives before his final one. Clearly he had passed through many bodily forms.

So we may well wonder why images of the Buddha began to appear when and where they did, in northern India during the 1st century C.E. One of the reasons has to do with changes in Buddhism itself. By this time, the Buddha was no longer thought of as an exemplary man but as a god, and his followers now wanted an image to help them focus their devotion. Another reason was the artistic heritage of Greece.

What does Greece have to do with India? During the 4th century B.C.E., the Macedonian Greek conqueror Alexander the Great led his armies not only through Egypt and the Persian Empire, but all the way to the Indus River in South Asia. For centuries afterward, regions bordering on India were part of the extensive Hellenistic world. Hellenistic culture was particularly vital in a region called Bactria, which bordered the mountains of the Hindu Kush. During the 1st century B.C.E., Bactria was conquered by a people of Chinese origin called the Kushans, who eventually established an empire that reached across northern India, where they encountered and embraced Buddhism. Having no monumental art of their own, the Kushans also embraced the Hellenistic culture of Bactria.

The Greeks had long envisioned their gods in sculpture as perfected humans. Under Kushan rulers, this Hellenistic heritage and the desire for an image of the Buddha merged in fascinating figures such as the one shown here. Modeled on statues of the Greek god Apollo, who was typically portrayed as a handsome youth, the Buddha stands in gentle contrapposto, the great contribution of the Greeks to art. His robe, reminiscent of a Roman toga, hangs in heavy folds over a naturalistically muscled body. The fragment of the relief illustrated to the right offers something even more surprising: a guardian of the Buddha dressed in a lion skin like the Greek hero Hercules and holding a thunderbolt like the Greek god Zeus! This fascinating Hellenistic-Indian hybrid style disappeared with the end of the Kushan Empire in the 3rd century C.E., but its effects were lasting. Contrapposto spread throughout India, where it is a prominent feature of later Hindu art. And the Buddha image was started on its long history.

(left) *Standing Buddha,* from Takht-i-Bahi, Gandhara. Kushan period, c. 100 C.E. Schist, height 35⅞". The British Museum, London. (right) *Vajrapani, Guardian of the Buddha, as Hercules.* Fragment of a relief from Gandhara. 1st century C.E. Stone, height 21¼". The British Museum, London.

19.6 (left) *The "Beautiful Bodhisattva,"* from Cave 1, Ajanta. c. 462–500 C.E. Fresco, detail.

19.7 (right) *Vishnu Dreaming the Universe,* relief panel, temple of Vishnu, Deogarh, Uttar Pradesh. Early 6th century C.E.

of these sculpted caves are among the earliest examples of Indian painting to have come down to us. The detail illustrated here depicts the bodhisattva Padmapani, an image so lovely that it has become known as *The "Beautiful Bodhisattva"* (**19.6**). Bodhisattvas are saintly beings who have delayed their own release in order to help others attain enlightenment. Padmapani is a special form of Avalokiteshvara, whom we met in Chapter 11 (see 11.4). Known as the Lotus-Giver, he is shown here holding a lotus blossom in his right hand and a begging bowl in his left. His hair is piled high, and he wears the jewels of a prince. His smooth, languorous body resembles that of the Buddha image from Sarnath (19.5), and it illustrates well the refined Gupta style in painting. The artist has given unforgettable form to the compassion a perfected being feels for the rest of humanity, still trapped in the world's illusions.

HINDUISM AND ITS ART

The Gupta rulers who patronized Buddhist art so lavishly were Hindu, as was the local dynasty that sponsored the creation of the magnificent Ajanta caves. Hinduism would become the dominant religion of India over the coming centuries, and Buddhism, having already spread to China and Southeast Asia, would virtually disappear from the land of its birth.

Hinduism developed as the older Vedic religion, with its brahmins and its emphasis on ritual sacrifice, evolved in its thinking and mingled with local Indian beliefs, probably including those hinted at in ancient Indus art. Like Buddhism, Hinduism has at its core a belief in the cyclical nature of time, including the cosmic cycles of the creation, destruction, and rebirth of the world and the briefer cycles of our own repeating lives within it. The ultimate goal is liberation from these cycles into a permanent state of pure consciousness. This liberation will be granted to us by a god in return for our devotion. Strictly speaking, Hinduism is not one religion but many related faiths, each one taking its own deity as supreme. We have met two of the three principal deities of Hinduism in earlier chapters of this book, the god

Shiva (see 1.9) and the goddess Devi or Shakti ("power"), whom we saw in her manifestation as Durga (see 11.14). The third principal deity is Vishnu.

Carved in stone, the relief illustrated here depicts Vishnu dreaming the world into existence (**19.7**). Wearing his characteristic cylindrical crown, he slumbers on the coiled serpent of infinity, Ananta. The goddess Lakshmi holds his foot. She represents the female side of his energy. Moved by her, Vishnu dreams the god Brahma into existence. Brahma appears at the center of the uppermost row of figures, sitting in a meditative pose on a lotus blossom that is understood to grow from Vishnu's navel. Brahma in turn will create the world of space and time by thinking, "May I become Many." In the smooth surfaces of Vishnu's body, delicately set with jewelry, we see the Gupta style in a Hindu setting.

This relief appears on the exterior of one of the earliest surviving Hindu stone temples, a small structure dating from around 500 C.E. Temple architecture evolved rapidly over the ensuing centuries, and by 1000 C.E. monumental forms had been perfected. A masterpiece of the monumental temple as it developed in northern India is the Kandariya Mahadeva (**19.8, 19.9**). Dedicated to Shiva, the temple rests on a stone platform that serves to mark out a sacred area and separate it from the everyday world. Visitors climb the stairs, visible to the right, and proceed through a series of three halls, each of which is distinguished on the exterior by a pyramidal roof. These roofs grow progressively taller, culminating in a majestic curving tower called a *shikhara*. Conceived as a cosmic mountain ringed around with lesser peaks, the *shikhara* rises over the heart of the temple, a small, dark, cavelike chamber called a *garbhagriha* ("womb-house"). The *garbhagriha* houses a statue of the deity, a statue in which the god is believed to be truly present.

Indian architects worked with post-and-lintel construction techniques, and thus the interior spaces of Hindu temples are not large. They do not need to be, for Hindu religious practice is not based in congregational worship. Instead, devotees approach the deity individually with such gifts as flowers, food, and incense. These are offered as sacrifices by a brahmin, who receives them at the entrance to the *garbhagriha*.

4.34
Ragamala
illustration

3.19 *Ramayana* illustration

19.8 (left) Kandariya Mahadeva temple, Khajuraho, Madhya Pradesh, India. c. 1000 C.E.

19.9 (right) Plan of the Kandariya Mahadeva temple.

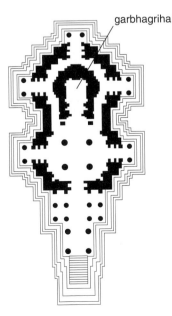

garbhagriha

Like the form of the temple itself, the sculptures on its exterior represent the energies of the god radiating outward into the world. The myriad Hindu gods and goddesses in their many guises are favorite subjects. On northern temples such as the Kandariya Mahadeva, voluptuous women and sensuous loving couples are depicted as well (**19.10**). The presence of women is mandated in the texts that guided northern architects, and it demonstrates how belief in such auspicious presences as *yakshi* (see 19.4) found a place in Hinduism.

From as early as the 2nd century B.C.E., India exerted an influence on developing cultures in Southeast Asia. Kingdoms of Southeast Asia adopted both Buddhism and Hinduism, and they created their own styles of the art forms that came with them. Among the greatest architectural treasures of Southeast Asia is Angkor, the capital of the Khmer kingdom. The Khmer kingdom dominated the region of present-day Cambodia and much of the surrounding area between the 9th and 15th centuries. Taking the title *devaraja*, "god-king," Khmer rulers identified themselves with a deity such as Vishnu, Shiva, or the bodhisattva Lokeshvara. A temple erected to the deity was also thus a temple erected to the king, who was viewed as one of the deity's earthly manifestations. The finest and largest example is the beautiful temple complex known as Angkor Wat (**19.11**).

Built in the early 12th century under the patronage of the god-king Suryavarman II and dedicated to Vishnu, Angkor Wat consists of five shrines on a raised, pyramidal stone "mountain." Each shrine houses a *garbhagriha*, the womblike dwelling place of the deity. Colonnaded galleries connect and enclose the five shrines, their walls carved with reliefs depicting dancing figures, celestial beings, and the many guises and adventures of Vishnu. Visitors approach the complex by a long walkway that originally crossed over a surrounding moat. Like Hindu temples in India, the plan of Angkor Wat is based in a mandala, a diagram of a cosmic realm, and thus the entire site reflects the meaning and order of the spiritual universe.

19.10 (left) Exterior detail of the Kandariya Mahadeva temple.

19.11 (right) Central temple complex at Angkor Wat, Cambodia. c. 1113–50 C.E.

PRESERVATION: ANGKOR WAT

HERE IS THE challenge: An ancient temple, magical in its beauty and thick with magnificent sculptures, is located deep inside a jungle. The climate is tropical—hot, humid, subject to monsoon rains. Algae and fungi grow unchecked, loving the moist atmosphere. Plants of all kinds flourish, boring their roots under and around temple stones, climbing the walls, penetrating every crevice. Bats proliferate, and their acidic droppings eat away the rock. Colonies of insects build their nests in the ground, in the cracks, in the delicate features of stone reliefs. When the rains come, water seeps through any opening, causing further erosion of the stone.

To make matters worse, the temple attracts other sorts of predators, predators encouraged not by the climate but by the treasures to be found inside. Because the temple complex is very large and difficult to guard, thieves regularly plunder the site for whatever artworks they can cut and carry away to sell to eager collectors. If a whole sculpture cannot be removed conveniently, looters simply slice off a portion. There are many headless statues in this temple.

Is that all? No, not quite. This temple happens to be located in Cambodia, in an area that has endured warfare variously involving government troops, the communist Khmer Rouge, the Vietnamese, and even the Americans. Bullet holes and mortar wounds give testimony to the fact that Angkor Wat stands in a battle zone.

The Khmer people abandoned their old capital at Angkor in the 15th century. Apparently, the site was more or less forgotten until 1861, when the French, who had colonized the region, rediscovered Angkor and literally hacked it out of the jungle. By then the jewel of the city, the temple called Angkor Wat, was in ruins. Sporadic attempts were made to preserve and restore the structures, but political turbulence over a long period made any real progress impossible. Finally, in the late 1980s, hostilities had declined to the point where restoration seemed feasible. A team of experts from India was selected for the project, but their task is daunting.

Some parts of Angkor Wat are so badly damaged that they must be completely dismantled and reassembled, stone by stone. Weed-killer and other chemicals will be used in great quantities to drive back the tropical growth. Ditches and conduits must be built to drain away excess water. And, of course, every inch of Angkor Wat and its sculptures will need to be scrubbed, to clean away centuries of nature's jungle coating. Recently, the restorers at Angkor Wat have drawn criticism from those who feel the scrubbing entails too much elbow grease and too little care—in other words, that untrained workers are throwing out the artworks with the algae. Angkor Wat, needless to say, is very fragile. As with any restoration project, it is hard to say when *enough* work is too much.

Perhaps the greatest challenge facing the restorers is one they cannot control. Unless peace can be maintained in the region, Angkor Wat is doomed. No temple, however magical, can survive the brutal assault of war.

Bas-relief sculpture at Angkor Wat, depicting the god Vishnu in the story called "Churning the Sea of Milk." The relief has been partially cleaned.

13.20 Interior, Jain temple

JAIN ART

The Jain religion traces its beginnings to a sage named Mahavira, who lived during the 6th century B.C.E. Like the Buddha, Mahavira left the comforts of home in his youth to pursue spiritual wisdom. Upon achieving enlightenment, he became known as the Jina, or "victor." In the religion developed by his followers, Mahavira is considered to have been the last in a line of twenty-four Jinas. Unlike Buddhism, the Jain religion did not become a world faith, yet within India it has remained an important presence.

In Chapter 13, we looked at the interior of a Jain temple (see 13.20). The hundreds of Jain temples constructed between the 11th and 16th centuries testify to the wealth of the merchants and traders who were the primary adherents of the Jain faith. Jains also commissioned thousands of illuminated manuscripts for donation to temple libraries (**19.12**). The scene reproduced here is from a manuscript of the *Kalpa Sutra*, a work that narrates the lives of the Jain saints. The restricted palette dominated by saturated red and blue is typical of Jain manuscripts. As in later Indian painting, position and overlap are the primary clues to spatial depth. The decorative flatness of the style alternates easily with passages of text, so readers pass from reading words to reading images with little sense of a shift in visual "gears." Wiry, linear drawing and oddly protruding eyes give the figures a sense of great alertness and spiritual energy.

MUGHAL ART AND INFLUENCE

A new culture developed in India with the arrival of the Mughals, an Islamic people from Central Asia who established an empire on the subcontinent beginning in the 16th century. Like most Islamic groups from Central Asia, the Mughals were influenced by Persian culture. In India, Persian forms mingled with Indian elements to create a uniquely Indian form of Islamic art. The most beloved work of Mughal architecture is the Taj Mahal (see 13.18). In Chapters 13 and 18, we pointed out the Persian aspects of the

19.12 (left) Detail of a leaf with *The Birth of Mahavira,* from the *Kalpa Sutra.* Gujarat, c. 1400 C.E. Opaque watercolor on paper, 3⅜ × 3″.
Prince of Wales Museum, Bombay.

19.13 (right) Ritual wine vessel, *jia.* Late Shang period. Bronze, height 13½″.
Nelson-Atkins Museum of Art, Kansas City, Missouri.

monument: its *iwan* entryways, its central domed interior, and its crowning ornamental onion-shaped dome. (To review the form of an *iwan*, see 18.3.) Looking at the building again, you can see that it rests on a stone platform in the manner of Hindu temples. The open, domed pavilions that sit on the roof and cap the four minarets are *chattri*, a traditional embellishment of Indian palaces.

Illustrated books were a second great Persian artistic tradition. The Mughal painting atelier was directed by Persian painters, who introduced new techniques, styles, subjects, and materials to the subcontinent. The influence of such Mughal masterpieces as the *Akbarnama* (see 3.12) was felt in Indian courts, where painters absorbed the Mughal love of detail and jewel-toned palette while retaining the decorative flatness and saturated color of earlier Indian manuscript painting (see 19.12). Examples of the new styles that resulted include *Lady with a Bird* (see 2.22) and the Manley *Ragamala* (see 4.34).

ARTS OF CHINA

Unlike India, China is not protected to the north by intimidating mountains. The vast and vulnerable northern frontier is one of the themes of Chinese history, for it resulted in a constant stream of influence and interaction. Peaceful contacts produced fruitful exchanges between China, India, Central Asia, and Persia. But repeated invasion and conquest from the north also shaped Chinese thinking and Chinese art.

Fundamental features of the Chinese landscape are the three great rivers that water its heartland, the Yellow in the north and the Yangtze and the Xi in the south. The Yellow River is traditionally spoken of as the "cradle of Chinese civilization." Advanced Neolithic cultures built settlements along the Yellow River from around 5000 B.C.E., yet recent archaeological research has found Neolithic sites together with artifacts in jade and ceramic over a much broader area, giving us a more complicated and still incomplete picture of the early stages of Chinese culture. All we can say now is that over time these many distinct Neolithic cultures seem to have merged.

THE FORMATIVE PERIOD: SHANG TO QIN

The history of China begins firmly with the Shang dynasty (c. 1500–c. 1050), whose kings ruled from a series of capitals in the Yellow River Valley. Archaeologists have discovered foundations of their palaces and walled cities, and excavations of royal tombs have yielded thousands of works in jade, lacquer, ivory, precious metals, and bronze. The illustration here shows a bronze *jia*, a vessel for wine (**19.13**). Valued and valuable possessions of elite families, bronze vessels were used at banquets for ritual offerings of food to ancestors. Visible on each side of the *jia* is the most famous and mysterious of Shang decorative motifs, the stylized animal or monster face known as *taotie*. Its two horns curling away from the raised center axis are clearly distinguishable, as are the staring eyes just beneath them. The *taotie* may relate to shamanism, the practice of communicating with the spirit world through animal go-betweens. Birds appear in a band above the *taotie*, the legs of the vessel are decorated with stylized dragons, and an animal of some kind sits on the lid. Whether directly associated with shamanism or not, animals both fantastic and real are a haunting presence in Shang art.

Around 1050 B.C.E. the Shang were conquered by their neighbors to the northwest, the Zhou, who ruled for the next 800 years. The first 300 years of this longest dynasty were peaceful. During later centuries, however, the

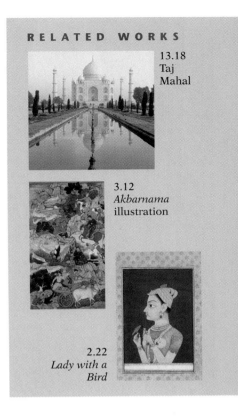

13.18
Taj
Mahal

3.12
Akbarnama
illustration

2.22
*Lady with a
Bird*

1.5
Gu beaker

19.14 View of Pit no. 1, part of the "terra-cotta army" surrounding the tomb-mound of the First Emperor of Qin (d. 210 B.C.E.).

states over which the Zhou presided grew increasingly independent and treacherous, finally descending into open warfare. The deteriorating situation inspired much thought about how a stable society could be organized. One of the philosophers of the day was Confucius, who lived around the turn of the 5th century B.C.E. His ideas about human conduct and just rule would later be placed at the very center of Chinese culture.

In 221 B.C.E., the state of Qin (pronounced "chin") claimed victory over the other states, uniting all of China into an empire for the first time. The first emperor, Shihuangdi, was obsessed with attaining immortality. Work on his underground burial site began even before he united China and continued until his death. The mound covering the burial itself has always been visible, but the accidental discovery in 1974 of a buried terra-cotta army guarding it was one of the most electrifying moments in 20th-century archaeology (**19.14**). Row upon row the lifesize figures stand in their thousands—soldiers, archers, cavalrymen, and charioteers—facing east, the direction from which danger was expected to come. Time has bleached them to a ghostly gray, but when they were new, they were painted in lifelike colors, for only by being as realistic as possible could they effectively protect the emperor's tomb behind them, about half a mile to the west.

CONFUCIANISM AND DAOISM: HAN AND SIX DYNASTIES

Our name for China comes from the first dynasty, Qin. Chinese historians, however, reviled the Qin for their brutal rule. Ethnic Chinese instead refer to themselves as Han people, after the dynasty that overthrew the Qin. Han rule endured, with one brief interruption, from 206 B.C.E. to 220 C.E. During these centuries many features of Chinese culture came into focus, including the central roles played by two systems of thought, Confucianism and Daoism.

The philosophy of Confucius is pragmatic; its principal concern is the creation of a peaceful society. Correct and respectful relations among people are the key, beginning within the family, then extending outward and upward all the way to the emperor. Han rulers adopted Confucianism as the offical state philosophy, in the process elaborating it into a sort of religion in which social order was linked to cosmic order.

Confucius urged people to honor ancestors and Heaven, as the Zhou deity was called. Apart from that, he had little to say about spiritual matters. For answers to questions about what lies beyond the physical world, the Chinese turned to Daoism. Daoism is concerned with bringing human life into harmony with nature. A *dao* is a "way" or "path." The Dao is the Way of the Universe, a current that flows through all creation. The goal of Daoism is to understand the Way and be carried along by it, and not to fight it by striving. The first Daoist text, the famous *Dao De Jing* ("the Way and its power") dates to around 500 B.C.E.; the materials it draws together are much older.

Among scholars, Daoism continued as a philosophy, but on a popular level it also became a religion; and in doing so it absorbed many folk beliefs, deities, and mystical concerns, including the search for immortality. The incense burner shown here, found in the tomb of a Han prince, portrays the Daoist paradise, the Isle of the Immortals in the Eastern Sea (**19.15**). A close look amid the crags of the mountainous island gradually reveals myriad small people, animals, and birds. They are the happy beings who have discovered the secret of immortality. Stylized waves inlaid in gold swirl around the base. Smoke from burning incense would have wreathed the island in clouds of fog, adding to its otherworldly appearance.

19.15 Incense burner from the tomb of Prince Liu Sheng, Mancheng, Hebei. Han dynasty, 113 B.C.E. Bronze with gold inlay, height 10¼". Hebei Provincial Museum, Shijiazhuang.

19.16 Attributed to Gu Kaizhi. *Admonitions of the Instructress to the Ladies of the Palace*, detail. Handscroll, ink and color on silk; height 9¾". Tang (?) copy after a 4th-century original.
The British Museum, London.

Not long after the end of the Han dynasty, invaders from inner Asia conquered the northern part of China. The imperial court fled to the south. For the next 250 years, China was divided. Numerous kingdoms—many under non-Chinese rulers—rose and fell in the north, while six weak dynasties succeeded each other in the south. For the educated elite, philosophical Daoism provided an escape route. To converse brilliantly, to wander the landscape, to drink and write poetry—these were suitable occupations for those who were alienated by debased times. Nevertheless, Confucianism, with its stern emphasis on duty to society, remained the official ideal, and Confucian themes continued to appear in art.

A famous example is the handscroll known as *Admonitions of the Instructress to the Ladies of the Palace*, attributed to the 4th-century painter Gu Kaizhi (**19.16**; to review the handscroll format see page 113). *Admonitions* illustrates a series of Confucian lessons in correct behavior for court ladies. In the very last scene, shown here, the instructress is portrayed writing down her words of wisdom. To the right, a court lady kneels in gratitude, her robe billowing out gracefully. To the left, two more court ladies flutter in to witness the event. With its thin, even lines and sparing use of color, the style of the painting is typical of the 4th century. There is no hint of a setting, and only the sensitive placement of the figures suggests depth.

THE AGE OF BUDDHISM: TANG

Buddhism had begun to filter into China during the Han dynasty, when missionaries from India arrived over the Silk Road. During the Six Dynasties period, it spread increasingly through the divided north and south. When China was reunited under the Sui dynasty (581–618 C.E.), the new emperor was a devout Buddhist; and during the first century of the Tang dynasty (618–906 C.E.), virtually the entire country adopted the Buddhist religion, and vast quantities of art were created for the thousands of monasteries, temples, and shrines that were founded.

The most popular form of Buddhism in China was the sect called Pure Land, named for the Western Paradise where the buddha Amitabha dwells. The fragment of a hanging scroll illustrated here (**19.17**) portrays a bodhisattva leading the soul of a fashionably plump, well-dressed little Tang lady to her eternal reward in the Western Paradise, imagined in the upper left corner as a Chinese palace. The magnificently attired bodhisattva is a Chinese fantasy of an Indian prince. In his right hand he holds an incense burner. His left hand holds a lotus flower and a white temple banner. Flowers fall about the couple, symbols of holiness and grace.

Much Buddhist art of the Tang dynasty was destroyed during the 9th century, when Buddhism was briefly persecuted as a "foreign" religion. One building that somehow escaped destruction is the Nanchan Temple (**19.18**). Little Chinese architecture has survived from before 1400, and thus the Nanchan Temple, though small, takes on added importance. Like all important buildings in China, the Nanchan Temple is raised above ground level by a stone platform. Wooden columns capped by bracket sets bear the weight of the tiled roof with its broad overhanging eaves. (To review the structural system of Chinese architecture, see page 299.) The gentle curve of the roof draws our eyes upward to the ridge, where two ornaments based on upsweeping fishtails serve symbolically to protect the building from fire.

The same basic principles and forms served Chinese architects for temples, palaces, and residences. Multiplied a hundredfold, this pleasing, sturdy temple lets us imagine the grandeur of the multistoried palaces of the Tang just as the painted bodhisattva, multiplied into a cast of hundreds, lets us imagine the vanished murals that were the glory of Tang Buddhist art.

THE RISE OF LANDSCAPE PAINTING: SONG

China again splintered after the fall of the Tang but was quickly reunited under the rulers of the Song dynasty (960–1279 C.E.). Artists during the Song continued to create works for Buddhist and Daoist temples and shrines. Sculpture played an important role in these contexts. The altar of a Buddhist

19.17 (left) *Bodhisattva Guide of Souls*. Tang dynasty, late 9th century C.E. Ink and colors on silk, height 31⅝". The British Museum, London.

19.18 (right) Nanchan Temple, Wutaishan, Shanxi. Tang dynasty, 782 C.E.

19.19 (left) *Guanyin.* Song dynasty, c. 1100. Painted wood, height 7'11".
The Nelson-Atkins Museum of Art, Kansas City, Missouri.

19.20 (right) Li Cheng (attrib.). *A Solitary Temple amid Clearing Peaks.* Northern Song dynasty, c. 960. Hanging scroll, ink and slight color on silk, height 44".
The Nelson-Atkins Museum of Art, Kansas City, Missouri.

shrine consists of figures from the Buddhist pantheon set on a platform and protected by a railing. A visitor to a large temple might find inside the entire assembly of heaven—buddhas, bodhisattvas, lesser deities, guardians, and other celestial beings—carved as life-size figures and arranged to reflect the hierarchy of paradise.

The bodhisattva Guanyin, known in India as Avalokiteshvara (see 11.4), became the object of special affection in China. As Guanyin of the Southern Seas, he was believed to reside high on a mountain and offer his special protection to all who traveled the sea. Carved from wood and richly painted and gilded, the sculpture here depicts Guanyin atop his sacred mountain (**19.19**). Left leg dangling down, right leg drawn up, he sits in a pose known as the pose of royal ease, as befits his princely nature. He would have been surrounded on his altar by attendants, making his high status even clearer. Cascading swags of drapery animate this serene figure, whose benevolent gaze is like the calm center within the storm, saving us from shipwreck, both at sea and in life.

We do not know who carved Guanyin with such virtuosity. Chinese thinking about art did not concern itself with sculpture and architecture but valued above all the "arts of the brush," calligraphy and painting. Often, paintings were preserved for future generations through the practice of copying. Many famous works of the Tang are known to us only through Song copies, such as Zhang Xuan's *Ladies Preparing Newly Woven Silk* (see 3.22) and Gu Hongzhong's *The Night Revels of Han Xizai* (see 4.47). The Tang dynasty was viewed by later writers as the great age of figure painting, and Song copies help us see why. Song painters, in turn, cast their own long shadow over the future with landscape.

The Song style of monumental landscape was largely the creation of Li Cheng, whose *A Solitary Temple amid Clearing Peaks* we illustrate here (**19.20**). Li built on the work of his predecessors of the early 10th century, when landscape first became an independent subject for painting. In his hands, the elements they had explored—mobile midair perspective, monochrome ink, vertical format, flowing water, shrouding mists, and a buildup of forms culminating in towering mountains—were gathered into a newly harmonious and spacious whole. Typically, paths are offered for us to walk in and people for us to identify with. Entering the painting with the traveler on the donkey at the lower left, we can cross the rustic bridge to a small village where people are talking and working. A glimpse of a stepped path farther up gives us access to the temple in the middle distance. But, also typically, there is a limit to how high we can climb. Mists separate the middle distance from the towering presences that rise up suddenly in the background. At this point, we must leave the painting and draw back, and when we do, we see a totality that is hidden from us in daily life: the whole of nature and our small place in it. Yet in this view of nature we seem to distinguish an ordering principle, and our place, though small, is in harmony with it: the temple raises its tower upward, and the mountains continue the gesture.

Li Cheng's vision of nature ordered by some higher force and human life in harmony with it clearly echoes the ideas of Daoism. In fact, some art historians believe that such paintings may originally have been understood to portray the Daoist Isle of the Immortals (see 19.15). Yet the painting can also be seen in a Confucian perspective as a mirror of the order of China itself, with the emperor towering above, surrounded by his officials, as well as through a Buddhist lens as the great example of the Buddha flanked by bodhisattvas.

SCHOLARS AND OTHERS: YUAN AND MING

During the Song dynasty, a new social class began to make itself felt in Chinese cultural life, scholars. Scholars were the product of an examination system designed to recruit the finest minds for government service. Candidates spent many years studying for the grueling test, which became the gateway to political power, social prestige, and wealth. Scholars did not study anything so practical as administration, however. Their education was in the classic texts of philosophy, literature, and history; and its purpose was to produce the Confucian ideal of a cultivated person, right-thinking and right-acting in all situations. Among their other accomplishments, scholars were expected to write poetry and practice calligraphy. During the Song dynasty, they also took an interest in painting.

The ideals of scholar painting were formed within the refined and cultivated Song court. During the ensuing Yuan dynasty, however, a split developed between scholars and the government. The Yuan (1279–1368 C.E.) was a foreign dynasty founded by the Mongols, a Central Asian people who had conquered China. The Mongol court continued to sponsor art, as had all of China's past rulers, but scholars regarded everything connected with the court as illegitimate. They viewed themselves as the true inheritors of China's past.

3.22 Hui-Zong, *Court Ladies*

4.47 Gu Hongzhong, *Night Revels*

Four scholar-painters of this time have come to be known as the Four Great Masters of Yuan. One is Huang Gongwang, whose *Dwelling in the Fuchun Mountains* is illustrated in Chapter 4 (see 4.45). Another was Ni Zan, whose best-known work is the beautiful, lonely *Rongxi Studio* (**19.21**). Typical of scholar paintings, the *Rongxi Studio* is painted in monochrome ink on paper. Vivid color and silk were both considered too pretentious, too professional. The brushwork is spare and delicate. Compared to the carefully drawn temple in Li Cheng's *A Solitary Temple amid Clearing Peaks* (see 19.20), Ni Zan's little studio is almost childlike. Like most scholar-painters, Ni Zan claimed that he painted merely to amuse himself, and that making a convincing likeness was the farthest thing from his mind. Also important is the inscription in Ni's own hand telling when, how, and for whom the picture was painted. Scholar-painters were not supposed to sell their work but to give it freely to each other as a token of friendship or in thanks for a favor. Their paintings almost always included an inscription and sometimes a poem as well. In their view, calligraphy and painting were closely related, for both consisted of brush strokes that revealed character.

The Ming dynasty (1368–1644) returned Chinese rulers to the imperial throne. The scholar-painter ideal retained enormous prestige during this and the ensuing Qing dynasty (1644–1911), and Chinese writing about art focused on it almost exclusively. The writers, of course, were themselves scholars. In truth, scholar-painting was only one of many types of art that

19.21 (left) Ni Zan. *The Rongxi Studio*. Yuan dynasty, 1372. Hanging scroll, ink on paper; height 29³⁄₈″.
National Palace Museum, Taipei.

19.22 (right) Lü Ji. *Cassia, Chrysanthemums, and Mountain Birds*. c. 1500. Hanging scroll, ink and color on silk.
Palace Museum, Beijing.

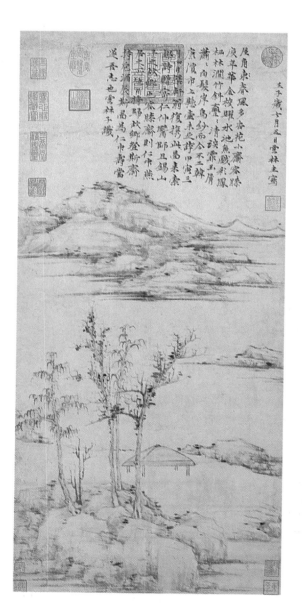

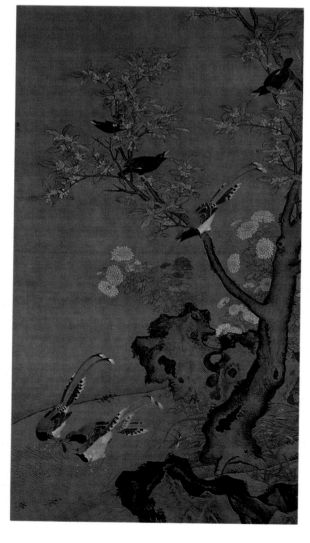

were being made. Workshops continued to turn out highly skilled sculptures and paintings for Buddhist and Daoist centers. The Ming imperial court favored more polished and splendid works such as Lü Ji's *Cassia, Chrysanthemums, and Mountain Birds* (**19.22**). Here is an exquisite example of the skill that scholar-painters claimed to disdain. Meticulously detailed, brilliantly colored, and brimming with contentment and good will, this painting asks only to be enjoyed.

Another sphere of artistic activity revolved around the large cities that had grown up during the late Song dynasty, especially in the south, and the wealthy middle-class patrons who lived in them. Thanks to these new markets for their work, numerous professional painters had thriving careers outside of the imperial court. The most admired professional painter of the Ming dynasty, Qiu Ying, lived and worked in the southern city of Suzhou. Even scholars respected this gifted painter, who was born into a poor family and died young: his knowledge of art history equaled theirs, he could imitate any number of ancient styles, his taste was impeccable, and his abilities were beyond question. No scholar would have tackled such an exacting composition as *Golden Valley Garden* (**19.23**). The subject, probably drawn from literary sources, is a host receiving his guest, and the painting itself would have been displayed in the reception hall of a well-to-do household. At the entrance to a pavilion set in a garden of rocks, trees, peonies, and peacocks, two men with a retinue of servants and musicians greet each other with utmost dignity. Undoubtedly they know the words of Confucius, who said, "If you study culture widely and sum it up in an orderly way of life, you may therefore avoid being uncivilized."[1]

19.23 Qiu Ying. *Golden Valley Garden.* First half 16th century. Hanging scroll, ink and color on silk, height 7′3/4″. Chion-in Temple, Kyoto.

ARTS OF JAPAN

12.1 *Haniwa* horse

Separated from the Asian landmass by the Sea of Japan, the islands of Japan form an arc curving northward from the tip of the Korean Peninsula. Neolithic cultures were established on the islands by 10,000 B.C.E. The ceramics they produced are not only the oldest known pottery in the world but some of the most fanciful as well, shaped with a seemingly playful streak that resurfaces regularly in Japanese art.

Japanese culture comes into clearer focus during the first centuries of our era. Large burial mounds from that time have yielded terra-cotta figures such as the horse illustrated in Chapter 12 (see 12.1). Called *haniwa*, they embody a taste for simple forms and natural materials that is one of the themes of Japanese art. We can see these characteristics again in the shrine at Ise (**19.24**). Erected during the first century C.E., the shrine has been ritually rebuilt on a regular basis since then, an unusual custom that allows this very early style to appear before our eyes in all its original freshness. The simple cylindrical shapes of the *haniwa* horse are echoed here in the wooden piles that raise the structure off the ground and the horizontal logs that hold the precisely trimmed thatch roof in place. The shrine is left unpainted, just as *haniwa* were left unglazed.

Housed in the shrine, which can only be entered by members of the imperial family and certain priests, are a sword, a mirror, and a jewel—the three sacred symbols of Shinto. Shinto is often described as the native religion of Japan, but religion is perhaps too formal a word. Shinto involves a belief in numerous nature deities that are felt to be present in such picturesque sites as gnarled trees, imposing mountains, and waterfalls. A simple, unpainted wooden gate may be erected to mark a particularly sacred site. The chief deity of Shinto is female, the sun goddess. Purification through

19.24 Inner shrine, Ise, Mie Prefecture. Early 1st century C.E.; rebuilt every 20 years; last rebuilding, 1993.

water plays an important role, as does the communion with and appease-ment of spirits, including spirits of the newly dead. The constant presence of nature in Japanese art, together with the respect for natural materials simply used, reflects the continuing influence of these ancient beliefs.

19.25 Horyu-ji Temple, Nara Pre-fecture. General view. Asuka pe-riod, 7th century C.E.

NEW IDEAS AND INFLUENCES: ASUKA

Japan was profoundly transformed during the Asuka period (552–646 C.E.), when elements of Chinese culture reached the islands through the interme-diary of Korea. One profound and lasting acquisition was the religion of Bud-dhism, accompanied by the art and architecture that China had developed to go with it. A perfected example of early Japanese Buddhist architecture is the temple compound Horyu-ji (**19.25**). Dating from the 7th century, Horyu-ji contains the oldest surviving wooden buildings in the world. The archi-tecture reflects the elegant style of the Six Dynasties period in China. We could imagine that Gu Kaizhi's ethereal palace ladies (see 19.16) would feel right at home here.

Inside the gateway and to the left stands a pagoda, a slender tower with multiple roof lines. The equivalent of an Indian stupa (see 19.3), a pagoda serves as a shrine for the relics of a buddha or saintly person. Its ancestors are the tall, multistoried watchtowers of Han dynasty China. When Bud-dhism entered China, Chinese architects adapted the watchtower form to this new sacred purpose. To the right of the pagoda is the *kondo* ("golden hall"). Used for worship, the *kondo* houses Tori Busshi's *Shaka Triad*, illustrated in Chapter 5 (see 5.9). Like the architecture around it, Busshi's sculpture is based in Chinese models.

Buddhism did not eclipse Shinto, which continued to exist alongside it. Similarly, the earlier architectural ideas that produced the shrine at Ise were continued along with the newer Chinese-inspired forms. This ability to absorb and transform new ideas while keeping older traditions vital is one of the enduring strengths of Japanese culture.

RELATED WORKS

5.9
Tori Busshi,
Shaka Triad

19.26 Illustration I from the "Azamaya" chapter of *The Tale of Genji*. Heian period, first half of 12th century. Handscroll (now preserved in sections), ink and color on paper; height 8½". Tokugawa Art Museum, Nagoya.

REFINEMENTS OF THE COURT: HEIAN

At the beginning of the Asuka period, Japan was ruled by powerful aristocratic clans, each of which controlled its own region. Inspired by the highly developed bureaucracy of China, the country moved toward unification under a centralized government. In 646 C.E., the first imperial capital was established at Nara. During the 8th century, the capital was moved to Kyoto, marking the beginning of the Heian period (794–1185 C.E.).

A highly refined and sophisticated culture developed around the court at Kyoto. Taste was paramount, and both men and women were expected to be accomplished in several arts. Perhaps the most important art was poetry. Through the miniature thirty-one-syllable form known as *tanka*, men and women communicated their feelings for each other, but always indirectly. The emphasis on literary accomplishment resulted in what many consider to be the greatest work of Japanese literature, *The Tale of Genji*, by Murasaki Shikibu. A lady of the court, Murasaki Shikibu wove aristocratic manners into a long narrative of love and loss that is often called the world's first novel.

Some of the earliest examples of secular painting in Japan survive in a copy of *The Tale of Genji* made during the 12th century (**19.26**). Written out and illustrated as a series of handscrolls (another imported Chinese idea), the monumental project brought together the specialized talents of a team of artists. The illustration here depicts a group of court ladies and their servants. As in all of the *Genji* paintings, we are given a bird's-eye view of an interior with the roof conveniently removed so we can see inside. The textile in the foreground, for example, is understood to be hanging from near the ceiling. Behind it, paper-covered sliding doors painted with a landscape lead to another room. To the left, a woman seated with her back to us is having her hair combed. Facing her across the alcove, in robes of green and orange, is Ukifune, the heroine of the last portion of *Genji*. She looks at a picture scroll while a nearby servant reads aloud.

Emerging from stylized renderings of starched and pleated robes, the women's white-powdered, masklike faces seem tranquil and composed. Yet in fact the scene has great underlying tension, for only hours before, Ukifune was the victim of a seduction attempt bordering on rape. Emotion is never betrayed by expressions or gestures in the *Genji* paintings. Just as Heian aristocrats conveyed their feelings indirectly through poems, the artists of the *Genji* scrolls conveyed emotions by other means, especially by the construction of space. Here, the characters are as hemmed in by their architectural setting as they are by their flawless manners. The room is closing in on them.

Buddhism remained central to Japanese life during the Heian period. Heian aristocrats at first favored esoteric Buddhism, an intellectually challenging faith that involved a hierarchy of deities as complicated as the hierarchy of the court itself. Later, as troubles grew, the simpler and more comforting message of Pure Land Buddhism became popular, as it had in China. In earlier chapters we looked at two of the loveliest masterpieces of Heian Pure Land Buddhist art, the temple Byodo-in (see 13.6) and the statue it houses, Jocho's *Amida Nyorai* (see 2.26). Amida is the Japanese name for Amitabha, the Buddha of the Western Paradise. One of the most delightful products of Heian art is also connected with Buddhism, Toba Sojo's *Frolicking Animals* (**19.27**). In the section of the handscroll illustrated here, a frog assumes the pose of a buddha while a monkey dressed in priests' robes ostentatiously prays aloud to it. Given the irreverent humor on display, it may come as a surprise to learn that the artist was an abbot of a Buddhist temple. Toba Sojo did not limit himself to religion but used his animals to poke fun at all levels of Heian society. The precise lines of his brush are as sharp as his wit. Not a stroke is wasted.

SAMURAI CULTURE: KAMAKURA AND MUROMACHI

The last decades of the Heian period were increasingly troubled by the rise of regional warriors, samurai. During the 12th century, civil war broke out as powerful regional clans, each with its army of samurai, battled for control of the country. With the triumph of the Minamoto clan in 1185, a military government was installed. The office of emperor was retained, but true power resided with the commander-in-chief, the shogun. A military capital was established at Kamakura, far from the distractions of the Heian court.

One of the great works of the Kamakura period (1185–1392) is the *Heiji Monogatari Emaki* ("the illustrated story of the Heiji era"), a set of handscrolls that tell of the wars between the Minamoto and their great rivals, the

13.6 Byodo-in

2.26 Jocho, *Amida Nyorai*

19.27 Attrib. Toba Sojo. *Monkeys Worshipping a Frog*, from *Frolicking Animals (Choju Jimbutsu Giga)*. Heian period, late 12th century. Handscroll, ink on paper; height 12½″.
Kozan-ji Temple, Kyoto.

19.28 *The Burning of Sanjo Palace*, detail from *Heiji Monogatari Emaki*. Kamakura period, late 13th century. Handscroll, ink and color on paper; height 16¼", overall length 22'9". Courtesy Museum of Fine Arts, Boston.

Taira. *The Burning of Sanjo Palace* (**19.28**) portrays a dramatic episode of 1159 when Taira forces abducted the emperor in a surprise nighttime attack. Never have the cinematic possibilities of the handscroll format been employed more effectively! Scene after scene scrolls by like an epic film with a cast of thousands: marshaling forces, surprise attack, spectacular conflagration, wild-eyed horses, streaming warriors, bloody hand-to-hand combat, and the emperor and his retinue fleeing in terror and disarray. In the detail shown here, mounted samurai archers surge toward a gate, the palace in flames behind them. The event is captured in minute and realistic detail, though the anonymous artists could only have known it through stories.

Just as dramatic in its own way is this Buddhist painting of a subject called *raigo* (**19.29**). Instead of samurai streaming through a gate in the light of a burning palace we see a buddha and his attendants streaming down from heaven in the light of their own glory. They flow toward a small house where an old man lies dying. Literally "welcoming approach," *raigo* depicts the buddha Amida arriving to escort a believer's soul to the Western Paradise. The gold on this *raigo* has dimmed with age, but when the painting was new, the heavenly procession shimmered into view over flowering mountains painted blue and green. Amida is preceded by numerous bodhisattvas; behind him celestial musicians play. Tiny saints hover like lanterns around the old man's cottage, while in the upper right is a distant view of the Western Paradise itself. *Raigo* were taken to the homes of the dying in the hopes that the vision they depicted might come true.

Pure Land Buddhism continued to win the hearts of ordinary people during the Kamakura period. The faith was spread through the countryside by wandering monks who taught a simple chant guaranteed to bring salvation. We saw a statue of one of these monks in Chapter 11, Koshi's affecting *Kuya Preaching* (see 11.19), carved in the new naturalistic style of the time.

Toward the end of the 14th century, the Ashikaga family gained control of the shogunate, and the military capital was moved to the Muromachi district of Kyoto. During the Muromachi period (1392–1568), a new type of Buddhism, Zen, became the leading cultural force in Japan. Zen reached

Japan from China, where it was already highly developed. Following the example of the historical Buddha, it stressed personal enlightenment through meditation. Centuries of accumulated writings and scripture were cast aside in favor of direct, one-on-one teaching, master to student. The best known Zen teaching tools are *koan*, irrational questions designed to "short-circuit" logical thought patterns. "What is the sound of one hand clapping?" is a well-known *koan*. Zen training was (and is) spartan and rigorous, qualities that appealed to the highly disciplined samurai.

Enlightenment in Zen is above all *sudden*. Zen priest-painters embodied this sudden appearance of meaning out of chaos in a painting technique called *haboku*, "splashed ink." Sesshu Toyo's *Landscape* (**19.30**) is a masterpiece of this difficult technique—difficult because most attempts end in a mess. Sesshu drew together his "splashes" with a few expertly placed dark strokes, giving us all the clues we need to see a forested hillside by the water. A small house nestles at the foot of the hill, and on the water floats a lone boat. While Sesshu Toyo was primarily a painter, he had trained as a Zen monk. He painted this work as a farewell gift for one of his pupils, and in the long inscription above he speaks of his own artistic path.

19.29 (below) *The Descent of Amida and the Twenty-five Bosatsu (Bodhisattvas).* Gold and color on silk, height 57". Kamakura period, early 13th century. Chion-in Temple, Kyoto.

19.30 (above) Sesshu Toyo. *Landscape* (in the *haboku* technique). 1495. Hanging scroll, ink on paper, width 12⅞". Tokyo National Museum.

SPLENDOR AND SILENCE: MOMOYAMA

The shogun's control over regional lords and their samurai weakened during the Muromachi period, and devastating civil wars broke out. After the Ashikaga family fell from power in 1568, three strong leaders controlled the shogunate in succession. The decades of their rule are known as the Momoyama period (1568–1603).

For all its turbulence, the Momoyama period was a time of splendor for the arts. Fortified castles and great residences were built by powerful regional lords, and their interiors were decorated by the finest painters. One of the most influential artists of this time was Kano Eitoku, who developed a bold and highly colored decorative style that was much imitated in later Japanese art (**19.31**). *Cypress Trees* was originally painted to decorate the paper-covered sliding doors of a large interior. It was later remounted as a folding screen—a portable partition that serves to mark off space within a larger room. A venerable cypress, gnarled and twisted with age, reaches from its roots at the right across the entire width of the screen. Stylized clouds of gold leaf float behind it over a blue and green landscape.

Golden screens, as they are known, represent only one side of Momoyama taste. The other side is almost the exact opposite: a hushed and understated monochrome such as we see in Hasegawa Tohaku's *Pine Wood*

19.31 (below, top) Attrib. Kano Eitoku. *Cypress Trees*. Momoyama period, late 16th century. Eight-fold screen; color, gold leaf, and ink on paper, 5'7" × 15'1½".
Tokyo National Museum.

19.32 (below) Hasegawa Tohaku. *Pine Wood*. Momoyama period, late 16th century. One of a pair of six-fold screens, ink on paper, height 5'1".
Tokyo National Museum.

(**19.32**). *Pine Wood* consists of a pair of six-panel folding screens, of which we show one. Painted with great simplicity in ink on paper, the ghostly trees appear through veils of mist. The paper itself, though technically blank, seems full of presences—trees we cannot see at the moment, or perhaps the edge of a lake. Tohaku's genius was to fashion monumental, decorative works from a fundamentally intimate style.

19.33 Hon'ami Koetsu. Teabowl. Momoyama–Edo period, late 16th–early 17th century. Raku ware, height 3⅜″.
Freer Gallery of Art, Smithsonian Institution, Washington, D.C.

ART FOR EVERYONE: EDO

Still another shift in the control of the shogunate signaled the beginning of the Edo period (1603–1868), named as before for the new capital city (present-day Tokyo). The many types of art that had been set in motion over the centuries continued during the Edo period. Decorative styles were carried on by such artists as Sakai Hoitsu, whose screen painting on silver paper is illustrated in Chapter 5 (see 5.14). The tradition of ink painting and the continuing influence of Zen produced such playful wonders as Nonomura Sotatsu's *The Zen Priest Choka* (see 5.15). The scholar painting of China inspired a parallel movement in Japan, and art was taken up by such amateurs as Yosa Buson, who was primarily a poet (see 6.15). But the great artistic event of the Edo period was the popularity of woodblock prints, a new form that made art available to everyone. Through the imagination of such masters as Hiroshige (see Crossing Cultures, page 101) and Hokusai (see 8.5), prints transcended their initial destiny as throwaway souvenirs to become lasting treasures of world art.

We end this look at Japanese art with a quiet and unassuming work, a teabowl by the calligrapher and tea-master Hon'ami Koetsu (**19.33**). The appreciation of tea in Japan grew up within the climate of Zen thought, and the rituals associated with it share Zen's appreciation for what is natural, spontaneous, and austere. Tea was prepared with a few intimates in a small room whose rustic simplicity was the product of sophisticated aesthetic choices. The objective was to clear the mind, to focus aesthetic attention on humble everyday objects, and to converse. Each utensil was regarded with the kind of rapt attention we might bring to an exceptionally well shaped piece of driftwood or a small, finely formed stone. When all is said and done, it isn't easy to make things as perfect and effortless as these. The uneven surfaces of Koetsu's bowl are designed to please both eye and hand, and the subtle glaze is drawn from nature's palette. We have come a long way in time from the *haniwa* figures and the shrine at Ise. In spirit, however, there is almost no distance at all.

RELATED WORKS

8.5 Hokusai, *The Great Wave*

p.101 Hiroshige, *Riverside Bamboo Market*

p.101 Hiroshige, *Fireworks at Ryogoku*

Arts of the Pacific and of the Americas

Continuing eastward around the world, we come to two regions that together cover almost half the globe: the vast ocean of the Pacific and the double continent of the Americas. We began the previous chapter by stressing the contacts that had linked India and China to the evolving Mediterranean world since ancient times. Here, we might do the opposite. From the end of the last Ice Age around 10,000 years ago, when rising waters submerged the land bridge that once linked Asia and Alaska, contact between Europe, Africa, and Asia on the one hand and the Americas and the Pacific Islands on the other was largely cut off.

In Chapter 16, there is a sign of the moment when one-half of the world rediscovered the other. If you look again at Holbein's *The Ambassadors* (see 16.24), painted in 1533, you will notice a globe on the lower shelf. Globes were all the rage in the early 16th century, spurred by Columbus' accidental discovery in 1492 of lands across the Atlantic Ocean and Vasco da Gama's discovery in 1498 that it was indeed possible to sail all the way around Africa and arrive in India. Holbein's globe is placed so that Europe is facing us. If you were to turn it around, you would see an emerging idea of the rest of the world. In this chapter, we fill in Holbein's map with a look at art as it had been developing in the cultures of the Pacific and the Americas.

PACIFIC CULTURES

The lands of the Pacific include the continent of Australia and the thousands of islands grouped together as Oceania, "lands of the ocean." Australia was settled by the ancestors of the peoples today known as Aborigines, who arrived by sea from Southeast Asia as early as 50,000 years ago. The neighboring island of New Guinea was settled around the same time. The peopling of the rest of the Pacific Islands was the result of centuries of maritime courage, as seafaring settlers set out across uncharted waters in search of land they could not have known existed. Among the first islands to be settled, beginning around 1500 B.C.E., were those to the east of New Guinea. These are grouped together with New Guinea as the cultural region of Melanesia. The last islands to be settled were the widely scattered islands of Polynesia,

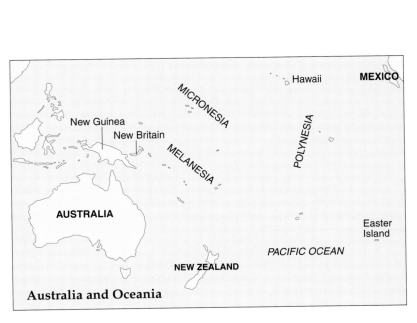

20.1 Lipundja. *Djalambu*. 1964.
Natural pigments on bark,
53 × 29¼".
National Gallery of Victoria,
Melbourne.

the easternmost cultural region of Oceania that includes Hawaii (settled around 500 C.E.) and New Zealand (settled between 800 and 1200 C.E.).

The oldest examples of Pacific art are the earliest rock engravings of the Aborigines, some of which may date to 30,000 B.C.E. The meanings of these images are not known, but more recent Aboriginal art is intimately connected with the religious beliefs known as Dreamtime or the Dreaming. Dreamtime includes the distant past, when ancestral beings emerged from the earth. Their actions shaped the landscape and gave rise to all forms of life within it, including humans. Dreamtime also exists in the present, and each individual is connected to it. With age a person draws closer to the realm of ancestors, and at death the spirit is reabsorbed into the Dreaming.

Ritual help for a spirit on its journey back to the Dreaming is the subject of Lipundja's *Djalambu* (**20.1**). Born in 1912, Lipundja was a member of the Yolngu, an Aboriginal people who live in Eastern Arnhem Land, in northern Australia. The Yolngu have many ways of talking about the journey back to the Dreaming. Often the soul is said to be carried by a current of water, in which case it may be thought of as a catfish that must avoid being eaten by diver birds. Catfish and diver birds are painted on Yolngu hollow-log coffins. During funerary rites, bullroarers (noisemakers) are whirled in the air to suggest diver birds in flight, while dancers painted as catfish scatter in fear. The central form of *Djalambu* is a log coffin, which is also understood to represent a catfish in the river. A diver bird and a long-neck tortoise appear near the base of the coffin-catfish, and seven bullroarers accompany it. The linear patterns of hatching and cross-hatching are characteristic of much Aboriginal art.

The most haunting elements of *Djalambu* are the two circular eyes of the coffin, the alert and otherworldly gaze of an ancestor looking into this world from the Dreamtime. Eyes from another realm meet our own again in this mask from the Tolai people of New Britain, one of the islands of Melanesia (**20.2**). Masks and masquerades play important roles in many Melanesian cultures. As in Africa (see Chapter 18), masks are used to materialize spirit beings. This mask is *tubuan*, the female spirit of a society called *duk duk*. *Duk duk* are male spirits, also danced by maskers, that punish lawbreakers at the bidding of the community's leaders. The male spirits are reborn each year from *tubuan*, who is immortal. With her costume of leaves, *tubuan* represents nature and the natural order of things, and she lends her support to the authority of the human community's leaders. Yet all is not so simple, for the powers of *tubuan* are volatile and potentially a force for chaos, and a true leader must show that he can control them.

Among the most well known works of the Pacific are the monumental stone figures of Easter Island, the most remote and isolated island of Polynesia (**20.3**). Almost 1,000 of the monolithic statues have been found. Scholars believe they were carved as memorials to dead rulers or other important ancestors. Whatever purpose the statues served, the islanders must have believed it to be vital to their community, for they went to heroic efforts to erect them. The stones were quarried and partially carved in the island's volcanic mountains. The average height of the figures is about 36 feet, and each one weighs tens of tons, yet somehow they were dragged for miles across the island and set upright on elevated stone platforms that probably served as altars.

Easter Islanders seem to have begun erecting the figures around 900 C.E. Six centuries later, conflicts apparently broke out on the island, and a period of warfare ensued. Most of the figures were knocked down and destroyed. The statues photographed here were restored in 1978, their heads crowned again with red stone topknots and their faces set with white coral eyes. Stones that had slumbered for centuries suddenly awoke. Lined up once more along the shoreline, they stare hypnotically out to sea in an eternal vigil whose purpose we may never fully understand.

Many Polynesian peoples imagined their deities as feathered beings. Rulers and other high-ranking members of society traced their descent from the gods, and they adorned themselves with feathered garments as a sign of their status. With their bold geometric designs and brilliant colors, the feather cloaks of Hawaii are the most spectacular products of this unique art form (**20.4**). While both men and women of the Hawaiian elite wore many types

20.2 (above) Female mask (*tubuan*) of the *duk duk* society. Tolai culture, New Britain, Papua New Guinea.
Museum der Kulturen, Basel.

20.3 (below) Stone figures on Ahu Naunau, Anakena, Easter Island (Rapanui), Chile.

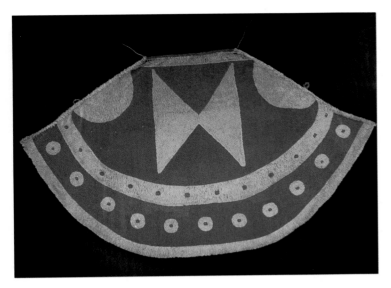

of feathered garments, majestic cloaks such as this, reaching from the shoulders to the ground, belonged exclusively to the highest-ranking men. The creation of such a cloak was itself a ritual activity limited to high-ranking men. As the makers wove and knotted the cloak's plant-fiber foundation, they chanted the names of the ancestors of the man who would eventually wear it. The names were thus captured in the cloak, imbuing it with protective spiritual power. Feathers were tied onto the completed fiber netting in overlapping rows. Feathers were collected by commoners, who offered them as part of their yearly tribute to their rulers.

The feather cloaks of Hawaii embody ideas about the order of society, the respective roles of men and women, the continuing presence of ancestors, and the protective power of the gods. Similar concerns are given architectural form in the men's meeting houses of the Maori people of New Zealand, the southernmost of the Polynesian islands (**20.5**). The house is understood as the body of the sky father, the supreme deity of the Maori. The ridgepole is his spine, and the rafters are his ribs. His face is carved on the exterior, where other elements symbolize his embracing arms. Meetings thus take place within the god, which is to say within his protection, sanction, and authority.

20.4 (above, top) Feather cloak. Hawaii. Feathers, fiber; height 5'9".
The British Museum, London.

20.5 (above) Raharuhi Rukupo, master carver. Meeting house, from Manutuke Poverty Bay, New Zealand. 1842–43, restored 1935. Wood, shell, grass, flax, pigments.
The Museum of New Zealand Te Papa Tongarewa, Wellington.

The two freestanding figures that support the ridgepole from inside portray ancestors. Their knees are bent in the aggressive posture of the war dance, reminding the living of their courage and great deeds. More stylized portrayals of snarling, powerful ancestors are carved in the series of reliefs that line the walls. Each relief panel meets a rafter whose lower portion is carved with still more ancestors. Everywhere, iridescent shell eyes gleam and glimmer as they catch the light. Ancestors were believed to participate in the discussions held in the house, and these sculptures make their watchful presence felt. The reliefs along the walls alternate with panels of lattice woven in symbolic patterns that relate to stories about Maori deities and heroes. The panels were woven by women. Women, however, are not permitted to enter the meeting house, and so they wove the panels from the back, standing outside.

The meeting house illustrated here shows the Maori carving style at its finest, with bold, massive forms covered in delicate, swirling detail. Master carver Raharuhi Rukupo worked with a team of eighteen wood carvers to create the house in memory of his brother in the mid-19th century. Restored in 1935 by carvers still working in traditional ways, the house is regarded by the Maori as a national treasure and is now sheltered in a New Zealand museum.

THE AMERICAS

No one knows for sure when humans first occupied the double continent of the Americas or where those people came from. The most widely accepted theory is that sometime before 12,000 years ago—and possibly as early as 30,000 years ago—migrating peoples crossed over a now-submerged land bridge linking Siberia with Alaska, then gradually pushed southward, seeking hospitable places in which to dwell. Firm evidence of human presence at the tip of South America has been dated to about 11,000 years ago, indicating that by then both continents were populated, if only sparsely.

By 3000 B.C.E. we can identify developed cultures in three important centers: the Northwest Coast of North America, the fertile plateaus and coastal lowlands of Mesoamerica, and the Pacific Coast of South America. During the ensuing centuries, peoples in these and other territories created rich and sophisticated artistic expressions. Their early art has sometimes been called "pre-Columbian," meaning that it was created before Columbus's voyages to the Americas. The term acknowledges that the arrival of Europeans changed everything, and that the civilizations of the Americas were interrupted as decisively as if they had been hit by a meteor. Yet it is best to approach them on their own terms and not to think of them as "before" something else. After all, they did not think of themselves as coming "before" anything, but rather *after* their many predecessors, whose achievements they knew and admired.

MESOAMERICA

"Mesoamerica" describes a region that extends from north of the Valley of Mexico (the location of present-day Mexico City) through the western portion of modern Honduras. Mesoamerica is a cultural and historical designation as well as a geographical one, for the civilizations that arose in this region shared many features, including the cultivation of corn, the building of pyramids, a 260-day calendar, similar deities, an important ritual ball game, and a belief in the role of human blood in sustaining the gods and the universe. Mesoamerican peoples themselves were conscious of their common cultural

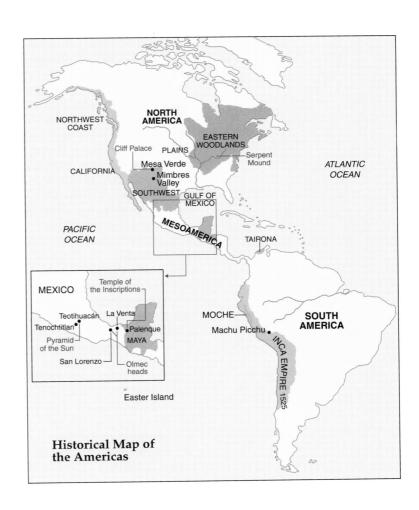

Historical Map of
the Americas

background. Thus the Aztecs, who were the most powerful culture in the region at the time of the Spanish conquests of the early 16th century, collected and admired jade sculptures by the Olmec, whose civilization had flourished over 2,000 years earlier.

Olmec civilization, which flourished between about 1500 and 300 B.C.E., is often called the "mother culture" of Mesoamerica, for it seems to have institutionalized the features that mark later civilizations of the region. The principal Olmec centers were concentrated in a small region on the Gulf Coast of Mexico, but the influence of Olmec culture extended over a much broader area. Chapter 11 illustrated one of the colossal stone heads carved by Olmec sculptors (see 11.8). Chapter 3 included a finely worked Olmec jade depicting a shaman (see 3.7). Olmec leaders may have derived their power by claiming ability as shamans. Rulers in later Mesoamerican societies were also expected to have privileged access to the sacred realm.

A few centuries after the decline of the Olmecs, the city of Teotihuacán, located to the northeast of present-day Mexico City, began its rise to prominence. At its height, between 350 and 650 C.E., Teotihuacán was one of the largest cities in the world. Laid out in a grid pattern with streets at right angles, the city covered 9 square miles and had a population of around 200,000. Teotihuacán exerted great influence over the rest of Mesoamerica, though whether this was through trade or conquest we do not know.

The heart of the city was its ceremonial center, a complex of pyramids and temples lining a 3-mile-long thoroughfare known as the Avenue of the Dead. To the Aztecs, who arrived in the region long after Teotihuacán had been abandoned, it seemed hardly possible that humans were capable of such wonders. They viewed the city as a sacred site where the gods had created the universe, and it was they who named its largest structure the

RELATED WORKS

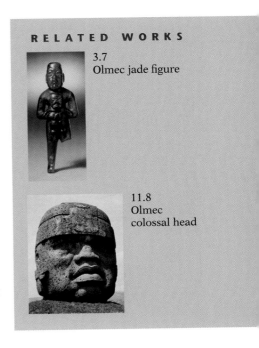

3.7
Olmec jade figure

11.8
Olmec
colossal head

Pyramid of the Sun (**20.6**). Made of stone and brick, the Pyramid of the Sun rises to a height of over 210 feet. A temple originally stood at its summit. Like the ziggurats of ancient Mesopotamia, Mesoamerican pyramids were symbolically understood as mountains. Excavations have discovered a tunnel leading to a natural cave containing a spring directly beneath the center of the Pyramid of the Sun. Perhaps it was this womblike source of water and life that was considered sacred by the city's original inhabitants.

Farther north along the Avenue of the Dead is a large sunken plaza surrounded by temple platforms. The focal point of this complex, the Temple of the Feathered Serpent, gives us our first look at a deity shared by many of the Mesoamerican civilizations (**20.7**). The Olmec pantheon included a feathered serpent, although its exact meaning is unclear. To the Aztecs, the feathered serpent was Quetzalcoatl, the god of windstorms that bring rain. Here, representations of the deity—its aggressive head emerging from a collar of feathers—alternate with the more abstract figure of the god of rain, distinguished by his goggle eyes. Rain, water, and the wind that brought them were essential to the agricultural societies of Mesoamerica.

One of the most fascinating of all Mesoamerican civilizations was that of the Maya, which arose in the southeastern portion of Mesoamerica, primarily in the Yucatán Peninsula and present-day Guatemala. Mayan culture began to form around 1000 B.C.E., probably under influence of the Olmecs. The Maya themselves come into focus just after the final decline of the Olmec civilization around 300 B.C.E. Mayan civilization flourished most spectacularly between 250 and 900 C.E. It was still in existence when the Spanish arrived in the early 16th century, however, and speakers of Mayan languages live in the region today.

Among their other accomplishments (including astronomy, biology, and the mathematical concept of zero), the Maya developed the most sophisticated version of the Mesoamerican calendar and the most advanced of the region's many writing systems. Scholars began to crack the code of Mayan writing in the 1960s, and since then the steady deciphering of inscriptions has provided new insights into Mayan civilization, in the process overturning much of what earlier scholars assumed.

The Maya were not a single state but a culture with many centers, each ruled by a hereditary lord and an elite class of nobles. Warfare between the

20.6 Pyramid of the Sun, Teotihuacán, Mexico. 50–200 C.E.

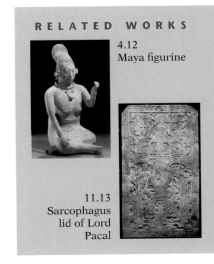

4.12
Maya figurine

11.13
Sarcophagus
lid of Lord
Pacal

centers was common, and its purpose was not conquest but capture: pris-oners of war were needed for the human sacrifices that were thought necessary to sustain the gods and maintain the universe. The official and cer-emonial architecture of the Maya was meant to impress, and it does (**20.8**). The photograph illustrated here shows the structures known as the Palace and the Temple of the Inscriptions at Palenque, in the Chiapas region of Mexico. The royal dynasty of Palenque was founded in 431 C.E. and rose to prominence under Lord Pacal, who died in 683 C.E. Pacal was buried in a small chamber deep beneath the Temple of the Inscriptions. The carved lid of his sarcophagus is illustrated in Chapter 11 (see 11.13).

The Palace probably served as an administrative and ceremonial center. Set on a raised terrace, it is constructed on two levels around three court-yards. Like the Temple of the Inscriptions atop the pyramid, the buildings of the Palace take the form of long, many-chambered galleries. The square pil-lars of their open porches support massive stone ceilings with corbelled vaulting. (To review corbelling, see page 308.)

20.7 (above, top) Temple of the Feathered Serpent, the Ciudadela, Teotihuacán, Mexico. 2nd century C.E.

20.8 (above) Palace and Temple of the Inscriptions, Palenque, Mexico. Maya, 7th century C.E.

20.9 East wall, Room 1, Bonampak, Mexico. Maya, 800 C.E. Polychromed stucco. Copy by Felipe Dávalos and Kees Grotenberg.
Florida State Museum, Gainesville.

A series of murals discovered at Bonampak, in Mexico, help us imagine the kinds of ceremonies that took place in Mayan palaces (**20.9**). Painted in 800 C.E., the original murals are today badly faded and crumbling, and we appreciate them best in this careful copy that restores their original colors. The murals depict events surrounding the presentation of an heir to the throne. In the upper band, nobles and lords gather. We can see four of the lords clearly in this view, with their white capes and feather-crowned headdresses. Vertical panels of writing next to them record their names. The assembly continues around the wall to the right and culminates with a view of the young heir himself (not visible here). In the lowest band, a colorful and evidently noisy procession winds around the walls against a vivid blue background. The jaguar pelts, finely woven textiles, abundant jewelry, and feathered ornaments of the Maya have not survived, but this mural and others like it allow us to restore a sense of color and pageantry to the deserted ruins we study today.

The first scholars to study the Maya believed that their art was primarily sacred and depicted cosmic events such as stories of the gods. Thanks to our understanding of Mayan writing, we now realize that Mayan art is almost entirely concerned with history. Like the murals at Bonampak, it memorializes rulers and portrays important moments of their reigns. Preeminent among Mayan arts are narrative stone relief carvings such as this lintel from a building in Yaxchilan, in Mexico (**20.10**). The scene is the second in a sequence of three compositions that portray a royal bloodletting ceremony. Bloodletting was a central Mayan practice, and almost every ritually important occasion was marked by it. Lady Xoc, the principal wife of Lord Shield Jaguar, is seated at the lower right. The previous panel showed her pulling a thorn-lined rope through her tongue in the presence of Shield Jaguar himself. Here, she experiences the hallucinatory vision that was the ceremony's purpose. From the bowl of blood and ritual implements on the floor before her there rises the Vision Serpent. A warrior, possibly one of Shield Jaguar's ancestors, issues from its gaping jaws. Dated with the Mayan equivalent of October 23, 681 C.E., the ceremony probably marked the accession of Shield Jaguar as ruler. Bloodletting and the visions it produced seem to have been the Mayan rulers' way of communicating with the spirits and gods. This communication was their privilege, their duty, and the source of their power.

The last Mesoamerican empire to arise before the arrival of European conquerors was built by the Aztecs. According to their own legends, the Aztecs migrated into the Valley of Mexico during the 13th century C.E. from their previous home near the mythical Lake Aztlan (hence Aztec). They settled finally on an island in Lake Tezcoco, and there they began to construct their capital, Tenochtitlán. Tenochtitlán grew to be a magnificent city, built on a cluster of islands connected by canals and linked by long causeways to cities on the surrounding shores. Massive pyramids and temple platforms towered over the ritual precincts, and in the market squares goods from all over Mesoamerica changed hands. By 1500 Aztec power reached its height, and much of central Mexico paid them tribute.

Almost nothing remains of Tenochtitlán. Spanish conquerors razed its pyramids, and Mexico City has since been built on the same site. Aztec books were consigned to the fire, and their arts in precious metals were melted down for gold and silver. Yet the Spaniards were deeply impressed by the arts they found, and many objects were sent back to Europe. The mask illustrated here (**20.11**) was probably made by Mixtec artists living in Tenochtitlán. Mixtec artists also made gold and silver objects for the Aztecs, who greatly admired their work. (For Diego Rivera's re-creation of a Mixtec artistic community, see 7.4.) Mosaic of turquoise painstakingly applied in minute squares follows every curve of the face. Pearl shell serves for teeth and eyes. Such a mask would have been worn in one of the numerous ceremonies of song and dance that were central to Aztec life. Masks had a long history in Mesoamerica. The Aztecs collected jade masks carved by the Olmecs and in Teotihuacán. Maya artists also carved ritual masks of jade.

20.10 (left) Lintel 25 (*The Vision of Lady Xoc*), Yaxchilan, Chiapas, Mexico. Maya, 725 C.E. Limestone, 51³⁄₁₆″ × 34″ × 4″. The British Museum, London.

20.11 (right) Ritual mask. Aztec, early 16th century C.E. Turquoise, pearl shell. The British Museum, London.

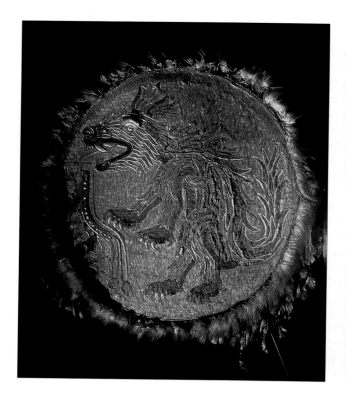

20.12 (left) Ceremonial shield. Aztec, early 16th century. Feather mosaic and gold on wicker base, diameter 27½".
Museum für Völkerkunde, Vienna.

20.13 (right) Stirrup vessel. Moche, 200–500 C.E. Earthenware with cream slip, height 9⅛".
The Metropolitan Museum of Art, New York.

Featherwork was greatly prized in Mesoamerica, and a specialized group of weavers in Tenochtitlán produced featherwork headdresses, cloaks, and other garments exclusively for nobles and high officials. The ceremonial shield here (**20.12**) shows their vivid sense of design and color. The heraldic coyote depicted in blue feathers edged in gold is the Aztec god of war. From his mouth issues the symbol for "water burning," an Aztec term for war. Rich in metaphors, Aztec speech also referred to warfare as "the song of the shields" and "flowers of the heart upon the plain." Feather shields such as this were part of the lavish dance costumes worn by warriors in ritual recreations of the warfare of the gods.

SOUTH AND CENTRAL AMERICA

Like Mesoamerica to the north, the region of the central Andes on the Pacific Coast of South America provided a setting in which numerous cultures developed. Pyramids, temple platforms, and other monuments have been found dating to the third millennium B.C.E., making them the oldest works of architecture in the Americas, contemporary with the pyramids of Egypt. Textiles of astonishing intricacy have also been found from this time.

Among the first South American peoples to leave a substantial record of art are the Moche, who dominated a large coastal area at the northern end of the central Andes during the first six centuries C.E. The Moche were exceptional potters and goldsmiths. Tens of thousands of Moche ceramics have been found, for one of their great innovations was the use of molds for mass production.

Kneeling warriors are a standard subject of Moche ceramic art (**20.13**). The large ear ornaments and elaborate headdress capped with a crescent-shaped element are typical of the costume on these figures. The warrior carries a shield and a war club; the heads of two more war clubs protrude from his headdress. His beaked nose probably links him to the barn owl, which was regarded as a warrior animal for its fierce and accurate nocturnal hunting abilities. Much of the finest Moche pottery takes the form of stirrup vessels, so called after the U-shaped spout (here attached to the warrior's back). The innovative spout pours well, can be carried easily, and minimizes evaporation. Yet such elaborate vessels cannot have been primarily practical.

One of the most spectacular archaeological sites in the world is the Inca city of Machu Picchu, in Peru (**20.14**). Beginning around 1430 and moving with amazing swiftness, the Incas created the largest empire of its time in the world. By 1500, Inca rule extended for some 3,400 miles along the Pacific Coast. Incan textiles are some of the finest in the long tradition of South American fiber work (see 12.13). Incan artists also excelled in sculptures and other objects of silver and gold. But the most original Incan genius expressed itself in stonework. Over 20,000 miles of stone-paved roads were built to speed communication and travel across the far-flung empire. Massive masonry walls of Incan buildings were constructed of large blocks of granite patiently shaped through abrasion until they fit together perfectly with no mortar.

Machu Picchu is set high in the Andes Mountains overlooking a hairpin turn in the Urubamba River thousands of feet below. Builders leveled off the site to create a small plateau and constructed terraces for houses and agriculture. Also visible at Machu Picchu is the wholly distinctive Incan sensitivity to the natural landscape. At the northern end of Machu Picchu, for example, a free-standing boulder was carved to resemble the silhouette of a peak that can be seen beyond it in the distance. Elsewhere a rounded building known as the Observatory accommodates a huge boulder into its walls

20.14 Machu Picchu, Peru. Inca, 15th–16th centuries.

and interior. Part of the boulder is subtly sculpted to create a staircase and chamber. The Inca believed stones and people to be equally alive and capable of changing into one another. This attitude seems to have resulted in their unique approach of relating architecture to its setting.

We end this section with an object made of the material that proved to be the Americas' undoing, gold (**20.15**). Fashioned of a gold and copper alloy called *tumbaga*, this pendant figure was made by artists of the Tairona culture, which flourished in northern Colombia after about 1000 C.E. The Tairona belong to the cultural region of Central America, which extends from the southern part of present-day Honduras into northwestern Colombia, where a mountain range called the Cordillera Oriental forms a natural boundary. The knowledge of extracting and working gold was first developed to the south, in Peru. Over generations it spread northward, with the goldsmith's art becoming increasingly refined and technically advanced.

Cast using the lost-wax technique, the pendant here portrays a ruler. He is probably also a shaman, and the birds that unfold like wings from either side of his head are the spirit alter egos that give him access to the other world. Tairona smiths added copper to the gold to lower its melting point and create a harder, more durable object. After casting, the pendant was bathed in acids that removed the outermost layer of copper particles, leaving the impression of solid gold. The taste for ornaments in precious metals

20.15 (left) Pendant depicting a ruler. Tairona culture, 1000–1300 C.E. Copper and gold alloy, height 2³/₄″.
Museu Barbier-Mueller d'Art Precolombí, Barcelona.

20.16 (right) Effigy pipe. Adena culture, 500–200 B.C.E. Stone, height 8″.
Ohio Historical Society, Columbus.

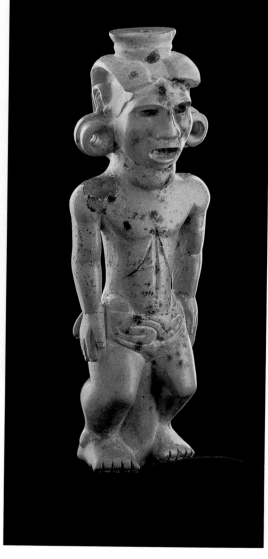

spread from Central America northward into Mesoamerica. There the finest artists in precious metals were the Mixtec, who supplied the Aztecs with their legendary and now lost works. Earlier cultures such as the Olmecs and the Maya had preferred jade.

NORTH AMERICA

It might be expected that those of us who live in North America would have a clear picture of the history of art on our own continent, since we are, after all, right here on the spot. Unfortunately, we do not. In general, the ancient arts of North America are much less available to us than those of many other parts of the world. Partly this is because the early inhabitants seem to have made their artifacts from perishable materials such as wood and fiber. Partly it is due to the absence of large urban centers. Patterns of life developed differently in the North.

Many arts of later North American peoples—Indians, as we have come to call them—are arts of daily life: portable objects such as baskets, clothing, and tools imbued with meanings that go far beyond their practical functions. In Chapter 3, we used as an example of such arts a basket from the Pomo of California (see 3.1). Pomo thought links the basket to the story of the sun's journey across the sky, and a flaw woven purposefully into the basket provides a way for spirits to enter and leave. The basket is thus connected to the sacred realm and to ritual. And yet it is also a basket.

The first clearly identifiable culture group of North America populated an area known as the Eastern Woodlands—in parts of what are now Ohio, Indiana, Kentucky, Pennsylvania, and West Virginia—starting about 700 B.C.E. Several Eastern Woodlands cultures are known collectively as the "mound builders," because they created earthworks, some of them burial mounds, in geometric forms or in the shapes of animals. The Serpent Mound in Ohio, illustrated in Chapter 11, is the most famous of the mounds still visible (see 11.29). Among the arts of daily life that have come down to us from early Eastern Woodlands cultures are pipes carved of stone (**20.16**). The pipe illustrated here was excavated in 1901 from an Adena burial mound. Like the Moche warrior earlier (see 20.13), the figure wears a crescent-shaped head ornament and large ornaments called ear spools. The gently rounded musculature and slightly bent knees convey a sense of movement and life.

Tobacco was considered a sacred substance by many North American peoples. First domesticated in the Andes around 3000 B.C.E., it made its way north by way of Mexico some 2,000 years later. In North America, smoking tobacco became viewed as a form of prayer. The rising smoke faded into the other world, bidding its spirits to come witness or sanction human events. Interestingly, while knowledge of tobacco arrived from the South, the stone pipe itself is a North American invention.

Europeans arriving in America introduced such new materials as glass beads, and Indian beadwork became justifiably famous. An older Indian art, however, is quillwork (**20.17**). Quills from porcupine or birds were softened by soaking, then dyed to produce a palette of colors and worked into a surface of deerskin or birch bark. The quillwork on the tabbed deerskin bag illustrated here portrays a thunderbird, a sky deity recognized by many Indian peoples. The thunderbird rises over a horizontal band that signifies earth. Below, two reptiles abstracted to diagonal lines are denizens of a symbolic underworld. The three levels of existence—sky, earth, and underworld—are summarized with great economy of means.

While Eastern Woodlands culture was based in a settled way of life, the Plains culture that formed to the west was nomadic, organized around the herds of buffalo that roamed the Great Plains. European explorers' greatest although accidental contribution to Plains culture was undoubtedly the horse, which was brought to America by Spanish colonists and spread throughout Indian cultures over the course of the 18th century.

11.29 Serpent mound

20.17 Tabbed skin bag. Ottowa(?) culture. Eastern Great Lakes, c. 1790. Black-dyed deerskin, porcupine quills, silk binding, hair tassels, tin cones; length 20½″. New York State Historical Association, Fenimore House Museum, Cooperstown.

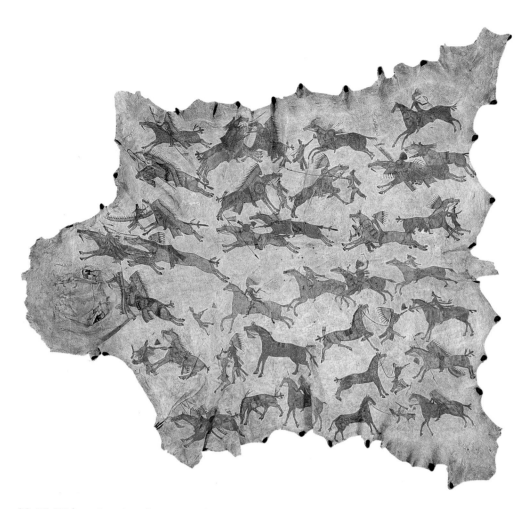

20.18 Hide painted with scenes of warfare. Western Lakota culture, North or South Dakota, c. 1880. Horsehide and pigments, branded; 8'2" × 7'9".
New York State Historical Association, Fenimore House Museum, Cooperstown.

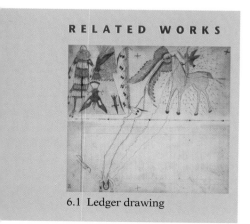
Buffalo hides provided not only clothing but also shelter in the form of covering for tents, tipis (also spelled "tepees"). Hides also provided a surface on which Plains men recorded their exploits as warriors (**20.18**). Drawn by Lakota warriors, the images here record a battle between the Lakota and the Crow, depicted with the vivid recall of participants. Such a hide would have been worn around the shoulders as a robe. Other garments such as shirts and leggings were also painted. Clearly visible are the feathered headdresses that were a distinctive feature of Plains costume. Headdresses were made from the tail feathers of eagles, which were identified with the thunderbird. Some offered protective spiritual power, while others were merely finery. Only a proven warrior was permitted to wear one in battle, however.

Urban life was not entirely absent from North America. The Anasazi people, who lived in the southwestern part of the continent, created ambitious communal dwelling sites. One such dwelling at Mesa Verde, in Colorado, has become known as Cliff Palace (**20.19**). The Anasazi had been present in the region from the first several centuries B.C.E. Around the 12th century C.E. they began clustering their buildings in protected sites on the undersides of cliffs. A complex system of handholds and footholds made access difficult. (Modern tourists have been provided an easier way in.) This arrangement allowed the Anasazi to ward off invaders and maintain a peaceful community life.

Cliff Palace, dated to about 1200 C.E., has more than 200 rooms organized in apartment-house style, most of them living quarters but some at the back meant for storage. In addition, there are twenty-three *kivas*—large, round chambers, mostly underground and originally roofed, used for religious or other ceremonial purposes. The structures are of stone or adobe with timber, and so harmonious is the overall plan that many scholars believe a single architect must have been in charge. Cliff Palace was occupied for about a hundred years before being mysteriously abandoned in the early 14th century.

The Anasazi's neighbors in the Southwest were a people we know only as the Mogollon culture, which flourished in the Mimbres Valley of what is now New Mexico between the 3rd and 12th centuries C.E. Today the word *Mimbres* is associated with a type of ceramic vessel developed about 1000 C.E. Mimbres jars and bowls were decorated with geometric designs or with stylized figures of animals or humans. Often these motifs appeared as paired figures (**20.20**). While Mimbres ceramics were probably used in households in some way, most examples that have come down to us have been recovered from burials. As grave goods the vessels often seem to have been ritually

20.19 (below, top) Cliff Palace, Mesa Verde, Colo. Anasazi culture, c. 1200 C.E.

20.20 (below) *Bowl with Two Human Figures*. Mimbres. 1000–1500 C.E. Ceramic, diameter 13″. Dallas Museum of Art.

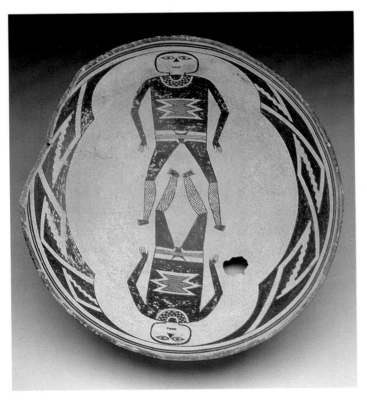

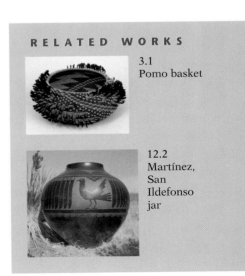

RELATED WORKS

3.1 Pomo basket

12.2 Martínez, San Ildefonso jar

"killed," either by shattering or, as here, by being pierced with a hole. The act draws a parallel with the human body, which is a vessel for a soul. In death, the vessel is broken and the soul released.

Masks and masking played important roles in some Indian cultures. The Pueblo cultures of the Southwest acknowledge numerous supernatural beings called kachina (from the Hopi *katsina*). Danced by maskers, kachina enter into the community at important times to bring blessings. They may appear, for example, early in the year as auspicious presences so that rain will follow for the new crops. Later, after a successful growing season, they dance at harvest ceremonies. Over 200 kachina have been identified, each with its own name, mask, character, dance movements, and powers.

Hopi and Zuni Indians make doll-size versions of kachina as educational playthings so that children may learn to identify and understand the numerous spirits (**20.21**). The kachina themselves often presented the dolls to the young members of the community during their appearances. The doll here portrays a kachina named *tamtam kushokta*. The spirit wears a white Hopi blanket around its waist and a bucket-shaped leather mask. A spectator who witnessed kachina maskers dancing in 1907 wrote, "In their right hands they carried a tortoise-shell rattle, which they shook with vigor when they danced, and in the left hand, a bundle of prayer sticks, tied up in corn

20.21 Kachina doll. Zuni culture. Before 1903. Wood, pigments, hair, fur hide, cotton, wool, yucca, height 19".
The Brooklyn Museum, New York.

20.22 Dance mask. Kwakiutl.
Late 19th century.
National Museum of Natural History,
Smithsonian Institution, Washington,
D.C.

husk, with a kind of handle attached by which it was held."[1] These handheld objects are faithfully represented on the doll. Kachina dolls were believed to contain some of the power of the spirit they represented. Early in the 20th century, admirers managed to purchase or commission kachina dolls, but this caused great unease among the Zuni, who believed that letting the dolls out of the community would result in crop failures or other disasters. Selling the dolls to outsiders was a crime subject to severe punishment, although it seems that some were indeed sold.

Masks are also danced by many peoples of the Pacific Northwest, including the Kwakiutl, who live along the southern coast of British Columbia. The flamboyant Kwakiutl mask illustrated here is Hokhokw, one of the four monstrous beings who live at the north end of the world and eat human flesh (**20.22**). During the winter, the four monsters invade the human community. They kidnap young men of noble families and turn them into cannibals. This kidnapping and transformation take place within the larger ceremony of potlatch, in which a host generously feeds guests from numerous villages over the course of many days. On the final day, the elders of the gathering ritually cure the young man of his cannibalism. The four masks dance as part of this ritual, after which they are banished for another year.

The long, pointed beak is hinged, and a skillful dancer can make it open and snap menacingly shut. Hokhokw masks are carved to this day, both for use and to be sold to collectors. Their tremendous formal variety shows how much room for creativity and individual expression an artist actually has within forms that are too often thought of as unchanging and "traditional."

CHAPTER 21

The Modern World: 1800–1945

For 19th-century artists and writers, walking through the teeming city streets was the equivalent of today's channel surfing—one sensation followed quickly on another, offering fleeting glimpses of thousands of lives. They found it overwhelming—sometimes thrilling, sometimes disturbing—but they recognized it as new and they called it "modern." Modernity reflected the emergence of a new kind of society in the wake of the three revolutions discussed at the end of Chapter 17: the French Revolution, the American Revolution, and the Industrial Revolution. Driven by technological progress and characterized by rapid change, the 19th century gave birth to our industrialized middle-class culture of mass production, mass advertising, and mass consumption, including the mass consumption of leisure activities such as shopping, going to entertainments, or visiting art museums.

Art museums themselves were a development of the 19th century, and they made art available to the public (including artists) in a way we now take for granted. The first national museum was the Louvre in Paris. Opened in 1793 during the fervor of the French Revolution, it placed the art that had been the private property of the kings of France on public view in what used to be the royal residence. Like everything else that used to belong to aristocrats, art was now for everybody, but what kind of art did everybody want? What kind of art was suited to a society no longer dominated by the Church or by the nobility, but by the middle class and its leaders of finance and industry? Debates about art and modernity began during the 19th century and continued into the 20th, resulting in the ever-increasing number of "isms" that appear in art history from this point on: Realism, Impressionism, Pointillism, Fauvism, Cubism, Futurism, Surrealism—each one staking out a different viewpoint about what art can be, what subjects it can treat, and how it can look. During this time as well, photography revolutionized the making of images. From the Chauvet cave paintings of 30,000 B.C.E. until the first successful daguerreotype in 1837, images had been made by hand. Suddenly, there was another way, and it posed profound questions about the nature and purpose of art even as it opened up new possibilities.

The changes of modernity occurred everywhere in Europe, but the debates they provoked in the visual arts played out most dramatically in France, especially in Paris, and this brief survey largely focuses there.

NEOCLASSICISM, ROMANTICISM, REALISM

As we have seen in earlier chapters, most periods in the history of art had one dominant style—the High Renaissance style or the Baroque style, for instance—that major artists of the time worked in. But French art of the early 19th century is not like that. It is customarily divided into three broad categories: classic, romantic, and realist. The fact that artists of the first rank were working in each of these styles gives a hint of the great diversity that was soon to come.

Representing the classic style was the work of Jean-Auguste-Dominique Ingres. Ingres was a pupil of Jacques-Louis David, the leading painter of Neoclassicism and the most influential teacher in France at the turn of the 19th century (see 17.17, 17.19). Ingres inherited his master's admiration of ancient Greek and Roman art, and he took to heart David's emphasis on clean contours, a smooth finish, and precise draftsmanship. He brought to these stylistic traits his own temperamental inclination toward emotional reserve, oddly mixed with a sensuous taste for the exotic. We see these qualities in *La Grande Odalisque* (**21.1**). *Odalisque* is a French word, derived from Turkish, meaning a concubine in a harem. The distant and aloof air of this odalisque is part of the cool "emotional temperature" of the Neoclassical style as practiced by Ingres, and the clarity of the drawing pays tribute to Raphael, a master of the High Renaissance whom Ingres particularly admired (see 4.10). Yet Ingres also willfully distorted the woman's body in pursuit of his own personal ideals of beauty, giving her an elongated back, an arm to match, and tiny, useless feet. In taking such freedoms he seems closer to Mannerist artists such as Bronzino (see 16.26) than to the idealizing spirit of the High Renaissance or the realism of Rome.

Ingres's lifelong rival was Eugène Delacroix, champion of the **Romantic** movement. The Romantic ideal stressed drama, turbulent emotions, and complex composition, all of which are evident in Delacroix's masterpiece,

21.1 Jean-Auguste-Dominique Ingres. *La Grande Odalisque*. 1814. Oil on canvas, 2′11¼″ × 5′3¾″. Musée du Louvre, Paris.

RELATED WORKS

4.8 Géricault, *Raft of the Medusa*

5.20 Goya, *Executions of the 3rd of May*

21.2 Eugène Delacroix. *Liberty Leading the People, 1830*. 1830. Oil on canvas, 8′6″ × 10′10″. Musée du Louvre, Paris.

Liberty Leading the People (**21.2**). In 1830 France was rocked by a brief uprising of the people, an aftershock of the French Revolution forty years earlier. Although not personally involved, Delacroix chose to depict an imaginary moment in this uprising as a statement of sympathy with the democratic ideals of the Revolution. Prominent in the composition is the figure of a woman, symbolizing Liberty and France—powerful, striding across the barricades, holding aloft the tricolor flag of France. Participants in the uprising stream behind her, following her lead—the artist does not tell us where, but presumably to the abstract goal of Freedom.

If we compare this passionate scene with the polished perfection of Ingres, the differences are obvious. Ingres's figure is motionless, languid; Delacroix's picture seethes with energy and violence. Ingres's *Odalisque* is beautifully contained within the frame of the picture, whereas Delacroix's figures marching toward us seem about to burst out of the composition, giving the impression of one frame in a continuous drama. Ingres's contours are clear and refined; Delacroix's free brush strokes give us a sense of blurred motion, of flickering light and confusion. Yet, in spite of its dynamism, Delacroix's painting is every bit as carefully composed as that of Ingres. The composition is stable, based on a triangle, with the apex in the hand and flag of Liberty, and the two sides moving down through the upraised rifle at left, the boy's arm and pistol at right. In their concern for the structure of painting Ingres and Delacroix were not as far apart as they appeared, but—because of the bitterness of their rivalry—neither would have admitted it.

The **Realist** movement in French art came somewhat later than Neoclassicism and Romanticism and was, in effect, a reaction against both. Realist artists sought to depict the everyday and the ordinary, rather than

the heroic or the exotic. Their concerns were very much rooted in the present. One of the leaders of the Realist movement was Gustave Courbet, who in 1855 exhibited a huge painting, *The Artist's Studio* (**21.3**), subtitled *A Real Allegory Summing Up Seven Years of My Life as an Artist.*

At the center of the canvas sits Courbet himself, at work on a landscape painting. Although a great many people crowd into the studio, the artist seems aloof from them, as though his aesthetic concerns are all-consuming. A little boy (usually identified as Innocence) gawks up at the work in progress. Behind the artist stands a nude model, whom some consider to be his Muse, or inspiration, others the personification of Truth (that is, the "naked truth"). All the figures to the left of the composition are common people; they are "types," not individuals, derived from Courbet's origins in a rural village. At right are the artist's "intellectual" friends, many of them identifiable figures—his patrons, other artists, writers, and so on. Perhaps Courbet is saying the artist represents a special elite, fed by his origins and by his comrades, but apart from them, alone with Innocence and Truth. We know from Courbet's work as a whole that here the artist was trying to make a particular point—that everyday activities, such as an artist working at his easel or peasants toiling in the fields, were fit subject matter for grand-scale art. In an age when only paintings of religious or historical or mythological scenes were considered "great art," this was a revolutionary idea.

All of the paintings we have considered so far in this chapter include a nude or seminude woman. Why are the women unclothed? Their nudity has a specific, accepted purpose—the exotic (Ingres' odalisque is a harem woman); the heroic (Delacroix's Liberty is bare-breasted as a mythical Amazon); the allegorical (Courbet's model may be the nude figure of Truth). These conventions satisfied contemporary tastes. But eight years after Courbet exhibited *The Artist's Studio*, a painting was placed on display in Paris that portrayed female nudity without any apparent justification at all. It caused a terrific scandal—the first of many artistic scandals that would shock the art world in the decades to come. The artist responsible for setting off this earthquake was a mild, conventional, well-to-do gentleman: Edouard Manet.

21.3 Gustave Courbet. *The Artist's Studio: A Real Allegory Summing Up Seven Years of My Life as an Artist.* 1855. Oil on canvas, 11'9¾" × 19'6⅝". Musée d'Orsay, Paris.

RELATED WORKS

5.17 Manet, *Bar at the Folies-Bergère*

8.12 Raimondi/Raphael, *Judgment of Paris*

16.17 Titian, *Fête Champêtre*

21.4 Edouard Manet. *Le Déjeuner sur l'herbe.* 1863. Oil on canvas, 7′ × 8′10″.
Musée d'Orsay, Paris.

MANET AND IMPRESSIONISM

In 19th-century France the mark of an artist's success was acceptance at the annual Salon, a state-sponsored exhibition of paintings. Artists submitted their work for consideration by an official jury, whose members varied from year to year but tended to be conservative, if not downright stodgy. In 1863 the Salon jury rejected almost 3,000 of the submitted works, which caused such an uproar among the spurned artists and their supporters that a second official exhibition was mounted—the "Salon des Refusés" (showing of those who had been refused). Among the works in the "refused" show—and very soon the most notorious among them—was Edouard Manet's painting *Le Déjeuner sur l'herbe* (**21.4**).

Luncheon on the Grass, as it is usually translated, shows a kind of outdoor picnic. Two men, dressed in the fashions of the day, relax and chat in a woodland setting. Their companion is a woman who has, for no apparent reason, taken off all her clothes. In the background another woman, wearing only a filmy garment, bathes in a stream.

Manet seems to have wanted to accomplish two goals with this work. The first was to join Courbet and other artists in painting modern life. But the other was to prove that modern life could produce eternal subjects worthy of the great masters of the museums. His solution was to "update" two famous Renaissance images, Titian's *Fête Champêtre* (see 16.17) and Raphael's *The Judgment of Paris* (see 8.12, lower right). The public saw what Manet was doing: the Titian, after all, was in the Louvre Museum close by, and the Raphael was routinely copied by art students. They saw what he was doing, and they didn't like it. Surely Manet was making fun of them. In place of Titian's idealized and dignified nudes, he had painted a common woman of loose morals: who else would sit there with no clothes on, meeting our gaze so frankly? The men in the painting, too, were completely undistinguished—not noble poets as in Titian, but ordinary students on holiday. One critic lamented that Manet was trying to achieve celebrity the easy way, by

EDOUARD MANET
1832–1883

E DOUARD MANET was a gentleman. That old-fashioned word aptly describes one of the most civilized, elegant figures in the history of art. Unfortunately for Manet, through most of his career he was also a gentleman scorned. Few artists have had to endure as much public derision and abuse as Manet did, and few have been as poorly equipped to tolerate abuse as he. To the end of his life he sought popular success for his art, but always it eluded him.

Manet was born in Paris of well-to-do parents. At first he contemplated a naval career, but after two unsuccessful attempts to gain admittance to the naval academy, he turned to painting. He studied at the Ecole des Beaux-Arts and also in the studio of the painter Thomas Couture, but the major influences on his work were Dutch and Spanish art, particularly the paintings of the great Spanish artist Diego Velázquez. In 1859, when he was just twenty-seven, Manet submitted work to the Salon, the annual government-sponsored art exhibition. This submission was rejected, but two years later Manet placed two paintings in the Salon, one of them a portrait of his parents.

Then in 1863 came the great scandal of *Le Déjeuner sur l'herbe,* which was rejected by the Salon, hung in the Salon des Refusés, called "immodest" by the French emperor, and heaped with abuse by critics and the public alike. Nevertheless, Manet continued to send paintings to the Salon each year, considering it the only true "field of battle" for an artist.

Surprisingly little is known about Manet's private life. He married Suzanne Leenhoff, who had been his piano teacher, in 1863. Though he earned little money from his art, his private means were sufficient to enable him to live comfortably. From time to time he traveled in Europe, but he always returned quickly to Paris, his spiritual as well as actual home. Manet was the quintessential Parisian. The well-dressed, well-mannered, well-spoken artist played an important role in intellectual society of the time. His closest friends were the writer-journalist Emile Zola and the poet Charles Baudelaire. Although he never exhibited with the Impressionist painters—most of whom were younger than he—Manet was considered by the Impressionists to be their natural leader and inspiration.

Sometime in the early 1880s Manet was struck by a serious illness, the exact nature of which is unknown. This illness resulted in the amputation of a gangrenous leg, and ultimately in his death at the age of fifty-one. As has happened with so many artists, recognition came to Manet just a bit too late. Seven years after his death, his painting *Olympia* was accepted by the Louvre.

Manet never got over his surprise at the public's contempt for his art, nor his bitterness about the rejection. In 1878 he wrote to Edgar Degas: "If there were no rewards, I wouldn't invent them: but they exist. And one should have everything that singles one out . . . when possible. It is another weapon. In this beastly life of ours, which is wholly struggle, one is never too well armed. I haven't been decorated? But it is not my fault, and I assure you that I shall be if I can and that I shall do everything necessary to that end."[1]

Henri Fantin-Latour. *Edouard Manet.*
1867. Oil on canvas, 46 × 35½".
The Art Institute of Chicago.

21.5 Berthe Morisot. *The Harbor at Lorient.* 1869. Oil on canvas, 17⅛ × 28¾".
National Gallery of Art, Washington D.C.

shocking his public. Others found the technique inept. Perhaps if Manet would learn something about perspective and drawing, they said, his taste might improve as well.

Manet's painting *is* odd, and art historians still debate just what he meant by it. In modeling his figures, Manet focused on the highest and lowest values, all but eliminating the middle, transitional tones. As a result, the forms appear flattened, as though illuminated by a sudden flash of light. The perspective is off: contemporary viewers were quite right. The bather is as far away as the rowboat, but if you imagine her standing in it, you see that she is a giantess. It was evidently more important to Manet to have her form the apex of his triangle of figures than to place her correctly in perspective. This, too, flattens the painting, for the bather seems to move forward to join the rest of the figures, compressing the space between foreground and background. The spatial tension plays out in the landscape itself: on the left side of the painting, the ground recedes convincingly into the distance, but on the right side there *is* no recession—just flat bright green. Nor do we believe for a minute that these people are really sitting outdoors. Clearly they are posing in a studio. The landscape is painted around them like a stage set or a photographer's backdrop. Finally, the borrowed composition *feels* borrowed, as though it were in quotation marks.

All of these qualities—the public scandal, the flatness, the artificiality, the ambiguity, and the self-conscious relation to art history—have made the painting a touchstone of modern art. Painting in the modern era could no longer be a simple, transparent window on the world. It would also be increasingly conscious of itself *as* a painting.

During the years following Manet's sensation in the Salon des Refusés, young French artists increasingly sought alternatives to the Salon. One group in particular looked to Manet as their philosophical leader, although he never consented to exhibit with them. They thought of themselves as Realists, for like Manet and Courbet they believed that modern life itself was the most suitable subject for modern art. In 1874 they organized their first exhibition as The Anonymous Society of Artists, Painters, Sculptors, Printmakers, etc. A painting in the exhibit by Claude Monet called *Impression: Sunrise,* however, earned the special scorn of one critic, who dubbed the whole endeavor Impressionism. The name stuck in the public imagination, and the artists largely accepted it: scenes glimpsed for a moment, sketched rapidly in paint as impressions of light and color on the eye—these were indeed some of their concerns.

With Impressionism, art moved outdoors—not the artificial outdoors of Manet, but the true outdoors. Painting up until then had been a studio product, in part because of the cumbersome materials it involved. Thanks to the new availability of portable oil colors in tubes (as they are still manufactured today), many of the Impressionists took their canvases, brushes, and paints outside to be part of the shifting light they wanted to depict. A lovely example of the new "open air" painting is Berthe Morisot's *The Harbor at Lorient* (**21.5**). The diagonal of a parapet leads our eyes into the composition to the demure figure of Morisot's sister Edma, who has been out for a stroll. Lost in a daydream, she does not return our gaze, which is now free to roam over the harbor with its milling people and accurately observed ships. The expanses of pale blue sky and water convey the feeling of a wide open space filled with light. Manet admired the painting so extravagantly that Morisot gave it to him.

The light in Renoir's enchanting *Le Moulin de la Galette* (**21.6**) is a light we have not seen before in painting, the dappled, shifting light that filters through leaves stirred by a breeze. Traditional chiaroscuro required a steady and even source of light for modeling form. But light in nature wasn't always like that. It moved, it shifted, it danced. And the forms it revealed weren't always clear. A house in the distance might just seem like a patch of yellow. A waltzing couple might be a blur. The desire to capture such optical sensations of perception required a new kind of painting technique. Instead of building a painting up from preliminary layers of drawing and modeling, Renoir began directly with paint, weaving individual brush strokes into an allover tapestry of colors that resolve into forms. The Impressionists surrendered the smooth surface of academic painting, with its layers of glazes and other studio refinements, for a straightforward painting technique devoted to capturing the fleeting sensations of perception. The resulting sketchiness disturbed Impressionism's critics; to them, the paintings looked unfinished and the forms not solid. Renoir would later adjust his style to create more solid figures and largely abandon modern life for "timeless" subjects, but here

21.6 Pierre-Auguste Renoir. *Le Moulin de la Galette.* 1876. Oil on canvas, 4'3½" × 5'9". Musée d'Orsay, Paris.

6.13 Degas, *Entrance of the Masked Dancers*

he is in his full Impressionist glory, capturing a moment's pleasure with flickering strokes of paint that record sensations of light, color, and movement.

Le Moulin de la Galette was an establishment on the outskirts of Paris where working people gathered on their day off to relax and enjoy themselves. Renoir paints a group of his own more elegant friends there, dancing and talking, drinking and flirting. The leisure activities of the emerging middle class were a favorite subject of the Impressionists, and we may be forgiven if because of them we picture 19th-century France as a land where there is always time to stroll in the country, where a waltz is always playing under the trees.

Another member of the Impressionist group was Edgar Degas. Degas' concerns were somewhat different from the rest of the Impressionists. He was not interested in painting outdoors, or in recording sensations of perception, or in landscape. A superb draftsman, his great interest was the human figure, and he was endlessly ingenious at finding subjects in contemporary life that allowed him to depict it (see 6.4, 6.13). Degas was a Parisian to the core and a keen observer of Parisian life. He was reported to be an excellent mimic, and he delighted in capturing the characteristic gestures of people he watched. We can be sure that the gesture of the woman biting the tip of her thumb in *Women At a Café, Evening* (**21.7**) was one he saw and filed away for use later. Typical of Degas, the composition seems as spontaneous as a snapshot, though it is actually carefully calculated. From Japanese prints, then widely collected in Paris, Degas borrowed the device of having an element such as a lamppost or pillar interrupt the composition and block our view. Such interruptions also reflect Degas' interest in photography, which lent itself naturally to intriguingly cropped views.

Degas drew the scene in black paint as a monotype, then worked over the print with pastels. Perhaps he felt such an improvised technique was better suited to the unstable nature of contemporary life than oil paint with its history of masterpieces and museums. Above all, the scene reflects Degas' fascination with the social levels of Paris, which were mingling in new ways during his lifetime. The women are prostitutes, gathered at a café to swap stories or wait for clients. The clues are lost on us today, but Degas' contemporaries had no trouble recognizing them, and they took the artist to task for depicting the women with what one critic called "terrifying realism."

21.7 Edgar Degas. *Women at a Café, Evening.* 1877. Pastel on monotype.
Musée d'Orsay, Paris.

PRESENTING THE PAST

the time. Folded back into the larger context of the era, the Impressionists would hang alongside the academic painters and forgotten favorites of the Salon. "Just the people they'd been trying to get away from all their lives," grumbled one Parisian painter.[2]

One of these people was the arch-academic William-Adolphe Bouguereau, whose *The Birth of Venus* is illustrated here. Bouguereau began his career painting tormented Romantic themes, yet he quickly discovered that what the public wanted was Venuses and Cupids, and that is what he gave them—slick, sentimental, and mildly titillating—until his death in 1905. It made him rich. Looking at this painting, with its clear contours and flawless finish, we can better understand the artistic debates of the day. No wonder Impressionist works looked sketchy and even vulgar! Suddenly our own position becomes less clear: what would we have preferred ourselves? Venus, or some uncouth students at a picnic? Stylish escape, or raw modern life? Which, honestly, do we prefer now?

In 1986, after a widely publicized battle of powerful public officials, critics, patrons, and artists, the Gare d'Orsay reopened as the Musée d'Orsay, now one of the most popular and visited showplaces of art in Europe. By blurring distinctions between high and low, academic and avant-garde, its inclusive collection has challenged some of our most accepted understandings of art history, while its user-friendly design has democratized and made accessible the stuffy and exclusive space of the fine arts museum. For these reasons, it is perhaps the first exhibition hall of our own Postmodern era.

GENERATIONS OF ART lovers have enjoyed the story of the triumph of Impressionism. So familiar have many of these paintings become, so central to our idea of "great art," that we find it hard to believe that critics and the public initially disliked them. Who could be so blind? Impressionism's important role in the history of modern art even earned the movement its very own museum in Paris, the intimate Jeu de Paume.

Many were horrified, then, when the French government announced in 1978 that it was going to move the Jeu de Paume's collection to the nearby Gare d'Orsay, a cavernous railway station that was to be renovated as a museum. There, the paintings would be united with works drawn from museums all over France and representing all the arts and artistic trends of the 19th century—not just progressive styles but conservative ones as well, not just painting and sculpture, but architecture, photography, popular arts and illustration, decorative arts such as furniture and porcelain, and exhibits about the political and social history of

---

(top) Interior of the Musée d'Orsay.
(center) William Bouguereau. *The Birth of Venus.* 1879. Oil on canvas, 9'10⅛" × 7'1⅜". Musée d'Orsay, Paris.

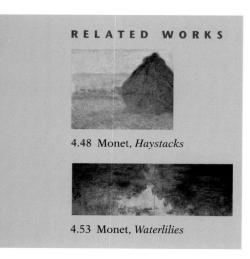
Modern life presented painters with subjects that had no precedent in art. How, for example, would you paint a railway station? These great structures in stone, iron, and glass were a prominent new feature of the cityscape. In *Gare Saint-Lazare* (**21.8**), Claude Monet used the technique of Impressionism to convey how new and how *modern* these cavernous structures felt. Railway stations have been called "the cathedrals of the 19th century," and Monet's painting shares something of this view. Our viewpoint is from inside one of the iron and glass sheds that received arriving trains. We look out its open end to the city beyond. Monet sets the opening symmetrically, underscoring its similarity to the pointed arch of Gothic architecture. Puffs of smoke and a suspended grid articulate the enclosed space, emphasizing how enormous it is. Sunlight entering through the glass roof lies on the ground in squares. Like Renoir in *Le Moulin de la Galette*, Monet created his image from a tapestry of individual strokes that gradually resolve into forms.

POST-IMPRESSIONISM

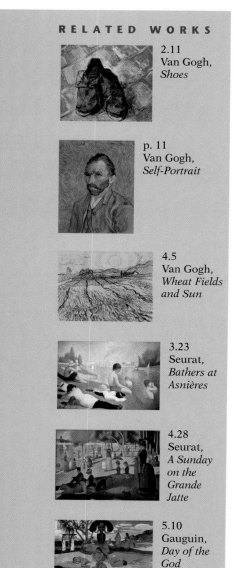
The next generation of artists admired many aspects of Impressionism, especially its brightened palette and direct painting technique. But they reacted in various ways to what they perceived as its shortcomings. Their styles are so highly personal that we commonly group them together under the neutral term *Post-Impressionists,* meaning simply the artists that came after Impressionism. They include Georges Seurat, Vincent van Gogh, Paul Gauguin, and Paul Cézanne.

Seurat wanted to place Impressionism's intuitive recording of optical sensations on a more scientific footing. His reading of the latest color theories led him to develop the technique of Pointillism, in which discrete dots and dashes of pure color were supposed to blend in the viewer's eye. Of all the Post-Impressionists, Seurat was the most faithful to the idea of painting modern life. In *A Sunday on La Grande Jatte* (see 4.28), he portrayed an ideal, harmonious society of common people enjoying their day off with ceremony and dignity, and *Bathers at Asnières* (see 3.23), set in the working-class outskirts of Paris, frankly acknowledged the factories that were now a part of the landscape.

For other Post-Impressionists, the industrialized modern world was not something that needed to be confronted but something that needed to be escaped. Vincent van Gogh arrived in Paris from Antwerp in 1886, but he stayed for only two years—just long enough to catch up with the latest developments in art. Van Gogh settled instead in Arles, a small, rural town in the south of France, where he painted the landscape, people, and things closest to him. The high-key colors, agitated brushwork, and emotional intensity of such works as *The Starry Night* (see 1.10) and *Shoes* (see 2.11) would have an enormous influence on the next generation of artists.

Paul Gauguin worked in an Impressionist style early in his career, but he soon became dissatisfied. He felt the need for more substance, more solidity of form than could be found in optical perceptions of light. Beyond this, Gauguin was interested in expressing a spiritual meaning in his art. All these he sought on the sun-drenched islands of the South Pacific, where he journeyed to escape what he called "the disease of civilization." The brilliant high-keyed colors of Gauguin's Tahitian paintings reveal his debt to Impressionism. To this lightened palette he added his own innovations: flattened forms and broad color areas, a strong outline, tertiary color harmonies, a taste for the exotic, an aura of mystery, and a quest for the "primitive."

Nafea Faaipoipo (When Are You To Be Married?) (**21.9**) was painted soon after the beginning of Gauguin's first long stay in Tahiti, and it shows all these characteristics. The figures of the two young women are so flat that we feel we almost could cut around them as if they were paper dolls and pull them out of the painting. Strong outlines define them; this is especially apparent in the skirt and face of the woman at left. The landscape is rendered in broad, flat color areas receding backward: green grass of the foreground, a large yellow middle ground, deep blue shadow under the trees, purple mountain in the background. We know that the women of Tahiti, especially the young girls, were usually slender and lithe. Gauguin has given them a heavy, monumental solidity in keeping with his interest in broad form, and perhaps also because it fulfilled his fantasies about what a "noble savage" ought to look like. Mystery and magic are conveyed by the stylized gesture of the woman at right and the secretive expressions of both women. Perhaps the magic was more in Gauguin's mind than in the subjects he painted. Nevertheless, in the South Pacific he found the ideal environment to foster his artistic vision.

In contrast to Gauguin's need for travel and exotic subjects, Paul Cézanne found everything he needed within walking distance of his home in the south of France. Cézanne admired the Impressionists' practice of working directly from nature, and he approved of their bright palette and their individual strokes of color. He was dissatisfied, though, with their casual compositions and their emphasis on what is transitory—the dappled sunlight on Renoir's spinning dancers or the clouds of steam in Monet's railway station. He felt that what had made painting great in the past was structure and order. He admired, for example, Poussin's majestic structuring of nature in such paintings as *The Ashes of Phokion* (see 17.8). Could the brush strokes that the Impressionists used to register optical sensations be used to build something more solid and durable? Could one paint directly from nature and find in it the order and clarity of Poussin? This was the goal that Cézanne set for himself.

21.8 (left) Claude Monet. *Gare Saint-Lazare*. 1877. Oil on canvas, 29½ × 50″.
Musee d'Orsay, Paris.

21.9 (right) Paul Gauguin. *Nafea Faaipoipo (When Are You To Be Married?)*. 1892. Oil on canvas, 41¼ × 30½″.
Rudolf Staechelin Foundation, Basel.

PAUL GAUGUIN
1848–1903

WHEN GAUGUIN SET sail from France in 1891, headed for the remote island of Tahiti in the South Pacific, he wrote a new chapter in the legend of the romantic, bohemian artist. To this day the legend persists. Many people want an artist to be—and Gauguin himself perhaps wanted to be—a dramatic, tormented soul who turns away from the comforts of modern civilization, who is not subject to society's conventions, who thrives in an exotic climate.

Paul Gauguin's origins gave but little hint of what was to come. Born in Paris, he spent part of his childhood in Peru, then returned with his family to France. After a stint in the merchant marine, he settled down and established himself as a stockbroker in Paris. When his career prospered, he married a young Danish woman, Mette Gad, who eventually bore him five children. Sometime in this period he took up painting as a hobby.

Over the years this hobby gradually came to be an obsession. In 1883, when he was thirty-five, Gauguin suddenly announced to his wife that he intended to quit his job and become a full-time painter. His attempts to support himself in this profession were not rewarding; eventually, Gauguin's wife rejoined her family in Denmark, taking the children, and the cou-

ple never lived together again. In 1886 Gauguin made the first of three visits to Brittany, the westernmost province of France. By this time he had already begun to establish his style of painting in broad shapes and flat color areas. A year later the artist journeyed to the island of Martinique, in the Caribbean, where the lush tropical colors heightened his palette even further. Late in 1888 Gauguin paid a brief—and disastrously unpleasant—visit to Van Gogh in the south of France. Finally, disillusioned with Western society and its values, Gauguin departed for Tahiti.

In Tahiti, Gauguin "went native." He lived in a grass hut and took as his *vahine*, or woman, a thirteen-year-old Tahitian girl, who gave birth to his son. At first all seemed idyllic, but even in the tropics one could not live for free, and Gauguin's finances were tight. He returned to Paris in 1893, hoping to sell his paintings, but the trip was not a success. Two years later Gauguin again set sail for Tahiti—never to return home.

During the second Tahitian period, Gauguin's fortunes went from bad to ghastly. He was wracked by a severe case of syphilis, suffered from a broken ankle that would not heal, and was desperately poor. At lowest ebb he attempted suicide, but the arsenic he swallowed was vomited up, causing him great agony. In 1901 he made his final voyage, to the Marquesas Islands, where—after a series of strokes—he died, penniless and completely alone. Three years after his death a memorial exhibition of Gauguin's work was organized in Paris. The show was a triumph. Gauguin was recognized as one of the great artists of his time.

Through all his ordeals, Gauguin seems to have considered the sacrifice worth it—necessary to achieve the vision he sought in art. As he wrote to his wife, "I am a great artist. . . . I am a great artist and know it. It is because of what I am that I have endured so many sufferings so as to pursue my vocation, otherwise I would consider myself a rogue."[3]

Paul Gauguin. *Les Miserables (Self-Portrait)*.
1888. Oil on canvas, 28 × 35".
Rijksmuseum Vincent van Gogh, Amsterdam.

A favorite subject of Cézanne's last years was Mont Sainte-Victoire, a mountain near his home (**21.10**). Altogether he made seventy-five painted or drawn versions of the scene. The broad outlines of the composition are simple and noble: a rectangular band of landscape surmounted by the irregular pyramid of the mountain. This underlying geometry emerges clearly from hundreds of small, vivid patches of color. Each patch is composed of the terse, precise, parallel strokes that Cézanne used to register what he called his "little sensations before nature"—the impressions that colors shimmering in the hot southern sun made on his eyes. Near the foreground, the red tile roofs of farmhouses are like ready-made color patches. The roof of the isolated house near the center reproduces exactly the silhouette of the mountain. To the left, the upward diagonal of the ocher area around the group of three farmhouses is exactly parallel to the upward slope of the mountain. These echoes are a key to Cézanne's way of thinking: Major structural lines are echoed everywhere. The line of the horizon, for example, is broken into segments, none of them quite horizontal. Segments of almost-horizontal lines appear throughout the painting, even in the sky, which is also painted in patches of color.

With paintings such as *Mont Sainte-Victoire*, Cézanne's treatment of nature grew increasingly abstract. Repetitions and echoes of key contour lines help unify the composition, but they have also begun to take on their own independent logic apart from the subject. Similarly, the terse strokes and color patches help unify the painting's surface, but they tend to fracture the image into facets. The next generation of painters would study these devices and build on them.

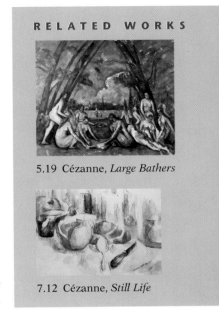

5.19 Cézanne, *Large Bathers*

7.12 Cézanne, *Still Life*

21.10 Paul Cézanne. *Mont Sainte-Victoire*. 1902–04. Oil on canvas, 27½ × 35¼". Philadelphia Museum of Art.

3.33 Cole, *The Oxbow*

4.44 Bierstadt, *Rocky Mts., Landers Peak*

21.11 George Caleb Bingham. *Fur Traders Descending the Missouri.* c. 1845. Oil on canvas, 29 × 36½". The Metropolitan Museum of Art, New York.

BRIDGING THE ATLANTIC: AMERICA IN THE 19TH CENTURY

Europe remained America's artistic touchstone during the 19th century, for America viewed itself then as a continuation of European culture. American artists often went to Europe for part of their training, not only to study with European teachers but also to see the collections of the great museums. In Europe, they could absorb more easily the history of their art at first hand. There was no American substitute, for example, for wandering through the ruins of ancient Rome or visiting a Gothic cathedral. Some American artists remained in Europe and spent their careers there. Similarly, some European artists emigrated to America, where opportunity seemed greater. Neoclassicism, Romanticism, Realism, and Impressionism were broad trends in America as they were in Europe, though without the intense battles they provoked in Paris.

Romanticism was a many-sided movement, and in America it expressed itself most clearly through an attitude toward landscape, an almost mystical reverence for the natural beauty of the unspoiled land itself. The broad vista and threatening storm of Thomas Cole's *The Oxbow* (see 3.33) display one aspect of American Romanticism. Cole was born in England, and his family emigrated to America when he was seventeen. His artistic training was in the United States, although he later spent two years looking at art in Europe.

In contrast to Cole, American-born George Caleb Bingham was largely self-taught. Bingham was the first major painter to live and work west of the Mississippi River. His *Fur Traders Descending the Missouri* (**21.11**), painted around 1845, portrays a French trapper and his son gliding down the Missouri River in a dugout canoe. The air is heavy with the golden light of dawn about to break. The son leans on their cargo, casually cradling a rifle. A duck

21.12 Mary Cassatt. *The Boating Party.* 1893–94. Oil on canvas, 35½ × 46⅛″. National Gallery of Art, Washington, D.C.

he has recently shot lies in front of him. Father and son both look our way. The son's gaze is open; his father's more guarded. But the strangest and most haunting gaze in the painting is one we can't decipher at all: that of a bear cub chained to the prow of the canoe. Stock still, doubled by its lengthening reflection in the river, the bear has an eerie presence, reminding us of how mysterious and unknowable nature truly is.

Realism found its finest American practitioner in Thomas Eakins, whose *The Biglin Brothers Racing* is illustrated in Chapter 4 (see 4.7). Eakins had studied in Paris and toured the museums of Europe, but he returned to Philadelphia to paint American lives. Eakins had a distinguished career as a teacher. Among his students was Henry Ossawa Tanner, whose *Banjo Lesson* is illustrated in Chapter 5 (see 5.18). One of the first important African American artists, Tanner moved to Paris in 1894, where he turned increasingly to religious subjects and exhibited regularly in the Salon.

Another American artist who traveled to Paris and remained there was Mary Cassatt. While her artistic training in America had been conservative and academic, her natural inclination drew her toward scenes from daily life, especially intimate domestic scenes of mothers and children—a world men rarely depicted in art. Degas was impressed by the paintings she exhibited at the Salon during the 1870s, and he invited her to show with the Impressionists instead. "Finally I could work with absolute independence without concern for the eventual opinion of a jury," Cassatt later wrote. "I admired Manet, Courbet, and Degas. I detested conventional art. I began to live."[4]

Painted in 1893, Cassatt's *The Boating Party* shows the joyous results of her artistic liberation (**21.12**). A well-to-do woman has hired a boatman to take her and her child on a pleasurable outing. The child, sprawled contentedly across her mother's lap, stares at the boatman with undisguised curiosity. The mother looks at him as well, pleasantly, but from a more polite distance. The bold, simplified forms and the broad areas of color reflect the influence of Japanese prints, which had been the subject of a major exhibition in Paris three years earlier. The straightforward color harmony of blue, yellow, and red is set singing by the boatman's black clothing and the boat's brilliant white gunwale.

RELATED WORKS

4.7
Eakins,
The Biglin Brothers Racing

5.18
Tanner,
Banjo Lesson

4.29
Whistler,
Nocturne

8.17
Cassatt,
Woman Bathing

INTO THE 20TH CENTURY: THE AVANT-GARDE

When you hear people talking about the newest, latest, most advanced art, you may hear them use the French term *avant-garde*. Avant-garde was originally a military term, referring to the detachment of soldiers that went first into battle. By the 1880s, younger artists began to refer to themselves as the avant-garde. They were the boldest artists, going first into uncharted territory and waiting for others to catch up. Their "battle" was to advance the progress of art against the resistance of conservative forces. Newness and change became artistic ideals. Each generation, even each group, believed it was their duty to go further than the one before. As the 20th century began, the idea of the avant-garde was firmly in place, and two of art's basic building blocks, form and color, were the focus of great innovation.

FREEING COLOR: FAUVISM AND EXPRESSIONISM

Though it no longer wielded the power it once did, the annual Salon of Paris was still a conservative force in artistic life, and movements regularly arose against it. In 1903, a group of young artists founded the Salon d'Automne, the "autumn salon," as a progressive alternative. From the exhibits they organized, it was clear who their heroes were. In 1904, the artists of the Salon d'Automne organized a large exhibition of Cézanne. In 1906, they mounted a major retrospective of Gauguin. But the most notorious exhibit of the Salon d'Automne was the one they organized for themselves in 1905. It was then that a critic dubbed them *fauves,* "wild beasts."

One of the paintings that earned the wild beasts their name was André Derain's *View of Collioure* (**21.13**). Collioure is a small port on the Mediterranean coast of France. Derain and his friend Henri Matisse had spent the summer painting there. Like many young artists, they had been experimenting with the Pointillism of Seurat, which seemed to embody the most advanced thinking of the day, but they found it too theoretical and constraining. The more instinctive works of Van Gogh and Gauguin offered a way out. Derain's debt to Van Gogh is clear in the whirlwinds of short brush strokes, but Van Gogh would never have considered a painting this bare to

21.13 André Derain. *View of Collioure.* 1905. Oil on canvas, 26 × 32⅜". Museum Folkwang, Essen, Germany.

be finished, nor would he have used pure, unmixed pigments, applied sometimes straight from the tube. The foreground, which Van Gogh would have labored over until it lay firmly underfoot, is nothing but swarms of brush strokes that register a kind of visual excitement. Most important, color is freed from its role in describing objects. Surely the distant hills and the near grasses were not orange! Derain painted them that way because orange, vibrating strongly near its complementary blue, seemed to convey the emotions he felt in the warmth, the sun, the sea air, the breeze.

Derain's fellow Fauve Henri Matisse took the liberation of color even further in a major work of the following year, *The Joy of Life* (**21.14**). Pink sky, yellow earth, orange foliage, blue tree trunks—in Matisse's hands, color itself became a world, a place to be. The discrete dots of color that were a legacy of Seurat are gone, as are the frantic brush strokes of Van Gogh. In their place is a radiant sense of well-being, a calm that Gauguin had often sought in his pictures of Tahiti.

Fauvism did not last long, a mere three years or so. *The Joy of Life* is already in some ways beyond it. But though brief, Fauvism was crucial for the development of modern art. Never again would artists feel they must confine themselves to replicating the "real" colors of the natural world. Freed from its descriptive role, color could be used as an independent expressive element.

Fauvism was part of a larger trend in Europe called expressionism, which arose as artists came to believe that the fundamental purpose of art was to express their intense feelings toward the world. Broadly speaking, **expressionism** describes any style where the artist's subjective feelings take precedence over objective observation. Spelled with a capital *E*, it refers especially to an art movement that developed in Germany in the early 20th century, where the expressive ideal had its greatest influence. Like the Fauves, Expressionist artists looked to Gauguin and Van Gogh as their predecessors. They admired as well the stark works of the Norwegian artist Edvard Munch, who was then living in Berlin (see 2.24, 2.25, 4.30).

One important Expressionist group was Die Brücke ("The Bridge"), founded in Dresden 1905, the same year as the Fauve exhibit in Paris. The bridge the artists had in mind was one they would build through their art to a better, more enlightened future. One of the founders was Ernst Ludwig

2.24 Munch, *Kiss by the Window*

4.30 Munch, *The Scream*

21.14 Henri Matisse. *The Joy of Life*. 1905–06. Oil on canvas, 5′8½″ × 7′9¾″. The Barnes Foundation, Merion, Pennsylvania.

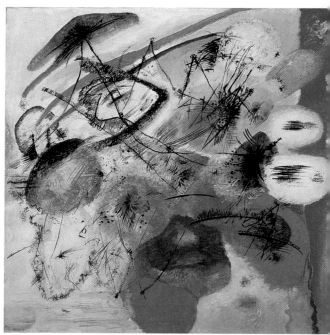

21.15 (left) Ernst Ludwig Kirchner. *Street, Dresden*. 1907. Oil on canvas, 4'11¼" × 6'6⅞". The Museum of Modern Art, New York.

21.16 (right) Vasili Kandinsky. *Black Lines*. 1913. Oil on canvas, 51 × 51⅝". Solomon R. Guggenheim Museum, New York.

Kirchner, whose *Street, Dresden* we illustrate here (**21.15**). The intense, arbitrary colors show Expressionism's link with Fauvism, and the wavering contours suggest the influence of Munch. To the right, a crowd moves toward us. Everyone seems to have a purpose—shopping, going to work, all of the usual reasons that keep city streets teeming with people. To the left, a crowd walks in the other direction. In the center is the small figure of a child. She stands isolated from the crowds, her feet planted apart, resisting the flow. Perhaps she is a stand-in for the artist, who also questions all this coming and going, what purpose it serves, and why everyone is alone.

Another Expressionist group was Der Blaue Reiter ("The Blue Rider"), organized in 1911 by the Russian painter Vasili Kandinsky. Kandinsky had been teaching law in Moscow when an exhibit of Impressionist painting so moved him that he abandoned his career and moved to Germany to study art. Kandinsky's early paintings were intensely colored, Fauve-like works on Russian mystical themes. He never abandoned his idea that spirituality and art were linked, but he became increasingly convinced that art's spiritual and communicative power lay in its own language of line, form, and color, and it was he who took the decisive step of eliminating representation altogether in such works as *Black Lines* (**21.16**). In his own telling, Kandinsky discovered the power of nonrepresentational art when he was struck by the beauty of a painting he didn't recognize in his studio. It turned out to be one of his own works, set the wrong way up. He realized then that subject matter was only incidental to art's impact. About color, Kandinsky wrote, "Generally speaking, color influences the soul. Color is the keyboard, the eyes are the hammers, the soul is the piano with many strings. The artists is the hand that plays, touching one key or another purposively, to cause vibrations in the soul."[5]

SHATTERING FORM: CUBISM

While artists associated with Europe's many expressionist tendencies were exploring the possibilities of color, two artists in Paris were reducing the role of color to a minimum in order to concentrate on the problem of representing form in space. One of these artists was a young Spanish painter, Pablo Picasso. In 1907, at age twenty-six, Picasso had already painted what is widely regarded as a pivotal work in the development of 20th-century art, *Les Demoiselles d'Avignon* (**21.17**).

Les Demoiselles d'Avignon was not Picasso's title but was given to the painting years later by a friend of his. It translates as "the young women of Avignon" and refers to the prostitutes of Avignon Street, a notorious district of Barcelona, Picasso's hometown. In early sketches for the painting Picasso included a sailor entering at left to purchase the prostitute's services, but as the composition evolved, the sailor was eliminated. Instead, the prostitutes display themselves to us.

If these are prostitutes, then how extraordinary they are! They are far from enticing. Picasso has chopped them up into planes—flat, angular segments that still hint at three-dimensionality but have no conventional modeling. Almost as an affront to traditional pictures of curvaceous nude bathers, the artist has defined his nudes in sharp geometric shapes. Figure and ground lose their importance as separate entities; the "background"—that is, whatever is not the five figures—is treated in much the same way as the women's bodies. As a result, the entire picture appears flattened; we have no sense of looking "through" the painting into a world beyond, as with Delacroix or even Manet.

To many people who see *Les Demoiselles* for the first time, the faces cause discomfort. The three at left seem like reasonable enough, if abstract, depictions of faces, except for the fact that the figure at far left, whose face is in profile, has an eye staring straight ahead, much as in an Egyptian painting. But the two faces at right are clearly masks—images borrowed from "primitive" art—and they create a disturbing effect when set atop the nude bodies of European females.

In *Les Demoiselles* Picasso was experimenting with several ideas that he would explore in his art for years to come. First, there is the inclusion of nontraditional elements. Picasso had recently seen sculptures from ancient Iberia (Spain before the Roman Empire), as well as art from Africa. In breaking with Western art conventions that reached back to ancient Greece and

21.17 Pablo Picasso. *Les Demoiselles d'Avignon*. 1907. Oil on canvas, 8′ × 7′8″.
The Museum of Modern Art, New York.

PABLO PICASSO
1881–1973

THE LIFE OF Picasso defies summary in a one-page biography. Few artists have lived so long; none have produced such an immense volume of work in so diverse a range of styles and media; and only a rare few can match him in richness and variety of personal history.

Pablo Ruiz y Picasso was born in the Spanish city of Málaga. He attended art schools in Barcelona and Madrid but became impatient with their rigid, academic approach and soon abandoned formal study. After two trips to Paris—where he saw the work of Van Gogh, Gauguin, and Lautrec—he settled permanently in that city in 1904 and never again lived outside France.

Although Picasso worked in many different styles throughout his life, much of his art is classifiable into the well-known "periods": the "Blue" period, when his paintings concentrated on images of poverty and emotional depression; the "Rose" period, whose paintings included depictions of harlequins and acrobats; the Cubist period, when he worked with the painter Georges Braque; and the "Neoclassical" period, in which the figures took on qualities resembling ancient Greek sculptures.

Success came early to Picasso. Except for brief periods when he was short of funds (usually because of some romantic entanglement), he lived well and comfortably and enjoyed a large circle of friends. His work was always in demand, whether in painting, sculpture, prints (of which he made thousands), theatrical design, murals, or ceramics (he took up ceramic art in 1947 and decorated some two thousand pieces in a single year).

It would be impossible to discuss Picasso's life without reference to the women who shared it, because they are a constant presence in his art. Picasso married only twice, but he maintained long, occasionally overlapping, liaisons with several other women. His attachments included Fernande Olivier; Eva Gouel; Olga Koklova, his first wife and the mother of his son Paulo; Marie-Thérèse Walter, mother of his daughter Maïa; Dora Maar; Françoise Gilot, who bore him Claude and Paloma, then later wrote a scandalous memoir of her years with the artist; and finally Jacqueline Roque, whom he married in 1961, in his eightieth year.

Despite his international celebrity, Picasso gave almost no interviews. One of the few took place in 1935 and included this insight into the nature of art: "Everyone wants to understand art. Why not try to understand the song of a bird? Why does one love the night, flowers, everything around one, without trying to understand them? But in the case of a painting people have to understand. If only they would realize above all that an artist works of necessity, that he himself is only a trifling bit of the world, and that no more importance should be attached to him than to plenty of other things which please us in the world, though we can't explain them. People who try to explain pictures are usually barking up the wrong tree."[6]

Pablo Picasso. *Self-Portrait with Palette.* 1906.
Oil on canvas, 36¼ × 28¾".
Philadelphia Museum of Art.

Rome, Picasso looked for inspiration from other, equally ancient, traditions. Second, there is the merging of figure and ground, reflecting the assumption that all portions of the work participate in its expression. And third, there is fragmenting of the figures and other elements into flat planes, especially evident in the breasts of the figure at upper right and the mask just below. This last factor proved especially significant for an artistic journey on which Picasso was soon to embark—the movement known as **Cubism.**

Picasso's partner in this venture was the artist Georges Braque. Braque was older than Picasso in years but younger as an artist. Picasso, after all, had been an artist since his early teens (see 2.14). He was one of the most naturally gifted artists in history, and his hand could produce any kind of style he asked it to. Braque was far less gifted, but because of that more disciplined and determined. He developed an intense personal identification with Cézanne, who also progressed from awkward beginnings to mastery. Picasso grew to share this interest, and for a time he renounced his natural gifts to pursue together with Braque this new line of investigation. Both artists emerged stronger for it.

Picasso and Braque began working together in 1909, and by 1910 their experiments were so closely intertwined that their styles became virtually identical. For a time, they even ceased signing their works. "We were prepared to efface our personalities in order to find originality,"[7] Braque later recalled. Illustrated here are two paintings by Braque that demonstrate how Cézanne's methods led to something new, *The Castle at La Roche-Guyon* (**21.18**) and *Le Portugais (The Emigrant)* (**21.19**).

Castle at La Roche-Guyon depicts a hillside town of houses surmounted by a castle. Following Cézanne's advice, Braque has reduced the architecture to its simplest geometric forms: cube, cylinder, cone. (It was a painting of similar hillside houses that prompted a visiting friend to remark, "Look, little cubes," thus accidentally and misleadingly naming the style.) We recognize Cézanne's parallel brush strokes and color patches, which seem to break

21.18 (left) Georges Braque. *The Castle at La Roche-Guyon.* 1909. Oil on canvas, 28¾ × 23¾". Musée d'Art Moderne, Villeneuve-d'Ascq.

21.19 (right) Georges Braque. *Le Portugais (The Emigrant).* 1911–12. Oil on canvas, 46 × 32". Kunstmuseum Basel.

7.15 Picasso, *Guitar, Sheet Music, and Glass*

the surface into facets (see 21.10). Also learned from Cézanne is the way the principal linear motifs of the composition echo outward to influence everything around them. Here, the earth around the castle and the surrounding green of nature all partake of the angles and facets of the houses. Braque has reined in Cézanne's bright Impressionist palette to a restricted range of gray, ocher, and green, allowing the forms to interpenetrate more easily. Some of the forms seem solid, but others shade off into transparency.

In *The Emigrant*, a fully Cubist work, these discoveries are taken to their logical conclusion. The figure of a seated man playing his guitar is broken into facets based in simple geometric shapes—triangle, circle, line. Because the forms are so basic, they easily echo throughout, unifying the composition. Color is reduced to gray warmed with ocher, allowing the shards of the foreground and background to interpenetrate at will. The principal lines of the composition suggest a classic Renaissance pyramid such as Leonardo used for *Mona Lisa* (see 16.8). Visual cues help viewers orient themselves: the open hole and strings of the guitar, the player's mustache, the rope to the right that sets the scene on a dock. The addition of stenciled letters, an intrusion from the "real world," was Braque's innovation. As Cubism progressed, the two artists experimented with incorporating other elements such as newspaper, wallpaper, and fabric. The psychological tension of merging the "real" with the "not real" (the illusory world of paint on canvas) would have important applications for later 20th-century art. Picasso and Braque also realized that the geometric rhythms of an object could be assembled from multiple views. For example, if you look at a pitcher from the front, the side, the top, the bottom, you will see a number of versions, but your true understanding of a pitcher is the sum of all of these. With Cubism, this sum of viewpoints could be painted. Cubism thus followed up on another discovery implicit in much of Cézanne's work: the eye is always moving, and motion is how we assimilate the world.

The great beauty of Cubism was that, like linear perspective, anyone could do it. Cubism offered the most original and powerful system for rethinking the representation of form and space since the Renaissance. Over the ensuing decade and more, many young artists in Europe passed through a Cubist phase in order to break free of the past.

FANTASY AND FUTURISM

Cubism poured all its energy into formal concerns. The subjects that Braque and Picasso treated while working out their discoveries were so traditional as to be neutral—a still life on a table top, a seated figure with a musical instrument, a landscape with some houses. Any of these subjects could have been painted in the 17th century. Other innovators, however, believed that art would move forward only through exploring new subjects. One of the most original and influential of these artists was the Italian painter Giorgio de Chirico. "It is most important that we should rid art of all that it has contained of *recognizable material* to date, all familiar subject matter, all traditional ideas, all popular symbols must be banished forthwith," he wrote. "To become truly immortal a work of art must escape all human limits: logic and common sense will only interfere. But once these barriers are broken it will enter the regions of childhood vision and dream."[8]

Dreams are what come to mind in front of *The Disquieting Muses* (**21.20**). The hot afternoon sun casts long shadows across an open plaza. There are no trees, no people. Nothing of nature at all. In the background, banners snap in the wind over an early Renaissance fortress. Next to the fortress is a factory. In the shade, a statue in classical garments stares (though her face is featureless) at the two presences in the foreground, the disquieting muses themselves: a pockmarked classical column, a sculpture with a hatmaker's dummy for a head, a tailor's dummy seated nearby. The painting is composed of fragments of Italy's own past and present—ancient

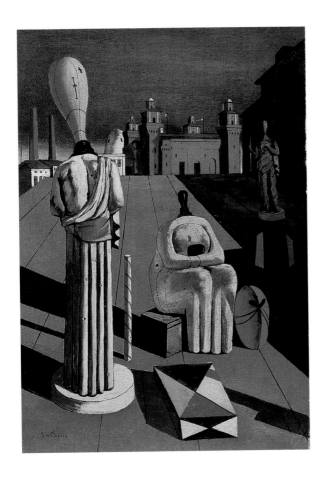

Rome, the Renaissance, the Industrial Revolution. How can we make any sense out of what history has left to us, it seems to ask? What do we do now?

In contrast to De Chirico's motionless dream world, a group of Italian artists calling themselves the Futurists decided that motion itself was the glory of the new 20th century, especially the motion of marvelous new machines. The view from an airplane, the feeling of racing through the countryside in an automobile—how could these new sensations not be reflected in art? In Chapter 4 we looked at a Futurist painting by Giacomo Balla (see 4.49). Here we illustrate a work by the movement's foremost sculptor, Umberto Boccioni (**21.21**). *Unique Forms of Continuity in Space* represents a striding human figure as the Futurist imagined it to be in the light of contemporary science: a field of energy interacting with everything around it. "Sculpture," wrote Boccioni, "must give life to objects by making their extension in space palpable, systematic, and plastic, since no one can any longer believe that an object ends where another begins and that our body is surrounded by anything . . . that does not cut through it and section it in an arabesque of directional curves."[9]

21.20 (left) Giorgio de Chirico. *The Disquieting Muses*. 1916. Oil on canvas 38¼ × 26″. Private Collection.

21.21 (right) Umberto Boccioni. *Unique Forms of Continuity in Space*. 1913. Bronze, height 43⅞″. The Museum of Modern Art, New York.

WORLD WAR I AND AFTER: DADA AND SURREALISM

In 1914, conflict broke out in the Balkan Peninsula. Soon, thanks to treaties and alliances, every major power in Europe was drawn into war. Soldiers with their heads full of gallant ideas about battle rushed headlong into the

RELATED WORKS

4.49 Balla, *Dog on a Leash*

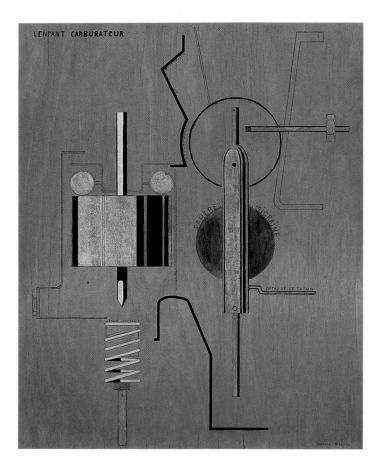

21.22 (left) Francis Picabia. *The Child Carburetor (L'Enfant Carburateur.)* 1919. Oil, enamel, metallic paint, gold leaf, pencil and crayon on stained plywood, 49¾ × 39⅞″. Solomon R. Guggenheim Museum, New York.

21.23 (right) Marcel Duchamp. *Bottle Dryer.* 1964 replica of 1914 original. Galvanized iron, height 23¼″.

RELATED WORKS

9.19 Hannah Höch, *Cut With the Kitchen Knife*

most horrible deaths imaginable. Trench warfare, poison gas, bombardment by air, machine guns, tanks, submarines—science and technology, in which the 19th century had put its faith, revealed their dark side. The ideal of progress was shown to be utterly hollow, and ten million people lost their lives in one of the bloodiest wars in history.

In 1916, a group of artists waiting out the war in Zurich, in neutral Switzerland, banded together as a protest art movement called Dada. What did Dada protest? Everything. Dada was anti. Anti art, anti middle-class society, anti politicians, anti good manners, anti business-as-usual, anti all that had brought about the war. In that sense, Dada was a big *no*. But Dada was also a big *yes*. Yes to creativity, to life, to silliness, to spontaneity. Dada was provocative and absurd. Above all, it refused to make sense or to be pinned down.

More an attitude than a coherent movement, Dada embraced as many different kinds of art as there were artists. In Germany, Dada developed a biting political edge in the work of Hannah Höch and others (see 9.19). In France, its absurd and philosophical aspects came to the fore. Picabia, a French artist who joined the Dada movement, delighted in the similarities between humans and machines, and he created paintings that looked like diagrams. *L'Enfant Carburateur (The Child Carburetor)* (21.22) would seem to offer a perfectly reasonable plan for constructing a child if the child you have in mind is part of an internal combustion engine. A carburetor is designed to produce an explosive mixture of fuel and air, and perhaps Picabia thought that children weren't so different. Labels point out such key areas as "Sphere of the Migraine" and "Destroy the Future." The materials include gold leaf, which gives the work a strangely precious and perhaps even sacred aura.

The Dadaist with the most lasting impact on American art in the 20th century was Marcel Duchamp, whose "ready-mades" probed the border between art and life in a way that later generations have returned to again and again. A ready-made is a work of art that the artist has not *made* but *designated*. One of Duchamp's strangest ready-mades is *Bottle Dryer*, a work of 1914 shown here in a signed replica of 1964 (**21.23**). *Bottle Dryer* is a replica because Duchamp never intended for his ready-mades to be permanent. His project was to find an object—he insisted that it be an object with no aesthetic interest whatsoever—and exhibit it as art. After the exhibition, the object was to be returned to life. After the 1914 exhibition, *Bottle Dryer* was sent back to the store. *Bottle Dryer* is just that, a rack on which bottles are set to dry. It looks strangely menacing, like a dress form with protective spikes.

Duchamp's ready-mades were pure provocation, and he pretended to be amazed that people took them seriously. Like many jokes, however, they raise interesting philosophical questions: Does art have to be made by an artist? Is art a form of attention? If we have spent our lives perfecting this form of attention on various acknowledged masterpieces, can we then bestow it on absolutely anything? If so, how is an art object different from any other kind of object? Does art depend on context, on being shown in an "art place" such as a museum or gallery? Can something be art in one place and not another? Is *Bottle Dryer* still art today, or was it only art for the time that Duchamp said it was? Duchamp thought that art and life could regularly trade places, and he suggested helpfully that one could use a Rembrandt as an ironing board.

A movement that grew out of Dada was Surrealism, which was formulated in Paris in the 1920s. Like Dada, Surrealism was not a style but a way of life. Fascinated by the theories of Sigmund Freud, who was then setting out his revolutionary ideas in Vienna, the Surrealists appreciated the logic of dreams, the mystery of the unconscious, and the lure of the bizarre, the irrational, the incongruous, and the marvelous. A central Surrealist practice, at least theoretically, was automatism—writing or drawing that flowed straight from the subconscious, uncontrolled by reason or by moral or ethical inhibitions. The combination of automatism and dream imagery resulted in paintings such as André Masson's *The Blood of the Birds* (**21.24**). Onto a surface of sand, Masson glued feathers collected during random walks. He

21.24 André Masson. *The Blood of the Birds*. 1925/26. Musée National d'Art Moderne, Centre Georges Pompidou, Paris.

RELATED WORKS

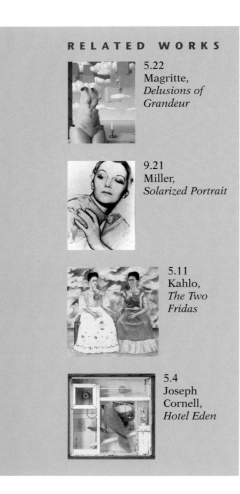

5.22
Magritte,
*Delusions of
Grandeur*

9.21
Miller,
Solarized Portrait

5.11
Kahlo,
*The Two
Fridas*

5.4
Joseph
Cornell,
Hotel Eden

then dripped and spattered paint across the surface in a series of "automatic" gestures. The American artist Jackson Pollock would later draw on these ideas to make his famous drip paintings, which also grew out of a Surrealist belief in the creative superiority of the unconscious (see 5.5, 22.1).

A distinctive contribution of Surrealism to art was the poetic object—not a sculpture as it had traditionally been understood but a *thing*. Surrealist objects often juxtapose incongruous elements in order to provoke a shiver of strangeness or disorientation. One of the most famous and unsettling Surrealist objects is Meret Oppenheim's *Object (Luncheon in Fur)* (**21.25**). Perhaps Oppenheim witnessed two ladies taking tea together in their best fur coats and melted them into a dreamlike object? Perhaps we really are supposed to imagine bringing the furry cup to our lips for lunch. Freud's theories famously claimed a large role for unconscious sexual desire, and Surrealist works often have erotic overtones.

Possibly the most famous of all Surrealist works is Salvador Dali's *The Persistence of Memory* (**21.26**), a small painting that many people call simply "the melted watches." Dali's art, especially here, offers a fascinating paradox: His rendering of forms is precise and meticulous—we might say *super*-realistic—yet the forms could not possibly be real. *The Persistence of Memory* shows a bleak, arid, decayed landscape populated by an odd, fetal-type creature (some think representative of the artist) and several limp watches—time not only stopped but melting away. Perhaps in this work Dali's fantasy, his dream, is to triumph once and for all over time.

Joan Miró's *Carnival of the Harlequin* (**21.27**), representing the abstract phase of Surrealism, shows us not the oddly distorted landscape of a Dali work but rather a completely invented landscape—and one teeming with life. Miró's fantasy world is aswarm with odd little creatures—animals and fish and insects and perhaps a snake or two—as well as nameless abstract forms that participate in the artist's madcap party. Much of Miró's imagery suggests a cheerful sexuality, as though the whole space of the universe were occupied with lighthearted erotic play and reproduction. In contrast to the utter stillness of Dali's *The Persistence of Memory*, Miró's *Carnival* is all movement. There are even a few musical notes at the top to accompany the dance. As interpreted by Miró, Surrealism's dreams are lively ones.

21.25 (left) Meret Oppenheim. *Object (Luncheon in Fur)*. 1936. Fur-covered cup, saucer and spoon, overall height 2⅞". The Museum of Modern Art, New York.

21.26 (right) Salvador Dali. *The Persistence of Memory*. 1931. Oil on canvas, 9½ × 13". The Museum of Modern Art, New York.

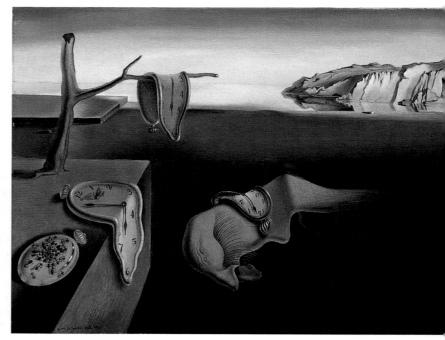

BETWEEN THE WARS: BUILDING NEW SOCIETIES

Surrealism offered a personal solution to life during the years following the trauma of World War I. But in the view of many artists, society, and possibly even human nature itself, had to be transformed so that such a horror would not happen again. That art could play a central role in bringing about a better society was a 19th-century idea, yet it found renewed application after World War I in a collective approach. It was not through the personal insights of individual artists that the world would change, but through the cooperative endeavors of artists, designers, and architects. Together, they could create a new environment for living, one that was completely modern, purged of associations with the past, and comfortable with the new spirit of the machine age.

Even more radical opportunities presented themselves in Russia and Mexico, where successful revolutions had toppled older governments. In these countries, new societies were being formed that embraced lofty ideals of social and economic equality for all and a concern for ordinary workers. In Chapter 7, we looked at a fresco commissioned from Diego Rivera by the revolutionary Mexican government (see 7.4). Prior to the Mexican Revolution, Rivera had been living in Paris and painting in an advanced Cubist style. On his return to Mexico, he developed a more accessible style for his murals, and he stayed with it for the rest of his career. His great desire was to communicate with everyone, to leave no one out. The demands of the European avant-garde must have seemed far away.

The Soviet government of Russia would eventually demand that its artists similarly turn their backs on modern tendencies, but during the first few years after the Russian Revolution of 1917, many artists believed that only the most revolutionary art could bring about a new world. One important movement was Constructivism, which had been founded by Vladimir Tatlin in 1913. Tatlin believed that advanced ideas about art should be put to practical use, and that artists should apply their talents to architecture,

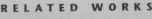

21.28 (left) Vladimir Tatlin. Model for the Monument to the Third International. 1919–1920. Wood, iron, and glass. Destroyed.

21.29 (right) Piet Mondrian. *Composition with Red, Yellow, and Blue.* Oil on canvas. Belgrade National Museum.

graphic design, theatrical productions, textiles, monuments, festivals, and all other visual forms. Tatlin's own design for the *Monument to the Third International* demonstrates what he thought could be done (**21.28**). Designed to house the Russian congress, the monument was never built, but what a work of architecture it would have been! An open steel framework would support the building from the outside, its spiral combining the industrial look of the Eiffel Tower (see 13.22) with a Futurist sense of motion. Suspended inside would be four chambers in pure geometric forms: a cube, a pyramid, a cone, and a sphere. The various branches of the government would meet in these rooms, which would rotate at speeds varying from one revolution per year (the large cube at the bottom) to one revolution per hour (the small sphere at the top).

When Constructivism was condemned by the Soviet regime in 1922, many of its artists left the Soviet Union to spread its ideals elsewhere. One of the European movements touched by Constructivist ideas was De Stijl, in the Netherlands. The most famous artist associated with De Stijl was Piet Mondrian, whose *Broadway Boogie-Woogie* we looked at in Chapter 5 (see 5.32). Mondrian painted *Broadway Boogie-Woogie* in response to the rhythm of life he discovered in New York, where he eventually emigrated late in his life. More typical of the work Mondrian painted in Europe is the tranquil *Composition with Red, Yellow, and Blue* (**21.29**). Beginning as a painter of flowers and landscapes, Mondrian distilled his art to what he considered to be the most universal signs of human order: vertical and horizontal lines, and the primary colors of red, yellow, and blue. To Mondrian, these formal elements radiated a kind of intellectual beauty that was humanity's greatest

achievement. Nature, with its irrationality and irregularity, encouraged humankind's primitive, animal instincts, resulting in such disasters as war. In Mondrian's vision of the world, people would be surrounded by rational beauty, and thus become balanced themselves.

Mondrian thought of his canvases as places where we could turn to stabilize ourselves and restore our calm. He also believed that they would not be necessary—no art would be necessary—in a future where people lived in environments such as Gerrit Rietveld's Schroeder House (**21.30**). Rietveld was the foremost architect of De Stijl, and Schroeder House looks very much like a Mondrian painting projected into three dimensions. Schroeder House is like an inhabitable sculpture—a construction in space of intersecting vertical and horizontal planes, color-coded inside and out in primary colors. As in Mondrian's painting, symmetrical elements are placed in subtle asymmetrical balance. No art hangs inside. Instead, the floor of one room is painted red, the wall of another is painted blue, and so on. Movable partitions allow the interior space to be reconfigured, and spaces flow into each other rather than being clearly separated.

Construction by intersecting planes in space is also the principle behind Marcel Breuer's famous armchair, designed in 1928 (**21.31**). Breuer was a teacher and a former student at the Bauhaus, a school of design founded in Germany in 1919 by the architect Walter Gropius. The Bauhaus was yet another incarnation of the ideal of collective artistic endeavor in the years following World War I. Students studied a variety of disciplines, and their education was designed to eliminate traditional divisions between painters, sculptors, architects, craft artists, graphic designers, and industrial designers. The word *Bauhaus* translates roughly as "building house," and its leaders sought to "build" new guiding principles of design compatible with 20th-century technology. Structures, rooms, furniture, and everyday household objects were stripped of superficial embellishment and pared down to clean lines. Breuer's armchair, made of canvas panels and steel tubing, was supposed to be economical to manufacture, making good design available to everyone. After the Nazis closed the Bauhaus in 1933, several of its key members emigrated to the United States, and the school's influence continued to be felt in all design disciplines for decades.

RELATED WORKS

2.21 Klee, *Monument in Fertile Country*

7.13 Klee, *Landscape with Birds*

The Bauhaus and De Stijl both sought to create harmony between individual lives and modern industry and technology. A man who painted visions of what this might be like was Fernand Léger (**21.32**). *Three Women (Le Grand Déjeuner)* presents us with a sort of 20th-century version of Ingres's *Grande Odalisque* (see 21.1). Léger has created a painting style that has the clean lines and forthright surfaces of industrial manufacture. The three women have come off a sort of artistic assembly line, fashioned of interchangeable parts. Yet the effect is not alienating at all. A cat dozes on the couch; the women take their meal. Their world is calm and ordered and content. In a lecture entitled "The Machine Aesthetic," Léger praised the beauty of industrial products and the dedication of those who made them. "A worker would never dare deliver a product other than clear-cut, polished, burnished," he later said. "The painter must aim at making a clear-cut picture, clean, with *finish*."[10] Léger had painted in a radical Cubist style before the war. After the war, he was not the only artist to step back from the avant-garde in what one French critic called "the return to order."

In the United States, the period following World War I also saw the flowering of art dedicated to building a better society. One of the most vibrant movements of the time arose in the New York neighborhood called Harlem. Harlem is the northeast section of Manhattan Island. It was and is home to many black Americans, of all economic classes. During the decade of the 1920s Harlem served as a magnet for some of the greatest talents of that generation—artists, musicians, composers, actors, writers, poets, scientists, and educators. Louis Armstrong came to Harlem, and so did Duke Ellington. The writer Langston Hughes and the poet Countee Cullen were in residence. Creative energy was in the air, and for a time it seemed as though almost every Harlemite was doing something wonderful—a book, a play, a Broadway show, a sculpture series, a jazz opera, a public mural. This phenomenon came to be called the Harlem Renaissance.

Much of the spirit embodied in the Harlem Renaissance had to do with merging three experiences: the rich heritage of Africa, the ugly legacy of slavery in America (ended barely more than fifty years earlier), and the realities of modern urban life. There is no single style associated with artists of the

21.32 Fernand Léger. *Three Women (Le Grand Déjeuner)*. 1921. Oil on canvas. 6′1¼″ × 8′3″. The Museum of Modern Art, New York.

Harlem Renaissance, but the work of the painter and illustrator Aaron Douglas is representative of the spirit and aspirations of the group. Douglas, who was born in Kansas, moved to Harlem in 1924. During the Harlem Renaissance years he gradually developed a style he called "geometric symbolism." He worked prolifically through the twenties but is perhaps most noted for a series of murals done a few years later, for the 135th Street branch of the New York Public Library. The series is called *Aspects of Negro Life*. Our illustration shows the segment that Douglas called *From Slavery Through Reconstruction* (**21.33**).

Several of Douglas' influences are evident in the mural. Douglas' simplification and stylization of forms surely derived from his studies of West African sculpture. Space is flattened, as in the paintings of modern masters like Gauguin (see 21.9), and the palette of colors is limited, as in Cubism (see 21.18, 21.19). This section of the mural shows a progression from left to right and (as the title implies) from slavery to freedom. At left, the silhouette figures seem bowed down and fearful. One plays a drum, symbolic of African heritage. At right, the figures are upright and proud and joyful. One plays a trumpet, symbolic of the Jazz Age and of black musical brilliance. The dominant center figure synthesizes these polarities. He points upward, toward freedom.

The Harlem Renaissance, as a movement, lasted only a decade. Its momentum was stopped by the stock market crash of 1929 and the ensuing Great Depression of the 1930s. Aaron Douglas' vision of a better society was actually painted during the early years of the Depression, as the dream of the Harlem Renaissance faded. It is nevertheless a vision of hope. Other artists continued to believe that art had a social mission during these difficult times. Dorothea Lange documented the dignity of ordinary people faced with extraordinary adversity in photographs such as *Heading West, Tulare Lake, California* (see 9.14). Rockwell Kent produced a stirring call to action in *Workers of the World, Unite!* (see 8.9). The Depression was in fact worldwide. In Europe, severe hardship fueled nationalist resentments against the unjust settlement of World War I. Anger swept the fascist regimes of Hitler and Mussolini into power in Germany and Italy. In 1939, the world was plunged again into war.

21.33 Aaron Douglas. *Aspects of Negro Life: From Slavery Through Reconstruction.* 1934. Oil on canvas, 5' × 11'7".
Schomburg Center for Research in Black Culture, The New York Public Library.

RELATED WORKS

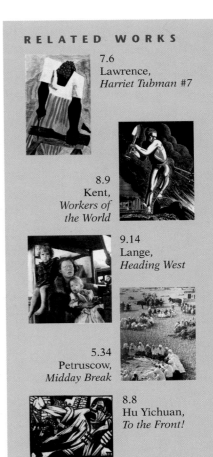

7.6 Lawrence, *Harriet Tubman #7*

8.9 Kent, *Workers of the World*

9.14 Lange, *Heading West*

5.34 Petruscow, *Midday Break*

8.8 Hu Yichuan, *To the Front!*

CHAPTER 22

Art Since 1945

The art made in Europe and North America since the end of World War II is dizzying in its variety and complexity. Nevertheless, we as viewers have one great advantage in approaching this art. We live now. All the artworks considered in this chapter were made during the lifetimes of people still alive today. While we can have only limited success in getting "inside" the minds of Michelangelo or Rembrandt, we inhabit the same world as contemporary artists. We have walked the same streets, watched the same movies and television programs, experienced the same world events. We share a culture with contemporary artists, and so this is *our* art. If we take the trouble to look and study, we may find it is the art with which we feel most connected.

The year 1945 is considered a turning point in the history of Western art. For long years most of the world had been preoccupied with killing and death and hardship—the horrors of World War II. When hostilities ended in late summer of 1945, there was a natural yearning to start afresh, to redirect energies toward creating rather than destroying. But another factor in this turning point was the shift in focus from the old world to the new. Since the time of the ancient Greeks the great centers of Western art had been in Europe—Athens, Rome, Florence, Paris, London. Now, suddenly, the art capital had crossed an ocean and settled in North America. Its hub was New York City.

THE NEW YORK SCHOOL

In the aftermath of World War II most of western Europe was completely devastated. The United States, while exhausted, was not. No bombs had fallen or battles been fought in New York, as they had in London and Paris and Amsterdam and most of the cities in Germany. When the time came to resume the normal activities of life, New York became the center of a vibrant art revival. Many of the most progressive European artists had immigrated to the United States, and they served as teachers and inspiration for a new generation of artists—most of them American—who gravitated to New York.

In fact, painters associated with the first major postwar art movement are referred to as the New York School.

Not a school in the sense of an institution or of instruction, the New York School was a convenient label under which to lump together a group of painters also known as the **Abstract Expressionists.** Primary among them were Jackson Pollock and Willem de Kooning. Abstract Expressionism had many sources, but the most direct influence was Surrealism, with its emphasis on the creative powers of the unconscious and its technique of automatism as a way to tap into them. The painters of the New York School developed highly individual and recognizable styles, but one element their paintings had in common was scale: Abstract Expressionist paintings are generally quite large, and this is important to their effect. Viewers are meant to be engulfed, to be swept into the world of the painting the way we may be swept into a film by sitting so close that the screen fills our entire field of vision.

The quintessential Abstract Expressionist was Jackson Pollock, who by the late 1940s had perfected his "drip technique." To create such works as *Number 1, 1949* (**22.1**), Pollock placed the unstretched canvas on the floor and painted on it indirectly, from above, by casting paint from a brush in controlled gestures or by dripping paint from a stir-stick. Layer after layer, color after color, the painting grew into an allover tangle of graceful arcs, dribbled lines, spatters, and pools of color. There is no focal point, no "composition." Instead we find ourselves in front of a field of energy like the spray of a crashing wave. A critic of the time coined the term **action painting** to describe the work of Pollock and others, for their paintings are not images in the traditional sense but traces of an act, the painter's dance of creation. Pollock said that his method of working allowed him to be "in" the painting, to forget himself in the act of painting, and that is also the best way to look at his works, to lose ourselves in them.

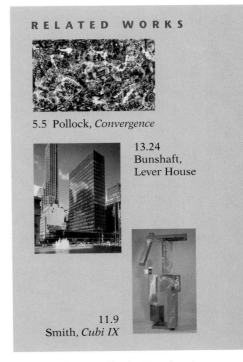

RELATED WORKS

5.5 Pollock, *Convergence*

13.24 Bunshaft, Lever House

11.9 Smith, *Cubi IX*

22.1 Jackson Pollock. *Number 1, 1949.* Enamel and metallic paint on canvas, 5'3" × 8'6". Museum of Contemporary Art, Los Angeles.

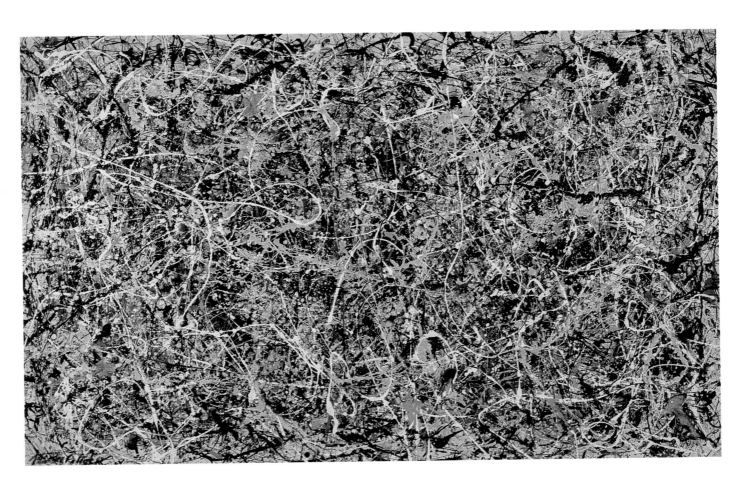

JACKSON POLLOCK
1912–1956

JACKSON POLLOCK was born on a sheep ranch in Cody, Wyoming, the youngest son in a family of five boys. During his youth the family moved around a good deal and led a fairly unstable existence. By the age of fifteen Jackson had begun to show signs of the alcoholism that would plague him all of his life.

In 1930 Pollock went to New York to study at the Art Students League. His principal teacher there was Thomas Hart Benton, a realistic painter of regional Americana, best known for his murals. Later, Pollock would say he was glad to have had the experience with Benton, because he then had to struggle all the harder to make art so very different from that of his mentor.

Money was a critical problem throughout the early years in New York. By 1935 Pollock was employed on the Federal Art Project of the Works Progress Administration—a Depression-era program meant to provide employment for artists. He was required to turn out, every four to eight weeks, one painting suitable for installation in public buildings, for which he was paid a stipend of about $100 a month. Frequent alcoholic binges often interfered with this work, and in 1937 Pollock began psychotherapy in an attempt to overcome his addiction.

Pollock's work was first exhibited in 1942, as part of a group show that also included the work of painter Lee Krasner. Krasner and Pollock soon formed a close relationship, and they were married in 1945. Gradually, Pollock's work began to change, to be freer and more spontaneous, to contain fewer and fewer figural elements. During the late 1940s he began exhibiting works in his mature style.

Some critics praised Pollock as the greatest of all American artists, but the general public was very slow to accept his revolutionary art. *Time* magazine epitomized the bewilderment of the popular press, dubbing him "Jack the Dripper." Nevertheless, there were some collectors willing to invest, so finances became less pressing.

The years 1948 to 1952—Pollock's late thirties—were the artist's prime, when he was at the height of his creative powers. After that, he seemed less sure where to go with his art, and even the sympathetic critics were not so responsive to the work. Pollock began to paint less and drink more. On the night of August 11, 1956, Pollock—along with two young women friends—was driving his convertible near his home when he lost control of the car and rammed into a clump of trees at high speed. Pollock and one of the women were killed instantly. The artist was only forty-four years old.

Pollock drunk could be violent and brutish; Pollock sober was shy, introverted, and uncommunicative. Few ever succeeded in getting him to talk about his art, but there is one quote, reprinted many times, that gives voice to his truly remarkable vision: "On the floor I am more at ease. I feel nearer, more a part of the painting, since this way I can walk around it, work from the four sides and literally be *in* the painting. . . . When I am *in* my painting, I am not aware of what I'm doing. It is only after a sort of 'get acquainted' period that I see what I have been about. I have no fears about making changes, destroying the image, etc., because the painting has a life of its own. I try to let it come through. It is only when I lose contact with the painting that the result is a mess. Otherwise there is pure harmony, an easy give and take, and the painting comes out well."[1]

Jackson Pollock in his studio at East Hampton, N.Y. 1950, photographed by Hans Namuth.

The energy of the artist's actions again supplies the expressive force in Kline's *Chief* (**22.2**). *Chief* is named after a locomotive that passed through the Pennsylvania town where the artist was born. Like a locomotive, the painting comes barreling straight toward us from parallel tracks in the upper right. *Chief* is typical in its "heroic" scale, and standing before it a viewer senses the involvement of the painter's entire body in the sweeping gestures of its creation. This sensation of primal release and physical freedom, transferred from artist to viewer through gesture, was part of what contemporary viewers found so exhilarating about the new type of painting.

Strictly speaking, the works we have looked at by Pollock and Kline are not abstract but nonrepresentational. As always, the terminology of art evolved haphazardly and inconsistently as people grasped for terms to speak about what was new. Critics and artists of the day used *abstract* and *nonrepresentational* interchangeably, and in casual speech and writing *abstract* is still the more common term. De Kooning's *Woman and Bicycle* (**22.3**) is abstract in our strict sense. Like Pollock and Kline, de Kooning had developed a nonrepresentational, gestural style during the 1940s. During the next decade, however, he returned to the human figure, most notoriously in the *Women* series.

Even today the *Women* paintings retain their power to disturb. De Kooning admitted that he began each painting from a magazine photograph of a beautiful woman, yet as he worked, they mutated into grimacing monsters. The artist was dismayed, for this wasn't his goal at all. We can see the paintings as reflecting de Kooning's conscious and unconscious feelings toward women. Yet they also record a struggle between two ways of thinking about art. Forceful gestures keep trying to establish a painting about the act of painting, but against this effort the image keeps reasserting itself, demanding to be recognized. Hovering in the background are the spirits of such great painters of human flesh as Rembrandt and Titian, who also used paint in an intensely physical way.

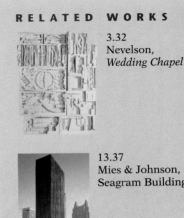
22.2 (left) Franz Kline. *Chief*. 1950. Oil on canvas, 4'10⅜" × 6'1½". The Museum of Modern Art, New York.

22.3 (right) Willem de Kooning. *Woman and Bicycle*. 1952–53. Oil on canvas, 6'4½" × 4'1". Whitney Museum of American Art, New York.

22.4 (left) Mark Rothko. *Orange and Yellow*. 1956. Oil on canvas, 7′7″ × 5′11″.
Collection Albright-Knox Art Gallery, Buffalo, N. Y.

22.5 (right) Robert Rauschenberg. *Factum II*. 1957. Combine painting: oil, ink, pencil, crayon, paper, fabric, newspaper, printed reproductions, and printed paper on canvas, 61⅜ × 35½″.
The Museum of Modern Art, New York.

Another form of abstraction that came into prominence in the postwar period is known as **Color Field** painting. As the name implies, imagery is reduced to a large "field" or area of color, in some cases one pure color filling the entire canvas. In contrast to the dynamic emotionalism of Abstract Expressionism, Color Field paintings have a meditative tranquility that draws the viewer in and invites contemplation. The work of Mark Rothko in the late forties through the sixties (**22.4**) usually features one or more soft-edged color rectangles floating in the larger color rectangle of the canvas. The inner rectangle has sides parallel to the canvas edges, and its boundaries are blurred and gently blended, causing the inner sections to float. Where Kline and De Kooning emphasized the physical presence of paint, Rothko did the opposite, thinning his paints so much that the pigment powder barely holds to the canvas. He wanted to communicate a sensation of pure dematerialized color, and in this sense one of his heirs is James Turrell, whose works such as *Milk Run II* (see 4.19) exist only as colored light.

Many of the next generation of artists continued to explore the directions opened up by Abstract Expressionism and Color Field painting. Helen Frankenthaler, for example, pioneered a staining technique, pouring thinned paint onto canvas and controlling its flow in various ways (see 7.14). Joan Mitchell took up the energetic brushwork of Abstract Expressionism and combined it with an interest in landscape filtered through the late paintings of Monet (see 4.53, 7.9).

INTO THE SIXTIES:
ASSEMBLAGE AND HAPPENINGS

By the middle of the 1950s, Abstract Expressionism had been the "new" style for fifteen years. Many artists felt it was time to move on. One of the most influential voices of the time was the composer John Cage, whose writings and speeches suggested a different path for art to follow. Music and art, Cage said, should be "an affirmation of life—not an attempt to bring order out of chaos nor to suggest improvements in creation, but simply a way of waking up to the very life we're living."[2] Like the Dadaists of forty years earlier, young artists began mixing art back up with life as they found it, sometimes literally and often humorously. Critics called the trend Neo-Dada ("new Dada").

An example of Neo-Dada is Robert Rauschenberg's witty *Factum II* (**22.5**). In the tradition of Dada artists such as Hannah Höch (see 9.19), Rauschenberg culled images from mass-printed sources such as magazines. The images relate to the idea of doubleness—a photograph of two trees, side-by-side photographs of a burning building, and even a **T** for "two." Rauschenberg pasted the images onto canvas and tied them together visually with paint applied in the gestures that Abstract Expressionism found so meaningful. Here, however, the gestures are not meant to express anything at all. Rauschenberg "found" them in Abstract Expressionist art just the way he found the images in magazines. Both were part of his life: why not throw them together? Rauschenberg carried his idea through to its logical conclusion by making the painting twice: there is a *Factum I* that looks just like this. In action painting, gestural brush strokes and drips were the spontaneous and authentic signs of a unique moment of creative frenzy. With sly humor, *Factum II* shows that they can be reproduced like any other image.

Rauschenberg referred to his works as combine paintings, but a more general term is **assemblage.** Another artist who made assemblages was Rauschenberg's friend Jasper Johns. Johns chose as his subjects some of the most familiar images one could imagine: the American flag, a map of the United States, numerals, letters of the alphabet, and targets (**22.6**). He said

22.6 Jasper Johns. *Target with Four Faces*. 1955. Assemblage: encaustic on newspaper and collage on canvas with objects, 26" square, surmounted by four tinted plaster faces in wood box with hinged front; overall dimensions with box open 33⅝ × 26 × 3". The Museum of Modern Art, New York.

that by choosing these motifs the work of composition had already been done for him, and he could concentrate on "other things." What other things? Paradoxes, for one. Painted in encaustic over newsprint, the target is textured, sensuous, and unique. Yet the idea of a target exists potentially in endless multiples. Above the target are portions of four faces. Johns took the casts from the same person, making a series of anonymous mechanical multiples from a unique individual. Like all of Johns' favorite motifs, a target is not only familiar but two-dimensional, abstract, and symbolic. Is the painting a representation of a target or a target? What is the difference? It also teases us into thinking about aesthetics and emotional distance. For example, if we appreciate the painting as an abstract composition of concentric circles, does that spare us from thinking about it as a target and the blindfolded victims of a firing squad?

An assemblage that passed quickly into legend was French artist Jean Tinguely's *Homage to New York* (**22.7**). *Homage to New York* was like an Abstract Expressionist painting in reverse. Instead of celebrating its own creation, it was designed to self-destruct. Tinguely assembled the convoluted and absurd mechanical sculpture in the garden of the Museum of Modern Art in New York. The scavenged materials included an upright piano, several fans, noisemakers, bicycle wheels, metal tubing, and a large orange weather bal-

22.7 (left) Jean Tinguely. *Homage to New York*. 1960. Self-destroying sculpture in the garden of The Museum of Modern Art, New York.

22.8 (right) Allan Kaprow. *The Courtyard*. 1962. Happening at the Mills Hotel, New York. Courtesy of the Library, Getty Research Institute, Los Angeles.

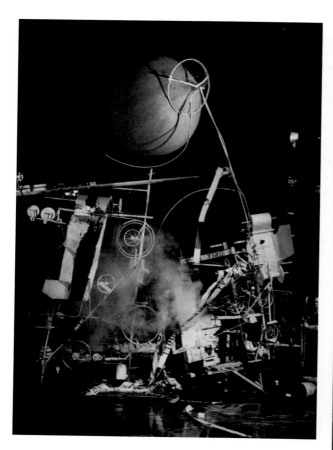

loon. On March 17, 1960, before an audience that included the governor of New York, Tinguely plugged the work in, and the sparks began to fly. Not all went according to plan, and in the end the fire department had to be called in to finish the sculpture off. *Homage to New York* was a parody of machines and the machine age, but it also allowed machines to do something they are rarely built to do: play. Art, Tinguely felt, should be fun.

Tinguely's sculpture existed as an object, but its act of self-destruction was the art. Art could be an event. John Cage, in fact, had suggested that the next move in art should be toward theater, the art that was most like life. The composer's friend Allan Kaprow followed through on this suggestion by eliminating the art object altogether and staging events he called **happenings.** Kaprow's *The Courtyard* (**22.8**) happened in the courtyard of a seedy hotel. Kaprow and his assistants erected a five-story "mountain" of scaffolding covered with black paper. On a platform atop it they set an "altar" of mattresses. Over the mattresses was suspended a large dome, also covered in black paper. After audience members helped sweep the space clean, black paper scraps were showered down from above. A woman in white danced around the base of the mountain and then climbed up to the mattresses. She was followed by photographers who took pictures of her as she continued to dance. Accompanied by shrieks, sirens, and thunder effects, the dome was lowered over them.

Among the spectators at *The Courtyard* was Hans Richter, one of the original members of Dada. None other than Marcel Duchamp, then living in New York, had drawn his attention to it. The Dadaists, too, had staged provocative events. "A Ritual!" Richter wrote. "It was a composition using space, color and movement, and the setting in which the Happening took place gave it a nightmarish, obsessive quality . . . ."[3] The Dadaists recognized their successors clearly. Just as Dada had created both art and anti-art as "shock therapy" for the complacent, conformist society that had produced World War I, this later generation was producing art and anti-art to jolt into awareness the complacent, conformist society of prosperous, postwar America.

ART OF THE SIXTIES AND SEVENTIES

Does art exist in its own aesthetic realm apart from life? Is it important for us to have art as an alternative to our social experience, a refuge from everyday concerns that keeps us in touch with spiritual or abstract matters? Or is art deeply involved with life? Is it important for us to see the lives we live, the issues that concern us, our sense of what it is like to be in the world here and now given form through art? These questions have animated the history of art since the beginning of the modern era. As viewers, we have the luxury of appreciating all types of art, but artists have to choose one path or the other. During the sixties and seventies, the directions that had been set out in the previous decade were continued, questioned, and complicated by new trends.

POP ART

Even the name is breezy: "pop," for popular. The artists of Pop found a gold mine of visual material in the mundane, mass-produced objects and images of America's popular culture—comic books, advertising, billboards, and packaging; the ever-expanding world of home appliances and other commodities; and photographic images from cinema, television, and newspapers. Like Neo-Dada, Pop drew art closer to life, but life as it had already been transformed into images by advertising and the media.

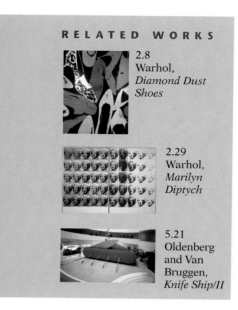

2.8
Warhol,
*Diamond Dust
Shoes*

2.29
Warhol,
*Marilyn
Diptych*

5.21
Oldenberg
and Van
Bruggen,
Knife Ship/II

22.9 (left) Andy Warhol. *100 Cans*. 1962. Oil on canvas, 6′ × 4′4″.
Collection Albright-Knox Art Gallery, Buffalo, N.Y.

22.10 (right) Roy Lichtenstein. *Masterpiece*. 1962. Oil on canvas, 4′6″ square.

The most enigmatic of Pop artists was Andy Warhol, who frustrated critics by refusing to explain what he meant by such painting as *100 Cans* (**22.9**). Was this a criticism of consumer culture? A celebration of it? Was Warhol saying "how awful" or "how wonderful"? Was he saying anything at all? Warhol even adopted the methods of mass production. He called his studio The Factory, and there he and his assistants manufactured his art. The use of photographic silkscreen gave the images a mechanical look removed from the personal touch of the artist's own hand. In a few years, Warhol's subjects grew to form a sort of portrait of America of the early sixties—products such as Campbell soup cans, Coca-Cola bottles, and Brillo boxes; people such as Marilyn Monroe, Jackie Kennedy, and Elvis Presley; symbols such as dollar bills and the Statue of Liberty; newspaper photos of car crashes, race riots, and an electric chair. All were repeated again and again across the surface of the canvas. Warhol's style was cool and detached. He said that everything that mattered, everything that was interesting, was right on the surface where you could see it, and he acted mystified when people wanted there to be more.

Roy Lichtenstein often based his imagery on the comic book. Many of Lichtenstein's paintings (**22.10**) are large, meticulously rendered frames adapted from comic strips, accurate down to the dialogue in the speech balloons and the dot pattern of crude newspaper reproduction. The artist did not hesitate to introduce a touch of irony by poking fun at himself and the art world in proclaiming this work a "masterpiece." Pop Art attempted to show that a detached look at the overfamiliar objects of daily life could give them new meaning as visual emblems.

The energies of Pop and Neo-Dada mingle in the work of Niki de Saint-Phalle. Among her early works were events called shootings, in which people gathered to watch the artist take aim at her own sculptures and assemblages with a pistol. Pouches of paint were hidden in the works, and each

successful shot produced an explosion of color. The combination of playfulness and violent aggression was intriguing, and the sight of a beautiful woman coolly firing a gun was part of the event. Beginning in 1965, Saint-Phalle affirmed the powers of women less ambiguously and more joyously in a series of Pop-inspired sculptures called *Nanas*, a French slang word for women. *Black Venus* (**22.11**), a painted polyester *Nana* more than 9 feet tall, exhibits a sexuality that is both powerful and buoyantly cheerful. The figure almost busts out of a sort of bathing suit gaily colored in hearts and flowers, clutching a beach ball. Her breasts and hips and thighs are enormous (remember the *Venus of Willendorf*, 14.2), but her pose is dynamic; she stands ready to run or jump or dance. Saint-Phalle's *Venus* is an earth mother, but an earth mother who wants to play.

MINIMAL ART AND SITE WORKS

Coexisting with Pop in the 1960s was a trend called Minimalism, which continued to explore the nonrepresentational directions that art could take. Minimalism was primarily concerned with three-dimensional art, but it was inspired by developments in painting such as Frank Stella's *Valparaiso Flesh and Green* (**22.12**). Abstract painting was certainly not new, but Stella's approach was fundamentally different in one important way: unlike the Abstract Expressionists and their heirs, he did not conceive of his work as a visual field that the viewer would see *into* but as an object the viewer would look *at*. The trapezoidal shape of *Valparaiso Flesh and Green* immediately signals that this painting is not a window onto anything—not a deep Renaissance perspective, not a shallow Cubist space, not an Abstract Expressionist infinity of tangled lines or hovering color. This painting is a *thing*.

Stella used color to divide the trapezoid into two equilateral triangles. His composition consists in repeating two of the three outlines of each triangle again and again, producing a series of chevrons (**V**s) of diminishing size in bands of color (the white between the colored chevrons is bare canvas). The reflective, metallic paint has an industrial look, and it further emphasizes the surface of the work. "What you see is what you see," Stella said about his painting, meaning that he did not intend anything by it other than what was there: the beauty of the color, the logic of the composition, the satisfaction of repetition. That was all there was, and he found it to be enough.

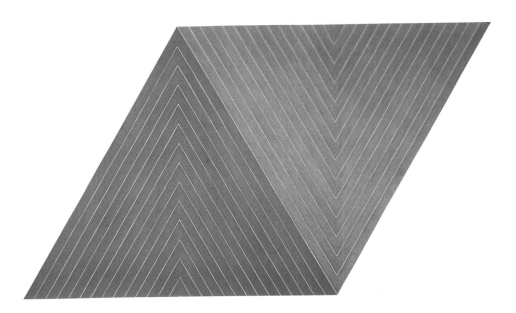

22.11 (above) Niki de Saint-Phalle. *Black Venus*. 1965–67. Painted polyester, 9'2" × 2'11" × 2'. Whitney Museum of American Art, New York.

22.12 (left) Frank Stella. *Valparaiso Flesh and Green*. 1963. Metallic paint on canvas, 6'6" × 11'3¼" × 3". Collection the artist.

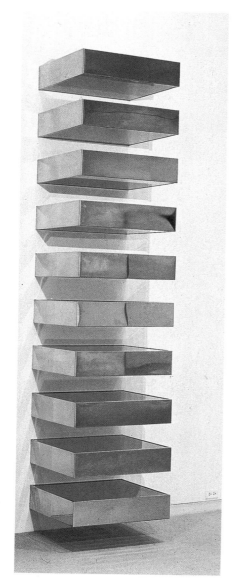

Considered purely as an object *Valparaiso Flesh and Green* becomes a kind of shallow, colored sculpture attached to the wall. This point was not lost on artists who were more interested in three-dimensional work, and they began to explore the implications. Donald Judd's *Untitled* (**22.13**) embodies many of the characteristics associated with Minimalism. It is made of common industrial and construction materials. These materials are used literally; they do not try to suggest or depict anything else. The composition is based in repeating units of simple geometric shapes. There is no trace of the artist's "hand" or "touch." Rather, the sculpture has the impersonal look of industrial fabrication. And yet it can be immensely satisfying to look at. The stacked boxes are like a lesson in seeing and perspective. The various shadows they cast, the even slices of space between them, the way the light filters through the red Plexiglas, the reflections of the polished brass—all give undeniable pleasure. The clear logic and straightforward repetition are strangely reassuring, like a nursery rhyme or a child counting its fingers, one to ten.

Minimalism was not a movement founded and defined by artists but a term invented by critics in an attempt to get a handle on the new art they were seeing. Many artists of the time were interested in simplified forms and honest materials, and the label Minimalism loosely includes a broad range of work. The organic fiberglass forms of Eva Hesse's *Repetition 19 III* (see 4.54) are an aspect of Minimalism. The sculptor Robert Smithson gradually abandoned industrial materials for natural ones and galleries for nature itself in site works such as *Spiral Jetty* (see 3.36). Like many site works of the 1970s, *Spiral Jetty* combines the aesthetics of Minimalism with the principles of Conceptualism (discussed below).

REAL, SUPER REAL

Still another trend that emerged around 1960, as the dominance of abstract art was increasingly challenged, was a revival of interest in the human figure. One of the most fruitful approaches to the figure was developed by George Segal. Segal began as an abstract painter during the late 1950s, but he grew to feel that too much of the world outside of the studio door had

22.13 (above) Donald Judd. *Untitled*. 1969. Brass and red fluorescent Plexiglas, ten units, 6⅛ × 24 × 7″ each, with 6″ intervals. Hirshhorn Museum and Sculpture Garden, Smithsonian Institution, Washington, D.C.

22.14 (right) George Segal. *The Parking Garage*. 1968. Plaster, wood, metal, electrical parts, and lightbulbs, 9′9¾″ × 12′8″ × 4′. The Newark Museum, New Jersey.

22.15 Don Eddy. *New Shoes for H*. 1973–74. Acrylic on canvas, 3′8″ × 4′.
The Cleveland Museum of Art.

to be ignored. He experimented with constructing plaster figures, but the technique he quickly came to prefer was making casts of live people by covering them with strips of plaster-soaked cloth.

Segal typically placed his figures in realistic, three-dimensional settings, as in *The Parking Garage* (**22.14**). Built like a stage set and including actual objects as props, the settings usually evoke an urban environment. The result is like a moment of theater with plaster actors. Segal's works capture a particular kind of city experience: the hundreds of people we come into contact with every day but do not know. We see them only for a moment, in passing. Yet they often leave an impression—the girl on the subway, the man waiting for the light to change, the woman in the restaurant window, or the boy in front of the parking garage. In some ways, they are the ghosts of our day, and Segal portrays them that way. The rough, unpainted plaster surfaces encourage us to experience his figures as anonymous types, but we see that they were cast directly from life and are thus individuals.

Like Neo-Dada and Minimalism, Segal's realism has a strong literal component, relying on ordinary materials that are what they are. The diverse painting trends of the time also share this trait in various ways. Pop artists, for example, took their inspiration from two-dimensional images, and Minimalist painters such as Frank Stella created paintings meant to be experienced as objects. At first glance, Don Eddy's *New Shoes for H*. would seem to be an exception (**22.15**). But in fact this is not a painting of a store window but a painting of a *photograph* of a store window. During the 1970s many painters became intrigued by the view through the lens. One of the trends this produced was known as **Photorealism,** meaning the particular kind of realism that the camera produces. *New Shoes for H*. depicts a photograph that Eddy took himself. He was interested in the double layer of information that windows offer by being both transparent and reflective. Photography's ability to capture a dizzying amount of detail for later study is on full view here. The painting, however, is not an exact copy of the photograph. First, the photograph was in black and white. More important, Eddy has given his painting and allover sharp focus that photographs do not possess. The result is a sort of hallucinatory superrealism.

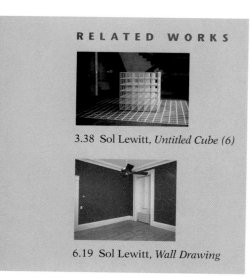

3.38 Sol Lewitt, *Untitled Cube (6)*

6.19 Sol Lewitt, *Wall Drawing*

22.16 Joseph Kosuth. *One and Three Chairs*. 1965. Folding wooden chair, photograph, blown-up dictionary definition.

CONCEPTUAL ART

Conceptual Art is art in which ideas are paramount and the form that realizes these ideas is secondary—often lightweight, ephemeral, unpretentious, cheap, ordinary, unremarkable. Arising in the mid-1960s as yet another echo of Dada, Conceptual Art is especially indebted to Marcel Duchamp, whose ready-mades such as *Bottle Rack* (see 21.23) can be considered as Conceptual works, though they made their appearance before the term was invented. In *Bottle Rack*, the idea of placing a bottle rack in a gallery for consideration as a work of art was paramount. The form the bottle rack took—whether it was tall or short, brass or steel, vertical or horizontal—did not matter, nor did Duchamp actually make the bottle rack himself.

Conceptualism is not a style but a way of thinking about art, and artists have put it to many different uses. Joseph Kosuth's *One and Three Chairs* (**22.16**) places three alternative representations of a chair together for comparison: an actual chair, a photograph of that chair, and a dictionary definition of the word *chair*. The definition is merely a blown-up photograph of a dictionary entry, and the chair a simple folding wooden chair. Kosuth did not even take the photograph of the chair himself. What we see is not a work of art but one of many possible ways to document a concept Kosuth had for raising questions about representation, and thus about art.

Like many early Conceptualists, Kosuth's desire to get rid of the art object was motivated by his opposition to the burgeoning art market, which implicitly equated art with luxury commodities such as antique furniture or designer clothing. He shifted his art into ideas and documented them in ways that had little or no perceived material value. Other artists enjoy the aesthetic liberation of Conceptualism. For Sol LeWitt, whose wall drawings consist solely of instructions to be executed by others (see 6.19), Conceptualism allows the artist to surrender direct control, open art up to chance, and involve other people.

FEMINISM AND FEMINIST ART

If you had been reading a book like this around 1968, the chapters of Part Five, "Arts in Time," would most likely not have introduced you to Sofonisba Anguissola (16.27), Artemisia Gentileschi (17.5), Judith Leyster (17.13), Elisabeth Vigée-Lebrun (17.18), Berthe Morisot (21.5), or Mary Cassatt (21.12). Art historians knew of works by these women. They just didn't make an effort to include them in their telling of the history of art. It was quite possible to come away from a course in art history or a visit to a museum believing that women had played little or no role in the art of the past. If you look forward in this book to the art of the eighties and nineties, you will find not only many more women but greater diversity in general. This diversity accurately reflects the makeup of the contemporary art world, and it is due in large measure to the impact of feminism and related social and political movements of the 1970s.

Feminist organizations had originally been formed around such issues as equal rights and equal pay. Because images are powerful and pervasive in contemporary society, visual culture quickly became a feminist concern, both in art and in the media. Women art professionals organized to recover women's art of the past, to push for more equitable representation in museums and galleries, and to nurture contemporary women artists. During this first phase of feminism, a project that intrigued many artists was the creation of a specifically female art. One of the most influential early feminist works was Judy Chicago's *Dinner Party* (see 12.19), which brought crafts media into art to honor the domestic realm, a feminine world through most of history. Chicago's colleague Miriam Schapiro also evokes the domestic realm in *Heartfelt* (**22.17**). Shaped like a schematic house, *Heartfelt* is layered

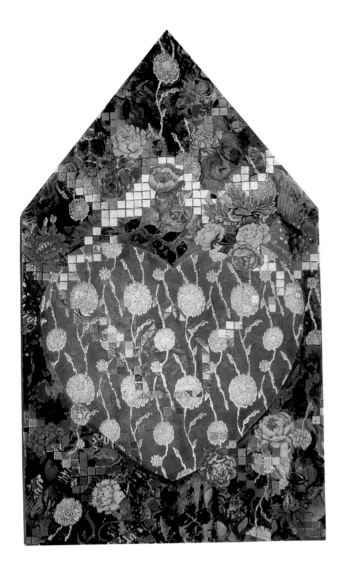

with mosaic and floral patterns, falling blossoms, and a big red heart. The crowded, unashamedly decorative surface and the popular, easily understood symbols of house and heart were intended as a female rebuke to the stripped-down industrial forms of Minimalism, which Schapiro considered typically male.

Feminist thought has since developed considerably, and most feminists today consider these early ideas about women's (and men's) essential natures to be too limiting. As for Minimalism, the organic work of Eva Hesse (see 4.54) has been at least as influential as any of the "male" versions. Nevertheless, the work of Chicago and Schapiro marked an important step in the full participation of women in contemporary artistic life. Early feminism also served to draw attention to many living women artists whose long careers had not received sufficient recognition. One of these was Alice Neel (**22.18**). Neel painted people. That was her interest. She was, it is now plain to see, one of the finest, most original, and most insightful painters of people of the 20th century. Unfortunately, her mature career overlapped almost exactly with the decades when abstract painting dominated the art world. She was far from the only artist to be pushed aside as irrelevant to the progress of art history as contemporary critics, curators, and gallery owners saw it. Later, when many younger artists began to explore figurative painting again, they discovered a master in their midst. Neel had been working all along.

22.17 (left) Miriam Schapiro. *Heartfelt*. 1979. Acrylic and fabric on canvas, 5'10" × 3'4". Collection the Norton Neuman Family.

22.18 (right) Alice Neel. *Virgil Thompson*. 1971. Oil on canvas. National Portrait Gallery, Washington, D.C.

RELATED WORKS

12.19 Chicago, *Dinner Party*

ALICE NEEL
1900–1984

WHEN AN ACQUAINTANCE once remarked that Alice Neel painted "like a man," the artist retorted, "No, I don't paint like a man; but I don't paint like they expect a woman to paint." As a matter of fact, this extraordinary woman spent a long lifetime doing the unexpected, with cheerful disregard for the prevailing mores and fashions.

Alice Neel was born in Merion Square, Pennsylvania, the daughter of a proper middle-class family that she described as "anti-bohemian." She studied at what was then the Philadelphia School of Design for Women—"a school where rich girls went before they got married"—and received a thorough, if conventional, grounding in art techniques.

Her personal life, too, was conventional up to that point, but soon it changed drastically. Neel referred to the men who played important roles in her life by stereotype, rather than by name. Upon leaving art school she married "the Cuban." The couple moved to Havana, where Neel continued to paint and had her first exhibition in 1926. The Cuban marriage

eventually broke up, after which Neel returned to New York and worked on the W.P.A. Art Project—the government-sponsored Depression program to help support artists. Along the way she took up with "the sailor," with whom she lived until he cut up and burned all her work. ("You know how men are, they get jealous, they're possessive.") There was also "the Puerto Rican singer." From these liaisons came four children, one of whom died in infancy. Later there would be several grandchildren, who became favorite subjects for Neel's art.

From the beginning Neel was a portraitist, although she preferred to call herself a "people painter," feeling that portraitists are looked down on. This assessment actually proved correct through most of her career. Just at the point when Neel should have been in her artistic prime—the 1940s and 1950s—abstraction had completely taken over the art world. The painter of figures was out of fashion and remained so for at least twenty years. Not until 1974, at the age of seventy-four, did Neel have her first important show—at the Whitney Museum in New York. The show included some fifteen pictures that had not previously been "off the shelf." Alice Neel waited a long time to hear an important critic name her as the best portrait painter of the 20th century, and then she herself did not contradict that statement. The pictures, however, have transcended portrait status in the sense of recording someone's looks. They are major paintings that happen to have people as their subjects.

Quite obviously, Alice Neel was an original, an exceptionally self-directed artist and human being. Neither her personal life nor her career was modeled after any example, nor did she follow anything but her own inclinations: "When they asked me if I had influences I said I never copy anybody. I never did, because I feel that the most important thing about art and in art—and I tell students this—is to find your own road."[4]

Alice Neel. *Self-Portrait*. 1980. Oil on canvas, 4'6" x 3'4". National Portrait Gallery, Smithsonian Institution, Washington, D.C.

ART SINCE THE EIGHTIES: POSTMODERN WORLD?

Over the course of the seventies, it became clear to many people that ideas about art that seemed to have been in place for much of the modern era were eroding and that something different was taking their place. This new climate of thought has come to be called Postmodernism. Whether Postmodernism is truly a new era or whether it is simply a new phase of Modernism is much debated. Future generations will no doubt decide; it is always difficult to understand and label one's own time.

The term *postmodern* was first used to describe architecture such as Renzo Piano and Richard Rodgers' Georges Pompidou National Center of Art and Culture (**22.19**). Designed in 1971 and completed six years later, the Pompidou Center created a sensation. Encased in scaffolding, pipes, tubes, and funnels—all color-coded according to function—it looks like a building turned inside out. The architects themselves likened it to "a Jules Verne spaceship that can't fly."[5] The Pompidou Center was one of many buildings of the time that turned away from the International style that had dominated Western architecture after World War II (see 13.24, 13.37). The International style had grown from the thinking of early-20th-century Modernist movements such as De Stijl and the Bauhaus (see pages 516–517). Its industrial materials, clean lines, and rectilinear forms sought not only to express the modern age but also to create a luminous, rational environment in which humanity itself would progress. By the mid-sixties, however, many began to find International style buildings oppressive and sterile. A new direction was called for, but instead of building on Modernist ideas and progressing *forward*, architects reached both *backward*—adapting ornaments and forms from traditions as distant as ancient Egypt—and *outward*—looking seriously at common, everyday architecture. Instead of the rational order of International style, they often emphasized other, equally human qualities such as playfulness, curiosity, and eccentricity.

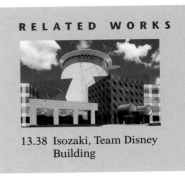

22.19 Renzo Piano and Richard Rodgers. Georges Pompidou National Center of Art and Culture, Paris. 1977.

The notion that there may be no such thing as "progress" in art is part of the web of related ideas that make up Postmodernism. Another is a more complex view of history. Feminism had clearly shown that within art history as it was usually told lay other histories that were untold. Art history was not the straightforward progression of one style to another that it had been made to seem. Rather, each historical moment was full of multiple directions, contradictions, and debates. Perhaps a fairer way to study history would be to study everything that happened, not just the "winners" whose style seemed to be part of "progress." This way of thinking led to the creation of museums such as the Gare d'Orsay in Paris. (See "Art Issues: Presenting the Past," page 497). Applying these ideas to the present moment logically leads to pluralism, the idea that art can take many directions at the same time, all of them equally valid. Historians of the future should no longer select one as "correct" and sweep the rest under the carpet. Pluralism in turn recognizes that there is no longer any single leading artistic center. Rather, the world of art consists of many centers and has many levels.

Sherrie Levine's 1991 *Fountain* may be the ultimate Postmodern statement (**22.20**). *Fountain* was the most notorious of Duchamp's ready-mades, an ordinary porcelain latrine that he contributed to an art exhibit in 1914. Levine presents a gleaming bronze version. Her *Fountain* is a valuable, even sacred object, suggesting that the original *Fountain* and all it stands for are now firmly enshrined in the thinking of contemporary artists. At the same time, we notice that she has not called her work *Homage to Duchamp*, or *After Duchamp*, or acknowledged Duchamp in any way. She presents the work as her own, a Postmodern practice known as **appropriation.** Loosely, appropriation refers to the artistic recycling of existing images. In this sense, it acknowledges that images circulate in such vast quantities through our society that they have become a kind of public resource that anyone can draw on. More strictly, appropriation is linked to Duchamp himself, who presented the creations of others (a latrine, a bottle rack) as his own and in doing so gave them a new meaning. In music, many of the same ideas lie behind the practice of sampling—taking bits of music from prerecorded songs and giving them new meaning by placing them in a new context. Both appropriation and sampling form part of larger theories that doubt whether

22.20 (left) Sherrie Levine. *Fountain*. 1991. Bronze, 14½ × 14¼ × 25″. Walker Art Center, Minneapolis.

22.21 (right) Anselm Kiefer. *Interior*. 1981. Oil, paper, and straw on canvas; 9′5¼″ × 10′2½″. Collection Stedelijk Museum, Amsterdam.

any artist is the sole creator of his or her work or the final authority about what it means. All artists borrow ideas in one way or another, and the meaning of a work is unstable and varies from viewer to viewer. The creation of meaning, and thus of art, is a communal project.

These, then, are some of the ideas that make up Postmodernism. This chapter closes with a brief look at the art of what may be the Postmodern era.

THE PAINTERLY IMAGE

For many observers, art history seemed to stop running forward in the mid-1970s, when one artist after another began to make paintings—not the minimal objects of Frank Stella (22.12) or the silkscreened ironies of Andy Warhol (22.9), but paintings where paint was freely manipulated as a sensuous material in order to make a recognizable, expressive image. That kind of painting was supposed to be over.

During the early 1980s some of these artists became known as Neo-Expressionists, for their work recalled the sincerity and emotional intensity of the Expressionist movements of early 20th-century Europe (see page 505). German artist Anselm Kiefer became one of the most talked about of this group, for his work often dealt directly with the great trauma of his country's past: the horrors of Nazi power under Adolf Hitler and the atrocities of World War II. *Interior* (**22.21**) was copied from a photograph of Hitler's Chancellery (office of state), a building designed by the ambitious Nazi architect Albert Speer. In Kiefer's work the Chancellery, rendered in dramatic perspective, is abandoned and decaying. A fire burns in the center of the room; perhaps it will destroy the building and the regime it represents. Most critics have read Kiefer's work as a kind of exorcism—an attempt to drive out the evil spirits of Germany's past. And, to be sure, the artist's vast theatrical spaces, almost like stage sets, are empty. The actors are gone.

An American artist who was associated at first with Neo-Expressionism is Eric Fischl. Fischl's early paintings explored the strangeness that lay just under the surface of ordinary suburban life. *Barbeque* (**22.22**) presents a slice of all-American normality in the vertiginous perspective of a wide-angle pho-

RELATED WORKS

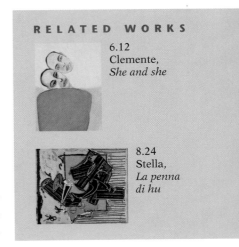

6.12
Clemente,
She and she

8.24
Stella,
La penna di hu

22.22 Eric Fischl. *Barbeque*. 1982. Oil on canvas. 5′5″ × 8′4″. Courtesy Mary Boone Gallery, New York.

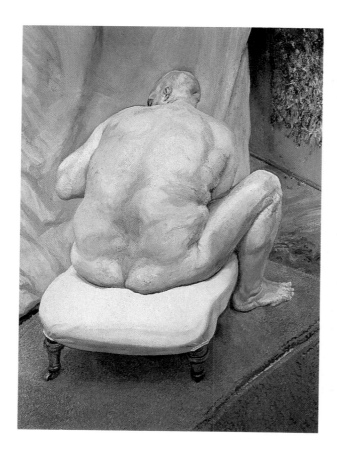

22.23 (left) Lucian Freud. *Naked Man, Back View*. 1991–92. Oil on canvas, 6′ × 4′6″.
Purchase, Lila Acheson Wallace Gift, 1993 (1993.71) and courtesy of the artist. Photograph © 1993 The Metropolitan Museum of Art.

22.24 (right) Jean-Michel Basquiat. *Gold Griot*. 1984. Oil and oil paintstick on wood. 9′9″ × 6′1″.
The Eli Broad Family Foundation, Santa Monica.

tograph. Objects in the foreground appear larger than they should, and the scene goes rushing into the distance as though it were being sucked down a wind tunnel. The father turns from his labors at the barbeque to smile approvingly at the hijinks of his son, who seems to be doing an amusing trick. But this is not a trick. The boy is breathing fire, smoldering in an adolescent rage that says GET ME OUT. He is an alien in their midst. In front of him, an arching fish seems to make a bid for freedom. It, too, is out of its element.

The new interest in figurative painting had the effect of drawing attention to some older painters who had been working with images all along. One of the most respected painters working today is the English artist Lucian Freud, a grandson of the pioneer psychoanalyst Sigmund Freud. Lucian Freud is best known for his nudes, which he paints with a candor that many find disturbing. Freud paints the mortality of the flesh. If we are to love the flesh, Freud's paintings seem to say, we must love it honestly and totally, in all its forms, even as it decays. *Naked Man, Back View* (**22.23**) is typical of his style. The huge body is so plastic that viewers feel they could actually reach out and squeeze the rubbery flesh, and that it would be warm to the touch. The sheer bulk of the subject, rendered in merciless detail, both fascinates and repels. The painter's honesty is matched by the honesty of his sitter, who agreed to pose for a series of works. The two are equally fearless and committed to truth, and the painting is in a sense their collaboration.

Freud formed his style from deep within the European figurative tradition. Younger painters in New York, however, often felt closer to street life and the highly stylized energy of the graffiti images that then were appearing on subways, storefronts, and almost every urban surface. One of these painters was Jean-Michel Basquiat, who began as a graffiti artist in the late 1970s. His work came to the attention of gallery owners when it was included in an exhibit of street art in 1980. Between his first gallery exhibit the following year and his death from a drug overdose at the age of twenty-eight, Basquiat blazed with amazing intensity, producing a large and compelling body of work. The subject of *Gold Griot* (**22.24**) is an African ceremonial storyteller, or *griot*. Painted on a gold background that indicates a sacred area and over a panel of wooden slats that evoke poor Caribbean dwellings, the *griot* shows Basquiat's purposefully "primitive" or "naive" style. In fact, Basquiat was anything but primitive. Growing up in a middle-class family in Brooklyn, son of a Haitian father and a Puerto Rican mother, Basquiat read widely and studied a broad range of art and artists. In his work he tried to encompass the many layers of the hybrid culture that he belonged to, the Afro–Caribbean–African American–New York culture that admired opera *and* jazz, that spoke Spanish *and* English, that danced the salsa *and* hip-hop, went to museums *and* clubs. Basquiat's death ended an astonishing career that straddled many worlds.

A 1978 exhibition at the Whitney Museum of American Art entitled "New Image Painting" was one of the events that first drew the public's attention to the fact that painting had become newly interesting to young artists. One of the painters included was Susan Rothenberg, whose paintings of ghostly horses—their dark outlines emerging from a web of white brush strokes—seemed to evoke the return of the image from abstraction itself. Then living in New York, Rothenberg painted horses from memory. Now living on a ranch in New Mexico, she draws her subjects from daily experience. As in her earliest work, fragments of images emerge from an allover flurry of brush strokes, often to poetic and haunting effect. *Calling the Dogs* (**22.25**) captures something of the sound of a lone voice carrying over vast open spaces. At the lower edge of the painting is a head; the blue area around its mouth may be sound. The yellow is perhaps indoors, home, the ranch. Above, a pair of arms reaches out and hands clap, calling the dogs who crowd in from the upper left corner.

Where Rothenberg evokes the mood of an experience through fragments of images, Elizabeth Murray typically explodes the painting itself into fragments in her unique approach to abstraction (**22.26**). *Painters Progress* illustrates the distinctive blend of goofiness and anxiety that pervade many of Murray's paintings. The central image depicts an artist's palette and brushes, a symbolic stand-in for the painter herself. Their swelling forms pay

22.25 (left) Susan Rothenberg. *Calling the Dogs*. 1993–94. Oil on canvas, 5′9½″ × 5′5¼″. Courtesy Sperone Westwater Gallery, New York.

22.26 (right) Elizabeth Murray. *Painters Progress*. 1981. Oil on canvas in 19 parts; 9′8″ × 7′9″. The Museum of Modern Art, New York.

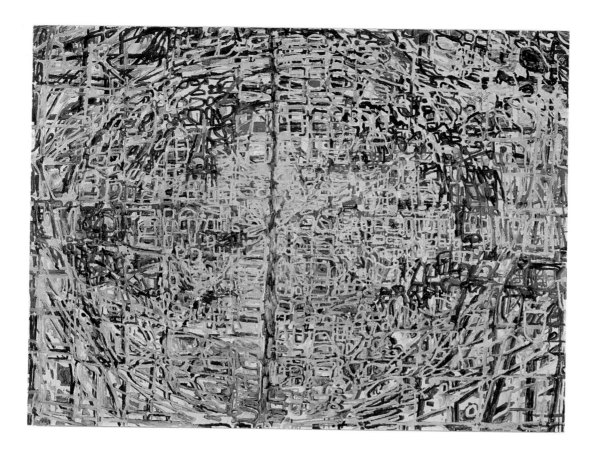

22.27 Terry Winters. *Color and Information*. 1998. Oil and alkyd resin on canvas, 9 × 12′. Courtesy Matthew Marks Gallery, New York.

equal tribute to the biomorphic dream images of Surrealist artists such as Miró (see 21.27) and Saturday morning cartoons. Similarly, the sharp, angular fragments of the painting remind us of the formal innovations of Cubism even as they suggest a psychological reading: a personality breaking up or trying to hold itself together. The painter's progress would seem to be fragile as she tries to make sense of the mix of popular culture, art history, and daily experience that surrounds her. But so far, so good.

The recent paintings of Terry Winters attempt to find a visual equivalent for the invisible, unquantifiable, overwhelming, abstract entity that is also the central reality of our time: information. *Color and Information* (**22.27**) defies conventional categories of representation and abstraction. Winters has developed a linear visual language whose basic markings of **I** and **O** reflect the on/off, if/then binary logic of computers. Just as streams of these simple choices generate complicated programs, so Winters uses them to create dense, layered paintings that seem to allude at once to a satellite photograph of a city, the twin lobes of the human brain, the circuitry of a computer, the explosion of a galaxy being born, the intricate maze of the World Wide Web, pure energy expanding outward. "I believe it is the first Millennium picture I have seen," wrote one critic.[6] Painting, long written off as dead, suddenly seems uniquely suited to carry us into the future.

WORDS AND IMAGES, ISSUES AND IDENTITIES

In works such as *Guitar, Sheet Music, and Glass* (7.15) and *The Emigrant* (21.19), Cubist artists at the beginning of the 20th century imported words into art. With the growth of advertising in the form of posters and newspapers, words had taken on a new visual presence in the environment, and Cubist paintings were the first to acknowledge this. During the 1960s, Conceptual Art often took the form of words or juxtaposed words and images in a critical spirit, as in Kosuth's *One and Three Chairs* (22.16). By the 1980s it had become clear to many that advertising was the prevalent visual reality of our time, and a number of artists adopted its techniques, most commonly to address political and social issues.

Jenny Holzer's *Protect Me from What I Want* (**22.28**) is one of a series of works in which the artist inserted words that closely resembled advertising slogans into public places. The photograph here shows the work installed at Caesar's Palace, a famous hotel and casino in Las Vegas. The photograph gives some idea of the dense advertising environment the sign was part of. Advertising, of course, is precisely about wanting, about creating desire. How many people noticed Holzer's prayerlike slogan shouting its warning amid the dazzling display of neon signs promoting hotels, casinos, restaurants, and other temptations? ("Win $5000 dollars!" reads a sign in the lower right.) We have no way of knowing, of course, but those who did may have paused for a moment.

Inserting an unexpected and dissonant element into the everyday visual environment is a Conceptualist strategy known as intervention. A gentler, more subtle Conceptual intervention was the image that Felix Gonzalez-Torres placed on twenty-four billboards around New York City of a rumpled bed that had clearly been slept in by two people (**22.29**). For Gonzalez-Torres, the image had a personal meaning: his lover had recently died of AIDS. Yet the artist did not expect anyone to know this, and no words appeared with the image to impose a meaning or even to tell viewers that the billboard was a gesture of art. Rather, Gonzalez-Torres offered an intimate image of love and absence to passersby and invited them, if they noticed it, to make their own meanings, to have their own thoughts.

22.28 (left) Jenny Holzer. *Survival*. 1983–85. Darktronics double-sided electronic sign, *Protect Me from What I Want*. Caesar's Palace.
Nevada Institute for Contemporary Art, Caesar's Palace, Las Vegas, Nevada, Sept. 2-6, 1986.

22.29 (right) Felix Gonzalez-Torres. *Untitled*. 1991. Billboard displayed in twenty-four locations in New York in 1992.
Courtesy Andrea Rosen Gallery, New York.

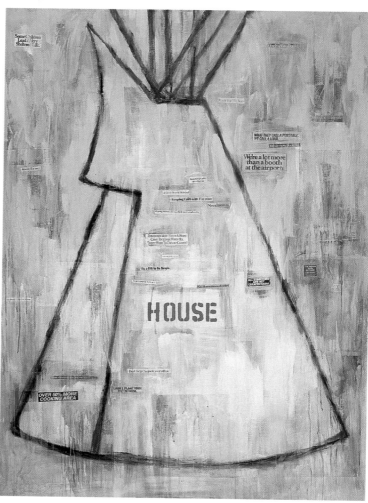

22.30 (left) Barbara Kruger. *Untitled (Are We Having Fun Yet?)*. 1987. Photographic silkscreen/vinyl, 12′3½″ × 8′7″. Courtesy Mary Boone Gallery, New York.

22.31 (right) Jaune Quick-to-See Smith. *House*. 1995. Acrylic and mixed media on canvas. 6′8″ × 5′. Courtesy Steinbaum Krauss Gallery, New York.

Barbara Kruger appropriates photographs from commercial sources such as magazines and newspapers and overlays them with messages drawn from advertising, politics, or popular jargon. Her works appear in sizes ranging from keychain to billboard and in locations ranging from galleries to magazine covers to public spaces. *Are We Having Fun Yet?* (**22.30**) juxtaposes that ironic question with a stark close-up of a woman's hands pressed to her face in anguish. The dissonance between the words and image creates a tension, a biting clash between what we see and mass-produced values like "having fun." Blown up to billboard size and yet displayed indoors, the effect is especially disturbing, like witnessing a nervous breakdown.

Much of Kruger's work is created from a feminist point of view—often a confrontational one. Artists associated with the feminist movement of the 1970s and the gay activism of the 1980s were instrumental in opening the art world to works that addressed human difference, just as American culture in general became more aware of the many identities it embraced and, all too often, silenced. Jaune Quick-to-See Smith's *House* makes its point quietly but firmly (**22.31**). On a textured yellow field that could itself be an abstract work about the landscape of the Great Plains the artist has drawn a simple, schematic tipi and stenciled the word "house" on it. We might see these elements of *House* as gentle rebuke to Miriam Schapiro's *Heartfelt* (see 22.17): not everyone has the same mental image of a house. Slogans culled from advertisements are pasted over the surface of the painting. Their juxtaposition with the image of a tipi produces delicate ironies. "Remember how

THE GUERRILLA GIRLS

WHO ARE THEY? That's a secret. How many of them are there? That's a secret too. How do you find them? You don't. You leave a message and, if they wish, they'll find you. If you are fostering sexism or racism in the art world, they'll find you whether you like it or not. They strike without warning, often by night, in the manner of guerrilla fighters, wearing the fierce, menacing head masks of gorillas. Each of them is a working artist, and together they have become a force to be reckoned with. They are the Guerrilla Girls.

The Guerrilla Girls came into being in 1985, shortly after the opening of a huge exhibition at New York's Museum of Modern Art. The show, entitled "International Survey of Contemporary Painting and Sculpture," included works by 169 artists, fewer than 10 percent of whom were women. One April morning residents of lower Manhattan, where many artists live and work, awakened to find copies of a distinctive poster plastered on outdoor walls. In bold type the poster inquired, "WHAT DO THESE ARTISTS HAVE IN COMMON?" Underneath were the names of 42 prominent artists—all male. The poster text continued, "They all allow their work to be shown in galleries that show no more than 10 percent women or none at all."

More posters followed. One asked, "DO WOMEN HAVE TO BE NAKED TO GET INTO THE MET. MUSEUM?" Another catalogued "THE ADVANTAGES OF BEING A WOMAN ARTIST," a sweetly sarcastic list that included such benefits as "Working without the pressure of success" and "Seeing your ideas live on in the work of others." Prime targets for the Guerrilla Girls' scorn were art critics, museums, and galleries that concentrate attention on white male artists, all but ignoring women and minority artists. The posters achieved almost instant chic, partly because of their excellent graphic design, partly because of the Guerrilla Girls' aura of mystery.

From posters, the Guerrilla Girls progressed to on-site appearances. Let a museum present a male-dominated exhibition, and the Guerrilla Girls were sure to turn up—wearing their gorilla masks (often with short skirts and lacy stockings), waving bananas, making street theater for an appreciative audience. Given such a cleverly designed campaign, media attention was inevitable. Scores of articles about the Guerrilla Girls have been published in newspapers and magazines. They have been interviewed on television and often speak at colleges.

For ease of communication, each of the Guerrilla Girls has taken the name of a noted woman artist who is dead. (Material for this essay was supplied to the author by "Alice Neel.") It is believed that several members of the group are quite well known artists, but this cannot be proved, because the women never appear in public as Guerrilla Girls without their masks.

The gorilla masks serve a double purpose. Of course, they protect the wearers' identities, but they also put everybody else at a disadvantage. One knows these are women, so it is more than a little disconcerting to be confronted with a ferocious, toothy ape face. This effect is no doubt intended. Individually, women artists may lack clout, but the Guerrilla Girls, as a group, know a thing or two about power.

There is no way to determine how much influence the Guerrilla Girls have had in improving prospects for women and minority artists. Still, as every reformer knows, the first step toward making a change is getting attention, and that has been taken care of. The Guerrilla Girls have a great many secrets. Just possibly, one of them may be the secret of success.

Some Guerrilla Girls (left) and one of their posters (right).

RELATED WORKS

8.21
Chagoya,
*What
Appropriation
Has Given Me*

9.26
Boltanski,
*Altar to the
Chases High
School*

9.24
Serrano,
*Black
Supper II*

22.32 Kerry James Marshall. *Past Times*. 1997. Acrylic and collage on canvas, 9′6″ × 13′. Metropolitan Pier and Exhibition Authority, Chicago.

easily a home came together when you didn't have to choose carpet?" reads one. "Keeping faith with function" claims another, a reference to the famous Modernist motto, "Form follows function."

In *Past Times* (**22.32**) Kerry James Marshall revisits Manet's *Déjeuner sur l'herbe* (see 21.4) and the Impressionist world of middle-class leisure. A family enjoys an outing by the lake with golf, croquet, music, boating, and waterskiing. Marshall has painted the skin tones flat black-brown, pointedly making his subjects as dark as possible. The composition alludes to Manet's famous work, but the most Manet-like element is the gaze of the three figures in the foreground. We see it time and again in Manet's paintings: the blank, mildly inquisitive gaze in our direction that makes us suddenly aware that we are staring. Like Manet's paintings, Marshall's painting looks back. When we move on, the three will return to their pleasures in the private space they have created temporarily in the public park.

In the background, the sun, a symbol of hope, rises next to a housing project. Blue birds of happiness twitter around a banner that proclaims bright sentiments for building the future. The golfer looks back at the city in much the same way that the central figure in Aaron Douglas' *From Slavery Through Reconstruction* (see 21.33) points upward to the "city on the hill" with its promise of freedom and justice. A housing project may not be paradise on earth, Marshall's painting suggests, but it can be a fine place, and good lives can be led there. With allusions to famous paintings, Marshall anchors his work firmly in the pastoral tradition that begins with Giorgione and Titian (see 16.16, 16.17) and passes through such visions of an ideal society as Seurat's *Sunday on La Grande Jatte* (see 4.28). Along the way, he claims a place for black faces and everyday life in the history of painting, long the most esteemed Western art.

South African artist William Kentridge faces different tasks as his country reorganizes and renews itself after the end of apartheid, the policy of racial segregation and white supremacy that was in place from 1948 until 1990. Kentridge's animated film *Stereoscope (and palimpsests)* turns around a character who has appeared in many of the artist's works, a white indus-

22.33 William Kentridge.
Drawing from *Stereoscope
(and palimpsests)*. 1998.
Courtesy Marian Goodman Gallery,
New York.

trialist named Soho Eckstein (**22.33**). Kentridge based Eckstein on memories of his own grandfather. The film opens with Eckstein in his office. Next, in a cavernous industrial space, a switchboard operator plugs in a call, sending blue lines of energy rushing in many directions. Blue connects all of the scenes that follow, many of which are shown on a split screen (hence "stereoscope"). Constantly transforming itself, blue appears as energy and as a strange electric cat that seems able to cross from one world to another—factories, city streets, homes. It seems that we are all connected in ways that we cannot fathom, and that Eckstein's company reaches everywhere and affects everyone as he piles up his riches. Finally the cat curls itself into a ball and explodes. The word *give* appears in blue, followed by the prefix *for*. Forgive. Eckstein stands alone in his office as we see him here, blue water pouring from his pockets. "What do you have to give in order to be forgiven?" the artist replied when asked about the work's meaning. "Is Soho Eckstein asking to be forgiven? What is the difference between the generosity of giving and the generosity of forgiving?"[7]

Kentridge created *Stereoscope* using a simple but painstaking technique. A single drawing in charcoal with blue pastel serves for each scene. The drawing is filmed for a few frames, then erased, modified, and photographed again for the next few frames. Each minute of film requires 1,400 images, and so each drawing is erased and redrawn up to 500 times. But the erasures are never quite complete. Ghostly lines of charcoal show what used to be. Each modification is a step forward, and yet the past shows through the present. Forgiveness will not be easy. The past is hard to erase.

TOWARD THEATER: PERFORMANCE AND INSTALLATION

"Where do we go from here?" the composer John Cage asked rhetorically in 1957. His answer: "Toward theater."[8] Cage believed that art's purpose was to heighten our awareness of being alive, and his suggestion for how this might be accomplished inspired the artists who created the happenings and events of the 1950s and 1960s. During the 1980s, this approach to art was developed considerably, and in a more sophisticated and self-aware form it became known as Performance Art.

One of the names most closely connected with Performance Art is Laurie Anderson. In *Empty Places,* a performance work first presented in 1989, the artist herself is at the center of the action (**22.34**). She tells stories and she sings, sometimes in her own clear soprano voice, sometimes through an electronic device that alters the sound. She plays a keyboard and a violin (Anderson is a classically trained violinist). Meanwhile, on a series of screens—two of them 20 feet tall—are projected still and moving images that change at a dizzying pace. The slides and films, most of which were shot by Anderson, may be keyed to the stories and the music (or they may not). In broadest terms, the theme of *Empty Places* is the American scene, but it is a scene filtered through the artist's own experience.

Like Conceptual Art, art that "happens" instead of being embodied in an object recognizes that art is fundamentally an experience. It may be the experience we have in front of a painting or a sculpture. It may be the experience we have as, rushing off late to work, we happen to notice a billboard with a picture of an unmade double bed. It may be the experience of having images flash and change before us as we watch a woman tell stories and play music. An artist is someone who creates the materials or conditions of a visual experience that he or she finds meaningful in the hope that others will find it meaningful as well.

Being in a room with art is a kind of experience. With Minimalism especially, artists began to take this experience into account. Part of the art was the experience of being in the same room with the object, of being aware of how it changed the feeling of space, and of becoming more intensely conscious (sometimes uncomfortably) of one's own body as an object in space as well. Building on this idea, artists began to think of the room itself as a work of art. The result was a new form known as **installation.** With installation, an artist creates an environment for the viewer to enter, move around, investigate, experience, reflect on, make sense of.

To enter an installation such as Robert Gober's untitled work at the Dia Center in New York is to be plunged into a mystery, like walking onto the set for a theatrical production after the actors are gone (**22.35**). The walls are painted in forest scenes copied from photographs Gober took. We are surrounded by nature, but it feels more like confinement than liberation. Painted paths lead out into the forest, but they keep circling back. There seems to be no escape. The feeling of imprisonment is reinforced by small

22.34 (above) Laurie Anderson in performance, *Empty Places*. 1989.

22.35 (below) Robert Gober. Installation at Dia Center for the Arts. New York, September 1992–June 1993.

windows cut high into the wall. Looking out, we can see a patch of sky, but no more. Sinks line the walls, their taps open, water running. Stacks of newspapers are tied up here and there. Observant viewers may notice eventually that the newspapers were not simply found but created. The photographs on the front page display happy couples, always a man and a woman. The headlines include "Vatican Condones Discrimination Against Homosexuals." All of the photographs and headlines were drawn from actual newspapers. Gober concentrated and juxtaposed them in newspapers bundled as trash, due for recycling. No meaning is imposed. We must examine our own responses.

Chinese artist Cai Guo Qiang combined installation and Performance Art in his recent *Venice's Rent Collection Courtyard* (**22.36**). Created for the Venice Biennale, a major international art exhibition that takes place every two years, *Venice's Rent Collection Courtyard* was based in a famous Chinese work of the 1960s, a tableau of 114 highly realistic, life-size clay figures depicting the many ways in which a heartless landlord exploited his poor peasant tenants. A team of artists created the original work collectively in the courtyard of a former landowner's home. As a work of propaganda art designed to remind viewers of the injustices that communism had put an end to, *Rent Collection Courtyard* toured China and other communist countries in fiberglass replicas. In Venice, Cai Guo Qiang staged the re-creation of part of *Rent Collection Courtyard* as a performance piece that he described as a meditation on the nature of time, sculpture, and history. Visitors watched Chinese and Italian artists molding the figures in clay over wooden armatures. As the figures dried, some of the parts cracked and fell off. Other figures were not yet begun. Clearly it was a project that would not be completed. When the Biennale was over, the re-creation in progress was destroyed.

In an unintended sequel, *Venice's Rent Collection Courtyard* has provoked controversy in China. Conservative artists, including members of the group who created the original work, are not familiar with the philosophy of appropriation or the ideas of Performance Art. To them, Cai Guo Qiang did not give their work another meaning by his gesture; he simply stole their idea. Younger Chinese artists in touch with Postmodern currents in art have staged demonstrations or private (and officially forbidden) performances in support of the work. As of this writing, the case is being studied by the Central Copyright Office in China.

22.36 Cai Guo Qiang. *Venice's Rent Collection Courtyard*. Performance installation at the 48th Venice Biennale, 1999. Courtesy the artist.

RELATED WORKS

9.40 Paik, *Fin de Siècle*

6.20 Borofsky, *Self-Portrait With Big Ears*

11.30 Christo and Jeanne-Claude, *Wrapped Reichstag*

11.31 Koons, *Puppy*

RELATED WORKS

5.3
Messager,
Mes Voeux

9.27
Canogar,
Alien Memory

11.25
Kiki Smith,
Honeywax

12.21
Kiki Smith,
Shed

BEING HUMAN: THE LIFE OF THE BODY

Our earthly life is the life of the body, a physical, animal existence in time. Contemporary artists have continued the long Western tradition of expressing the human experience through works that portray the body. Each generation has its own questions to ask about our physical nature, and each generation of artists expands the boundaries of art as they seek a formal language that lets them address new concerns. Chapter 12 illustrated Kiki Smith's 1996 glasswork *Shed* (see 12.21). Like much contemporary art, *Shed* is ambiguous and invites viewers to construct their own meanings. Many today will think first of the blood-borne disease of AIDS and the personal, social, and political issues that it brought into focus. Daniel Canogar's 1998 installation *Alien Memory* (see 9.27) focuses on our contemporary concerns about the body and technology. Like *Shed*, it also probes how comfortable we are with the full extent of our physical natures, inside and out. Annette Messager's assemblage *Mes Voeux* (see 5.3) is concerned with the body as a location of desire, identity, and shame.

Another artist whose work has often explored questions surrounding our physical existence, especially our nature as sexual beings, is Matthew Barney. Since 1991, Barney has used his own body as an expressive instrument in the manner of an actor, dancer, or athlete, but with the visual imagination of an artist (**22.37**). The illustration here is from Barney's film *Cremaster 5*, one of the series of five *Cremaster* films that have been the artist's principal focus since 1994. Cremaster is the name of the muscle that regulates the height of the testicles in the male body. Barney uses the word to refer metaphorically to the idea of genders merging, especially to the first weeks of the development of the human embryo, when the child is neither male nor female. *Cremaster 5* is a hypnotic, dreamlike film set in the lavish splendor of 19th-century Budapest. Barney plays a character called The

22.37 Matthew Barney. *Cremaster 5: Her Giant*. 1997. C-print in acrylic frame, 52¾ × 42⅝ × 1″. Courtesy Barbara Gladstone Gallery, New York.

22.38 Louise Bourgeois. *Untitled*. 1996. Cloth, bone, rubber, and steel; height 9′3½″. Courtesy Cheim and Read Gallery, New York.

Magician, who loves and is loved by a woman called The Queen of Chain. He also plays The Giant, illustrated here, who likewise attends on the Queen and seems, in his not-quite-male state, to embody ideas of sexual becoming or transformation. The doves along his outstretched arms remind us of magic tricks of transformation, as when a magician produces a bouquet of flowers or a fistful of white silks that suddenly become a pair of fluttering doves. Budapest is the birthplace of Harry Houdini, a magician whose great physical strength enabled him to perform astonishing daredevil escape tricks. Barney himself was an athlete, and his interest in the transformative powers of physical cultivation and bodily ordeals is one of the many themes of his work. In *Cremaster 5*, The Magician's death is imagined as a failed escape trick: naked and shackled, The Magician plunges from a bridge into the icy waters of a river far below. But he does not resurface in triumph. Perhaps, however, he has transformed himself one final time into something wholly new. Perhaps the escape was from our physical limits on earth.

It is commonplace that cutting-edge art is made by younger artists, yet the example of Louise Bourgeois demonstrates dramatically that youth has no monopoly on newness. Born in 1911, Bourgeois has been making challenging art since the 1930s. *Untitled* (**22.38**) is one of a number of recent works in which the artist's own clothes from decades gone by are used to evoke the passing of time, the decay of the body, and the many versions of the self that we discard or outgrow as we journey through life. The hanging dress is spread out as though it had a life of its own. Other items of clothing are stuffed less flatteringly, as though in our fleshly existence we were all so much meat in a butcher shop. Bourgeois came to her first artistic maturity in the artistic environment of Surrealism, and her works today combine the Surrealists' fondness for disturbing dream images with a constantly evolving formal approach that has renewed her art for each generation of viewers.

22.39 (left) Luis Jiménez. *Fiesta Dancers (Jarabe)*. 1996. Fiberglass with urethane finish, 9'6" × 8' × 5'11".
Collection University of New Mexico, Albuquerque. Courtesy the artist.

22.40 (right) Christian Marclay. *Amplification*. 1995. Ink-jet prints on cotton scrim, found photographs, as installed at San Stae Church, Venice.
Courtesy Paula Cooper Gallery, New York.

RELATED WORKS

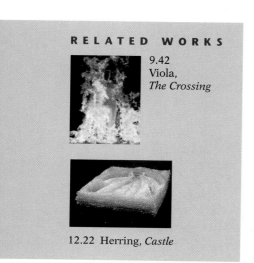

9.42 Viola, *The Crossing*

12.22 Herring, *Castle*

BEING HUMAN: THE LIFE OF THE SPIRIT

We have no proof that the body is not all there is to us. Yet for as long as humans have been expressing themselves through art, an idea that recurs again and again is that there is something more, something we agree to call spirit, or soul, or essence. Art itself is deeply entwined with our faith that there is something that transcends our physical nature, for through art we communicate meanings that go beyond their materials. We believe that an image can carry some kind of meaning beyond the subject it literally depicts; that in dance, we can use our bodies in order to forget them, soaring for a moment beyond physical limits; that in music, pure sound with no material existence at all, we can communicate feelings that go beyond words.

In *Fiesta Dancers (Jarabe)* (**22.39**) Luis Jiménez celebrates the art of dance and the spirit of Mexican immigrants who have made new homes and new lives in the border states of the United States. The dancers are ordinary people, not beauties, no longer young. Yet their dancing has pride and dignity as they shed, if only for a brief time, their everyday concerns. In *Amplifications* (**22.40**) Christian Marclay also takes ordinary people for his subject. The images were enlarged from photographs that Marclay found in attics, in flea markets, in old scrapbooks. We no longer know who they are, nor does it matter. They are just people making music together. Enlarged, printed on translucent fabric, and displayed in church, they are indeed amplified, as the title suggests. Marclay has lifted them up to the light that shines through the sacred space, creating a moving tribute to all who have nourished their spirit by living with art.

PRONUNCIATION GUIDE

This guide is meant to provide the reader with an acceptable pronunciation for names and other words that may be unfamiliar to native speakers of English. It is not perfect. It ignores the nasal sounds of the French *en, in, ain*, as well as the guttural German consonants, giving instead the nearest English equivalents. These sounds are difficult to render phonetically and difficult to pronounce for those who have not studied the languages. But no reader should be embarrassed by using these pronunciations.

In many cases there are two or more pronunciations for a particular artist's name, both or all of which are in common use and considered "correct." The pronunciations in this guide are those most often heard among English-speaking North Americans, and a few alternates have been provided. Some instructors may prefer variant pronunciations of certain artists' names; these may be equally correct but inadvertently omitted from the list.

The phonetic system employed for this guide is meant to be as simple as possible. Its conventions include those listed in the margin.

an—plan, tan
ay—play, day, stay
ah—spa, hurrah
eh—pet, get
er—her, fur
oh—toe, show, go
ohn—phone, moan
ow—cow, how
uh—bus, fuss
ye—pie, sky

Aachen AHK-en
Abakanowicz, Magdalena mahg-dah-LAY-nuh ah-bah-kah-NOH-vich
Akan AH-kahn
Akhenaten AH-keh-NAH-ten
Alberti, Leon Battista LAY-on bah-TEES-tuh ahl-BAIR-tee
Alhambra ahl-AHM-bruh
Alvarez-Bravo, Manuel mahn-WELL AHL-vah-rez BRAH-vo
Amida Nyorai ah-MEE-duh nyoh-RYE
Amitayus AH-mi-TYE-OOS
Angkor Wat ANG-kohr WAHT, or ANG-kohr VAHT
Anguissola, Sofonisba soh-foh-NEES-bah ahn-gwee-SOH-lah
Antoni, Janine jah-NEEN an-TOH-nee
Aphrodite aph-roh-DYE-tee
Apoxyomenos ah-POX-ee-oh-MEN-ohs
Athena Nike uh-THEE-nuh NYE-kee
auteur oh-TER
Avalokiteśvara ah-vah-loh-kih-TESH-vahr-uh
avant garde AH-vawn GARD
Balla, Giacomo JAH-koh-moh BAH-lah
Basquiat, Jean-Michel ZHAWN-mee-SHELL BAHS-kyah
bas-relief BAH ree-leef
Baule BOW-lay
Bayeux bye-YE(r)
Bellini, Giovanni joh-VAHN-ee bell-EE-nee
Benin beh-NEEN
Bernini, Gianlorenzo jahn-loh-REN-zoh bayr-NEE-nee
Bierstadt, Albert BEER-shtaht
Bilbao bil-BAH-oh
Boccioni, Umberto oom-BAIR-toh boh-CHO-nee
bodhisattva boh-dih-SAHT-vuh
Borromini, Francesco frahn-CHESS-koh boh-roh-MEE-nee
Bosch, Hieronymus heer-AHN-ih-mus BOSH
Botticelli, Sandro SAN-droh bot-ee-CHEL-ee

Bourgeois, Louise boorzh-WAH
Brancusi, Constantin KAHN-stan-teen BRAHN-koosh (more often in the U.S.: brahn-KOO-see)
Braque, Georges zhorzh BRAHK
Breuer, Marcel mahr-SELL BROY-er
Bronzino, Agnolo AHN-yoh-loh brahn-ZEE-noh
Bruegel, Pieter PEE-tur BROO-g'l (often: BROY-g'l)
buon fresco boo-OHN FRES-koh
Byodo-in BYOH-doh-een
Cai Guo-Qiang KYE gwoh-CHANG
Camara, Fodé foh-day kah-MAH-rah
camera obscura KAM-er-uh ob-SKOOR-uh
Campin, Robert roh-BAYR kahn-PAN
Caravaggio kah-rah-VAH-jyoh
Cartier-Bresson, Henri awn-ree KAR-tee-ay bress-AWN
Cellini, Benvenuto ben-veh-NOO-toh cheh-LEE-nee
Cézanne, Paul POHL say-ZAN
Chagall, Marc shah-GAHL
Chagoya, Enrique en-REE-kay chah-GOY-ah
Chartres SHAR-tr'
Chauvet cave shoh-VAY
chiaroscuro kee-ah-roh-SKOOR-oh
Cimabue chee-mah-BOO-ay
cire perdue seer payr-DOO
contrapposto kohn-trah-POH-stoh
Copley, John Singleton KOP-lee
Córdoba KOR-doh-buh
Courbet, Gustave goos-TAHV koor-BAY
Daguerre, Louis Jacques Mandé loo-ee ZHAHK man-DAY dah-GAYR
Dali, Salvador sal-vah-DOHR DAH-lee, or dah-LEE
Daumier, Honoré ohn-ohr-AY dohm-YAY
David, Jacques Louis zhahk loo-EE dah-VEED
De Chirico, Giorgio DJOR-djoh deh-KEER-ee-koh
Degas, Edgar ed-GAHR deh-GAH
de Kooning, Willem VILL-um duh KOON-ing
Delacroix, Eugène uh-ZHEN duh-lah-KRWAH
Derain, André ahn-DRAY deh-RAN
diptych DIP-tik

551

dipylon DI-pi-lon
Dogon doh-GAWN
Donatello dohn-ah-TELL-oh
Duccio DOO-cho
Duchamp, Marcel mahr-SELL doo-SHAHN
Dufy, Raoul rah-OOL doo-FEE
Dürer, Albrecht AHL-brekht DOOR-er
Eakins, Thomas AY-kins
facade fuh-SAHD
Fante FAHN-tay
Fauve fohv
Fragonard, Jean-Honoré jawn AW-nor-ay
FRA-goh-nahr
Frankenthaler, Helen FRANK-en-thahl-er
fresco secco FRES-koh SEK-oh
Garduño, Flor gar-DOON-yoh
Gauguin, Paul POHL goh-GAN
Genji Monogatari GEHN-jee mohn-oh-geh-TAHR-ee
Gentileschi, Artemisia ahr-tuh-MEE-zhyuh
jen-till-ESS-kee
Géricault, Théodore tay-oh-DOHR zheh-ree-COH
Ghiberti, Lorenzo loh-REN-zoh ghee-BAYR-tee
Giacometti, Alberto ahl-BAYR-toh jah-coh-MET-ee
Giorgione johr-JOHN-ay
Giotto JOH-toh
Gonzales-Torres, Felix gawn-ZAH-layss TOH-rayss
gouache gwahsh
Goya, Francisco de frahn-SISS-coh day GOY-ah
(in Spain: frahn-THEES-coh)
Grien, Hans Baldung GREEN
Grünewald, Matthias mah-TEE-ess GROON-eh-vahlt
Gu Hongzhong GOO hong-ZHUNG
Gu Kaizhi goo kye-ZHR
Guanyin gwahn-YEEN
Guernica GWAIR-nih-kuh
Hagia Sophia HYE-uh soh-FEE-uh
Han Xizai HAHN shee-ZYE
Hasegawa Tohaku HA-suh-gah-wuh TOH-hah-koo
haut-relief OH ree-leef
Heian hay-AHN
Heiji Monogatari HAY-jee mohn-oh-geh-TAHR-ee
Hesse, Eva AY-vuh HESS-uh
Hiroshige, Ando AHN-doh heer-oh-SHEE-gay
Hokusai, Katsushika kat-s'-SHEE-kah HOH-k'-sye
Holbein, Hans HAHNS HOHL-byne
Hon'ami Koetsu HOH-nah-mee ko-EH-tsoo
Horyu-ji hor-YOO-jee
Hu Yichuan HOO yee-CHWAN
Huang Gongwang HWANG gung-WANG
Hui-zong hway-DZUNG
hypostyle HYE-poh-styel
Ife EE-fay
ijele ee-JAY-lay
Inca ING-keh
Iktinos IK-tin-ohs
Ingres, Jean-Auguste-Dominique zhahn oh-GOOST
dohm-een-EEK AN-gr'
intaglio in-TAHL-yoh (sometimes anglicized to
in-TAG-lee-oh)

Ise EE-say
iwan EE-wahn
Jain JAYN
Jiménez, Luis loo-EES hee-MAY-nez
Jocho DJOH-CHOH
Kairouan KAIR-wahn
Kallikrates kah-LIK-rah-teez
Kandariya Mahadeva kahn-DAHR-yuh
mah-hah-DAY-vuh
Kandinsky, Vasili vah-SEE-lee kan-DIN-skee
Kangxi kang-SHEE
Kano Eitoku KAH-no ay-TOH-koo
Keïta, Seydou SAY-doo KAY-tuh
Kiefer, Anselm AHN-zelm KEE-fur
Kirchner, Ernst Ludwig AYRNST LOOT-vik
KEERSH-nur
Klee, Paul KLAY
Klimt, Gustav goos-TAHV KLEEMT
Knossos NAW-sis
Kokoschka, Oskar koh-KOHSH-kah
Kollwitz, Käthe KAY-tuh KOHL-vitz
Lakshmana LAHK-shmah-nah
Laocoön lay-AH-coh-un
Lascaux las-COH
Le Corbusier luh KOHR-boo-(zee)-AY
Léger, Fernand fayr-NAHN lay-ZHAY
Li Cheng lee CHENG
Leonardo da Vinci lay-oh-NAHR-doh dah VEEN-chee
(often in U.S.: lee-oh-NAHR-doh)
Leyster, Judith YOO-dit LYE-stur
Limbourg lam-BOOR
Louvre LOOV-r'
Lü Ji lee-OO ZHEE
Lysippos lye-SIP-os
Machu Picchu MAH-choo PEEK-choo
Maeda, John MAY-duh
Magritte, René reh-NAY ma-GREET
Mahavira mah-hah-VEE-ruh
Malevich, Kasimir kah-ZEE-meer mah-LAY-vitch
Manet, Edouard ayd-WAHR ma-NAY
Mapplethorpe, Robert MAY-p'l-thorp
Martínez, María & Julian mah-REE-uh & HOO-(lee)-ahn
mahr-TEE-nez
Masaccio mah-ZAH-choh
Masson, André ahn-DRAY mah-SAWN
Massys, Quinten KWIN-ten MASS-ees
Matisse, Henri ahn-REE ma-TEES
Maya MAH-yah
Menkaure men-KOW-ray
Mesa Verde MAY-suh VAIR-day
Messager, Annette MESS-ah-JAY
mezzotint MET-zoh-tint
Michelangelo mye-kel-AN-jel-oh, or mee-kel-AHN-jel-oh
Mies van der Rohe, Ludwig LOOT-fik mees van der
ROH-eh
mihrab MI-hrahb
Mimbres MIM-bres
Miró, Joan HWAHN meer-OH
Moche MOH-chay

Modersohn-Becker, Paula MOH-der-zun BEK-er
Mondrian, Piet PEET MOHN-dree-ahn
Monet, Claude CLOHD moh-NAY
Morisot, Berthe BAYR-t' mohr-ee-ZOH
mosque mahsk
Mughal MOO-gahl
Munch, Edvard ED-vahrd MOONK
Muromachi MOOR-oh-MAH-chee
Muybridge, Eadweard ED-werd MY-bridj
Mycenae my-SEEN-ay, or my-SEEN-ee
Nefertiti NEF-er-TEE-tee
Ni Zan nee DZAHN
Nicephore Niepce NEE-say-for n'YEPS
nkisi nkondi en-KEE-see en-KOHN-dee
Noguchi, Isamu EE-sah-moo noh-GOO-chee
Nolde, Emil AY-meel NOHL-duh
Notre-Dame-du-Haut NOH-tr' DAHM doo OH
Olmec OHL-mek
Olowe of Ise OH-loh-way of EE-say
Paik, Nam June nahm djoon PYEK
Palenque pah-LENG-kay
Pantokrator pan-TAW-kruh-ter
Pei, Ieoh Ming ee-OH ming PAY
Perugino PAIR-oo-DJEE-noh
Petruscow, Georgij DJOR-djee peh-TROO-scof
Pfaff, Judy FAFF
Picabia, Francis frahn-SEES pee-KAH-byuh
pointillism PWAN-teel-ism (sometimes anglicized to POYN-till-izm)
Pollock, Jackson PAHL-uck
Polyclitus pahl-ee-KLY-tus
Pompeii pahm-PAY, or pohm-PAY
Pont du Gard pohn dyu GAHR
Poussin, Nicolas nee-coh-LAH poo-SAN
Praxiteles prak-SIT-uh-leez
qibla KIB-luh
Qiu Ying chyoo YING
Qur'an koor-'AHN
Raetz, Markus MAHR-koos RETS
Ragamala RAH-gah-mah-lah
raigo rye-GOH
Raimondi, Marcantonio MAHRK-ahn-TOH-nee-oh rye-MOHN-dee
Rama RAH-mah
Raphael RAFF-yell, or RAF-fye-ell, or raf-fye-ELL
Rauschenberg, Robert ROW-shen-burg
Renoir, Pierre-Auguste pyayr oh-GOOST rehn-WAHR
repoussé reh-poo-SAY
Rheims RANS
rhyton RYE-ton
Riemenschneider, Tilman TEEL-mahn REE-men-shnye-der
Rietveld, Gerrit GAY-rit REET-velt
Rivera, Diego dee-AY-goh ree-VAIR-uh
Rococo roh-coh-COH
Rodin, Auguste oh-GOOST roh-DAN

Rogier van der Weyden roh-JEER van dur VYE-den
Rongxi rong-HSEE
Rousseau, Henri (le Douanier) ahn-REE roo-SOH (luh dwahn-YAY)
Ryoan-ji RYOH-ahn-jee
Saint-Phalle, Niki de nee-kee duh san-FAHL
Sainte-Chapelle sant shah-PELL
Sainte-Foy sant FWAH
Sainte-Madeleine sant mah-d'LEN
Sakai Hoitsu SAH-kye HOY-ts'
Salgado, Sebastião seh-BAHS-(tee)-ow sahl-GAH-doh
San Vitale san vee-TAHL-ay
Sassetta sah-SEH-tuh
Sesshu SESS-yoo
Seurat, Georges zhorzh sur-RAH
sfumato sfoo-MAH-toh
Shiva Nataraja SHEE-vuh NAH-tah-rah-juh
Singh, Raghubir RAH-goo-beer SING
Sotatsu, Nonomura noh-noh-MOOR-ah SOH-taht-s'
Stieglitz, Alfred STEEG-litz
stupa STOO-puh
Taj Mahal tahzh meh-HAHL
tathagata tah-tah-GAH-tah
Teotihuacán tay-OH-tee-hwah-CAHN
Tinguely, Jean ZHAWN TANG-uh-lee
Titian TISH-an, or TEE-shan
Todai-ji toh-DYE-jee
Tori Busshi toh-ree BOO-shee
Toulouse-Lautrec, Henri de awn-REE duh too-LOOZ loh-TREK
Tutankhamun toot-an-KAH-mun
Van Eyck, Jan YAHN van IKE
Van Gogh, Vincent van GOH (in the U.S.; the Dutch pronunciation is nearly impossible to render phonetically for English speakers)
Van Ruisdael, Jacob YAH-cub van ROYS-dahl
Vasari, Giorgio JOHR-joh va-ZAHR-ee
Velázquez, Diego DYAY-goh vay-LASS-kess (usually in the U.S.; in Spain, vay-LATH-keth)
Vermeer, Johannes yoh-HAH-ness vair-MAYR or vair-MEER
Versailles vayr-SYE
Vigée-Lebrun, Elisabeth ay-leez-eh-BETT vee-ZHAY leh-BRUN
Vishnu VISH-noo
Wang Hui wang HWAY
Wang Jian wang ZHYAHN
Watteau, Antoine ahn-TWAHN wah-TOH, or vah-TOH
Willendorf VILL-en-dohrf
Xoc shawk
Yoruba YAW-roo-buh
Yosa Buson yoh-sah BOO-sohn
Yucatán yoo-cuh-TAN
Zhao Mengfu zhow meng-FOO
Zhou Dynasty ZHOH
ziggurat ZIG-oor-aht

BIBLIOGRAPHY AND SUGGESTED READINGS

GENERAL REFERENCES

Adams, Laurie Schneider. *History of Western Art*, 3rd ed. New York: McGraw-Hill, 2001. • ———. *Art across Time*, 2nd ed. New York: McGraw-Hill, 2002. • Beardsley, John, and Jane Livingston. *Hispanic Art in the United States.* New York: Abbeville Press, 1987. • Chadwick, Whitney. *Women, Art, and Society.* London: Thames and Hudson, 1990. • Chipp, Hershell B. *Theories of Modern Art: A Source Book by Artists and Critics.* Berkeley and Los Angeles: University of California Press, 1968. • Cummings, Paul. *Artists in Their Own Words.* New York: St. Martin's, 1982. • Fleming, William. *Arts & Ideas*, 9th ed. Fort Worth, TX: Harcourt Brace, 1995. • Goldwater, Robert, and Marco Treves, eds. *Artists on Art: From the Fourteenth to the Twentieth Century.* New York: Pantheon, 1974. • Gombrich, E. H. *The Story of Art*, 16th ed. Englewood Cliffs, NJ: Prentice Hall, 1996. • Harris, Ann Sutherland, and Linda Nochlin. *Women Artists: 1550–1950.* New York: Knopf, 1997. • Heller, Nancy G. *Women Artists: An Illustrated History.* New York: Abbeville, 1987. • Honour, Hugh, and John Fleming. *The Visual Arts: A History*, 5th ed. Englewood Cliffs, NJ: Prentice Hall, 2000. • Janson, H. W. *History of Art*, 6th ed. rev. by Anthony Janson. Englewood Cliffs, NJ: Prentice Hall, 2001. • Jones, Lois Swan. *Art and Information on the Internet.* Phoenix, AZ: Oryx Press, 1999. • Kleiner, Fred S., et al. *Gardner's Art through the Ages*, 11th ed. Fort Worth, TX: Harcourt Brace, 2001. • Patton, Sharon F. *African-American Art.* Oxford: Oxford University Press, 1998. • Piper, David, ed. *Random House Library of Painting and Sculpture*, 4 vols. New York: Random House, 1981. • Stangos, Nikos. *The Thames and Hudson Dictionary of Art and Artists*, rev. ed. New York: Thames and Hudson, 1994. • Stokstad, Marilyn, with the collaboration of David Cateforis. *Art History*, 2nd ed. New York: H. N. Abrams, 2002.

CHAPTER 1
LIVING WITH ART

CHAPTER 2
WHAT IS ART?

Arnheim, Rudolf. *Visual Thinking.* Berkeley and Los Angeles: University of California Press, 1980. • Ashton, Dore, ed. *Picasso on Art: A Selection of Views.* New York: Viking, 1972. • Belting, Hans. *Likeness and Presence: A History of the Image before the Era of Art.* Chicago: University of Chicago Press, 1994. • *Brancusi.* Philadelphia: Philadelphia Museum of Art, 1995. • Buchloh, Benjamin, and Judith Rodenbeck. *Experiments in the Everyday: Allan Kaprow and Robert Watts—Events, Objects, Documents.* New York: Wallach Art Gallery, Columbia University, 1999. • Carroll, Noel, ed. *Theories of Art Today,* Madison: University of Wisconsin Press, 2000. • Hall, Edwin. *The Arnolfini Betrothal: Medieval Marriage and the Enigma of Van Eyck's Double Portrait.* Berkeley and Los Angeles: University of California Press, 1994. • Hammacher, A. M., and Renilde Hammacher. *Van Gogh: A Documentary Biography.* New York: Macmillan, 1982. • Lipman, Jean, and Tom Armstrong, eds. *American Folk Painters of Three Centuries.* New York: Hudson Hills and Whitney Museum of American Art, 1980. • McShine, Kynaston, ed. *Andy Warhol: A Retrospective.* New York: Museum of Modern Art, 1989. • Mendelowitz, Daniel M. *Children Are Artists.* Stanford, CA: Stanford University Press, 1963. • Moorman, Margaret. "Rebecca Purdham: In a Mysterious Light." *Art News,* March 1988. • Nelson, George. *How to See: A Guide to Reaching Our Manmade Environments.* Boston: Little, Brown, 1979. • Roskill, Mark, ed. *The Letters of Vincent van Gogh.* New York: Atheneum, 1977. • Silver, Larry. *The Paintings of Quentin Massys.* Montclair, NJ: Allanheld & Schram, 1984. • Sonnenburg, Hubert von, et al. *Rembrandt/Not Rembrandt.* New York: Metropolitan Museum of Art, 1995. • Wollheim, Richard. *Painting as an Art.* Princeton, NJ: Princeton University Press, 1987.

CHAPTER 3
THEMES AND PURPOSES OF ART

Bradley, William. *Art: Magic, Impulse, and Control: A Guide to Viewing.* Englewood Cliffs, NJ: Prentice Hall, 1973. • Clark, Kenneth M. *Civilization: A Personal View.* New York: Harper & Row, 1970. • Elsen, Albert E. *Purposes of Art,* 4th ed. New York: Holt, Rinehart and Winston, 1981. • Lin, Maya. *Boundaries.* New York: Simon & Schuster, 2000. • *The Spiritual in Art: Abstract Painting, 1890–1985.* New York: Abbeville, 1986. • White, Christopher. *Rembrandt.* London: Thames and Hudson, 1984.

CHAPTER 4
THE VISUAL ELEMENTS

CHAPTER 5
PRINCIPLES OF DESIGN

Albers, Josef. *Interaction of Color,* rev. ed. New Haven, CT: Yale University Press, 1975. • Frayling, Christopher, Helen Frayling, and Ron van der Meer. *The Art Pack.* New York: Knopf, 1992. • Gill, Robert W. *Basic Perspective.* London: Thames and Hudson, 1980. • Guiton, Jacques. *The Ideas of Le Corbusier on Architecture and Urban Planning.* New York: George Braziller, 1981. • Itten, Johannes. *The Art of Color.* New York: Van Nostrand Reinhold, 1973. • ———. *Design and Form: The Basic Course at the Bauhaus and Later.* New York: Van Nostrand Reinhold, 1975. • Jones, Roger, and Nicholas Penny. *Raphael.* New Haven, CT: Yale University Press, 1983. • Kossak, Steven. *Indian Court Painting: 16th–19th Century.* New York: Metropolitan Museum of Art, 1997. • Lauer, David. *Design Basics,* 3rd ed. Fort Worth, TX: Harcourt Brace, 1990. • Lisle, Laurie. *Portrait of an Artist: Georgia O'Keeffe.* New York: Seaview Books, 1980. • Puttfarken, Thomas. *The Discovery of Pictorial Composition.* New Haven, CT: Yale University Press, 2000. • Sullivan, Michael. *The Meeting of Eastern and Western Art,* revised and expanded ed. Berkeley and

Los Angeles: University of California Press, 1989. • *James Turrell: Spirit and Light*. Houston, TX: Contemporary Arts Museum, 1998.

CHAPTER 6
DRAWING

Berlo, Catherine, ed. *Plains Indian Drawings 1865–1935*. New York: H. N. Abrams, 1996. • Betti, Claudia, and Teel Sale. *Drawing: A Contemporary Approach*, 3rd ed. Fort Worth, TX: Harcourt Brace, 1992. • Chaet, Bernard. *The Art of Drawing*, 2nd ed. New York: Holt, Rinehart and Winston, 1983. • Edwards, Betty. *Drawing on the Right Side of the Brain*, rev. ed. Los Angeles: Tarcher, 1989. • Goldstein, Nathan. *The Art of Responsive Drawing*, 4th ed. Englewood Cliffs, NJ: Prentice Hall, 1991. • *Sol Lewitt: A Retrospective*. San Francisco: San Francisco Museum of Modern Art, 2000. • Mendelowitz, Daniel M., and Duane Wakeham. *A Guide to Darwing*, 4th ed. Forth Worth, TX: Harcourt Brace, 1988. • Nicolaides, Kimon. *The Natural Way to Draw*. Boston: Houghton Mifflin, 1975.

CHAPTER 7
PAINTING

Chaet, Bernard. *An Artist's Notebook: Techniques and Materials*. New York: Holt, Rinehart and Winston, 1979. • Goldstein, Nathan. *Painting: Visual and Technical Fundamentals*. Englewood Cliffs, NJ: Prentice Hall, 1979. • Hoopes, Donelson F. *Winslow Homer Watercolors*. New York: Watson-Guptill, 1976. • Mayer, Ralph. *The Artist's Handbook of Materials and Techniques*, 5th ed. New York: Viking, 1991. • Rewald, John. *Cézanne: A Biography*. New York: H. N. Abrams, 1990. • Vogel, Susan. *Africa Explores: 20th Century African Art*. New York: The Center for African Art; Munich: Prestel, 1991. • Wheat, Ellen Harkins. *Jacob Lawrence: American Painter*. Seattle: Seattle Art Museum, 1986.

CHAPTER 8
PRINTS

Ackley, Clifford S. *PhotoImage: Printmaking 60s to 90s*. Boston: Museum of Fine Arts, 1998. • Fine, Ruth E., and Mary Lee Corlett. *Graphicstudio*. Washington, D.C.: National Gallery of Art, 1991. • Getlein, Frank, and Dorothy Getlein. *The Bite of the Print*. New York: C. N. Potter, 1963. • *Hokusai and Hi-roshige: Great Prints from the James A. Michener Collection*. San Francisco: Asian Art Museum of San Francisco, 1998. • Mayfield, Signe. *Directions in Bay Area Printmaking: Three Decades*. Palo Alto, CA: Palo Alto Cultural Center, 1992. • Mayor, A. Hyatt. *Prints and People*. Princeton, NJ: Princeton University Press, 1980. • Onus, Lin. *Urban Dingo: The Art and Life of Lin Onus 1948–1996*. South Brisbane: Queensland Art Gallery, 2000. • Panofsky, Erwin. *The Life and Art of Albrecht Dürer*. Princeton, NJ: Princeton University Press, 1955. • Peterdi, Gabor. *Printmaking*. New York: Macmillan, 1986. • Rauschenberg, Robert. *An Interview with Robert Rauschenberg by Barbara Rose*. New York: Elizabeth Avedon Editions, 1987. • Saff, Donald, and Deli Sacilotto. *Printmaking: History and Process*. New York: Holt, Rinehart and Winston, 1978. • Tallman, Susan. *The Contemporary Print: From Pre-Pop to Postmodern*. London: Thames and Hudson, 1996.

CHAPTER 9
THE CAMERA ARTS: PHOTOGRAPHY, FILM, AND VIDEO

Bernard, Bruce. *Photodiscovery: Masterworks of Photography 1840–1940*. New York: Abrams, 1980. • Danto, Arthur. "Pas de Deux, en Masse: Shirin Neshat's *Rapture*." *The Nation*, 28 June 1999. • Galassi, Peter. *Henri-Cartier Bresson, the Early Work*. New York: Museum of Modern Art, 1987. • Gumpert, Lynn. *Christian Boltanski*. Paris: Flammarion, 1994. • Hirsch, Robert. *Seizing the Light: A History of Photography*. New York: McGraw-Hill, 2000. • Horan, James D. *Mathew Brady: Historian with a Camera*. New York: Bonanza, 1955. • Kirkland, Douglas. *Icons: Creativity with Camera and Computer*. San Francisco: Collins, 1993. • Kismaric, Susan. *Manuel Alvarez Bravo*. New York: Museum of Modern Art, 1997. • Livingston, Jane. *Lee Miller: Photographer*. New York: The California/International Arts Foundation, 1989. • London, Barbara, with John Upton. *Photography*, 5th ed. New York: Harper/Collins, 1993. • Newhall, Beaumont, and Nancy Newhall, eds. *Masters of Photography*. New York: A & W, 1983. • *The Photomontages of Hannah Höch*. Minneapolis: Walker Art Center, 1996. • Ross, David A., et al. *Bill Viola/with contributions by Lewis Hyde*. New York: Whitney Museum of American Art in association with Flammarion, Paris, 1997. • *Sebastião Salgado: Workers, an Archaeology of the Industrial Age*. New York: Aperture, in association with the Philadelphia Museum of Art, 1993. • *Andres Serrano: Works 1983–1993*. Philadelphia: Institute of Contemporary Art, University of Philadelphia, 1994. • Shipman, David. *The Story of Cinema*. New York: St. Martin's Press, 1986. • Spoto, Donald. *The Dark Side of Genius: The Life of Alfred Hitchcock*. Boston: Little, Brown, 1983.

CHAPTER 10
GRAPHIC DESIGN AND ILLUSTRATION

Bellatoni, Jeff, and Matt Woolman. *Type in Motion: Innovations in Digital Graphics*. New York: Rizzoli, 1999. • Blackwell, Lewis, and David Carson. *The End of Print: The Graphic Design of David Carson*. San Francisco: Chronicle Books, 1995. • Glaser, Milton. *Graphic Design*. Woodstock, NY: Overlook, 1983. • Heller, Steven. *Paul Rand*. London: Phaidon, 1999. • Lupton, Ellen. *Mixing Messages: Graphic Design in Contemporary Culture*. New York: Cooper-Hewitt National Design Museum, 1996. • Meggs, Philip B. *A History of Graphic Design*, 3rd ed. New York: John Wiley, 1998. • Neuenschwander, Brody. *Letterwork*. London: Phaidon, 1993. • *Paul Rand: A Designer's Art*. New Haven, CT: Yale University Press, 1985. • *Stenberg Brothers: Constructing a Revolution in Soviet Design*. New York: Museum of Modern Art, 1997.

CHAPTER 11
SCULPTURE

The Autobiography of Benvenuto Cellini, revised ed. London: Penguin, 1998. • Beardsley, John. *A Landscape for Modern Sculpture: Storm King Art Center*. New York: Abbeville, 1985. • ———. *Earthworks and Beyond*. New York: Abbeville, 1989. • Chapuis, Julien, et al. *Tilman Riemenschneider: Master Sculptor of the Late Middle Ages*. Washington, DC: National Gallery of Art; New York: Metropolitan Museum of Art, 1999. • Clifford, James. *The Predicament of Culture: Twentieth-Century Ethnography, Literature, and Art*. Cambridge, MA: Harvard University Press, 1988. • Gray, Cleve, ed. *David Smith by David Smith*. New York: Holt, Rinehart and Winston, 1968. • Posner, Helaine. *Kiki Smith*. Boston: Bullfinch, 1998. • Prather, Marla. *Alexander Calder: 1898–1976*. Washington, DC: National Gallery of

Art; New Haven, CT: Yale University Press, 1998. • Rhodes, Colin. *Primitivism and Modern Art.* London: Thames and Hudson, 1994. • *The Sculpture of Nancy Graves: A Catalogue Raisonné.* New York: Hudson Hills Press in association with the Fort Worth Art Museum, 1987. • Walker, Roslyn A. *Olowe of Ise: A Yoruba Sculptor to Kings.* Washington, DC: National Museum of African Art, Smithsonian Institution, 1998.

CHAPTER 12

CRAFTS

Charleston, Robert J., ed. *World Ceramics.* Avenal, NJ: Outlet, 1991. • Chicago, Judy. *The Dinner Party: A Symbol of Our Heritage.* Garden City, NY: Doubleday, 1979. • Nelson, Glenn C. *Ceramics: A Potter's Handbook,* 5th ed. New York: Holt, Rinehart and Winston, 1984. • Nordness, Lee. *Object U.S.A.* New York: Viking, 1970. • Waller, Irene. *Textile Sculptures.* London: Studio Vista, 1977.

CHAPTER 13

ARCHITECTURE

Bennett, Corwin. *Spaces for People: Human Factors in Design.* Englewood Cliffs, NJ: Prentice Hall, 1977. • Bruggen, Coosje van. *Frank O. Gehry: Guggenheim Museum Bilbao.* New York: Guggenheim Museum Publications, 1997. • Dunlop, Beth. *Building a Dream: The Art of Disney Architecture.* New York: Abrams, 1996. • Fuller, R. Buckminster, and Robert W. Marks. *The Dymaxion World of R. Buckminster Fuller.* New York: Reinhold, 1960. • Hitchcock, Henry Russell. *In the Nature of Materials: The Buildings of Frank Lloyd Wright, 1887–1941.* New York: Da Capo, 1975. • Mehrabian, Albert. *Public Places and Private Spaces: The Psychology of Work, Play and Living Environments.* New York: Basic Books, 1980. • Rudofsky, Bernard. *Streets for People: A Primer for Americans.* New York: Doubleday, 1969. • Safdie, Moshe. *Form and Purpose: Is the Emperor Naked?* Boston: Houghton Mifflin, 1982.

CHAPTER 14

ANCIENT MEDITERRANEAN WORLDS

Boardman, John. *The Parthenon and Its Sculptures.* Austin, TX: University of Texas Press, 1985. • Chauvet, Jean-

Marie, et al. *Dawn of Art: The Chauvet Cave.* New York: Abrams, 1996. • Malek, Jaromir. *Egyptian Art.* London: Phaidon, 1999. • Osborne, Robin. *Archaic and Classical Greek Art.* Oxford: Oxford University Press, 1998. • Pedley, John Griffiths. *Greek Art and Archaeology.* New York: Abrams, 1993. • Spivey, Nigel. *Greek Art.* London: Phaidon, 1997. • Strouhal, Eugen. *Life of the Ancient Egyptians.* Norman, OK: University of Oklahoma Press, 1992. • Walker, Susan, ed. *Ancient Faces: Mummy Portraits from Roman Egypt.* New York: Metropolitan Museum of Art, 2000.

CHAPTER 15

CHRISTIANITY AND THE FORMATION OF EUROPE

Chastel, André. *French Art: Prehistory to the Middle Ages.* Paris and New York: Flammarion, 1994. • Evans, Helen C., and William D. Wixom, eds. *The Glory of Byzantium.* New York: Metropolitan Museum of Art, 1997. • Flanagan, Sabina. *Hildegard of Bingen: A Visionary Life.* London and New York: Routledge, 1989. • Holme, Bryan. *Medieval Pageant.* New York: Thames and Hudson 1987. • *Illuminations of Hildegard of Bingen,* with commentary by Matthew Fox. Santa Fe, NM: Bear & Company, 1985. • Lowden, John. *Early Christian & Byzantine Art.* London: Phaidon, 1997. • Stokstad, Marilyn. *Medieval Art.* New York: Harper & Row, 1986. • Swaan, Wim. *The Gothic Cathedral.* Garden City, NY: Doubleday, 1969.

CHAPTER 16

THE RENAISSANCE

Boase, T. S. R. *Giorgio Vasari: The Man and the Book.* Princeton, NJ: Princeton University Press, 1979. • Ferino-Pagden, Sylvia, and Maria Kusche. *Sofonisba Anguissola: A Renaissance Woman.* Washington, DC: National Museum of Women in the Arts, 1995. • Harbison, Craig. *The Mirror of the Artist: Northern Renaissance Art in Perspective.* New York: H. N. Abrams, 1995. • Hartt, Frederick. *History of Italian Renaissance Art,* 4th ed. Englewood Cliffs, NJ: Prentice Hall, 1994. • Paoletti, John, and Gary M. Radke. *Art in Renaissance Italy.* New York: H. N. Abrams, 1997. • Snyder, James. *Northern Renaissance Art: Painting, Sculpture, the Graphic Arts from 1350 to*

1575. New York: H. N. Abrams, 1984. • Vasari, Giorgio. *Lives of the Artists,* trans. George Bull. New York: Penguin, 1966.

CHAPTER 17

THE 17TH AND 18TH CENTURIES

Held, Julius S., and Donald Posner. *17th and 18th Century Art.* New York: Abrams, 1979. • Levey, Michael. *Rococo to Revolution.* New York: Praeger, 1966. • Minor, Vernon Hyde. *Baroque and Rococo: Art and Culture.* New York: H. N. Abrams, 1999. • Walton, Guy. *Louis XIV's Versailles.* Chicago: University of Chicago Press, 1986.

CHAPTER 18

ARTS OF ISLAM AND OF AFRICA

Blier, Suzanne Preston. *The Royal Arts of Africa: The Majesty of Form.* New York: H. N. Abrams; Upper Saddle River, NJ: Prentice Hall, 1998. • Bloom, Jonathan, and Sheila Blair. *Islamic Arts.* London: Phaidon, 1997. • ————. *The Art and Architecture of Islam, 1250–1800.* New Haven, CT: Yale University Press, 1994. • Brend, Barbara. *Islamic Art.* Cambridge, MA: Harvard University Press, 1991. • Phillips, Tom, ed. *Africa: The Art of a Continent.* Munich and London: Prestel Verlag, 1999. • Thompson, Robert Farris. *African Art in Motion.* Berkeley and Los Angeles: University of California Press, 1974. • Visonà, Monica Blackmun, et al., *A History of Art in Africa.* New York: H. N. Abrams, 2001.

CHAPTER 19

ARTS OF EAST ASIA: INDIA, CHINA, AND JAPAN

Barnhardt, Richard M., et al. *Three Thousand Years of Chinese Painting.* New Haven, CT: Yale University Press; Beijing: Foreign Languages Press, 1997. • Blurton, T. Richard. *Hindu Art.* Cambridge, MA: Harvard University Press, 1993. • Clunas, Craig. *Art in China.* Oxford: Oxford University Press, 1997. • Dehejia, Vidya. *Indian Art.* London: Phaidon, 1997. • Lee, Sherman. *A History of Far Eastern Art,* 5th ed. New York: H. N. Abrams, 1994. • Mason, Penelope. *History of Japanese Art.* New York: H. N. Abrams, 1993. • Sullivan, Michael. *The Arts of China,* 3rd ed. Berkeley and Los Angeles: University of California Press, 1984. •

Thorp, Robert L., and Richard Ellis Vinograd. *Chinese Art and Culture*. New York: H. N. Abrams, 2001.

CHAPTER 20
ARTS OF THE PACIFIC AND OF THE AMERICAS

Arts of the South Seas: Island Southeast Asia, Melanesia, Polynesia, Micronesia; The Collection of the Musée Barbier-Mueller. Munich and New York: Prestel, 1999. • Berlo, Janet. *Native North American Art*. Oxford: Oxford University Press, 1998. • Berlo, Janet, et al. *Native Paths: American Indian Art from the Collection of Charles and Valerie Diker*. New York: Metropolitan Museum of Art, 1998. • Coe, Michael D., et al. *The Olmec World: Ritual and Rulership*, Princeton, NJ: The Art Museum, Princeton University, 1995. • D'Alleva, Anne. *Art of the Pacific*. London: Weidenfeld and Nicolson, 1998. • Miller, Mary Ellen. *Maya Art and Architecture*. London: Thames and Hudson, 1999. • Miller, Rebecca Stone. *Art of the Andes: From Chavin to Inca*. London: Thames and Hudson, 1995. • Morphy, Howard. *Aboriginal Art*. London: Phaidon, 1998. • Penny, David W. *Art of the American Indian Frontier: The Chandler-Pohrt Collection*. Seattle: University of Washington Press in association with the Detroit Institute of Arts, 1992. • ———. *Native American Art*. New York: Hugh Lauter Levin, 1994. • Schele, Linda, and Mary Ellen Miller. *The Blood of Kings: Dynasty and Ritual in Maya Art*. New York: George Braziller, in association with the Kimbell Art Museum, Fort Worth, TX: 1986. • Townsend, Richard F. *The Aztecs*. London: Thames and Hudson, 1992.

CHAPTER 21
THE MODERN WORLD: 1800–1945

Arnason, H. H., and Marla F. Prather. *History of Modern Art: Painting, Sculpture, Architecture, and Photography*, 4th ed. New York: H. N. Abrams, 1997. • Brettell, Richard, et al. *The Art of Paul Gauguin*. Washington, DC: National Gallery of Art, 1988. • Clark, T. J., *The Painting of Modern Life: Paris in the Art of Manet and His Followers*, rev. ed. Princeton, NJ: Princeton University Press, 1999. • Clark, Toby. *Art and Propaganda in the 20th Century*. New York: H. N. Abrams, 1997. • Dachy, Marc. *The Dada Movement*. New York: Rizzoli, 1990. • Eisenman, Stephen. *Nineteenth-Century Art: A Critical History*. London: Thames and Hudson, 1994. • Gale, Matthew. *Dada & Surrealism*. London: Phaidon, 1997. • Getlein, Frank. *Mary Cassatt: Paintings and Prints*. New York: Abbeville, 1980. • Green, Christopher. *Cubism and Its Enemies*. New Haven, CT: Yale University Press, 1987. • *Harlem Renaissance: Art of Black America*. New York: The Studio Museum and Abrams, 1987. • Herbert, Robert L. *Impressionism: Art, Leisure, and Parisian Society*. New Haven, CT: Yale University Press, 1991. • Hughes, Robert. *The Shock of the New*. New York: McGraw-Hill, 1991. • Lanchner, Carolyn. *Joan Miró*. New York: Museum of Modern Art, 1993. • Nochlin, Linda. *Realism: Style and Civilization*. New York: Viking, 1993. • Rewald, John. *A History of Impressionism*, 4th ed. rev. New York: Museum of Modern Art, 1973. • Richter, Hans. *Dada: Art and Anti-Art*. New York: McGraw-Hill, 1965. • Rosenblum, Robert, and H. W. Janson. *19th-Century Art*. New York: H. N. Abrams, 1984. • Rubin, William. *Picasso and Braque: Pioneering Cubism*. New York: Museum of Modern Art, 1989.

CHAPTER 22
ART SINCE 1945

Anderson, Laurie. *United States*. New York: Harper & Row, 1984. • Ashton, Dore. *The New York School: A Cultural Reckoning*. New York: Penguin, 1980. • Batchelor, David. *Minimalism*. Cambridge: Cambridge University Press, 1997. • Battcock, Gregory. *Super Realism: A Critical Anthology*. New York: Dutton, 1975. • ———. *Minimal Art: A Critical Anthology*. New York: Dutton, 1968. • Crow, Thomas. *Modern Art in the Common Culture*. New Haven, CT: Yale University Press, 1996. • Danto, Arthur. *The Philosophical Disenfranchisement of Art*. New York: Columbia University Press, 1986. • Dawtrey, Liz, et al., eds. *Investigating Modern Art*. New Haven, CT: Yale University Press in association with the Open University, 1996. • Fineberg, Jonathan. *Art Since 1940: Strategies of Being*. Upper Saddle River, NJ: Prentice Hall, 1996. • Godfrey, Tony. *Conceptual Art*. London: Phaidon, 1998. • Guilbaut, Serge. *How New York Stole the Idea of Modern Art: Abstract Expressionism, Freedom, and the Cold War*. Chicago: University of Chicago Press, 1983. • Hills, Patricia. *Alice Neel*. New York: H. N. Abrams, 1983. • Kaprow, Allan. *Assemblage, Environments, and Happenings*. New York: H. N. Abrams, 1966. • Ratcliff, Carter. *Andy Warhol*. New York: Abbeville Press, 1983. • Rogers, Sarah. *Body Mécanique: Artistic Explorations of Digital Realms*. Columbus, OH: Wexner Center for the Arts, Ohio State University, 1998. • Seitz, William C. *Abstract Expressionist Painting in America*. Cambridge, MA: Harvard University Press, 1983. • Stella, Frank. *Working Space*. Cambridge, MA: Harvard University Press, 1986. • Varnedoe, Kirk. *Jasper Johns: A Retrospective*. New York: Museum of Modern Art, 1996.

NOTES TO THE TEXT

CHAPTER 1

1. Quoted in Friedrich Teja Bach, "Brancusi: The Reality of Sculpture," *Brancusi* (Philadelphia Museum of Art, 1995), p. 24.

2. Quoted in Dawtrey et al., *Investigating Modern Art* (London: Yale University Press in association with The Open University, 1996), p. 139.

3. Mark Roskill, ed., *The Letters of Vincent van Gogh* (New York : Atheneum, 1977), p. 188.

4. Adapted from Sidney J. Parnes and Harold F. Harding, eds., *A Source Book for Creative Thinking* (New York: Scribner's, 1962); and Daniel M. Mendelowitz, *Children Are Artists*, 2nd ed. (Stanford, Calif.: Stanford University Press, 1963).

5. Quoted in Robert Goldwater and Marco Treves, eds., *Artists on Art : From the Fourteenth to the Twentieth Century* (New York: Pantheon, 1972), p. 308.

6. Quoted in "An Artist's Work Blurs Lines between Art and Science," *The New York Times* (August 10, 1999), p. F5.

7. Quoted in Marilyn Stokstad, *Art History* (New York: H. N. Abrams Inc., 1995), p. 1037.

CHAPTER 2

1. For more detail about *The Polish Rider* and the Rembrandt Research Project, see Anthony Bailey, "A Young Man on Horseback," *The New Yorker* (March 5, 1990), pp. 45–77.

2. Quoted in Carter Ratcliff, *Warhol* (New York: Abbeville Press, 1983), p. 109.

3. Gretchen Berg, "Andy: My True Story," *Los Angeles Free Press* (March 17, 1967), p. 3; quoted in Knaston McShine, ed., *Andy Warhol: A Retrospective* (New York: Museum of Modern Art, 1989), p. 460.

4. Vincent van Gogh, *The Complete Letters*; quoted in Ronald Pickvance, *Van Gogh in Saint-Rémy and Auvers* (New York: The Metropolitan Museum of Art and Harry N. Abrams, Inc., 1986), p. 219.

5. John Cage, "On Robert Rauschenberg, Artist, and His Work," *Silence* (Middletown, Conn.: Wesleyan University Press, 1961) p. 108.

6. Quoted in Margarete Moorman, "Rebecca Purdham: In a Mysterious Light," *ARTNews*, March 1988, p. 106.

7. From "Two Statements by Picasso" in Dore Ashton, ed., *Picasso on Art: A Selection of Views* (New York: Da Capo Press, 1988), p. 4.

CHAPTER 3

1. All quotes in this essay are from Maya Lin, *Boundaries* (New York: Simon & Schuster, 2000).

2. Joan Kinneir, *The Artist by Himself* (New York: St. Martin's, 1980), p. 101.

CHAPTER 4

1. Robert Goldwater and Marco Treves, eds., *Artists on Art: From the Fourteenth to the Twentieth Century* (New York: Pantheon, 1972), p. 413.

2. Ibid., p. 74.

3. Quoted in Marilyn Stokstad, *Art History* (New York: H. N. Abrams, 1995), p. 1038.

4. John McCoubrey, ed., *American Art, 1700–1960: Sources and Documents* (Englewood Cliffs, NJ: Prentice Hall, 1965), p. 184.

5. Quoted in Ken Shulman, "Monumental Toil to Restore the Magnificent," *The New York Times* (July 2, 1995), pp. 31, 34.

6. F. T. Marinetti, "Futurist Painting: Technical Manifesto" in Hershell Chipp, *Theories of Modern Art* (Berkeley and Los Angeles: University of California Press, 1968), p. 289.

CHAPTER 5

1. Exhibition catalogue statement, Anderson Galleries, January 29, 1923; quoted in Laurie Lisle, *Portrait of an Artist: Georgia O'Keeffe* (New York: Seaview Books, 1980), p. 66.

2. Robert Goldwater and Marco Treves, eds., *Artists on Art: From the Fourteenth to the Twentieth Century* (New York: Pantheon, 1972), pp. 203–204.

CHAPTER 6

1. Quoted in Robert Wallace and the Editors of Time-Life Books, eds., *The World of Leonardo* (New York: Time Incorporated, 1966), p. 17.

2. Martha Kearns, *Käthe Kollwitz: Woman and Artist* (Old Westbury, N.Y.: Feminist Press, 1976), p. 48.

3. Ibid., p. 164.

4. Quoted in Michael Aupig, *Drawing Rooms: Jonathan Borofsky, Sol LeWitt, Richard Serra* (Fort Worth, Texas: Modern Art Museum of Fort Worth, 1994), p. 38.

CHAPTER 7

1. Black Mountain College Records, 1946; quoted in Ellen Harkins Wheat, *Jacob Lawrence: American Painter* (Seattle: Seattle Art Museum, 1986), p. 73.

2. Gerstle Mack, *Paul Cézanne* (New York: Knopf, 1936), p. 199.

3. Quoted in Sharon F. Patton, *African-American Art* (Oxford: Oxford University Press, 1998), p. 188.

CHAPTER 8

1. Robert Goldwater and Marco Treves, eds., *Artists on Art: From the Fourteenth to the Twentieth Century* (New York: Pantheon, 1972), p. 82.

2. Elizabeth Ripley, *Hokusai: A Biography* (Philadelphia: Lippincott, 1968), p. 24.

3. Ibid., pp. 62, 68.

4. Robert Rauschenberg, *An Interview with Robert Rauschenberg by Barbara Rose* (New York: Elizabeth Avedon Editions, 1987), p. 59. Information in this biography is adapted from *Robert Rauschenberg* (Washington, D.C.: National Collection of Fine Arts, 1976).

CHAPTER 9

1. *Victorian Photographs of Famous Men and Fair Women by Julia Margaret Cameron* (Boston: Godine, 1973), p. 13.

2. Ibid., p. 18.

3. Ibid., p. 19.

4. Helmut Gernsheim, *Julia Margaret Cameron* (New York: Aperture, 1975), p. 180.

5. Quoted in a press release from Alinder Gallery, Gualala, California, August 1998.

6. Sue Davidson Lowe, *Stieglitz: A Memorial Biography* (New York: Farrar, Straus & Giroux, 1983), pp. xxiii, 441.

7. Richard Huelsenbeck's "Dadaist Manifesto" quoted in Matthew Gale, *Dada & Surrealism* (London: Phaidon Press Ltd, 1997), p. 121.

8. Jane Livingston, *Lee Miller: Photographer* (New York: The California/International Arts Foundation, 1989), p. 35.

9. Quoted from an e-mail exchange with the author, July 2000.

10. Quoted in "Berenice Abbott's Revelatory Science Photographs on View at the New York Public Library," NYPL press release, Fall 1999.

11. *The New York Times Film Reviews 1913–1970* (New York: Arno Press, 1971), p. 6.

12. François Truffaut, *Hitchcock*, rev. ed. (New York: Simon and Schuster, 1983), p. 256.

13. Quoted in John Lahr, "The Imperfectionist," *The New Yorker* (December 9, 1996), pp. 68, 70, 73.

14. Kerry Green, "Nam June Paik," *Video Systems* (July 1982), p. 53.

15. *Bill Viola* (New York: Whitney Museum of American Art in association with Flammarion, Paris–New York, 1997), p. 65.

CHAPTER 10

1. Quoted in Claudia Dreifus, "A Conversation with John Maeda: When M.I.T. Artist Shouts, His 'Painting' Listens," *The New York Times*, July 27, 1999.

CHAPTER 11

1. Benvenuto Cellini, *Autobiography* (London: Penguin Books Ltd., 1956, rev. ed. 1998, translation © George Bull), p. 350.

2. Robert Hughes, "Dark Visions of Primal Myth," *Time* (June 7, 1993), p. 64.

3. Quoted in Helaine Posner, *Kiki Smith/Helaine Posner*; interview by David Frankel (Boston: Bulfinch, 1998), p. 12.

4. Ibid., p. 32.

5. Douglas C. McGill, "Artists and Officials Argue over Removing Sculpture," *The New York Times* (March 7, 1985), p. B1.

6. "Intrusive Arc," *The New York Times* (May 31, 1985), p. A26.

7. Steven R. Weisman, "Christo's Intercontinental Umbrella Project," *The New York Times* (November 13, 1990), p. C13.

CHAPTER 12

1. Susan Peterson, *The Living Tradition of María Martínez* (New York: Kodansha International, 1977), p. 191.

2. Quoted in Clark Garth, *The Mad Potter of Biloxi: The Art and Life of George E. Ohr* (New York: Abbeville Press, 1989), p. 131.

CHAPTER 13

1. Quoted in Stanley Meisler, "Long Live Paris, with Her Pleasures and Complexities," *Smithsonian* (August 1991), p. 44.

2. *The New York Times* (July 3, 1983), p. 17.

3. Quoted in *A Profile of the East Building: Ten Years at the National Gallery of Art* (Washington, D.C.: The National Gallery of Art), p. 31.

4. Frank Lloyd Wright, *A Testament* (New York: Horizon Press, 1957), p. 64.

CHAPTER 14

1. *Life Stories of Men Who Shaped History, from Plutarch's Lives*, Eduard C. Lindeman, ed. (New York: The New American Library, 1950), p. 73.

2. Thucydides, *The Peloponnesian War*, trans. Rex Warner (Baltimore: Penguin, 1954), pp. 118, 121.

CHAPTER 16

1. Quoted in R. Goldwater and M. Treves, eds., *Artists on Art: From the Fourteenth to the Twentieth Century* (New York: Pantheon, 1972), p. 69.

2. Ibid., p. 70.

3. Ibid., p. 52.

4. Ibid., p. 82.

5. Ibid., p. 30.

6. Ibid., p. 60–61.

7. Quoted in Hans Belting, *Likeness and Presence: A History of the Image before the Era of Art* (London and Chicago: The University of Chicago Press, 1994), p. 465.

CHAPTER 17

1. Robert Goldwater and Marco Treves, eds., *Artists on Art: From the Fourteenth to the Twentieth Century* (New York: Pantheon, 1972), p. 134.

2. Ibid., pp. 145–146.

3. *Memoirs of Madame Vigée-Lebrun*, trans. Lionel Strachey (New York: Braziller, 1989), pp. 20, 21, 214.

CHAPTER 19

1. Quoted from Thomas Clearly, trans., *The Essential Confucius* (San Francisco: HarperSanFrancisco, c. 1992), p. 31.

CHAPTER 20

1. Quoted in Diana Fane, *Objects of Myth and Memory: American Indian Art at the Brooklyn Museum* (Brooklyn, N.Y.: The Museum in association with the University of Washington Press, 1991), p. 107.

CHAPTER 21

1. Nicholas Wadley, *Manet* (London: Paul Hamlyn, 1967), pp. 25–26.

2. Simon Hantaï, in a conversation reported to the author.

3. Daniel Guerin, ed., *The Writings of a Savage: Paul Gauguin* (New York: Viking, 1974), p. 54.

4. Quoted in Ian Dunlop, *Degas* (New York: Galley Press, 1979), p. 168.

5. Quoted in Hershel B. Chipp, *Theories of Modern Art: A Source Book by Artists and Critics* (Berkeley: University of California Press, 1968), pp. 154–155.

6. Robert Goldwater and Marco Treves, eds., *Artists on Art: From the Fourteenth to the Twentieth Century* (New York: Pantheon, 1972), p. 417.

7. Quoted in William Rubin, *Picasso and Braque: Pioneering Cubism* (New York: The Museum of Modern Art, 1989), p. 19.

8. Quoted in Chipp, pp. 401–402.

9. Ibid., p. 300.

10. Quoted in Christopher Green, *Cubism and Its Enemies* (New Haven and London: Yale University Press, 1987), p. 147.

CHAPTER 22

1. Quoted in Irving Sandler, *The Triumph of American Painting: A History of Abstract Expressionism* (New York: Harper & Row, 1976).

2. John Cage, "Experimental Music" (1957) in *Silences* (Middletown, Conn.: Wesleyan University Press, 1961), p. 12.

3. Hans Richter, *Dada: Art and Anti-Art* (New York, Toronto: McGraw-Hill Book Company, 1965), p. 213.

4. Barbaralee Diamonstein, *Inside New York's Art World* (New York: Rizzoli, 1979), pp. 261–262.

5. Quoted in Alan Riding, "Showcasing a Rise from Rebellion to Respectability," *The New York Times*, March 5, 2000.

6. Ronald Jones, "Notebook," in *Terry Winters: Graphic Primitives* (New York: Matthew Marks Gallery, 1999), p. 44.

7. Quoted in Kathryn Smith, "William Kentridge at the Goodman," *Artthrob*, October 1999 (www.artthrob.co.za).

8. Cage, "Experimental Music," p. 12.

GLOSSARY

Words in *italics* are also defined in the glossary. Numbers in **boldface** following the definitions refer to the numbers of figures in the text that best illustrate the definitions.

abstract   Characteristic of art in which natural forms are not rendered in a *naturalistic* or *representational* way, but instead are simplified or distorted to some extent, often in an attempt to convey the essence of form. Compare *nonobjective*. **(2.16)**

Abstract Expressionism   Painting style of the late 1940s and 1950s in which *abstract* or *nonobjective forms* were used to convey emotional content. Abstract Expressionism emphasized spontaneity and often employed bold colors and/or strong *value* contrasts; the paintings were usually quite large in *scale*. Because this art often involved energetic physical movement by the artist, it is also referred to as *action painting*. **(22.1)**

acrylic   A plastic substance commonly used as a *binder* for paints and as a *casting* material for sculpture. **(7.14)**

action painting   Any painting style calling for vigorous physical activity; specifically, *Abstract Expressionism*. **(22.1)**

adobe   Sun-dried (as opposed to furnace-baked) brick made of clay mixed with straw. **(13.1)**

aesthetic   Pertaining to the beautiful, as opposed to the useful, scientific, or emotional. An aesthetic response is an appreciation of such beauty.

aisle   Generally, a passageway flanking a central area. In a basilica or cathedral, aisles flank the *nave*. **(15.4)**

ambulatory   In church architecture, a vaulted passageway for walking (ambulating) around the *apse*. An ambulatory allows visitors to walk around the altar and choir areas without disturbing devotions in progress. **(15.14)**

analogous harmony   The juxtaposition of hues that contain the same color in differing proportions, such as red-violet, pink, and yellow-orange, all of which contain red. **(4.24)**

animal style   A style in European and western Asian art in ancient and medieval times based in linear, stylized animal forms. Animal style is often found in metalwork. **(15.10)**

appropriation   A postmodern practice in which one artist reproduces an image created by another artist and claims it as his or her own. In postmodern thought, appropriation is felt to challenge traditional ideas about authenticity and individuality, the location of meaning within a work of art, and copyright issues involving intellectual property. **(22.20)**

apse   The semicircular, protruding niche at one or both ends of the *nave* of a Roman *basilica*. In basilica-based church architecture, an apse houses the altar and may be elongated to include a choir. **(15.4)**

aquatint   An *intaglio* printmaking method in which areas of tone are created by dusting resin particles on a plate and then allowing acid to bite around the particles. Also, a *print* made by this method. **(8.17)**

arch   A curving architectural *form* usually made of bricks or other masonry, often in the shape of a semicircle but sometimes rising to a point at the top. **(13.9)**

Archaic style   In Greek art, the style prevalent from the 8th to the 6th century B.C.E. **(14.21)**

architrave   In *Classical* architecture, the lowest band of the *entablature*. **(13.5)**

Art Deco   An art style of the 1920s and 1930s based on modern materials (steel, chrome, glass) and repetitive geometric patterns.

assemblage   The technique of creating a sculpture by joining together individual pieces or segments, sometimes "found" objects that originally served another purpose. Also, a sculpture made by this method. **(11.09)**

asymmetrical   Not *symmetrical*. **(5.13)**

atmospheric perspective   See *perspective*. **(4.44)**

auteur   A filmmaker who exercises maximum control over a film's production and imparts an individual style to a film, often drawing upon personal imagery, dreams, obsessions, fears, memories, or loves as subject matter. **(9.34)**

axis   A straight line, often an imaginary vertical line. **(5.06)**

Baroque   A style dominant in European art during the 17th century, characterized by strong colors and *value* contrasts, bold *scale*, dramatic use of light, elaborate ornamentation, great emotionalism, even theatricality. **(17.5)**

barrel vault   See *vault*. **(13.10)**

basilica   In Roman architecture, a standard type of rectangular building with a large, open interior. Generally used for administrative and judicial purposes, the basilica was adapted for early church architecture. Principal elements of a basilica are *nave*, *clerestory*, *aisle*, and *apse*. **(15.4)**

bas-relief   See *relief*. **(11.13)**

Bauhaus   A school of design in Germany from 1919 to 1933, best known for its attempts to adapt design principles to machine technology. **(21.31)**

bay In architecture, a modular unit of space, generally cubic and generally defined by four supporting *piers* or columns. **(13.10)**

binder A substance in paints that causes particles of *pigment* to adhere to one another and to a *support.*

buttress, buttressing In architecture, an exterior support that counteracts the outward thrust of an arch, dome, or wall. A **flying buttress** consists of a strut or arch segment running from a freestanding *pier* to an outer wall. **(13.12)**

calligraphy The art of "beautiful writing." Specifically, writing considered as an art form in East Asian and Islamic cultures. **(2.3)**

cantilever A horizontal architectural *form* projecting beyond its supports. **(13.40)**

capital In architecture, the decorative sculpted block surmounting a column. In *Classical* architecture, the form of the capital is the most distinctive element of the various *orders.* **(13.3)**

Carolingian The period in medieval European history dominated by the Frankish rulers of the Carolingian dynasty, roughly 750–850 C.E. In art, the term refers especially to the artistic flowering sponsored by Charlemagne (ruled 800–840). **(15.12)**

cartoon 1. A simple drawing with humorous or satirical content. 2. A preparatory drawing for a *mural, fresco,* or other large work.

casting The process of making a sculpture or other object by pouring liquid material—clay, metal, plastic—into a mold and allowing it to harden. **(11.5)**

ceramic Made from fired ("baked") clay. **(12.1)**

chiaroscuro Literally, "light-dark." In two-dimensional art, the use of different *values* to create *modeling* and to simulate the effects of light and shadow in nature. **(4.15)**

chroma See *intensity.* **(4.22)**

cire-perdue See *lost-wax casting.* **(11.5)**

Classical style In Greek art, the style of the 5th century B.C.E. Loosely, the term "classical" is often applied to all the art of ancient Greece and Rome, as well as to any art based on logical, rational principles and deliberate *composition.* **(14.25)**

clerestory The topmost part of a wall, extending above flanking elements such as *aisles.* and set with windows to admit light. In a *basilica* or church, the clerestory is the topmost zone of the *nave.* **(15.2)**

coffer A recessed, geometrical panel in a ceiling, often used in multiples as a decorative element. **(13.15)**

collage A work of art made by pasting bits of paper, cloth, or other material onto a flat surface. **(7.15)**

Color Field painting A style of painting prominent from the 1950s through the 1970s, featuring large "fields" or areas of color, meant to evoke an *aesthetic* or emotional response through the color alone. **(22.4)**

color wheel A circular arrangement of *hues* based on some particular color theory. Often, an arrangement of the hues in a rainbow, plus intermediary colors. **(4.21)**

complementary colors *Hues* directly opposite one another on the *color wheel* and therefore assumed to be as different from one another as possible. When placed side by side, complementary colors are intensified; when mixed together, they produce a *neutral.* **(4.21)**

composition The organization of lines, shapes, colors, and other art elements in a work of art. More often applied to two-dimensional art; the broader term is design.

Conceptual Art An art form in which the underlying idea or concept and the process by which it is achieved are more important than any tangible product. **(22.16)**

Constructivism A Russian art movement of the early 20th century. Based in the principles of geometric abstraction, Constructivism was founded around 1913 by Vladimir Tatlin and condemned in 1922 by the Soviet government. **(21.28)**

contour The perceived edges of a three-dimensional form such as the human body. Contour lines are lines used to indicate these perceived edges in two-dimensional art. **(4.4)**

contrapposto Literally, "counterpoise." A method of portraying the human figure, especially in sculpture, so that it is apparently relaxed and mobile. The result is often a graceful S-curve. **(11.21)**

Corinthian order See *order.* **(13.3)**

cornice In *Classical* architecture, the uppermost element of an *entablature;* a raking cornice frames the upper, slanting edges of a *pediment.* More generally, a horizontal, projecting element, usually molded and usually at the top of a wall. **(13.5)**

cross-cutting In filmmaking, a technique of alternating two or more scenes or shots to advance the action.

cross-hatching An area of closely spaced lines intersecting one another, used to create a sense of three-dimensionality on a flat surface, especially in drawing and printmaking. See also *hatching, stippling.* **(4.16, 4.17)**

Cubism A style of art pioneered in the early 20th century by Pablo Picasso and Georges Braque. In the most developed type of Cubism, *forms* are fragmented into *planes* or geometric facets, like the facets in a diamond; these planes are rearranged to foster a pictorial, but not *naturalistic,* reality; forms may be viewed simultaneously from several vantage points; figure and background have equal importance; and colors are deliberately restricted to a range of *neutrals.* **(21.19)**

Dada A movement that emerged during World War I in Europe that purported to be anti-everything, even anti art. Dada poked fun at all the established traditions and tastes in art with works that were deliberately shocking, vulgar, and nonsensical. **(21.23)**

daguerreotype The earliest form of photograph, invented by Louis Jacques Mandé Daguerre, in which the photographic image is made permanent on a copper plate. **(9.5)**

design The planned organization of lines, shapes and masses, colors, textures, and space in a work of art. In two-dimensional art, often called *composition.*

diptych A composition consisting of two panels side by side, often hinged to open and close like a book. **(2.29)**

direct casting A casting technique in which molten metal incinerates and replaces the object itself instead of a wax intermediary. **(11.10)**

dome An architectural structure generally in the shape of a hemisphere or half globe; theoretically, an arch rotated 360 degrees on its vertical *axis.* **(13.13)**

Doric order See *order.* **(13.3)**

drum In architecture, a cylindrical wall used as a base for a dome. **(13.18)**

drypoint An *intaglio* printmaking technique, similar to *engraving,* in which a sharp needle is used to draw on a metal plate, raising a thin ridge of metal that creates a soft line when the plate is printed. Also, the resultant *print.* **(8.13)**

edition In printmaking, the number of images made from a single plate and authorized by the artist.

embroidery A technique of needlework in which designs or figures are stitched into a textile ground with colored thread or yarn. **(15.16)**

encaustic A painting *medium* in which the *binder* is hot beeswax. **(7.1)**

engraving An *intaglio* printmaking method in which a sharp tool called a burin is used to scratch lines into a metal plate. Also, the resultant *print*. **(8.12)**

entablature In *Classical* architecture, the horizontal structure supported by capitals and supporting in turn the pediment or roof. An entablature consists of three horizontal bands: *architrave, frieze,* and *cornice.* **(13.5)**

entasis In *Classical* architecture, the slight swelling or bulge built into the center of a column to make the column seem straight visually. **(14.24)**

environmental art 1. Art that is large enough for viewers to enter and move about in. 2. Art designed for display in the outdoor environment. 3. Art that actually transforms the natural landscape. **(11.29)**

etching An *intaglio* printmaking method in which lines and image areas are created by first coating a plate with an acid-resistant substance, then scratching through the substance with a sharp needle, and finally immersing the plate in acid, which "bites" depressions into the exposed sections. Also the resultant *print*. **(8.15)**

Expressionism Any art that stresses the artist's emotional and psychological expression, often with bold colors and distortions of form. Specifically, an art style of the early 20th century followed principally by certain German artists. See also *Abstract Expressionism.* **(21.15)**

Fauvism A short-lived painting style in early-20th-century France, which featured bold, clashing, arbitrary colors. **(21.13)**

ferroconcrete Reinforced concrete; a building material that has metal rods or steel mesh embedded in concrete to provide strength. **(13.26)**

figure-ground relationship In two-dimensional art, the relationship between the principal *forms* and the background. Figure-ground ambiguity suggests equal importance for the two. **(1.14)**

flashback In filmmaking, a cut to a scene or episode that is supposed to have taken place before the main action of the film.

flying buttress See *buttress*. **(13.12)**

foreshortening A method of portraying *forms* on a two dimensional surface so that they appear to project or recede from the *picture plane*. **(4.42)**

forging Shaping metal with hammers while it is hot; the method for making wrought iron.

form 1. The physical appearance of a work of art—its materials, style, and *composition*. 2. Any identifiable shape or mass, as a "geometric form."

fresco A painting medium in which colors are applied to a plaster ground, usually a wall *(mural)* or ceiling. In **buon fresco,** also called **true fresco,** colors are applied before the plaster dries and thus bond with the surface. In *fresco secco* ("dry fresco") colors are applied to dry plaster. **(7.4)**

frieze Generally, any horizontal band of *relief* sculpture or painted decoration. In *Classical* architecture, the middle band of an *entablature,* between the *architrave* and *cornice,* often decorated with relief sculpture. **(13.5)**

Futurism Art movement founded in Italy in 1909 and lasting only a few years. Futurism concentrated on the dynamic quality of modern technological life, emphasizing speed and movement. **(4.49)**

genre Art that depicts the casual moments of everyday life and its surroundings. **(17.13)**

geodesic dome An architectural structure invented by R. Buckminster Fuller, based on triangles arranged into tetrahedrons (or four-faceted solids). **(13.27)**

gesso A brilliant white undercoating made of inert pigment such as chalk or plaster and used as *ground* for paint, especially for *tempera*.

glaze In oil painting, a thin, translucent layer of color, generally applied over another color. (For example, blue glaze can be applied over yellow to create green.) In ceramics, a liquid that, upon firing, fuses into a vitreous (glasslike) coating, sealing the porous clay surface. Colored glazes are used to decorate ceramics. **(12.4)**

Gothic Style of art and architecture that succeeded *Romanesque* and flourished in Europe, especially northern Europe, from the mid-12th century to the 16th century. The pointed *arch* and *flying buttress* are typical elements of Gothic architecture. **(15.17)**

groin vault See *vault*. **(13.10)**

ground 1. A substance applied to a painting or drawing *support* in preparation for the pigmented material. 2. The preparatory substance used as a coating for a printmaking plate. 3. The background in a work of two-dimensional art. See also *primer, figure-ground relationship*.

happening An event performed by artists, usually spontaneous and unrehearsed, that may include music, dance, mime, art, reading, or any combination of these. **(22.8)**

hatching An area of closely spaced parallel lines used to create a sense of three-dimensionality on a flat surface, especially in drawing and printmaking. See also *cross-hatching, stippling*. **(4.16, 4.17)**

haut-relief See *relief*. **(11.14)**

Hellenistic style In Greek art, the style of the 3rd to 1st centuries B.C.E., characterized by drama and emotionalism and, in sculpture, a tendency for *forms* to push out boldly into space. **(14.29)**

hierarchical scale The representation of more important figures as larger than less important figures, as when a king is portrayed on a larger scale than his attendants. **(5.24)**

high relief See *relief*. **(11.14)**

hue The property of a color that distinguishes it from others in the *color wheel;* the name of a color. **(4.21)**

hypostyle An interior space filled with rows of columns that serve to support the roof. **(3.4)**

icon In Byzantine and later Orthodox Christian art, an image of a holy person such as Jesus, the Virgin Mary, or a saint. Generally small in scale and painted in a highly stylized manner on a gold ground over a wooden support, icons are often themselves held to be sacred. **(15.9)**

iconography The identification, description, and interpretation of subject matter in art. **(2.27)**

illumination Hand-drawn decoration or illustration in a manuscript, especially prevalent in medieval art. **(15.11)**

impasto A thick application of paint to canvas or other *support*. **(7.8)**

Impressionism An art style of the late 19th century, principally in France, in which artists tried to capture in paint the fleeting effects—or impressions—of light, shade, and color on natural *forms*. **(21.6)**

installation An art form in which an entire room or similar space is treated as a work of art to be entered and experienced. More broadly, the placing of a work of art in a specific location, usually for a limited time. **(22.35)**

intaglio   Any printmaking technique in which the lines or image areas to be printed are recessed below the surface of the printing plate. The intaglio techniques are *aquatint*, *drypoint*, *etching*, *engraving*, and *mezzotint*. **(8.11)**

intarsia   A technique in which an image is created from pieces of variously colored woods inlaid into a wooden surface. **(12.10)**

intensity   The degree of purity or brilliance of a color. Also known as *chroma* or *saturation*. **(4.22)**

interlace   Decoration composed of intricately intertwined strips or ribbons. Interlace was especially popular in medieval Celtic and Scandinavian art. **(15.11)**

International style   A style that prevailed after World War II as the aesthetic of earlier Modernist movements such as de Stijl and the Bauhaus spread throughout the West and beyond. International style buildings are generally characterized by clean lines, rectangular geometric shapes, minimal ornamentation, and steel-and-glass construction. **(13.24)**

Ionic order   See *order*. **(13.3)**

isometric perspective   See *perspective*. **(4.46)**

keystone   The wedge-shaped, central stone in an arch. Inserted last, the keystone locks the other stones in place. **(13.9)**

kinetic   Of or relating to movement. Kinetic art is art that incorporates movement as part of its expression. **(4.50)**

kore   Greek for "maiden"; an ancient Greek sculpture of a young woman, usually clothed.

kouros   Greek for "youth" or "boy"; an ancient Greek sculpture of a nude young man. **(14.26)**

layout   In graphic art, the disposition of text and images on a page, or the overall design of *typographic* elements on page, spread, or book. **(10.9)**

linear perspective   See *perspective*. **(4.39)**

linocut   Also known as linoleum cut, a *relief* printmaking technique in which a block of linoleum is carved so as to leave image areas raised above the surface of the block; in function, similar to a common rubber stamp. Also, the resultant *print*. **(8.10)**

lintel   A beam; a horizontal architectural member usually supported by vertical posts. See also *post-and-lintel*. **(13.2)**

lithography   A *planographic* (or flat-surface) printmaking technique, based on the premise that oil and water do not mix. Image areas are drawn in greasy crayon on a stone or plate, and the greasy ink used in this method adheres to those areas. **(8.18)**

lost-wax casting   Also known by the French term *cire-perdue*, a method for *casting* metal sculptures and other objects. Positive and negative *molds* are built around a layer of wax that exactly duplicates the shape and size of the desired sculpture. When this arrangement is heated, the wax melts out (is "lost") and then molten metal is poured into the mold to replace it. **(11.5)**

low relief   See *relief*. **(11.13)**

Mannerism   A term sometimes applied to art of late 16th and early 17th-century Europe, characterized by a dramatic use of space and light and a tendency toward elongated figures. **(16.26)**

mass   Three-dimensional *form*, often implying bulk, density, and weight. **(4.12)**

medium   1. The material used to create a work of art. 2. The *binder* for a paint, such as oil. 3. An expressive art form, such as painting, drawing, or sculpture.

megalith   A very large stone. **(1.4)**

metalpoint   A drawing technique, especially popular in the *Renaissance*, in which the drawing material is a thin wire of metal. See also *silverpoint*. **(6.8)**

mezzotint   An *intaglio* printmaking method in which the printing plate is first roughened all over with a sharp tool called a rocker to create a pattern of burrs. *Values* from light to medium dark are created by smoothing away the burrs in relative degree. Also, the resultant *print*. **(8.14)**

minaret   A tower forming part of a mosque and serving as a place from which the faithful are called to prayer. **(18.1)**

Minimalism   A style of painting and sculpture in the mid 20th century in which the art elements are restricted to an extreme "minimum"—lines, simple (often geometric) shapes, and sometimes color. **(3.38)**

mixed media   Descriptive of any work of art employing more than one *medium*—for example, a work that combines painting, *collage*, and *screenprinting*. **(12.19)**

modeling   1. In sculpture, shaping a *form* in some *plastic* material, such as clay, wax, or plaster. 2. In drawing, painting, or printmaking, the illusion of three-dimensionality on a flat surface created by simulating effects of light and shadow. **(11.3, 4.15)**

mold   A hollow or negative *shape* used for *casting* liquid clay, metal, or *plastic*. **(11.5)**

monochromatic   Having only one color. Descriptive of work in which one *hue*—perhaps with variations of *value* and *intensity*—predominates. **(4.29)**

monotype   A printmaking method in which only one impression results. **(8.23)**

mosaic   An art form in which small pieces of tile, glass, or stone are fitted together and embedded into a background to make a pattern or image. Often used for floor and wall decoration. **(7.17)**

mural   Any large-*scale* wall decoration in painting, *fresco*, *mosaic*, or other *medium*. **(20.19)**

narthex   In early Christian architecture, the porch or vestibule serving as an entryway to a church. **(15.4)**

naturalistic   Descriptive of a work of art that closely resembles *forms* in the natural world. Sometimes used synonymously with *realistic*. **(2.1)**

nave   The long central section of a church or cathedral where the congregation stands or sits. **(13.11)**

Neoclassicism   "New" classicism—a style in 19th-century Western art that referred back to the *Classical* styles of Greece and Rome. Neoclassical painting is marked by sharp outline, reserved emotions, deliberate (often geometric) *composition*, and cool colors. **(17.17)**

neutral   Having no *hue*—black, white, or gray; sometimes a tannish color achieved by mixing two *complementary colors*.

nonobjective   Descriptive of works of art that have no reference to the natural world of images. Composed of lines, shapes, and sometimes colors, chosen and arranged for their own expressive potential. Synonymous with *nonrepresentational*. Compare *abstract*, *stylized*. **(3.9)**

nonrepresentational   See *nonobjective*. **(3.9)**

oculus   A circular opening in a wall or at the top of a dome. **(13.13)**

open palette   See *palette*. **(4.25)**

optical color mixture   The tendency of the eyes to blend patches of individual colors placed near one another so as to perceive a different, combined color. Also, any art style that exploits this tendency, especially the *pointillism* of Georges Seurat. **(1.19)**

order In *Classical* architecture, a system of standardized types. In ancient Greek architecture, three orders pertain: Doric, Ionic, and Corinthian. The orders are most easily distinguished by their columns. **Doric:** The shaft of the column may be smooth or fluted. It does not have a base. The capital is a rounded stone disk supporting a plain rectangular slab. **Ionic:** The shaft is fluted and rests on a stepped base. The capital is carved in graceful scrolling forms called volutes. **Corinthian:** The shaft is fluted and rests on a more detailed stepped base. The elaborate capital is carved with motifs based on stylized acanthus leaves. **(13.3)**

palette 1. A surface used for mixing paints. 2. The range of colors used by an artist or group of artists, either generally or in a specific work. An **open palette** is one in which all colors are permitted. A **restricted palette** is limited to a few colors and their mixtures, tints, and shades. **(4.24, 4.25)**

pastel 1. A soft, chalky crayon used for drawing; also, the resultant drawing. 2. A light-*value* color. **(6.13)**

pediment The triangular area above the porch on a Greek temple, often decorated with sculptures. **(13.5)**

pendentive In architecture, a curving, triangular section that serves as a transition between a *dome* and the four walls of a rectangular building. **(13.16)**

performance art Similar to a *happening*, art in which there is no concrete object but, rather, a series of events performed by the artist in front of an audience, possibly including music, recitation, audio-visual presentations, or other elements. **(22.34)**

perspective A system for portraying the visual impression of three-dimensional space and objects in it on a two-dimensional surface. **Linear perspective** is based on the observation that parallel lines appear to converge as they recede from the viewer, finally meeting at a vanishing point on the horizon. Linear perspective relies on a fixed viewpoint. **Atmospheric perspective** is based on the observation that distant objects appear less distinct, paler, and bluer than nearby objects due to the way moisture in the intervening atmosphere scatters light. **Isometric perspective** uses diagonal lines to convey recession, but parallel lines do not converge. It is principally used in East Asian art, which is not based in a fixed viewpoint. **(4.40)**

Photorealism A painting style of the mid-20th century in which people, objects, and scenes are depicted with such naturalism that the paintings resemble photographs. **(22.15)**

picture plane An imaginary flat surface that is assumed to be identical with the surface of a painting. *Forms* in a painting meant to be perceived in deep three-dimensional space are said to be "behind" the picture plane. The picture plane is commonly associated with the foreground of a painting.

pier A vertical support, often square or rectangular, used to bear the heaviest loads in an arched or vaulted structure. A pier may be styled to resemble a bundle of columns. **(13.11)**

pigment A coloring material made from various organic or chemical substances. When mixed with a *binder*, it creates a drawing or painting *medium*.

plane A flat surface. See *picture plane*.

planography A printmaking technique in which the image areas are level with the surface of the printing plate; *lithography*. **(8.19)**

plastic 1. Capable of being molded or shaped, as clay. 2. Any synthetic polymer substance, such as *acrylic*.

pointillism An art style of the late 19th century, particularly associated with Georges Seurat, in which small patches or "points" of color are placed close together to build *form*. See also *optical color mixture*. **(4.28)**

Pop Art An art style of the 1960s, deriving its imagery from the popular, mass-produced culture. Deliberately mundane, Pop Art focused on the overfamiliar objects of daily life to give them new meanings as visual emblems. **(2.29)**

porcelain A *ceramic* ware, usually white, firing in the highest temperature ranges and often used for fine dinnerware, vases, and sculpture. **(12.3)**

portico A projecting porch with a roof supported by columns, often marking the entrance to a building. **(13.13)**

post-and-lintel In architecture, a structural system based on two or more uprights (posts) supporting a horizontal crosspiece (lintel or beam). **(13.6)**

Post-Impressionism A term applied to the work of several artists—French or living in France—from about 1885 to 1905. Although all painted in highly personal styles, the Post-Impressionists were united in rejecting the relative absence of *form* characteristic of *Impressionism*. The group included Vincent van Gogh, Paul Cézanne, Paul Gauguin, and Georges Seurat. **(1.10)**

primary color A *hue* that, in theory, cannot be created by a mixture of other hues. Varying combinations of the primary hues can be used to create all the other hues of the spectrum. In pigment the primaries are red, yellow, and blue. **(4.21)**

primer A preliminary coating applied to a painting *support* to improve adhesion of paints or to create special effects. A traditional primer is gesso, consisting of a chalky substance mixed with glue and water. Also called a *ground*.

print An image created from a master wood block, stone, plate, or screen, usually on paper. Prints are referred to as multiples, because as a rule many identical or similar impressions are made from the same printing surface, the number of impressions being called an *edition*. See *relief intaglio, lithography, screenprinting*. **(8.4)**

proportion Size relationships between parts of a whole, or between two or more items perceived as a unit; also, the size relationship between an object and its surroundings. Compare *scale*. **(5.28)**

Realism Broadly, any art in which the goal is to portray forms in the natural world in a highly faithful manner; *naturalism*. Specifically, an art style of the mid-19th century, identified especially with Gustave Courbet, which fostered the idea that everyday people and events are fit subjects for important art. **(21.3)**

refraction The bending of a ray of light, for example, when it passes through a prism. **(4.20)**

registration In printmaking, the precise alignment of impressions made by two or more printing blocks or plates on the same sheet of paper, as when printing an image in several colors. **(8.5)**

relief Anything that projects from a background. 1. Sculpture in which figures are attached to a background and project from it to some degree. In **bas-relief,** also called **low relief,** the figures project minimally, as on a coin. In **haut-relief,** also called **high relief,** figures project substantially from the background, often by half their full depth or more. In **sunken relief,** outlines are carved *into* the surface and the figure is modeled within them, from the surface down. 2. In printmaking, techniques in which portions of a block meant to be printed are raised. See *woodcut, linocut, wood engraving*. **(16.2, 8.1)**

Renaissance The period in Europe from the 14th to the 16th century, characterized by a renewed interest in *Classical* art, architecture, literature, and philosophy. The Renaissance began in Italy and gradually spread to the rest of Europe. In art, it is most closely associated with Leonardo da Vinci, Michelangelo, and Raphael. **(7.3)**

representational Descriptive of a work of art that depicts *forms* in the natural world. **(2.6)**

restricted palette See *palette*. **(4.24)**

ribbed vault See *vault*. **(13.11)**

Rococo A style of art popular in Europe in the first three quarters of the 18th century. Rococo architecture and furnishings emphasized ornate but small-*scale* decoration, curvilinear *forms*, and *pastel* colors. Rococo painting, also tending toward the use of pastels, has a playful, light-hearted, romantic quality and often pictures the aristocracy at leisure. **(17.15)**

Romanesque A style of architecture and art dominant in Europe from the 9th to the 12th century. Romanesque architecture, based on ancient Roman precedents, emphasizes the round *arch* and *barrel vault*. **(13.10)**

Romanticism A movement in Western art of the 19th century, generally assumed to be in opposition to *Neoclassicism*. Romantic works are marked by intense colors, turbulent emotions, complex *composition*, soft outlines, and sometimes heroic subject matter. **(4.8)**

rotunda An open, cylindrical interior space, usually covered by a dome. **(13.15)**

saturation See *intensity*. **(4.22)**

scale Size in relation to some "normal" or constant size. Compare *proportion*. **(5.21)**

screenprinting A printmaking method in which the image is transferred to paper by forcing ink through a fine mesh in which the areas not meant to print have been blocked; a stencil technique. **(8.21)**

secondary color A *hue* created by combining two *primary colors*, as yellow and blue mixed together yield green. In pigment the secondary colors are orange, green, and violet. **(4.21)**

serigraphy See *screenprinting*. **(8.21)**

sfumato From the Italian word for "smoke," a technique of painting in thin *glazes* to achieve a hazy, cloudy atmosphere, often to represent objects or landscape meant to be perceived as distant from the *picture plane*. **(16.8)**

shade A color darker than a hue's normal value. Maroon is a shade of red. **(4.22)**

shape A two-dimensional area having identifiable boundaries, created by lines, color or *value* changes, or some combination of these. Broadly, *form*. **(4.11)**

silkscreen See *screenprinting*. **(8.21)**

silverpoint A variation of *metalpoint* in which the drawing material is a thin silver wire. **(6.8)**

simultaneous contrast The tendency of *complementary colors* to seem brighter and more intense when placed side by side. **(4.23)**

stained glass The technique of creating images or decorations from precisely cut pieces of colored glass held together with strips of lead. **(12.5)**

still life A painting or other two-dimensional work in which the subject matter is an arrangement of objects—fruit,

flowers, tableware, pottery, and so forth—brought together for their pleasing contrasts of shape, color, and texture. Also, the arrangement of objects itself. **(7.12)**

stippling A pattern of closely spaced dots or small marks used to create a sense of three-dimensionality on a flat surface, especially in drawing and printmaking. See also *cross-hatching, hatching*. **(4.17)**

stupa A shrine, usually dome-shaped, associated with Buddhism. **(19.3)**

style A characteristic, or a number of characteristics, that we can identify as constant, recurring, or coherent. In art, the sum of such characteristics associated with a particular artist, group, or culture, or with an artist's work at a specific time.

stylized Descriptive of works based on *forms* in the natural world, but simplified or conventionalized for *design* purposes. See also *abstract*. **(5.9)**

sunken relief See *relief*. **(14.16)**

support The surface on which a work of two-dimensional art is made; for example, canvas, paper, or wood.

Surrealism A movement of the early 20th century that emphasized imagery from dreams and fantasies. **(21.25)**

suspension A structural system in architecture, most common in bridges, in which the weight of a horizontal member is suspended from steel cables supported by uprights called pylons. **(13.25)**

symbol An image or sign that represents something else, because of convention, association, or resemblance. **(10.1)**

symmetrical Descriptive of a design in which the two halves of a composition on either side of an imaginary central vertical *axis* correspond to one another in size, shape, and placement. **(5.8)**

tapestry An elaborate textile meant to be hung from a wall and featuring images and motifs produced by various weaving techniques. **(12.14)**

tempera Paint in which the pigment is compounded with an aqueous, emulsified *vehicle* such as egg yolk. **(7.5)**

tensile strength In architecture, the ability of a material to span horizontal distances with minimum support from underneath.

terra cotta Italian for "baked earth." A *ceramic* ware, usually reddish, fired in the low temperature ranges and somewhat porous and fragile; earthenware. **(11.3)**

tertiary colors Colors made by mixing a primary color and an adjacent secondary color (for example, red and violet). **(4.21)**

tint A color lighter than a hue's normal value. Pink is a tint of red. **(4.22)**

transept The arm of a cruciform church perpendicular to the *nave*. The transept often marks the beginning of the *apse*. **(15.14)**

triptych A composition consisting of three panels side by side, generally hinged in such a way that the outer two panels can close like shutters over the central one. **(16.21)**

typeface In graphic design, a style of type. **(10.6)**

typography In graphic design, the arrangement and appearance of printed letter forms (type). **(10.8)**

value The relative lightness or darkness of a *hue*, or of a *neutral* varying from white to black. **(4.22)**

vanishing point In *linear perspective*, the point on the horizon where parallel lines appear to converge. **(4.39)**

vault An arched masonry structure or roof that spans an interior space. A **barrel vault** is half-round arch extended in depth. A **groin vault** is formed by the intersection of two barrel vaults of equal size at right angles. A **ribbed vault** is a groin vault in which the lines marking the intersection of the vaults are reinforced with a raised rib. A **corbelled vault** is a vault made with the technique of **corbelling,** in which each course of stone projects slightly beyond the one below to create an arch form (but not a true, weight-bearing arch). **(13.10)**

vehicle Another term for *medium,* in the sense of a liquid compounded with pigment to make paint.

visual weight The apparent "heaviness" or "lightness" of the forms arranged in a composition, as gauged by how insistently they draw the viewer's eye. **(5.12)**

volume Similar to *mass,* a three-dimensional *form* implying bulk, density, and weight; but also a void or empty, enclosed space. **(4.37)**

volute In architecture, a spiral, scroll-like ornament such as the *capital* of a column in the *Ionic order.* **(13.4)**

wash Ink or *watercolor* paint thinned so as to flow freely onto a *support.* **(6.14)**

watercolor A painting *medium* in which the *binder* is gum Arabic. **(7.11)**

woodcut A *relief* printmaking method in which a block of wood is carved so as to leave the image areas raised from the background. Also, the resultant *print.* **(8.8)**

wood engraving Similar to *woodcut,* a *relief* printmaking process in which the image is cut on the end grain of a wood plank, resulting in a "white-line" impression. **(8.9)**

ziggurat In ancient Mesopotamian architecture, a monumental stepped structure symbolically understood as a mountain and serving as a platform for one or more temples. **(14.4)**

PHOTOGRAPHIC CREDITS

Chapter 14: 14.1 Colorphoto Hans Hinz; **14.2** L/AR; **14.3** Bruce Coleman, Inc./F. Jackson; **14.4** Erwin Boehm, Mainz; **14.5** University of Pennsylvania Museum (neg. #T4.1000c); **14.6, 14.17, 14.24, 14.27, 14.28, 14.30, 14.31, 14.32** S/AR; **14.7** Gift of John D. Rockefeller, Jr., 1932 (32.143.2). Photograph © 1981 The Metropolitan Museum of Art; **14.8, 14.25, 14.34** © The British Museum, London; **14.9** Staatliche Museen zu Berlin, Bildarchiv Preussischer Kulturbesitz, Vorderasiatisches Museum/VABAb. Foto: Klaus Göken, ©1992; **14.10** Spectrum Colour Library; **14.11, 14.12, 14.22** G/AR; **14.13** Bruce Coleman, Inc.; **14.14** Werner Forman/AR; **14.15** Staatliche Museen zu Berlin, Ägyptisches Museum. Bildarchiv Preussischer Kulturbesitz. Foto: Margarete Büsing; **14.16** Bildarchiv Preussischer Kulturbesitz, Photo: Margarete Büsing; **14.18** Gift of Christos G. Bastis, 1968 (68.148). Photograph © 1996 The Metropolitan Museum of Art; **14.19, 14.20, 14.29** Nimatallah/AR; **14.21** Rogers Fund, 1914 (14.130.14). Photograph © 1996 The Metropolitan Museum of Art; **14.23** Photograph courtesy of the Royal Ontario Museum, ©ROM; **14.26** Fletcher Fund, 1932 (32.11.1). Photograph © 1997 The Metropolitan Museum of Art; **14.33** Photo Researchers, Inc./C. Seghers.

p. 345 S/AR;
p. 350 Photography by Egyptian Expedition, The Metropolitan Museum of Art.

Chapter 15: 15.1, 15.5, 15.16, 15.24 S/AR; **15.3** The New York Public Library, Miriam and Ira D. Wallack Division of Art, Prints and Photographs; **15.6** AKG, London/Heiner Heine; **15.8** G/AR; **15.9** © 1997 The Metropolitan Museum of Art. Photo: Bruce White; **15.10** The British Museum, London; **15.11** Library of Trinity College, Dublin, MS. 57, fol. 191v. The Board of Trinity College Dublin; **15.12** AKG, London/Hilbich; **15.13** L/AR; **15.15** © Paul M.R. Maeyaert; **15.17** Adam Woolfitt/Woodfin Camp & Associates; **15.18** John Elk III/Bruce Coleman, Inc.; **15.20, 15.21** © James Austin, Bourn, Cambridge; **15.22** Roger-Viollet/Liaison Agency, Inc.; **15.23** The Pierpont Morgan Library/AR; **15.25** Alinari/AR.

p. 370 L/AR.

Chapter 16: 16.1, 16.2, 16.3, 16.4, 16.6, 16.9, 16.13, 16.16, 16.28 S/AR; **16.7** © The Frick Collection, New York; **16.8, 16.22** RMN/AR; **16.10** Monumenti Musei e Gallerie Pontificie, Vatican, Rome, Italy, Photo Vatican Museums: A. Bracchetti. P. Zigrossi, Mar. 2000; **16.11, 16.12** Nippon Television Network Corporation, Tokyo; **16.15** Nicolo Orsi Battaglini/AR; **16.18** Samuel H. Kress Collection. Photograph ©2001 Board of Trustees, National Gallery of Art, Washington; **16.19, 16.27** L/AR; **16.20, 16.23** G/AR; **16.21** The Cloisters Collection, 1956 (56.70). Photograph © 1996 The Metropolitan Museum of Art; **16.22** Gift of Mr. and Mrs. Henry Lee Higginson, 93.153. Courtesy, Museum of Fine Arts, Boston. Reproduced with permission. © 2000 Museum of Fine Arts, Boston. All Rights Reserved; **16.24, 16.26** ©National Gallery, London; **16.25** Rogers Fund, 1919 (19.164). Photograph © 1998 The Metropolitan Museum of Art.

p. 382 © Bettmann/CORBIS;
p. 387 L/AR;
p. 389 S/AR.

Chapter 17: 17.1 Nimatallah/AR; **17.2, 17.4, 17.6, 17.13** S/AR; **17.5** Photograph © 1984 The Detroit Institute of Arts. Gift of Mr. Leslie H. Green; **17.7** Onze Lieve Vrouwkerk, Antwerp Cathedral, Belgium/Peter Willi/Bridgeman Art Library; **17.8** Courtesy the Board of Trustees of the National Museums and Art Galleries on Merseyside (Walker Art Gallery, Liverpool); **17.9, 17.18** G/AR; **17.10, 17.17** RMN/AR; **17.11** Institut Amatller d'Art Hispanic. © Museo del Prado. All rights reserved; **17.12** Rijksmuseum, Amsterdam; **17.14** Artothek; **17.15** L/AR; **17.16** ©The Frick Collection, New York; **17.19** Musées Royeaux des Beaux-Arts de Belgique, Brussels; **17.20** Gift of Joseph W., William B., and Edward H.R. Revere, 30.781. Courtesy, Museum of Fine Arts, Boston. Reproduced with permission. © 2000 Museum of Fine Arts, Boston. All Rights Reserved.

p. 408 S/AR;
p. 412 S/AR;
p. 425 S/AR.

Chapter 18: 18.1 © Roger Wood/CORBIS; **18.2** Institut Amatller d'Art Hispanic; **18.3** Credit: Courtesy of the World of Islam Festival Trust; **18.4** Robert Harding Picture Library LTD; **18.5** Adam Lubroth/AR; **18.6** By Permission of the British Library, London, MS. Add. 22412; **18.7** Courtesy of the Freer Gallery of Art, Smithsonian Institution, Washington, DC (F1956.14 folio 22r); **18.8, 18.13** © The British Museum, London; **18.9** Staatliche Sammlungen Aegyptischer Kunst, Munich; **18.10** © 1979 Dirk Bakker; **18.11** Photo: Eliot Elisofon, 1970. Image no. 7590. Eliot Elisofon Photographic Archives, National Museum of African Art, Smithsonian Institution, Washington, DC; **18.12** © John Pemberton III, Amherst, MA; **18.14** Gift of Lester Wunderman, 1977 (1977.394.15). Photograph © 1993 The Metropolitan Museum of Art; **18.15** The Michael C. Rockefeller Memorial Collection, Bequest of Nelson A. Rockefeller, 1979 (1979.206.121). Photograph © 1992 The Metropolitan Museum of Art; **18.16** © Africa-Museum Tervuren, Belgium. Photo Plusj; **18.17** Photo by Frederick Lamp; **18.18** Photo courtesy Elizabeth Evanoff Etchepare.

p. 437 Photo courtesy of Professor Herbert M. Cole.

Chapter 19: 19.1, 19.7, 19.8, 19.10 Borromeo/AR; **19.2** National Museum of India, New Delhi, India/Bridgeman Art Library; **19.3, 19.4** S/AR; **19.5, 19.6, 19.12** AKG, London/ Jean-Louis Nou; **19.11** Paul Miller/Black Star; **19.13, 19.19, 19.20** The Nelson-Atkins Museum of Art, Kansas City, Missouri (Purchase: Nelson Trust); **19.14** © Wolfgang Kaehler/CORBIS; **19.15, 19.18, 19.22** Cultural Relics Publishing House, Beijing; **19.16, 19.17** © The British Museum, London; **19.21** National Palace Museum, Taipei, Taiwan, Republic of China; **19.23** Kyoto National Museum; **19.24** Photo credit: Kyodo News, Tokyo; **19.25** Photo credit: Shogakukan, Tokyo; **19.26** Tokugawa Art Museum, Nagoya; **19.27, 19.30, 19.31, 19.32** Tokyo National Museum; **19.28** Fenollosa-Weld Collection, 11.4000. Courtesy, Museum of Fine Arts, Boston. Reproduced with permission. © 2000 Museum of Fine Arts, Boston. All Rights Reserved; **19.29** Photo credit: Sakamoto Photo Laboratory, Tokyo; **19.33** Courtesy of the Freer Gallery of Art, Smithsonian Institution, Washington, DC (F1899.34).

p. 447 © The British Museum, London;
p. 451 © Michael Freeman.

Chapter 20: 20.1 Lipundja, 1912.1968, Daygurr-gurr clan, Gopapuyngu language, Milingimbi, central Arnhem Land. Djalambu, 1964. Earth pigments on bark. 134.5 x 74.5 cm. Purchased through the Art Foundation of Victoria with the assistance of Esso Australia Ltd. Fellow 1989. National Gallery of Victoria, Melbourne, Australia; **20.2** ©Museum der Kulturen, Basel. Photo Peter Horner; **20.3** Georgia Lee, Rapa Nui Journal-Easter Island Foundation, CA; **20.4** © The British Museum, London; **20.5** Interior of Te Hau ki Turanga, a meeting house from Manutuke, Poverty Bay, New Zealand. Carved by Raharuhi Rukupo, master carver, 1842.43. Restored 1935, wood, shell, grass, flax, pigments. The Museum of New Zealand Te Papa Tongarewa, Wellington. Neg. B18358; **20.6** Photo Researchers, Inc./Carl Frank; **20.7** SEF/AR; **20.8** J. G. Sidaner/AR; **20.9** Courtesy Florida Museum of Natural History, Gainesville, FL; **20.10** © Justin Kerr; **20.11** Werner Forman/AR; **20.12** L/AR; **20.13** Gift of Nathan Cummings, 1963 (63.226.8). Photograph © 1994 The Metropolitan Museum of Art; **20.14** Nick Saunders/Barbara Heller Photo Library, London/ AR; **20.15** Photo: Pierre-Alain Ferrazzini, Musée Barbier-Mueller, Genève; **20.16** Ohio Historical Society, Columbus; **20.17, 20.18** New York State Historical Association, Cooperstown, New York. Fenimore Art Museum, The Eugene and Clare Thaw Collection. Photo: John Bigelow Taylor, NYC; **20.19** © Ed Bohon/Corbis Stock Market; **20.20** Dallas Museum of Art, Foundation for the Arts Collection, anonymous gift; **20.21** Brooklyn Museum of Art, Museum Collection Fund, 03.325.4653; **20.22** Catalogue No. 169106, Department of Anthropology, Smithsonian Institution.

Chapter 21: 21.1, 21.7, 21.8 L/AR; **21.2, 21.4, 21.6** RMN/AR; **21.3** G/AR; **21.5** Ailsa Mellon Bruce Collection. Photograph ©2001 Board of Trustees, National Gallery of Art, Washington; **21.9** Hans Hinz - Artothek; **21.10** Philadelphia Museum of Art: George W. Elkins Collection. Photo: Graydon Wood; **21.11** Morris K. Jesup Fund, 1933 (33.61). Photograph © 1992 The Metropolitan Museum of Art; **21.12** Chester Dale Collection. Photograph ©2001 Board of Trustees, National Gallery of Art, Washington; **21.13** Artothek, NY/ADAGP, Paris; **21.14** BF#719 © Reproduced with the permission of The Barnes Foundation, All Rights Reserved. © 2001 Succession H. Matisse, Paris/ARS, NY; **21.15** Ernst Ludwig Kirchner, The Street, Dresden, 1908 dated on painting 1907. Oil on canvas. The Museum of Modern Art, New York. Purchase. Photograph © 2001 The Museum of Modern Art, New York. © (for works by E. L. Kirchner) by Ingeborg & Dr. Wolfgang Henze-Ketterer, Wichtrach/Bern; **21.16** Photo: David Heald © Solomon R. Guggenheim Foundation, New York. © 2001 ARS, NY/ADAGP, Paris; **21.17** Acquired through the Lillie P. Bliss Bequest. Photograph © 2001 The Museum of Modern Art, New York. © 2001 Estate of Pablo Picasso/ARS, NY; **21.18** Gift of Geneviève and Jean Masurel. Musée d'art moderne de Lille Métropole, Villeneuve d'Ascq © Muriel Anssens. © 2001 ARS, NY/ADAGP, Paris; **21.19** Hans Hinz - Artothek, © 2001 ARS, NY/ADAGP, Paris; **21.20** S/AR. © 2001 ARS, NY/SIAE, Rome; **21.21** Acquired through the Lillie P. Bliss Bequest. Photograph © 2001 The Museum of Modern Art, New York; **21.22** Photo: David Heald © Solomon R. Guggenheim Foundation, New York. © 2001 ARS, NY/ADAGP, Paris; **21.23** AR. © 2001 ARS, NY/ADAGP, Paris/Estate of Marcel Duchamp; **21.24** CNAC/MNAM/Dist Réunion des Musées Nationaux/AR © 2001 ARS, NY/ ADAGP, Paris; **21.25** Purchase. Photograph © 2001 The Museum of Modern Art. © 2001 ARS, NY/Pro-Litteris, Zürich; **21.26** Given anonymously. Photograph ©2001 The Museum of Modern Art, New York. © 2001 Kingdom of Spain, Gala-Salvador Dali Foundation/ARS, NY; **21.27** Collection Albright-Knox Art Gallery, Buffalo, New York, Room of Contemporary Art Fund, 1940. © 2001 ARS, NY/ADAGP, Paris; **21.28** Photo: Sovfoto/Eastfoto. © Esatate of Vladimir Tatlin/Licensed by VAGA,

New York, NY; **21.29** S/AR. © 2001 ARS, NY/Beeldrecht, Amsterdam; **21.30** Centraal Museum, Utrecht; **21.31** The Museum of Modern Art, New York. Gift of Herbert Bayer. Photograph © 2001 The Museum of Modern Art, New York; **21.32** The Museum of Modern Art, New York. Mrs. Solomon Guggenheim Fund. Photograph © 2001 The Museum of Modern Art, New York. © 2001 ARS, NY/ADAGP, Paris; **21.33** Schomburg Center, The New York Public Library/AR.

p. 493 The Stickney Fund. © 2001 The Art Institute of Chicago. All rights reserved;
p. 497 left AKG, London/Robert O'Dea;
p. 497 right L/AR;
p. 500 Amsterdam, Van Gogh Museum (Vincent van Gogh Foundation);
p. 508 Philadelphia Museum of Art: A. E. Gallatin Collection. Photo: Graydon Wood. © 2001 Estate of Pablo Picasso/ARS, NY.

Chapter 22: 22.1 The Museum of Contemporary Art, Los Angeles, The Rita and Taft Schreiber Collection. Photo: Fredrik Nilsen. © 2001 The Pollock-Krasner Foundation/ARS, NY; **22.2** Gift of Mr. and Mrs. David M. Solinger. Photograph © 2001 The Museum of Modern Art, New York. © 2001 The Franz Kline Estate/ARS, NY; **22.3** Purchase. 55.35. Photograph Copyright © 2000: Whitney Museum of American Art. © 2001 Willem de Kooning Revocable Trust/ARS, NY; **22.4** Collection Albright-Knox Art Gallery, Buffalo (gift of Seymour H. Knox, 1956) © 1998 Kate Rothko Prizel & Christopher Rothko/ARS, NY; **22.5** Purchase and an anonymous gift and Louise Reinhardt Smith Bequest. Photograph © 2001 The Museum of Modern Art, New York. ©Robert Rauschenberg/Licensed by VAGA, New York, NY; **22.6** Gift of Mr. and Mrs. Robert C. Scull. Photograph © 2001 The Museum of Modern Art, New York. © Jasper Johns/Licensed by VAGA, New

York, NY; **22.7** Photo David Gahr, NY. © 2001 ARS, NY/ADAGP, Paris; **22.8** © Allan Kaprow, courtesy of the Library, Getty Research Institute, Los Angeles. Photo: Lawrence Shustak; **22.9** Andy Warhol, 100 Campbell Soup Cans, 1962, oil on canvas, 6' × 4'4″. Collection Albright-Knox Art Gallery, Buffalo, New York, Gift of Seymour H. Knox, 1963. © 2001 Andy Warhol Foundaton/ARS, NY/TM Licensed by Campbell's Soup Co. All rights reserved; **22.10** © Estate of Roy Lichtenstein. Photo: Robert McKeever; **22.11** Gift of the Howard and Jean Lipman Foundation, Inc. Photograph Copyright © 2000: Whitney Museum of American Art. © 2001 ARS, NY/ADAGP, Paris; **22.12** © ARS, NY, Collection of the Artist. Art Resource, NY. © 2001 Frank Stella/ARS, NY; **22.13** Hirshhorn Museum and Sculpture Garden, Smithsonian Institution, Washington, DC. Gift of Joseph H. Hirshhorn, 1972. Photo: Lee Stalsworth. Art © Donald Judd Foundation/Licensed by VAGA, New York, NY; **22.14** The Newark Museum/AR. ©The George and Helen Segal Foundation/Licensed by VAGA, New York, NY; **22.15** © The Cleveland Museum of Art, 2000, Purchase with a grant from the National Endowment for the Arts and matched by gifts from members of The Cleveland Society for Contemporary Art, 1974.53. Courtesy of the artist and Nancy Hoffman Gallery, New York; **22.16** Courtesy of Joseph Kosuth. © 2001 Joseph Kosuth/ARS, NY; **22.17** Courtesy the artist and Bernice Steinbaum Gallery, Miami, FL; **22.18** National Portrait Gallery, Smithsonian Institution/ AR. © The Estate of Alice Neel. Courtesy Robert Miller Gallery, New York; **22.19** © Gordon R. Gainer/ Corbis Stock Market; **22.20** Collection Walker Art Center, Minneapolis. T.B. Walker Acquisition Fund, 1992. Courtesy of the artist; **22.21** AR; **22.22** Courtesy the artist and Mary Boone Gallery, New York; **22.23** Purchase, Lila Acheson Wallace Gift, 1993 (1993.71). Courtesy of the artist. Photograph

© 1993 The Metropolitan Museum of Art. **22.24** The Broad Art Foundation, Santa Monica. Photo credit: Zindman/Fremont. © 2001 ARS, NY/ADAGP, Paris; **22.25** Courtesy Sperone Westwater, New York. © Susan Rothenberg/Photo: Thomas Powel. © 2001 Susan Rothenberg/ARS, NY; **22.26** Acquired through the Bernhill Fund and gift of Agnes Gund. Photograph © 2001 The Museum of Modern Art, New York. © Elizabeth Murray; **22.27** Courtesy of the artist and Matthew Marks Gallery, New York; **22.28** © Jenny Holzer, Photo: Thomas Holder. © 2001 Jenny Holzer/ARS, NY; **22.29** (The Museum of Modern Art, NYC, Projects 34: Felix Gonzalez-Torres May 16–June 30, 1992; Location #11: 31-33 2nd Ave. at East 2nd St.). Courtesy of Andrea Rosen Gallery, New York, in representation of The Estate of Felix Gonzalez-Torres. Photo Peter Muscato; **22.30** Courtesy the artist and Mary Boone Gallery, New York; **22.31** Courtesy the artist and Bernice Steinbaum Gallery, Miami, FL; **22.32** Photo courtesy of Jack Shainman Gallery, New York; **22.33** Courtesy of Marian Goodman Gallery/©William Kentridge; **22.34** Martha Swope/ TimePix/© Laurie Anderson; **22.35** © Robert Gober. Courtesy Dia Center for the Arts. Photo: Bill Jacobson; **22.36** Courtesy of the artist, Photo: Elio Montanari; **22.37** © 1997 Matthew Barney, Photo: Michael James O'Brien. Courtesy Barbara Gladstone Gallery; **22.38** Cheim and Reid Gallery. Photo: Allan Finkelman. © Louise Bourgeois/Licensed by VAGA, New York, NY; **22.39** Courtesy: the artist, © 2001 Luis Jiminez/ARS, NY; **22.40** Courtesy Paula Cooper Gallery, New York. Photo: P.A Grisoni and J. Staub.

p. 522 Center for Creative Photography, University of Arizona, Tucson;
p. 534 National Portrait Gallery, Smithsonian Institution/AR. © The Estate of Alice Neel. Courtesy Robert Miller Gallery, New York;
p. 543 © Guerrilla Girls.

INDEX

All references are to page numbers.
Numbers in **boldface** indicate an illustration on that page.